USAF HISTORICAL STUDIES: NO. 97

Airborne Operations In World War II, European Theater

By
Dr. John C. Warren

USAF Historical Division
Research Studies Institute
Air University
September 1956

Published by Books Express Publishing
Copyright © Books Express, 2011
ISBN 978-1-78039-503-6

Books Express publications are available from all good retail and online booksellers. For publishing proposals and direct ordering please contact us at: info@books-express.com

Personal views or opinions expressed or implied in this publication are not to be construed as carrying official sanction of the Department of the Air Force or the Air University.

Published at
Maxwell Air Force Base, Alabama
September 1956
Air University USAF Historical Division Study
(AU-97-53-RSI)

Foreword

This monograph describes the planning and execution of airborne operations by the Army Air Forces in the European Theater during World War II. Intended to serve as a case history of large-scale airborne operations, it seeks to analyze and evaluate them as a basis for doctrine and for the information of future planners. This history was written by Dr. John C. Warren of the USAF Historical Division.

Like other Historical Division studies this history is subject to revision, and additional information or suggested corrections will be welcomed.

Contents

I	THE AIRBORNE INVASION OF NORMANDY—PLANS AND PREPARATIONS .	1
	Background	1
	Early Planning—The COSSAC Phase	2
	Shaping the Outline Plans	6
	Detailed Planning	9
	The Buildup	17
	Deployment and Training	20
	Final Preparations	26
	Deception and Diversion	28
II	THE ASSAULT	32
	The Pathfinders	32
	ALBANY Mission and the Paratroop Operations of the 101st Division	33
	BOSTON Mission and the Paratroop Operations of the 82d Division	48
	Evaluation of the Paratroop Operations	58
	CHICAGO and DETROIT—The Initial Glider Missions	61
	KEOKUK and ELMIRA Glider Missions	65
	The Glider Missions on D plus 1—GALVESTON and HACKENSACK	69
	Evaluation of the Glider Missions	72
	Parachute Resupply Missions	74
	The British Missions and WILDOATS	78
III	FROM NEPTUNE TO MARKET	81
	Organizational Changes	81
	Plans and Operations during the Campaign in France	83
	The Planning of MARKET	88
	Resources and Preparations	97
	Preliminary Support Operations	100
IV	MARKET—THE AIRBORNE INVASION OF HOLLAND	101
	D-day, the Pathfinders	101
	D-day, Operations in the Eindhoven Sector	102
	D-day, Operations in the Nijmegen Sector	107
	D-day, Operations in the Arnhem Sector	112
	The Balance for D-day	115
	D plus 1, Plans and Auxiliary Air Action	117
	D plus 1, Eindhoven Sector	118
	D plus 1, Nijmegen Sector	120
	D plus 1, Resupply by Bomber	123
	D plus 1, Arnhem Sector	125
	The Balance for D plus 1	127
	D plus 2, Plans and Auxiliary Air Action	127

D plus 2, Eindhoven Sector		129
D plus 2, Nijmegen Sector		130
D plus 2, Arnhem Sector		131
The Balance for D plus 2		133
D plus 3		133
D plus 4		136
D plus 5		140
D plus 6		141
D plus 7		145
D plus 8		145
D plus 9 and After		146
Conclusions		149
V	Varsity—The Airborne Assault Across the Rhine	156
	Preliminary Planning	156
	Development of the Assault Plan	157
	Planning for Auxiliary Air and Artillery Action	166
	Training	168
	Briefing and Security Measures	170
	Auxiliary Air Operations	171
	The Final Decision and the Ground Assault	173
	The Lift and Initial Operations of the British Airborne Division	174
	The Lift and Initial Operations of the American Paratroops	177
	The Lift and Initial Operations of the American Glider Troops	181
	Resupply	188
	The Exploitation of VARSITY	190
	Special Features of VARSITY	191
	Conclusions	192
VI	Conclusions Regarding Large-scale Airborne Operations	196
	Footnotes	203
	Appendix	224
	1. Statistical Tables—Operation NEPTUNE	224
	2. Statistical Tables—Operation MARKET	226
	3. Statistical Tables—Operation VARSITY	228
	Glossary	230
	Index	234

Maps

No.		Page
1.	Operation NEPTUNE: Routes of Troop Carrier Missions	13
2.	Operation NEPTUNE: Approach and Assault Area of Airborne Missions	34
3.	Operation NEPTUNE: Assault Area	37
4.	Operation NEPTUNE: Paratroop Drop of 101st Airborne Division	44
5.	Operation NEPTUNE: Paratroop Drop of 82d Airborne Division	49
6.	Operation MARKET: Routes of Initial Troop Carrier Missions	92
7.	Operation MARKET: Assault Area, 101st Airborne Division	104
8.	Operation MARKET: Assault Area, 82d Airborne Division	108
9.	Operation MARKET: Assault Area, British and Polish Airborne Troops	113
10.	Operation MARKET-GARDEN: Battle Area	116
11.	Operation VARSITY: Troop Carrier Routes	162
12.	Operation VARSITY: Assault Area	175

Charts

1.	Operational Chain of Command for Airborne Operations, Allied Expeditionary Force, 5 June 1944	31
2.	Chain of Command for Operation MARKET, 17 September 1944	84

Illustrations

Figure		Page
	Waco Gliders on Landing Zone Near Wesel, Germany, After Operation VARSITY	Frontispiece
1.	Paratrooper Boarding a C-47	20
2.	Paratroop Officer Demonstrates Jump Position	20
3.	Cockpit of a Waco Glider	21
4.	Jeep Emerging from Nose of Waco Glider	21
5.	Waco Gliders Landing in Normandy	62
6.	Remnants of Gliders in a Normandy Hedge-row	63
7.	Pick-up of a Waco Glider from a Field in Normandy	73
8.	Horsa Glider of IX Troop Carrier Command after Landing in Normandy	74
9.	Paratroop Drop near Grave, Holland, during Operation MARKET, 23 September 1944	127
10.	Resupply Drop from B-24's over Holland during Operation MARKET, 18 September 1944	128
11.	Troop Carrier Aircraft Carrying Paratroops in Operation VARSITY, 24 March 1945	182
12	Paratroop Drop near Wesel, Germany, during Operation VARSITY, 24 March 1945	183

Waco Gliders on Landing Zone near Wesel Germany after Operation VARSITY.

The Airborne Invasion of Normandy - Plans and Preparations

Background

THE FIRST combat airborne missions in history were flown by the Germans in 1940. Recognizing the possibilities of such operations, the British and Americans followed suit. The first British mission was flown in February 1941, and the first American mission was flown from England to Oran, Algeria, on 8 November 1942 as part of the Anglo-American invasion of North Africa. Other, later missions, principally in the Mediterranean region, provided the American troop carriers with an apprenticeship in airborne warfare.* However, until the summer of 1944 no force larger than a reinforced regimental combat team was flown into action in any Allied mission. In World War II the only Allied airborne operations employing more than one division took place in the invasion of Normandy, the unsuccessful attempt to win a bridgehead across the Rhine at Arnhem, and the successful crossing of the Rhine at Wesel.† Consequently the study of airborne missions in the European Theater of Operations is of particular importance for the light it throws on the planning and performance of large-scale airborne assaults.

The invasion of Normandy occurred on 6 June 1944, but preparations for that event had begun long before. British planning for an invasion of the Continent had been carried on as early as 1941, and after the United States entered the war, President Roosevelt and his Chief of Staff, General George C. Marshall, concentrated unswervingly on that objective as the decisive action of the war. Actual preparations for such an invasion were begun early in 1942 under the code name of BOLERO. The BOLERO plans called for creation of a mighty airborne force, for which the 51st Troop Carrier Wing and a paratroop battalion were sent to England that summer as the first American installment.

The decision at the end of July 1942 to launch an invasion of North Africa before attempting an attack on Festung Europa postponed further planning of the latter operation for several months. It also resulted in a sweeping diversion to Africa of men and materiel needed for an invasion of Europe. In the spring of 1943 only one American division and no American airborne units remained in the British Isles. American airpower in the United Kingdom consisted of less than 12 operational combat groups of all types, including half of a troop carrier group.[1] British striking power was similarly depleted.

In May 1943 when the TRIDENT conference was held in Washington, it was obvious that between the invasion of Sicily, scheduled for 10 July, and the end of the summer there would not be time to concentrate an invasion force in the United Kingdom. Therefore, although at TRIDENT the Allies sanctioned renewed preparations for an invasion of Northwest Europe, they gave it a target date of 1 May 1944. To this crucial operation they gave the name OVERLORD. On 25 May 1943 the Combined Chiefs of Staff pledged a build-up to 29 divisions, two of them airborne, before the target date.

---

*See USAF Historical Study 74, Airborne Missions in the Mediterranean, 1942-1945. For airborne operations in Burma and New Guinea, see W. F. Craven and J. L. Cate, *The Army Air Forces in World War II*, IV (Chicago, 1950), 181, 184-86, 503-7, 516-17, 658-59.

†In DRAGOON, the invasion of southern France, the troop carriers delivered one provisional airborne division of approximately 9,000 men.

Early Planning—The COSSAC Phase

These decisions were received by a planning headquarters, already in existence. Pending appointment of a Supreme Allied Commander for the invasion, Lt. Gen. Frederick E. Morgan, a British officer, had been appointed on 12 March as Chief of Staff to the Supreme Allied Commander. During April Morgan had set up at Norfolk House in London a headquarters which shared with its chief the code name of COSSAC (taken from the initials of his title). On 14 April Brig. Gen. Robert C. Candee, Commanding General of VIII Air Support Command, reported to Morgan for additional duty as Principal Staff Officer of the AAF Branch of COSSAC. On 26 April, just before TRIDENT, the Combined Chiefs of Staff gave COSSAC a directive including in its responsibilities the planning of a full-scale invasion of the Continent in 1944.[2]

At that time the AAF commanders in England were struggling with the problem of working out a proper buildup for their forces, and the AAF Branch of COSSAC began its career by participating in this task. General Candee, convinced of the importance of airborne operations, recommended a buildup to 23 American troop carrier groups with an assigned strength of 1,196 planes as being "the minimum necessary" for airborne operations in the invasion. Since that was almost as many troop carrier craft as the entire AAF possessed at that time, Candee's proposal seemed impracticable and had no immediate effect. A chart brought by General Stratemeyer from the United States indicated that only nine groups would be available. That estimate was favored by the bomber men in the Theater and endorsed by Maj. Gen. Follett Bradley, Air Inspector of the AAF, who arrived in England in May to assess the overall requirements of the AAF for the invasion. On 25 May the Combined Chiefs of Staff decreed a troop carrier buildup of 8½ American groups and 7 British squadrons, a total of 634 troop carrier aircraft. This figure remained unchanged for the next four months.[3]

General Morgan was convinced that OVERLORD should be based on all available information, but designed without reference to previous plans. Therefore his staff surveyed the whole west coast of Europe before deciding late in June (as some British planners had done before them) that the grand assault should be launched against the coast of Normandy between the Caen area and the Cotentin Peninsula. Unlike its most favored rival, the Pas de Calais, Normandy had not been heavily fortified by the Germans. It had good beaches within fighter range of England, a great port in Cherbourg, and adequate sites for airfields.

On 15 July a preliminary study on the proposed invasion was submitted to the British Chiefs of Staff, and on the 30th, COSSAC issued a rather vague and tentative outline plan for an invasion of Normandy. In essence the plan called for an amphibious assault by three divisions against beaches between the mouths of the Orne and the Vire. The initial objective was a line running between Grandcamp, Bayeux and Caen. Morgan would have preferred to land another division further west on the beaches of the Cotentin, but he had been promised barely enough landing craft to carry three in the initial assault.

At first COSSAC had been inclined to employ its airborne forces on the right flank near Carentan rather than to risk them in the Caen area. The 634 troop carrier aircraft promised for the invasion could carry only two-thirds of a division at a time, and it was thought that at least a whole division would be needed to take Caen. On the other hand, Caen was the gateway to Normandy. In Allied possession it would be a barrier to enemy troops seeking to enter the invasion area from the east or northeast. It could also provide an entry into central France when the Allies were ready to attack out of the beachhead. So tempting a prize persuaded Morgan to approve an airborne assault against Caen.

Between 21 and 28 July COSSAC decided on an initial assault by two-thirds of a British airborne division to take Caen and, less definitely, on assaults by seven American paratroop battalions* against coastal batteries and river crossings on the right flank of the beachhead. The minimum number of troop carrier aircraft needed to carry out the program was estimated to be 799 planes. COSSAC therefore requested at least 13 American troop carrier groups (of 52 planes each) plus a reserve of 120 aircraft and crews.

Room for additional troop carrier units would have to be found on Britain's crowded airfields.

---

*The May estimate of airborne forces for OVERLORD had been increased by five American paratroop regiments.

Fortunately, higher echelons proved sympathetic. For example, Lt. Gen. Ira C. Eaker, Commander of Eighth Air Force, wrote on 3 August that he believed the proposed increment could be squeezed in. The next step was to present the COSSAC plan to the Allied leaders who convened at Quebec on 17 August 1943 for the QUADRANT conference. They not only approved the plan but also intimated that it might be possible to expand it. They offered little prospect of increasing the buildup of troop carrier units from the United States, but COSSAC was already exploring the possibility of getting them from other theaters of operations.

The Mediterranean theater was a promising source for all kinds of reinforcements for OVERLORD. Because the British were loath to halt major operations in that area, decisive action to divert its resources was not taken at Quebec. However, such action was contemplated and was already regarded as almost certain. Soon after the QUADRANT meetings, negotiations to obtain four additional troop carrier groups from the Mediterranean were in full swing. By November the four groups were included in flow charts, and fields were earmarked for their use. At Cairo in December the Chiefs of Staff officially allocated 13½ American troop carrier groups with 880 aircraft for use in OVERLORD. This level was to be achieved by taking from Italy the 52d Troop Carrier Wing with four groups plus two squadrons of the 315th Troop Carrier Group. Preparations for their transfer to the ETO were initiated on 8 January 1944.[4]

While the size of the airborne forces to be used in OVERLORD was being determined, the doctrine which was to govern their employment was just beginning to take shape. Indeed, written doctrine for airborne operations scarcely existed in July 1943 when the Allies invaded Sicily (Operation HUSKY). Allied experience in the field was too recent and limited. Operations in HUSKY had been expected to serve as a guide, but initial reports on them were incomplete and contradictory. As the summer progressed it became evident that the execution of the airborne missions in Sicily had been poor and their success rather limited. The conclusion was drawn that unless planning, equipment, and training could be markedly improved the premises of the COSSAC plan were too optimistic.[5]

Planning for HUSKY had not been well coordinated, partly because the headquarters of many of the commands involved had been widely separated. Great pains were taken to see that the several headquarters planning OVERLORD would work closely together. In HUSKY the routes selected for the troop carriers had been much too complicated and difficult. The planners resolved to make them as simple as possible for OVERLORD. Fire from Allied guns had disrupted two airborne missions to Sicily in spite of the establishment of safety zones and in spite of warnings to the surface forces. Henceforth the necessity for ample precautions against such mishaps and particularly for keeping as far away as possible from convoys and naval vessels was consistently stressed.

The principal glider mission in HUSKY had been a fiasco, largely because the gliders had been released at night over the open sea. Because of the glider's ability to deliver men and materiel in concentrated packets, COSSAC had hitherto favored it over the parachute and had planned to use 350 gliders in the initial assault.

However, all agreed that the initial airborne assault in OVERLORD would require the protection of darkness, and HUSKY had confirmed earlier opinions that glider missions should not be flown at night except perhaps in fair weather under a full moon. Chances of getting fair weather and a full moon simultaneously for OVERLORD were less than 50 percent. These circumstances explain why responsibility for the initial assault came to rest with the paratroops.

Faulty navigation at night in the Sicilian missions had caused dispersion of the paratroop drops over the entire southeastern portion of the island. These errors stimulated a search for means to guide the troop carriers to their objectives in spite of darkness or bad weather. One remedy was the dropping of pathfinder troops before the arrival of an airborne mission to mark drop or landing zones. Some experimentation with pathfinder teams using visual aids had been done, and the need to provide guidance for formations which otherwise might pass many miles outside visual range led to consideration of radio and radar beacons for pathfinder use. Most promising of these was the Eureka, a simple, light, durable instrument which could be dropped by parachute and be put into operation within five minutes. Its responses to the signals of an airborne interrogator called Rebecca gave an accurate bearing and a fair indication of distance at ranges which varied considerably with conditions but were generally over 10 miles. After pathfinder teams equipped with Eureka proved effective in guiding airborne missions during the invasion of Italy it was generally accepted that pathfinder tactics would be employed in OVERLORD.

The American CG-4A glider, commonly known as the Waco, had proved combat-worthy in Sicily, but it was small, unable either to carry over 3,750 pounds or to take a gun and its prime mover in one load. Made of fabric with a tubular steel frame, the Waco was durable except for its nose, which was weak and easily crushed. Also, the nose, which was hinged to swing outward and up, was the only door, so that if the glider skidded into an obstacle, as commonly happened in Sicily, the cargo would be sealed in.

The British had developed a plywood glider, the Horsa, which could carry 6,700 pounds and could contain both a 75-mm. howitzer and a jeep to tow it. Early models had two passenger doors and a cargo door in the sides. The Horsa, although liable to break loose in flight and to splinter on landing, did well enough in Sicily to interest the Americans in adopting it. This interest grew after tests conducted in August proved that a C-47 could tow a Horsa, albeit with some difficulty. The British also had a giant glider, the Hamilcar, with a capacity of 17,500 pounds. Few in numbers and as yet untested in combat, the Hamilcar required an exceptionally powerful four-engined airplane to tow it. The American troop carriers consequently regarded it as unsuitable for their use.

HUSKY had revealed at least as much about the troop carrier crews as about their equipment. Some analysts considered that the greatest single lesson of the airborne operations in Sicily was that troop carrier crews needed far more training in night flying, especially night flying in formation. Weakness in this field had caused a tremendous amount of straggling and excessively loose formations. Almost all aspects of glider training had been shown to need improvement.

These shortcomings and others should have been revealed by a rehearsal, but there had been no rehearsal and few realistic exercises by the troop carriers before HUSKY.* The planners resolved that before OVERLORD the troop carriers would be thoroughly trained in night flying and glider work and that their proficiency would be tested by numerous exercises capped by a realistic rehearsal.[6]

The command structure under which troop carrier operations in the European theater were to be conducted developed gradually. In June 1943 Air Marshal Trafford Leigh-Mallory, chief of the RAF Fighter Command, had been named provisionally to head the air planners of COSSAC, and at Quebec in August the Allies had agreed to designate him as commander in chief of their tactical air forces in OVERLORD. After a period of discussion over the extent of its authority, his command, the Allied Expeditionary Air Force, was established in November. Headquarters, AEAF was located at Stanmore, a dozen miles northwest of London, but a delegation was left at Norfolk House to collaborate with COSSAC.

Immediate, full, and direct control of the Second Tactical Air Force, RAF, Air Defense of Great Britain, and the RAF 38 Group was given to AEAF as of 15 November. All British troop carrier operations were in the hands of 38 Group. Equivalent in size to an American wing, it was equipped with converted bombers good for glider work but ill-suited for paratroop operations. The British planned to expand 38 Group to 9 squadrons with 180 aircraft in time for OVERLORD. In December, as a result of pressure to enlarge the airborne assault, the RAF decided to establish another troop carrier group. The tactical air commanders had asked the Air Ministry for a loan of 150 Dakotas (British C-47's) from the RAF Transport Command and at least 150 bombers from Bomber Command for use in OVERLORD. The bombers were not forthcoming, but the Dakotas were. On 17 January 1944 this new force was organized as the RAF 46 Group. It was to be under operational control of 38 Group until after OVERLORD and would then revert to Transport Command.[7]

American tactical air units in England had been organized on 16 October 1943 into the Ninth Air Force under the command of Maj. Gen. Lewis H. Brereton, a veteran who within the past two years had commanded air forces in a wide variety of combat activities in four theaters of operations. Simultaneously with the creation of Ninth Air Force, IX Troop Carrier Command was activated as one of its components, replacing a provisional

---

*The reasons for this situation are explained in USAF Historical Study 74, Airborne Missions in the Mediterranean, 1942-1945, Chap. III.

command set up by the Eighth Air Force in September. Its commander was Brig. Gen. Benjamin F. Giles. However, even before General Giles assumed his command, it was understood that Brig. Gen. Paul L. Williams, who had directed the troop carriers during almost all the Allied airborne operations in the Mediterranean theater, would take over IX Troop Carrier Command before intensive preparation for OVERLORD was begun.[8] When activated the troop carrier command had under it only one recently arrived troop carrier group, the 434th, and a detachment of the 315th Group with two or three planes.* The 435th Group and the headquarters of the 50th Troop Carrier Wing arrived from the United States before the end of the year.[9]

On 15 December AEAF received operational control of Ninth Air Force and its components. In the case of the troop carriers this control was to be unusually direct and complete. Leigh-Mallory regarded the coming airborne operations as subject to his special prerogative. He stated as a matter of course that planning for airborne operations would be done between his headquarters and 21 Army Group, which was to command the ground forces in the assault phase of OVERLORD. Coordination of plans for such operations with other outside agencies was also to be handled by AEAF, and it was to have the final say in arrangements for fighter protection, routing, altitude, timing, and recognition procedure in airborne missions. Although subordinate commands would participate, all of the planning except such details as could be worked out between troop carrier wings and the ground units they were to carry was to be concentrated in AEAF headquarters.

On 6 December Leigh-Mallory announced that the launching of airborne forces would be the responsibility of his headquarters. At a conference three days later he asserted that AEAF should have direct operational control, not only of 38 Group, but also of Ninth Air Force's subsidiary, IX Troop Carrier Command, and he got an expression of agreement on this point from Brereton.[10]

Debatable points in the airborne planning were ironed out at meetings of the Airborne-Air Planning Committee. This organization, established in December, included Leigh-Mallory, the British and American troop carrier commanders, the principal British and American airborne commanders, and such other persons as might be needed on a given occasion. At its meetings Leigh-Mallory presided and usually played a dominant role.[11]

At times the AEAF commander acted as though his operational and planning authority included the right to direct supervision of troop carrier training. Brereton insisted sharply that such supervision be exercised indirectly through the Ninth Air Force. Even this indirect authority was challenged by USSTAF which, as the highest AAF headquarters in the United Kingdom in 1944, claimed to have sole authority over the training of Ninth Air Force. In practice the troop carrier command was in constant close consultation with both AEAF and the Ninth Air Force in training matters, but had very little to do with USSTAF.[12]

One important link in the chain of command controlling airborne operations in Normandy was not forged until the spring of 1944. On 27 January the Airborne-Air Planning Committee recommended that a joint troop carrier operations room and command post be set up for IX Troop Carrier Command, 38 Group, and 46 Group in the Uxbridge area near AEAF headquarters for use during large-scale exercises and operations. Leigh-Mallory favored the idea, and on 21 February it was agreed that such a post should be established. A suitable room was found at Eastcote Place, and on 9 April IX Troop Carrier Command set up an advance command post there. The facilities at Eastcote were tested in a subsequent exercise and proved very satisfactory. Under the title of Troop Carrier Command Post this was the point from which troop carrier operations in the invasion were directed.[13]

During the autumn of 1943 Leigh-Mallory played the leading part in an interesting episode affecting airborne planning. In October General Morgan had visited Washington to discuss OVERLORD with American military leaders. There Lt. Gen. H. H. Arnold, Chief of the United States Army Air Forces, presented him with a plan, supported by the chief of staff, General George C. Marshall, to make OVERLORD predominantly an airborne operation. As many as three airborne and air transported divisions were to be delivered to a

---

*At that time an American troop carrier group was composed of a headquarters with 4 aircraft and 4 squadrons with 12 planes apiece. About half of the 315th Group had reached England early in 1943, but most of the planes and crews had been flown to North Africa in May to supplement the troop carrier forces committed to HUSKY and had been kept there.

strategic point well inland from the French coast. This force was to sever enemy communications and strike out in all directions until such time as sea-landed forces made contact with it.

Feeling the need for assistance in so momentous a matter, the COSSAC commander called for Leigh-Mallory. He arrived about the end of October and after examining the project gave his verdict against it. In the first place, Leigh-Mallory observed, the allotted troop carrier aircraft could not lift much more than one division at a time. Secondly, Leigh-Mallory had a somewhat exaggerated idea of what German guns and planes could do to an airborne mission. Thirdly, he believed, in company with most experts at that time, that airborne units should not be expected to operate against a strong enemy for more than a day or two before junction with friendly ground forces. Tailored to the limited capacity of the C-47, an American airborne division had no armor, no vehicle bigger than a jeep and less than half the firepower of an infantry division. Some consideration had been given to using Hamilcar gliders to carry tanks or big guns in OVERLORD, but the Hamilcars were few in number, and only one squadron in 38 Group had planes capable of towing them. Resupply by air was still in the experimental stage and was viewed with some skepticism. For instance, on 1 January 1944 the AEAF Chief of Operations wrote that he did not believe large ground forces in action would ever be wholly supplied by air. The number of aircraft required would, he thought, be prohibitive. On such grounds as these the AAF plan was rejected. However, the exponents of "vertical envelopment" were not discouraged. They revised their plans and bided their time to make a new proposal.[14]

It appeared settled that the airborne troops would not be used independently; but exploration of how they would be used had barely begun. In December, 21 Army Group had initiated preparation of a plan for OVERLORD. Syndicates representing appropriate ground, air, and naval commands were set up at the army group headquarters, St. Paul's School, in London to examine various aspects of the invasion.

One syndicate, analyzing the threat of counterattack by German armored forces, observed that the roads to the proposed beachhead converged on Caen at its eastern end and on Bayeux in the center of the area. Consequently plans were laid for the employment of a British airborne brigade at points east of Caen to block the crossings of the Orne and for drops and landings southeast and southwest of Bayeux by American airborne units to cut highways leading to that town.

Airborne operations around Bayeux had one grave drawback. The terrain outside the town was open with few obstacles to deter enemy armor from overrunning the positions of the lightly armed airborne troops. However, within a few days the problem became academic when the accession of new commanders produced fundamental changes in the nature of OVERLORD.[15]

Shaping the Outline Plans

Firm planning for OVERLORD could not begin until the Supreme Commander of the Allied Expeditionary Force (SCAEF)* was chosen. On 5 December the choice fell on Lt. Gen. Dwight D. Eisenhower, who had commanded the Allied forces in the Mediterranean theater ever since their first landings in North Africa. Shortly thereafter General Bernard L. Montgomery, who was famed for his victory at El Alamein and who had served under Eisenhower as commander of the British Eighth Army in the Tunisian, Sicilian, and Italian campaigns, was named commander of 21 Army Group. Under him two other veterans of the Mediterranean campaigns, Lt. Gen. Omar N. Bradley and Lt. Gen. Miles C. Dempsey respectively, were to command the First United States Army and the British Second Army.

These appointments were the harbingers of change, for on learning of the COSSAC plan both Eisenhower and Montgomery immediately became convinced that the assault was too weak and on too narrow a front. On 2 January 1944, Montgomery arrived in England to act as Eisenhower's representative pending the latter's arrival. No sooner had he been briefed on the COSSAC program than he threw all the weight of his strong personality and great prestige into an effort to expand the initial assault to a strength of five divisions, even threatening to resign his command if the change were not made. By 6 January planning on the old basis had been halted, and ways

---

*Eisenhower's headquarters was commonly known as SHAEF, an abbreviation of its full title, Supreme Headquarters, Allied Expeditionary Force.

and means to mount the larger assault were under consideration at COSSAC.[16]

On 14 January Eisenhower arrived in England to support the new dispensation, and to take over from COSSAC the responsibility for OVERLORD. On the 21st Eisenhower held at Norfolk House the first two meetings of his principal commanders. There Montgomery presented the case for a five-division assault on a front extended westward onto the Cotentin peninsula. The United States First Army would drive ashore with two divisions, one a little way northwest of Bayeux, the other at the base of the Cotentin. Three divisions of British Second Army would land between Bayeux and Ouistreham. The meeting endorsed the proposal, and, accordingly, on the night of 23 January a message was sent to the Combined Chiefs of Staff asking their assent. This was given on the 31st.

Obtaining the additional landing craft required for the enlarged assault was to prove extremely difficult. To get more time to obtain these boats the CCS on 31 January postponed the target date for OVERLORD from 1 May to 1 June,* but not until 21 March did they finally make up their minds to meet the needs of OVERLORD by taking from the Mediterranean assault craft hitherto earmarked for ANVIL, an invasion of southern France.

Planning could not be postponed to await this decision. On 15 January 21 Army Group, assuming that the five-division plan would receive both official approval and the necessary shipping, had set up new interservice syndicates. They were directed to produce by the end of the month an initial joint plan from which further planning on Army-Air Force levels could proceed.[17]

The situation of the American division which was to land on the Cotentin peninsula was perilous enough to warrant special attention. Its beach, a mile of hard sand later christened UTAH, near the village of St. Martin-de-Varreville, was fenced in by two natural barriers. Behind it lay a swampy area which the Germans had flooded. Four causeways which crossed this flooded land had to be taken if the Americans were not to be confined to the beach. On the left was a second barrier, the marshy valleys of the Douve, Vire, and Taute, which lay between the Cotentin and the rest of the invasion area. Since practically all routes across those valleys centered on the town of Carentan, the Germans by holding that town could isolate the UTAH force,* which might then be defeated or at least effectively contained.

On the other hand, if airborne troops seized the causeways and cleared the way for an advance across the Douve, the UTAH force might take Carentan on D-day and establish contact with the other assault divisions. It would then be free to make a quick stab northward toward the valuable port of Cherbourg.

An airborne mission in the UTAH area was both feasible and relatively safe. Ample drop zones were available. The marshy, stream-girt meadows behind the coast were full of obstacles to enemy armor. No strong German forces were known to be in the vicinity, and the airborne troops could be reinforced within a few hours by guns and tanks from the beaches.

These considerations had led First Army to conclude almost as soon as it began planning the UTAH operation that an American airborne division should be employed behind the beaches to support the UTAH landing. Montgomery so far approved the plan as to include it in his presentation on 21 January, and at first Leigh-Mallory welcomed it as a change from the airborne operations in the Caen area for which, he said, he had never cared.[18]

Thus endorsed, the drop behind UTAH Beach was duly established in the NEPTUNE† Initial Joint Plan issued on 1 February. According to that plan a second airborne division would attack within twenty-four hours after the first, but whether its objective would be in the British or the American sector was still under discussion. The British continued to want an operation near Caen to hold the line of the Orne, and General Bradley was much interested in plans to place an American airborne division on the west side of the Cotentin. Plans for a third airborne operation were left indefinite because, although four airborne divisions and several smaller units were on hand, it was very doubtful whether there would be enough troop carrier aircraft for three large-scale lifts. On

---

*This postponement was welcome to Leigh-Mallory, who had already requested such a delay to provide more time for troop carrier training.

*See Map No. 3, p. 37.
†About this time the code word NEPTUNE came to be used for the assault on Normandy, the term OVERLORD being restricted to later phases of the invasion or to the invasion as a whole.

24 January Leigh-Mallory had pointed out the hard fact that he had only enough planes to carry one division at a time. The attrition of two hazardous operations might reduce the number of troop carriers operational to a much lower level.[19]

As a result of this situation renewed efforts to get additional troop carrier strength had been made during January. Proposals for expansion of 38 Group won support from the Prime Minister, Winston Churchill, and by 23 February had been approved by the Air Ministry. The Group was to be raised in time for NEPTUNE to a strength of 212 first-line aircraft and 36 reserves.

Meanwhile Eisenhower had appealed to Washington for aircraft and crews sufficient to provide IX Troop Carrier Command with a striking force of 832 planes plus 208 reserves. The AAF had a shortage of trained crews and barely enough C-47's in prospect to meet his request after filling existing commitments. Nevertheless, on 31 January the Operational Plans Division of AAF Headquarters worked out a solution. The departure of the last troop carrier group scheduled for spring delivery would be speeded so that it would have time to participate in preparations for OVERLORD. The troop carrier groups in England would be expanded by 1 April from 52 aircraft and crews apiece to a recently established T/O strength of 64 plus 9 in reserve. Thus IX Troop Carrier Command would have 13½ groups with 986 aircraft available for OVERLORD. On 19 February the War Department formally notified Eisenhower that these measures had been approved.

Ultimately Washington found it possible to send enough additional crews so that over 1,100 were in England at the time of the invasion, but the basic planning for the airborne operations in NEPTUNE was on the basis of the February estimates.[20]

While the wheels of the War Department were turning to supply additional troop carriers for OVERLORD, AAF Headquarters produced a plan for a large-scale airborne operation deep in enemy territory. Prepared by Brig. Gen. Frederick W. Evans, head of I Troop Carrier Command, and Col. Bruce W. Bidwell of the Operational Plans Division, this plan was approved by General Marshall, on 7 February and flown to England a few days later.

With it went a letter from Marshall in which, while disclaiming any desire to exert undue pressure, he expressed to Eisenhower his strong personal support of the project. He criticized previous airborne operations as piecemeal, indecisive, and narrowly conceived. As for objections to the plan on grounds that nothing like it had been done before, he commented ". . . frankly that reaction makes me tired."[21]

The enterprise which so appealed to him was a parachute and glider assault between Evreux and Dreux by two reinforced airborne divisions on the night of D minus 1. In that area, some 70 miles east of Caen and 40 miles west of Paris were four large airfields. These would be seized and used for airlanding of two additional reinforced divisions before daylight on D plus 1. At least 1,250 tons a day of supplies would be delivered by 600 C-47's flying by night and 200 heavy bombers operating by day. The initial objective of the airborne troops after consolidating their position would be the Seine crossings below Paris. All of these were within striking distance of the airhead.

General Eisenhower gave the plan full consideration, but at a meeting with his subordinate commanders on 18 February he went on record as rejecting it. His objections were based on the immobility of the airborne troops after landing. This, together with their limited firepower and lack of armor, might permit the Germans to surround and destroy them if the forces in the amphibious assault were not able to move rapidly to their assistance. He also feared that their aerial resupply might be seriously interrupted by weather or enemy action. Eisenhower's view was that the time for such massed and deep penetrations by airborne forces would come when the Allies were established on the Continent and in position for a breakthrough.[22]

Since in actuality the Allies were unable to break out of their Normandy beachhead for a month and a half after D-day, Eisenhower's fear that under the Evans plan his airborne forces might be destroyed before ground assistance could reach them seems justified by events.

After 1 February planning responsibility for NEPTUNE passed from SHAEF to the appropriate army and air force commanders. The proposals of the former for airborne operations were presented at an interservice meeting on 23 February. There General Bradley won a second decision in favor of the use of an airborne division behind UTAH Beach. His emphatic statement that seizure of the exits from the beach was vital to his assault plan outweighed protests from Leigh-Mallory that the area near UTAH was not well suited to glider operations and was defended by perilously large numbers of antiaircraft installations.

The lift of an American airborne division to take the UTAH causeways would require 800 of the 1,154 troop carrier aircraft which were to be available.* The commanders agreed on the 23d that the remaining 354 planes should go to the British for missions carrying two brigades on D minus 1 to take or destroy bridges east of Caen. The two brigades (each roughly equivalent to an American regiment) would have a very tight squeeze.

Both Bradley and Dempsey wanted their airborne troops delivered on the night of D minus 1. Leigh-Mallory conceded that paratroop operations would be possible by moonlight but reserved judgment on the feasibility of glider landings at night. He also disliked the idea of having to furnish fighter escorts for two simultaneous airborne operations.

General Bradley had proposed that a second American airborne division be dropped and landed in an area on the west side of the Cotentin northwest of La Haye du Puits after the first two airborne missions were completed. Leigh-Mallory argued that zones south of La Haye were preferable, and decision on that point was postponed. On 2 March the Initial Joint Plan was amended to provide specifically for three airborne operations, but the exact timing and location of the second American assault was left open.[23]

Shortly thereafter it was settled that this operation would take place, as Bradley desired, northwest of La Haye du Puits on the night of D-day/D plus 1. North of La Haye, entrance to the west side of the Cotentin had to be gained through a four mile strip of dry land west of the Douve marshes or over a causeway two miles east of St. Sauveur de Pierre Pont. If one airborne division could block that bottleneck, while another seized or destroyed the bridges over the Douve in the UTAH area, the Cotentin would be effectively sealed against either the reinforcement or the escape of its Nazi garrison. However, since the La Haye area was more than 20 miles away from UTAH Beach, it might be several days before American ground forces could reach it. Because of this prospect of hard fighting in an isolated position the experienced 82d Airborne Division was chosen to strike there, and the operation in the UTAH sector was given to the 101st Airborne Division.

The commanders agreed that the British airborne operation east of Caen could be handled by 38 Group and 46 Group. However, because of the small size of the British troop carrier force, IX Troop Carrier Command might have to assist it if further missions by the British airborne were undertaken. Later it was planned that the troop carrier command might help carry the British 1 Airborne Division in an operation after D plus 6 or make an emergency drop of a British paratroop brigade to reinforce the beachhead. However, it was never called upon to carry out those missions.*[24]

Detailed Planning

After 23 February detailed study of the proposed airborne operations was begun by the Airborne Operations Staff, AEAF and by the staffs of IX Troop Carrier Command, 38 Group, and the airborne divisions, with the Airborne-Air Planning Committee serving as a central forum. The most heated controversy arose over the question of whether to attempt glider missions at night.

The troop carriers and Leigh-Mallory stood together against this and against landings at daybreak as involving excessive operational difficulties. They proposed that the gliders of the 101st Division be landed at dusk on D minus 1, but this was ruled out as forewarning the enemy of the main operation. On the other hand, General Bradley insisted on having 260 gliders landed by early morning of D-day to facilitate the capture of Carentan. Impatient with objections of the air commanders, he declared that if gliders could not carry out missions in the proposed areas they were of no value as weapons of war, and that if the

---

*Assuming a force of 986 American and 398 British planes of which 230 planes would be held in reserve.

*Since the British and American airborne missions to Normandy were geographically and tactically separate, and since the Americans did not participate in the British missions, further discussion of British operations will be limited to matters of mutual concern and to brief comments for purposes of comparison.

For accounts of the British airborne operations in Normandy see Air Ministry (A.H.B.) *Airborne Forces* (London, 1951); Richard N. Gale, *With the 6th Airborne Division in Normandy* (London, 1948); and Hilary St. G. Saunders, *The Red Beret* (London, 1950).

glider troops of the 101st could not be delivered and ready for action before noon on D-day, he would prefer to take them in by boat. Maj. Gen. Matthew B. Ridgway, commander of the 82d Division, also wanted his glider echelon brought in as early as possible, preferably with the paratroops, to provide artillery* against possible panzer attacks.[25]

Up to the middle of April it appeared that Bradley and Ridgway would have their way, that 260 gliders would land at dawn in the 101st Division's operation and 410 gliders would participate in the initial assault of the 82d Division. However, doubt was cast on the feasibility of this procedure by a test landing under realistic conditions at dawn on 18 April. Although only one major accident occurred there were many minor ones, and only half of the 48 gliders involved in the test could be flown away. On the 24th the issue was still in doubt, but by the 28th all gliders had been omitted from the initial missions and a new plan established under which the paratroops of both divisions would go in on the night of D minus 1. At dawn on D-day each division would be reinforced by about 50 gliders. Such small missions would be easy to escort, could be landed quickly and would not crowd small landing areas. Another glider mission would be delivered at dusk for the 82d Division and others thereafter at times as yet undetermined.[26]

The number of gliders to be sent in the evening on D-day was the subject of some misunderstanding and dispute. At first General Williams supposed it had been set at 150, while Bradley's staff held out for 200. Finally, late in May, it was decided that 176 gliders should be sent at that time for the 82d Division and 32 for the 101st. Later missions to the 82d Division, being both safer and less urgent, had been agreed on by the end of April. One mission of 100 gliders would go early on the morning of D plus 1, and another 100 would arrive at dusk. A parachute resupply mission by 185 planes would be flown on the night of D plus 1, and another parachute or glider mission of indefinite size would be flown on the next night.[27]

The main features of the American airborne operations seemed to have been settled; however, late in May they had to be radically revised as a result of defensive measures taken by the enemy. Until the spring of 1944 the Germans had concentrated on defense of the Pas de Calais and neglected Normandy. Then Hitler in one of his flashes of intuition called attention to the likelihood of Allied invasion of Normandy or Brittany, and in April German intelligence analysts substantiated his suggestion. While still inclined to think that the main assault would be elsewhere, the High Command recognized that Normandy was in danger and that the Cotentin was peculiarly suitable for an airborne operation.[28]

One answer to this threat was to fortify Normandy to the point of impregnability. Fortunately for the Allies the Germans lacked time, men, and materials to do the job thoroughly, but the Cotentin did break out with a rash of entrenchments and obstacles. These were particularly dangerous to the 82d Division. One of the drop zones originally selected by it was later described by Brig. Gen. James M. Gavin, as "the most thorough job of anti-airborne organization I have ever seen."[29]

Photographic reconnaissance confirming these developments caused anxiety but no change in plan. Late in May came more serious news. The Germans had reinforced the 243d and 709th Divisions, already known to be in the Cotentin, with the 91st Infantry Division, the 6th Parachute Regiment and some lesser units. Thus German reinforcements, which it was the mission of the 82d Airborne to bar from the Cotentin, were already there in sufficient strength to give the 82d a very hard fight. The move also increased the chances that the 101st Airborne would meet strong opposition. If so, that division, which had been assigned to take an area of some 40 square miles containing 14 important objectives, might need some assistance.[30]

The possibility of such a situation had not been entirely unforeseen, and obviously the solution was to shift the 82d Division into a position where it and the 101st would be mutually supporting. On 26 May the old plan was canceled. On the 27th a meeting was held at Bristol to make a new one. First Army proposed that the 82d Division be dropped near the town of Ste Mère Eglise to cover the right flank of the 101st, but VII Corps, which was in charge of the UTAH assault, preferred to have the division placed west of the Merderet to establish bridgeheads over that river.

---

*Only two or three battalions of parachute field artillery were available and events in Sicily had raised doubts as to whether they could be used effectively.

This had the virtue of keeping the two divisions far enough apart to avoid confusion during the paratroop drops, but there were not enough good drop and landing zones on the west side of the Merderet for a whole division. The outcome was a compromise by which two paratroop regiments of the 82d would drop on the west side of the river and one near Ste Mère Eglise. At first all gliders of the 82d Division were to land southeast of Ste Mère Eglise, close to the paratroops of the 101st, but later it was arranged that the initial glider mission of the division should land northwest of that town in position to make quick contact with the paratroop regiment there. Only one change was made in the plans of the 101st Division, but that was important. Hitherto a single battalion of the 506th Parachute Infantry Regiment (PIR) had been assigned to cover the southern perimeter of the division. Now the 501st PIR, previously assigned to take Ste Mère Eglise, was shifted south to reinforce that sector. It had proved possible to change drop and landing zones without changing loading plans, but the timing and route of the missions had to be revised.[31]

The staff of the 82d Division, well aware of the increasingly hazardous nature of their original operation, welcomed the new one "without a single regret."[32] On the other hand, the situation led the already pessimistic Leigh-Mallory to lose all faith in the chances of the American airborne operations. The AEAF commander appealed to Eisenhower in person and in writing to cancel the missions on the ground that enemy antiaircraft might shoot down half the parachute force and 70 percent of the gliders, and that the reinforced German troops would overwhelm such airborne forces as succeeded in landing. Eisenhower, though much perturbed, refused to accept the recommendation. He considered that the airborne missions were feasible and that their risks were warranted by their value. Without them the UTAH landing might fail, and its failure would cripple the whole assault. Therefore the Supreme Commander took the responsibility for having the missions carried out.[33]

Until May, planning for the protection of the airborne missions had of necessity remained unsettled pending decisions on the nature and timing of the missions themselves. The Allied commanders, particularly Leigh-Mallory, had been anxiously aware throughout their planning of the danger presented by German aircraft and antiaircraft. It was conservatively estimated during the spring that the Germans would have at least 850 usable aircraft in northwest France on D-day and that over 200 of them would be first-line fighters.* This later proved an accurate estimate. Allied airmen hoped to cripple these forces by pounding their airfields, but had little expectation of knocking them out. They anticipated that as many as 1,000 sorties a day might be made by the GAF. Since German warning radar was capable of picking up the troop carrier formations more than 30 miles off the coast, the risk of fighter interception in daylight missions, particularly glider missions, appeared great. German night fighters were not numerous in Normandy but had to be watched for. Antiaircraft fire was considered very dangerous. The whole tip of the Cotentin north of a line from les Pieux to Quineville was known to be infested with light and heavy guns, and intense fire was to be expected all along the east coast.[34]

To protect the airborne operations against these perils the Allies relied on avoidance, deception, and powerful air support. By 12 April IX Troop Carrier Command had planned and won approval for a route which avoided most antiaircraft concentrations by entering the Cotentin through the back door.

The assembly point of the 52d Troop Carrier Wing was to be about 20 miles east of Birmingham. From there the serials of that wing would fly southwest for 60 miles to the head of the Severn estuary and south for another 60 miles to the Command Assembly Point ELKO. The assembly points of the 50th and 53d Wings were respectively 23 miles west-southwest and 28 miles northeast of ELKO. From the Command Assembly Point all units would fly south-southwest for 30 miles to the Command Departure Point (FLATBUSH), at the tip of the sandy cape called Portland Bill. Thence they would go straight on over the sea for 57 miles to a point at 49° 45' 30" N, 02° 56' 30" W (HOBOKEN) at which they would make a 90 degree turn to the left and fly a 54-mile leg between Alderney and Guernsey, just out of range of the antiaircraft on either island, to the Initial Point

---

*Some later estimates, based on German efforts to conserve strength during the spring, were more pessimistic. On 5 June Ninth Air Force calculated that the Germans had 1,099 usable aircraft, including 634 fighters, in position for employment against OVERLORD by D plus 1. (Ltr, Hq 9th AF Adv to CG 9th AF, Subj: Estimated Scale of Effort of the G.A.F. Against Operation "OVERLORD," 5 Jun 44, in 533.451-632A.)

(PEORIA) on the west coast of the Cotentin about six miles north of the towns of Carteret and Barneville. Although the coastline there was not particularly distinctive, PEORIA was on the straightest possible route to the objectives. Directly ahead about 11 miles away was the area northwest of La Haye which was then the destination of the 82d Division. A slight turn to the left at the IP and a 25-mile flight would bring the 101st Division to its drop and landing zones behind UTAH Beach. Rather than risk passing over the antiaircraft batteries along the east coast and the Allied convoys off UTAH Beach all serials were to turn to the right after accomplishing their mission and return on a reciprocal course.

Discovery by German warning radar was to be delayed as long as possible by keeping below 1,500 feet over England and descending to 500 feet over the Channel. On reaching Normandy the troop carrier formations would climb to 1,500 feet to reduce the effectiveness of small arms fire. The route had the added virtues of avoiding the dense concentrations of aircraft operating from eastern and central England and giving a wide berth to the Allied convoys headed for Normandy.

The Allied naval commander agreed to set up a 10-mile safety corridor along the route, to notify his forces of the missions, and to instruct them that troop carrier formations on proper course and schedule were to be allowed to pass without challenge. Important as this precaution was, it was considered secondary to keeping the troop carriers out of range of the convoys.[35]

The revolution in troop carrier plans at the end of May necessitated certain changes in route. The concentration of German troops near the neck of the Cotentin, and the shift of the 82d Division's zones to the east exposed the troop carrier formations to greatly increased risks from ground fire during their flight across Normandy. With surprise and darkness in their favor the groups carrying paratroops could risk crossing the peninsula on the way in, but it was tempting providence to have them return the same way. Consequently, between 27 and 30 May they were given a new homeward route out over the east coast to the St. Marcouf Islands (PADUCAH), then over the water northward for 16 miles and west-northwest for 78 miles to rejoin the outward route at a check-point (GALLUP) 28 miles from Portland Bill. Such a course had been proposed previously by troop carrier planners but had been vetoed by naval representatives.

In order to separate the approach routes of the two divisions and thereby give the paratroops of the 82d Division a better chance to achieve surprise, the route of the 101st Division's paratroop mission from HOBOKEN to the mainland was swung slightly southward so that landfall would be made at an IP (MULESHOE) near the village of Portbail. The village and the inlet on which it was located provided excellent checkpoints. The run from MULESHOE to the drop zones of the 101st was 22 miles straight ahead with the Douve and Merderet rivers providing several landmarks along the way.

Later, after strenuous discussion, the planners agreed that the glider missions of the 82d and 101st at dawn on D-day should follow the same routes as the paratroop missions. The dim light of the early morning was relied on to protect their approach. Not until 31 May was it decided that subsequent glider and resupply missions, rather than fly across the Cotentin by daylight, were to approach their zones from the east side of the peninsula, following the route by which the earlier missions had returned, and that they would go back the same way.[36]

The new course entailed new risks. While it avoided the convoys as much as possible, some missions would pass over the UTAH assault area. The troop carrier spokesmen, fearing a barrage from the ships, asked for an absolute prohibition on naval antiaircraft fire at times when airborne missions were scheduled to pass overhead. The admirals objected on the grounds that a German air raid on the convoys might coincide with the passage of troop carrier formations. However, because of the importance attached to the airborne missions, the Allied naval commander did accept the new routes and imposed on the naval gunners the prohibition requested by IX Troop Carrier Command.[37]

While under the revised plans the close proximity of troop carrier and naval operations made aircraft recognition very important, the troop carriers were limited to the use of visual recognition procedure. In case of challenge they could respond with Very pistols and Aldis lights, but they were forbidden to use IFF except when ditching. Early in April SHAEF had established a committee to study the possibility that the huge number of Al-

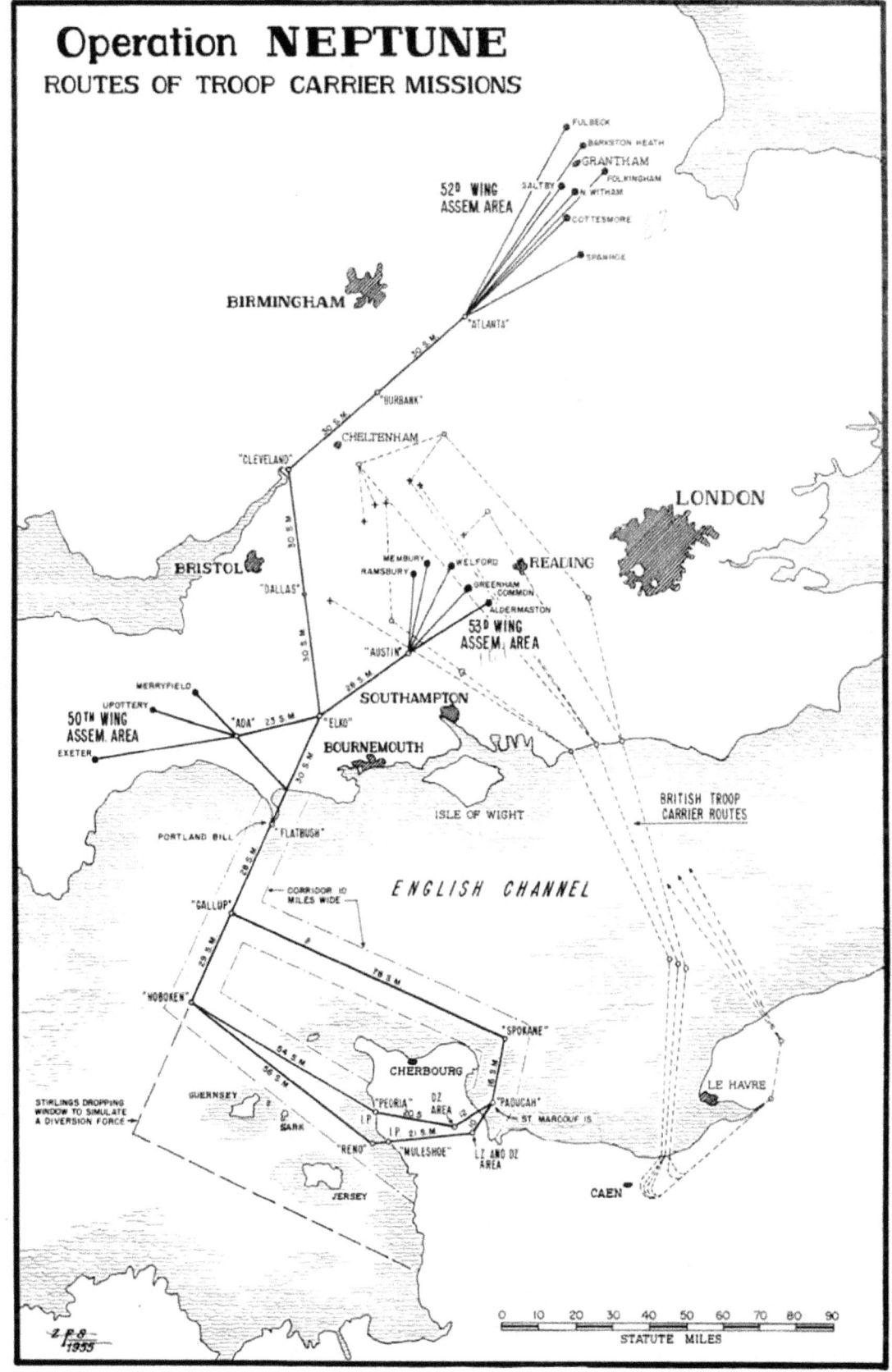

Map 1.

lied aircraft employed in the invasion might saturate the IFF system and cause it to break down. The committee reported on 2 May that without severe restrictions on the use of IFF such a result was to be expected. Consequently an interservice meeting on 9 May agreed to limit the use of IFF in the invasion mainly to night-fighters and carrier-based planes.[38]

One way to distinguish Allied aircraft from those of the enemy was to paint them with distinctive markings. In early May IX Troop Carrier Command was still thinking of camouflaging its planes, but since the decision not to use IFF made visual identification almost essential, it was ruled that certain types of aircraft including the troop carriers would be marked. Some SHAEF experts questioned whether it would be worthwhile to paint gliders as well as aircraft, but on 17 May Leigh-Mallory decreed that this, too, would be done. The pattern chosen for troop carrier craft consisted of three white and two black stripes, each two feet wide, around the fuselage back of the door and from front to back on the wings. To familiarize the naval forces with these markings an exercise was held on 1 June in which marked aircraft were flown over the invasion fleets. However, for security's sake, general marking of planes and gliders was not ordered until 3 June (D minus 2). It proved an arduous task which in many groups occupied all available troop carrier personnel far into the night.[39]

Security dictated that the paratroop missions arrive under cover of darkness. However, to help the troop carriers keep formation and enable the airborne troops to assemble after jumping, bright moonlight was considered highly desirable. This consideration, together with others relating to the amphibious assault had led Eisenhower early in May to pick 5 June as D-day. It was the first day after the 1 June target date that would be preceded by a moonlit night. Should a postponement prove necessary, the light on the next two nights would also be satisfactory.

To conceal themselves as far as possible, the paratroop formations were to reduce their lighting to a minimum, particularly over enemy territory. It was agreed in April that navigation lights would be turned off 10 miles from the British coast, downward recognition lights off at HOBOKEN, and formation lights dimmed at HOBOKEN until barely visible. They would be turned on again at the same points on the way back. After the homeward route was changed GALLUP replaced HOBOKEN as the place where recognition and formation lights would be turned on again. Flame dampeners were relied on to hide the light from the exhaust.[40]

Leigh-Mallory had suggested in March that smoke might be used to shield the troop carrier formations. A test held on 12 April indicated to at least one observer that laying sufficient smoke to protect large missions would take more effort than it was worth. However, at the wish of the airborne commanders plans were made to lay smoke for the relatively small glider missions to be flown at dawn on D-day. On 17 May the Ninth Fighter Command agreed to provide six A-20's at that time to blanket five miles of coast north of Cape Carteret for ten minutes. A strafing of enemy positions was to precede the smoke-laying.[41]

The employment of deception and diversionary operations in support of OVERLORD had been considered by Allied planners as early as 1943, but not until 14 April 1944 did 21 Army Group present the AEAF commanders with a definite plan. A force of Stirlings was to simulate paratroop drops in coastal areas north of the Seine at about the time of the first British airborne missions on the night of D minus 1. WINDOW would be used to give the effect of a large force of aircraft to enemy radar, and dummy paratroops, rifle fire simulators and pintail bombs would be dropped. It was later agreed that a few SAS troops* would be dropped to add realism. Meanwhile a dozen Stirlings were to screen the actual operations by jamming enemy warning radar all along the north coast of Normandy and six others would jam fighter control stations. While 38 Group was given control of the diversions, it had no planes to spare, so the necessary units were to be obtained from RAF Bomber Command.[42]

The American airborne commanders showed little interest in diversionary operations. However, by early May plans had been formulated to fly six Stirlings with the first paratroop mission. One would accompany the lead ship of each of the first six serials as far as HOBOKEN. Instead of turning there they would continue straight to the cost of Brittany, dropping WINDOW as they went to simulate a force of six troop carrier serials.

---

*Specialists dropped to perform demolitions or to work with Resistance forces.

Late in the month a decision was made to screen this operation by jamming enemy radar on the northwest corner of the Cotentin and in the Channel Islands. Accordingly, on 3 June, AEAF requested the 803d Special Squadron from the Eighth Air Force to do the jamming.[43]

Final coordination of all plans for radio countermeasures was supervised by an advisory group directly under the British Air Ministry. This was established by SHAEF on 15 May, too late for major changes of plan. However, the simulated British airborne missions were later integrated with naval feints at Cap d'Antifer and the Boulogne area to give the effect of a coordinated airborne and amphibious assault. Also, the Stirling feint in conjunction with the first American mission was altered. It was to turn left a few miles after passing HOBOKEN and head for the Coutances area in Normandy instead of Brittany. By thus closely paralleling the troop carrier route the feint was more likely to achieve deception and to distract the German garrison of Normandy. Responsibility for radio countermeasures during the critical 30 hours preceding H-hour was delegated by SHAEF to the Allied Naval Commander of the Expeditionary Force.[44]

In early May plans for air support of the American airborne missions called for preliminary bombing, halted at twilight on D minus 1 to avoid hampering the troop carriers by fire or heavy smoke along the route. The paratroop missions that night would be protected by 15 British night fighters attacking searchlights and gun positions, 6 patrolling the coast around the IP, and 8 acting as escort. Similar protection was to be given the dawn glider missions on D-day. In addition all the glider missions were to be given daylight escort on a ratio of one fighter group for every 50 gliders.

By the end of the month changes had been made. Night fighters were to provide cover for the paratroop missions over the Channel. In the interval between the pathfinder drop and the arrival of the main force in the first paratroop mission, bombers would attack points in the Cotentin to draw flak and searchlights, and the positions thus revealed would be attacked by a dozen night fighters. While the paratroop missions were over Normandy interceptors equipped with AI radar would patrol in relays of six between enemy airfields and the troop carrier route at altitudes of 5,000 to 8,000 feet, and two or three squadrons of intruders would orbit over the enemy airfields. All these tasks were to be performed by the RAF.

On 22 May VIII Fighter Command accepted responsibility for support of the first two glider missions, but when the route of those missions was changed at the end of May it was apparently released from that task. About the middle of May IX Fighter Command agreed to provide three fighter groups as close escort for the twilight glider mission on D-day and to support glider and resupply missions on D plus 1 on a similar basis.

Coordination of planning and control of air support for the airborne missions was in the hands of a Combined Control Center at Uxbridge to which AEAF had delegated control of all fighter operations in the initial phase of the invasion. Controllers from RAF 11 Group would direct the British, and IX Fighter Command would provide controllers for the Americans.[45]

The planners, vividly remembering how missions to Sicily had been thwarted by faulty navigation, were almost more afraid of that than of enemy guns. They saw to it that the troop carrier route was marked like an avenue as far as HOBOKEN, and they sought to provide as much guidance as possible from there to the zones.

The British Navy had promised to provide a 110-foot MT boat and a smaller craft to act as markers, one at GALLUP, the other at HOBOKEN. The boats were to keep in position by using a radar system called Gee.* Navigational aids in England and on the boats were to be set up and operated by IX Troop Carrier Command.

For visual guidance aerial lighthouses known as occults were to be put at 30-mile intervals from the 52d Wing's assembly point to Portland Bill, and the marker ships were to have green holophane lights. Eureka beacons would be placed at all wing assembly points, the head of the Severn estuary, ELKO, FLATBUSH, and the marker boats. This list includes all points outside enemy territory at which there would be a change of course. In addition a beacon known as the BUPS, would mark the English coast at FLATBUSH and the important over-water turn at HOBOKEN.[46]

To guide the missions across Normandy much reliance was placed on navigational aids to be set up on the zones by teams of pathfinder troops flown in half an hour ahead of the main serials.

*See below, p. 16.

The pathfinder planes were to locate the zones by conventional navigation assisted by Gee (PPF) and SCR-717C (PPI) radar.

Gee, which had been used successfully by RAF bombers in 1943, was a British radio system in which position was determined by triangulation. Navigators observed the sequences of pulses received from three stations and checked their results against a map on which the lattice lines marked the distribution of pulse patterns. Gee was effective to ranges of over 100 miles, ample for the Normandy missions. However, very precise interpolation was needed. Some experts held that errors of over 2,000 feet in range and 1,500 feet in deflection were to be expected, but troop carrier plans for NEPTUNE assumed a probable error of 400 yards. More anxiety was felt about Gee's vulnerability to jamming, which would be effective at distances up to 15 miles.

The SCR-717, an American product, was an airborne radar sender-receiver, which scanned the landscape with its beams. The reflected beams produced on the scope a crude outline map in which water seemed black, while land and shipping appeared lighter. It would thus provide a recognizable map of the Channel Islands and the Normandy coast.

The first installation of Gee on an American troop carrier aircraft was made in mid-January 1944. By the end of the month the command had decided to use it, and by 23 February the Ninth Air Force agreed to equip 108 troop carrier planes fully and 44 others partially with Gee. It is interesting that on 25 February General Williams, who had no experience with Gee in the Mediterranean but was full of confidence in Rebecca, offered to give up all or most of the Gee equipment if it were needed for bombing. This concession was not called for, and IX Troop Carrier Command got its quota of Gee sets.

On 8 January 1944 the command had requested samples of SCR-717, and on 4 February the War Department promised to give it 16 sets by the middle of March, including 5 which were already installed on planes of the 52d Wing. More were to be sent thereafter as they became available. However, because of production difficulties IX Troop Carrier Command had only 11 planes with this equipment on 9 April, and only about 50 sets arrived in time for use in the invasion. The first experimental installation of Gee in a C-47 having SCR-717 was made on 9 April. By fast work all or most of the other planes with SCR-717 had also been equipped with Gee before D-day. Even so, there were only enough such planes for the pathfinders and for one or two of the leaders in each serial.[47]

The aids to be set up by the pathfinder teams on the zones consisted of BUPS and Eureka beacons, lights, panels, and smoke.

The BUPS, a supplement to the SCR-717, was a responsor beacon designed to react to the beam of the SCR-717 as a Eureka beacon did to that of Rebecca. The blip produced by its response on the scope of a SCR-717 provided an orientation point from which a navigator could get his bearings and to some extent his range. Six BUPS beacons arrived in England in April and May. Tests made in England indicated that the BUPS could be dropped with pathfinder troops and used by them. Consequently, besides the two at FLATBUSH and HOBOKEN, arrangements were made to send in two with the pathfinders. One was to be set up on the most central zone (DZ C) and used throughout the paratroop jumps and the dawn glider missions as an orientation point for the entire drop and landing area. Another was to be used to guide resupply missions for the 82d Division.[48]

While the BUPS was regarded as an experiment, Rebecca-Eureka was heavily relied on to guide the approach of night missions. Eureka beacons were to be set up on every zone, and all aircraft employed by IX Troop Carrier Command were equipped with Rebecca. In February IX Troop Carrier Command had expected to have 650 Rebecca sets. A month later it was counting on 750. On 22 March word came from Washington that 200 more sets would be delivered by 1 May and 300 by 1 June. This pledge was fulfilled.

Though the supply of Rebecca was ample, its employment was restricted by technical considerations. Experts decided that simultaneous use of several hundred sets would cause failure through oversaturation. Therefore, its use in the airborne missions was to be limited to flight leaders, that is to about one pilot in nine in the paratroop formations. Even these were to turn off their sets between HOBOKEN and points 20 miles short of their zones and between the zones and points 30 miles out on the return trip. Stragglers and leaders of straggling elements were authorized to use Rebecca but only in emergency, presumably if they were lost or hopelessly separated from their serial.

Radar experts also feared that interference and confusion might arise among the Eurekas, since six closely grouped beacons were to be used in rapid succession. Transmitting and receiving channels for the Eurekas were carefully chosen to minimize the chance of interference, and their signals were coded so that if received by the Rebeccas of a serial for which they were not intended, they could be distinguished from those of the correct beacon. As a further precaution, each Eureka was to be turned on at a specified time, in most cases 15 minutes before planes were due at its zone, and turned off 20 minutes after the pathfinders considered that the drop or release on that zone was completed.

One weakness of the Rebecca-Eureka was a tendency of the transmitter pulse on the scope of the Rebecca to merge with the blip from the Eureka a mile or two before the beacon was reached, thus ending the instrument's effectiveness and causing premature drops and releases. For this reason the troop carriers in NEPTUNE were directed to determine their drop or release point not by Rebecca but by visual observation of lights, panels and smoke, set up to mark the zones.[49]

For night missions lights were to be used. They were to be set up on each zone in the shape of a T with the stem 30 yards long, parallel to the line of flight of approaching serials, and head 20 yards across. The pathfinders would place a Eureka 25 yards beyond the head of the T. Each T was to be lit by 5 specially designed holophane lights which shot narrow beams of light about 2 degrees above the horizon in the direction from which the planes would come. They were also visible from above through frosted panes in the top of each light. The lights on the three drop zones of the 101st Division were to be green, red, and amber respectively; so were those on the zones of the 82d Division; while all of the three glider landing zones were to have green lights. Both for security and to prevent confusion, the lights on a given zone were not to be turned on until six minutes before planes were due there and were to be turned off as soon as the drop or release on that zone was considered complete. The scheduling of the serials was such that there seemed hardly a chance that two T's of like color would be on at the same time for the paratroop missions. There was, however, a strong likelihood that green lights for different glider missions would be on simultaneously, since at dawn and dusk on D-day missions for both airborne divisions were to arrive in quick succession. This opportunity for error may have been discounted because it seemed settled that those missions would have some sunlight to assist them. As an additional means of identification, the lights on each drop or landing zone were to flash in code the letter identifying that zone.

For daylight missions, zones were to be marked by fluorescent panels 3 feet by 15 feet in size, arranged to form T's and identifying letters, and by colored smoke. Each zone would have its own color combination of panels and smoke.

Emergency resupply missions were to be called for by placing one long and one short panel in line pointing toward the desired zone. Such missions could also be requested by radio by an air support party through Ninth Air Force Headquarters at Uxbridge. No provision was made for direct radio contact between the airborne troops in Normandy and the planes engaged in follow-up missions. Moreover, to provide maximum security for the airborne and amphibious landings, complete radio silence was imposed from the start of the invasion until H-hour, which was ultimately set at 0630 on D-day.[50]

Thus stood the plans at the end of May, a carefully constructed and comprehensive structure. Flaws there might be, but until revealed by combat experience they were scarcely visible.

The Buildup

The preparations of IX Troop Carrier Command for OVERLORD were favorably affected by a strong transfusion of experienced officers into its headquarters and adversely affected by an influx of new and green personnel into its flying units.

The command expanded its staff from about 100 officers in January to over 150 by the middle of March. Most of the newcomers had served in the Mediterranean either with the 52d Troop Carrier Wing or on the staff of the XII Troop Carrier Command, which had been dissolved on 20 February, the cream of its officers being sent to England. About half of them went into the A-3 Section, which grew from 17 to 33 officers, and into Communications, which expanded from 13 to 21 officers.[51] Man for man, the experience of the contingent from the MTO in handling airborne missions was unparalleled in the AAF or, indeed, in any other air force with the possible exception of the German Luftwaffe. Naturally, the already strong influence of Mediterranean doctrine and methods on IX Troop Carrier Command became increasingly dominant.*

Most important of the personnel changes was the assumption of command on 25 February by General Williams, former chief of XII Troop Carrier Command, in place of General Giles. Lt. Col. James C. Pruitt, who had been Williams' Signal Officer in the MTO, had arrived ahead of him and had been installed as Communications Officer early in February. Within a week after taking command General Williams named a new A-1, Lt. Col. Owen G. Birtwistle, formerly with the 52d Wing, and a new Deputy Chief of Staff, Col. Peter S. Rask, who had held a corresponding post in XII Troop Carrier Command.

Col. Ralph E. Fisher, who joined the command in April and became A-3, was a comparative outsider, though favorably known to Williams. With Fisher in the A-3 Section were two veterans from the MTO, Col. Glynne M. Jones, former A-3 of XII Troop Carrier Command, and Lt. Col. John W. Oberdorf, who had also held that position for a time. Both played an active and influential role in planning the coming airborne operations. In close contact with them was Col. Ralph B. Bagby, former Chief of Staff of XII Troop Carrier Command. He had been assigned to Headquarters AEAF, put in their Operations Section, and given charge of their troop carrier planning.

Three major holdovers provided IX Troop Carrier Command with an element of continuity and a valuable knowledge of the administrative intricacies of the ETO. The Chief of Staff, Col. James E. Duke, Jr., had held his post since December 1943. The A-2, Lt. Col. Paul S. Zuckerman, and the A-4, Col. Robert M. Graham, had held theirs since October 1943 when the command was in its infancy.[52]

When Williams took command the field strength of IX Troop Carrier Command was growing fast. What had been little more than an advance party in 1943 was being built up to a point where it could undertake large-scale training in March 1944. In the first two months of the year the 436th, 437th, and 438th Troop Carrier Groups, part of the 439th, and Headquarters, 53d Troop Carrier Wing had come from the United States. In addition most of the air echelon of the 61st, 313th, 314th, and 316th Groups and Headquarters, 52d Wing, which commanded them, had flown up from the Mediterranean. By the end of March the rest of the 439th, the 440th, 441st and 442d Groups had arrived from the United States, and all of the 52d Wing and its four groups had come from the MTO, as had 47 planes and crews for the 315th Group. The command had attained its full complement of 13½ groups and 3 wing headquarters.

However, at that time it had on hand only about 760 crews and 845 aircraft. Its strength was built up to 1,076 qualified crews and 1,062 operational aircraft by the end of April, and raised to 1,116 qualified crews, and 1,207 operational aircraft at the end of May by flying in additional crews and planes from the United States. This action provided a sufficient force and reserve for all airborne missions to be undertaken by IX Troop Carrier Command in NEPTUNE. However, it should be remembered that of 924 crews which IX Troop Carrier Command was committed to send on missions before H-hour on D-day about 20 percent would have to be inexperienced filler personnel who had been overseas less than two months.[53]

The groups from the United States brought with them their T/O complement of 104 glider pilots apiece, so, although the 52d Wing was somewhat short of glider personnel when it arrived in the United Kingdom, IX Troop Carrier Command had pilots and co-pilots for 618 gliders by 31 March, not counting the glider pilots of the 442d Group, then en route from the United States. As it turned out, this was enough. However, had the large glider operations which First Army desired been approved and others tentatively arranged with the British been carried out, the supply of glider pilots would certainly have run low. In view of such a situation IX Troop Carrier Command had requested late in January that an additional 700 glider pilots be sent from the United States as replacements. Drastic steps were taken to step up the rate of advanced glider training and some pilots were diverted from other theaters with the result that 380 pilots reached the United Kingdom in late March and early April and 215 more

---

*However, policy was shaped by experts from all possible sources. For example, Lt. Col. M. C. Murphy, formerly director of the Advanced Tactical Glider School, was an active and helpful adviser in glider matters.

arrived in May, giving IX Troop Carrier Command enough for 951 gliders on the eve of OVERLORD.[54]

One potentially grave personnel shortage existed in IX Troop Carrier Command. With planes and combat crews more than a third overstrength, ground personnel had been left at T/O level. However, because the ground crews were mostly fresh and enthusiastic and materiel mostly new and in good condition, this situation, although it caused some anxiety, did not appreciably impede operations in OVERLORD.[55]

Of the planes themselves over three-quarters were less than a year old as of 1 June, and all were in fine condition. All old engines had been replaced, thus eliminating a prime cause of abortive sorties. During the winter, supply shortages had been frequent, but by late May, time, effort, and high priorities had given the troop carriers all the items they needed for their planes with one exception, self-sealing fuel tanks.

The command had asked in February for personnel armor and self-sealing tanks. Thanks in part to lend-lease assistance from the British they got armored seat-pads for their pilots and co-pilots, and flak helmets, armored vests and aprons for all crew members. Seat-pads and armored clothing were also procured for the pilots and co-pilots of the gliders. The request for self-sealing tanks was turned down; General Arnold, himself, ruled in February that they could not be spared for troop carrier use. Information in April that about 75 such tanks might be available roused IX Troop Carrier Command to new efforts to get at least enough to equip its pathfinders, but these attempts, too, were in vain.[56]

The troop carriers had plenty of gliders on hand before the end of April 1944, largely because provision for them had been made well in advance. Before the end of July 1943 General Arnold, who then believed that gliders would be a decisive factor in the assault, had ordered the shipment of 1,441 Waco gliders to the United Kingdom. About the same time the British, who expected to have some 1,600 Horsa gliders on hand by the spring of 1944, had pledged a minimum of 300 of them to the AAF. These quotas were later made even larger. By February 1944, 2,100 Waco gliders had been shipped to England.

On 31 May, after considerable attrition in training IX Troop Carrier Command had 1,118 operational Waco gliders and 301 operational Horsas.[57] However, before so many gliders had been made available delays in the assembly of the Wacos had threatened to upset the troop carrier training program. Except for the first shipment of Waco gliders, which had arrived unexpectedly in the United Kingdom in May 1943, Wacos were stored at Crookham Common about 40 miles southwest of London. Attempts to use the nearby base of Aldermaston for assembly proved unsatisfactory because of transportation difficulties, so Crookham came to be the center for assembly as well as storage of Waco gliders. While spacious and fairly well located, Crookham Common lacked facilities for efficient glider assembly and was so windswept that completed gliders were in constant danger of being wrecked.

During the summer of 1943 Eighth Air Force delegated the care and assembly of incoming gliders to untrained British civilian workers with the result that of the first 62 gliders they attempted to put together 51 were unflyable. In September the 26th Mobile Reclamation and Repair Squadron was given the assembly job. In October the IX Air Force Service Command took over the base and unit. Inexperienced, ill-equipped, and undermanned, the squadron managed to assembly about 200 gliders out of a quota of 600 before the end of 1943. It failed to speed up appreciably during the next three months and was set back by storms, which damaged over 100 completed gliders. On 26 March 1944 IX Troop Carrier Command, which even then had less than 300 usable Wacos, appealed to IX Air Force Service Command to raise glider output to 20 a day. The response was a promise to produce 30 a day. Many additional personnel, including an experienced engineer officer who was to reorganize assembly methods, were sent to Crookham Common. For its part the troop carrier command arranged to have the gliders flown away promptly after completion to prevent them from accumulating. Working a seven-day week, the men at Crookham assembled 910 Wacos in April, and the danger of a glider shortage vanished.[58]

During late April attention shifted to glider modification, including the installation of parachute arrestors, landing lights, glider-plane intercommunication sets, and especially the Griswold nose, a framework designed to protect the Waco and its contents in a crash-landing. On 29 April

IX Troop Carrier Command requested that the Griswold nose be installed in all of 500 Wacos still awaiting assembly at Crookham. Later it agreed to have production reduced to 10 gliders a day in order to get that modification done. In addition it sent out service teams to put the Griswold reinforcement on gliders at its own bases. By 27 May 288 Griswold noses had been installed. Two or three days later work at Crookham was halted and the mechanics there were sent to the troop carrier bases to help the overburdened glider mechanics in their final preparations.[59]

Although British lashings for Horsa cargoes arrived late, the only important Horsa equipment not received in time for the invasion was $15/16$-inch nylon tow ropes, of which 960 had been ordered from the United States on 10 February. Three months later none had arrived, and the troop carriers urgently requested that 100 sets be sent by air. Only a few incomplete sets arrived, and $11/16$-inch rope had to be used. Fortunately, it proved to be a satisfactory substitute.*

Late in April, inspections revealed decay around

---

*Unlike the Waco, which was towed by a single rope hitched to the nose, the Horsa had a Y-shaped tow rope with 350-foot stem and 75-foot arms hitched to either wing.

Figure 2. *Paratroop Officer Demonstrates Jump Position.*

the stern posts of many Horsas, and a crew of 100 civilians was hastily set to repairing them. Also during the late spring the Horsas were being modified so that their tails could be removed if the doors were jammed or blocked. By the end of May mechanics of IX Air Force Service Command had made this change on 257 of the Horsas in American possession.[60]

Deployment and Training

On 6 February SHAEF had directed IX Troop Carrier Command to prepare in conjunction with the airborne commanders an intensive training program to culminate early in May in exercises with an airborne division. The goal of the training was to enable the troop carriers to fly night paratroop missions to within a mile of an objective and to fly glider missions by twilight or moonlight to a given landing zone in formation and within a minute of schedule. By 26 February such a program had been worked out. It called for intensive joint training with airborne troops to begin on 15 March. Later the plan was revised

Figure 1. *Paratrooper Boarding a C-47.*

to meet General Williams' feeling that training should be made more realistic and that a larger proportion of the program should be devoted to exercises with American airborne units, since all scheduled missions were to be with them.[61]

Until 1944 it had been assumed that IX Troop Carrier Command would fly its missions from fields in the northeast of England. Its headquarters had been established at Grantham in Lincolnshire, and the bases it was to use in the invasion were grouped around that town. There its units could practice in relative security from enemy air raids and would not interfere with the bomber and fighter units so tightly packed in the southeast of the island.

However, preliminary studies had shown that glider missions would stand a much better chance if based near the south coast, because they would be less exposed to bad weather and nearer to their objectives. These points applied particularly to Horsa missions, since towing them taxed a C-47 to the limit. Accordingly arrangements were made in January to move a wing containing five groups to fields in southern England. Ramsbury and Welford Park were quickly obtained, and by 17 February authority had been given to take over the neighboring fields of Greenham Common, Membury, and Aldermaston. All five were excellent bases. They were located about 50 miles from the south coast and between 50 and 70 miles west of London. The 53d Troop Carrier Wing was picked to occupy them.

Up to the end of February 1944 IX Troop Carrier Command had no intention of seeking more

Figure 4. Jeep Emerging from Nose of Waco Glider.

than five southern fields. The decision to lift two American divisions and the requests of those divisions for glider missions produced a change. On 3 March General Williams announced at a meeting of Ninth Air Force commanders that if his command was to fly 400 gliders in the assault phase of OVERLORD, it would need five additional fields in southern England from which to launch them. Within a week the RAF had agreed to provide five fields in the southwest near Exeter, and on 16 March a meeting at AEAF Headquarters selected Exeter, Upottery, Merryfield, and Weston Zoyland for use by the American troop carriers as tenants of the RAF. The 50th Wing was designated to occupy them. No suitable fifth field was found, although several were proposed then and later.[62]

Throughout the training period, the 52d and 53d Wings were closely paired with the divisions they were to carry in NEPTUNE.* When the 53d moved to its southern bases it found its partner, the 101st Division already established close-by. Divisional headquarters was at Greenham Lodge, only a mile or so from wing headquarters at Greenham Common. The divisional commander, Maj. Gen. William C. Lee, one of the pioneers of airborne warfare, was incapacitated by illness in March. His place was taken by Brig. Gen. Maxwell D. Taylor, Divisional Artillery Commander of the 82d Division, an officer who had won much experience and a fine reputation in the Mediterranean. In mid-February the 82d Division had

Figure 3. Cockpit of a Waco Glider.

---

*The 50th Wing was able to work with the 82d Division until it moved south in April, but its southern fields had been acquired too late to make good arrangements for training there with the airborne.

moved from Northern Ireland to the Leicester area within easy commuting distance of the bases into which its partner, the 52d Wing, was then moving. Divisional headquarters was set up at Braunstone Park in Leicestershire. The 82d's commander was Maj. Gen. Matthew B. Ridgway, who had directed the 82d throughout its campaigns in the Mediterranean.

Both divisions were remodeled to provide the powerful paratroop punch expected of them in Normandy. The 101st had come overseas with one parachute regiment, the 502d. Now it had the 506th PIR assigned and the 501st PIR attached to it; it lost one of its two glider regiments, retaining the 327th.

The 82d Division had left one of its two parachute regiments in Italy. This unit, the 504th PIR, which had suffered severely at Anzio, did not reach the United Kingdom until May and was not ready for use in the invasion. However, as compensation, the 507th and 508th PIR's were attached to the division in January to supplement its veterans, the 505th PIR and the 325th Glider Infantry.[63] Thus the airborne divisions, as used in Normandy, were in effect quadrangular with three parachute and one glider regiment apiece.

The joint training program could not be uniform. It had to be adjusted to the missions and proficiencies of the various troop carrier units as well as to the training policies and geographic accessibility of the airborne troops. As a result each wing and to some extent each group of troop carriers received different training.

The 53d Wing had been selected to specialize in glider operations but would have to be ready for possible paratroop commitments. To aid its preparation for this dual role, it was given the only four groups in the command which were intact and fully operational at the end of February. Of these, the 434th and 435th Groups had already flown many paratroop and glider exercises in the United Kingdom. The 436th and 437th were well qualified for paratroop work but had had only rudimentary training with gliders. By 3 March these four groups had been assigned to the wing and moved to their tactical bases, Aldermaston, Welford Park, Membury, and Ramsbury. The 438th Group, which joined the Wing at Greenham Common on 16 March, was not operational until April.[64]

During early March the 53d Wing put its fliers through a series of paratroop exercises with simulated drops, and on the night of 12 March executed a successful drop of a parachute regiment. The wing made a spectacularly good drop on 23 March in the presence of Eisenhower, Brereton, and Churchill and a still better one on the night of 12 April. These performances won the confidence of IX Troop Carrier Command in spite of the fact that in a night exercise on 4 April heavy clouds with bases at 1,000 feet had caused three out of four serials of the 53d to abort and the other to disperse and to drop inaccurately. The wing ended its work with paratroops on 18 April, because its partner, the 101st Division, decided its troops had jumped enough.

All groups of the 53d Wing did some training with gliders during March, and the 434th and 437th Groups, which were picked to specialize in glider operations, reached the point where they could fly glider formations at night. After some experimentation the 437th concluded that the most satisfactory formation was the pair of pairs in echelon to the right. Glider training in the 53d Wing rose to such intensity during April that the wing logged 6,965 hours of glider towing that month. The effects of this work were shown in an exercise on 21 April when pilots, most of whom had towed a Horsa for the first time less than seven weeks before, released 241 out of 245 Horsas at their proper landing zones after a long flight. For the first three weeks of May the wing continued glider training with increasing emphasis on night formations and on landings at dawn in areas less than 400 yards in length. The final verdict of IX Troop Carrier Command was that it was fully qualified for its coming role.[65]

Between 11 February and 5 March almost all the air echelon of the 52d Wing, including the flying personnel of the 61st, 313th, 314th, and 316th Groups flew from Sicily to England via Marrakech and Gibraltar with a loss of only one out of 221 planes. The rear echelon arrived by boat on 18 March. The remnant of the 315th Group in England was assigned to the 52d Wing on 17 February. In March the 315th's two squadrons in North Africa returned to the ETO and the group also received 26 aircraft with experienced crews transferred from troop carrier units in the Mediterranean to bring it up to strength. These crews later were organized into two new squadrons. Attached to the 52d Wing in May for operations and training was the 442d Group, which had arrived from the United States between 26 and 29 March and had been assigned to the 50th Wing.

During the training phase the groups of the 52d Wing were concentrated within a 15-mile radius of Grantham, except for the 315th, which was at Spanhoe 22 miles away. Wing headquarters and the 316th Group were at Cottesmore, the 61st at Barkston Heath, the 313th at Folkingham, the 314th at Saltby and the 442d at Fulbeck. All bases were connected by good English roads and when completed had all necessary facilities including hard-surface runways in the 6,000-foot class. The notoriously bad spring weather of northern England often interfered with flying. However, enough time had been provided so that the training of all but the 315th and 442d Groups was completed with time to spare.

The quality of the 315th and 442d Groups was very different from that of the other four. The others had flown so much that there was a danger they would go stale. Their pilots had an average flying time of well over 1,500 hours when training began. Most of them had been overseas for more than ten months and had flown paratroop missions. The fliers of the 315th Group had equally impressive amounts of overseas and flying time, but its two original squadrons had been employed for ten months on routine transport work and never had had much training for airborne operations. Also, the group, having been built up from various sources, needed time to develop teamwork. The 442d was a very green unit. Activated in September 1943, it had had only one or two C-47's per squadron until December. Its training in the United States, hampered by winter weather, and curtailed to meet the schedule for OVERLORD, had included almost no night formation flying or dropping of paratroops.[66]

The 52d Wing had been selected to fly the paratroops of the 82d Division into Normandy. Since its bases were too far north to be suitable for glider missions, the wing concentrated on paratroop work. Nevertheless, it spent 4,207 hours in April and May towing gliders and demonstrated in a daylight glider exercise on 29 May that it could fly glider missions if necessary.

The 61st and 316th Groups were able to make actual drops of paratroop battalions on 18 March. The 313th and 314th Groups, hampered by construction at their fields, flew no exercises until April. By the end of that month all four were considered ready, although the 313th and 314th had done badly in three night drops.

Meanwhile the 315th and 442d had not begun training programs until 3 April, and had spent that month mostly in formation flying. They flew no exercises and dropped no troops until May. By then the American airborne divisions had almost wound up their jumping program and were not eager to risk accidents by further parachuting. Fortunately, the 82d Division had some men who had not completed their quota of jumps, and additional exercises were scheduled for the nights of the 5th and 7th of May. In the former both groups had loose formations and the 315th drifted off course. In the latter, flown in cloudy weather by the 315th, assembly, formation and drop were all unsatisfactory.

EAGLE, the command rehearsal on 11-12 May, had been intended as the final exercise of the training period, but IX Troop Carrier Command recognized that the 315th and 442d Groups needed more work and felt that the 314th had not yet proved itself in night operations. The performance of the three groups in EAGLE bore out this opinion. Accordingly the 314th was given another night paratroop exercise on 14/15 May, and the training periods of the 315th and 442d were extended to 26 May at which date they, too, made night paratroop drops on a token basis. The three exercises were so completely successful as to indicate that even the least experienced groups would be ready for NEPTUNE.[67]

Last of the troop carrier wings to enter intensive training was the 50th. During the winter it had been at Bottesford in command of the groups subsequently given to the 53d Wing. In their place it received the 439th Group on 25 February and the 440th and 441st Groups on 21 March.* None of these groups had been in existence for more than nine months. All had arrived from the United States within a few days of their assignment to the wing. The 439th was stationed at Balderton, the 440th at Bottesford, the 441st at Langar. The three fields were in the northern group and were all within about five miles of IX Troop Carrier Command headquarters at Grantham. Some formation flying was done in daytime during March, despite wintry weather, but the

---

*The 442d Group was also assigned to the 50th Wing but its training has been discussed in connection with the 52d Wing.

wing's training program did not really get under way until the beginning of April. At that time an inspector observed that all groups in the 50th lacked practice in night formation flying and that most of the navigators were inexperienced and ignorant of all radar aids, even Rebecca.[68]

During April each of the groups had a different program. The 439th specialized in glider towing and became skillful enough to fly night formations with gliders. It carried out four glider exercises by daylight with good results. In its only paratroop exercise everything went wrong, and the drop was far from the DZ. The 440th flew one successful daytime glider exercise, and executed four paratroop drops, the last three of which were very good. The 441st Group, which had dropped paratroops only twice in its short life, carried none in April. It concentrated on day formation flying until the tenth and on night formations thereafter but did make a very accurate resupply drop on the afternoon of the 21st.

During the last week of April the 50th moved to southwest England. Wing headquarters and the 440th Group went to Exeter, the 439th to Upottery about 15 miles northeast of Exeter, and the 441st to Merryfield some ten miles northeast of Upottery. All were fine large bases with long hard-surface runways. Although some construction was still going on at all three fields, they were ready for use.

During early May the 50th Wing carried on intensive training, including two simulated wing paratroop drops at night. No troops were actually dropped, because the 101st Division had finished its jump training except for EAGLE and was averse to doing more. Although the wing did well in EAGLE, it was considered to be in need of further practice. Since there were no paratroops to drop, it flew four more night exercises with simulated drops between 18 and 29 May. These were carefully designed to resemble actual operations, and lights were flashed to indicate when the jump signal would have been given. The results were good. Besides these exercises a heavy schedule of other flying training was continued until the 29th of May. By then the 50th Wing, too, was rated as ready for action.[69]

Besides the three wings, another organization, the Command Pathfinder School, was engaged in an even more exacting training program. The development of a separate pathfinder organization seems to have been a gradual process. The success of RAF bombers led by Gee-equipped pathfinders inspired the command to begin training navigators at Bottesford in the use of Gee about the end of January. The school had one radar officer, a second lieutenant, and four instructors with one Gee ground trainer, three Gee ground sets, and two Gee-equipped aircraft. Early in February the arrival of five planes from the MTO equipped with SCR-717C made it possible to begin training with that instrument. By 12 February IX Troop Carrier Command had decided to include both Gee and SCR-717 training in one Command Pathfinder School.

To secure more room and better facilities the school was moved to Cottesmore. On 26 February Lt. Col. Joel L. Crouch, who had planned and led pathfinder operations in Italy, was named as Commandant (one of General Williams' first appointments in IX Troop Carrier Command), and on the 28th the school officially opened. Cottesmore, which also housed the 316th Group and 52d Wing headquarters, proved to be too congested, so on 22 March the pathfinders were moved to North Witham, about ten miles south of Grantham.[70]

Early plans for large-scale radar training had to be whittled down for lack of equipment and instructors. Aircraft with SCR-717 already installed trickled in one by one from the United States. Men trained to use or repair the SCR-717 were scarce and tools with which to repair it were scarcer.* Although Gee was more plentiful, and the RAF had provided instructors and mechanics to help the Americans get started, test equipment and parts for it were hard to get. Consequently the first class had to be limited to 24 crews, 3 from each of the 8 troop carrier groups then in England. A few more were included after the course started. These were to be trained intensively for 60 days. If time and facilities permitted, another class would be trained later in the spring. Whole crews were enrolled on the grounds that much better results could be attained by a team working together than by a trained navigator whose comrades were ignorant and perhaps skeptical of his new techniques.

---

*The first shipment of materiel for installation of SCR-717 did not arrive in England until 18 May, and 18 trained radar officers requested by IX Troop Carrier Command in March did not arrive until 28 May. (Journal, IX TCC Comm Off, 18, 28 May 44 in 546.901A; Rpt, IX TCC Comm Off, 20 May 44, in 546.116.)

By the end of March the students had completed ground training and had an average of 60 hours flight instruction and practice with the new instruments. Most of them were deemed skillful enough to graduate from basic instruction and to concentrate on perfecting their technique in practice missions. Therefore on 6 April, 24 more crews were called in for training. Since this expansion required additional equipment, IX Troop Carrier Command decided to allot the pathfinders 52 aircraft, including the 11 equipped with SCR-717 which were then on hand and all of the same type subsequently received by the command. The rest of the 52 planes were to be equipped with Gee and, after the successful installation of a Gee set in a plane with SCR-717, all aircraft so equipped were also provided with Gee.

As early as 18 March pathfinder planes had participated in exercises and dropped paratroops with Eureka beacons and visual aids. However, in several early exercises the Rebeccas in the troop carrier aircraft were ineffective because they were badly tuned or even set for the wrong channel. The pathfinder school requested and was given the responsibility for designating channels and for the tuning of Rebecca-Eureka equipment. With precise tuning this radar improved remarkably thereafter in reliability and in range. Some poor performances had occurred because the paratroop pathfinder teams dropped to operate the Eurekas had only limited knowledge of their instruments and were ignorant of troop carrier plans and procedure. Therefore 300 pathfinder personnel from the American airborne divisions were sent to North Witham to study and work with the troop carrier pathfinders. This also produced dividends in greater efficiency and better teamwork.

By 10 May the second batch of crews had completed their basic training, and 14 fully trained crews were returned to the groups to lead serials in EAGLE. Lack of coordination in EAGLE between those 14 crews and the serials they were supposed to lead resulted in a decision to keep at North Witham only 24 crews for further training and return the rest to the groups to get practice as leaders. The aircraft of the 28 crews which were returned had to fly to North Witham every three days for servicing and current radar data, but the move was probably a wise one. Reintegrated into their groups, and usually with group commanders or executive officers as pilots, most of these ex-pathfinders did well in NEPTUNE.

By D-day, all navigators at the pathfinder school had operated Gee for at least 25 hours and were considered qualified operators. Most had had from 15 to 45 hours training with the SCR-717C and could easily identify the image of a coastline on its scope. However, using the SCR-717 to orient oneself over inland areas was much more difficult and few if any were prepared to do this with assurance.[71]

The command exercise, EAGLE, deserves attention both as the nearest thing to a true rehearsal held for any American airborne operation in World War II, and as a test to determine whether IX Troop Carrier Command could carry out its controversial and perilous role in NEPTUNE. EAGLE was originally an exercise of the 50th and 53d Wings with the 101st Division, but late in April after the 82d Division paratroop mission was moved up to follow immediately after that of the 101st, the exercise was revised to include the 52d Wing and the 82d Division and to correspond as closely as possible to the whole sequence of pre-H-hour airborne missions as then planned. It was also postponed from the 7th to the 11th and 12th of May so that all units would be ready to participate.

The main route to be flown ran from March, the 52d Wing assembly point, westward for 159 miles to Cefn Llechid in Wales, then south for 50 miles to a marker boat in the Bristol Channel, and east for 55 miles to Devizes, which was the IP. Eurekas and beacon lights were spaced at intervals along the way, including all assembly points and turns. In addition BUPS beacons were provided on the marker boat and at Devizes. Drop zones were to be marked by pathfinder troops essentially as they would be in the invasion. Simulated glider landing zones in the tactical area were to be marked by T's, but after some debate, it had been settled that the gliders would simply be towed over these zones and land in comparable areas marked out on airfields, thus avoiding possible crashes and recovery problems.

The rehearsal began on the night of 11 May with the take-off of seven pathfinder serials from North Witham half an hour ahead of the main serials. Four pathfinder serials got excellent results; two did well; one lost its way in a haze, which in places limited the visibility to three miles. When it did reach its zone it was so late that the troops it carried were unable to get their equipment into action in time to direct the 315th Group, which was the first scheduled to drop there.

After the pathfinders came 19 paratroop serials spaced at 6-minute intervals. The parachute echelon of the 101st Division was flown by 432 aircraft in 10 serials, half from the 53d Group and half from the 50th. The first jump was to take place at 0033. The serials of the 53d Wing were uniformly successful. Those of the 50th also did creditably, except that one flight from the 440th Group fell out of formation, missed its drop zone in the haze and returned without making a drop.

The paratroops of the 82d Division were carried by 369 planes of the 52d Wing in nine serials. Unlike the 101st Division which, having prepared the operation long in advance, sent over 6,000 jumpers, the 82d was able to provide only token loads of two jumpers per plane. One serial, that of the 442d Group, broke up on the way. Only 16 of its 45 aircraft got to the vicinity of the drop zone and dropped troops. The rest, lost in the haze, returned to base on orders from group headquarters and tried again at dawn. The Eurekas and lights on the zone were off at the time and the 442d, baffled, dropped its paratroops 10 miles away. The other serials reached the drop area approximately on course and on schedule, and six did well. However, the aids on the zones of the 314th and 315th Groups were not on when they arrived. Most of the 314th made a second pass, saw the T, which by then had been lighted, and dropped troops on it. However, nine pilots had given up and gone home, and another nine made drops by guesswork far from the zone. The 315th Group, although it finally received some signals, was too disoriented to make use of them and returned without making any drop.

Only two glider serials were flown in EAGLE. They were spaced 10 minutes apart from head to head and consisted of 52 planes each from the 434th and 437th Groups, towing a mixture of Wacos and Horsas. The first glider was to be released at 0529, ten minutes before civil twilight.* Seven pilots of the 434th lost their way in the dark, but the 437th released all but one of its gliders at the proper point. The landings were considered good.

---

*Civil twilight begins in the morning when there is enough sunlight to see by. The sun is then about 6 degrees below the horizon.

The effect of EAGLE was to induce a mood of optimism as far as troop carrier capabilities were concerned. Williams, who had already declared that, barring unexpectedly heavy flak or failure by the pathfinders, 90-100 percent of the paratroops in IX Troop Carrier Command's Normandy missions would land in the correct area, was confirmed in his opinion. Even Leigh-Mallory stated that he was highly impressed.[72]

Since in general the experienced groups had done very well, and the only serious failures were by the inexperienced 315th and 442d Groups, the lesson seemed to be that further training of the weak sisters was the only thing needed to insure good performance, at least as far as the paratroop operations were concerned. (The attitude toward the initial glider missions remained a mixture of opposition and fatalistic resignation.) This optimism was related to neglect of a major variable in the situation, namely the weather. Time and time again in big and little exercises during the past two months, and in several previous missions, wind and low visibility, particularly at night, had scattered troop carrier formations, twisted them off course or spoiled their drops. Yet the halcyon weather in EAGLE seems to have pushed all this into the background. The field orders for EAGLE had contained full and specific precautions against bad weather. Those for NEPTUNE were to be notably lacking in such precautions. Even the requirements of security and the need to send in the NEPTUNE missions under almost any conditions cannot fully explain this neglect.

Final Preparations

Final troop carrier preparations began with the completion by IX Troop Carrier Command of Field Order 1, NEPTUNE-BIGOT, at 1500 on 31 May. Although as yet few knew it, D-day had been set for 5 June, and the first planes were to be on their way over the Channel before midnight on the 4th. The 52d Wing at Cottesmore was so close it could pick up the orders almost immediately and have its own order out next day. Copies for the 50th and 53d Wings were flown to them, those for the 53d arriving at Greenham Common about 2300 on the 31st. Working continuously the staff of the 53d Wing issued the first part of its order at 0800 on 1 June. The 50th Wing issued its field order at 0800 on 2 June. By 1400 that afternoon the 53d had the last annexes to its order ready for distribution. Group field orders, being hardly more than extracted copies of the command and wing orders, came out almost immediately after the wing orders. Some groups relied on wing orders and issued none of their own.

The troop carrier command had obtained ample supplies of maps from First Army and distributed them to the wings. The maps of Normandy were on a scale of 1:50,000, those of the troop carrier routes and objective areas on a scale of 1:25,000. One innovation was the addition of 1:25,000 photographic maps of routes and zones as they would appear at night.

The wings received photographs from IX Troop Carrier Command at about the same time as the field orders. Coverage included run-in strips, obliques of landfall areas, and mosaics of drop zones and landing zones. These were identical with the photographs used by the airborne units. An agreement had been reached in March to consolidate airborne and troop carrier requests for photographic reconnaissance and to have photographs and overlays standardized so that they could be used interchangeably by both parties.

On 29 April, just after completion of the Tactical Air Plan, IX Troop Carrier Command had arranged to have experts from Ninth Air Force make terrain models of run-in and objective areas on a scale of 1:25,000 and of some particularly important places on a scale of 1:5,000. They had begun work on 4 May. Changes in plans after 26 May had required additional models, particularly for the new zones of the 82d Division, but by 1500 on 3 June all models were ready, and copies were on their way to the wings, which in turn loaned them out to their groups for briefing purposes.[73]

Except that one officer representative from each wing had participated in planning since about the beginning of March, IX Troop Carrier Command had carefully restricted information on its impending missions to a small group of specially cleared officers on its own staff. A high-level briefing of troop carrier officers was scheduled for 20 May but was postponed, and during the last five days of the month the unsettled state of planning made briefing impossible. On the 31st Leigh-Mallory announced that high-level briefing could begin and Williams called a meeting for the next day. This was held at Northolt in the briefing room of Advance Troop Carrier Headquarters and was attended by wing and group commanders plus four or five key staff officers from each wing and two or three, usually the S-2, S-3, and Communications Officer, from each group. The briefing was thorough, possibly too much so, since there were no less than a dozen speakers including Williams, Brereton, Ridgway, a British representative, a naval representative, and various other experts.

After returning from Northolt the group commanders of the 50th Wing held briefings for additional members of their staffs and for squadron commanders, S-2's and S-3's on 2 June. With minor differences most other groups appear to have done likewise.

Formal briefing of flying personnel was done on a group basis, although additional briefing was done by squadrons. Each group had its own schedule and procedure. Some began briefing on 3 June, some on the 4th, and some, learning that operations had been postponed 24 hours, set back their schedules accordingly and began briefing on the 5th.

When a single group was sending out 90 planes and some 400 men it was obviously undesirable to brief all its crews at once. In general, groups sending two serials briefed each separately, and the pilots, co-pilots and navigators of a serial were usually briefed separately from the radiomen and crew chiefs, who were given only limited and special information. Many of the pilots' briefings were addressed by airborne officers and attended by jumpmasters of the units they were to carry. To avoid unduly long meetings some groups split their data and saved part of it for later sessions. On the evening of D minus 1 final briefings were held from which in most cases the crews went directly to their planes. Not until those last meetings was the time of the mission announced. The briefings were generally rated as very good and the information in them thorough and accurate, as might be expected considering the unparalleled time and effort devoted to collecting it. During the last two or three days General Williams flew from group to group giving short talks to staff members and flight leaders. These, however, were "pep talks" rather than briefings.[74]

Between 28 May and 1 June the airborne divisions had moved onto the airfields from which they were to be flown. There they bivouacked in the most isolated spots available behind heavily guarded barbed wire. The service troops keeping house for them were also isolated. On the arrival of the airborne units the troop carrier men were restricted, and so were the large numbers of British civilians living in the base areas. Current business provided pretexts for a surprising number of special passes, but the movement of military and civilian gossips and possible spies was successfully halted. Before briefing began, the bases were sealed to almost all personnel. Personal phone calls were prohibited, and all calls were monitored; pay phones were discontinued, and personal mail was put in special bags and stored until after D-day. All briefed personnel were segregated in special quarters under officer guards who escorted them even on trips to the latrine. Wing and group war rooms were also put under 24-hour guard, and so were the marshalling areas during the servicing and loading before take-off.

The need for strict security in connection with airborne missions had always been recognized, but these measures were the strictest yet imposed. The fact that restrictions had been ordered during EAGLE and on several other occasions kept the uninitiated from realizing that something unusual was going on. Those who knew what was planned could not talk to those who did not, and many men at the bases learned with surprise after the planes were in the air that the long-awaited invasion had begun. While some surmised what was coming, they were unable to verify their surmises or to disseminate them outside the bases.[75]

English weather, famed for its unpredictability, nearly upset the entire invasion. Transports were at sea, the troop carrier bases had been sealed and the crews and their airborne passengers were being briefed when the high command found itself faced with the agonizing necessity of postponing NEPTUNE perhaps indefinitely.

The SHAEF weather forecast on 3 June for the 5th, which was to be D-day, was unexpectedly bad. It predicted winds of 17 to 22 knots, thick clouds below 500 feet and a four-foot surf on the Normandy beaches. Such winds were too high for paratroop drops. The low visibility would make the towing and landing of gliders next to impossible. Even amphibious landings would be hazardous in the high surf. Two anxious meetings by the principal Allied commanders ended with Eisenhower deciding to wait six hours for a new forecast. This was worse than the last, and about 0415 on the 4th he ordered the invasion postponed for 24 hours.

At 2115 on the 4th the commanders met again and were told that a sudden shift in the weather pattern gave promise of an interval of relatively good weather for the next two days. Beyond that the outlook was dubious. There remained a certainty of heavy surf, and a likelihood of high winds and low clouds. However, waiting another day was more likely to forfeit what opportunity there was than to gain better conditions, while further postponement was an appalling prospect because the next date suitable for the amphibious operations would be the 19th, which fell at a phase of the moon unsuitable for airborne missions. Moreover, the problems involved in keeping the force in readiness for two weeks more and still maintaining secrecy were staggering. It seemed better to gamble on the 6th. "I don't like it," said Eisenhower, "but I don't see how we can possibly do anything else." Leigh-Mallory liked it even less. Stormy weather and low visibility could play hob with all the missions assigned the AEAF. However, he conceded that given the expected lull, air support could be provided and airborne missions would be practicable. Thus the invasion was set to take place on 6 June unless some new and extraordinary difficulty arose. The paratroops, its advance guard, would set out on the night of the 5th.

Deception and Diversion

In return for the trouble it gave them, the weather rewarded the Allies a hundredfold by giving them an extraordinary opportunity for tactical surprise. Since the Germans had no outposts in the Atlantic to report the coming lull, they believed that storm conditions would shield them from invasion for several days. Consequently they were caught with their patrol boats in harbor and their reconnaissance planes on the ground.[76] The only means by which they could know of the approaching armadas was by radar.* Along the invasion coast they had warning stations at average intervals of approximately ten miles. The best of these had a maximum range of 150 miles at high altitudes and could pick up low-flying aircraft

---
*They did intercept BBC messages alerting the French resistance, but Rommel's army group staff, which was responsible for the defense of Normandy did not take them seriously and apparently did nothing to alert its subordinates.

at a distance of 30 to 35 miles. In the normal course of things the operators would discover the troop carriers at least half an hour before they reached their objectives.

Beginning on 10 May, the AEAF, occasionally assisted by Eighth Air Force and Bomber Command, RAF, had conducted a bombing campaign to knock out these radar stations. They were hard to hit, and the effort devoted to them was limited by other and heavy commitments and by a rule that, to preserve security, two stations outside Normandy would be hit for every one inside it. On the other hand the stations were only moderately defended and scantily camouflaged, and none of the long-range sets were mobile. By D minus 1 the system had been hammered until, according to subsequent Allied estimates, it was no more than 18 percent operative and few, if any, sets were functioning between Le Havre and Barfleur. In addition, the headquarters of German signal intelligence in northwest France had been bombed out on the night of D minus 3.

Against the punch-drunk remnant of the German warning system the Allies employed a three-point program of countermeasures, jamming of warning and night fighter radar in the invasion area, simulation of an invasion north of the Seine, and simulated paratroop drops just far enough from the American and British drop areas to confuse the enemy as to the true location of his airborne assailants. In these operations 105 planes, mostly RAF bombers, were employed and three were lost.

Despite bombing and jamming, German radar apparently caught brief, ambiguous glimpses of mine-sweepers off the cost and troop carrier formations off Cherbourg, but was unable to see enough to recognize their full significance. Some troops may have been alerted as a result, but no general alarm was given until a majority of the airborne troops had landed.

The fake invasion consisted of a few ships and planes using WINDOW and other devices to simulate two large convoys headed respectively for the Le Havre and Boulogne areas and troop carrier serials making a drop a few miles from Le Havre. The airborne and seaborne feints at Le Havre, though well executed, had little effect, but that at Boulogne drew a violent reaction. The Germans opened up with searchlights and guns on the supposed convoy and between 0100 and 0400 sent 24 night fighters against a patrol of 29 WINDOW-dropping bombers which was simulating air cover for the convoy. Thus at the very time when they might have been slashing at the troop carrier columns over Normandy, most of the Nazis' small stock of night fighters in northwest France were chasing will o' the wisps off the mouth of the Somme.

The influence of these threats of invasion between the Seine and the Straits of Dover in helping convince the German high command that the main Allied effort was going there rather than to Normandy was probably of substantial strategic value in delaying the movement of German reserves into Normandy. It did not, however, affect the German forces already in the vicinity of the American airborne objectives.

It is very doubtful whether the simulated mission near Coutances designed to divert the enemy from the true American drop area had much effect. During the night, reports were received of landings in that area, but the Germans apparently reserved judgment on them pending reports of actual fighting. Postwar German assertions that their signal intelligence distinguished the true drops from the false by the presence or absence of radio activity seem questionable because for various reasons there was scarcely any radio activity that night in the genuine drop areas.

Seventh Army, which commanded the German forces in Normandy, had a rough idea of the situation by 0220, an hour and half after the main American drops began. Before 0300 it had identified the Caen area and the eastern Cotentin as areas of concentration. By 0340 its chief of staff was convinced that a major operation involving those sectors was in progress, and by 0500 he had recognized that Ste Mère Eglise was the focal point in the American drop area and had guessed that the Allies meant to cut the narrow base of the Cotentin.

What prevented Seventh Army for several hours from identifying the precise objectives of the American airborne missions was the accidental dispersion of the troops, who, as will be seen, had been spread over a 20-mile strip of the eastern Cotentin between Carentan and Valognes with some elements even more scattered. In the darkness even units in contact with them could only guess at their strength and distribution. Such information as was obtained filtered in slowly to

German higher headquarters, since paratroops were cutting wires and blocking roads at scores of places, and the French resistance forces were doing likewise all over Normandy. An extraordinary demonstration of the blindfold thus imposed on the Germans is the fact that as late as 1720 on D-day Seventh Army headquarters was still ignorant of the amphibious landings on UTAH Beach, which had begun 13 hours before, and supposed that in the Cotentin it had only airborne troops to deal with.[77]

In summary, aside from the diversion of German night fighters, Allied efforts at deception had at most a slight effect on German opposition to the American airborne missions and, despite all attempts at secrecy, the Germans had some inkling of the impending invasion before midnight on D minus 1. However, it was too little, and too late for them to redeploy or even to issue a general alert before fighting began. They learned the general location of the assaults very quickly after that, but communication difficulties and the accidental dispersion of the paratroops prevented Seventh Army for four hours from making a precise estimate of their positions and objectives. Indeed, all through D-day German headquarters outside the invasion area had very little idea of what was going on inside it.

---★---

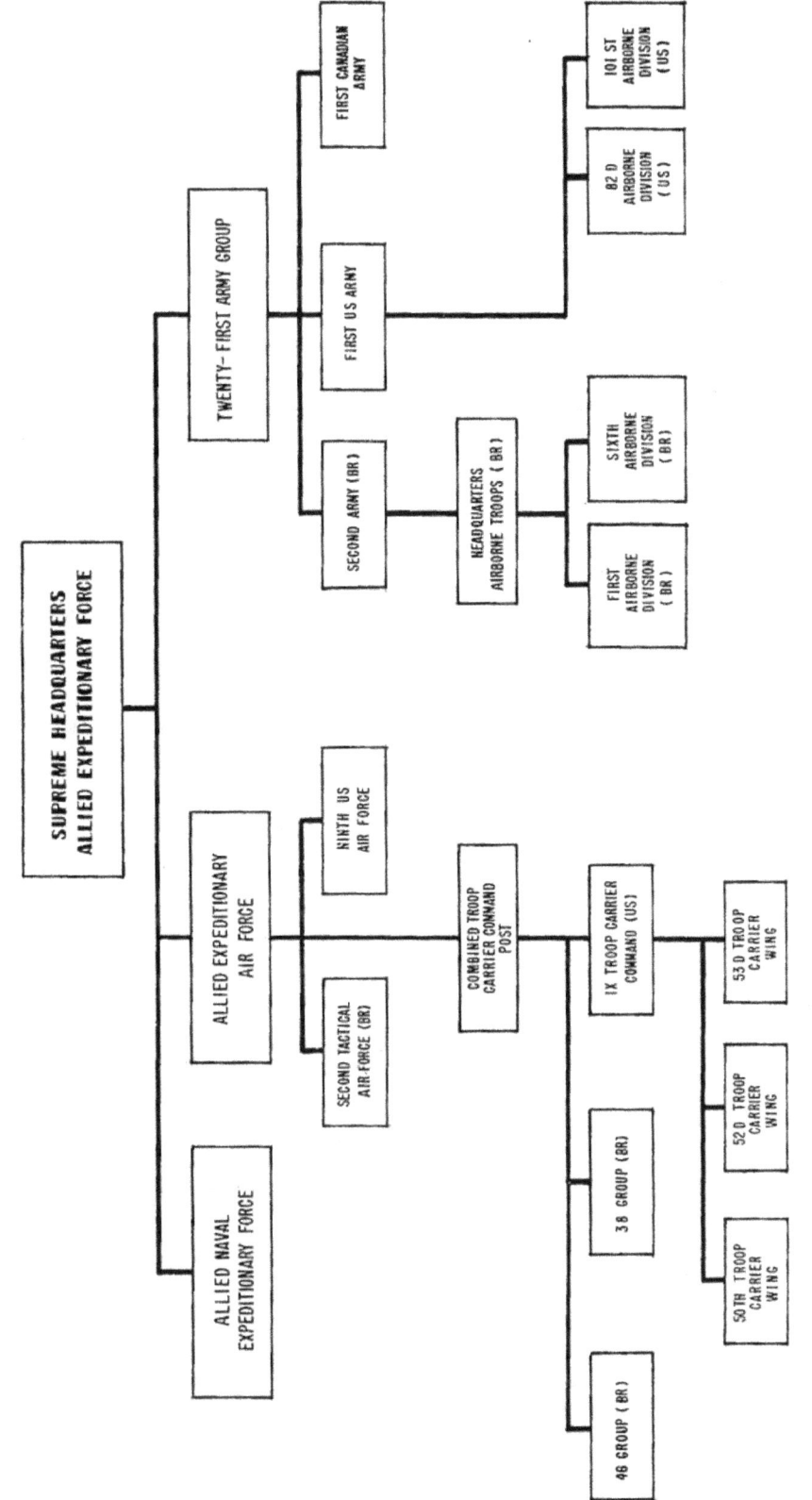

Chart 1

CHAPTER II

The Assault*

The Pathfinders

THE PATHFINDER force which was to blaze a way for the airborne missions of IX Troop Carrier Command consisted of 6 three-plane serials, one for each of the 6 drop zones, and another serial of 2 aircraft added in accordance with a late decision. The troops carried by this serial were to jump on Drop Zone C, move about a quarter-mile west and set up aids for the 101st Division's first glider mission. Each plane carried panels, holophane lights, two Eureka beacons, and a team of pathfinder troops averaging 13 in number. In addition the pathfinders brought the two BUPS beacons.

The pathfinder drops in the 101st Division area were to begin at 0020 and those for the 82d Division at 0121, Double British Summer Time, which was the time used throughout the operation. Mass drops by the respective divisions were to begin half an hour after their first pathfinders landed. It was estimated that at least one team from each serial would be in operation on its zone in time to guide them.

The first pathfinder serial for the 101st Division took off from North Witham shortly before 2200 with Colonel Crouch flying the lead plane. It crossed Portland Bill slightly ahead of scheduled time of 2324. Twilight still glimmered in the western sky as the planes crossed the English coast.

The expert pathfinder pilots and navigators had no trouble reaching Normandy. They crossed the Channel in good formation "on the deck," risking collision with Allied shipping, in order to conceal themselves from German warning radar. A favoring wind brought them to HOBOKEN about five minutes ahead of schedule. After turning there, they relied on the outline of the coast and islands displayed on the scope of the SCR-717 to guide them safely between the antiaircraft guns of Alderney and Guernsey and to show them the proper points at which to make landfall. In this they were successful, although radar maps prepared to help them interpret the SCR-717 had not arrived in time to be used. After reaching Normandy the fliers relied on Gee and dead reckoning, supplemented to the limited extent feasible by SCR-717 and visual recognition of the terrain.

The pathfinders for the 101st Division had been given a special course in order to facilitate their use of Gee. After passing Jersey they were to swing south of the main route, make a 90 degree turn to the left five miles offshore and fly east-northeast to points 2 or 3 miles south of Montebourg. There they would strike the Gee Chart lattice lines which passed through their respective drop zones, and make a 90 degree turn to the right to run down the lines to the zones.

On approaching the Continent the pathfinders found their navigation impeded by a layer of clouds which extended from the western shores of the Cotentin almost to the drop area. Sporadic German fire, mostly from small arms, damaged eight planes slightly but had no serious effect. Planners had feared that the Germans might jam the Gee sets, but interference was negligible.*

The lead serial navigated by Gee from landfall to destination, although it did get a visual check at the final turn. At 0016 the jump signal was given. The troops came down about a mile northeast of

---

*For route and assault area orientation in this chapter refer respectively to Map No. 1, p. 13, and Map No. 2, p. 34, and Map No. 3, p. 37.

*To prevent jamming, new bands had been chosen at the last moment and each Gee set was put on a different frequency.

the objective, Drop Zone A, northernmost zone of the 101st Division. Unable to reach DZ A in time, they set up their navigational aids near the village of St. Germain-de-Varreville.

In the first serial for DZ C, the 101st Division's center drop zone, one plane was ditched with engine trouble before reaching Normandy. All aboard were rescued, the first of many to be picked up that day. The other two aircraft in the serial made their drop at 0025, having depended on Gee entirely except for some visual checks at the turn and a glimpse of Ste Mère Eglise by one crew. One stick of troops hit close to the zone and the other about half a mile southeast of it. The pathfinder equipment was put up on the zone, but about a quarter-mile southeast of its planned position.

The second serial to DZ C overshot the final turn but dropped its troops at 0027 between one and two miles south of the zone. However, the equipment brought by that serial was not to be used until dawn—for the glider missions—so the pathfinder troops had plenty of time to move into position.

The serial which was headed for DZ D, the third and southernmost of the 101st Division zones, misjudged its position because the Gee in the lead aircraft had not been properly set, failed to recognize its final turning point, and ran out over the east coast before discovering its mistake. It made a sweeping circle to the right and approached the DZ from the southeast over the Carentan estuary. The drop, believed to be accurate, was made at 0045; the troops actually landed about a mile from the zone.

The three pathfinder serials scheduled for the drop zones of the 82d Division were to go straight from PEORIA to their zones, just as the main paratroop serials of the division were to do. This course cut diagonally across the lattice lines of the Gee charts, a satisfactory if not ideal arrangement. An approach down the lattice lines was not feasible for them, since it would have required passing close to German antiaircraft concentrations.

The pathfinder serial bound for DZ O, the zone outside Ste Mère Eglise, attempted to cross the Cotentin on Gee but swerved north, passed close to Valognes and made its final run parallel to the lattice lines. It was fired on but surprise and the cloudy weather saved it from serious damage. At 1115, six minutes ahead of schedule, it dropped its teams on the basis of Gee indications supplemented by a visual check. All troops landed on or close to the zone.

Of the two DZ's on the west side of the Merderet, the northernmost was called DZ T, the southern one DZ N. The three planes bound for DZ N made their approach according to plan at 0138 and had a good look at the DZ area. Their navigators were sure the drop had been accurate, but the troops landed over a mile southeast of the zone.

The pathfinder serial for DZ T made landfall appreciably north of PEORIA, but made accurate use of Gee, sighted some landmarks near the zone, and dropped its team with precision. Unlike the other serials it had come in considerably above the prescribed altitude of 600 feet.

The fact that most of the pathfinder pilots who supposed they had pinpointed their DZ's with Gee had actually missed them by over a mile was attributed by an AEAF radar expert to the navigators' relatively limited experience with Gee and to the combat conditions under which they worked. He thought the normal margin of error in such cases would be about three times as great as under favorable conditions. However, other factors besides Gee should be considered. Difficulty in allowing for the brisk northwest wind probably contributed to the deflection of some teams, and slight delays in jumping might account for an apparent tendency to overshoot.

At any rate, though only two serials achieved the degree of accuracy prescribed in the directives, all teams were put near enough their zones to perform their missions in spite of cloudy weather which might easily have caused the pilots to lose their way completely had they not had Gee to help them.[1]

ALBANY Mission and The Paratroop Operations of The 101st Division

Half an hour after the first pathfinders jumped, the main paratroop drops began. These were ALBANY, a mission by 432 aircraft carrying troops of the 101st Division, and BOSTON, a 369-plane mission for the 82d Division. The missions were divided into serials, most of which contained 36 or 45 planes. In 1943 it would have

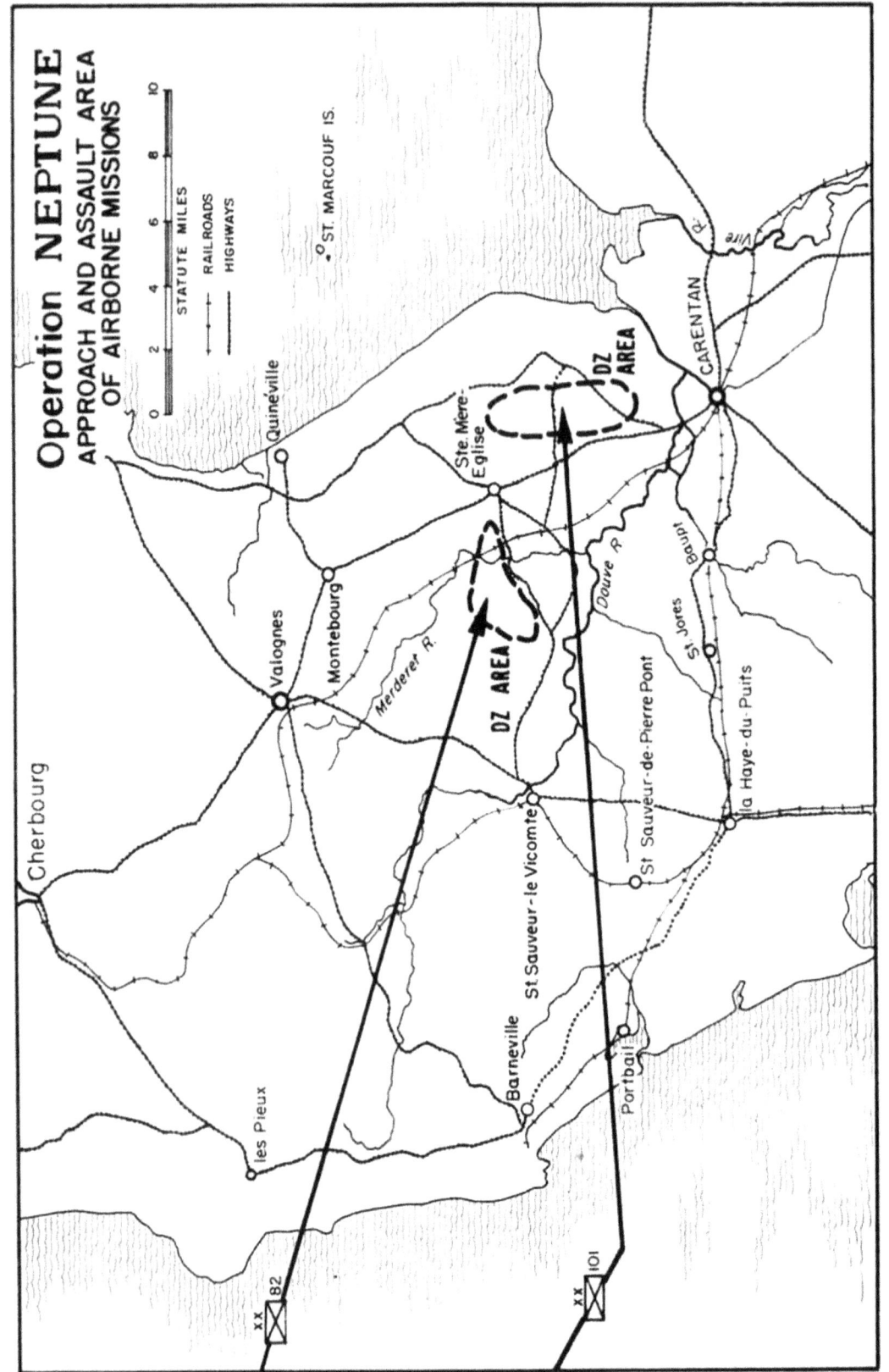

Map 2.

been all a group could do to contribute one such serial. Having been raised to almost double the 1943 strength, all IX TCC's groups except the 315th, the 442d, and the two groups responsible for the morning glider missions, were able to send two serials.

Within the missions the interval between successive serials was to be six minutes from head to head. With two minor exceptions, each was made up entirely of nine-aircraft V's of V's in trail, with the leader of each nine-ship flight keeping 1,000 feet behind the rear of the preceding flight. The leaders of the wing elements in each flight were to fly 200 feet behind and 200 feet to the right and left respectively of the rear planes in the lead element. Within each three-plane element the wingmen were to hold positions 100 feet back and 100 feet to the left and right of their leader. This was a tight formation at night for aircraft approximately 65 feet long and 95 feet from wingtip to wingtip.

A preliminary warning would be given to the paratroops when their plane was 20 minutes from its zone, and the door cover would then be removed. When four minutes from the DZ the lead pilot of each serial was to flash a red warning light by the door to alert the troops. They would then line up for the jump and would hitch their parachutes to the static line. An order to flash the red light would be transmitted to the rest of the serial with a red Aldis lamp displayed by the radio operator from the astrodome and would be passed on by the other flight leaders to the pilots behind them. Approaching the zone the formations would descend to 700 feet and slow down from the cruising speed of 140 miles an hour prescribed for the outward route to 110 miles an hour to give the paratroops the best possible drop. When in position over the drop zone the serial leader would give the green light which was the signal for an immediate jump. The signal would be passed back as before by a green Aldis lamp, with the flight leaders repeating the signal when they found themselves at their jump point. Before the men jumped the crew chief and the paratroops nearest the door were to shove out bundles of supplies and equipment.* References in unit histories indicate that these procedures were generally followed.

All pilots were adjured to drop all their troops. Evasive action prior to dropping was prohibited lest it disrupt formations or throw the paratroops into confusion. Planes missing a drop zone on the first pass were to drop near it if possible. If they overshot so far as to find themselves over the east coast, they were to circle to the right and drop their loads on DZ D. Stragglers would be held responsible for finding their own way to their zones, using Rebecca if necessary.

After completing the drop, the pilots were to dive down onto the deck and fly out over the coast to the St. Marcouf Islands at an altitude of 100 feet as a precaution against antiaircraft and other ground fire in the coastal area. They would proceed home at a cruising speed of 150 miles an hour by way of GALLUP, and Portland Bill, climbing to 3,000 feet at GALLUP in accordance with agreements with the naval commander. Over England they would retrace the routes taken on the way out, except that the 50th Wing was authorized to take a 20-mile short cut from the coast to its wing assembly point.[2]

The loading, take-off and assembly of the troop carrier serials in ALBANY was accomplished as the 101st Division later reported with "notable efficiency."[3] This was the well-earned result of the many months spent in planning, training and preparation of equipment.

It is true that both troops and planes were loaded to the limit. Some paratroops when fully laden weighed as much as 325 pounds and had to be boosted aboard their planes much as 14th century knights were hoisted onto their horses. Partly as a result of this individual overloading, some planes contained more than the 5,850 pounds prescribed in the field orders as the maximum. Also, several carried more than 18 paratroops, although this was considered the maximum for a good drop from a C-47. These overloads, generally slight, did not hinder the flight of the planes but may have created some delay and confusion in the drops.

Take-off went rapidly and smoothly despite the ban on use of radios. Blinker lights were used to control taxiing and take-offs. Not one plane had an accident, and none had to turn back. At Greenham Common the 438th Group, which was to fly the lead serials, got 81 planes in the air between 2232 and 2256, an average of 18 seconds per plane. The 441st at Merryfield reported that its aircraft took off at average intervals of 10 seconds apiece. Other groups made similar time. Such

---
*The usual number of bundles was two.

speed was made possible by high proficiency and the excellence of the British airfields.

Assembly, never an easy matter at night, was handled with equal success. All serials spiraled into formation over their home fields and swung onto course over ELKO at approximately the prescribed six-minute intervals.[4]

The weather over England was then in process of changing and varied from hour to hour, and from base to base. The wind ranged from 10 to 30 miles per hour from the north and west. Cloudiness ran the gamut from none to 10/10, the overcast, fortunately, being above 4,000 feet. However, over the Channel the sky was generally clear and visibility excellent. As one pilot put it "It was a beautiful night. You could fly formation by moonlight."[5]

Under these conditions navigation was easy as far as HOBOKEN. Apparently all the serials in ALBANY approached Normandy on course and in good formation. Almost all were four or five minutes ahead of schedule, probably because of the wind, but the condition was so general that they kept their relative positions and did not overrun each other.

The coastline at the IP was visible, but immediately beyond it the mission ran into an unforeseen obstacle which disrupted its formations and very nearly caused it to fail. This was the cloudbank already encountered by the pathfinders. It extended solidly for 10 or 12 miles inland, becoming progressively thinner and more broken between the center of the peninsula and the east coast. Near the IP the base of this layer was at an altitude of 1,100 feet and its top at about 2,000 feet. With any sort of warning the troop carriers could have flown over or under it, but no provision for such a warning had been made, and radio silence was in effect. Thus the pilots, flying at 1,500 feet as prescribed, did not know of the overcast until it loomed up close ahead, and most of the formations plunged into the heart of it.

The first four ALBANY serials, two from the 438th Group at Greenham Common and two from the 436th Group at Membury, consisted of 36, 45, 36, and 54 aircraft respectively. They had been given the task of bringing the 502d Parachute Infantry Regiment and the 377th Parachute Field Artillery Battalion to DZ A. The lead plane of the first serial was flown by Lt. Col. John M. Donalson, commander of the 438th. DZ A was a rough oval about a mile and a half long from west to east and about a mile wide, situated 2½ miles east of Ste Mère Eglise and half a mile southwest of St. Martin-de-Varreville. Only a mile east of the zone were the flooded areas behind UTAH Beach, a hazard to troops who were slow to jump or whose pilot overshot. Like all zones of the 101st, DZ A was on low, flat land broken into small fields and orchards.

These four lead serials had the easiest approach of any. They reported light, scattered clouds over Normandy but apparently had little trouble keeping clear of them. They had greater difficulty with a ground fog which limited visibility in the drop area to about three miles. Moreover, they achieved a degree of surprise which gave them substantial protection from the enemy. The lead flight reached the drop area without being under fire; the second was near Ste Mère Eglise when first shot at; and all the rest of the 438th was several miles inland before the enemy went into action. The serials of the 436th came under fire soon after landfall, but it was inaccurate, sporadic and mostly from small arms. So feeble was the opposition that the two groups lost no aircraft, suffered no serious damage, and had no casualties. In the 438th Group five or six planes received slight damage, mostly bullet holes, and 11 in the 436th had similar petty damage.

The pathfinder troops allotted to DZ A had been unable to get their beacons in operation in time for the arrival of the first serial of the 438th Group, so Colonel Donalson made his approach and drop on Gee. His passengers jumped at 0048,* two minutes ahead of time, from the prescribed altitude. By 0058 the Group had completed its drop, although several planes had had to circle back for a second pass. Of 1,430 troops carried in the first two serials all jumped but one man who had been stunned by a fall.

About the time the second serial of the 438th reached the drop area, the pathfinders got a Eureka beacon and an amber T into operation near St. Germain-de-Varreville, a mile north of the zone. The 436th Group obtained responses from the Eureka at a point 10 miles away, probably at the moment the set was switched on. Some pilots also sighted the amber T. Several pilots had to make extra passes, and one made three to get all

---

*So states the operations report. The group history gives the time as 0044.

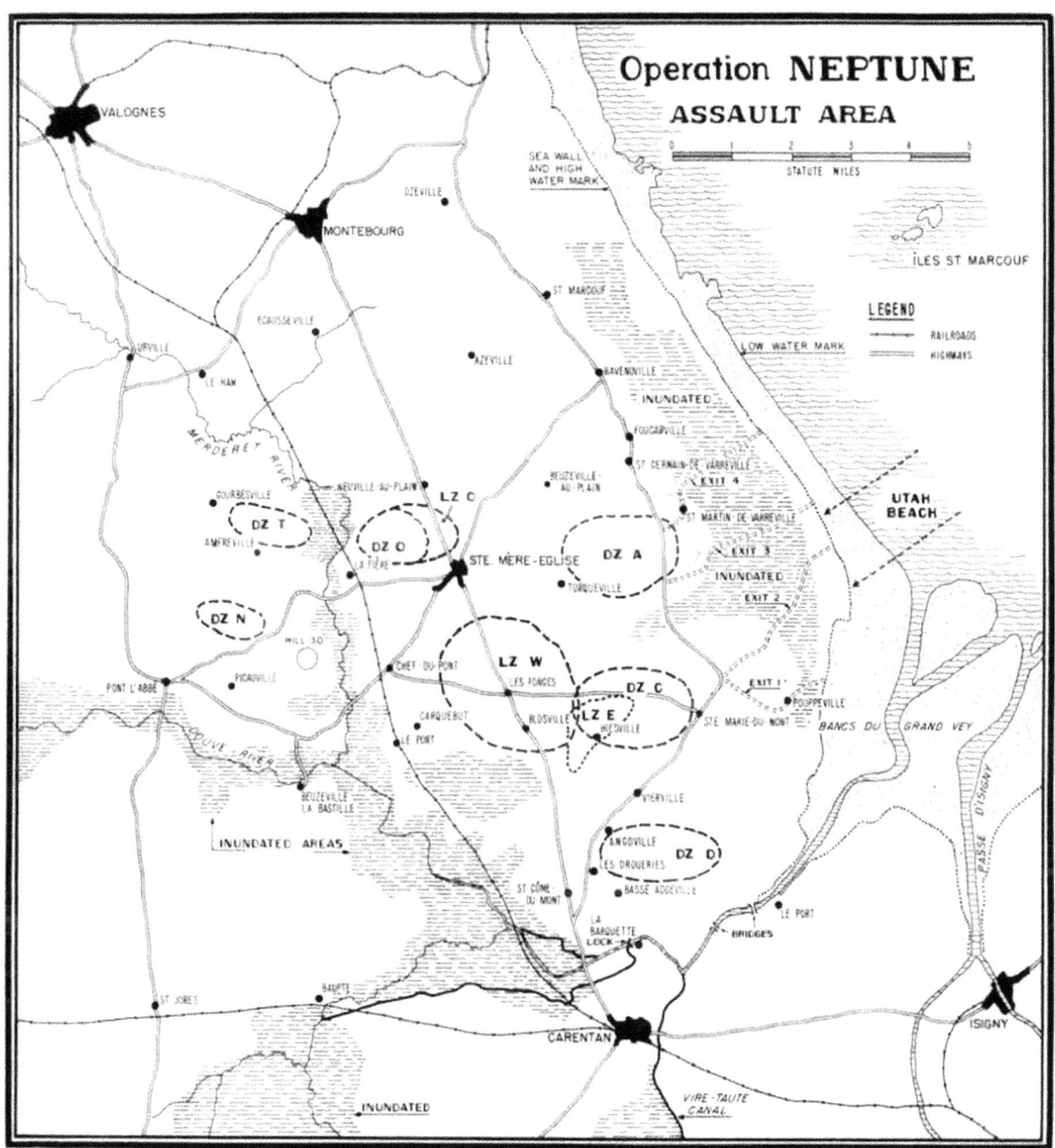

Map 3.

his troops out; a bundle had stuck in the door on his first run. The 436th had carried 1,084 men and 12 guns and dropped all but two or three injured men and one who refused to jump.

Both groups reported their drops as ranging from good to excellent, and unit histories, written some three weeks later, reiterate assertions that the drops were both accurate and compact.[6] Actually, none of the four serials had done very well, and one had done very badly.* Colonel Donalson's lead serial had dropped the 2d Battalion of the 502d PIR compactly but inaccurately. Through some maladjustment or misinterpretation of his Gee set, Donalson gave his troops the green light on the far edge of DZ C, three miles south of DZ A, and 26 of his pilots in tight formation followed his example. Six others dropped within a mile of this concentration. One straggler in the serial put his load within a mile of DZ A; one dropped five miles northwest of that zone; and one stick was missing.†

The second serial of the 438th was more accurate than its predecessor, but seems to have flown a rather loose formation. Its leader dropped his troops, members of the 3d Battalion of the 502d, near the south side of DZ A, but none of his flight dropped with him. He may have relied on Gee, while the others homed on the Eureka near St. Germain. At any rate, 36 of the pilots put their sticks in an area about four miles long from west to east and about two miles wide, with the pathfinder aids at its center. Three others, including the leader, dropped within two miles of the zone; five impatient pilots dumped their men three or four miles short of the DZ, and one stick went unaccounted for.

The lead serial of the 436th Group, which carried the 1st Battalion of the 502d PIR, placed 20 of its 36 loads, including those of the leader and his two wingmen, within about a mile of the beacons. These can be considered as dropped from a loose formation onto what appeared to be the drop zone. Of the rest, 4 were within a mile of the original zone and 6 between one and 2 miles from it. Presumably their pilots had straggled slightly and had used landmarks or dead reckoning to pick their drop points. Another 4 sticks landed between 2 and 4 miles from DZ A; one load fell in the Channel; and one was listed as missing.

In contrast to this respectable performance was that of the second serial of the 436th, which was supposed to deliver the 377th Parachute Field Artillery and 12 of its guns, a planeload of medics, and 5 planes of supplies. All the flights in this formation missed the DZ by a wide margin, and all but the first 2 flights had become badly dispersed before they made their drops. Those 2 flights followed a line of approach which passed about 3 miles north of the DZ. The first did drop its troops about 3 miles away near St. Marcouf, a village near the coastal marshes which might have been mistaken for St. Martin-de-Varreville. The second flight dropped prematurely from 5 to 7 miles northwest of the zone. The last four flights in the serial got thoroughly lost and badly dispersed. How they did so, and why hardly any of them recognized and corrected their errors is anybody's guess. Most made a pronounced deviation to the north, with the result that 5 sticks were dropped beyond Valognes at points between 10 and 20 miles northwest of the zone; and 21 loads came down between 5 and 10 miles north of it; and 2 sticks went unaccounted for. Of the 8 sticks which landed within a 5-mile radius of the zone, only one was within a mile of it and one other within 2 miles. If the 2 pilots delivering them knew approximately where they were, they were the only ones in the serial who did.[7]

The mission of the units dropped on DZ A was to seize the exits of Causeways 3 and 4 which were a little more than a mile away to the southeast and northeast respectively. In addition the paratroops were to clean up German positions near St. Martin-de-Varreville and to establish a defense on the north flank of the 101st Division on a line running from the marshes near St. Germain-de-Varreville to a contact-point with the 82d Division near Beuzeville-au-Plain.

The 2d Battalion of the 502d Parachute Infantry Regiment, despite its excellent concentration, had such trouble in assembling and orienting itself in its unexpected location that it played little part

---

*Discussions of drop accuracy in NEPTUNE must be regarded as approximations. General Taylor and his staff, though dropped comparatively close to their zone, did not know where they were until dawn, and this apparently was true of a majority of the paratroops. Since they moved about constantly in zigzags during the night attempting to assemble, to gather equipment, to engage or avoid the enemy and to reach their objectives, they might at dawn be several miles from where they had come down and with only a vague idea of the direction and extent of their wanderings.

†Sticks described as missing were so listed in reports a month or more after D-day. In most cases that means that no member of the stick had returned to duty at that time.

in the action on D-day. This difficulty was in part caused by the dense hedges which split most of that part of Normandy into a maze of little fields known as the bocage.

The 3d Battalion, scattered as it was, achieved its objectives. It was scheduled to help the 2d Battalion if necessary in neutralizing a coastal battery west of St. Martin-de-Varreville, but its principal task was to capture the causeway exits. Lt. Col. Robert G. Cole, the battalion commander, hit the ground about half a mile west of the drop zone, made a false start toward Ste Mère Eglise, discovered where he was, and headed eastward across the zone toward his objectives. On the way he picked up about 75 men including some from the 82d Division and several others who did not belong to his battalion. They reconnoitered the coastal battery about 0400 and found that it had been dismantled and abandoned as a result of damage recently inflicted by the RAF. Already at the battery were the commander of the 2d Battalion and a dozen of his men waiting in vain for the rest of their unit. With the battery disposed of, Cole decided to attack the causeways. He divided his men into groups, one to take Exit 4,* another Exit 3, and another to go to DZ C and make contact with the 506th PIR. Exit 4 was found unoccupied but unusable, because German guns to the northwest could rake the causeway. Cole led the assault on Exit 3 and took it easily before 0730. When, about two hours later, German forces driven from the beaches began retreating across that causeway, they were easy game for the entrenched paratroops, who killed over 50 of them without losing a man. At 1300 the first American patrol from the beaches arrived at the exit. Following the patrol came the 1st Battalion, 8th Infantry Regiment, which moved inland from the causeway and bivouacked that night about two miles east of it. At the end of the day Cole's battalion, then numbering about 250 men, was ordered into regimental reserve. It had accomplished its mission.

The 1st Battalion of the 502d, which was supposed first to destroy the German troops quartered on the outskirts of St. Martin-de-Varreville and then to establish a defensive line on the northern flank of the division, achieved even more spectacular results than the 3d, and with even fewer men. Its commander, Lt. Col. Patrick J. Cassidy,

landed near the pathfinder beacons outside St. Germain,* collected a small force, composed mostly of his own men, and marched on St. Martin. By 0630 he had reached there and set up a command post. Keeping part of C Company in reserve, he first checked the situation at Exits 3 and 4, then sent about 15 men to attack the German quarters. With a few later additions this handful of men with tommy guns, bazookas and grenades took the massive stone buildings in which the Germans had barricaded themselves. Before they finished the job at 1530 they had killed or captured over 150 of the enemy.

Meanwhile some 45 men of A Company had undertaken the task of defending the division's northern perimeter. During the morning they seized the village of Foucarville and by early afternoon had established four roadblocks in that area. The Germans around Foucarville greatly outnumbered them, but contented themselves with unaggressive patrolling. Late in the afternoon the arrival of 200 more paratroops at Cassidy's CP enabled him to move reinforcements onto the northern flank. He thereupon sent his reserve, C Company, to occupy the Beuzeville sector of the perimeter, two miles inland from Foucarville. The company encountered such stiff resistance that Cassidy hastily dispatched B Company, which had assembled during the afternoon, to move into line on C's left flank. As yet there was no contact with the 82d Division and the thinly held perimeter seemed for a time to be in danger. However, the low quality and morale of the enemy and the advance of Allied forces from UTAH Beach saved the day.

The German forces facing A Company lost their nerve and shortly before midnight at least 137 of them hoisted the white flag. About the same time two battalions of the 22d Infantry Regiment, which, unable to cross on Causeway 4, had spent seven hours wading through the marshes, were plodding into St. Germain-de-Varreville, and the 12th Infantry Regiment, which had also waded the marshes, was moving into position in the Beuzeville sector ready to take the offensive next day. Thus the independent operations of the 502d were successfully concluded within 24 hours after its jump.

---

*See Map No. 3, p. 37.

*One statement that he landed "in the middle of the battalion drop zone near St. Germain-de-Varreville" is self-contradictory. (UTAH Beach to Cherbourg, (Washington, 1948) p. 18.)

As for the 377th Field Artillery Battalion, only a handful of its men played a significant part in the fighting on D-day, and only one of its 12 guns supported the operations of the 101st Division. Scattered many miles north and west of the drop area, the artillerymen engaged the enemy in innumerable little fights and showed great resourcefulness in regaining the Allied lines, but their actions had at best a nuisance value.[8]

The next three serials in ALBANY were 45 aircraft of the 439th Group from Upottery carrying the headquarters and 1st Battalion of the 506th Parachute Infantry Regiment, 36 from the group carrying the 2d Battalion of the 506th, and 45 planes of the 435th Group from Welford with the 3d Battalion of the 501st PIR plus divisional headquarters and artillery and signal personnel. The lead plane of the 439th was flown by the group commander, Lt. Col. Charles H. Young, and had on board Col. Robert L. Sink, commander of the 506th PIR. In the lead aircraft of the 435th Group, which was flown by the group commander, Col. Frank J. MacNees, were General Taylor and several of his staff, and the second plane of that group carried the 101st Division's artillery commander, Brig. Gen. Anthony C. McAuliffe.

The destination of these serials was DZ C, an oval 1½ miles long from west to east and over a mile wide. It was 2½ miles south of DZ A and a mile east of the highway from Carentan to Ste Mère Eglise. Through it went a road running east from the hamlet of les Forges on the highway to the village of Ste Marie-du-Mont. A large flooded area just southwest of les Forges provided a landmark to guide the troop carriers' approach.

The formations of the 439th and 435th reached Normandy in good shape, only to run squarely and unexpectedly into the cloudbank which covered the western Cotentin. Colonel Young climbed through the overcast on instruments, descended through a hole in the clouds 11 miles inland, and headed for the drop zone using Gee and Rebecca. The pathfinders responsible for DZ C had managed to get a Eureka beacon in operation a few moments earlier. However, loss of lights and the presence of enemy troops had prevented them from setting up a T. All they could do was to flash a single green Aldis lamp. Young apparently did not see this, but he did recognize the principal landmarks around the DZ and dropped accurately at a bend in the road to Ste Marie-du-Mont on the northeast side of the zone at or slightly before his scheduled time of 0114.

All but a few of Colonel Young's serial had lost contact with him in the clouds and their formation had loosened and broken. The other two serials disintegrated. This was natural, since in the overcast pilots generally lost sight of the dimmed lights of planes in other flights and were often unable to see even the planes in their own element. In addition, they had reacted to the situation in different ways, some going stubbornly ahead, others climbing to get above the clouds or diving to get under them.

On emerging from the overcast they were harassed by light flak and small arms fire which was moderately severe over the last eight miles of the route. Its effect was intensified by the fact that many stragglers passed over danger spots such as Pont l'Abbé (Etienville) a mile or two off the proper course. Three planes in the 439th Group were shot down and crashed with their crews. The pilot of one of them, Lt. Marvin F. Muir, saved his paratroops at the cost of his own life by holding his burning craft steady while they jumped. The group had a total of 27 aircraft damaged, but only 3 severely enough to need the attentions of a service unit later. Three planes in the serial from the 435th Group blew up or went down in flames before reaching the drop zone; the only survivors were a few troops who were lining up at the door of one plane when it was hit. Seven other planes in the group were hit, but not seriously damaged.

In spite of its difficulties, Colonel Young's serial managed to give its troops a fairly good drop. Only two or three serials in NEPTUNE did better. Besides Young himself 14 pilots put their loads on or almost on DZ C. Another 13 bunched their sticks within a mile and a half east and southeast of the zone. The rest straggled. Six dropped troops from three to five miles north of DZ C; another dropped seven miles north, and four did so about five miles south on the far side of the Douve river. Very much on the debit side were a pilot who ended up 17 miles to the north and a three-plane element which dropped its unfortunate troops 21 miles to the northwest.

The second serial of the 439th, besides becoming rather dispersed, had swung three or four degrees to the north onto a line of flight which brought it over Ste Mère Eglise. The paratroops, seeing beneath them green T's, which had been set up for the 82d Division on DZ O, clamored that they were being taken past their zone. The pilots in the front of the serial knew this was not the case and flew straight on, headed perhaps for the Eureka outside St. Germain-de-Varreville. A dozen dropped troops in a loose pattern in the general vicinity of St. Germain, and another five placed their sticks slightly south of there near DZ A. In the rear of the serial, 14 well-bunched planes made their drop prematurely close to Ste Mère Eglise. Either their pilots had mistaken DZ O for DZ C or they had yielded to the demands of the paratroops for an immediate drop. One plane in the serial put its stick within a mile of DZ C and 2 others came within 2 miles of it. Only one stick, 6 miles to the north, was outside a five-mile radius of the zone. One was missing.

The 435th Group made its first drops about 0120, six minutes ahead of schedule. Its serial had scattered so widely that at least 25 stragglers felt justified in using Rebecca. This action was probably decisive in enabling most of them to make a good drop. The Eureka signals came through strong and only slightly cluttered despite the heavy use. With their aid about 20 pilots came close enough to the pathfinders to see their green light blinking. However, several overshot the zone and had to circle for a second try.

None of the group hit DZ C, but 25 dropped troops or supplies within 1½ miles of it. Of these, 16 bunched their loads close to the east end of the zone near the pathfinder aids. All but one of that bunch were from the first 21 planes in the serial, and among them were the first two sticks with Generals Taylor and McAuliffe. Another six sticks came down between 1½ and 3 miles from the DZ. For some strange reason eight pilots of various flights concentrated their loads near St. Jores about eight miles southwest of DZ C on the south side of the Douve. Since it is unlikely that they would make the same gross mistake independently, the presumption is that these pilots had formed an improvised flight after emerging from the overcast and made their erroneous approach in formation behind a pilot who either did not use radar or could not use it properly. Three other loads were dropped between 5 and 10 miles from the zone, and one bewildered pilot of the 435th returned to base with his troops.*

In all, the 439th Group had carried 1.357 troops to Normandy and dropped all but about 33 —those whose planes were shot down, one wounded man, and one who refused to jump. The 435th had carried 677 and dropped 626. Of the others, 36 were shot down, 13 were with the pilot who lost his way, and 2 had equipment trouble.[9]

The paratroops on DZ C had been assigned to take the exits of the two southern causeways and to clear the Germans from the vicinity. Exit 1† was near the hamlet of Pouppeville, two miles east of the DZ, and Exit 2 was two miles northeast of the zone. Unable to assemble more than a fraction of their men, the paratroop commanders found it difficult to reach their objectives in the face of opposition.

The taking of the exits had been entrusted to the 2d Battalion of the 506th PIR, but few of its men landed near the drop zone, its main concentrations being near Ste Mère Eglise and St. Germain-de-Varreville. By 0330 almost 200 of its troops and 20 from the 82d Division had assembled near St. Germain under the battalion commander. They set out about 0430 for the causeways, but machine gun nests and interdictory artillery fire so slowed their progress that not until 1330 did a few men work their way around the German strongpoints to Exit 2. They found it already in American hands and crowded with troops, tanks and guns. The 8th Infantry Regiment had made its way across from UTAH beach before noon and secured the exit. The paratroops enlisted the aid of some of the soldiers and tanks at the exit to mop up the German strongpoints blocking the progress of the main body of the 2d Battalion. This was quickly done, and by 1530 the battalion was in position at Exit 2 with about 300 men at its disposal.

Despite the relatively good drop given by Colonel Young's serial to Regimental Headquarters and the 1st Battalion of the 506th, they were unable to assemble quickly. One reason for this was lack of communications. Most of the signal equipment and all the operators had come down many miles outside the drop area. Two hours after the drop only about 45 men from head-

---
*He tried again next night with the 435th's glider serial and made a successful drop.
†See Map No. 3, p. 37.

quarters and 50 from the 1st Battalion had gathered under Colonel Sink at Culoville on the south side of the zone. These troops had been designated as regimental reserve, but at dawn Sink, having heard nothing from the other battalions, sent what he had of the 1st Battalion to take Exit 1. Delayed by a series of skirmishes, they were unable to reach the exit until mid-afternoon. They found the 3d Battalion of the 501st PIR already in possession.

About 90 men of that battalion under their commander, Lt. Col. Julian Ewell, and 60 members of divisional headquarters, including Generals Taylor and McAuliffe, had managed to assemble during the night. Though only a short distance southeast of the drop zone, none of them knew where they were until the rising sun revealed the church tower of Ste Marie-du-Mont looming above the trees. Soon after daybreak General Taylor ordered an attack on Exit 1 by the headquarters troops and Ewell's battalion, which had been intended for divisional reserve. Ignorant of how the rest of his division was faring and aware that American possession of the causeways was essential, Taylor was staking everything on a bid to take one.

At 0600 some 60 paratroops of the 501st under Ewell and 25 from divisional headquarters, including the two generals, set out for Pouppeville. The little force was top heavy with rank. Taylor remarked dryly that never were so few led by so many. Except for one brief encounter they advanced unopposed to Pouppeville, picking up about 60 more men along the way. About 0900 on the outskirts of Pouppeville they ran into stubborn resistance from Germans of the 1058th Grenadier Regiment, part of the 91st Division. The attackers lacked men and firepower for a real assault and had to squeeze the Nazis out in house-to-house fighting which lasted until noon. Casualties numbered 18 paratroops and 25 Germans, and 38 Germans were taken prisoner. A few minutes after the village was taken elements of the 8th Infantry Regiment crossed the causeway and established contact between airborne and seaborne forces.

Meanwhile the situation back at DZ C was difficult and dangerous. About 150 paratroops gathered during the morning at a divisional headquarters set up at Hiesville by a few men Taylor had left behind. At noon they were reinforced by over 100 troops who had landed at dawn in the CHICAGO glider mission. Colonel Sink's CP at Culoville was also reinforced by more than 70 additional men of the 1st Battalion of the 506th PIR who had found their way to the DZ. These, however, seemed all too few. The enemy were swarming around like hornets and twice pushed attacks close enough to threaten the Culoville position. Unknown to the Allies, the Germans had installed an entire battalion of the 191st Artillery Regiment in and around Ste Marie-du-Mont. Many paratroops who landed near their positions had been shot before they could get free of their chutes. The rest gave a good account of themselves and even took one of the German batteries, but it was not until after 1420 when elements of the 8th Infantry Regiment pushed into the town that the issue was decided and German resistance in Ste Marie was broken.

At the end of the afternoon the portions of the 1st and 2d Battalions of the 506th PIR which had been at the causeways returned to DZ C, giving Colonel Sink a total of some 650 men, including a few from other units. Their initial task had been accomplished, and the 2d and 3d Battalions of the 8th Infantry Regiment had moved into positions around les Forges thus shielding the 506th from the west. However, efforts to seal off and occupy the area between them and the Douve had not succeeded, and the situation there was so chaotic that General Taylor, returning from Pouppeville, ordered the 506th to make a reconnaissance in force into this no-man's land next morning.[10]

The last serials of ALBANY were two of 45 aircraft apiece, flown by the 441st Group from Merryfield, and one of like size by the 440th Group from Exeter. The first serial carried the 1st Battalion, part of the 2d Battalion, and Regimental Headquarters of the 501st Parachute Infantry Regiment. In its lead plane were Lt. Col. Theodore Kershaw, the group commander, and Col. Howard R. Johnson, the regimental commander. The second serial contained most of the 2d Battalion of the 501st, half an engineer company, and some medical personnel. The last serial carried the 3d Battalion of the 506th PIR and the rest of the engineer company. The destination of these serials was DZ D.

Ten days before the invasion this zone had been located about three quarters of a mile southwest of DZ C, and only the 3d Battalion, 506th

PIR, was scheduled to drop on it, the battalion's mission being to secure the southern perimeter of the 101st Division along the Douve. At that time the 501st PIR (less the 3d Battalion) was supposed to jump on DZ B, 1½ miles south of Ste Mère Eglise for the purpose of taking that town and the bridges over the Merderet at la Fière and Chef-du-Pont. On 27 May when those tasks were transferred to the 82d Division, the 501st was shifted to DZ D to help hold the Douve line.[11]

Since new objectives of the 501st were about 2½ miles south of DZ D, the zone was relocated about a mile further south at the request of the regimental commander. Its new position was between Angoville-au-Plain and Basse Addeville, a hamlet 1,200 yards east of St. Côme-du-Mont. Somewhat smaller than the other DZ's, it was less than 1¼ miles long from east to west and slightly under a mile across.

In making their final approach to the zone, the pilots would have four landmarks to guide them: the junction of the Douve and Merderet, 4½ miles from the zone; the railway, 2½ miles from the zone, the flooded area which lay east of the railroad north of the line of flight; and the north-south highway to Carentan, which they would cross less than a mile before reaching the DZ. A secondary road to Ste Marie-du-Mont skirted the west end of the zone.

The 441st and 440th Groups, like their predecessors, had little trouble reaching Normandy, but over the French coast the first serial of the 441st ran into the clouds and broke up. The two lead flights of the second serial ducked under the overcast and kept formation, but its other flights hit the cloud-bank and dispersed. The serial from the 440th appears to have avoided the clouds and held together.

Little fire was encountered over the western part of the Cotentin. The 441st reported considerable shooting near St. Sauveur de Pierre Pont and at other points between there and the DZ. The 440th had scant opposition until it was within six miles of the zone. Then it received intense light flak and automatic fire which caused many pilots to take evasive action and drop out of formation. Searchlights and magnesium flares further loosened the formations by dazzling pilots and forcing them to dodge. Some searchlights were quickly attacked and extinguished by Allied night-fighters but others survived long enough to cause trouble. Very intense flak and automatic weapons fire was encountered on DZ D and immediately west and east of it.* The Germans had spotted the area as a likely one for airborne use and were present in force. Fortunately their fire was not accurate, and the actual number of antiaircraft guns was probably small. The rate of aircraft losses for the three serials was less than 5 percent. One plane of the 441st blew up before reaching the drop area, and another crashed soon after dropping its load. A third, hit by antiaircraft fire as it left the DZ, made a forced landing near Cherbourg, its crew ultimately reaching the Allied lines in safety. One plane limped home good for nothing but salvage, and 14 others in the 441st were damaged.† In the 440th two planes were shot down by intense machine-gun fire over the DZ, and another, hit as it left the zone, plunged into the sea. A dozen other craft of the 440th suffered damage but were quickly repaired.

A Eureka which the pathfinders had set up west of the zone was received up to 17 miles away. Signals from the beacon on DZ A were also received, but were readily distinguished from the correct ones by their coding and by their position on the Rebecca scope. The lighted T supposed to mark the zone was not observed. The enemy thereabout were so numerous and active that the pathfinder troops had been unable to operate the lights. Except that the lead pilot of the 441st made some use of Gee to check his position, the three serials relied on Rebecca-Eureka or on visual recognition to locate the zone. The Rebecca was a poor guide at close range, and the cloud-swept landscape proved hard to identify. Many stragglers from the first serial of the 441st and some from other serials had to make two or three passes to orient themselves. Some of them grew completely confused and ended up by making drops many miles from the drop area. However, most pilots believed that they had achieved accuracy, and only one, a member of the 441st Group, gave up after three attempts and went home with his load.

At 0126, five minutes ahead of schedule, the first serial of the 441st started its drop. The next began at 0134. Between them they carried 1,475

---
*One account states that some planes had not turned off all their lights and so attracted fire. (Hist 302d TC Sq, Jun 44.)

†One aircraft had collided with a bundle dropped by a plane ahead of it. (Hist 301st TC Sq, Jun 44.) Considering the huge number of planes and the general failure to keep formation, it is almost miraculous that there were not more accidents of this sort.

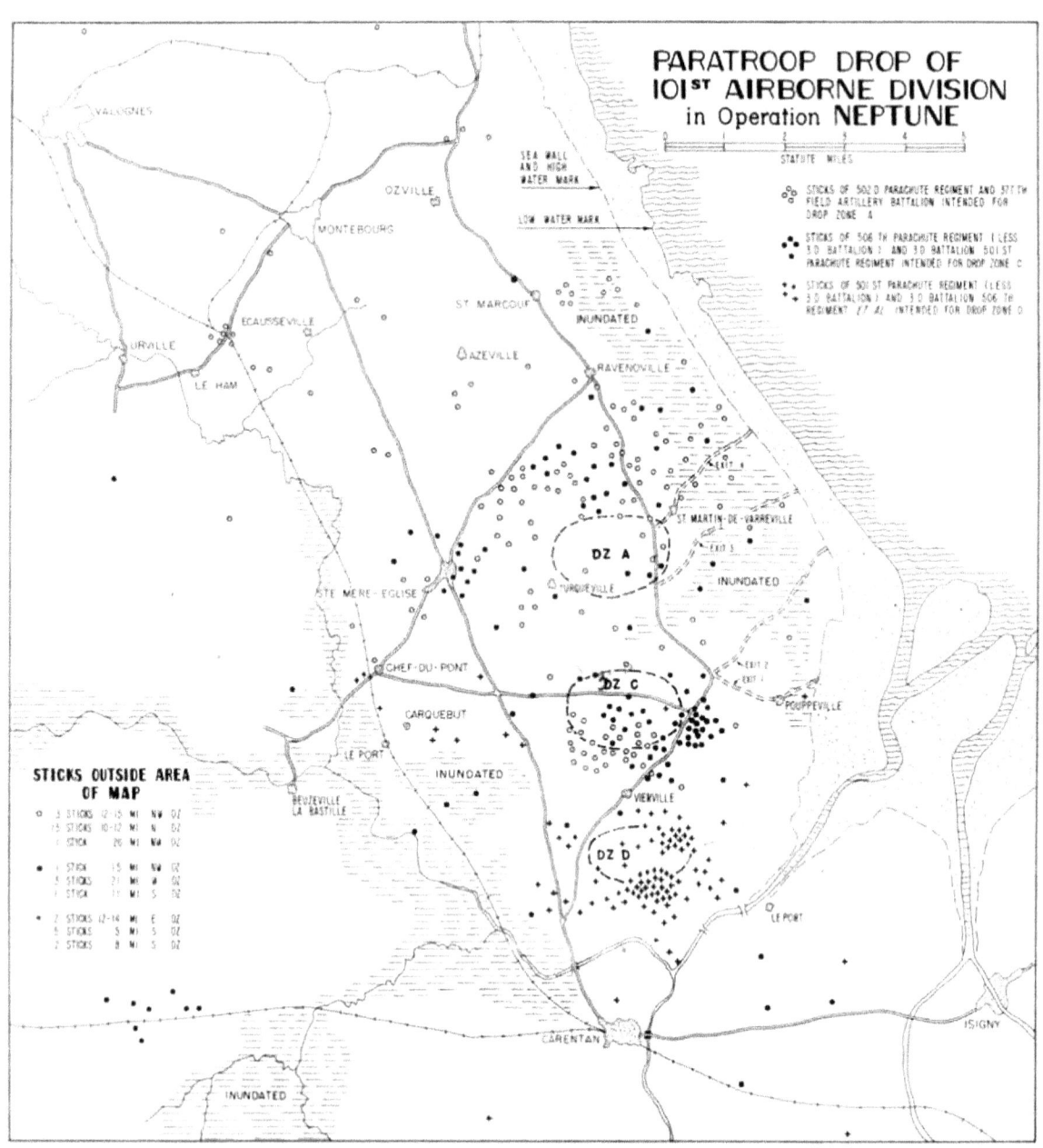

Map 4.

troops, of which they dropped at least 1,429. Returned were one soldier who had fainted and 12 who had slipped in vomit and had become entangled. The drop by the 440th Group began at 0140. Out of 723 troops carried 719 jumped. Flak had wounded one man, and he had blocked the exit of the other three.

The return of the ALBANY serials was generally uneventful after they left Normandy. Over the Channel the sky was becoming overcast, but the clouds were above 4,000 feet, and visibility was good. In southern England there were scattered squalls, one of which caused returning planes to stack up for a time over Membury. Except in the 438th and 440th Groups most of the pilots returned singly or in small formations. Some must have wandered far and wide, for the flow of returnees lasted from 0210 when the first plane reached Greenham Common until about 0430.[12]

The airborne units which the 440th and 441st Groups had been responsible for dropping on DZ D had been assigned to cover the left flank of VII Corps by holding or destroying all crossings of the Douve below its junction with the Merderet. Although protected by the river from German forces to the south, they were six long miles away from UTAH Beach, and their task turned out to be much more difficult than had been expected.

The 1st Battalion, 501st PIR, was to seize and hold a lock at la Barquette half a mile south of DZ D and only a mile and a half north of Carentan. Besides its utility as a crossing, the lock was valued as a means of controlling the tidal flooding of the Douve marshes.* The 2d Battalion and engineers with it were to seize and demolish the bridges over the Douve on the north-south highway to Carentan about a mile southwest of la Barquette. The 501st had as secondary objectives the taking of St. Côme-du-Mont and the destruction of a railroad bridge across the river about a mile west of the highway. The 3d Battalion, 506th PIR, was to take two wooden bridges in the le Port area a mile and a half east of la Barquette.

The headquarters and first battalion of the 501st PIR had received only a partially satisfactory drop. Some 19 planes, including the three in the lead element of the serial put their sticks on DZ D or close to its southern edge. Two others came within a couple of miles of it. On the other hand, the whole last flight veered north of course onto a line passing close to DZ C. Eight of its nine loads landed between two and four miles northwest of DZ D between Chef-du-Pont and DZ C, and the other was about three miles further east on the same line of flight. One stick came down about seven miles north of the proper zone. These sticks at least landed within the 101st's prescribed perimeter, but another nine had been scattered from 4 to 10 miles south of DZ D in the Carentan area on the far side of the Douve. One stick probably went down with its plane, and four others carried by the serial are unaccounted for.

Those troops who did come down near the zone were involved in fighting from the start. The battalion commander was killed and his executive officer was captured. None of the company commanders were on hand. Through a fortunate accident the regimental commander, Colonel Johnson, was present to take charge. His pilot had given the green light a little too soon, but a bundle stuck in the door had delayed the jump until the plane was exactly over the zone.

Johnson gathered men from various units until he had about 150, and worked his way toward la Barquette. At dawn his men rushed the lock, found it undefended, and were dug in before enemy sentries on the other bank realized they were there. The German guards, few in numbers, made no attempt to counterattack, but as a result of their observations German artillery soon began shelling the lock area. Once established at the lock, Johnson sent patrols westward in hopes that the highway bridges could be taken with equal ease, but every advance in that direction was halted by intense fire. Clearly the bridges could not be taken without a hard fight.

The colonel therefore returned to the drop zone with about 50 men to seek reinforcements. At 0900 outside Basse Addeville he found his S-3 with about 100 miscellaneous troops already engaged with enemy forces north and west of them. Most of Johnson's regiment seemed to have vanished, but he learned presently that half his 2d Battalion was fighting less than a mile to the north near the hamlet of les Droueries. This force twice tried to break through to him but was stopped both times by the enemy. In contrast to intelligence reports which had indicated that the only German unit in the area was a single platoon, the entire

---

*This flooding never became necessary. It probably would not have been quick enough to be effective had the Germans launched a sudden assault.

3d Battalion of the enemy's 1058th Regiment was there and was fighting tenaciously.

No word was received from division or corps, but at noon an encouraging bulletin from the BBC led Colonel Johnson to attempt a second advance on the highway bridges by way of la Barquette. He left 50 men to hold Basse Addeville, and marched off about 1330 toward the lock. This movement drew heavy artillery and mortar fire from the south near Carentan and from the northwest near St. Côme-du-Mont. A naval fire-control officer who had dropped with the regiment made radio contact with the fleet, and accurate naval gun fire subdued the mortars around St. Côme. Nevertheless stiff resistance blocked every effort to push toward the bridges. All that could be done was to consolidate the postion around the lock.

After receiving one of the best drops in either ALBANY or BOSTON the 2d Battalion of the 501st had a hard and seemingly fruitless day. At least 40 of its 45 sticks had come down on or within a mile of the drop zone, mainly near its southern edge.* The battalion commander, Lt. Col. Robert A. Ballard, was able to collect about 250 men for an attack on St Côme-du-Mont, but unexpectedly strong and determined enemy forces threw back his attacks at the hamlet of les Droueries, half a mile from St. Côme. They also blocked his subsequent attempts to join forces with Colonel Johnson. Even after the control officer with Johnson had called down naval gunfire on the hostile positions Ballard's men were unable to make much headway. On the other hand, by keeping the Germans around St. Côme on the defensive, his battalion may have prevented a counterattack against the exposed positions of the paratroops at la Barquette.

The 3d Battalion, 506th PIR, had been given a good drop by the 440th Group. About eight of its sticks landed on the zone and 26 more within a mile of it, the principal concentration being near the eastern end. Only two sticks, dropped some 13 miles to the south are known to have landed far from their goal.

Unfortunately the Germans were ready and waiting and had converted the drop area into a deathtrap. The moment the jump began an oil-soaked building burst into flame, and by its light machine guns and mortars mowed down the paratroops before they could get clear of their chutes.

Both the battalion commander and his executive were among the slain. The survivors had all they could do to assemble and maintain themselves.

The battalion S-3, Capt. Charles G. Shettle, descended in slightly safer territory in the southern part of the zone. After only a momentary pause to assess the situation he hurried off toward the le Port bridges with only 15 men, leaving the rest of the battalion to follow if it could. This seemingly reckless haste paid high dividends, and was to exercise a considerable influence on paratroop tactics. Picking up another 18 men along the way, Shettle reached the bridges at 0430 and quickly occupied their western ends. After 20 more paratroops joined his group he sent patrols across to the far bank. However, German pressure forced them to withdraw two hours later largely for lack of ammunition. With only about 30 rounds apiece the paratroops had to husband their resources. Contact was made during the day with Johnson's force at the lock, but he was in no position to provide assistance.

That night 40 more troops, said to have been dropped near Carentan, managed to reach Shettle's position. At 0200 the Germans attempted to cross one of the bridges, but recoiled when the paratroops poured a volley into them at close range. Thereafter the enemy contented themselves with keeping Shettle's group under constant harassing fire from across the river. However, the Americans prepared the bridges for demolition in case of a more formidable attack. Thus at dawn on D plus 1 Shettle and Johnson held defensive positions at the lock and the two wooden bridges with the equivalent of less than two companies of troops almost without ammunition, food and water. Colonel Johnson put out panel signals at dawn for aerial resupply. Supplies were dropped at 0630, but they fell in the marshes or in areas exposed to German fire and could not be recovered.

About noon Shettle sighted some P-47's and set out signal panels requesting a bombing mission against the enemy positions across the river. The mission arrived about 0430, but, through some misunderstanding, strafed the American position and destroyed both bridges by accurate skip bombing before frantic waving of orange identification panels led the fliers to shift their attacks to the other side of the Douve.

What had been achieved was important. What had not been done could have been disastrous.

---

*One was 1½ and another 2½ miles away.

The paratroops on DZ D had failed in their overall objective, the sealing off of the southern flank of the UTAH beachhead. From Carentan to beyond St. Côme-du-Mont the north-south highway and its bridges over the Douve remained in German hands. Through this gateway the Nazis could and did, launch a counterattack.

At about 0600 on D-day the commander of the German 6th Parachute Regiment, stationed near Périers, southwest of Carentan, had received orders to attack northward toward Ste Mère Eglise. He moved his regiment to the vicinity of Carentan, reconnoitered the situation at St. Côme, and about noon ordered two of his battalions to join him there. They crossed the river during the afternoon and struck northward from St. Côme about 1900. With many skirmishes, but no major engagements, the first battalion reached the vicinity of Ste Marie-du-Mont before midnight. The second, somehow slipping behind American positions around les Forges, may have come within a mile of Ste Mère Eglise, which was its objective.

The size of the American buildup had already been such that it would have taken two regiments of Germans rather than two battalions to create a threat to the UTAH operation. Nevertheless, by resolute action these thrusts could have caused enough trouble to delay VII Corps for many days. Actually they accomplished little. During the night the German regimental commander, gradually realizing the odds against his men, ordered them back. The second battalion got the order and returned safely to St. Côme. The first battalion, which did not acknowledge the order, and may not have received it, retired southward next morning. Unable to make contact with its comrades, it marched without reconnoitering toward the crossings at la Barquette and le Port in apparent ignorance that the Americans held those points. About 1600 the battalion approached the river.

It was disconcerting to the Americans to see such large forces advancing unexpectedly on their rear, but it was doubtless more so for the Germans to receive rifle and machine-gun fire from ambush at close range and to find their retreat suddenly cut off. In the ensuing battles some 800 German paratroops were defeated by about 250 American paratroops under Johnson and about 100 under Shettle. Shettle made adroit and aggressive use of patrols to convince the Germans in his sector that his force was too much for them. They trickled in squad by squad until he had 255 prisoners. In the lock area such disintegration was checked by Nazi officers who shot anyone who showed signs of surrender and wounded Colonel Johnson himself, when he advanced to offer terms after hearing cries of "Kamerad." Later Johnson did succeed in conferring between the lines with a German enlisted man and sent him back with an ultimatum to surrender in 30 minutes or be "annihilated by our superior forces." Almost on the deadline the Germans began surrendering. This capitulation, also, was a piecemeal process with officers coming in last a little after nightfall. The force at the lock had inflicted about 150 casualties and taken 350 prisoners at a cost of 10 men killed and 30 wounded. It was an extraordinary victory for courage and bluff over a unit supposedly better than most the Germans then had in Normandy.[13]

While this success was being won, a relief column was fighting its way south from the vicinity of DZ C. Late on D-day General Taylor, out of contact with his forces on the Douve front, had directed Colonel Sink to take the 506th PIR (less the 3d Battalion) on a reconnaissance in force through Vierville to the river. The 506th marched south on the morning of the 7th with more than 600 men. They encountered stiff resistance after passing through Vierville, and only with the aid of two platoons of tanks, which proved invaluable in knocking out machine-gun nests, were they able to fight their way to the vicinity of Angoville, where Sink and one battalion managed to join forces with Colonel Ballard's group. Together they drove salients north and south of les Droueries but were unable to take the strongly defended positions around that hamlet.

The attack by V Corps in the OMAHA Beach sector south of the Vire was not going well, and on the 7th General Bradley, on orders from Eisenhower, gave VII Corps as its primary goal the taking of Carentan, since this was the one point essential to a link-up of the two corps. The best and shortest way to Carentan was blocked by two German battalions holding les Droueries and St. Côme. In order to crush their resistance Colonel Sink was heavily reinforced. On the night of the 7th he received the 3d Battalion, 501st PIR, a battalion of glider troops (brought in over the beaches), eight light tanks, and a battalion of field artillery with 105 mm. guns.

At 0500 on the 8th Sink launched an attack by

the four airborne battalions. This was preceded by artillery preparation and a rolling barrage ahead of the troops. After hard fighting the enemy withdrew during the afternoon, hammered back the 3d Battalion of the 501st, which had pushed into their path, and retreated across the Douve, blowing up one of the highway bridges and the railway bridge as they went. The 101st Division had accomplished its initial mission and had consolidated its lines along the Douve. However, to do so against the opposition of two battalions had required two and a half days and the help of tanks and artillery brought in by sea.

On the 9th the division paused to reorganize for its drive toward Carentan. This pause may be taken as the end of the airborne stage of its operations. The subsequent attack by the 101st which made contact with V Corps on 10 June and took Carentan on 12 June was made as a ground unit striking out of an organized beachhead.[14]

BOSTON Mission and the Paratroop Operations of the 82d Division

The 82d Division's paratroop mission, BOSTON, was flown by the 52d Wing and the attached 442d Group from their bases around Grantham in the north of England. The serials were to assemble over their bases according to group SOP's, pass over the wing assembly point at six-minute intervals, and fly the course already taken by the pathfinders from there to HOBOKEN, PEORIA, and the drop zones. Between the command assembly point and the IP the lead plane in BOSTON was to fly 10 minutes behind the leader of the last serial in ALBANY.

The first plane took off about 2300, and by 0002 all were in the air except one in the 315th Group which did not go because a paratrooper's grenade had exploded before take-off, making a shambles of the rear of the aircraft. The fastest departure appears to have been that of the 61st Group from Barkston Heath. Taking off in elements of 3 at 7-second intervals, it put two 36-plane serials in the air in 2½ minutes apiece.

The weather was favorable. The moon shone brightly through high, scattered clouds and visibility was generally excellent. Under these conditions the Eureka beacons and flashing aerial lighthouses at 30-mile intervals made it easy to stay on course, and the bright lights on the planes made it easy to keep formation during the trip to the south coast. One pilot said it seemed as though they were following a lighted highway. The marker ships proved equally efficacious, and, as in ALBANY, all serials appear to have approached Normandy on course and in formation.

The first three serials in BOSTON were to drop the 505th Parachute Regiment between 0151 and 0208. The lead serial, 36 planes of the 316th Group, carried the 2d Battalion. Another 36 from that group took the 3d Battalion of the 505th, two 75 mm. howitzers, and 20 artillerymen of the 456th Parachute Field Artillery Battalion. Then came 47 planes of the 315th Group bearing the Headquarters and 1st Battalion of the 505th and a platoon of engineers. With them was General Ridgway, who had decided a few days earlier to parachute in rather than come, as previously planned, by glider.

The destination of these serials, DZ O, was an oval about a mile long from west to east and half a mile wide from north to south extending from half a mile northwest of Ste Mère Eglise almost to the east bank of the Merderet. It was to be marked by Eureka beacons and green T's. From a pilot's viewpoint it was conveniently boxed in on the west by the Merderet, on the south by a road running west from Ste Mère Eglise, and on the east by the north-south highway.

All three serials carrying the 505th apparently sighted the cloudbank over the western Cotentin soon enough for most of the planes to climb over it without losing formation. The clouds shielded them from observation, and by following a different route from ALBANY they achieved a degree of surprise. All three crossed the coast without opposition and even the last was four miles inland before it was fired upon. Such fire as was encountered was sporadic and ineffectual and was mostly from rifles and machine guns. No planes were lost. The 316th had a dozen slightly damaged, and 11 in the 315th required minor repairs. One flak burst which wounded seven paratroops aboard a plane of the 315th prevented that stick from jumping. However, the clouds above the zone were more of a hindrance than the enemy.

The pathfinder troops on DZ O had put their Eureka in operation by 0125. The first serial received its responses clearly when 15 miles away,

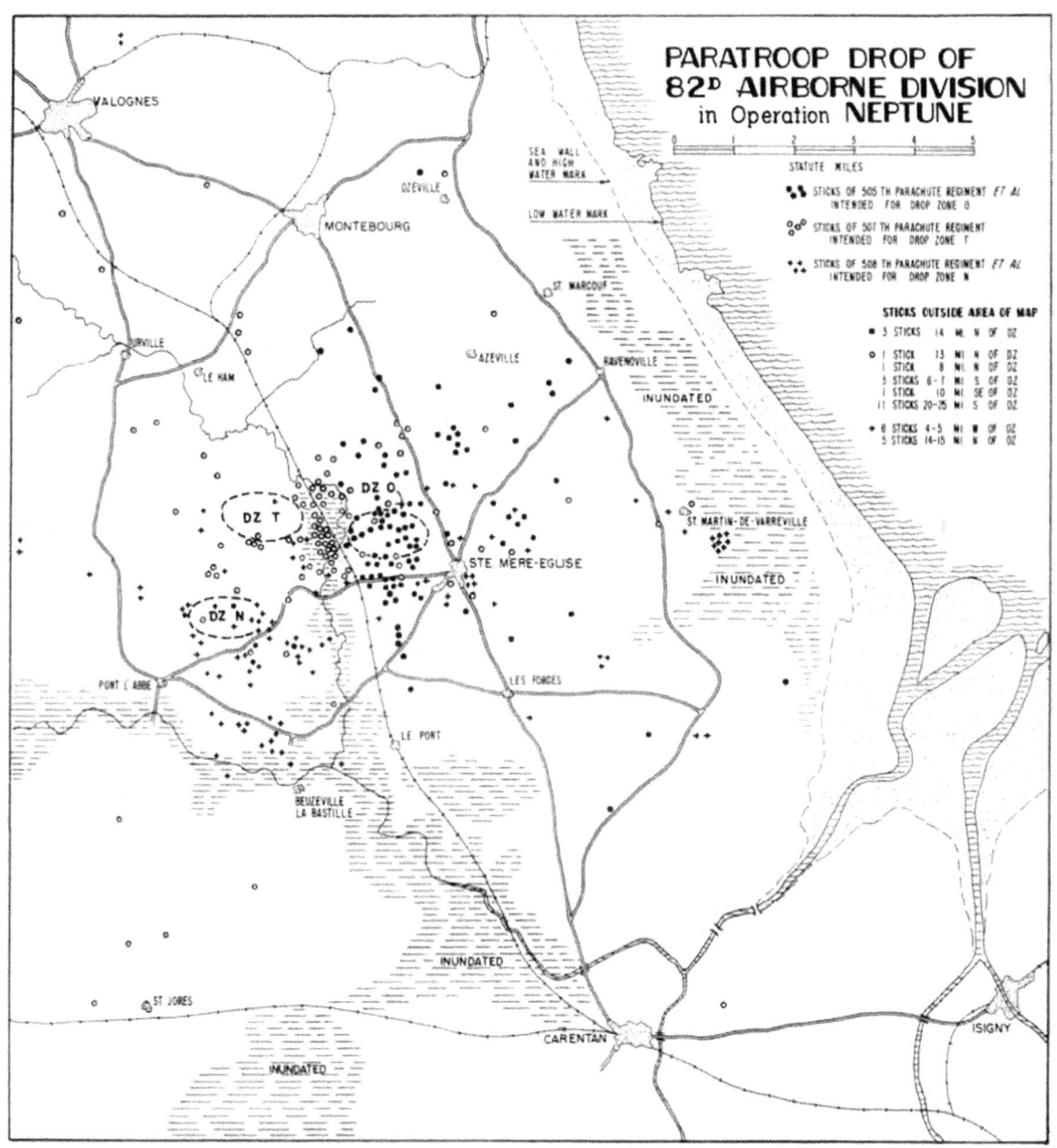

Map 5.

and the third did so at distances up to 21 miles. The pathfinders also had three T's of green lights gleaming on the zone, one for each battalion, but not until it was almost on top of the lights did the lead serial see them through a break in the clouds. In consequence it made a high drop from about 1,000 feet. Some pilots overshot and dropped troops east of the zone. Others who overshot or straggled off course made another pass. The second serial had begun a descent through the clouds on Rebecca before reaching the DZ and dropped on the T. The 315th Group's serial had to change its course and lose altitude rapidly after it sighted the T but was able to drop over the zone from about the proper height. At least one of its pilots missed the zone in the overcast, turned back at the coast and dropped at what he believed to be the alternate zone, DZ D. Although accounts differ, the first drops were probably made about 0145 and the last about 0204. As in so many other cases the arrival had been slightly ahead of schedule.

Of 1,276 troops aboard planes of the 316th Group, all but two jumped, and all but 28 out of 844 carried by the 315th did so. Of those brought back, 7 paratroopers had been wounded by a flak burst on one plane of the 315th, and 4 had refused to jump.[15]

The drops at DZ O were, taken together, the best at any zone by IX TCC in NEPTUNE. Half the troops dropped were assembled and ready for action within eight hours. Among the factors contributing to this were the success of the 316th and 315th Groups in climbing over the cloudbank and descending to the DZ without losing formation, the absence of intense enemy fire during the approach and over the zone, and the lighted T. This last was an aid not available on the other zones, except at DZ A where the lights went on too late for the first serials. Its presence at O appears to have been important, since after seeing it two of the serials had to make hasty changes in course and altitude in order to drop correctly.

Of 118 sticks delivered in Normandy and intended for DZ O, 31 landed on or barely outside the zone, approximately 29 more came within a mile, and at least an additional 20 were within two miles of it. Some 17 were scattered within or just outside a 5-mile radius. Only three sticks, dropped 14 miles north of the zone, were certainly outside the objective area, but several were missing or unreported.[16]

The 505th Regiment was responsible for an area extending westward from the 101st Division sector at Beuzeville-au-Plain to the Merderet and from les Forges, initially a 101st Division responsibility, northward to include Neuville-au-Plain. In the center of this area was Ste Mère Eglise, next to the causeways the most important objective of the airborne troops. In American hands it would be the hub of communications within the beachhead. Without it the line of the Merderet would scarcely be tenable, and units on the west bank of that river would probably be cut off.

The 2d Battalion of the 505th was to hold the northern perimeter from Beuzeville to the river. The 3d Battalion was to take Ste Mère Eglise. The 1st Battalion was to send one company to seize the Merderet crossings at la Fière, 2 miles west of Ste Mère, and at Chef-du-Pont, which was about 2 miles west of les Forges. The rest of the battalion was to be in reserve.

Almost no initial opposition was met on DZ O, so the well-concentrated troops were able to assemble quickly. By 0820 32 officers and 303 men of the 2d Battalion were organized and ready for action. The battalion commander, Lt. Col. Benjamin H. Vandervoort, had broken his leg in the drop but continued in charge of his unit. Soon after dawn he gave orders to set out northward toward Neuville-au-Plain, but the movement was halted by the regimental commander, who had not heard from the 3d Battalion and was worried about the situation in Ste Mère Eglise. After three hours of uncertainty Vandervoort's men were ordered to advance into that town. Arriving shortly before 1000 they found the 3d Battalion already in full control of Ste Mère Eglise, but hard pressed by counterattacks from the south.

The 3d Battalion had also received a good drop. Lt. Col. Edward C. Krause, the battalion commander, after descending, exactly as planned, beside his unit's assembly point on the south side of DZ O, had organized a system of search parties which within 45 minutes gathered in 180 men from his own battalion plus some from other units. They were just starting for Ste Mère Eglise when they met a Frenchman who told them that most of the German garrison had been moved to positions outside the town for fear of Allied bombing, and that he could lead them in safely by a back road. He was as good as his word. Moving silently and swiftly, with strict orders from Krause not to use firearms, the battalion stole into Ste Mère Eglise and before dawn had occupied all key points and manned a ring of roadblocks around it. Krause himself cut the Cherbourg-Carentan cable. The garrison, mostly antiaircraft artillerymen, had been so surprised that their resistance was negligible. About 30 of the enemy were taken prisoner, including some captured in bed; 10 were killed; and the rest fled southward. A runner with news of this success reached General Ridgway, but, in the excitement, failed to report to the regimental commander.

Krause had instructed his troops to follow him to Ste Mère if they missed him on the drop zone, and by 0900 enough had joined him to bring his strength to over 300 men. He needed every one of them, for at 0930 the Germans attacked from the south with about two companies of infantry supported by guns and tanks. The situation was eased by the arrival of Vandervoort's battalion. It took over the northern and eastern sides of town, while Krause's men concentrated on the south.

By 1130 the attackers had been stopped, and Krause ordered 80 men to strike at their western flank. This show of strength, intimidated the enemy into making a substantial withdrawal. They made no further attacks until dusk when they advanced again after a preliminary shelling. The 505th turned them back easily and classed the fight as hardly more than a strong patrol action. The enemy forces involved were the 795th Georgian Battalion, 91st Division, and some other elements of that division. The paratroopers task was eased by the fact that the Georgians were not eager to fight and their German officers, cut off from higher headquarters, were uneasy and hesitant.

Not until late on D-day did the Germans exert much pressure on the northern perimeter of Ste Mère Eglise. In the morning about two companies of the 1058th Grenadier Regiment had attempted an attack down the north-south highway, but they had been held up from 1030 to about 1700 by the heroic action of a single platoon which Vandervoort had sent that morning to serve as outpost at Neuville. Only 16 out of 44 men in the platoon got back, but their stand had cost the Germans time which they could ill afford to lose.

The last drop on DZ O, that of Headquarters and the 1st Battalion of the 505th PIR by the 315th Group was on a par with those by the first two serials. By 0600 the regimental CP was in operation in an orchard 1,200 yards west of Ste Mère Eglise, and with it was the divisional CP, established by General Ridgway, who had been given a most accurate drop by Capt. Chester A. Baucke of the 52d Wing. By 0930 the 1st Battalion had assembled 22 officers and 338 men, and by then or a little later regimental headquarters had mustered 12 officers and 61 men.

Two hours after the drop Company A, which then numbered 11 officers and 132 men, was dispatched to take the crossing at la Fière. At daybreak as it was approaching its objective it met large bodies of troops from the 507th and 508th Regiments. Together they attempted to reach the bridge but were held short of it throughout the morning by machine-gun fire from a small detachment which the Germans were said to have put there for the first time a day or two before. Early in the afternoon contingents of the other regiments rushed the bridge but the attack failed, and as a result Company A, which had remained on the east bank in a support role, was left almost alone to face an impending counterattack. The rest of the 1st Battalion of the 505th was hastily called to la Fière to meet this threat.

The Germans hammered the battalion for the rest of the day with mortars and artillery and attacked twice across the bridge using infantry of the 1057th Grenadier Regiment and light tanks of the 100th Panzer Replacement Battalion. Both attacks were repulsed but, in the first two, tanks got almost across the causeway before being knocked out by bazookas. The second attack crossed the river, overran the 1st Battalion CP and forced the battalion to drop back temporarily. Needless to say, the 505th had been unable to spare any men for its mission to Chef-du-Pont. Instead, about 1500 hours, some 200 men of the 507th and 508th Regiments who had been attempting to take the crossing there had to be rushed north to la Fière to assist the 505th, leaving only a platoon at Chef-du-Pont. With their help the Germans at la Fière were pushed back west of the river.

Thanks to the good drop they had received, more than three quarters of the troops in the 505th PIR had reported to their units by nightfall on D-day. They were needed, for casualties had been heavy, and no relief was in sight. The troops at Ste Mère Eglise had 44 dead, 130 wounded in hospital, and many wounded still fighting, including Colonels Krause and Vandervoort. At la Fière the 1st Battalion had 20 dead and over 150 other casualties. For artillery the 505th had only one of the two howitzers dropped in BOSTON* and 6 out of 16 antitank guns brought in DETROIT, the predawn glider mission. Ammunition of all types was running very low. However, the rank and file of the 505th, battle-hardened in Mediterranean campaigns, felt themselves equal to the situation. "We're staying right here," they told the French that night.

The commanders of the paratroops were more worried than their men. Radio contact with headquarters in England had not been established, although one large radio was available, and attempts were made to use it. More serious was the inability of the 82d to get in touch with VII Corps, 4th Division or even the 101st until late on D-day. The first radio contact was made with 4th Division about 2100. About the same time a patrol of the 505th PIR met one from the 4th Division near Beuzeville, but it brought back little information. Not until the morning of the 7th when a staff officer of the 82d who had gotten through to the 4th Division CP returned from a midnight conference there did Ridgway know that his east flank was secure and that help was coming.

Equally welcome was the news that the enemy south of the 505th was no longer a serious threat. On the afternoon of D-day the 8th Infantry Regiment, whose progress from UTAH Beach through the 101st Division sector has already been described,† had pushed one of its battalions to the vicinity of Turqueville 1½ miles southeast of Ste Mère Eglise and its other two battalions beyond les Forges, one company almost reaching Chef-du-Pont. The advance penned the 795th Georgian Battalion and other enemy troops on a strip of high ground stretching about two miles southwest from Turqueville across the north-south highway. Others, separated from the rest by the 8th Infantry salient, held out further south at Carquebut.

The 8th Infantry preferred to consolidate its gains rather than risk further action that day, and a seaborne detachment of 93 men of the 325th Glider Infantry, reinforced by a cavalry reconnaissance platoon and a company of light tanks, which had been detailed to clear the les Forges area for glider landings, proved too weak to make much headway. Thus the encircled enemy west of Turqueville was able to play hob with the glider missions.*

On the morning of D plus 1 the 8th Infantry and the detachment from the 82d Division attacked the Turqueville wedge. At Turqueville most of the German officers pulled out as the attack started, and over 150 Slavic and Asiatic conscripts were then talked into surrender by American prisoners.† At other points resistance was stiff, but by 1030 the wedge had been wiped out. A battalion of the 325th Glider Infantry, which had landed near les Forges early in the morning, was sent about noon to deal with the Germans at Carquebut. It found the place deserted. The enemy had fled. However, they reinfiltrated later and had to be driven out again next day.

North of Ste Mère Eglise the Germans were able to launch a formidable attack on 7 June, employing the 1058th Grenadiers, reinforced by the Seventh Army Sturm Battalion, approximately three battalions of artillery, and some tanks or self-propelled guns. This action created such concern that the commander of VII Corps detached a reinforced tank company from 4th Division reserve to protect the 82d Division from attacks by enemy tanks. This force engaged an enemy column just north of Ste Mère Eglise, then swung northeast around its flank toward Neuville-au-Plain, causing the Germans to withdraw their guns and vehicles hastily for fear of being cut off. German infantry remained ensconced in ditches and hedges northwest of town until in mid-afternoon the 2d Battalion of the 505th and the 2d Battalion, 8th Infantry, which had moved up to Ste Mère Eglise, launched a coordinated attack supported by tanks. They outflanked the Germans and defeated them, inflicting heavy casualties.[17]

Thus by the end of D plus 1 the 505th PIR was part of a solid beachhead extending inland to the Merderet. All regimental objectives east of the river had been taken except Neuville-au-Plain, which fell next day, and troops from the beaches were moving up to take over most of its northern front. Behind it in divisional reserve were over 1,700 officers and men of the 325th Glider Infantry Regiment, brought in that morning by gliders

---

*The breechblock of the other landed on ground swept by enemy fire and was not recovered.
†See above, pp. 41-42.

*See below, p. 67.
†Capt. William J. Adams, a captured glider pilot, was later awarded the Silver Star for his part in persuading them to give up.

in GALVESTON and HACKENSACK missions. Divisional artillery was still weak. Only 6 out of 13 antitank guns and 3 out of 24 howitzers brought by the ELMIRA glider mission on the evening of D-day went into action on D plus 1. However, adequate ammunition supplies had been retrieved from the gliders, and next day 11 more of the glider-borne howitzers were hauled to the 505th's sector and began firing. Meanwhile, beyond the Merderet things had not gone so well. Not only had the 507th and 508th Regiments failed to achieve their objectives, but large portions of them were in danger of destruction.

The 508th Parachute Infantry Regiment and a detachment of divisional headquarters had been carried by serials of 36 and 24 aircraft from the 314th Troop Carrier Group and by two serials of 36 planes each from the 313th Group. The lead serial was scheduled to make its drop at 0208. The regimental mission was to hold the southern half of the bridgehead which the 508th and the 507th were supposed to establish beyond the Merderet. The sector assigned to the 508th was a rough quadrangle extending about three miles west of the Merderet and about two miles north from the Douve. The bridge over the Merderet at la Fière was just outside the northern edge of this area.

All four serials were to drop on DZ N, a relatively small zone, about a mile long on the axis of approach and half a mile wide from north to south. It lay 1½ miles west of the Merderet and almost two miles north of the Douve in flat country checkered with hedgerows. Touching its southern edge was a highway running southwest from la Fière to Pont l'Abbé, a town on the Douve about 1½ miles southwest of the zone. About a mile south of DZ N was the hamlet of Picauville. Unknown to the Allies, the German 91st Division had recently established its headquarters a little way north of Picauville and had stationed considerable forces in that area.

Less fortunate than the serials going to DZ O, those intended for DZ N had run headlong into the cloudbank a moment after crossing the coast at PEORIA. Most of the 314th Group apparently stayed in the clouds until within three miles of the zone. Near the DZ they met with some flak and much machine-gun fire, but, thanks to the protecting clouds, only 18 aircraft were damaged, almost all lightly. However, one plane was shot down over the zone after making three passes to drop its troops. The jumpmaster had called the first pass too low, and flak had spoiled the second. The crew survived and reached the Allied lines that night. The pilot of another plane was killed on his second pass, but the co-pilot completed the sortie.

The 313th Group was harder hit than its predecessor, mostly by accurate small-arms fire. One plane crashed in flames after making its drop. Another, burning and with damaged engines, ditched on the way back. A third was missing. The group brought back 21 planes with slight damage, 11 needing moderate repairs, and one badly damaged.

Flying blind until almost at the DZ and harassed by enemy fire as they emerged from the clouds, these four serials were peculiarly in need of pathfinder assistance. They got very little. The pathfinder troops had landed more than a mile southeast of DZ N and found enemy forces blocking their way to the zone. In this dangerous situation all they could do was to operate a Eureka and two amber lights. They reported later that the Eureka was on in ample time and was "triggered" by Rebecca signals at 0156 when the first planes of the 314th were still over 12 miles away. However, only the first serial of the 313th Group reported receiving usable signals from the Rebecca. Some members of other formations picked it up but had poor reception, possibly due to jamming. A few pilots did see the amber lights and used them as a guide. Although the pathfinders turned on their BUPS beacon, there is no evidence that any of the few navigators who had SCR-717 made use of it in selecting their drop point.

The leaders of both serials of the 314th and the rear serial of the 313th Group relied on Gee to establish their position and obtained fairly good results. The most successful was Lt. Col. Clayton Styles, commander of the 314th Group, who placed his stick in good position on the south side of the zone. In the stick was Lt. Col. Thomas J. B. Shanley, commander of the 508th's 2d Battalion, an officer destined to play an important part in the coming battle. The leader of the second serial made his drop about two miles north of DZ N. The leader of the third, using Rebecca-Eureka gave the jump signal in the vicinity of the pathfinders. The fourth leader made a fairly accurate drop on Gee. Thus, if the serials had held together, about half the paratroops intended for DZ N would have come down on or close to it and almost all would have been within two miles of it. In fact all four serials had disintegrated leaving only a small minority in formation behind the leaders.

Of 2,188 paratroops slated for DZ N, 2,183 had been dropped. Two had refused to jump, two had fouled chutes and one was wounded. Over 95 percent of the 63 tons of supplies and equipment carried had been delivered, but a large part of the men and materiel landed far away from the drop zone. About 17 out of 132 sticks did land on or very near to DZ N, and another 16 were within a mile of it. Most of the latter were located beyond the zone, indicating that the pilots had been a little slow in recognizing their position. Perhaps they had seen parachutes beneath them or the Merderet ahead. Some 30 additional planeloads came down within a two-mile radius of the zone. Half of these were in the general vicinity of the pathfinders. The pathfinder beacons were near the Douve, and several sticks fell into the river. No less than 34 pilots went past DZ N, crossed the Merderet, and dropped their loads between DZ O and the coast. At least three of these set their drops by the green T on DZ O, 9 put their sticks near Ste Mère Eglise, and 10 dropped near St. Martin-de-Varreville, which was six miles east of DZ N. Most of the troops dropped east of the river fought on D-day with the 505th PIR or the 101st Division, then assembled on the 7th, and reported to their regimental commander, on the east side of the Merderet near DZ O. A number of jumps were made prematurely with the result that eight sticks descended between three and five miles short of DZ N. Through gross errors two sticks were dropped near Valognes, nine miles north of DZ N and five were dropped about 15 miles north of the zone. The directional error in those cases is so great that it seems as though the pilots must either have gone off course before reaching PEORIA or circled for a second run and lost their bearings completely. Approximately 20 sticks went unaccounted for.

Broadly speaking, then, about a quarter of the 508th Parachute Regiment was dropped within a mile of its zone; one quarter was within two miles of it; another quarter was unable to perform its assigned mission because it had been flown past DZ N and dropped on the wrong side of the Merderet, and most of the remainder was ineffective because of dispersed drops in remote or dangerous places.[18]

The regimental commander, Col. Roy Lindquist, and the divisional paratroop commander, Brig. Gen. James M. Gavin, were dropped by the second serial of the 314th Group, came down about two miles north of DZ N within the territory of the 507th PIR, and joined forces with elements of that regiment. Their activities, can best be discussed later in connection with the 507th. The only important operations on D-day west of the Merderet by members of the 508th were conducted by a group which coalesced gradually around Lieutenant Colonel Shanley on the south side of the drop zone.

After his jump Shanley had quickly collected 30 men by hanging bundle lights in a tree, and then had sent out patrols for more. The next morning he made radio contact with two other groups of platoon size or less. It is a striking fact that although both were within a mile of him, neither was able to join him until the middle of the afternoon. They had had to feel their way cautiously through a maze of thick, high, almost impenetrable hedges, stopping at intervals to skirmish with enemy patrols. The hedges were both an impediment and a shield. The German 91st Division had a battalion of the 1057th Grenadier Regiment in that area and other units nearby with artillery and tanks, enough to have treated the scattered bands of paratroops very roughly in open country. As it was, the Nazis' movements were blind and hesitant.

Shanley's battalion had had the mission of moving south to destroy the highway bridge across the Douve at Pont l'Abbé and defend the north bank of that river from Pont l'Abbé to the Mederet, but after finding his way to the Douve blocked by superior forces Shanley decided to take defensive positions on Hill 30, a partially wooded rise about a mile to the east of him. The hill overlooked the Merderet half way between the la Fière bridge and that at Chef-du-Pont. It took him from late afternoon until almost midnight to cover that one mile. Near the hill he picked up a body of about 200 leaderless and bewildered paratroops. Had those troops attacked the bridge at Chef-du-Pont earlier in the day they could probably have taken it and saved the division much trouble. In the interim the Germans had manned the approaches to the crossing, but they had not yet occupied the hill. Shanley beat them to that. There for the next three days he and his men acted as a kind of shock absorber on which the Germans expended much of their striking power. Shanley had radio contact with divisional headquarters, and was able to get some artillery support. Aside from that his group held out unassisted.[19]

The last phase of the BOSTON paratroop mission was to be the dropping of the 507th Parachute Regiment on DZ T beginning at 0232. The regiment was carried by two serials of 36 planes each from the 61st Troop Carrier Group and one of 45 aircraft from the 442d Group. Five miles before reaching the zone these serials would cross the upper Douve at a point where it was spanned by a long causeway. After that there were no distinctive landmarks short of the Merderet, which flowed just beyond the east end of the DZ, much too close as it turned out. The zone itself was an oval about 1¼ miles long on the axis of approach and half a mile wide, lying on flat alluvial ground 1½ miles north of DZ N, and about the same distance northwest of the la Fière bridge. A thousand yards northeast of the DZ loomed the embankment of the Valognes-Carentan railway slanting southeastward across the Merderet to la Fière.

The 61st Group had some trouble with the clouds, but most of its lead serial held together. The Group suffered little from ground fire. One pilot whose plane was hit within sight of the zone dropped his troops but crashed later. He and his crew bailed out safely. Only six other aircraft of those two serials were hit, and none seriously. The 442d Group had a harder time. Its formation ran into the overcast and dispersed. It was also the target of more fire, principally medium to intense light flak and small-arms fire near the drop zone. One plane was hit over western Normandy and had to crash-land after first dropping its troops many miles short of their goal. Another was missing with all aboard. One with both engines dead was ditched successfully on the way home. Among those returning were 28 with slight and 3 with medium damage.

The pathfinders on DZ T had scored a bulls-eye on their zone, but they found enemy units so near them that they dared not use their lights. They did turn on their Eureka at 0212 and received Rebecca signals at 0217. The incoming serials received the responses very well, and relied on Rebecca in making their drop. The leader of the 442d Group also picked up the responses of the Eureka south of DZ N. Checking it by Gee, he recognized that its location was wrong and also noted the difference in coding. However, about half of his formation were straggling, and there is reason to believe that some of them did drop troops on the wrong beacon. The first plane of the 61st Group made its drop at 0226 and the last at 0245 or later. The main body of the 442d dropped its troops between 0239 and 0242. Of 1,187 troops carried by the 61st Group all but one man, who refused to jump, were deposited in Normandy. Of 750 carried by the 442d Group, all jumped with the possible exception of the one stick aboard a missing plane.

On the whole the drop was better than that of the 508th Regiment. Two or three sticks landed on the zone, and about 50 more came within a mile of it. Unfortunately many pilots had overshot, by between 1,000 and 1,500 yards, causing their troops to land in the swampy backwaters of the Merderet. The water was shallow at most points and few men were drowned, but the rest, floundering in the water with most of their equipment at the bottom of the river were in sorry state to start a battle.

Another 22 sticks came down within approximately two miles of DZ T. The rest, with one odd exception, were scattered. About 16 landed between 2 and 5 miles from the zone, 11 more within a 10-mile radius of it, one 13 miles to the north, and one 25 miles to the south. The only concentrated drop away from the zone was made by 10 pilots in the second serial of the 61st Group who wandered to the vicinity of Montmartin-en-Graignes, 18 miles southeast of DZ T, and dropped about 160 paratroops of the 3d Battalion of the 507th Regiment there. This was the worst error by a formation of such size in either ALBANY or BOSTON. Once again the most plausible explanation is that after some mix-up in the clouds the pilots had fallen in behind a straggler who was not using radar. That they followed their false leader unquestioningly on such a wild-goose chase may be considered a triumph of discipline over common sense.[20]

The most impressive feature of the return from BOSTON Mission was the splendid formation in which the first serial of the 316th Group reached Cottesmore at 0400. This achievement, unique in NEPTUNE, indicates that the serial had at no time been badly scattered. On the other hand, the 313th and 314th Groups returned singly or in driblets. Also some elements of the 61st Group left their corridor and cut straight across from Normandy to Portland Bill. The last stragglers to reach British soil did so about 0540. Their arrival ended the troop carriers' role in the paratroop missions.

The 507th Parachute Regiment was supposed to hold the northern half of the 82d Division's bridgehead over the Merderet. It was to defend a perimeter curving from the northwest corner of the 508th's territory to a point on the Merderet two miles north of la Fière. One battalion was to take the western approaches to the la Fière bridge. By a curious combination of circumstances much more than a battalion gathered at that crossing, but on the wrong side, the eastern shore of the river.

Elements of G Company of the 507th under Capt. F. V. Schwartzwalder came down on the east side of the Merderet north of the bridge, moved toward it, and at dawn joined with A Company of the 505th PIR in a fight against Germans in houses near the bridge. Later they were joined by most of the forty-odd sticks of the 507th and 508th which had dropped into the marshes of the Merderet east of DZ T. Many of those troops had headed straight for the railway embankment which was the nearest and most obvious dry ground and had moved southeast along the embankment and across the river to la Fière. Others had tried to move down the west bank of the river, were halted by enemy forces of superior strength, and likewise decided on the embankment as the best way to the bridge. First came 130 men under Lindquist, then more than 100 under Gavin, then about 150 collected by Lt. Col. Arthur Maloney and Lt. Col. Edwin J. Ostberg of the 507th. Others followed in smaller groups. By midmorning about 600 paratroops were massed near la Fière.

Since this force seemed more than sufficient to take the bridge, Gavin sent 75 paratroops under Maloney to reconnoiter southward and later, on hearing that Chef-du-Pont was undefended, set out with Colonel Ostberg and 75 men to take the bridge there. The east end of the Chef-du-Pont crossing was readily secured, but a few stubborn Germans with some very effective artillery assistance barred the bridge, even though during the afternoon Ostberg and Maloney employed nearly 250 troops in attempts to cross.

Meanwhile, Colonel Lindquist, left in command at la Fière, prepared to force a crossing at that point. One company did not get the order, but the rest cleared the east end of the bridge, and Schwartzwalder dashed across with about 80 men. On the far side they met a patrol sent out by Lt. Col. Charles J. Timmes, commander of the 2d Battalion of the 507th. He had assembled about 50 of his men east of Amfreville near their prescribed zone. Most unfortunately, Captain Schwartzwalder, instead of consolidating his bridgehead, decided that he ought to join Timmes, and did so, leaving only a dozen men behind at the bridge. Before adequate reinforcements could join them, the Germans counterattacked with tank and artillery support, retook the west end of the bridge and soon established themselves there in strength.

In this manner the 82d Division lost its bridgehead west of the Merderet and the paratroops on that side of the river were cut off. Some 300 of them were with Shanley and 120 with Timmes and Schwartzwalder. A larger group gradually concentrated around Col. George V. Millett, Jr., the commander of the 507th PIR. On D-day about 75 men assembled with him near the west end of DZ T. As more converged on that area his force grew until finally he had about 400 men under his command.

Though relatively strong in numbers, Millett's group was without artillery and almost without ammunition. Pinned down among the hedgerows it was unable even to reach Timmes, who was less than a mile away. The Germans, gradually realizing Millett's weakness, pressed him harder and harder, until on the 8th he sent out a series of radio messages declaring that the situation was very critical and that he could hardly hold out another day unaided. Timmes' position, too, was highly precarious, and Shanley, though resisting staunchly, was nearing the end of his resources. The propect of the paratroops west of the Merderet looked dark indeed.

Certainly part of the responsibility of this situation must rest on the troop carriers. Only about a third of the 507th and 508th PIR's had landed in their assigned operational area. At full strength they would have been more than a match for their principal opponent, the 1057th Grenadier Regiment. Instead, they were outnumbered, scattered, and handicapped by the loss of much of their equipment. Whether the movement of several hundred paratroops along the embankment to the east side of the river was an inevitable result of the inaccurate drop may be doubted. Nor were the results of that move necessarily bad. Since the initial German garrisons at the la Fière and Chef-du-Pont bridges were very small, the former might conceivably have been taken before dawn by Schwartzwalder's men and the latter by the paratroops dropped near Hill 30. In that case Company A of the 505th PIR, reinforced by the troops which arrived later from the embankment, would probably have sufficed to defend them. Even as it was, a foothold on the west bank was won by Captain Schwartzwalder and with better coordination might have been held. Although such a bridgehead could not have been exploited immediately, it would have spared the 82d Division the necessity for a bloody assault later to secure a crossing and would thereby have speeded both the relief of the encircled paratroops and the Allied advance across Normandy.

For two days after the D-day battles the situation along the Merderet remained practically unchanged. On 7 June the Germans made fierce but unsuccessful attacks at la Fière. Both sides spent the 8th in reorganizing and skirmishing. On the evening of the 8th Ridgway decided to strike across the river and rescue his encircled men. He had available about 850 men of the 508th PIR and perhaps 500 of the 507th, but they were tired, and short of equipment. He therefore picked for his assault fresh troops of the 325th Glider Infantry Regiment, which had arrived by glider on D plus 1.

The 1st Battalion of the 325th crossed the Merderet via the embankment about midnight on 8/9 June, waded along a submerged road through the marshes, turned south after reaching dry ground and attacked toward the la Fière bridge, picking up Timmes' force on the way. Half a mile from the bridge they ran into strong opposition and fell back. Millett's group, which had been directed to fight its way east and join Timmes, attempted to do so but broke up in confused fighting north of Amfreville. Millett himself was missing in action, and half his men were captured or killed. The rest filtered north around the flank of the German positions and ultimately reached the east side of the river, presumably by way of the embankment.

The 3d Battalion of the 325th had been held in reserve.* On learning that the flank attack had been stopped, General Gavin ordered the battalion to rush the la Fière bridge. With the enemy present in strength this was a difficult and hazardous business, since, though the bridge itself was short, it was approached at either end by a long, narrow causeway completely exposed throughout its length. The attack jumped off at 1045 on the 9th after a 15-minute artillery preparation by a few howitzers and medium tanks. The first rush carried most of a company across, although bullets were beating on the bridge like hail. Then some men faltered and a jam developed; a tank sent to hearten the infantry struck a mine and slewed sideways across the causeway; and heavy-weapons men, unable to get through set up machine guns on the road, increasing the congestion. After an hour of strenuous efforts in which Ridgway personally participated, the causeway was made passable, and the rest of the 3d Battalion of the 325th crossed in spasmodic rushes together with a company of the 507th PIR, which had been thrown in to assist them. About noon the heavy weapons platoon and three Sherman tanks got across to provide the infantry with very welcome fire support, and the 3d Battalion of the 508th PIR was committed to take over the southern flank of the bridgehead.

Throughout the afternoon the Americans, greatly hampered by lack of communications, not only with their artillery, tanks and higher headquarters, but even between company and company, advanced slowly through the hedgerows in hard fighting. At 1530 contact was made with Timmes and the 1st Battalion of the 325th. A little later the 3d Battalion of the 508th reached Shanley's positions on Hill 30. By evening the 82d Division held a bridgehead two miles wide extending three-quarters of a mile west of the Merderet to the village of le Motey.

The battle seemed won, but the 1057th Grenadiers, though terribly mauled, were still dangerous. At 1900 they launched a counterattack so savage that it almost broke through to the river. The 1st Battalion of the 325th Glider Infantry was cut off for a time. The regimental commander was evacu-

---

*The 2d Battalion of the 325th was assisting the 505th PIR in its attack northward from Ste Mère Eglise.

ated with combat fatigue, and the executive sent word that he did not think he could hold. The rest of the 507th PIR, about 350 men, was hastily thrown into the line, and by 2045 the situation was stabilized. Casualties had been very heavy, the 325th having lost half its strength during the day. Exclusive of the 2d Battalion, it had 60 men dead, 283 seriously wounded, and 246 who were still missing two days later.

At dawn on 10 June two regiments of the 90th Division passed through the bridgehead to relieve the airborne troops holding it and take up the attack westward across the peninsula. The 82d Division, except for the 505th PIR and one glider battalion which were attacking northward toward le Ham in collaboration with the 8th Infantry, was withdrawn to rest and reorganize. The initial phase of its operations was over.[21]

Evaluation of the Paratroop Operations

As D-day drew to a close, the feeling in IX TCC and 9th AF was that the delivery of the paratroops had been an outstanding success. Losses and aborts had been negligible, and mission reports indicated that all serials had done well. On 10 June came the reaction. General Quesada returned from a visit to Normandy with news that the paratroops had been badly scattered and that General Bradley was much disappointed.[22]

To put the matter in perspective, it is well to summarize just what had been accomplished. The troop carriers had undertaken to bring 13,348 paratroops to Normandy. Of these, about 90 were brought back for one reason or another and 18 were in a plane ditched before reaching the Continent. About 100 in ALBANY and perhaps 30 or 40 in BOSTON were killed when the planes carrying them were shot down. The rest jumped. Of the jumpers over 10 percent landed on their drop zones, between 25 and 30 percent landed within a mile of their zone or pathfinder beacon, and between 15 and 20 percent were from 1 to 2 miles away. At least 55 percent of the pilots made drops within 2 miles of their goals. About 25 percent of the troops came down between 2 and 5 miles away from their zones or beacons. With few exceptions these landed east of Pont l'Abbé and north of the Douve, seemingly within reach of the combat area. About 10 percent were from 5 to 10 miles off the mark, and 4 percent were scattered between 10 and 25 miles from their zones. The remaining 6 percent were unaccounted for.*

The question arises why, if over 10,000 men were dropped within five miles of their zones, the 101st Division had only about 1,100 troops and the 82d Division about 1,500 troops near their divisional objectives at H-hour (0630) four hours after the end of the drop. Why, too, did the 101st Division have only 2,500 paratroops under divisional control and the 82d Division about 2,000 at midnight of D-day? The matter is important, for if the troops had been able to concentrate on their zones at even the rate of one mile an hour, three-quarters of the force dispatched would have gone into action against its objectives on the morning of D-day and General Bradley would have had slight reason to complain of dispersion.

Colonel Shanley's experiences and those of a multitude of others demonstrate that it often took most of a day to move a single mile in the hedgerow country, particularly if there was the slightest trace of opposition. This circumstance caused drop dispersion to seem much greater than it was and to have more serious consequences than would otherwise have been the case.† The isolation of large bodies of paratroops west of the Merderet and in the vicinity of DZ D accentuated the impression of weakness and dispersion which prevailed in higher headquarters on D plus 2 and D plus 3. Recognition that such groups as those under Shanley and Johnson had received good drops and had done valuable work did not come until later.

On the other hand, it must be said that only six serials in the two paratroop missions achieved anything like compact drops. A map of the other drops looks as though a pepper shaker had been waved three or four times over each zone. Since the zones were all close together and the number of troops was great, these scatterings overlapped, blanketing the battle area. For miles around bands of paratroops attacked outposts and small troop movements and cut communications with paralyz-

---

*Many of those were badly dropped, but undoubtedly some well-placed sticks went unreported because of battle losses.
†The 101st Division used the metal snappers known as crickets for recognition and assembly. In the bocage these proved helpful even by daylight. The 82d Division had relied on lights and patrol for assembly and did not have the crickets.

ing effect.* The Germans even suspected that they were faced with a new tactic of saturation drops.

Such a tactic, however, would be of dubious value, partly because of the vulnerability of scattered troops, and partly because of the need to concentrate decisive numbers at decisive points. The whole history of war shows that a good fighting team can usually beat the best individual fighters, and the effective mopping up of several hundred outlying paratroops in Normandy by quite small German units bears out this rule. The 101st Division reported that it could not have held out in its scattered state for much more than 24 hours without support from the beaches, and it seems doubtful whether even the veteran 82d Division could have lasted 48 hours without such help. If the 505th PIR had not been able to function as a unit close to full strength because of its concentrated drop the plight of the 82d would have been disastrous. The ability of the airborne to clear causeways from the beaches and establish a perimeter of sorts from the sea to the Merderet was derived, not from dispersion but, on the contrary, from the presence of barely enough men in the right place at the right time. If anyone had tried to tell Shettle's men at the le Port bridges or Company A of the 505th at la Fière about the advantages of scattering troops the answers would surely have been unprintable.

Having assessed the paratroop missions as better than sometimes supposed, but still only barely successful, the next step is to determine why they fell short of expectations. The evidence indicates that except for slight errors in timing, troop carrier performance was almost flawless until the Normandy coast was reached, and that with one exception most subsequent difficulties may be traced to three factors, clouds, enemy action, and the limitations of navigational aids.

Of these, the cloudbank over the western Cotentin was the most damaging. At least 9 of the 20 main serials had plunged into the clouds and were badly dispersed as a result. All of the six making reasonably compact drops appear to have avoided the cloudbank. Since the clouds were over a thousand feet up and less than a thousand feet in thickness it would have been easy to go over or under them with a minimum of warning. If only a weather plane had been sent to test conditions, if only radio silence rules had not prohibited one serial from warning those that followed, troop carrier performance would have been immensely improved. Masses of low clouds were known to be over Normandy on three June nights out of four, and it must be rated as a serious planning error that no safeguard against their presence was made.

Enemy fire had considerable effect, but it had been minimized as far as could reasonably be expected. Thanks to excellent intelligence, planes staying on course encountered very little flak. Thanks to effective tactical surprise and the protection of the cloud bank, fire of any sort was slight until the planes were within five miles of the drop zones. Even then it was wild and ineffective, causing losses of under 2½ percent. Although the pilots had been warned against evasive action many of them did indulge in it. After all, about a fifth of them had had only a minimum of training and three-quarters of them had never been under fire before. Later, in MARKET and VARSITY, they were to do better in this respect under much greater hazards. It should be remembered to their credit that all but two stuck to their task and dropped their troops, many making repeated passes under fire in attempts to correct errors. Another adverse effect of ground fire was to interfere with navigation by distracting attention and concealing signals. A pilot whose plane was tossed about by a bursting shell might be a mile off course before he knew it. Light signals from formation leaders or from pathfinder troops on the ground could be hidden in a welter of flares, tracers and smoke.

The pilots were forced to rely heavily on radar because for most of their way across Normandy the clouds rendered visual navigation nearly impossible. In NEPTUNE radar proved to be a much less effective guide than radar enthusiasts had supposed. It did guide planes to the general vicinity of their zones, but it could not be relied on to produce an accurate drop.

As already noted, SCR-717 was of little value in locating inland objectives. Gee was successful enough to rouse uncritical enthusiasm, but its margin of error in Normandy averaged about a mile.[23] Miscalculations or faulty adjustment could cause a three-mile error like that of the lead serial of the 438th Group. Although it had a bad repu-

---

*Most notable of their exploits was that of six paratroops of the 508th PIR who ambushed and killed Generalleutnant Wilhelm Falley, commander of the 91st Division, just as he was setting out by car at 0600 on D-day from his headquarters near Picauville. (James M. Gavin, *Airborne Warfare* (Washington, 1947), p. 65; statement by POW Baumann, 11 Jun 44, in 82d Abn Div, G-2 File in Microfilm Box 2007, Item 2029.)

tation for breakdowns and vulnerability to jamming, Gee was 98 percent serviceable and almost unaffected by jamming in NEPTUNE. However, since only the pathfinders and one or two planes in each serial were equipped with Gee, it was of no help to the multitude of pilots whose formations had broken up.

Rebecca-Eureka, prescribed as the primary aid to be employed in approaching the drop zones, was so used in a majority of cases. Responses from the Eurekas on the zones were picked up clearly at an average distance of 16 miles, except at DZ A and DZ N. In the former case the beacon was turned on too late for the first one or two serials, and in the latter, either because of jamming or because of malfunction, the reception was unsatisfactory. Had some beacons and some Rebecca sets been turned on sooner the average reception distance might have increased to about 20 miles. The average range of the Eurekas in England and on the marker boats was 22 miles, but in part this was achieved because the missions flew higher over England than during their approach to Normandy. As anticipated, precision dropping with Rebecca proved very difficult because the blips representing plane and beacon merged well before the plane reached its zone. This may have been the main reason why so many of the pilots came within 2 miles of their zones, but were unable to hit them.

Another weakness of Rebecca-Eureka was that, when many beacons were used in a small area, a Rebecca was likely to trigger the wrong beacon and receive its responses. Available channels were too few and too close together, and the sets were insufficiently selective to prevent such reception. Many pilots in NEPTUNE are known to have picked up the wrong beacon, and there is circumstantial evidence that others made drops on the wrong beacon, despite the fact that each had its own distinctive coding.

Most serious of all was the liability of Rebecca-Eureka to saturation if more than about 40 sets were in use at once. For this reason its use had been limited to flight leaders except in case of emergency. Although used by an estimated 150 stragglers, and by as many as 30 of them at one time on one beacon, the Rebecca system did not become saturated. What did happen was that at least 150 pilots who needed to use it did not do so. In this category may be placed most of those who dropped their loads more than five miles from their zones. With few exceptions pilots making such drops had become separated from their flight-leaders. We may surmise that most of them had lost track of their position either because of evasive action or because they had overshot and had to make an additional pass. Once disoriented, it was fatally easy for them to make a wrong guess as to where they were and proceed to the wrong destination, or, like the St. Jores group, to fall in behind others who were doing so. Cautious pilots used Rebecca and succeeded. Confident or overconscientious pilots hesitated to use it and went astray. Since the sets were 97 percent serviceable and had sufficient range to cover most of the Cotentin, almost every one of these wanderers could have reached the drop area by using them. The error lay in the wording of the field orders which should have enjoined all individual stragglers and all leaders of straggling elements to make use of Rebecca, as soon as they became separated from their flight.* Admittedly this would have involved some risk of saturation, but the alternative course denied radar guidance to those who needed it most.

Another handicap which fell especially on the inexperienced pilots who lost contact with their formations was that only two planes in five carried navigators. This number, all that the tables of organization permitted, was ample for formation flying by daylight, but stragglers on a difficult flight over enemy territory at night would have benefitted by having trained men to compute their positions.

One major episode, the bad drop made by the second serial of the 436th Group, is difficult to explain in the above terms. The three or four mile deviation of the lead elements might possibly have resulted from radar misuse or malfunction, but how a majority of the serial, could have dropped north of Montebourg is an enigma.

If all had gone according to plan, formations guided by Gee or Rebecca to the vicinity of their zones would have seen lighted T's showing them exactly where to drop. However, on four zones out of six enemy action or the nearness of enemy troops prevented display of anything but an occasional surreptitious light. At a fifth zone, DZ A, the T was put out too late for two serials, one probably never came in sight of it, and the other

---

*It is significant that field orders for airborne missions after NEPTUNE were worded to this effect.

one slated to use it was scattered. On DZ O where T's were put out as planned the best drops in either ALBANY or BOSTON were achieved, and they were the best precisely because of corrections made after the T's were sighted. Since of all the other serials only two or three made even comparably good drops, the case for use of lighted T's seems strong, if not conclusive.

The difficulties encountered in NEPTUNE once again raised the question of whether night paratroop operations were worth while. Given the vulnerability of lighted beacons, the limitations of radar, and the difficulty of keeping formation at night, the advantage of being able to see one's way might more than balance the hazards of ground fire and air interception incurred by daytime missions—provided the enemy were not too strong. So General Williams decided prior to DRAGOON, and so General Brereton decided before MARKET and VARSITY. Never again in World War II did any considerable number of Allied paratroops make a night drop.

CHICAGO and DETROIT — The Initial Glider Missions

For reasons already noted the follow-up missions in NEPTUNE were comparatively small. They played only a minor part in the operations of the 101st Division because of its quick link-up with the seaborne forces. They were of real but limited assistance to the 82d Division. Their greatest value lay in the experience they provided in the little-known fields of aerial reinforcement and re-supply.

The first reinforcements, consisting principally of artillery, were to be delivered by two glider missions, CHICAGO and DETROIT, about dawn on D-day. Late in May the time of the two missions had been changed from civil twilight to before daybreak to give the glider men greater safety from ground fire. Release time for CHICAGO was to be 0400 and that for DETROIT 0407. In vain did both the troop carrier and airborne commanders protest to Leigh-Mallory that they were once more being committed to night landings and that such landings on the small fields of the Cotentin might cost half the force in crashes alone.* Fear of German guns outweighed their objections and the decision stood. However, as a concession, about two days before D-day IX TCC was authorized to use Waco gliders exclusively in those two missions in place of the heavier, less maneuverable and less familiar Horsas. The change entailed a hasty revision of loading plans and a substantial reduction in the amount carried. Since the two serials were to approach under cover of darkness, they could safely follow the same routes as the paratroops. CHICAGO, which was in support of the 101st Division, would follow the course of ALBANY, and DETROIT, which was to serve the 82d Airborne, would follow the path of BOSTON.[24]

CHICAGO began at 0119 when 52 planes of the 434th Group, each towing a Waco, began their take-off from Aldermaston. Occupying 44 of the gliders were Batteries A and B of the 81st Airborne AA Battalion. Aboard the others were medics, engineers, signal men, and a few staff personnel, including Brig. Gen. Don F. Pratt,* assistant commander of the 101st Division. In all, the serial carried 155 airborne troops. The cargo consisted of sixteen 57-mm (6-pounder) antitank guns, 25 vehicles, including a small bulldozer for the engineers, 2½ tons of ammunition and 11 tons of miscellaneous equipment.

The destination was LZ E, a roughly triangular area overlapping the west side of DZ C. Its northern side, a mile long, ran beside the road which connected Ste Marie-du-Mont and les Forges. Its western boundary was about 1½ miles long. The slightly concave hypotenuse passed through the village of Hiesville, two miles west of Ste Marie. Like the rest of that region, the LZ was flat and divided into fields, of which most of those on the zone were between 300 and 400 yards long. Outside the zone the average field was considerably shorter, many being only 200 yards in length. Early intelligence reports had described the fields as bordered by trees averaging 40 feet in height. These trees had not shown up well on reconnaissance photographs, and their presence received little or no mention in the briefings of the glider pilots, who assumed that the borders were merely large hedges.

The 434th made a good take-off, and with bright moonlight to assist it readily assembled

---

*It will be recalled that the glider training program of IX TCC had not included tactical landings at night.

*Pratt's inclusion in the glider mission was an afterthought. He had originally been designated to command the seaborne echelon of the division.

Figure 5. Waco Gliders Landing in Normandy.

into columns of four in echelon to the right. Shortly thereafter a glider broke loose and landed four miles from the base. In it was a SCR-499 radio by which the 101st Division was to have communicated with higher headquarters. The equipment was retrieved and sent that evening in KEOKUK Mission, but together with the loss of communications personnel and equipment in ALBANY this accident prevented the Division from communicating with the outside world until after noon on D-day.

The rest of the serial reached Normandy without incident, but encountered sporadic fire, mostly from small arms, while crossing the peninsula. The enemy shot down one plane and glider near Pont l'Abbé and inflicted minor damage on seven planes. Some slight damage was also done to the gliders. The weather over the Cotentin was cloudy but not enough so to cause dispersion. Only one pilot straggled out of formation. He released his glider south of Carentan, about eight miles from the LZ. The other 49 pilots reached the release area, split into two columns as prescribed to avoid congestion during the landings, and released their gliders from an altitude of 450 feet at 0354, six minutes ahead of schedule. They had been guided for the last 20 miles by a Eureka set up by the pathfinders and could see the green lights of the T flashing beneath them. After releasing they headed out over the St. Marcouf islands. All arrived safely at Aldermaston soon after 0530.

Their portion of the operation had been successful, but the glider pilots ran into difficulties. They swept into the prescribed 270 degree left turn and in the process most of them apparently lost sight of the T. Without it in the dim light of a setting moon obscured by clouds they could not recognize their landing zone. Only 6 landed on the zone and 15 within about half a mile of it. Ten were neatly concentrated near les Forges, west of LZ E, and the other 18 scattered east and southeast of the zone, all but one landing within two miles of it.

Most of the gliders made crash landings. This was to be expected. The Waco was capable of clearing the highest trees around the zones and landing within 300 yards, but in doing so there was almost no margin for error. Pilots attempting the feat in semi-darkness were likely to overshoot and ram into a tree or ditch at the far end of the field. The unexpectedness of the obstacles greatly

Figure 6. Remnants of Gliders in a Normandy Hedgerow.

increased the hazard. On smaller fields outside the zone a crash was inevitable, and the T had been misplaced somewhat west of its proper location, causing some glider pilots to mistake their position and land on unsuitable fields.

Nevertheless the landings were successful. Darkness minimized the amount of effectiveness of enemy fire, and all but a handful of glider pilots managed to bring their craft to a stop without harming the passengers and contents, even though the gliders themselves were mostly crumpled beyond repair. Five of the airborne, including General Pratt, were killed, 17 were injured, and 7 were missing.

It took time to pry equipment out of smashed gliders, and more time to assemble, with occasional interruptions by rifle fire or mortar shells. A detachment sent out at dawn by the 101st Division to meet the mission at the LZ and guide the reinforcements to Hiesville did not return until noon, but when it came back it brought with it 3 jeeps, 6 antitank guns, 115 glider troops, and 35 prisoners to boot. Because of the bad drop of the 377th FA Battalion, the division had for artillery only one 75-mm. pack howitzer on the northern perimeter near Foucarville and one captured German gun at the 506th's Culoville CP, so the gliderborne antitank guns were particularly welcome. On D plus 1 and D plus 2, they provided valuable support for Colonel Sink's thrusts southward against the Germans at St. Côme-du-Mont. CHICAGO Mission had succeeded beyond expectation.[25]

The 82d Division's initial glider mission, DETROIT, was flown from Ramsbury by the 437th Group. It was to follow 10 minutes after CHICAGO. The same Eureka beacon and T of green lights which had been provided for the paratroop drop on that zone would be used as aids for the gliders. The serial was made up of 52 C-47's and 52 Wacos. It carried Batteries A and B of the 80th Airborne Antiaircraft Battalion, part of the divisional staff, and a signal detachment, 220 troops in all. Its cargo was 22 jeeps, 5 trailers, sixteen 57-mm antitank guns, and 10 tons of other equipment and supplies.

The 437th Group began taking off at 0159 and had its serial in the air by 0223 with the exception of one plane which lost its glider, returned for a substitute, and delivered it to the LZ about half an hour behind the rest. The weather over England and the Channel was reported as favorable with visibility over 10 miles at most points. The Eurekas at the checkpoints were picked up at 10 to 12 miles distance, and the lights at GALLUP and HOBOKEN were visible from afar. Unaffected by distant fire from Alderney and Guernsey, the formation reached PEORIA intact. Then, like so many of its predecessors in the paratroop missions, it ran into the cloudbank, which at that time and place extended from an altitude of about 800 feet to approximately 1,400 feet.

The leader and many others climbed to 1,500 feet, went over the clouds, and let down two or three minutes later through breaks in the overcast. They emerged somewhat scattered and slightly north of course. However, a substantial portion of the serial plunged into the clouds and found itself in such dense obscurity that the glider pilots could not see their own tow planes. Inevitably that part of the formation broke up, although most of the pilots remained approximately on course.

While in the cloudbank seven gliders broke loose, were released, or were cut loose by enemy fire. Two were later located in western Normandy, but the rest were still unaccounted for a month later. Further inland the clouds became thinner and more broken, but visibility was still bad enough to cause the premature release of seven more gliders on the west side of the Merderet. It appears that one or two pilots, catching a glimpse of the flooded valley ahead of them, mistook it for the sea and hastily gave the signal for release. Others behind them saw their gliders descending, assumed the zone had been reached, and likewise released their gliders.

Once out of the clouds, the serial was harassed by small-arms and machine-gun fire. One plane was lost, 13 received enough damage to ground them temporarily on their return, and 25 more were decorated with bullet and shell holes. The gliders, too, incurred some damage and the troops suffered a number of casualties.

About 37 pilots surmounted all difficulties and reached the vicinity of the LZ between 0401 and 0410. The Eureka on LZ O was functioning and had been picked up by the leaders at a distance of 15 miles. The T was not in operation, and certain glider pilots who reported seeing a green T south of Ste Mère Eglise had probably sighted the one on LZ E.

Loose and disorganized as the serial was, part of it did make a concerted release in two columns with the left-hand column some 200 yards north of the LZ and the right-hand one heading over the center of the zone at altitudes between 400 and 500 feet. Most of the stragglers released in that general area and at roughly the same altitude. After releasing, all planes dived down to about 100 feet, skimmed out over the coast through a spatter of small-arms fire, and headed home. The first reached the runway at Ramsbury at 0522, and the last straggler was back by 0610.

While the descent of the gliders in DETROIT was marked by no such confusion as had marred the big glider mission to Sicily, it was certainly not according to plan. Instead of spiralling smoothly into their appointed fields, the gliders came down by ones and by twos with each pilot following the pattern that seemed best to him. Several were under fire on their way down, and one glider pilot claimed to have been attacked by an enemy fighter (probably another glider), but the main difficulty was the inability of glider pilots to identify their proper fields or, in some cases, to orient themselves at all. The railway and the town of Ste Mère Eglise seem to have been the only landmarks that most could recognize in the dim light. Nevertheless, between 17 and 23 managed to land on or near LZ O.* The best concentration among these was achieved by 5 pilots of the 84th Troop Carrier Squadron who landed their Wacos in adjoining fields at the western end of the LZ. Nine other gliders, including 2 which crash-landed in Ste Mère Eglise, were within two miles of the zone. Three, which came down near Hiesville, may have followed aids set out on LZ E for CHICAGO.

As in CHICAGO safe landings were the exception rather than the rule. Some 22 of the gliders were destroyed, and all but about a dozen were badly smashed. Again the principal cause of crashes was the smallness of the fields and the height of the trees surrounding them, but other hazards such as swamps, and the rows of posts known as "Rommel's asparagus," accounted for nearly half the crack-ups. One glider ran into a herd of cattle. The rough landings produced fewer casualties than might have been expected. Only three of the airborne troops were killed and 23 injured. Several jeeps broke loose and 11 of them were unusable. The guns were more durable. Of 8 landed within two miles of the zone all remained intact.

One effect of the dispersion of the paratroops was to provide friendly reception committees on the spot for most of the gliders even in cases where they missed the zone by a considerable distance. Overjoyed to get artillery, these men were of great assistance in unloading. They blasted down a wall to get one gun out of an orchard in St Mère Eglise and ripped another out of a Waco which had wrapped itself around a tree. By noon four of the guns were in action at la Fière and two or three others on the outskirts of Ste Mère Eglise. Though hardly more than 50 percent effective, the mission had given the airborne troops some badly needed firepower.[26]

KEOKUK and ELMIRA Glider Missions

Between dawn and early evening on D-day the troop carriers undertook no further operations, but about 2100, two hours before sunset two more glider missions, KEOKUK and ELMIRA, arrived over Normandy. As already noted, these and subsequent missions were heavily escorted and minimized their exposure to German antiaircraft by approaching their objectives from the east coast over the UTAH beachhead.

KEOKUK was flown from Aldermaston for the 101st Division by 32 planes of the 434th Group, each towing a Horsa. The big gliders carried 157* signal, medical, and staff personnel, 40 vehicles, 6 guns, and about 19 tons of other equipment and supplies. Release was to be made at 2100 hours over LZ E. At 1830 the first tug and glider took off on what proved to be an incredibly easy mission as far as the aircraft crews were concerned. With good weather and daylight all the way everyone kept on course and in formation. No enemy aircraft were encountered and virtually no ground fire. Battle damage consisted of a few nicks in one plane. A detachment of glider pilots had been busy clearing the drop zone and cutting down trees, and the pathfinders had marked it with a yellow panel T and green smoke.

The serial, like most of its predecessors, arrived

---

*Interrogations of the glider pilots indicate that 23 were in the vicinity, but some of them are very vague as to their exact location.

*Given as 165 in Leonard Rapport and Arthur Northwood, Jr., *Rendezvous With Destiny* (Washington, 1948), p. 133.

ahead of schedule, and the gliders were released at 2053. The pilots then circled and returned as they had come over the St. Marcouf islands, and GALLUP. They reached Aldermaston at 2228.

The glider pilots had a harder time than the plane crews. The Germans still had considerable forces around Turqueville, two miles north of LZ E, and St. Côme, two miles south of the zone, and had not been entirely cleared from the area between. After holding fire as the planes passed over, the enemy concentrated it on the descending gliders but were not near enough to do much harm. Operating in daylight, most of the glider pilots were able to land the Horsas with no more than moderate damage, a fact worth noting in view of what was to happen later in ELMIRA Mission.* However, bullets and accidents combined to kill 14 troops and cause 30 other casualties. Ten of the airborne were missing. They had been in two gliders which landed within the German lines near les Droueries.

The distribution of the landings indicates that most of the serial had released its gliders at least a mile short of the proper point. Fourteen gliders were concentrated in a few fields about 2½ miles northeast of LZ E; five were at points several hundred yards further east; eight were scattered southeast of the zone at distances up to two miles from it; and only five landed on the LZ itself.

KEOKUK was helpful rather than essential to the operations of the 101st Division. However, it is important as the Allies' first tactical glider operation in daylight. It indicated that gliders, when not exposed to fire at close range, could be landed in daytime without excessive losses.[27]

ELMIRA, the other glider mission on the evening of D-day was to reinforce the 82d Division. In order to limit the glider columns to a defensible length and to reduce congestion during the glider landings it was split into two echelons. One, towing 76 gliders, was to be 10 minutes behind KEOKUK, the other, towing 100 gliders, would go two hours later.

The goal of the mission was LZ W, an oval about 2,800 yards long from north to south and over 2,000 yards wide on terrain much like that of LZ E. The northern tip of the oval was about a mile south of Ste Mère Eglise, and the highway from that town to Carentan ran through the middle of the zone. About 1,000 yards inside the southern end of the LZ, the highway was intersected at les Forges by the east-west road from Ste Marie-du-Mont.

The first echelon contained two serials, one of 26 planes of the 437th Group, towing 8 Wacos and 18 Horsas, and a second of 50 from the 438th Group with 14 Wacos and 36 Horsas. The Wacos were segregated in separate flights to reduce the problem of flying two types of glider in one formation. Within the gliders of the first echelon were Battery C of the 80th Airborne AA Battalion, contingents of medics, signal men and divisional headquarters personnel, a reconnaissance platoon and an air support party—437 men in all. The cargo comprised 64 vehicles, mostly jeeps, 13 antitank guns (57-mm.), and 24½ tons of other supplies and equipment.

The 437th took off from Ramsbury between 1907 and 1921, and the 438th from Greenham Common between 1848 and 1916. Climbing with the heavily laden Horsas was a slow business, but all planes succeeded in assembling and setting out in formation. Over England squally weather made the gliders hard to handle; they veered and pitched on their long ropes. From then on the weather was excellent with unlimited visibility and scattered clouds overhead at 3,000 feet. At Portland Bill the escort appeared. The sky seemed full of P-47's, P-51's and P-38's, an impressive array. Besides "delousing" patrols ahead of the column, fighters were flying close cover on both sides and high cover at between 3,000 and 5,000 feet. No German planes appeared to challenge them, and the columns flew in serenely over UTAH Beach.

Not until the release point was almost reached did ground fire begin. This rapidly increased in intensity and did considerable damage. The volume of fire was moderate, the period of exposure was short, and the weapons employed were small arms and machine guns with a little 20-mm. flak, but the shooting was unpleasantly accurate. Enemy troops were close to the line of flight, and the mission had neither surprise nor darkness to protect it. Two aircraft were shot down after releasing their gliders, but only two or three injuries resulted. One of the two planes, its engines dead, dived between two trees, stripping off both wings and engines, yet skidded safely to rest. Some 37 aircraft returned to England with slight or moderate damage. Two had dead engines, one had 65 bullet holes, and one limped in with the crew

---
*See below, pp. 67-68.

chief holding its shattered feed lines together. Three men had been slightly wounded.

LZ W, a short six miles from the coast, should have been easy to locate. The landscape was still plainly visible, and some pilots saw a panel T and green smoke, near which a Eureka beacon was sending out signals, clearly received on the Rebecca sets in the planes. However, because of an emergency as yet unknown to IX TCC, the T, smoke and radar were not on LZ W but two miles northwest of it. A potential source of further confusion was the presence of the panel T and green smoke set out for KEOKUK in the vicinity of LZ E, which was two miles east of les Forges.

Guided by Gee and by visual identification of the terrain, the leader of the 437th Group headed straight for LZ W and released his glider there at 2104, followed, it appears, by almost all his serial. Ten minutes later planes of the 438th Group appeared over the zone and made their release, but, part of the serial had erroneously loosed their gliders over LZ E. Release altitudes were generally between 500 and 750 feet. From such heights a Waco could glide more than two miles, a Horsa less than a mile. After releasing their gliders, the troop carrier pilots swung their planes into a 180 degree left turn, thereby exposing themselves to fire from the Germans around St. Côme-du-Mont, and headed out over UTAH Beach. They were back at their bases within two hours.

No one who knew the situation on LZ W at that moment would have recommended landing gliders on it. The wedge of German resistance between Turqueville and Carquebut extended across the northern part of the zone and isolated it from the territory taken by the 505th Parachute Regiment. The paratroops around Ste Mère Eglise could not get through the belt of German territory to reconnoiter LZ W, let alone to set up beacons there, and until late in the day General Ridgway had every reason to believe that the entire zone was in German hands. Hence he had decided to place the beacons and markers in the vicinity of LZ O. He had attempted to get word of the situation to IX TCC, first by radio and later by panels laid out for a reconnaissance plane, but the message was not received, and the panels were not observed.

During the afternoon of the 6th two battalions of the 8th Infantry Regiment had driven the enemy from the southern portion of LZ W, and small seaborne elements of the 82d Division under Col. Edson D. Raff made two unsuccessful attempts later to push the Nazis from the rest of the zone. However, when the gliders arrived the Germans still held approximately the northern quarter of the LZ. From their lines southward almost to les Forges the zone was a no-man's land, full of snipers, traversed by German patrols, and under observed fire from mortars and an 88-mm. gun on high ground near Fauville. Raff's men did their best to steer the gliders to safety by waving yellow flags and making an F of orange smoke, but the glider pilots either did not see them or did not know what to make of the unexpected signals.*

As a final hazard, landings had to be made in the face of obstacles greater than those on the other zones. Not only were there "postage stamp" fields 200 yards long, bordered by 50-foot trees, but also some of the designated fields turned out to be flooded and others were studded with poles more than 5 inches thick and 10 feet or more in height. Trip-wires for mines had been attached to many of the poles but fortunately, the mines themselves had not been installed.

A fairly typical landing was that of the Horsa carrying Capt. William W. Bates of the 53d Wing. Unable to reach a large field, the pilot picked a small one, lowered his flaps, and landed at about 70 miles an hour. The glider bounced twice and when about 10 feet off the ground on its second bounce crashed through a row of trees which stripped it of its wings and landing gear. The craft scraped to a stop 10 yards behind Raff's forward positions. There were plenty of bullet holes in the tail, but the only casualty was a soldier who suffered a broken leg as a result of leaving his safety belt unbuckled during the landing. The cargo, an ammunition trailer, was intact and was unloaded in 20 minutes. The episode illustrates the surprising degree to which the passengers and cargoes of the gliders survived crash landings.

All things considered, the glider pilots did fairly well under difficult circumstances. Only two gliders in the first serial landed on LZ W, but 12 came within a mile and all but one or two were within two miles of it. In the second serial all but one of the 14 Wacos, flown by the 88th Troop Carrier Squadron, landed on or very near the zone, 9

---

*Orange smoke and yellow panels were supposed to indicate friendly troops, but there was no plan to have them mark landing zones.

Horsas hit the zone, and 6 came within a mile of it. On the other hand, a dozen Horsas in that serial landed near LZ E, and 4 Horsas missed the zone by about three miles. Few, if any, followed the pathfinder aids to LZ O, and the 82d Division therefore considered the release inaccurate.

Thanks to greater durability and their longer gliding range the Wacos made a much better safety record than the Horsas. Over half of them landed intact, while only about 20 percent of the Horsas were undamaged. Three Wacos and 21 Horsas were destroyed, but much of the destruction was caused by enemy action. Particularly in the case of landings north of les Forges, the lives of the men often depended on their jumping out of the glider and into the nearest ditch before the Germans could bring artillery, mortars or machine guns to bear on them. Unloading had to wait until nightfall or until it was clear the glider was not being used as a target. However, within a few hours most of the men and materiel which had landed in friendly territory on or near the LZ had been brought to Colonel Raff's command post on the north side of les Forges. Of the glider pilots 5 had been killed, 4 were missing and 17 had been wounded or injured. The airborne had five killed and 18 injured or wounded. None of them were missing for long.[28]

The second echelon of ELMIRA contained one 50-plane serial from the 436th Group at Membury with two Wacos and 48 Horsas, and another from the 435th Group at Welford with 12 Wacos and 38 Horsas. With them went a paratroop plane of the 435th which had failed to drop its troops on the previous night. The great capacity of the Horsas, one of which could carry a 75-mm howitzer, a jeep and five men, enabled these serials to carry much more than those in the morning missions. The first serial carried the 319th Field Artillery Battalion and a few other artillerymen, medics and engineers, a total of 418 airborne troops. As cargo it had 31 jeeps, twelve 75-mm. howitzers, 26 tons of ammunition and 25 tons of other equipment. The second serial was occupied exclusively by the 320th Field Artillery Battalion with 319 troops, twelve 105-mm. howitzers, 28 jeeps, 33 tons of ammunition and 23 tons of other equipment.*

The troop carriers set out still unaware that the 82d Division was marking LZ O instead of LZ W. They did receive a last-minute phone call from the 53d Wing directing them to make a 180 degree right turn after releasing their gliders instead of the left turn prescribed in their orders. Presumably IX TCC had learned that the Germans still held the St. Côme area in strength.

The lead plane of the 436th took off at 2037 and that of the 435th about 2040. As the 435th circled upward to form its column of fours, one Horsa broke loose, and one plane turned back with its generators burned out. Both loads were towed in next morning with the 437th Group as part of GALVESTON mission. The trip to the east coast of Normandy was uneventful. The weather was favorable and the fighter cover lavish, but, presumably because of the impending darkness, the escort turned back at the St. Marcouf islands.

The sun set a few minutes before the serials reached UTAH Beach, and as they passed over Normandy the landscape lay in deepening shadow. The pathfinder troops on LZ E had long since ceased operations. Undistracted by landmarks or rival beacons, the second installment of ELMIRA headed for the Eureka and the visual aids set up by the 82d Division in the vicinity of LZ O.

To their surprise, about three miles inland the serials ran into fire bad enough to make the 435th's paratroop operation seem like a milk run. The fire grew more intense as they approached the LZ, and continued during their 180 degree turn to the right and, in some cases at least, all the way back to the coast. The explanation is simple when one realizes that a course from UTAH to LZ O would pass over or just north of the German positions at Turqueville, that the LZ area was within range of German forces north of Ste Mère Eglise, and that a right turn after release would bring the planes directly over those forces. A wide turn or a slight deviation to the north would put a pilot over German-held territory clear to the beaches. German marksmanship was also aided by the American flame-dampeners which became white hot and shone brightly in the semidarkness.

The barrage was less deadly than it appeared. The harm it caused aboard the planes was proportionately about the same as that inflicted on the previous echelon. In the first serial 33 aircraft received some slight damage, and two troop carrier men were wounded. In the other, three aircraft had to be ditched on the way back because of

---

*According to the report of the 82d Division, the 12 Waco gliders in that serial each carried a 105-mm. howitzer.

hits on engines or fuel systems. All personnel aboard them were rescued. Two planes had to make emergency landings in England, and 20 more were damaged but readily repairable. One member of the 435th Group was killed and one wounded. Both groups scattered and returned in driblets, some arriving as late as 0300 next morning.

The initial glider release in this part of ELMIRA occurred at 2255, five minutes ahead of schedule. The second serial loosed its first glider at 2305. Most of the lead serial released their gliders over a mile short of LZ O, and six gliders were released at least five miles east of the zone.* The main body of the second serial was quite accurate, but five of its pilots went to LZ W by mistake. Either they were not using Rebecca or they trusted their briefing more than the beacon.

Once again small fields and enemy fire played havoc with the glider landings. The fire in some places was intense, and many men were killed or wounded in the one or two minutes before their gliders reached the ground. Some pilots, despite strict orders for a slow landing, slammed their Horsas into the landing fields at 100 miles an hour. Since the fields were short, some being only 100 yards long, and since the twilight made a precise approach over the hedgerows increasingly difficult, even the most careful pilots were lucky to escape a crash.

Counting some damage done after landing by enemy fire, only 13 of 84 Horsas were left intact, and 56 of them were totally destroyed. There was a widespread feeling among the glider pilots that the Wacos, with their gentler glide and tougher frames would have done better, but none of the 14 Wacos which were sent survived intact and 8 of them were destroyed. Of 196 glider pilots 10 were killed, 29 or more were wounded or injured, and 7 were still missing at the end of the month. The airborne had 28 killed and 106 wounded or injured, but hardly any were missing for more than two days.

Once again the occupants of most of the gliders had to take cover immediately after landing, and unloading was postponed until after dark. The cargoes had come through surprisingly well. The 435th Group estimated that 39 of its 48 loads were usable, and this is confirmed by estimates from glider units that 42 out of 59 jeeps, 28 out of 39 trailers and 15 out of 24 howitzers were serviceable. However, much of the materiel could not be collected or used immediately.*[29]

The focal point of the landings of the gliders in the first serial was almost two miles northeast of LZ O. This put them near to and in some cases within the German positions. A member of the divisional artillery staff, who had come with the serial, gathered about 200 men of the 319th and led them during the night into the lines of the 4th Division east of Ste Mère Eglise. Other groups made their way back with more or less difficulty, and at 1715 on 8 June the 319th Field Artillery went into action near Chef-du-Pont with almost all its men and 6 of its howitzers.

In the second serial, carrying the 320th Field Artillery, all gliders but the five released near LZ W and one or two released a few seconds too soon northeast of Ste Mère Eglise landed within a mile of LZ O. Maj. Robert M. Silvey of the 320th, who had landed in DETROIT Mission that morning, was waiting beside the pathfinders on the zone and soon gathered slightly less than half the battalion with two usable howitzers. These began firing at 0930 on the 7th from positions 400 yards west of Ste Mère Eglise. Thereafter patrols brought in a steady stream of troops and materiel from outlying gliders, and by evening of 8 June the battalion had eight of its howitzers in action, including two landed in the vicinity of LZ W, and had accounted for practically all of its personnel.[30]

Glider Missions on D plus 1 — GALVESTON and HACKENSACK

Reports of the hazards and confusion which plagued ELMIRA prompted the 53d Wing to make certain changes in GALVESTON, the first glider mission scheduled for D plus 1. Landfall was to be made four miles south of UTAH Beach on the north side of the Douve estuary. Instead of using LZ W the pilots were to release their gliders in the vicinity of LZ E about a mile west of Ste Marie-du-Mont, and their homeward turn after release would be made to the left, instead of the right. These changes would keep the serials out of

---

*Some sanction to these premature releases was provided by the field orders, which prescribed release short of the zone but within gliding range of it to minimize exposure of aircraft to enemy fire.

*There are substantial differences between the two chief sources for these figures. (Hq 82d Abn Div, Action in Normandy, Annex 5; Table on Landings of the 320th Gl FA Bn, in Box 2029 AGO microfilm, Item 2101.)

range of the enemy north of Ste Mère Eglise and in the Turqueville enclave.

GALVESTON was designed to reinforce the 82d Division with guns, vehicles and glider infantry. Its first serial, flown by the 437th Group from Ramsbury, consisted of 50 planes towing 32 Wacos and 18 Horsas. In the gliders were the 1st Battalion of the 325th Glider Infantry, and part of an engineer company, a total of 717 troops with 17 vehicles, 9 pieces of artillery and 20 tons of equipment. The second serial was made up of 50 planes and 50 Wacos, flown by the 434th Group from Aldermaston. Aboard were the headquarters of the 325th Glider Infantry, the Reconnaissance Platoon of the 82d Division and sundry engineers and artillerymen, in all, 251 men with 24 vehicles, 11 guns, 5 tons of ammunition and 1½ tons of other materiel. With the mission went two planes of the 435th Group towing Horsas which had aborted in ELMIRA.

Take-offs at the two fields began at 0439 and 0432 respectively, more than half an hour before dawn, in conditions of poor visibility, rain, and gusty wind. One Horsa of the 437th with a 1000-pound overload wouldn't budge off the ground. Another was accidentally released during assembly, but its tug plane returned and picked up a substitute. One glider of the 434th Group likewise was released over the field and was replaced by a substitute. Another broke loose near Portland Bill, too far away to transfer its load.

Over the Channel and over Normandy the weather improved. The rain gave way to thin, high, broken clouds and the visibility became excellent. The mission followed the beacons to GALLUP, turned there and proceeded by pilotage and dead reckoning to the St. Marcouf Islands, and the mouth of the Douve. Since the sun was up and the Normandy coast plainly visible most of the way after GALLUP, navigation was not difficult. The serials passed over or near many Allied ships, but by daylight the glider formations and their identifying stripes were recognized in all cases. Some of the gliders, sluggish because of overloads, were hard to manage, and some formations became scrambled. One glider pilot reported seeing C-47's above and beneath him as he approached Normandy.

Between the coast and the LZ both serials reported small arms fire of medium intensity, probably from German elements pushed south from the UTAH area on the previous day and not yet mopped up. The 437th was also fired on after its turn, which probably brought it over the German salient around St. Côme. In the 437th's serial 8 planes received moderate damage and 18 in the 434th were hit, none of them seriously.

The 437th Group arrived at 0655, five minutes ahead of schedule. Its serial came in low and released most of its gliders from between 200 and 300 feet and a few of them even lower. Release at such altitudes meant that the gliders could not glide much more than half a mile or stay in the air over half a minute. It decreased exposure to enemy fire but increased the chance of accidents. All but five or six of the gliders were released too soon and landed between the two southern causeways and LZ E, the greatest concentration being a mile northeast of Ste Marie-du-Mont.

The gliders landing east of LZ E had only an occasional sniper or mortar shell to harass them, but suffered many accidents. No less than 10 of the Horsas were destroyed and 7 damaged with 17 troops killed and 63 injured. Of the Wacos 9 were destroyed and 15 were damaged, but only 22 of their passengers were injured and none killed. The glider pilots apparently had no deaths and few injuries.

The 434th Group, flying second in GALVESTON, reached its release area at 0701, nine minutes ahead of time. Unlike the first serial it appears to have released on LZ W and, despite lack of beacons and markers, to have done so very accurately. The 82d Division credited it with 20 gliders landed on the zone, 19 within a mile of it and 8 within 2 miles. One was 2½ miles off and one 4½ miles away. Accidents destroyed 16 Wacos and damaged 26, but no troops were killed and only 13 injured. Moreover, at least 19 jeeps, 6 trailers and 7 guns were found in usable condition. The enemy around Turqueville still kept LZ W under fire, but in spite of them the gliders were unloaded in fairly good time and the glider troops assembled near les Forges.[31]

The last glider mission in NEPTUNE was HACKENSACK, which was flown to LZ W two hours after GALVESTON. Its lead serial, 50 planes towing 30 Horsas and 20 Wacos, was provided by the 439th Group at Upottery. This carried the 2d Battalion, 325th Glider Infantry and most of the 2d Battalion, 401st Glider Infantry, which was attached to the 325th and acted as its third battalion. These numbered 968 troops,* of which Horsas carried over 800. The cargo included 5 vehicles, 11 tons of ammunition and 10 tons of other supplies. The other serial consisted of 50 planes and 50 Wacos of the 441st Group from Merryfield. They carried 363 troops,† mostly service personnel of the 325th and 401st, and 18 tons of equipment, including twelve 81-mm. mortars, 20 jeeps, 9 trailers and 6 tons of ammunition. A pathfinder aircraft, piloted by Col. Julian M. Chappell, commander of the 50th Wing, and Lt. Colonel Kershaw of the 441st, accompanied the serial to guide it to the zone.

Take-off, conducted from static hook-up, was begun at 0647 from Upottery and about 0717 from Merryfield. Some of the troop carriers complained that the airborne had seriously overloaded their gliders, making them difficult to handle. The sky was leaden and the air so rough that spectators on the ground could easily observe the pitching of the gliders. After England was left behind, conditions improved. The ceiling rose from 2,000 to 8,000 feet and the clouds thinned out. Over France they were scattered with bases over 3,000 feet, and visibility was excellent. Like the daylight missions of the day before, HACKENSACK was accompanied from the English coast by a large escort which the troop carriers described as excellent and very reassuring. The approach was made by the east-coast route over the St. Marcouf Islands and UTAH to LZ W. No enemy planes were seen, and ground fire was negligible until the LZ was reached. Even there it was directed mostly at the gliders. The lead serial began its release at 0851, nine minutes ahead of schedule, and the other released its first gliders at 0859, eleven minutes early. They then turned to the right, and went home as they had come except for the authorized short cut from the English coast to the wing assembly area. Meager small-arms fire during and after the homeward turn scored some hits. Three planes in the 439th and eight in the 441st were damaged, but none were lost. In general the flights held together during the return. Between about 1000 and 1038 all pilots arrived at their bases, except one who landed at Warmwell with a dead engine.

Release had been made from about 600 feet. The 439th Group seems to have released by squadrons, rather than as a unit, and, since there was no marking on the zone to guide them, the glider pilots headed wherever they saw a promising spot. A dozen gliders from one squadron came down near the northern end of the zone under intense fire which killed several of the troops before they reached the ground. Most of the gliders in another squadron came down about a mile west of the zone, while a third had several land about 2½ miles east of it. The last squadron's gliders were released over the southwest side of LZ W with the result that some came down in the flooded area, which at that point extended very close to the zone, if not actually into it. Of 29 Horsas accounted for, 12 landed within a mile of the zone, 7 more within 2 miles of it, 9 from 2 to 4 miles away, and one 9 miles off. Of the Wacos, 7 were within a mile, 6 more within 2 miles, and 6 between 2 and 4 miles away, one location being unspecified.

Small fields, high trees, flooded marshland, poles and wires set up by the Germans, debris from previous glider landings, enemy fire caused numerous accidents. No less than 16 Horsas were destroyed and 10 damaged in landing, 15 of the troops aboard them being killed and 59 injured. Of the Wacos only 4 were destroyed and 10 damaged, apparently without casualties. Two glider pilots in the serial were killed, and 10 or 11 injured.

For no obvious reason the comparatively inexperienced 441st Group did vastly better than the three preceding serials. It made a concerted release over the northern part of LZ W, and its gliders started down in the approved spiral pattern. The hazards and obstacles already described forced many glider pilots to zig-zag about, looking for a safe landing place, but by daylight in Wacos released above 600 feet they could pick and choose in an area of several square miles. At least 25 gliders in this serial hit the zone, another 19 were within about a mile of it, and the remaining 6 were probably not far off. Although 8 Wacos were destroyed and 28 damaged, only one of the airborne occupants was killed and 15 injured; while 18 out of 20 jeeps and 8 out of 9 trailers came through unscathed. One glider pilot was killed and five injured. Highly accurate, with few casualties and with cargoes almost intact, this one serial reached

---
*According to the 82d Division, the number was 982. (Hq 82d Abn Div, Action in Normandy, Annex 5.)
†The operations report of the 441st Group lists 463 troops, but this figure appears to include the pilots and co-pilots of the gliders.

the standard that glider enthusiasts had dreamed of.

By about 1015 all battalions of the glider regiment had reported in and were ready to support the 82d Division. The glider men's first task was to send a battalion westward to Carquebut to deal with the Germans who had held out so stubbornly there on the previous night against the 8th Infantry.

The unit arrived early in the afternoon only to find the area deserted. The Germans had fled. It then followed the rest of the 325th to Chef-du-Pont where the regiment was to report for duty as divisional reserve of the 82d Division. That evening the 1st Battalion had 545 officers and men fit for duty, the 2d Battalion had 624, and the 3d had 550. Only 57 of their troops were missing, all but one of those being from the 1st Battalion. Despite the death or injury of 7.5 percent of its men during landing about 90 percent of the regiment was ready for action.[32]

Evaluation of the Glider Missions

The glider operations had gone as well as most experts expected and vastly better than some had predicted. The predawn missions had demonstrated that gliders could deliver artillery to difficult terrain in bad weather and semidarkness and put 40 to 50 percent of it in usable condition within two miles of a given point. The missions on D plus 1 had shown that by day infantry units could be landed within artillery range of an enemy and have 90 percent of their men assembled and ready for action within a couple of hours. While some felt that CHICAGO and DETROIT proved the feasibility of flying glider missions at night, the general consensus was that landing in daytime or at least about sun-up had proven to be much more accurate and much less subject to accidents and that the vulnerability of gliders to ground fire had been overrated.

Many of the difficulties encountered had been unavoidable, particularly those of terrain and of weather. However, the glider pilots were convinced that they would have made better landings if provided with low-level oblique photographs plainly showing the tree-studded hedges. Also DETROIT would have benefitted from a warning to avoid the cloud-bank on the west coast.

In ELMIRA and GALVESTON confusion and casualties resulted from German occupation of LZ W and from the inability of the 82d Division to inform the troop carriers of the situation. One solution proposed to avert such crises was to send an advance party with ground-air radio to talk the gliders in. Since such a party might itself fall prey to enemy action or to accident, it seems that provision might also have been made for alternate zones and for standardized visual signals to indicate that zones had been changed. As will be seen, this problem could also arise in parachute resupply missions and played a serious part in MARKET.

American experience in Normandy indicated that the Waco was easier to fly, much easier to land, and very much more durable than the Horsa. Such a conclusion was not entirely warranted, since the unfamiliarity of their American pilots, the low release altitudes of the American missions, and the use of fields of minimum size for landings had combined to show the Horsas in an unfavorable light. In Normandy and in other operations later the British got good results with the big gliders.

The IX Troop Carrier Command was also convinced that its operations in NEPTUNE had proved the superiority of the Griswold nose, designed to protect gliders against vertical obstacles like trees and posts, as compared to the Corey nose which enabled gliders to ride up over logs or other low, horizontal obstructions. Again the verdict was premature. Had the Germans felled trees instead of erecting posts as obstacles the Corey nose might have been preferable.

In hopes of recovering a substantial proportion of the gliders used in NEPTUNE the AAF had sent to England 108 sets of glider pick-up equipment. In essence this apparatus was simply a hook underneath an aircraft fuselage. As the plane flew low over a stranded glider the hook would engage a loop of tow rope raised on a light frame and snatch the glider into the air. Since an empty Waco weighed less than 3,700 pounds, the shock of the pick-up was not excessive.

Although IX Troop Carrier Command had put half its pick-up sets in storage, damaged 20 others, and had only a limited number of crews qualified for pick-up operations, its resources proved to be more than sufficient. The American Horsas in Normandy were practically all unflyable.* All but

---
*The British retrieved some of their Horsas late in the summer, using Dakotas with American pick-up equipment.

Figure 7. Pick-up of a Waco Glider from a Field in Normandy.

about 40 of the Wacos were also found to be unserviceable or inaccessible to pick-up planes. Many of the remainder were damaged by vandals before they could be picked up. Some gliders in marginal condition might have been repaired on the spot or after a short flight to some base in Normandy. However, the troop carriers did not and could not have guards, bases or repair units in Normandy for many weeks after NEPTUNE. The ground forces, hard put to it to sustain their fighting men, opposed the landing of any unessential personnel, and the few bases in the beachhead were jammed to capacity with fighters. Bad weather and the combat situation combined to delay recovery operations until 23 June. After that, 15 gliders were picked up and flown back to England. The technique worked well. However, 97 percent of the gliders used by American forces in Normandy had had to be left to rot.[33]

The status of the glider pilots after landing was anomalous. They were troop carrier personnel, and, while they had been given some training in infantry tactics, it had been short and relatively sketchy. Yet they constituted 20 percent of the approximately 5,000 men brought into the battle area by glider. Plans called for them to assist in the unloading of the gliders and the clearing of the landing areas, to assemble under the senior glider pilot in their vicinity, and to report to the headquarters of the airborne divisions for such duties as might be required of them. It was contemplated that they would guard command posts and prisoners until a firm link-up with the amphibious forces was made and then be evacuated as soon as possible.

A majority of the glider pilots followed this pattern, and on the whole did very well. About 300 gathered at Raff's headquarters near les Forges and 270 of them were evacuated to the beaches on the afternoon of the 7th. About 170 others who had been guarding the headquarters and prisoners of the 82d Division west of Ste Mère Eglise departed for the beaches with 362 prisoners at noon on 8 June after General Ridgway had addressed them in a speech, later embodied in a commendation, which thanked them warmly for their good service in Normandy. Most of the rest were collected and evacuated within three days after they landed.

While many glider pilots, particularly those landed in outlying areas, had attached themselves as individuals to airborne units and fought with them for a day or two, combat participation by the great majority was limited to a short period

Figure 8. Horsa Glider of IX Troop Carrier Command after Landing in Normandy.

during unloading and assembly. There are few cases in which glider pilots were killed or wounded after leaving the vicinity of their gliders.

Out of 1,030 American glider pilots reaching Normandy all but 197 had been accounted for by 13 June. What had happened to most of those missing at that time is indicated by a rise in known casualties from 28 on 13 June to 147 on 23 July. Of the latter total 25 were dead, 31 wounded and 91 injured. An additional 33 who were still missing were probably prisoners.

The discipline and ground combat training of the glider pilots were criticized by the airborne and by some of their own members. However, the policy of quick evacuation had worked well in Normandy and had won general acceptance. As long as it was assumed that glider pilots could and should be quickly evacuated there was no justification for giving them extensive infantry training. It seemed much more important to improve their proficiency in tactical landings.[34]

Parachute Resupply Missions

Two large parachute resupply missions were flown on the morning of D plus 1. The first, FREEPORT, was performed by the 52d Wing for the 82d Division. It was a scheduled mission with the time of the initial drop set at 0611. The other, MEMPHIS, conducted by the 50th Wing for the 101st Division, was set up to drop at 0635, but only if specifically called for. The formations and speeds to be flown in these missions were like those in the paratroop serials, except that speed during the drops would be 120 miles an hour instead of 110 miles an hour. The route was that taken by the daylight glider missions with approach and return over the St. Marcouf Islands. The altitudes to be maintained were 1,500 feet over England, 1,000 feet over Portland Bill, 500 feet to the drop zone, and beneath 500 feet from the zone back to GALLUP. If possible the zones were to be marked with panels, smoke and beacons, but it was understood these might not be available and that zones might have to be changed to suit the ground situation.

Cargoes were to consist of 6 bundles in each plane and six more carried in pararacks in all planes but those equipped with SCR-717. The normal load thus carried was only slightly over a ton, although a C-47 could carry almost three tons. The difference lay in the need to get the cargo out within half a minute so that it would all land on the DZ. More might have been delivered had British roller coveyers been used, but the canvas covers of American containers were apt to jam the conveyers, and a decision had been made in March not to use British wicker containers.[35] The 2d Quartermaster Depot Supply Company, a unit of IX Air Force Service Command, was supposed to manage the loading of planes for aerial resupply operations and to provide dropmasters to handle the actual dropping with the assistance of crew chiefs and radio operators. That company had neither enough men nor enough training to do the job. Made up of soldiers without previous experience in supply work, it had received its first personnel on 25 April. Although it had been exposed to a two-week course in aerial resupply, only 98 of its members had qualified as supply droppers and been placed on flying status in time for NEPTUNE.

Under pressure of the supply needs of the airborne troops FREEPORT had grown during May from a 185-plane mission to one of 196 and finally of 208 planes. These were drawn from the 61st, 313th, 314th and 316th Groups, each of which contributed a 52-plane serial. The 82d Division had asked for 250 tons of supplies. Because some items were not obtainable the mission carried only 234 tons, about half of it ammunition, plus 22 paratroops who had been brought back on the previous night. The lead serial carried 54 quartermaster personnel to act as dropmasters. In the other formations the crew chief and radioman would have to shove out the bundles in the planes. As for the bundles in the pararacks, they would salvo like bombs at the touch of a switch, providing the mechanism worked.

The first take-off was made by the 313th Group at 0310. The 316th Group was delayed for 15 minutes when two of its planes collided as they taxied into position. Both aircraft were badly damaged and one pilot was killed. The other 206 planes chosen for the mission all took off successfully. Among them were 11 C-53's, although these had smaller doors than the C-47 and were not designed to carry cargo.

There was no light of sun or moon to help the planes assemble, and layers of heavy cloud covered the sky, the lowest being considerably under 1,500 feet. However, the layers were broken in places, and there was space enough between them at about the 1,500-foot level for the groups to form their serials. Having been assured at briefing that the weather, though unfavorable, would not require instrument flying, the troop carriers set out boldly into the murk.

Instead of improving as they proceeded, the weather grew rapidly worse. Over the route for most of the 120 miles between ATLANTA, the wing departure point, and ELKO, the command assembly point, hung a solid mass of clouds with bases as low as 300 feet and tops as high as 10,000 feet. Icing conditions prevented flight over the clouds. Passage through the narrow crack between clouds and ground was hazardous, though many pilots tried it. Most flew into the clouds and attempted to continue individually on instruments. In spite of the Rebecca beacons along the course a majority of these pilots lost their way at least temporarily. Radio channels to the troop carrier CP at Eastcote were swamped by requests for information and instructions. Some planes, particularly in the rear flights of the 316th Group turned back under orders. Others flew around until they ran short of fuel and had to land at fields in southern England. While some pilots took off to try again, at least 14 were refused permission to go on. In all, 51 planes failed to leave England and one other crashed, killing everyone aboard, in an attempt to land at Oxford.

Over southern England the weather was better, and over the channel there were only high scattered clouds, giving about $\frac{3}{10}$ cover at 8,000 feet. Also, by the time the first planes reached Portland Bill the sun was rising. It was thus possible to re-form off the south coast. This was certainly done by most of the 61st Group and by portions of later serials. However, many pilots failed to recover contact with any large formation and went on alone or in small bunches.

From England to Normandy the mission was given the same powerful escort and fighter cover as the daylight glider missions. No enemy planes attempted to penetrate this screen. One straggler in the 314th Group received a blast of antiaircraft fire from Allied shipping off the St. Marcouf Islands which induced him to give up and go home. A pilot in the 313th also reported naval fire, but it stopped when he signaled his identity.

FREEPORT, like GALVESTON, made landfall on the north side of the Douve estuary. There a perplexing discrepancy appeared. The orders and briefing of the pilots had called for a drop on DZ N, a mile north of Picauville on the west side of the Merderet. However, as the main body of the 61st Group approached the shore, it received the prescribed signals from a Eureka beacon near

Ste Mère Eglise, 2½ miles northeast of DZ N. The 82d Division, cut off from its units on the west bank of the river, had ordered the beacon to go into action on DZ O. Apparently no smoke or panels were used.

The 61st Group formation followed the radar signals to DZ O and dropped its bundles in that general vicinity at about 0603 from between 400 and 600 feet. It reported that the dropmasters provided by the quartermaster company were for the most part awkward, timid, and airsick and of little help in kicking out the bundles.*

After this initial drop the situation became chaotic. Stragglers and small groups, often drawn from several different flights kept arriving at irregular intervals until 0815. A few of them received the radar signals and dropped their loads on or near DZ O. Elements of the 313th and 316th Groups totalling at least a dozen planes made their drops on LZ W. Nearly half the pilots followed their maps and their instructions to DZ N. Perhaps the objective seemed too obvious to require use of Rebecca; perhaps the policy of restricting the use of radar to serial and flight leaders was still exercising its baneful influence; certainly a four-man crew without a dropmaster to help them would be too busy preparing to dispose of their load to tinker with a Rebecca in the last minutes of their run unless it seemed necessary.

In all, at least 148 planes dropped approximately 156 tons of supplies. Since the Germans held DZ N and most of the territory west of the Merderet, very little of what was dropped beyond the river could be collected at that time. Less than 100 tons were retrieved that day, and although ultimately about 140 tons were recovered,† the paratroops on D plus 2 were very short of food and ammunition and subsisted largely on a captured trainload of cheese.

The planes going to DZ O passed over the Germans in the Turqueville-Fauville pocket during their approach and swung over German-held territory west of the Merderet before completing their homeward turn. Those heading for DZ N had to fly for two or three miles over enemy positions. This proved costly enough to show that those who had predicted heavy troop carrier losses in NEPTUNE were not mere alarmists. The Germans put up only moderate small arms fire with little or no antiaircraft, but this was sufficient to bring down 10 planes. Among those attempting to use DZ N the loss rate was probably over 10 percent. Of the downed aircraft, four crashed in Normandy, one was still missing a month later, and five were successfully ditched off the Normandy coast. Only one casualty was caused by ditching, while aboard the crashed planes 11 troop carrier men were killed and the rest of their crews were hospitalized or missing. All of these planes appear to have dropped at least part of their cargoes; one, piloted by Capt. Howard W. Sass, was already ablaze when the bundles went out.*

Of about 140 planes which got back after being in the drop area almost all reached their bases singularly or in small groups between 0815 and 1050. Ninety-two were damaged, some very badly. Every squadron had its tale of hazardous returns. One aircraft, barely controllable and with one engine dead, had been coaxed back to Folkingham by way of the North Sea and the Wash so that it could ditch instantaneously if necessary. Between 15 and 20 had made forced landings at Warmwell and other points in southern England. None of the damaged craft had to be salvaged, but many required several days' work by service units. At the end of the month casualties in FREEPORT were listed as 15 dead, 20 wounded and 17 missing. It is not suprising that pilots reporting in after their return swore that second missions were jinxed.[36]

While MEMPHIS, the supply mission to the 101st Division, was less costly than FREEPORT, it was even less successful. Why it was sent at all is a mystery. The Headquarters of the 101st Division had not called for it, did not expect it, and had set out no markers or beacons to guide it. The mission thus had two strikes on it from the start.

MEMPHIS was to be flown by two serials, each of 63 aircraft, from the 440th and 442d Groups respectively. No facilities for air re-supply had been established at their bases, so the mission had to stage from Welford and Membury. The

---

*There is very little evidence on the efficiency with which the supply dropping was conducted. One squadron reported that it took an average of 12 seconds per plane to get out its bundles. Others had trouble with bundles stuck in pararacks or jammed in doors, but the percentage not dropped for those reasons was very low, in the neighborhood of 1 percent. (CMR, Hq 48th TC Sq Mission "NEPTUNE" II, Resupply, 7 Jun 44, in unit hist file.)

†Probably including some delivered in MEMPHIS.

*Sass went down with his burning plane, was catapulted into a hedge when it crashed, and survived with comparatively minor injuries.

planes were supposed to be there by 2130 on D-day for loading. The 440th began take-off from Exeter at 2020 and most of its aircraft reached Welford by 2130. The 442d did not depart from Fulbeck until about 2120, and sent only 56 planes. The 439th had sent six to Membury to complete the serial, but through some misunderstanding those planes had not come properly prepared and therefore could not go on the mission. Dropmasters from the quartermaster company took part in MEMPHIS, but the number involved is unspecified.

The 442d Group took off with 56 planes between 0421 and 0428 in the dim twilight before dawn. The 440th, perhaps more confident of its ability to assemble quickly, did not take off until about 20 minutes later. One of its 63 planes aborted because of a flat tire and was not replaced. A substitute had been on hand when the group left Exeter, but none was ready at Welford.

Fortunately for the 442d Group, the take-off bases lay south of the disturbance which upset FREEPORT, but the weather at the start was bad enough to make assembly difficult. An unbroken blanket of cloud covered the sky 1,500 feet up and northwest winds, blowing aloft at 27 miles an hour, drove rain squalls across the fields. However, beyond Portland Bill weather ceased to be an obstacle. The overcast became thin and broken with bases above 2,500 feet, and the wind abated. Over Normandy the clouds lay lower and thicker, but not seriously so.

The fighter protection over the Channel won, as in the other daylight missions, the enthusiastic admiration of the troop carriers. One pilot described his serial as surrounded above, below, and on all sides by fighters and declared that he had never seen so many at once as during that operation. Oddly enough, the first loss was caused by a friendly plane. Near UTAH Beach a bomb-cluster, accidentally dropped by a P–47, hit a plane of the 440th Group and set off ammunition in its cargo. The pilot managed to ditch his plane, but the explosion had killed two crewmen, a dropmaster, and a correspondent. Gunners on Allied ships off the St. Marcouf Islands fired at or near some planes in MEMPHIS, but briefly and without effect.

The 440th Group dropped its load, 63 tons of ammunition, 10½ tons of rations and 21 tons of combat equipment, between 0632 and 0639. Only one pararack pack and seven bundles, which had damaged chutes, were brought back. The 442d Group, which had carried 678 pararacks and bundles with a gross weight of 126 tons, dropped 652 of them about 0638 from between 500 and 1,000 feet. The rest had stuck or were damaged. One dangling parapack was pried loose by a crew chief hanging out of the plane with the radio operator holding his ankles.

The supplies were supposed to land on LZ E near Hiesville, but Headquarters, 101st Division, located in that area, asserted that it saw no drop and recovered no bundles. The 442d Group reported that it deposited its cargoes near Blosville, 1½ miles west of Hiesville on LZ W. That zone, strewn with parachutes and gliders, would seem a logical objective to anxious pilots who had received no radar signals and seen no markers. The 82d Division, to which LZ W was assigned, presumably retrieved these supplies along with those dropped there about the same time by formations in FREEPORT. The embattled paratroops were doing very little paper work that day and probably went on the principle of all supplies gratefully received and no questions asked. The 8th Infantry may also have taken a share.

The course taken by the 440th Group is less certain, but most of its planes probably dropped between St. Côme and la Barquette. Colonel Johnson of the 501st PIR reported a supply drop in sight of his position at la Barquette about 0630. The drop was made some distance to the west of him, most of the bundles landing in no-man's land, behind the German lines, or in the Douve marshes. This in all likelihood was the work of the 440th Group. The group encountered heavy flak, of which there was hardly any north of St. Côme, and the history of one of its squadrons, the 98th, refers explicitly to observations made in the Douve area. Flying in from the northeast over UTAH Beach, as it was supposed to do, the 440th had only to persist on course after passing LZ E to come within sighting distance of the panels Johnson had put out requesting supplies and had only to veer a few degrees to the south to reach the Douve at the point where the drop was actually made. The failure to release the supplies over Johnson's position may be explained by assuming that the leader saw the panels too late to head directly over them and chose to drop west of the signals on his first run rather than make a second pass.

Some planes in both groups may have dropped at other points, particularly northwest of Ste Mère Eglise near DZ O. Elements of the 440th reported picking up a Eureka signal and following it in, although it was poorly received. The only Eureka known to have been in operation at the time was that on DZ O to guide FREEPORT. Its signals would naturally have seemed poor, since the Rebecca sets of the 440th were tuned to a different channel. At DZ O, as at LZ W, such supplies as were dropped would have been picked up by the 82d Division and, if accounted for at all, would probably be credited to FREEPORT.

MEMPHIS suffered much less from enemy action than its predecessor. Small arms fire at the 442d Group just after it made its drop caused minor damage to 21 planes and wounded two men. As the 440th Group turned left after its drop, flak smashed engines on two planes, forcing them to ditch. Fourteen others in the serial were damaged, 11 of them severely enough to need 2d and 3d echelon repairs. Two men were wounded. The groups returned to their home bases, not those from which they had staged. The 440th, reached Exeter at or about 0828. All planes of the 442d except one, which had landed at Warmwell, were back at Fulbeck by 0905.[37]

The ineffectiveness of FREEPORT and MEMPHIS was primarily due to lack of radio contact between the airborne commanders and IX TCC. With such contact MEMPHIS would either not have been sent or would have been given adequate instructions and a zone equipped with navigational aids. With such contact the pilots in FREEPORT would not have been dispatched to a zone which was wholly in enemy hands. The atrocious weather which broke up the formations in FREEPORT and forced a quarter of the pilots to turn back was pure bad luck. It was also fair warning that in Western Europe operations relying on aerial resupply would have to gamble on the weather. The losses caused by enemy fire in FREEPORT were a reminder, if one were needed, that troop carrier formations were vulnerable and that passage over alerted enemy troops could be costly.

By noon on 7 June all major airborne missions in NEPTUNE had been completed. However, six small parachute and glider resupply missions were flown later on call. All of them went smoothly without enemy opposition and without appreciable hindrance from weather. On the 8th a single aircraft of the 441st Group, staging from Greenham Common, took off at 0700 hours with 150 pounds of medical supplies for the 101st Division. Escorted by four P-38's, it flew over the route used in HACKENSACK, made its drop, probably on LZ E, and returned unmolested. Next day two gliders with badly needed signal equipment landed successfully near Ste Mère Eglise about 1845. The recipient in this and the four following missions was the 82d Division. On the 10th the 436th Group dispatched six aircraft from Membury with Wacos. The gliders held 2 jeeps, 2 soldiers, and 6½ tons of combat equipment. Released at 1740 near Ste Mère Eglise, they made excellent landings in the area designated. On 12 June nine planes of the 436th Group flew a paradrop re-supply mission, carrying 2 tons of 60-mm. and 81-mm. mortars and 5 tons of ammunition stowed in 54 parapacks and 25 bundles. At 0802 they made an accurate drop of all but one parapack from an altitude of 300 feet on a zone just east of Ste Mère Eglise. Five aircraft of that Group towed Waco gliders to the same zone that evening. Aboard the gliders were 2 jeeps and 42 airborne troops, and one of the planes carried 15 paratroops.* The gliders were released and the paratroops then jumped about 2021, all landing safely on the zone. The Germans, who still held positions within four miles of Ste Mère Eglise, responded to the landing by shelling the area. The last of these missions was flown on the 13th by 11 planes of the 436th Group. Escorted by 12 P-38's they towed 11 Wacos to Ste Mère Eglise. The gliders contained 1½ tons of ammunition and 13 tons of equipment. Release was made at 1913 from a height of 600 feet and the landings were thoroughly successful.[38]

The British Missions and WILDOATS

The British airborne operations in NEPTUNE provide a useful, if imperfect, yardstick by which to rate American performance. Their paratroop missions were unquestionably more accurate than those of IX Troop Carrier Command, although their pathfinders had been rather less successful. One of their three zones was almost without pathfinder aids because one team intended for it had

---
*Such a dual role was unusual because paratroops preferred to jump from a tight formation rather than a long glider column, and because of the restriction of gliders to follow-up operations.

been dropped out of reach and the other had lost its equipment. Another team inaccurately dropped set up its beacons on the wrong zone, two miles from its own. Nevertheless, in the main paratroop drop, which was to begin 0050 hours on D-day about 30 percent of the 237 pilots dispatched hit their zones, 25 percent came within a mile and 10 percent dropped their sticks within two miles. Most of the drops farther away could be blamed on the lack or misplacing of pathfinder aids. On the one zone where the aids were wholly satisfactory at least 75 percent put their sticks within a one-mile radius, and the units dropped there mustered about 60 percent of their strength in the initial assembly.

This superior performance convinced the British that the American troop carrier tactic of flying in serials was inferior to their own method of individual navigation. The glider-towing planes of 38 Group flew in loose pairs at 20-second intervals, and 46 Group flew in V's of three aircraft at 30-second intervals. General Browning was so sure that the technique of 38 Group was better that he recommended that IX TCC adopt it.

Actually, the British had had certain advantages which made the comparison misleading. They encountered no serious cloud obstacle such as that which upset the American missions. Their drop zones, which they approached directly from the Channel coast, were respectively 2, 3, and 5 miles inland. Thus, although enemy fire was intense enough to bring down seven planes, a ratio comparable to that in ALBANY and BOSTON, it had little time to affect navigation. Most important, all their planes had Gee and about 90 percent of the crews used it effectively. Rebecca was relegated to a supplementary role. The Americans simply did not have enough Gee sets to go around. If ALBANY and BOSTON had flown the British route, and if stragglers in those missions had had both Gee and Rebecca sets with qualified operators and freedom to use them, IX TCC would certainly have made a much better showing than it did. However, it does seem that the American serials, even when accurately led and substantially intact, as in the drops of the 505th PIR, put more men outside a one-mile radius of their zone than did the British system of individual drops—presumably because darkness and bad weather had loosened the formations.

The British also flew glider missions before dawn on D-day, and in these, too, Gee served them well. Despite strong winds and low clouds which caused about 20 of the 98 gliders dispatched to break loose or be cast loose prematurely, they landed 52 on their zones and 6 more within a mile of them. Landing accidents were numerous, further proof of the costly nature of night glider operations. On the evening of D-day the British dispatched their main glider mission with 256 Horsas and Hamilcars* in tow. Their landings, beginning at 2051, were highly successful. Only one or two gliders were shot down, and 246 landed on or very near their zones. However, the risk of antiaircraft fire in this twilight operation had been minimized, since by then the British had full possession of the terrain over which the approach was made and had pushed their front well beyond the landing zones.

The only large British resupply drop was to be made by 50 planes of 46 Group at midnight of D-day. Once again, as in the invasion of Sicily, jittery naval gunners loosed a barrage on an airborne mission with the result that six planes were lost and only 20 percent of the supplies dispatched were received by the airborne troops. Four small resupply missions flown in daylight by 38 Group were fairly successful, although in one of them 7 out of 12 planes were recalled because of low clouds like those that forced recalls in FREEPORT.

One important respect in which the British pioneered was the dropping of heavy equipment. On D plus 4 they successfully dropped six 6-pounder guns and six jeeps into Normandy from the bomb bays of six Halifaxes flying at a height of 1,000 feet. Each item was packed in a protective frame and provided with a cluster of twelve 32-foot parachutes to cushion its descent. Only one jeep was damaged enough to be unserviceable. To understand what an advance this was, it should be observed that the Americans at that time were still breaking down their pack howitzer into seven bundles to get it out the door of the C-47.[39]

Another important airborne operation was planned but did not take place. After its missions with the 82d Division the 52d Wing had been held on the alert for missions with English troops. The British ground commanders asked for an operation called WILDOATS to achieve a breakthrough by dropping and landing the British First

---
*The Hamilcars successfully brought in Tetrarch tanks, an item which would have been invaluable to the 82d Division.

Airborne Division near Evrecy ahead of an attack by 7 Armored Division. The paratroops would be dropped by the 52d Wing, after which the glider echelon would be delivered by British troop carriers, assisted by the 435th, 438th, 440th and 441st Groups. Leigh-Mallory presided over a meeting at Stanmore on 11 June to consider this enterprise. There troop carrier and airborne representatives voiced strong objections to WILDOATS. If flown in from the east coast of Normandy it would go over the invasion fleets (the commander of which refused to prohibit antiaircraft fire during the missions), over the beachhead, and over the German front lines. An approach from the other side of the peninsula required a flight of more than 50 miles over enemy territory, much of it out of range of navigational aids. During most of the night there would be no moon. By day the risks from enemy fire would be very great whatever the route. Nevertheless, the ground forces were so insistent that the critics reluctantly accepted the operation.

WILDOATS was to be launched on 14 June with the first paratroops jumping at 0420. The gliders would follow close behind the jumpers and begin landing at 0530. The route, excepting certain minor variations, ran from Portland Bill to a point off Cape Barfleur, thence to the St. Marcouf Islands and from there to Bayeux, the IP, which was about 16 miles north-northwest of the drop and landing zones. Return would be made by a reciprocal route.

On 12 June wing commanders and key staff officers were briefed at Eastcote. On the 13th group commanders and staffs were briefed and the briefing of crews was begun. That very day, however, a German armored division hurled back the British at Villers Bocage and took the initiative in that sector. Under those circumstances WILDOATS would have been extremely dangerous. Accordingly it was postponed on the evening of the 13th and was formally cancelled on the 17th. This decision put an end to airborne operations in NEPTUNE.[40]

★

CHAPTER III

From Neptune to Market

Organizational Changes

THE INTERVAL of three months between NEPTUNE and MARKET, the next airborne operation in the European Theater, was marked by important organizational changes and by unprecedented fluctuations in the extent and character of troop carrier utilization.

The principal change was the creation of First Allied Airborne Army. Even before NEPTUNE was launched the British, who had set up a command known as Headquarters Airborne Troops for their own airborne in 1943, had recommended the establishment of a headquarters to command all Allied airborne units in the Theater. This was not necessary in Normandy because British and American airborne operations there were separate. However, future operations involving several airborne divisions of different nationalities might need central control. The British intimated that their existing airborne headquarters might well provide a commander and cadre for the one proposed.

Eisenhower on 20 June approved the idea of a unified command for the airborne troops, but coupled with his approval a more sweeping proposal for a command which would control troop carriers as well. In this he was in accord with the ideas of General Marshall and General Arnold. The latter had written to Spaatz in December 1943 urging that both airborne and troop carrier forces in England be placed under one headquarters for training and operations. He had favored placing such a command under the Ninth Air Force.

Except for Leigh-Mallory, who favored an airborne headquarters but argued that to place the troop carriers under its authority was unnecessary, inefficient, and contrary to the principle of unity of command for air forces, there was little opposition to Eisenhower's counterproposal. However, the British felt strongly that, whichever pattern was followed, their airborne commander, Lt. Gen. F.A.M. Browning, should be chosen to head the new command. The Americans, thought it proper to name an American, since they were contributing most of the troop carrier forces and a majority of the airborne, but they found it difficult to produce a candidate who was a match for Browning. Lieutenant generals with suitable experience were scarce indeed. Finally Eisenhower's choice fell on General Brereton. Although junior to Browning by a few months,* he had a length and variety of service unsurpassed in the AAF, had commanded air forces in the Far East, North Africa, and England, and as commander of the Ninth Air Force had acquired a working knowledge of IX Troop Carrier Command. On 16 July Brereton was informed that he had been nominated to command the new airborne-troop carrier organization.

On 2 August he received notice of his appointment from SHAEF and with it a personal note from Eisenhower asking him to pay particular attention to improving troop carrier navigation. That day Brig. Gen. Floyd L. Parks reported for duty as his Chief of Staff. Next day Brereton named Brig. Gen. Ralph S. Stearley as G-3, Operations, and Brig. Gen. Stuart L. Cutler, formerly on the staff of First US Army Group, as Deputy C/S, Plans. On 4 August he accepted General Browning as his deputy commander. Also on the 4th he obtained a loan of buildings formerly used by Headquarters, Ninth Air Force, at Sunnyhill Park near Ascot to house his new headquarters.

---
*He was made lieutenant general in April 1944; Browning had held the rank since December 1943.

On the 5th the embryonic organization was plunged into the planning of an operation.[1]

Not until 8 August did SHAEF officially announce the establishment of Combined Airborne Headquarters with General Brereton in command. On 16 August this organization was redesignated First Allied Airborne Army. It was placed directly under SHAEF and was given command of all Allied airborne troops and operational control of British and American troop carriers.

The principal functions of Airborne Army were to supervise training, prepare plans for airborne operations, including resupply, and control such operations until junction of the airborne with the ground forces. It was to prepare outline plans for airborne operations in conjunction with SHAEF, consult with the naval and air commanders-in-chief on matters touching them, and conduct detailed planning in conjunction with the ground force and air force commanders.[2]

In practice, Airborne Army initiated planning in response to requests from the Army Group Commanders, Bradley and Montgomery,* without waiting for a SHAEF directive, and the staff of the army group sponsoring a given operation participated in formulating an outline plan or staff study for it. Not until the army group commander had approved this initial plan was detailed planning undertaken. In some cases, notably BOXER and LINNET II, Brereton apparently called for preliminary planning on his own initiative.[3]

Airborne Army exercised command of the British airborne troops through Headquarters, Airborne Troops (subsequently redesignated 1 Airborne Corps) under Browning and command of the American airborne through XVIII Airborne Corps, a new headquarters under the command of General Ridgway.† It took over operational control of IX TCC from AEAF despite spirited protests from Leigh-Mallory. Inclusion of 38 Group and 46 Group was impeded by involvement of the former in special operations with resistance groups on the Continent and by the desire of the RAF to keep at least part of 46 Group for its own use in air supply. In this regard the RAF could point out that Ninth Air Force and USSTAF each had an American air transport group assigned to it and serving it almost exclusively. For these reasons the status of 38 Group and 46 Group was left open, and Airborne Army was only given control of "such Royal Air Force Troop Carrier formations" as might be allocated to it "from time to time." Because of their ambiguous position, the British troop carriers were not at first represented on Brereton's staff. However, it was understood from the first that they would be needed for any big airborne operation, and they soon found themselves in the inconvenient position of being committed to operations in the initial planning of which they had not been represented. Therefore on 31 August the commander of 38 Group, AVM L. N. Hollinghurst, asked the inclusion of an RAF element in Brereton's headquarters. Brereton agreed; an organization plan was drafted on 6 September; and the RAF side of the headquarters was officially formed on 13 September, thus correcting a situation which was certainly irregular and could have been dangerous.*

Many subsequent headaches of Airborne Army arose from its acquisition on 16 August of an obscure little agency named the Combined Air Transport Operations Room and generally known as CATOR. This had been set up under AEAF at Stanmore on 1 June 1944 to serve as a central agency for air supply. Unfortunately, its only instrument for carrying supplies was IX TCC. Ninth Air Force and USSTAF kept their air transport groups, and when CATOR was transferred from AEAF to Airborne Army, the RAF, following their example, kept control of the supply activities of 46 Group. As for 38 Group, it was not included because, aside from its work in special operations, its converted bombers were ill-suited to supply work.[4]

As long as demands on CATOR were small, Airborne Army could almost always spare planes to satisfy them, but if heavy demands for air supply coincided with requests for large-scale airborne operations, someone would have to be disappointed. The troop carriers could not do two things at once.

On 25 August, as a sequel to the creation of Airborne Army, IX TCC was relieved from assign-

---

*Montgomery ceased to be ground commander-in-chief on 1 August when 12th Army Group under Bradley took over control of the American armies from 21 Army Group. However, he continued to exercise some authority over all ground operations as Eisenhower's deputy until the latter moved to France and on 1 September assumed the role of ground commander in addition to that of supreme commander.

†General Gavin succeeded Ridgway as commander of the 82d Division.

*When MARKET was decided on Airborne Army had to request that 38 Group and 46 Group be allocated to it for that operation. (Ltr, Hq FAAA to Lt Gen F. A. M. Browning, subj: Task Force for Operation "MARKET," 11 Sep 44, in 520.452.)

ment to Ninth Air Force and was placed under administrative control of USSTAF. As of 26 August all the service units working for IX TCC, including the glider assembly workers at Crookham Common, were transferred from IX AFSC to the troop carrier command and were placed under a new organization, the IX Troop Carrier Service Wing (Provisional). The troop carriers probably benefitted in the long run by having direct control of their service units, but some mistakes and confusion in the preparations for MARKET resulted from the fact that the new system was not yet well established.[5]

Another change was the transformation of the Pathfinder School on 14 September 1944 into the IX Troop Carrier Pathfinder Group (Provisional). Lieutenant Colonel Crouch continued in command. The change reflected growing recognition of the value of pathfinder tactics in airborne missions and also Crouch's conviction that the pathfinders would be more efficient as an independent organization.[6]

A few significant changes were made in the staff of IX TCC during the summer. Lt. Col. Grant W. Ernst became A-2. Col. Glynne M. Jones took Fisher's place as A-3, and Lt. Col. Francis A. McBride succeeded Graham as A-4. The latter two new staff officers had served on Williams' staff in North Africa and Italy. Ernst and Colonel Duke, the Chief of Staff, were the only officers in major staff positions who were not veterans of the Mediterranean campaigns. One other notable event was the promotion of General Williams on 26 August to the rank of major general.[7]

Plans and Operations During the Campaign in France

Troop Carrier planning between NEPTUNE and MARKET falls into three phases, one of inactivity from 13 June to 29 July, one of readjustment to a rapidly changing situation between 29 July and 17 August, and a period of heavy and conflicting commitments from 17 August to 17 September.

During the first stage, which began with the calling off of WILDOATS, the ground forces did not ask for airborne operations, and air supply was on a relatively small scale. Plans were conceived and elaborated at SHAEF and AEAF for combined airborne and amphibious operations in the Quiberon Bay area, at St. Malo, or at Brest to secure seaports. Since the allied armies were still being supplied over open beaches, even a small port was regarded as a great prize. Although outline plans were completed for the first two operations, HANDS UP and BENEFICIARY, the former was tabled, largely because of naval objections, and the latter was rejected on 15 July because St. Malo was too strongly defended. SWORDHILT, an attack on Brest, seemed more promising but was cancelled on 29 July as a result of the breakthrough at St. Lô, which seemed to ensure the speedy capture of ports without the risks of an airborne venture.[8]

The only large airborne units available for missions up to the end of July were the British First Airborne Division and a Polish airborne brigade, which was not fully trained. The consensus early in July was that none of the three airborne divisions committed in Normandy would be ready for another flight into battle until after at least 75 days of training and refitting. The 101st Division had been kept in action until 27 June, the 82d until 8 July. As for the British Sixth Airborne Division, it was not relieved until 26 August. The American divisions recuperated sooner than expected, but winter came before 6 Airborne was again fit for an airborne operation.[9]

A further reduction in airborne capabilities came when about a third of the American troop carriers were sent to the Mediterranean Theater at the request of the Allied Commander in that theater for an airborne operation in the invasion of southern France.

In the middle of July 413 troop carrier planes left England for Italy, carrying with them a small staff, headed by General Williams, and 225 glider pilots. Another 375 glider pilots were flown there later. This force did not return until about the 25th of August. While they were away IX TCC had at its disposal the 52d Wing and three provisional groups from the 50th and 53d Wings with about 870 planes.[10]

At first this reduced strength was more than enough to meet the supply needs of the ground forces. Half a million tons of supplies had been delivered to the Normandy beaches in June and vastly more during July, so much that large surpluses accumulated. As long as the front was near the beaches the ground forces would have little need of air supply. At the same time, as long

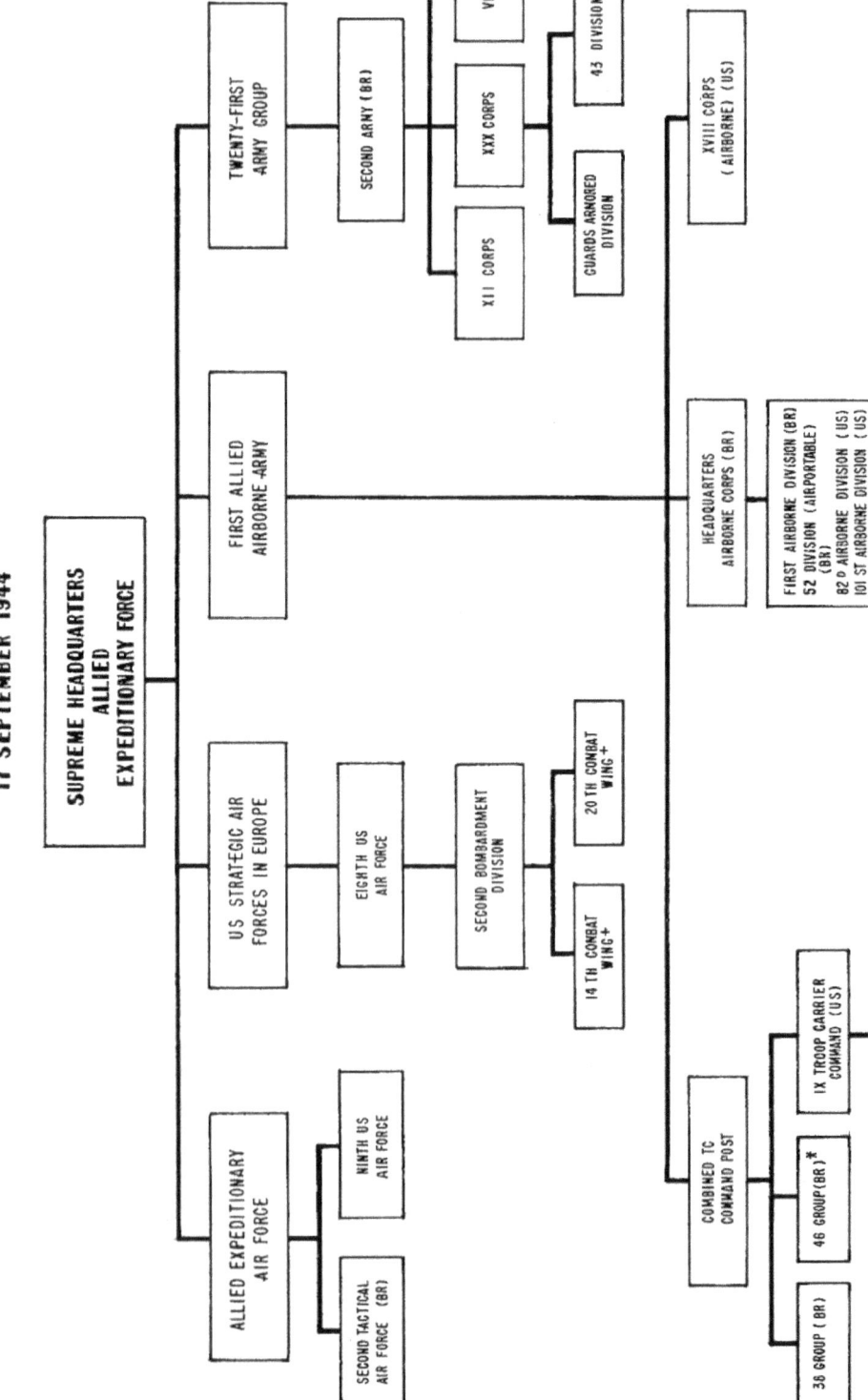

Chart 2

as the beachhead was small, they preferred to have its few airfields used by fighters and fighter-bombers rather than by cargo planes. Two big supply missions were flown in June after storms halted the flow of seaborne supplies. Otherwise until August the American troop carriers usually flew less than 50 sorties a day to France to carry special items and to evacuate casualties.

When the lull began General Williams had directed that the time be used for further training, but never at any time in the war did the troop carriers have less need or desire for training. In fact up to the end of July very little training was done. For six weeks the aircraft of IX TCC averaged less than an hour of flight per plane per day for all purposes.[11]

The American breakthrough at St. Lô transformed a stable situation into an extremely fluid one. By 30 July a gaping hole had been created in the German lines through which armored units drove to Avranches at the base of the Norman peninsula, 30 miles south of St. Lô. From Avranches Lt. Gen. George Patton's Third Army swept southeast around the left flank of the German Seventh Army, covered 100 miles in a week, and reached Le Mans on 8 August. On the 6th SHAEF and Airborne Army, anticipating that this threat would soon force the Germans to retreat, agreed on an airborne operation called TRANSFIGURE. At the outset Eisenhower was strongly in favor of this operation and is said to have called it the blow most likely to end the war in Europe.

The purpose of TRANSFIGURE was to destroy a large part of the German Seventh Army by trapping it south of Paris. As Patton approached Orleans, airborne troops would spring the trap by blocking the roads over which the enemy intended to retreat. In its final form the plan called for parachute and glider operations by the 101st Division near St. Arnoult-en-Yvelines and by the British First Airborne Division and the Polish Parachute Brigade in the vicinity of Rambouillet. By 13 August the operation had been worked out, and the troops moved to the airfields. On the 15th General Brereton approved the plans in their final form, and field orders were cut. On the 16th almost every usable troop carrier plane was marshalled and ready.[12]

The operation was scheduled to take place on 17 August, but swiftly as TRANSFIGURE had been prepared, Patton's tanks had moved faster.

On the 16th one of his columns, far ahead of schedule, approached Rambouillet. Next morning TRANSFIGURE was postponed, and on the afternoon of the 17th it was cancelled. For the next two days attention was given to alternative airborne operations to take one or another of the Seine crossings, but on the 19th units of Third Army crossed the Seine near Mantes-Gassicourt, making these projects, too, obsolete.[13]

Meanwhile the headlong Allied advance had created a need for air supply so urgent that this task threatened to take priority even over airborne operations. Hitherto, the use of the troop carriers for other than high priority or emergency supply operations had hardly been considered. Apart from the fact that it had not been needed, it was very wasteful and could not in any case provide for more than a fraction of the Allied needs. A C-47 carrying gasoline to France used about a gallon for every two gallons carried. Without forward bases on the Continent and with less than 900 C-47's on hand the Troop Carrier Command could not possibly deliver to the advancing armies enough to keep five divisions in action at the accepted consumption rate of 600 tons of supplies per division per day. Finally, embodied in manuals and regulations was the rule that the primary mission of troop carrier units was to carry airborne troops in operations and training.

However, the situation had become such that all supply to the forward divisions was emergency supply. The French railroads, shattered by sabotage and bombing, took many weeks to repair. Throughout August and early September the front was usually over 100 and occasionally over 200 miles beyond the railheads. Truck transport could deliver no more than 7,000 tons a day to the Americans and perhaps 4,000 to the British. That was enough to sustain approximately 20 divisions, and the Germans were thought to have just about 20 divisions left to hold their western front. In these circumstances air supply might provide the margin for a decisive thrust before the enemy could rally.

Eisenhower, therefore, gave air supply precedence over training for airborne operations. On 12 August SHAEF proposed a supply lift of 1,000 tons a day, and on the 14th it raised the proposed quota to 2,000 tons a day. This would have required an all-out effort by IX TCC with everything it had and perhaps some help from 46

Group. General Brereton accepted the 2,000 ton lift, but with qualifications intended to give IX TCC freedom of action. On 18 August, immediately after TRANSFIGURE was cancelled, Brig. Gen. Harold L. Clark, who was commanding the troop carriers in Williams' absence, committed them to a lift of 750 tons a day to the Continent, a level which he believed compatible with adequate training. On 25 August SHAEF directed that after the return of the contingent in Italy, IX TCC should provide 400 planes a day for air supply. Protests by Airborne Army were met by the statement that General Bradley had to have the supplies and could get them in no other way. On 4 September General Williams agreed to increase the supply lift to a level of 600 planes a day from IX TCC and the RAF pledged 30 a day from 46 Group.* It was understood, however, that if orders were issued for an airborne mission, the planes needed for that mission would have to be grounded for servicing, loading, and marshalling.

In the month between the cancellation of TRANSFIGURE and the launching of MARKET, IX TCC by an all-out effort under ideal conditions might have hauled about 80,000 tons of supplies to the front. Assuming there were no interruptions, it was pledged to haul nearly 40,000 tons. Actually it carried slightly over 20,000 tons. One school of thought blamed this result on the grounding of planes for projected airborne operations. However, many other factors were involved. It is true that on each of 13 days a wing or more was grounded for that reason, but on four of those days the command met its supply obligations and on five other days weather would have grounded the bulk of the planes anyway. On nine days during that month the weather was generally unsatisfactory for supply flights to the Continent Another handicap which, although hard to measure, was certainly great, was the scarcity of forward airfields available for air supply. Because almost all good bases near the front were preempted by fighter and fighter-bomber units, the troop carriers were seldom able to use all the planes they had available and sometimes had to stop the flow of supplies to certain sectors because they had no place to land them.

---

*The Eighth Air Force also participated in the supply effort. Liberators of the Second Bombardment Wing hauled 1,900 tons of freight between 29 August and 17 September. However, the bombers had to be modified for supply work and could only land on good, hard-surfaced bases. (Hq IX TCC, Supply By Air, App A, Air Supply and Resupply By B-24 Aircraft, Nov 44, in 546.461.)

Besides these major factors were a multitude of minor difficulties which sprang from the unprecedented and unexpected size of the supply requirements and the rapid advance of the armies. CATOR was at first somewhat inefficient in handling its huge new responsibilities. Ground force supply organizations sometimes delivered supplies late or to the wrong place, so that a mission had to be postponed for lack of a load. Some missions to captured enemy air bases had to be briefed from target folders and target books because no other data was yet available. Usually the destination was a sod or dirt strip less than 4,000 feet long with a minimum of control and unloading facilities. The normal capacity of such strips when all went smoothly was between 36 and 72 planes an hour.* Unloading was done by whatever ground units happened to be available. Occasionally none showed up, and the crews unloaded their own planes.

Although the unstinted efforts of the troop carrier men under such conditions won several commendations, some American ground commanders, seeking a scapegoat for their inability to get greater tonnage by air, felt that all troop carrier planes should have been withdrawn from airborne operations and training and committed entirely to supply. On the other hand, General Brereton felt that even the air supply effort actually made was an unwise diversion of his forces from their primary mission. SHAEF alone could decide between the contending viewpoints, and on the whole its compromise course seems wise. The complete diversion of effort desired by the ground forces could not have increased supply deliveries appreciably unless the troop carrier units had either been given bases in France (as was finally done) or had been provided with more and better forward landing fields. In any case it seems unlikely that it would have produced enough tonnage to warrant the sacrifice of the airborne weapon.[14]

As Patton's men crossed the Seine on 19 August it was evident that the German armies in France were shattered and could make no effective stand short of the Siegfried Line in the east and the Rhine in the north. General Bradley recommended a drive eastward through the Siegfried Line. General Montgomery favored a thrust

---

*In most cases nothing bigger than a C-47 could have been used. Even had the C-46 been available it would have bogged down on soft surfaces. Moreover, it stood so high that it could not be unloaded without special equipment.

through the Low Countries and across the Rhine onto the plains of northern Germany. This would breach the last possible barrier between the Allies and Berlin and would also help solve the supply problem through capture of the Channel ports and Antwerp. The transportation shortage made it impossible to deliver a major effort in both directions at once. On 23 August Eisenhower approved Montgomery's proposal of a drive northward. It was to be made by the British 21 Army Group with the United States First Army on its right, while Third Army conducted a limited secondary offensive eastward to the Marne and farther if convenient.[15]

The first airborne operation considered for use in the northward drive was BOXER, a drop and landing about 30 miles inland from Boulogne to take that port and harass the German retreat. Approved by SHAEF on 24 August, it was turned down by 21 Army Group at a conference next day as an indecisive operation off the main line of advance.

At the same meeting General Brereton and Montgomery's chief of staff agreed on an operation in the Lille-Arras-Douai area directly ahead of the British thrust for the purpose of cutting off the retreating enemy. By the 26th, Airborne Army had picked Tournai and vicinity as objectives for the operation, which was christened LINNET. On the 27th preliminary instructions were given to the troop carrier and airborne commanders, and the troop carriers were relieved from supply operations effective the 28th. On 29 August Airborne Army issued its outline plan, and both SHAEF and 21 Army Group approved 3 September as target date. On the 31st IX TCC issued its field order, and the troops arrived at the airfields. By the evening of 2 September marshalling was completed.

Once again, however, the rapid advance of the ground forces forestalled an airborne venture. On the night of 2 September British and American troops met in Tournai, and at 2224 Montgomery's headquarters sent word that LINNET was cancelled.

LINNET would have been a major operation, carrying the 82d and 101st Divisions, the British 1 Airborne, and the Polish Brigade. It seems questionable whether the results would have been worth the effort, even if the Allies had not been close to Tournai. It offered nothing decisive, nothing not quickly obtainable by ground action, only a few miles more ground, a few thousand more prisoners and an unimportant river crossing. Probably because of this, proposals had been made on 1 September that the operation be cancelled, and General Brereton had set about looking for an alternative. He found one and suggested it next day.

On the afternoon of 2 September, foreseeing that LINNET would not take place, since stormy weather was predicted for 3 September, and the Allies would surely be in Tournai by the 4th, Brereton asked SHAEF to approve a substitute, LINNET II, to secure crossings over the Meuse north of Liége on 4 September. Eisenhower left the decision to Montgomery, who ruled against it, presumably because it lay on the path of an advance eastward through Aachen and the Siegfried Line, while his intention was to drive north across the Rhine. The verdict against LINNET II was telephoned to Airborne Army at 2125 on 3 September and reached the troop carriers next morning.

Had the mission been flown on 4 September it might have been seriously disrupted for lack of maps, photographs and other information, which there was not time to obtain. General Browning was so agitated over the effect of these shortages on the airborne as to offer his resignation, though he later withdrew it. The troop carriers' attitude is unknown, but they might have had a hard time locating their zones, especially since navigational aids between England and the objective area would probably have been limited to one marker boat in the Channel.[16]

On the evening of 3 September, after cancelling LINNET II, Montgomery asked Airborne Army for an operation by the British 1 Airborne Division and the Polish Parachute Brigade to secure a crossing of the Rhine in the stretch between Arnhem and Wesel on the afternoon of the 6th or the morning of the 7th. Next day Montgomery's staff selected Arnhem as the crossing point, largely because the flak around Wesel was considered prohibitively thick.

Airborne Army began on the 4th to prepare for this operation, which was christened COMET. On the 6th troop carrier plans were substantially complete, except for the timing which was settled that afternoon in a conference at Stanmore. A *coup de main* party in 18 gliders was to seize the Arnhem bridge at 0430 on 8 September. Pathfinder troops carried in 12 Stirlings were to begin dropping at 0645. At 0715 the main force would arrive, a column of 340 British gliders, towed by 38 and 46 Groups, followed by 269 planes of the 52d Wing with paratroops. In the afternoon, missions would be flown by 320 British planes with gliders, 114 paratroop aircraft of the 52d Troop Carrier Wing, and 144 with supplies to drop. Next day, if feasible, 157 gliders towed by the 61st and 442d Groups would bring in the American 878th Aviation Engineer Battalion to prepare an airfield on which the British 52 Light Division, which had been made air transportable, might be landed as reinforcements.

The troops who were to take the bridge at Arnhem were to be flown in over a route very similar to the northern route later used in MARKET, to a drop zone and a landing zone five miles northwest of Arnhem which were practically identical with zones used on MARKET. In these respects MARKET was simply COMET, slightly revised. The rest of the troops were to be flown over a more southern route to zones south of Nijmegen to take bridges over the Waal at Nijmegen and over the Maas at Grave. While these objectives were retained in MARKET, the planning in relation to them was drastically changed.

By 7 September COMET plans were complete and field orders were issued. The 52d Wing called in its group commanders and their staffs at 1300 for briefing. However, storm warnings forced a 24-hour postponement. On the 8th Montgomery got word that German resistance along the Albert and Meuse-Escaut canals west of Antwerp was stiffening. He therefore asked another postponement. Further news of effective German resistance and even counterattacks caused him to delay COMET again on the 9th and to cancel it on the 10th. The Nijmegen-Arnhem area was more than 50 miles behind the German front, and in between were seven canals and rivers at which the Germans might be able to hold. If they did so the predicament of the airborne would be very dangerous; just how dangerous, events were to show.

Between 8 and 10 September Montgomery also considered an airborne operation against Walcheren Island to open the Scheldt, but Brereton rejected this, asserting that the terrain was very unsuitable and flak sure to be intense.[17]

The Planning of MARKET

On the morning of 10 September General Eisenhower flew to Brussels to confer with Montgomery on the strategy they would use in the coming weeks. In a stormy session aboard Eisenhower's plane Montgomery won his superior's approval for an expanded version of COMET. This operation, MARKET, was to lay an airborne carpet, comprising not only the First Airborne Division and the Polish airborne but also the American 82d and 101st Divisions, along the road to Arnhem. To lift this force would require all available British and American troop carrier aircraft in a series of missions lasting at least two days.

Montgomery also wanted ground operations outside Belgium brought to a standstill so that he could put maximum force into Operation GARDEN, a ground assault from his front along the Meuse-Escaut Canal up the Hasselt-Arnhem highway. In this respect he got by no means all he desired, but on the 12th SHAEF did promise to divert to his service enough American trucks and planes to bring 1,000 tons a day to Brussels for GARDEN. Satisfied that this met his minimum requirements, Montgomery then set 17 September as D-day for MARKET-GARDEN.[18]

At 1430 on 10 September General Browning, who had just flown back to England with news of the Brussels conference, notified Airborne Army of the decision on MARKET. At 1800 General Brereton held a conference of his troop carrier and airborne commanders and their staffs* at Airborne Army Headquarters in Sunnyhill Park. There Browning sketched out Montgomery's conception of MARKET, and a short discussion was held on the main points of the operation.

Before anything else could be settled, the objectives had to be determined. The commanders agreed that the British and Polish airborne should be concentrated for the Arnhem assault, that the 82d Division should take over the Nijmegen-Grave area, and that the 101st Division should seize crossings over the principal waterways south of Grave. This decision ensured that missions carrying the 82d Division from the Grantham area would not cross the path of missions bearing the 101st from southern England. It also ensured that the less seasoned 101st would be the first to make contact with the Allied ground forces.

---

*Except General Ridgway who was in France.

Agreement as to just where and how the 101st was to be used was not so easy. Montgomery's proposal called for it to be strung out like a kite-string over a 30-mile stretch extending to within artillery range of the Second Army front. General Taylor protested against such extreme dispersion of his division and was strongly supported by Brereton. No decision on the matter was reached at the Sunnyhill Park meeting, but Brereton took the matter up with Montgomery, who agreed after a rather sharp exchange of views to let the matter be settled by direct discussion between General Taylor and Lt. Gen. Miles C. Dempsey, commander of the British Second Army. They met at Montgomery's headquarters on 12 September. Since both were good diplomats, and General Dempsey was confident that his army could slice through unaided as far as Eindhoven, they readily reached a solution. The 101st was to be responsible for the crossings in a 16-mile area between Veghel and Eindhoven, and could postpone the taking of Eindhoven until two hours after its initial operations. Thus drops near Eindhoven would not be necessary, and the division could concentrate its drops and landings further north.

Another basic decision made on 10 September was that the allocation of aircraft and bases for MARKET would be essentially that planned for LINNET.* This decision was adhered to, and comparison of the air movement tables for the two operations reveals that very little change was made in the paratroop serials.† In the glider serials the LINNET teaming of airborne and troop carrier units was retained, but instead of towing two gliders apiece, as would have been done in the former operation, tug aircraft in MARKET were restricted to single-tow. This made it necessary to add a couple of glider serials to the original sequence and to schedule additional missions on D plus 2 and D plus 3 to bring in the displaced gliders. While it was difficult and hazardous for a C-47 to tow two Wacos at once, bad weather on D plus 2 was to make the decision on single-tow a costly one. Another addition, obvious and inevitable from the start, was a series of resupply missions on D plus 2 and thereafter. Unnecessary in LINNET, they were to play an important and tragic part in MARKET.

The signal plan set up for LINNET was also adopted for MARKET and was later incorporated into the field orders with a minimum of change. One reason for this borrowing from previous plans was to save time. Unaware of the extent of Montgomery's supply difficulties, Brereton and his commanders expected that MARKET might have to go as early as the 14th. The only way to do that was to make maximum use of existing arrangements. Similar use of plans for cancelled operations had made possible the hasty launching of the Salerno missions in Italy. These cases indicate the possibility and value of having stand-by plans prepared for various sizes and types of airborne operation and adapting them to the needs of the moment instead of having to construct each new plan from the ground up.

One limiting factor in the speed with which the operation could be launched was the need to secure and distribute photographic intelligence. In this instance General Brereton seems to have agreed that H-hour should not be less than 72 hours after receipt of photographic coverage.

During the meeting at Sunnyhill Park, Brereton named General Williams as air commander for MARKET with operational control not only of IX TCC but also of 38 Group, 46 Group, and such bomber aircraft as might be used for resupply. He would exercise control through the Command Post at Eastcote. General Browning was designated as airborne commander. He was to be flown in by glider with a small staff to direct operations in the airhead until firm contact was made with the ground forces.

Brereton also ruled that MARKET would be flown in daylight. This decision was bold, but not unprecedented. During the invasion of southern France Williams had sent in paratroop missions at dawn and gliders by daylight with negligible losses. Moreover, TRANSFIGURE, LINNET, and COMET had all been planned as daylight operations. In COMET, however, the decision had been made on the assumption that neither German fighters nor German antiaircraft could do the missions much harm. Intelligence estimates indicated that the Luftwaffe would not be a serious threat to MARKET, but that the flak around Arnhem was much more plentiful than when COMET was conceived and was increasing to the point where it might present a serious threat.

Whatever the danger from flak, a night mission was virtually out of the question once D-day was

---
*See above, p. 87.
†The 437th and 442d Groups did exchange assignments.

set for 17 September, because that date fell at the dark of the moon. Postponement would not help, since on the following nights the moon would not rise until about dawn. Both doctrine and experience warned against attempting airborne missions in total darkness. The warning was reinforced by the fact that the objectives in MARKET, deep in enemy territory, and some 200 miles from the nearest Gee chain, would be much more difficult to locate by radar than those in Normandy had been. The question was whether flak could be avoided or neutralized sufficiently so that MARKET could be flown safely by day. Brereton with his exceptional experience in tactical air operations judged that it could.

On 12 or 13 September, H-hour, the moment when the initial troop carrier serials, exclusive of pathfinders, would arrive over their zones, was set at 1300 hours, Zone A Time.* This timing gave ample opportunity for preliminary anti-flak operations between dawn and H-hour. It was also considered early enough to enable armored units of Second Army to begin their attack after H-hour and still make contact with the airborne troops in the Eindhoven area before sundown.[19]

The troop carrier and airborne staffs spent the night of 10 September in preparation for a conference at Eastcote at 0900 the next morning. The troop carrier wings were alerted that night and their commanders were summoned to Eastcote to attend the discussion. The principal items on the agenda were selection of routes, selection of zones, and preliminary decisions on the loading plan. Routes were worked out by a troop carrier planning committee and presented to the airborne for approval. Each airborne division selected drop and landing zones for itself and submitted them to the meeting for acceptance. Once routes and zones were chosen the conferees could proceed to the allocation of units to missions and of lift to troops, fundamental pairings on which detailed loading tables would later be based. Tentative decisions on all these matters had been made by the time the conference broke up at noon on the 11th. However, major changes were made on the 12th and several minor ones were introduced later.[20]

The choice of routes lay between a northern course similar to one planned for COMET and a southern route across Belgium. The former traversed enemy territory for 80 miles, but it was almost straight and was believed to be relatively free from flak. The latter involved the shortest possible flight over enemy territory but would necessitate flying over the battle lines. The troop carriers favored the northern route because they feared the massed artillery of an active front. However, the final decision was to use both routes. Since the supply of fighter escorts was ample and the number of German fighters few, this dispersion would actually facilitate the defense of the missions. Also the operation gained in flexibility. With maps on hand and navigational aids set up for two routes, it would be possible to shift from one to the other as circumstances dictated. All serials going to Arnhem and Nijmegen on D-day would use the northern route. Those for the Eindhoven area would take the southern route. Because their objectives were relatively near the Allied lines, use of that route would cut their time over enemy territory by more than half.

A noteworthy innovation, planned for LINNET but first used in MARKET, was the massing of serials in three parallel lanes 1½ miles apart. The plan for MARKET did not call for simultaneous use of more than two of those lanes on a given route, but all could be used at once if need arose. In addition 38 Group and 46 Group were to fly gliders over the northern route at a level 1,000 feet above the Americans, making that a four-lane skyway.

Further concentration was achieved by spacing the American parachute serials at four-minute intervals and glider serials at seven-minute intervals instead of the six and ten-minute intervals prescribed by IX TCC in Normandy. This tightening of the column was possible because MARKET was to be flown in daylight instead of darkness or twilight. By these means, the use of two routes, each with three or four lanes for traffic, and the closer spacing of serials, 1,055 planeloads of paratroops and 478 gliders were to be delivered in the initial lift within 65 minutes, the same time it took to bring in 369 sticks of paratroops for the 82d Division in NEPTUNE.

The northern route began at the seaside town of Aldeburgh beside the Alde estuary, ran for 94 miles straight across the North Sea to the west end of Schouwen Island, a distinctive landfall

---

*This was one hour ahead of Greenwich Mean Time. It came into effect at 0300 on the 17th.

point, and on without turning for 18 miles to the eastern tip of the island. From there it ran for 52 miles to the IP, which was christened ELLIS. This was about three miles south of 's Hertogenbosch and could be readily identified by several highway intersections in its vicinity. It was about 30 miles southwest of the zones in the Arnhem area, about 25 miles west-southwest of those in the Nijmegen section. The northernmost of the zones eventually selected in the Eindhoven sector was about 10 miles east-southeast of it.

The southern route started at Bradwell Bay (ATTU) and cut across the Thames estuary for 34 miles to the tip of the North Foreland. This involved a detour for the 53d Wing, but a more direct course would have brought the wing over the antiaircraft batteries and barrage balloons of the London metropolitan area and would have required special permission. From the North Foreland the route ran for 159 miles to the IP (DELOS), a point in Belgium where it crossed the Albert canal. The Eindhoven group of zones was slightly over 30 miles northeast of DELOS. An approach on this heading would cut neatly between known flak concentrations around Eindhoven and Tilburg. On 16 September General Williams decided to bend the route slightly southward to avoid a pocket of German troops who were holding out south of the Scheldt. As revised it ran from CATALINA, a landfall point four miles northeast of Ostend, to the outskirts of Ghent airfield and from there to DELOS.

After passing their zones the American troop carriers were to turn 180° to left or right, depending on the position of the zone, and return by the way they had come. They were to fly at 1,500 feet on the trip out, descend to 500 feet to make their drop or release, and return at 3,000 feet to avoid the incoming traffic. American paratroop formations would be the usual 9-plane V of V's in serials of from 27 to 45 planes. American glider formations again would be columns made up of pairs of pairs in echelon to the right in serials of from 30 to 50. British tow-planes and gliders would proceed in a loose column of pairs at 10-second intervals, flying at 2,500 feet on the way to their zones, and returning at 5,000-7,000 feet.[21]

Selection of drop and landing zones was facilitated by the previous planning for COMET and by the fact that the terrain was more favorable than that in the Normandy operations. In the north, especially around Arnhem, the land was rolling and in many places wooded. Between the Rhine and the Waal and everywhere in the Eindhoven sector it was flat, open, and interlaced with rivers, canals and ditches, which could shield the airborne troops against attacks by enemy armor. Fields varied from very large to less than 200 yards in length but were bordered by low, weak fences and small hedges instead of the formidable barriers encountered in the Cotentin.

The great prize, the *sine qua non* of the whole enterprise, was the single-span steel bridge by which the highway running north from Hasselt crossed the Lower Rhine into the city of Arnhem. The river at that point was about a tenth of a mile across. The south side was low-lying and scantily settled. The north side was a thriving urban area, Arnhem being a modern city of over 100,000 persons with several good-sized suburbs. A second highway bridge into the city had been destroyed, but a railway bridge 2½ miles east of the highway was still intact. At Heveadorp, a mile below the railroad bridge, there was a ferry. The Germans were known to have built a pontoon bridge near the highway.

To take and hold one or more of these crossings was the task of the British First Airborne Division. Its initial paratroop drop was to be made in essentially the same place selected for the first paratroops in COMET. This zone, DZ X lay about six miles northwest of the center of Arnhem, north of the village of Heelsum, and just south of the Amsterdam-Arnhem railway.* It was an irregular area containing about a square mile. As in COMET the first British gliders were to land on LZ S, a narrow strip over a mile long and about half a mile wide, a little way northeast of DZ X and on the other side of the railroad. The next contingent of gliders, which in the COMET plan had been slated for the Nijmegen area, was now assigned a new zone, LZ Z, adjoining DZ X and extending about half a mile east of it. All three zones were made up of fields, pasture and heath bordered by pine woods.

While the zones were good enough in themselves and provided a tight initial concentration, they were all over five miles away from the highway bridge which was the chief objective of the troops. American airborne doctrine, confirmed by Allied

---
*For British and Polish landing and drop zones see Map No. 9, p. 113.

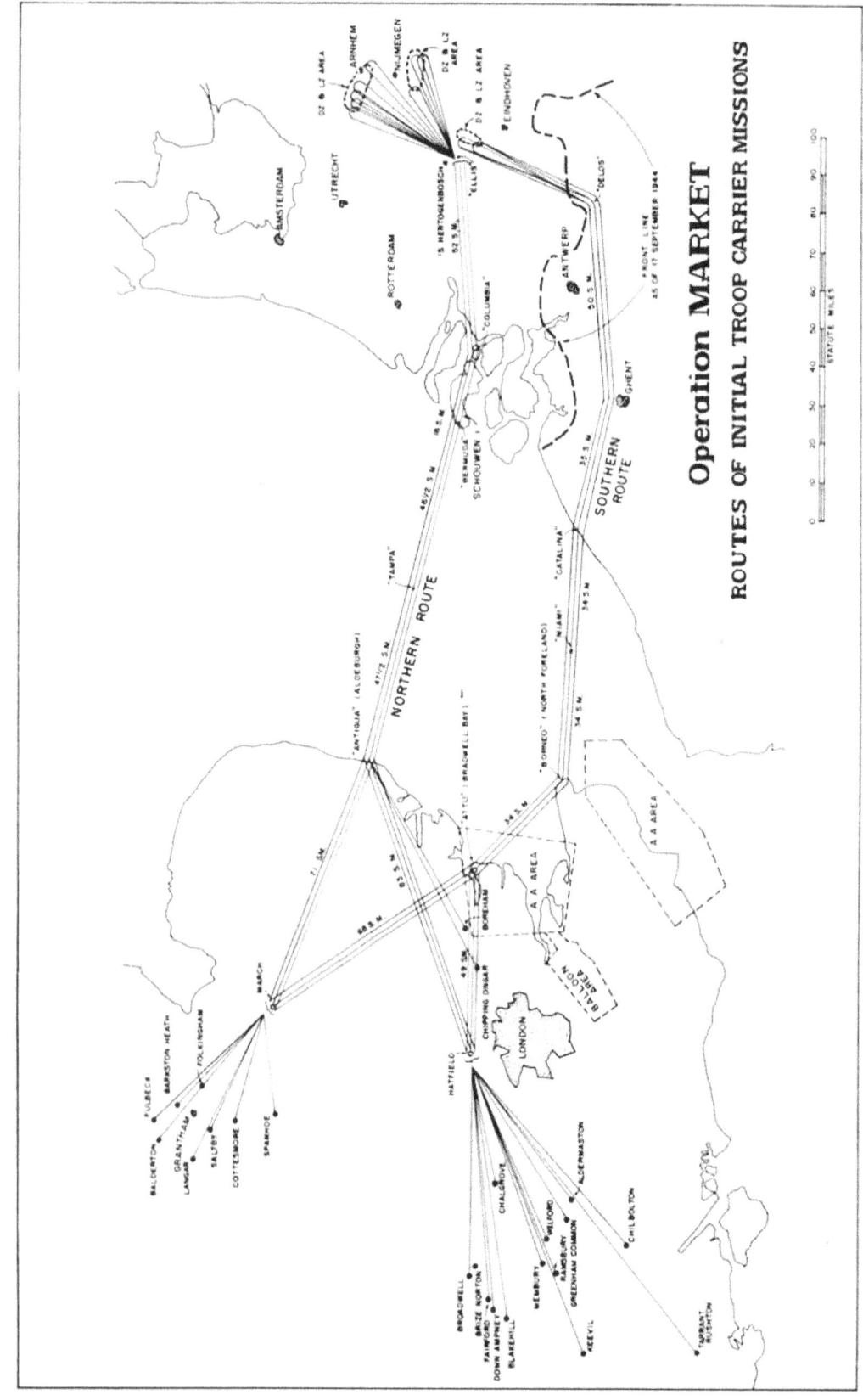

Map 6.

experience in Normandy, held that this was too far. Precious time would be consumed merely in marching to the bridge. The risk of delay by roadblocks was great. In addition, part of the force would have to be left behind to hold zones for use by other missions on D plus 1.

The British airborne staff officers were not unaware of these handicaps but Maj. Gen. R. E. Urquhart, Commander of First Airborne Division, preferred good zones at a distance to bad zones near his objectives. North of the river there were no large open areas near the city, though some smaller ones might have been used. Dutch reports as to the topography of the south shore of the river were pessimistic, indicating that it was swampy, dissected by ditches, and easily swept by gun fire from the opposite bank. Moreover, the area was said to be subject to flooding, a most unpleasant possibility to men who remembered British and American drops into swamps in Normandy. Another consideration was fear of antiaircraft guns, great numbers of which were said to be massed near the bridge. Consequently no D-day drops or landings were to be made near Arnhem. The *coup de main* contemplated for COMET was abandoned, and nothing was put in its place.

On D plus 1 a second installment of paratroops, originally slated in COMET for the Nijmegen area, were to drop on DZ Y, a splendid open quadrangle containing well over a mile of ground but about eight miles away from the highway bridge. It lay north of the Amsterdam railway about a mile west of LZ S. Gliders that day would use DZ X as a landing zone, and supplies were to be dropped on DZ L, an area containing less than a square quarter-mile, located about half a mile east of LZ S. The success of this plan depended on maintaining fairly complete control over a strip of land 8 miles long and up to 3 miles in width extending from DZ Y to the bridge, a very large task for half an airborne division.

On D plus 2 the outlying areas would be abandoned to shorten the line of defense. The principal airborne operation, a drop by paratroops of the Polish Brigade, would be directed at DZ K, a circular zone three-quarters of a mile in diameter on the south side of the Rhine about a mile south of the highway bridge. Other troops and materiel of the brigade and of the American 878th Aviation Engineer Battalion would land by glider on DZ/LZ L.* If all went well the engineers were to prepare landing strips on which planes in subsequent missions could air-land the British 52 Light Division. Supply drops on D plus 2 were to be made at Supply Drop Point (SDP) V, a quadrant containing about a quarter-mile of ground at a road junction less than a mile west of the outskirts of Arnhem.[22]

The 82d Division in contrast to the British, placed its zones on an average about a mile from its initial objectives.† Its staff spent the night of 10-11 September selecting zones, and next morning after discussion and some revision to meet troop carrier objections its choices were approved at the Eastcote meeting.

The task of the 82d was to take and hold a bridge over the Maas outside the village of Grave five miles southwest of Nijmegen, at least one of four bridges over the Maas-Waal Canal between Grave and Nijmegen, and the bridge over the Waal at Nijmegen itself. Success in holding these crossings was dependent on possession of another objective, the Groesbeek heights, a ridge some 300 feet high about two miles southeast of Nijmegen. This ridge was the only high ground for miles around and dominated the whole region. Nijmegen, a town of some 82,000 population on the south side of the Waal, was reported to have around it at least 22 heavy antiaircraft guns and 86 lighter pieces, and was thought likely to contain a large garrison. South of the town between the canal and the ridge the country was wooded, so drops to take objectives other than the Nijmegen bridge would have to be made west of the canal or southeast of the ridge.

Units put down near Nijmegen on D-day might suffer heavily from flak on the way in, would be quickly engaged by fairly strong enemy forces, and would have to deal with those forces for many hours in isolation from the rest of the division. Furthermore, without the ridge and crossings over the Maas and the canal, the Nijmegen bridge would be worthless. General Gavin and his staff therefore determined to put first things first and leave Nijmegen to be taken by ground attack after the other objectives were secured. This decision was later confirmed in very explicit terms by General Browning.

Gavin chose to bring in most of the division to

---

*See the British and Polish assault area, Map No. 9, p. 113.
†See the 82d Division assault area, Map No. 8, p. 108.

a belt of drop and landing zones between 3 and 4 miles southeast of Nijmegen on the far side of the Groesbeek heights so that he could attack the ridge as quickly as possible with maximum force and then set up a defensive perimeter including both ridge and zones. This seemed to minimize the risk of an enemy occupation of the landing area such as had happened in Normandy.

At the northern end of the belt was DZ T, an oval 3,000 yards long from east to west and three-quarters of a mile wide, framed in a neat triangle by a railroad along its south side and by two roads which intersected at the village of Wyler a few hundred yards north of the zone. Approaching serials would pass close to the bridge at Grave about 7 miles short of the zone and over the Maas-Waal Canal about three miles before reaching the zone. Some 3,000 yards southwest of DZ T was a slightly smaller oval, DZ N, bordered on its western and northern sides by the woods of the Groesbeek ridge. The junction of the canal with the Maas river a mile and a half east of DZ N made an excellent landmark on the line of approach.

Between and overlapping both DZ's was a rough oblong averaging 3½ miles from north to south and 1½ miles from east to west, which had been selected for glider landings. This was split into a northern half, LZ T and a southern half, LZ N. The latter had small fields averaging 200 yards in some sections. However, there were few high obstacles and the Germans did not seem to be erecting any. Experts calculated that by daylight the two zones could receive between 700 and 900 gliders, all the 82d would need. LZ N was also selected as destination for parachute resupply missions to the 82d Division.

One regiment had to be put within striking distance of the bridge at Grave, and for this purpose DZ O, an oval drop zone over 1¾ miles long from west to east and almost a mile wide, was marked out on flat, open land astride the Eindhoven-Nijmegen highway halfway between the Grave bridge and the Maas-Waal Canal. The troops dropped there were to attack both the Grave bridge a mile to their west and three bridges over the canal between one and two miles east of them. Gavin laid great stress on taking at least one bridge over the canal to ensure contact between this outlying regiment and the main force in the Groesbeek area. He had a horror of having men cut off as Millett had been.

Convinced that the big bridge at Grave would be defended and prepared for demolition, Colonel Reuben Tucker, commander of the 504th Parachute Regiment, which was picked for the mission to DZ O, urged that the proper way to attack the structure was to drop men on the south bank of the Maas and rush the bridge from both ends. Just 36 hours before MARKET began, Tucker's proposal was accepted, and orders were given that a company of his paratroops be dropped on a special DZ on the south side of the river half a mile from the end of the bridge. The ground there was low, marshy, and heavily ditched, a bad drop zone, chosen deliberately to achieve quick access to the objective.

One general point in regard to the zones of the 82d Division is that the network of waterways, highways and railroads south of Nijmegen was particularly distinctive. If a pilot could come within sighting distance of Grave, he would have an abundance of landmarks thereafter.[28]

The 101st Division may have chosen the zones it wanted even before General Taylor's meeting with Dempsey. Certainly it had them ready for detailed description in field orders on 13 September.* As redefined by Taylor and Dempsey the initial tasks of the division were to take a bridge over the Wilhelmina Canal at Zon five airline miles north of Eindhoven, a bridge over the Dommel River at St. Oedenrode four miles north of Zon, and four bridges over the Aa River and the Willems Canal at Veghel, which was five miles northeast of St. Oedenrode and 13 miles southwest of Grave. After that, but before nightfall if possible, the 101st was to take Eindhoven and four bridges there over the upper Dommel. Of these objectives the two canal bridges were much the most important, since the canals were 60 feet across and too deep for tanks; none of the rivers were over 25 feet wide, and the Dommel at Eindhoven was a mere creek.

Faced with the problem of taking objectives strung out over more than 15 miles of highway Taylor decided to bring in most of his division to a single area midway between St. Oedenrode and Zon from which he could strike quickly against both places and then move readily against Eindhoven. Available for his purpose was a large open

---
*See Map No. 7, p. 104.

tract on the west side of the north-south highway about 1½ miles north of Zon. South of the open land lay a belt of woods, known as the Zonsche Forest, extending to the Wilhelmina Canal, which ran east and west from Zon. A road and a railroad running northwest from Eindhoven crossed the canal about a mile southwest of the tract and a mile southeast of the little town of Best.

On the open area the divisional staff marked out an oblong 4,000 yards long and 2,800 yards wide, which it split longitudinally into two equal drop zones, DZ's B and C. The long axes of these zones ran east-northeast. Troop carriers approaching them by the southern route would be on a heading of north-northeast. A landing zone, LZ W, was drawn to include most of the oblong but was slightly narrower from north to south and extended 1,000 yards further west. The zone was considered more than sufficient for 400 gliders, and most of its fields were over 300 yards in length.

One parachute regiment had to be dropped farther north for the taking of Veghel. The spot chosen for its jump was a potbellied oval, DZ A, which was about two miles long from east to west, up to 2,000 yards wide, and about a mile southwest of the town. North of the zone was a railroad running east to Veghel. Southeast of the zone was the Eindhoven-Arnhem highway. The bridges over the Willems Canal were only a few hundred yards northeast of DZ A, but the Aa River was a mile further on. Thus the paratroops would have to secure a crossing over the canal and move through a populated area before attacking the road and railway bridges over the river. This difficulty led to a change in plan similar to that initiated by Tucker at Grave.

Lt. Col. W. O. Kinnard, a battalion commander, proposed that his unit be dropped north of the Willems Canal in position to move against the river bridges immediately after assembling. His idea was approved, and his battalion was given a new zone DZ A-1. This was a flat, open, area on the northeast side of the canal about a mile north of DZ A.[24]

Experience having indicated that bad navigation was the factor most likely to spoil a troop carrier mission, the planners took care to provide navigational aids, even though MARKET was to be flown by day. Eureka beacons and M/F (CRN-4) beacons for use with radio compasses were placed at the wing assembly points, and Eurekas, M/F beacons, and the aerial lighthouses known as occults were put at the points of departure from the British coast.

About half way between England and the Continent on both the northern and the southern route were stationed marker boats with Eureka beacons and green holophane lights. The boat on the northern route had been obtained for COMET, but the other had to be borrowed and put in position on short notice. Their code names were TAMPA and MIAMI. All the above beacons except the occults were operated by troop carrier personnel.

No beacons were to be provided on the northern route between TAMPA and the zones because that 150-mile stretch was all over water or enemy territory. At first the southern route was similarly devoid of aids between marker boat and zones. However, at a meeting on 14 September between Williams, Hollinghurst, and representatives of 21 Army Group and Second Army, the latter agreed that at a point near Gheel about 5,000 yards behind the front and about 3 miles north of DELOS CENTER their troops would set out a white panel T with head and stem 100 yards long and set yellow smoke generators at 100-yard intervals for 500 yards beyond the tips of the T. The British soldiers were also to take such measures as they could to mark the front itself with fluorescent panels, yellow smoke generators, yellow celanese triangles and lights. By 16 September the troop carriers had arranged to mark the IP. DELOS was to have a Eureka beacon, a green holophane light and green smoke.

The American planes in MARKET were all equipped with radio compasses and Rebecca. As in NEPTUNE, only flight leaders were to operate Rebecca. However, this time it was explicitly stated that if formations broke up, the lead ship in each element would operate its set. Enthusiastic about the performance of Gee and SCR-717 in NEPTUNE, IX TCC had asked on 18 June that half its aircraft be equipped with both SCR-717 and either Gee or Loran. Its request for SCR-717 was considered excessive, but its quota was raised to two and then three sets per squadron. The command had also won authorization to install Gee equipment on all its planes. However, so long as a serial held together only its leader would have much occasion to use SCR-717 or Gee.

The planes of 38 and 46 Group were equipped with both Rebecca and Gee, and all crews were authorized to use them. Under the British system of flying in column the risk of interference was small enough to permit such general use of sets. The British did not have radio compasses or SCR-717. The bombers employed for resupply had radio compasses, but no Rebecca sets.

Pathfinder assistance, though less needed than in a night operation, was not to be dispensed with. The Americans planned to employ six sticks of pathfinder troops. A pair of teams with one officer and nine enlisted men apiece were to be dropped on DZ's O, A, and B-C respectively. Each pair was to be responsible for setting up a Eureka, an M/F beacon, panel T's and letters and smoke signals. Each zone had its distinctive color combination of panels and smoke. At first the pathfinder drop was scheduled for 1230, half an hour before the main force arrived, but on the 16th it was shifted to 1245. These changes represent a balancing of two considerations, the need of the pathfinders for enough time to begin operations before the other serials approached, and the fact that every extra minute given them was a minute more warning given the enemy, a minute more in which the isolated pathfinder troops might be attacked and destroyed.

The smallness of the pathfinder effort was made possible by provisos that early serials for DZ's N and T would utilize the aids on DZ O, which lay almost on their line of approach, and that those bound for the two contiguous zones, B and C, would all rely on a single set of beacons and markers. As soon as possible DZ's N and T were to be marked by paratroops with smoke signals, and if feasible, with panel T's in time for use of those aids by the glider serials. Likewise, DZ's B and C were to be distinguished as soon as possible by different smoke signals and colored panels. The transformation of zones B and C into LZ W was to be accomplished simply by recoding the two beacons from B to W and rearranging the panels there to form a W in place of a B. Since the pathfinders could not carry enough equipment with them to operate for all the missions scheduled, additional equipment, mostly smoke and batteries was to be dropped onto LZ N and LZ W at 0630 on D plus 1 from a single pathfinder plane.

The British were to dispatch a dozen modified Stirling bombers of 38 Group to drop pathfinder teams 20 minutes before H-hour, half on DZ X and half on LZ S. The teams were to set up Eurekas, panel letters and smoke on both zones, put out a panel T on DZ X, and fire Very lights on LZ S. On the following days they would use the same set of aids on the other British zones, reserving Very lights for landing zones and T's for drop zones and drop points.[25]

Protection of MARKET from friendly fire was simplified by the fact that there were no invasion convoys anywhere about. Absent, too, were their attendant swarms of fighters, and their absence left IFF channels open to troop carrier use. The field orders directed that in MARKET flight-leaders and stragglers should keep their IFF sets on. As further protection from naval antiaircraft, the Allied navies were given full information on the initial missions. However, in subsequent missions some changes had to be made too late to get word to ships at sea. The principal risk of friendly fire came from front-line troops on the southern route, and on this point the British ground forces agreed on 14 September that no antiaircraft fire by day would be permitted during MARKET and that only such as was specially authorized would be allowed at night.[26]

Air support for MARKET was coordinated through AEAF Rear at Stanmore. On 11 September Leigh-Mallory called representatives of all commands concerned to meet at Stanmore at 1600 on the 12th to deal with the matter. Since prior discussions for LINNET and COMET had paved the way to agreement, the roles of the various air forces were quickly decided. Eighth Air Force and Air Defense of Great Britain would fly escort and cover for the missions and protect them from antiaircraft. If desired, Ninth Air Force would help with the latter task. Between missions the Second Tactical Air Force, RAF, whose planes lacked staying power for escort work, would protect the airborne troops from enemy aircraft and be available for close support missions. At night Second TAF would be assisted by night fighters of ADGB.

Measures were also prescribed to neutralize in advance, as far as possible, those enemy flak batteries and air bases which were in a position to endanger MARKET. For this purpose Eighth Air Force was directed to reconnoiter the troop carrier routes to locate flak positions and to bombard those positions with its heavy bombers at the latest possible time before H-hour, and RAF Bomber Command was to attack enemy airfields on the night of D minus 1.

Deception was not as much stressed as it had been in the Normandy missions, partly because the possibilities of surprise in daylight missions to objectives deep in enemy territory were relatively limited. However, RAF Coastal Command was requested to fly diversionary missions outside the Arnhem area, and Bomber Command was designated to make diversionary drops of dummy paratroops.

Tentative plans were also made for a resupply mission by about 250 heavy bombers of Eighth Air Force on D plus 1. This was requested by the troop carriers to free their planes from resupply work in order that they might be devoted to bringing in more airborne troops.

The decision to pick 17 September as D-day gave time for another meeting at Stanmore at 1600 on 15 September to refine and revise support plans. Arrangements were made on the assumption that both routes would be used on D-day. Escort and flak-suppression on the northern route between England and the IP was entrusted to ADGB. Beyond the IP, Eighth Air Force would perform those tasks. On the southern route Eighth Air Force was to fly escort between the Belgian coast and the zones. It also agreed to provide perimeter patrols to intercept enemy air-aircraft approaching the MARKET area from the east or north. At the meeting, Airborne Army asked that four groups of fighter-bombers be provided to neutralize flak and ground fire on the southern route between the IP and the DZ during the missions. That responsibility was given to Ninth Air Force, which apparently was not represented at the meeting. Its operations section was first informed of the decision by phone from AEAF at 2020 on the night of the 15th. A great deal of preliminary notification on assignments in MARKET appears to have been done by telephone from Eastcote or Stanmore.

Another request by Airborne Army was for rocket-firing aircraft to break up possible attacks on the 82d Division by tanks reported lurking in the Reichswald Forest, which lay two or three miles southeast of the zones of that division. On 16 September Ninth Air Force was asked to provide a group of rocket-equipped fighters, but it had only one squadron of such planes and was unable to make that available in time for use on D-day. However, the squadron was used later to good effect.

The meeting also specified the tasks to be performed before H-hour by Eighth Air Force and Bomber Command. The former was supposed to deal with German garrisons in Arnhem and Nijmegen but objected to employing its high-level, heavy-bomber formations over towns with friendly populations, so medium bombers of Second TAF were given the job of attacking German barracks in those towns on the morning of D-day. Either at the meeting or about the same time the details of the diversionary operations were specified. Dummy drops were to be made from 40 planes of Bomber Command on the night of D-day at points west of Utrecht, east of Arnhem and at Emmerich. The purpose was to delay, if only momentarily, the movement of German ground reinforcements from Holland and the Rhineland against the airheads at Arnhem and Nijmegen.

The resupply mission on D plus 1 was definitely to be undertaken by Eighth Air Force. Weather permitting, it would send 252 B-24's with turrets removed.[27]

Resources and Preparations

Almost without exception the troop carrier units in MARKET had flown missions before, an advantage which should not be underestimated. The Ninth Troop Carrier Command had the same 3 wings, 14 groups, and pathfinder unit that it had had in NEPTUNE, and all wings and all groups but the 315th and 434th had participated in at least one other airborne operation, either in 1943 or during the invasion of southern France. The British had in 38 Group the same 10 squadrons which they had used in June but had increased 46 Group from 5 to 6 squadrons.

In most cases the troop carriers were located at good bases, at which they were well established, and were teamed with troops which were stationed nearby and had flown with them before from those bases. The British had made no changes of station since June. Their squadrons were located in pairs at eight bases, six of which were bunched about 80 miles west of London and 30 miles northwest of Greenham Common. The others, Keevil and

Tarrant Rushton lay respectively 30 and 60 miles south of the rest. From these eight fields would fly the glider echelon of the British 1 Airborne Division, which had been in readiness with gliders loaded since the marshalling for LINNET on 2 September.

The 53d Wing and its groups still held the bases at and around Greenham Common that they had occupied during NEPTUNE. Once again they were to lift the 101st Division, which was in its old billets nearby. The 442d Group, which had been attached to the 52d Wing for COMET, was attached to the 53d Wing on 11 September for MARKET. The group moved that same day from Boreham to Chilbolton, a field 20 miles south of Greenham Common. Chilbolton had not hitherto been occupied by troop carriers, but the 442d had made large-scale supply flights from there on the 12th.

The 52d Wing and its groups were on the same bases around Grantham which they had held since March. The only change needed was the addition of pierced steel plank for glider marshalling on muddy ground at Cottesmore, Fulbeck and Barkston Heath. Begun for LINNET, this work was completed in plenty of time. Besides carrying its old teammate and neighbor, the 82d Division, the wing was also to lift the British paratroops of First Division and the Polish Brigade. The 50th Wing was to assist it in carrying the American troops.

These assignments were essentially those made for LINNET, and the 50th Wing and the 439th, 440th, and 441st Groups had been moved to Balderton, Fulbeck, and Langar in the Grantham area in preparation for that operation. However, on 8 September, they had been ordered to France to concentrate on air supply operations for the ground forces. By 10 September the air echelons of the 439th and 441st Groups and a detachment of wing headquarters were actually in operation in the Reims area,* and most of the wing's equipment and all its refueling units were either already in France or in transit to France. At 2330 on 10 September the wing was alerted for MARKET and ordered to be at its LINNET bases ready to operate by 2400 on the 11th. The bases were then being closed out for release to the British. Strenuous efforts by supply and engineering officers of the wing and IX TCC set Balderton, Langar, and Fulbeck functioning again and provided necessary unit equipment, including refueling units borrowed from the 52d Wing. The deadline was met, a remarkable achievement, but one for which the excellent communications and ample supplies in England should be given some credit.

The pathfinders had moved early in September from North Witham to Chalgrove, which was about 20 miles north of Greenham Common. The change gave them a base of their own with climatic conditions better than those in the Grantham area.[28]

The IX TCC went into MARKET with much the same resources it had had for NEPTUNE. Losses of aircraft and crews had been replaced, and on 16 September the command had 1,274 operational aircraft and 1,284 assigned and available crews. The British had 321 converted bombers in 38 Group and 164 Dakotas (C-47's) in 46 Group.

The supply of gliders had increased despite the loss of almost all of those used in Normandy. On 1 July IX TCC had had 1,045 operational Wacos. These were only enough to lift the glider echelon of one division, so on 8 August in anticipation of operations involving several divisions a new glider assembly program had been inaugurated at Crookham Common with the objective of producing at least 40 completed Wacos a day. This time IX AFSC employed 26 officers and over 900 men under direction of the 26th Mobile Repair and Reclamation Squadron. Well organized and adequately equipped, they proved capable of assembling 60 (and once even 100) gliders in a day. By the end of August IX TCC had 1,629 operational Wacos, and by 16 September it had 2,160 of them. Plans called for the employment of about 90 percent of these gliders in MARKET. The British had 812 Horsas, the Americans only 104 of them. However, the latter had acquired a distaste for the Horsa and did not intend to use it. In addition to its Horsas 38 Group possessed 64 of the huge Hamilcar gliders, which were capable of carrying tanks.

About 1,900 American glider pilots were on hand at the end of August, but the arrival of 200 more by air a few days later gave IX TCC a total of 2,060 on the eve of MARKET. Since General Williams and General Brereton had decided not to use co-pilots on American gliders, they had enough

---

*Rear echelons of both the wing and its groups were still functioning at Exeter, Upottery, and Merryfield.

glider pilots for the proposed missions, but they would have virtually no reserves.[29]

As in June, the aircraft of IX TCC were without armor or self-sealing fuel tanks. The long struggle for safer fuel tanks had appeared to be won when, while in England on a tour of inspection in the latter part of June, Robert A. Lovett, Assistant Secretary of War for Air, promised that IX TCC would get at least enough for its pathfinders. However, the tanks were then very scarce; AAF Headquarters was unwilling to reallocate them; and the troop carriers got none. Some were shipped in September but did not arrive in time for MARKET.

Only about 400 of the Wacos had nose reinforcements of either the Corey or the Griswold type, and only about 900 had parachute arrestors. Large orders for arrestors and protective noses had been sent to the United States long before MARKET, but delivery had been slow. One cause of delay had been disagreement and vacillation in the United States as to which type of nose should be produced.[30]

MARKET is unique as the only large American airborne operation during World War II for which there was no training program, no rehearsal, almost no exercises, and a generally low level of tactical training activity. During the first two weeks of August intensive training had been resumed, and (counting that done by the units in Italy) there was more tactical training done in those two weeks than in all the rest of the summer. After that training declined sharply, and in September it sank even lower. In the month before MARKET only two paratroop exercises, totalling 288 sorties, were flown and no glider exercises at all. Less formal tactical training was also on a very low level. Only 306 airborne troops were carried during the two weeks before MARKET. Night flying training of all sorts generally amounted to less than an hour a week per pilot, and even daylight formation flying by more than a few planes at a time was a rare occurrence.[31]

Only half of the responsibility for this situation rests on the supply effort. Bad weather washed out some training and some was cancelled by alerts for airborne missions, but the constant expectation of such missions seems to have been an even greater hindrance. From 12 August to 17 September there were only five days on which FAAA did not believe that an airborne operation was just around the corner. This belief made training plans seem superfluous and realistic exercises a rash commitment.

On 14 September the troop carrier units were alerted and restricted, and American airborne troops began moving into bivouac at the bases. Early in the evening on the 15th wing commanders and key members of their staffs were fully briefed at Eastcote. On their return that night they briefed the wing staffs and the group commanders. About the same time field orders for the operation arrived at the wings from troop carrier headquarters. Early next morning rigid restrictions and security measures, such as had been in force before NEPTUNE, were imposed at all bases. During the day group staffs were briefed and wing and group field orders were issued.

In the afternoon and evening of 16 September, D minus 1, the groups briefed their combat crews. The briefings were generally regarded as well organized and comprehensive. However, detailed maps (1:50,000 and 1:25,000) were in such short supply that there were hardly enough for the group staffs, and as usual there was an acute lack of low-level photographs of the zones and run-in areas. The final briefings, held on the morning of the 17th just before the crews went to their planes, were short and were concerned mainly with weather conditions.[32]

While General Brereton was the final judge of routes and timing for MARKET, the verdict really lay in the hands of the weathermen. It was a heavy responsibility, for weather in the North Sea area was notoriously changeable, and MARKET needed three days in a row of good flying weather to give it a reasonable chance of success. The evaluation was to be made by the Staff Weather Officer of IX TCC and the Senior Meteorological Officer of 38 Group, acting at Ascot as joint weather officers for Airborne Army. Besides IX TCC's own weather service, run by detachments of 21 Weather Squadron, they could draw on all the extraordinary array of weather experts then gathered in the British Isles. They held two conferences a day with the long-range forecasters of USSTAF, the weather section of AEAF Rear at Stanmore, and the combined weather staffs of IX TCC and 38 Group at Eastcote. Meteorologists of several other commands were consulted from time to time. A constant informal exchange of information and opinions on changing conditions was maintained with the troop carrier weathermen at Eastcote.

Every day at 1630 the weather officers of Airborne Army issued a four-day forecast for use by the commanders and their operations staffs at Ascot and Eastcote. They also issued daily 24-hour forecasts which were sent to all troop carrier wings and groups by teletype or telephone. Actual conditions over Belgium were checked before each day's operations by three flights by planes of the 325th Reconnaissance Wing of the Eighth Air Force, timed so that telephone reports could be made to Airborne Army and Eighth Air Force at H-8, H-6, and H-4. This was intended to prevent such unpleasant surprises as the cloud bank which upset operations in Normandy.

At 1630 on 16 September (D minus 1) the experts delivered a favorable report on the coming four-day period. A high-pressure system was approaching Belgium from the southwest and would be over it next day. Fair weather with little cloud and gentle winds would prevail until the 20th. The forecast did predict fog on and after D plus 1, but only during the early morning.

With auspices so favorable Brereton gave orders at 1900 hours that next day the airborne carpet would be laid along the road to Arnhem. As previously planned H-hour would be at 1300, the 53d Wing mission to the Eindhoven area would take the southern route, and missions to Nijmegen and Arnhem would fly the northern route.[33]

Preliminary Support Operations

Before the carpet could be laid, the ground had to be cleared. This work was begun by 282 RAF bombers which on the night of D minus 1 attacked airfields at Leeuwarden, Steewijk-Havelte, Hopsten, and Salzbergen within fighter range of MARKET objectives and formidable flak installations around a bridge at Moerdijk which menaced planes flying the northern route. Though the bombers were shielded from enemy interceptors by six RAF planes and five from Eighth Air Force with radar jamming equipment, two were lost, presumably to flak or fighters. About 1,180 tons of bombs were dropped during the operation and the effects were considered generally good.

On the morning of 17 September Eighth Air Force dispatched 872 B-17's to attack 117 installations, mostly antiaircraft batteries, along the troop carrier routes. Scheduled to arrive at 0900, they were delayed for 30 minutes, but did their bombing between 0930 and 1130 and were clear of the Continent before the troop carriers appeared. In order to cope with their obscure, small targets, they flew in formations of 4 or 6 and relied principally on 260-pound fragmentation bombs, which they dropped from altitudes of 10,000 to 22,000 feet. All told, 852 bombers dropped 2,888 tons of fragmentation bombs and 29 tons of high explosive. Analyses of the results indicated that about 45 percent of the bombs came within 1,000 feet of their targets and that good results were achieved in 43 of the 117 cases. Visibility was good; no enemy planes appeared; and there was little flak except around Arnhem, where it was reported as moderate but inaccurate. Two bombers were brought down and 112 damaged, only four seriously. They had been given area support during the operation by 147 P-51's under MEW control. One of these failed to return.

Another operation that morning was an attack by 85 Lancasters and 15 Mosquitoes of the RAF, escorted by 53 Spitfires of ADGB, against coastal defenses on Walcheren Island. It was presumably intended to mislead the Germans into thinking that Walcheren, which lay between the two troop carrier routes, was the objective of the initial troop carrier missions.

The last preliminary operation on the morning of the 17th was the dispatch of 50 Mosquitoes, 48 Mitchells (British B-25's) and 24 Bostons (British A-20's) of Second TAF against German barracks at Nijmegen, at Arnhem, and at Ede ten miles northwest of Arnhem. Six Mosquitoes made low-level attacks on the barracks at Nijmegen with four tons of high explosive. Thirty-four Mosquitoes dropped 27 tons of bombs on Arnhem at a price of three planes lost to flak. At Ede 30 Mitchells and 13 Bostons bombed from medium altitude with 63 tons of high explosive. Because of cloud conditions and other difficulties 23 or more pilots returned without bombing and the remainder hit targets of opportunity. In retrospect it appears that these attacks on barracks did not have much effect on the enemy's power to resist.[34]

CHAPTER IV

Market--The Airborne Invasion of Holland

THE COMPLEX COURSE of operations in MARKET can best be followed from day to day with the narrative for each day subdivided so as to treat separately the course of events in each of the three main battle areas, Eindhoven, Nijmegen, and Arnhem. Although the Arnhem area was primarily a British responsibility, operations there will be discussed in considerable detail, since they were decisive for the whole of MARKET, and since American troop carriers flew several of the Arnhem missions.

D-day, The Pathfinders

At 1025 on D-day the first pair of American pathfinder planes took off from Chalgrove, followed at ten-minute intervals by the other two pairs. A final briefing had been held at 0830 after which crews and troops reported to their planes. Both fliers and airborne had been working as teams for almost six months, and nearly all were veterans of the Normandy drops. They knew their business, and they knew each other.

From Chalgrove the pathfinder serials flew eastward to the coast and appear to have followed the southern route from there on. They had a P-47 escort over the Channel but none over the Continent. The pathfinders of the 82d Division, flying in the lead, had an easy trip as far as Grave where antiaircraft batteries opened up on them. They were under intense fire as they made their drop on DZ O, but fighters of the 78th Fighter Group, which were in the area on a flak-busting mission, dived on the guns and silenced them. The drop was made at 1247 from an altitude of 500 feet. The two pathfinder teams landed side by side in open fields about 500 yards north of DZ O.

While the second team stood guard, the first set up its equipment. Except for a sniper or two there was no resistance, and within three minutes the team had spread its panels and put both radar and radio beacons in operation.

The pathfinders of the 101st Division had a harder time. Their two serials made landfall together, but over the Belgian coast the rear pair circled to reestablish its time interval while the lead pair flew on to DZ A. Both pairs sighted the orange smoke set out near Gheel to mark the front, and both ran into heavy fire over the German lines. Evasive action being forbidden, all the pilots could do was to speed their lumbering planes to 180 miles an hour. Near Ratie one of the pair bound for DZ A was hit in the left engine and wing tank and crashed in flames. The loss shows the particular value of leakproof tanks in pathfinder work. Had anything happened to the other plane in that pair, DZ A would have gone unmarked. Fortunately the surviving craft flew safely and accurately to Veghel, sighted the railway which bounded the zone on the north, turned parallel to the tracks and made its run right over the zone. At 1247 it dropped its troops on DZ A from standard altitude at minimum speed. The paratroops met no resistance and were able to put the Eureka in operation in a minute and to lay out the panels in 2½ minutes. They had trouble with the radio antenna but had that set working within five minutes. The smoke signals were not set off till the main serials were sighted.

The pair of planes slated for DZ's B and C dropped their teams side by side with pinpoint accuracy at 1254. They had slowed to less than 90 miles per hour for the jump, and the men landed so close together that no assembly was necessary. The Eureka was in action in less than a minute, and panels and radio were ready within four minutes. Although a few enemy troops were in the vicinity, they were readily disposed of without affecting the pathfinders' work.[1]

The 12 Stirlings of 38 Group which were to deliver British pathfinder teams to LZ S and DZ X took off from Fairford with six airborne officers and 180 enlisted men aboard. They located their zones without difficulty and made accurate drops about 1240. Some flak was met and one Stirling was damaged, but none of the troops were injured. Every stick was dropped successfully on its proper zone. The teams assembled quickly, accepted the surrender of 15 Germans, and had their equipment functioning several minutes before the main serials arrived.[2]

D-day, Operations in the Eindhoven Sector*

Shortly after 1000 on the 17th, even before their pathfinders had left the ground, the formations of the 53d Troop Carrier Wing which were to fly the paratroops of the 101st Division began taking off from their bases around Greenham Common. Up to the previous day they had been slated to send 432 planes, but a late change reduced the total to 424 by eliminating 8 from the 435th Group. Aboard those 424 planes were 6,695 paratroops of the 101st Division.

Take-off and assembly went smoothly and swiftly. One serial of the 442d Group got its 45 planes in the air in five minutes, and a quarter hour later swept over the field in formation on its way to Hatfield, the wing assembly point. The 435th Group got a 32-plane serial into the air and into formation in 15 minutes.

The weather was almost exactly as promised. Fog, present in the early morning, had cleared by 0900. A little thin, low stratus persisted longer but had dissipated by take-off time. Over the channel the weather was excellent, and over Belgium and Holland it was generally good with visibility of from 3 to 7 miles. In places masses of cumulus clouds gave as much as $8/10$ cover but, since their bases were at altitudes of 2,500 to 3,000 feet, they presented no obstacle to the Americans.

*For orientation in this Sector, refer to Map No. 7, p. 104.

From Hatfield, where the serials swung into line at four-minute intervals in a column 80 miles long, the 53d Wing flew 49 miles to Bradwell; from there it proceeded over the revised southern route, including the detour to Ghent airport. DELOS was reached accurately and approximately on schedule by means of visual navigation assisted by Rebecca and Gee. The Rebecca beacons at the turns and on the marker boat were received at distances of 30 and even 40 miles. Gee was used occasionally by formation leaders to check position, but there were some who reported it unusable because of jamming. The aids at the IP were not in operation in time for the first serials and perhaps not for any, but the T and yellow smoke set out near Gheel by the ground forces were clearly visible.[3]

From the time they arrived at the Belgian coast the troop carriers were given area cover by six groups of P-51's from Eighth Air Force. These flew in two layers, half at 2,500 feet and half at 5,000 feet, flying lower in cloudy areas to keep below the cloud-base. To the east between Hasselt and Wesel a P-51 group, directed by MEW, was sweeping back and forth on perimeter patrol, and another was patrolling along a semicircular line between Wesel and the Zuider Zee. No enemy aircraft came in sight of the troop carriers or their escorts. The only efforts by the Luftwaffe to penetrate the MARKET area on D-day were met and turned back by the two groups on perimeter patrol. Pilots of the 4th Fighter Group, patrolling northwest of Wesel, intercepted 15 uncommonly aggressive and persistent FW-190's near Bocholt and claimed to have destroyed five of them and probably a sixth while losing one plane. The 361st Group southwest of Wesel had a brush with 15 ME-109's and shot down one.

As had been expected, ground fire was a real danger to the missions and one which was difficult to eradicate. Flak suppression between the IP and the drop zones had been entrusted to two Ninth Air Force fighter groups with P-47's and two with P-38's. These planes were considered more suitable than the P-51 for anti-flak operations because of their heavy striking power and their ability to take punishment. They carried two 500-pound general purpose bombs apiece.

A total of 142 fighter-bomber sorties were made. The four fighter groups arrived in the Eindhoven area at 1230, 1300, 1330 and 1350 and stayed slightly under an hour apiece.* Thus during the period of the main paratroop drop between 1300 and 1340 there were generally two groups in action between the front and the drop zones. The 474th Fighter Group, first to arrive, was much the most effective. It reported the destruction of 7 gun positions and the probable destruction of 18 more. The next two groups claimed only 9 positions destroyed or silenced, and the last group arrived as the last troop carriers were leaving. Because of hazy weather, low clouds, and the inconspicuousness of the targets, dive-bombing of antiaircraft guns was almost impossible. In fact any bombing was so difficult that the first three groups used only 61 bombs and relied largely on strafing. Two P-38's were reported shot down or missing.[4]

The troop carriers reported that the fighter-bombers had done an effective job against enemy positions in the open but achieved little in wooded areas. As the serials crossed the German lines near Rethy they were met with intense flak and small-arms fire. The 18 miles from Rethy to the Wilhelmina Canal were fairly free of opposition, but several flak installations along the canal were still sending up moderate to intense fire as the first few serials went over. Intense and persistent flak came from the village of Best, a mile southwest of DZ's B and C, and from the woods surrounding the drop zones there was light flak and small arms fire which even the last serials rated as moderate to intense. After their drop the troop carriers made 360° left turns. These turns brought some of them over intense flak from the villages of Boxtel and Schijndel, causing a few losses and considerable damage. Probably the best measure of the work done by the flak-busters is that of 16 planes destroyed on the mission only 2 came from the last four serials, although the number of planes damaged in those serials was greater than in the early ones. The inference is that, while small arms and machine-gun fire may actually have increased as the Germans mobilized their forces, most of the antiaircraft guns had been silenced.

Besides the 16 troop carrier planes shot down, 14 were badly damaged and 84 received moderate or light damage. Of the badly damaged aircraft, 4 had to make emergency landings in Belgium, and several others barely reached England. The 53d Wing had 26 men dead or missing and 15 wounded or injured.[5]

This time enemy fire had almost no effect on the delivery of the paratroops. The formations held tightly together, and the pilots of the damaged planes coaxed them along with a skill and a courage which had the paratroops open-mouthed. One colonel was so absorbed in watching the struggle of a badly damaged plane to reach its zone that he almost forgot to jump.

"Don't worry about me," the pilot of a burning plane* told his flight leader. "I'm going to drop these troops in the DZ." He kept his word—and crashed in flames immediately after the drop. At least three other pilots† stayed at the controls of burning aircraft and gave their lives to give their paratroops an accurate drop. Every one of the 424 sticks was dropped, and, except for those of two planes shot down near Rethy, not one was dropped prematurely.

The first three serials, 90 aircraft of the 434th Group and 45 from the 442d were to deliver the 501st Parachute Regiment and a few other troops, about 2,050 in all, to DZ's A and A-1 outside Veghel. They began their run-in at Oirchot on the Wilhelmina Canal about 12 miles southwest of the zones. The flak at Oirchot was particularly thick, which may account for the one bad drop given the 101st. The lead serial, which was carrying the 1st Battalion of the 501st to DZ A-1, swerved west of its true course and at 1301 dropped 42 sticks of troops in fields about three miles northwest of the zone. No pathfinders were slated to operate on DZ A-1, but it seems as though the Rebecca on DZ A should have shown the serial its error.

The lapse in accuracy was offset by an excellent drop pattern. The battalion was able to assemble 90 percent of its men and materiel inside 45 minutes. It then marched down a straight, open road to Veghel, preceded by an advance guard in requisitioned trucks and on bicycles, overcame token resistance by about 30 rear-echelon troops, and by 1600 had taken its objectives, the two bridges over the Aa river just southeast of the town.

The second serial dropped at 1306 in an excel-

---

*Late in the afternoons the 365th Fighter Group made a sweep over the Eindhoven area in search of enemy planes reported there but found none. (Oprep 365th Ftr Gp, 17 Sep 44, in unit hist file.)

*2d Lt Herbert E. Shulman.
†Maj Dan Elam, 1st Lt John Gurecki, 1st Lt Robert S. Stoddart, Jr.

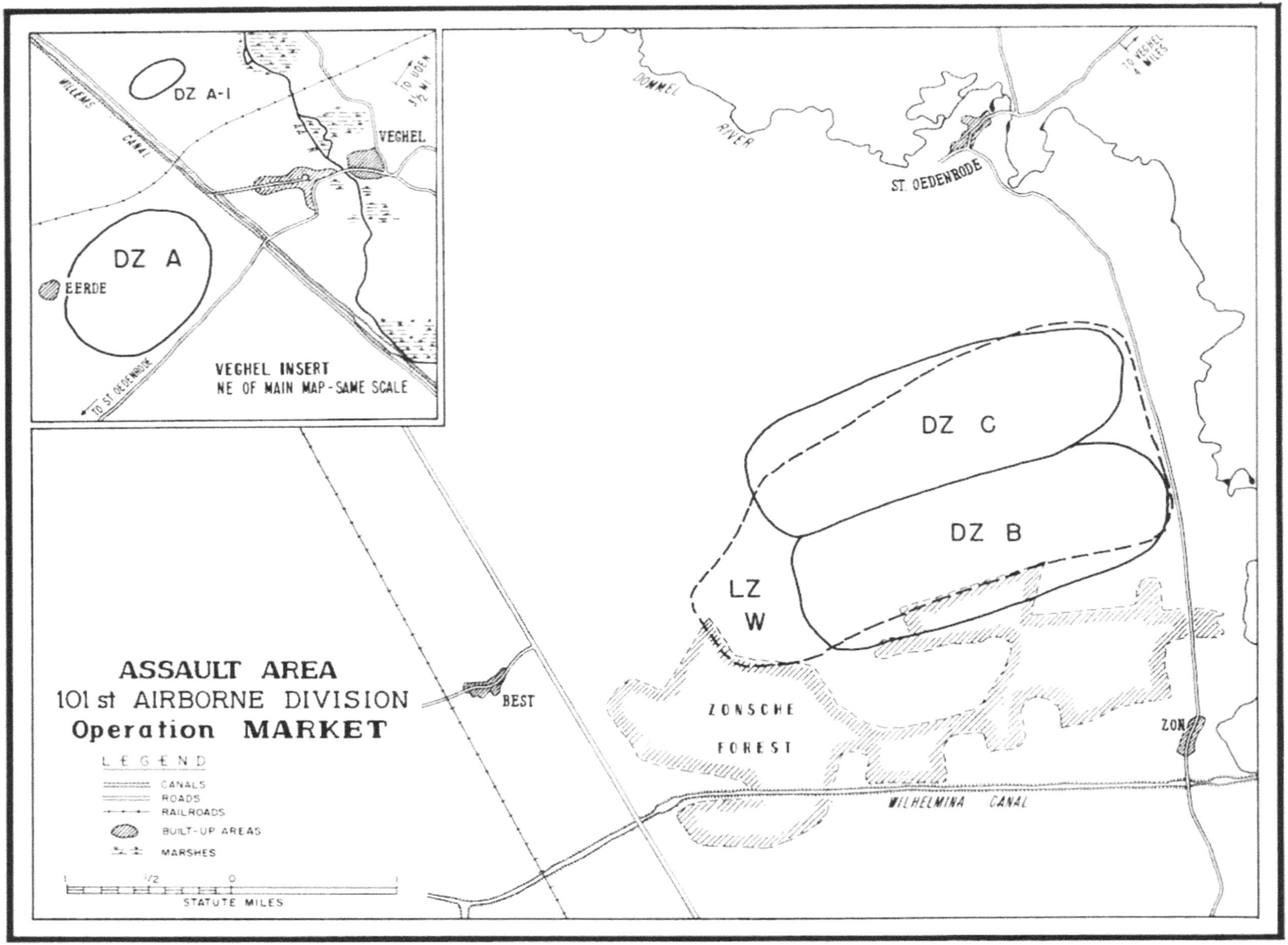
ASSAULT AREA
101 st AIRBORNE DIVISION
Operation MARKET
LEGEND
CANALS
ROADS
RAILROADS
BUILT-UP AREAS
MARSHES
1/2
0
1
STATUTE MILES
VEGHEL INSERT
NE OF MAIN MAP-SAME SCALE
DZ A-I
DZ A
EERDE
VEGHEL
WILLEMS CANAL
TO UDEN 3½ MI
TO ST OEDENRODE
DOMMEL RIVER
ST. OEDENRODE
TO VEGHEL 4 MILES
DZ C
DZ B
LZ W
ZONSCHE FOREST
BEST
ZON
WILHELMINA CANAL

Map 7.

lent pattern at the western end of DZ A, and at 1311 the third serial put its troops in an equally fine pattern centered about 1,500 yards west of the zone. Three stragglers from the first serial also dropped near DZ A. The regiment assembled 95 percent of its men and material in 45 minutes without any opposition and dispatched its battalions to their assigned objectives. By 1515 the 2d Battalion had secured the road and railroad bridges over the Willems Canal and the 3d Battalion had taken Eerde and set up positions south of the drop zone on the Eindhoven-Arnhem highway. Within another hour contact was established with the 1st Battalion and Veghel was occupied. About 1800 the 3d Battalion made contact with patrols of the 502d PIR moving up from DZ C.

The 501st PIR had taken all its D-day objectives intact and 32 prisoners besides at a cost of 10 jump casualties and apparently no battle casualties. It was in touch with airborne units dropped south of it and had encountered very few of the enemy. No operation could have begun more auspiciously.[6]

The next three serials, 45 planes of the 442d Group and 90 from the 436th, were to deliver the 506th PIR and a platoon of engineers, about 2,200 men in all, to DZ B, the southern member of the pair of drop zones a mile northwest of Zon.* Except for one aircraft which was shot down early, those serials dropped their paratroops with great accuracy from tight formations at 1312, 1315 and 1324.

The regimental CP was set up at 1345, and within an hour after the jump assembly was 80 percent complete. Only 24 men had been hurt in the drop. The journal of the 506th calls it "an ideal jump, better than any combat or practice jump [we] executed," and its after action report likewise described the drop as "the best the unit ever had."

The 1st Battalion had the urgent task of taking the highway bridge and two small bridges over the canal at Zon before they could be blown up. Guided by experience in Normandy, it made a quick assembly on the south side of the DZ and started. Troops too late for the initial assembly formed groups of 15 to 25 under an officer and set out after the rest. Thus most of the unit was well on its way within 45 minutes. In hopes of taking the bridges by surprise the battalion moved due south through the woods from the drop zone to the canal and then turned left along the canal bank to Zon, but it was observed and its advance was halted by fire from two 88-mm. guns.

The 2d Battalion, which was to assemble at the east end of the zone and advance down the highway against Zon an hour after its jump with the rest of the regiment following, was half an hour late in getting started. It had lost some time because of confusion with assembly signals of the 502d PIR on the neighboring zone, and more in assisting the glider serial which landed after it and in waiting for its commanding officer, who was missing. The battalion met no opposition on the road. Of at least four German tanks which might have attacked it, Allied fighters had destroyed two and driven off the rest. The 2d Battalion like the 1st was held up temporarily by German fire in Zon. By 1600 resistance had been broken, but as the two battalions converged on the highway bridge it blew up in their faces. The other bridges had been destroyed a day or two before. Some paratroops swam across and secured the far side of the canal while engineers built a footbridge across it. This was ready by 1730 but was so small and weak that the 506th did not get completely across until 0100 and then had to halt for the night about 1,500 yards south of the canal.

The regiment had been supposed to take Eindhoven and its bridges by 2000, but its inability to do so did not matter, since the British Guards Division which was to use those bridges had to stop for the night six miles short of them at Valkenswaard. The division had jumped off at 1435 behind a rolling barrage from 400 guns with close support from 100 Typhoons working in relays but had had to fight its way past anti-tank weapons set near the highway in swampy woods into which tanks could not go and pilots could not see. Somehow the Germans had gathered five battalions of tough troops to man those positions.

In any case, the crossings at Eindhoven were not difficult. What was essential was to have a crossing over the wide Wilhelmina Canal ready for the British tanks. For that purpose the airborne engineers dropped with the 506th worked frantically all night on the center trestle of the Zon highway bridge, the piers and underpinnings of which fortunately had not been much damaged by the blast.[7]

---

*The troop carriers called the southern zone B and the northern one C while the airborne sometimes reversed this usage. (See Hq IX TCC, FO 4, 13 Sep 44 and Hq 101st Abn Div, Report on Operation MARKET, 12 Oct 44.)

The last parachute serials flown by the 53d Wing were two of 36 and 28 planes respectively from the 435th Group and two of 45 each from the 438th Group bearing the 502d PIR, the advance echelon of Divisional Headquarters, and a company of engineers, a total of 2,434 men, to be dropped on DZ C. The lead plane of the 435th was flown by Colonel Frank J. MacNees the Group Commander with General Taylor and the regimental commander as passengers.

These serials kept the prescribed formation, route and timing all the way to the drop zone. When they were between 10 and 20 miles away they picked up the signals of the pathfinders' Eureka set. They reported seeing a B of white panels spread out on one of the zones but no T. As the first serial of the 435th approached the zone, the last serial of the 436th, slightly off course and four minutes late, cut across its path forcing it to climb to avoid a collision. As a result the 435th had to make a high drop from between 900 and 1,200 feet. Otherwise the drops were orthodox and very successful. Between about 1324 and 1338 the four serials dropped 2,391 of their paratroops on or very near DZ C. One stick had been dropped near Rethy when its plane was fatally hit, and another overshot slightly because a trooper was slow to jump. Ten men were returned for various reasons.

The 502d Regiment considered its jump fully as good as that of the 506th. It was able to assemble within an hour. The 3d Battalion, which rated its drop as very good and its assembly as excellent, had gathered 85 percent of its strength by 1440.

The function of the 502d PIR was to act as a connecting link between the 501st on the north and the 506th on the south and to act as divisional reserve. Its 1st Battalion marched north up the highway, easily captured St. Oedenrode, halfway between Zon and Veghel, and about nightfall made brief contact with the 501st north of St. Oederode. A bridge over the Dommel in the town was taken intact.

One company of the 3d Battalion was sent to seize a bridge over the Wilhelmina Canal nearly a mile southwest of DZ C. It set out at 1440 and took the bridge without much trouble, but German forces counterattacked out of Best, drove the paratroops from the bridge and almost cut them off. The rest of the battalion moved to their aid at 1845 but was engaged by an approximately equal force of Germans and had to dig in short of the bridge. The rest of the 502d Regiment spent the night near the drop zone.[8]

Following the paratroop formations to the Zon area came two serials from the 437th Group with 35 planes apiece towing Waco gliders. The gliders contained 43 jeeps, 18 trailers, and 311 airborne troops, mainly from the 101st Division's signal company and reconnaissance platoon plus some headquarters, artillery and medical personnel, and a Phantom* detachment. The large number of vehicles and the complete lack of artillery pieces shows that the 101st expected to need mobility more than firepower. Also, its planners had supposed that British artillery would very quickly come within supporting distance.

Three of the gliders aborted over England; one ditched safely in the Channel; and two broke loose or were released over friendly Belgium. The Germans, who found the glider formations a splendid target, brought down 6 of the 64 planes which crossed their lines and damaged 46 more, 6 so badly they were fit for nothing but salvage. The troop carriers had 18 men missing and 3 wounded. Aircraft losses of 9 percent (19 percent counting salvaged planes) and a damage rate of 70 percent contrast painfully with the corresponding ratios of 4 and 23 percent in the paratroop serials. Glider missions had flown in daylight with impunity on D plus 1 in NEPTUNE and in the invasion of southern France. MARKET was a different story.

Seven gliders came down between the IP and LZ W. At least three and perhaps five of these premature releases were made because the tug plane was hit and about to crash. One of the seven gliders plummeted into the ground; one was unaccounted for. The rest landed safely and all the men and materiel aboard them reached the division in a day or two with the help of friendly Belgians.

The first serial released its gliders at 1348, and the second did so at 1355. Three Wacos, two of which had collided in flight, crashlanded on the zone, killing a pilot, injuring five men, and damaging the cargoes. The remaining 53 gliders found ample room on the zone and landed safely with 252 troops, 32 jeeps and 13 trailers. In one instance a soldier took the controls after the pilot was wounded and steered the glider down. The glider operation had been costly, but it had successfully delivered to the landing zone about 80

---

*British liaison and combat communications unit.

percent of the personnel and about 75 percent of the heavy equipment and vehicles carried.[9]

D-day, Operations in the Nijmegen Sector*

The mission bearing the paratroops of the 82d Division began its take-offs at 1019 on the 17th. Six groups of the 52d and 50th Wings based in the Grantham area contributed 480 planes organized in 11 serials. Aboard the aircraft were about 7,250 paratroops. Take-off and assembly went smoothly and without serious mishaps, although one soldier went violently insane after take-off and had to be landed. The 313th Group put its planes in the air at five-second intervals and the rest likewise did well.

That part of England was enjoying a warm, hazy autumn morning. Only at Langar did weather present any difficulties. There, overcast forced the 441st Group to climb above 2,500 feet before assembling. Along the route, cloud cover varied from $3/10$ to $8/10$ with the base of the clouds between 2,000 and 3,000 feet, and there was a slight haze, thickest at the Dutch coast, where it limited visibility to three or four miles. Conditions at the destination were favorable with cloud bases above 2,500 feet and visibility of seven miles or more.

After reassembling over the bases the serials flew to March, the assembly point, and swung into line at the appointed intervals. From March they proceeded for 71 miles to Aldeburgh, the starting point on the northern route, and over that route to the IP south of 's Hertogenbosch. The Eurekas in England and on the marker boat worked well, and so did the Gee sets of the leaders. All of the 480 planes made an accurate landfall on Schouwen Island.[10]

Besides the perimeter patrols, which protected both routes, the northern route had heavy protection of its own. Escort and area cover from England to the IP was provided by 18 squadrons of Spitfires from ADGB. Between the IP and the Nijmegen area two P-51 groups sent by Eighth Air Force handled cover and escort duties, using the same tactics as the groups on the southern route. Although a few enemy planes were sighted, no air action occurred.

Flak suppression from the coast to the IP was in the hands of eight Tempest, three Mustang, and two Spitfire squadrons of ADGB, all of which did an excellent job. One Mustang was lost during sweeps against armed barges, pillboxes, and batteries. Beyond the IP the Nijmegen column had only the 78th Fighter Group of the Eighth Air Force with 50 P-47's to sweep flak out of its path. This group went into action about half an hour before the troop carriers arrived. By flying low to draw antiaircraft fire and then strafing and dive-bombing, it knocked out an estimated eight guns and silenced six more. It also hit other targets including a flak barge and a Messerschmitt on the ground at Gilze-Rijn. Most of this work was done in 15 minutes. Then the Nazi gunners stopped firing. Unable to find targets, the 78th flew out to meet the troop carrier formations near the IP and accompanied them to the drop zones. The group lost one plane and had a dozen damaged during its mission.[11]

The troop carriers had a quiet trip until they reached Grave. The route proved to have been well-chosen, and effective preliminary bombing combined with splendid work by the flak-busters to reduce ground fire over most of the route to a negligible quantity. However, one plane was shot down and a few damaged by gunners near Zevenbergen and Oosterhout. As the mission neared its drop zones enemy fire began to thicken. The most intense and accurate light flak and small arms fire came up from bridges and wooded areas, especially the Reichswald Forest, over which passed the eight serials which made left turns after completing their drops. One plane crashed and another crash-landed shortly before reaching their zones, but all their troops had been able to jump. Soon after leaving DZ T four more were shot down by guns near that zone or in the Reichswald. On the way back two aircraft went down over Holland and one had to ditch, but two of these losses were caused primarily by collision rather than by flak. All aboard the ditched plane were rescued, and 15 other troop carrier men landed or parachuted safely and reached the Allied lines. Most spectacular was the case of Lt. Col. Frank X. Krebs, commander of the 440th Group. He and his crew got back after being hidden for more than a month by the Dutch underground. Total losses in the mission were 10 planes destroyed and 25 troop carrier men dead or still missing at the end of

---

*For orientation in this Sector, refer to Map No. 8, p. 108.

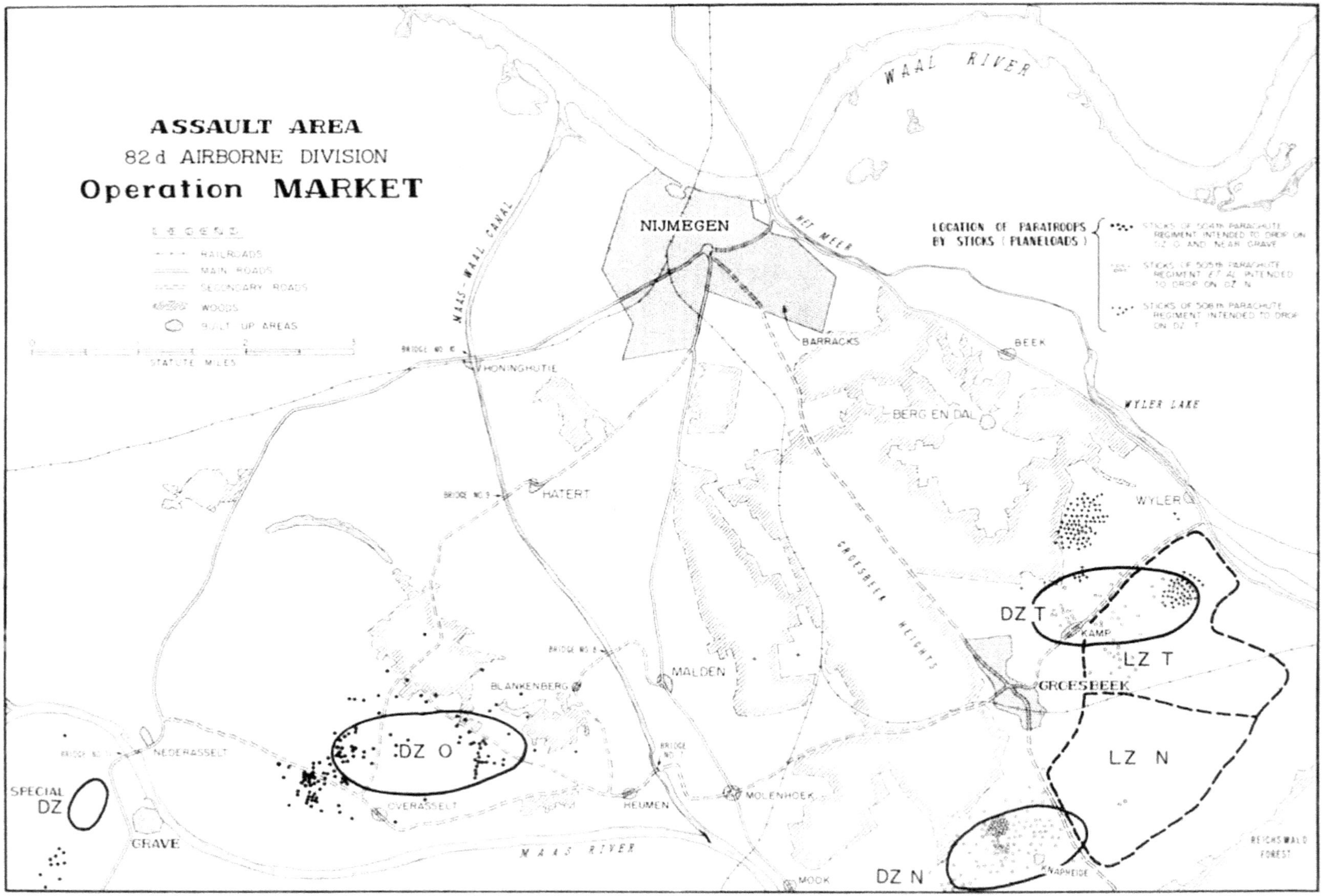
ASSAULT AREA
82d AIRBORNE DIVISION
Operation MARKET
LEGEND
RAILROADS
MAIN ROADS
SECONDARY ROADS
WOODS
BUILT UP AREAS
STATUTE MILES
LOCATION OF PARATROOPS BY STICKS (PLANELOADS)
STICKS OF 504th PARACHUTE REGIMENT INTENDED TO DROP ON DZ O AND NEAR GRAVE
STICKS OF 505th PARACHUTE REGIMENT ET AL INTENDED TO DROP ON DZ N
STICKS OF 508th PARACHUTE REGIMENT INTENDED TO DROP ON DZ T
WAAL RIVER
NIJMEGEN
HET MEER
BARRACKS
MAAS-WAAL CANAL
HONINGHUTIE
BEEK
WYLER LAKE
BERG EN DAL
HATERT
WYLER
GROESBEEK HEIGHTS
DZ T
KAMP
LZ T
GROESBEEK
MALDEN
BLANKENBERG
DZ O
NEDERASSELT
LZ N
SPECIAL DZ
OVERASSELT
HEUMEN
MOLENHOEK
GRAVE
MAAS RIVER
REICHSWALD FOREST
KNAPHEIDE
MOOK
DZ N

Map 8.

October. Six men were wounded or injured and 118 planes were damaged, about 20 badly enough to require salvage or lengthy repairs. About 80 percent of the damage was concentrated in three serials which dropped on DZ T, evidence that the area around that zone was the most hazardous traversed on the mission.[12]

The first drops were to be made on DZ N by two 45-plane serials of the 313th Group and one of the same size from the 316th Group. Aboard them were 2,281 paratroops of which 2,151 were from the 505th PIR, and in their pararacks were 756 containers with 70 tons of supplies and equipment. In accordance with plan, DZ N and DZ T were unmarked, but the pathfinders had their beacons and signals in full operation on DZ O.

Through an error in marshalling the 313th Group's second serial had exchanged places with the first. This formation, accidentally in the lead, appears to have sighted the smoke and panels on DZ O. Nevertheless, it swerved north of course and under intense fire dropped almost all of the second battalion of the 505th between 1½ and 3 miles northeast of DZ N.* Only six pilots carrying regimental headquarters and signal men did locate their zone and drop their troops on or near it. This performance in broad daylight shows the folly of economizing on pathfinders. Had radar and visual aids been functioning on DZ N such a mistake could hardly have happened.

The first seven planes in the 313th Group's other serial followed the lead of their predecessors and dropped half of regimental headquarters between two and three miles north of DZ N at 1308. The rest, carrying the 3d Battalion, gave it an excellent drop. The third serial, which brought Division Headquarters and the 1st Battalion of the 505th, had gotten so far south of its course that it actually passed over the lead serial of the 53d Wing while the latter was making its drop nothwest of Veghel. It quickly reoriented itself and by careful observation of landmarks achieved a perfect drop on DZ N at 1312.

The 2d Battalion of the 505th was supposed to occupy the west side of the regiment's perimeter, make contact with the 504th along the Maas-Waal Canal, reconnoiter a railroad bridge over the Maas between Molenhoek and Mook, and occupy high ground west of Groesbeek. Although their drop was neither accurate nor compact, most of the battalion had come down fairly close together near the village of Kamp about a mile northeast of Groesbeek. Using an observatory as a rallying point, they assembled a strong nucleus within half an hour and at 1415 set out to take their objectives. Against feeble opposition they pushed through the northern part of Groesbeek and seized the hill beyond it without a struggle at 1545.

The battalion then sent a strong patrol south to the railway bridge, which it found destroyed. Two patrols were dispatched westward to the canal to make contact with the 504th. At 1930 one of these reached Bridge 8 over the canal near Malden. The bridge had been blown, but the men could see elements of the 504th on the far side. At 2100 the other patrol made contact with the 504th at the southernmost canal crossing, Bridge 7 between Heumen and Molenhoek, which the 504th had taken intact.

The 3d Battalion of the 505th had assembled and set up its CP by 1345. Two companies then marched on Groesbeek, which was less than a mile north of the zone, and took it easily about 1500. The other company patrolled southeastward toward the Reichswald Forest. The enemy halted its probing in several sharp encounters near the edge of the forest but showed no aggressive tendencies. The tanks rumored to be in the forest did not appear.

The 1st Battalion, which was to hold the division's southern perimeter from the railroad bridge to the Reichswald, assembled about 90 percent of its strength on DZ N before 1330—in less than 20 minutes. It proceeded to occupy positions at the southern end of the Groesbeek ridge, and then sent detachments west to Mook and the railroad bridge, south to Riethorst, and east to the edge of the Reichswald. They took 30 prisoners at Mook, and found the enemy in the Reichswald much weaker than expected, but at Riethorst on the main road running along the Maas to Gennep the Germans attacked with motley forces of somewhat more than company strength. By nightfall they had been beaten off with heavy losses and the front was quiet.

Thus by 2100 the 505th PIR had taken all its objectives and held a strong semi-circular perimeter extending from the canal on the west to Riethorst in the south and Heikant in the east. A

---

*Probably because of this heavy fire the drop was made from between 800 and 900 feet above sea level instead of about 600 feet as specified in the orders.

summary of battalion strength reports at 2200 gave the 1st Battalion 43 officers and 614 men, the 2d 42 officers and 552 men and the 3d 40 officers and 592 men. The regiment had at its disposal over 95 percent of those who had made the drop. Jump casualties from accidents and wounds combined had put only 14 of its men out of action, and battle losses had been very small.[13]

The second trio of serials, also of 45 planes apiece, carried 2,031 troops of the 504th PIR. One planeload carried by the 315th Group went down over western Holland. Three soldiers refused to jump, and two wounded were brought back. The rest jumped in the vicinity of DZ O.

The first of these serials, flown by the 316th Group, was to put down the 1st Battalion of the 504th at the east end of DZ O, a mile northeast of the village of Overasselt and 1½ miles west of the Maas-Waal Canal. The battalion had the task of taking the bridges over the canal, and its drop point had therefore been set as close to them as was feasible. The drop was good, though about five minutes late. At 1315 some 32 sticks landed on the prescribed spot and the rest within a mile of it.

The 315th Group, flying the other two serials, was to drop all but 11 sticks a short distance northwest of Overasselt. Doing what the 504th's commander called a splendid job, it put all 78 sticks within 1,500 yards of the pathfinder beacons. In this area landed all of the 504th PIR except the 1st Battalion and Company E. That company had been detailed to drop in heavily ditched fields on the far side of the river to take that end of the Grave bridge. The highway, river and bridge marked the spot unmistakably, but 10 of the 11 sticks landed between 500 and 1,200 yards south of the zone, possibly because the pilots feared they might drop the men in the river.

The 504th had its CP open by 1330 and had radio contact with all its units by 1340. First in action was Company A, which assembled within 15 minutes and moved rapidly on its objective, Bridge 8. However, as the troops came in sight of the bridge the Germans blew it up. More fortunate was Company B, which managed to approach Bridge 7 at Heumen unseen and kept it under such fire that the enemy was unable to explode the charges. About 1800 the company seized the Heumen bridge intact. Company C reached Bridge 9 at Hattert about 1940 after a march of nearly three miles only to have it blow up as the unit approached. Only one bridge over the canal had been taken, but that was all that was needed, and the west side of the canal had been secured up to Bridge 9.

Far more important than the canal bridges was the 640-foot structure over the Maas at Grave. That had to be taken intact if the British armor was to get through on schedule. Recognizing the need for haste, the platoon of E Company dropped nearest the bridge attacked it without waiting for the rest of the company. The paratroops worked their way down drainage ditches until they were close to the span. Then they raked its approaches with machine-gun fire, used a bazooka to put a flak tower at the south end of the bridge out of action, rushed the tower, and took over the gun. Meanwhile, the rest of the 2d Battalion, having assembled within half an hour, was hurrying up to the north end of the bridge. They took it easily, and at 1650 the battalion commander jubilantly reported "Bridge 11 is ours."[14] Before midnight the battalion had pushed several hundred Germans out of Grave and had established a perimeter about a mile in radius around the south end of the bridge.

The 3d Battalion of the 504th had been designated as regimental reserve. Part of it was used to clear the area northwest of DZ O. About three miles away beyond the village of Alverna the detachment ran into some resistance but nothing very formidable.

At the end of the day the 504th was established securely on all its objectives at about 95 percent of full strength. Enemy action and jump injuries had produced 57 casualties. A slightly larger number of men, all of whom were later accounted for, were still missing.[15]

The seventh serial in the 82d's mission, 30 planes of the 439th Group, arrived at its destination, DZ N, at 1321, slightly ahead of schedule. The group gave a near perfect drop to 47 headquarters artillery personnel and 388 men of the 307th Engineer Battalion. All the troops landed on the zone with only 6 injured and 1 man wounded. There being no immediate call for engineers, the 307th was used initially to provide security for divisional headquarters and later to guard the 82d's CP, which was set up at 1700 about 1,000 yards west of Groesbeek.[16]

Next to drop were 1,922 men of the 508th PIR and 40 pathfinders of the 325th Glider Regiment, transported by two 45-plane serials of the 441st Group and one of 42 planes from the 440th Group with DZ T as their destination. One stick had to jump near DZ O and another went out half a mile short of the zone because the planes carrying them were about to crash. Two or three other sticks jumped between DZ O and DZ T because of over-eagerness. Two pilots overshot the zone by 1,000 yards and dropped their loads east of it near Wyler. About 25 paratroops, a majority of whom had been wounded, were brought back to England.

The zone was unmarked, and hopes that the first troops to land could set off smoke signals for later serials were not fulfilled. Nevertheless, although the fire around DZ T was severe, headquarters and two battalions of the 508th were put down in excellent tight patterns just outside the northern edge of the zone and the 3d Battalion, also well massed, was placed within its eastern end. The drop had begun at 1326 and by 1500 the regiment was 90 percent assembled. The commander of the 3d Battalion wrote 'We could not have landed better under any circumstances."

The first task of the 508th was to clear the vicinity of its drop zone. This was quickly accomplished. One German antiaircraft battery on the edge of the zone was overwhelmed by troops jumping directly on it, and 20 men who had dropped near Wyler surprised and wiped out the crew of another battery. The next step, seizure of the northern portion of the Groesbeek ridge and establishment of roadblocks in the hamlets of De Ploeg and Berg en Dal on either side of the ridge was accomplished before 1900 over light resistance. General Gavin had directed that if all went well in these operations a battalion should be sent as soon as possible to take the Nijmegen bridge. More than 4,000 SS troops had been reported in Nijmegen, but the bridge was essential* and a bold stroke might take it. With surprise and darkness to aid them the attackers might bypass the main German garrison and reach the bridge, which was on the eastern edge of the town.

Accordingly the 1st Battalion of the 508th was directed to take the Nijmegen bridge, and at 2030 A and B Companies marched north up the road from De Ploeg, while the 3d Battalion assisted by sending G Company forward from Berg en Dal to cover their right. Guided by members of the Dutch underground A and B Companies reached Nijmegen at 0015 on the 18th and penetrated to within 400 yards of the bridge before the Germans closed in on them. That ended the first bid for the bridge. The paratroop vanguard, heavily outnumbered, held their ground until morning but could not advance. However, by seizing and destroying the building which housed the controls, they had upset German arrangements for demolition of the span.[17]

The 376th Parachute Field Artillery Battalion had been sent in the eleventh and last of the division's paratroop serials, a 48-plane formation of the 440th Group, to drop on DZ N at 1340. This gave the 505th about half an hour to clear the enemy from the vicinity and mark the zone with smoke as insurance against the inaccuracy and heavy losses which had plagued artillery drops in the past. The serial carried 544 troops and 42 tons of materiel, including twelve 75-mm. howitzers. It reached the zone at 1333, about seven minutes early.

This time the artillery got an almost perfect drop. Every stick landed on or very close to the zone. At least 24 men were injured or wounded but hardly a one was missing. In slightly over an hour the battalion was assembled and had 10 of its howitzers ready for action. Another gun was firing before nightfall. According to General Gavin these weapons were of very great assistance in breaking up attacks by low-caliber German troops thrown against his division in the 24 hours after it landed.[18]

After the paratroops of the 82d Division came a single glider serial from the 439th Group bound for LZ N with 50 planes towing Wacos. In the first 22 gliders were 86 men of Battery A, 80th Airborne Antitank Battalion, with eight 57-mm. guns, nine jeeps, and two trailers of ammunition to provide some insurance against attacks by enemy armor. In the rear were elements of divisional headquarters, divisional artillery headquarters, the divisional signal company, the reconnaissance platoon, and an air support party, which all together numbered 130 men and 18 jeeps.

The serial began its take-off from Balderton at 1112 and began assembling at low altitude while

---

*It was a five-span steel bridge 1,960 feet long with a 35-foot roadway fit for heavy vehicles and tanks. Beside it the Germans had set up a pontoon bridge. There was also a railroad bridge across the Waal west of Nijmegen, but this had only a 10-foot roadway unsuitable for vehicles. The Waal at Nijmegen was between 800 and 1,800 feet across. To build a bridge across it capable of carrying tanks and guns would be a slow business requiring great quantities of engineer supplies.

the 439th's paratroop serial was still circling overhead. Soon afterwards the serials of the 440th Group swept over the field causing some confusion. Two gliders broke their towropes at take-off and had to start over, and another, brought back because its load started to shift, was towed to Holland alone some time after the rest. One Waco carrying a jeep began to disintegrate over the Channel, was released, and ditched safely. Antiaircraft guns on Schouwen Island brought down one plane and its glider, putting 6 troop carrier men and two of the airborne in the missing column. Five planes were damaged by antiaircraft fire.

With these exceptions the flight was successful and comparatively uneventful. Release was made at 1347 about a mile short of the proper point. This error probably prevented some losses by enabling the serial to make its turn without going over enemy positions in the Reichswald Forest. Only six of the gliders reached LZ N, but 40 came down within a mile to the west, and the other one in the formation landed about 1½ miles west of the zone. The terrain on which they landed, though hillier than that within the zone, was otherwise favorable. Two of the gliders were destroyed in landing and 14 were damaged, but only seven of the airborne troops were injured and four of the jeeps seriously damaged. All the guns came through intact.[19]

One other glider mission to the 82d Division's sector was made by the RAF to bring the Headquarters of 1 Airborne Corps to LZ N. Dispatched were 38 planes of 38 Group towing 32 Horsas and 6 Hadrian (Waco) gliders which contained 105 airborne personnel and great quantities of equipment. One Horsa aborted over England, one over the sea, and one broke loose over Holland. The other 35 gliders had a rather uneventful trip and landed safely in the Groesbeek area shortly after 1400. Photographs later established that 28 of the Horsas had landed on LZ N. The first attempt to fly a corps headquarters into combat had succeeded.

The British troops assembled quickly and by 1530 had a corps CP functioning on the wooded slopes of the Groesbeek ridge near the northern edge of DZ N. Unfortunately corps communications functioned very badly. Although radio contact was soon made with rear headquarters in England and with Second Army, no effective communication with First Airborne Division or with the 101st Division was achieved that day. Some improvement occurred on the 18th, and some information was obtained by telephone, since Dutch patriots operated the exchanges in Arnhem and Nijmegen. Nevertheless, Browning's first full and reliable information on the situation at Arnhem was a SITREP received at 0800 on the 19th, and until that day he had little knowledge of or influence on operations outside the Nijmegen area.[20]

D-day, Operations in the Arnhem Sector*

The British airborne troops were to be delivered in four missions, three to Arnhem and one to Nijmegen. First, 130 planes of 46 Group and 23 of 38 Group were to release Horsa gliders on LZ S beginning at 1300 hours. Then 167 aircraft of 38 Group would loose 154 Horsas and 13 Hamilcar gliders on LZ Z. The gliders would bring in troops of 1 Airlanding Brigade Group, including an antitank battery with 17-pounder guns aboard the big Hamilcars. Next in line were the 38 planes which, as described earlier, were to turn aside at Nijmegen and deliver British Corps Headquarters to LZ N. Finally, 143 American aircraft of the 52d Wing would fly to DZ X and drop 1 Parachute Brigade there at 1355.

The glider missions to LZ's S and Z began inauspiciously with one glider grounded by damage before take-off and 23 gliders breaking loose over England. The British, flying at 2,500 feet, had run into clouds which the Americans a thousand feet below them had not encountered. Beyond the English coast the clouds were mostly above 2,500 feet, but even under these improved conditions one more glider broke loose over the Channel and seven over Holland. Engine trouble caused one combination to turn back and forced the release of three gliders, two of them over the sea and one over Schouwen. All occupants of the ditched gliders were rescued. A total of 39 gliders were unable to reach their zones.

In their flight over the northern route the two missions suffered even less from enemy action than did the American paratroop mission to Nijmegen, which accompanied them much of the way. Nearing the coast they encountered some flak from batteries and a barge. They saw very little flak

---
*For orientation in the Sector, refer to Map No. 9, p. 113.

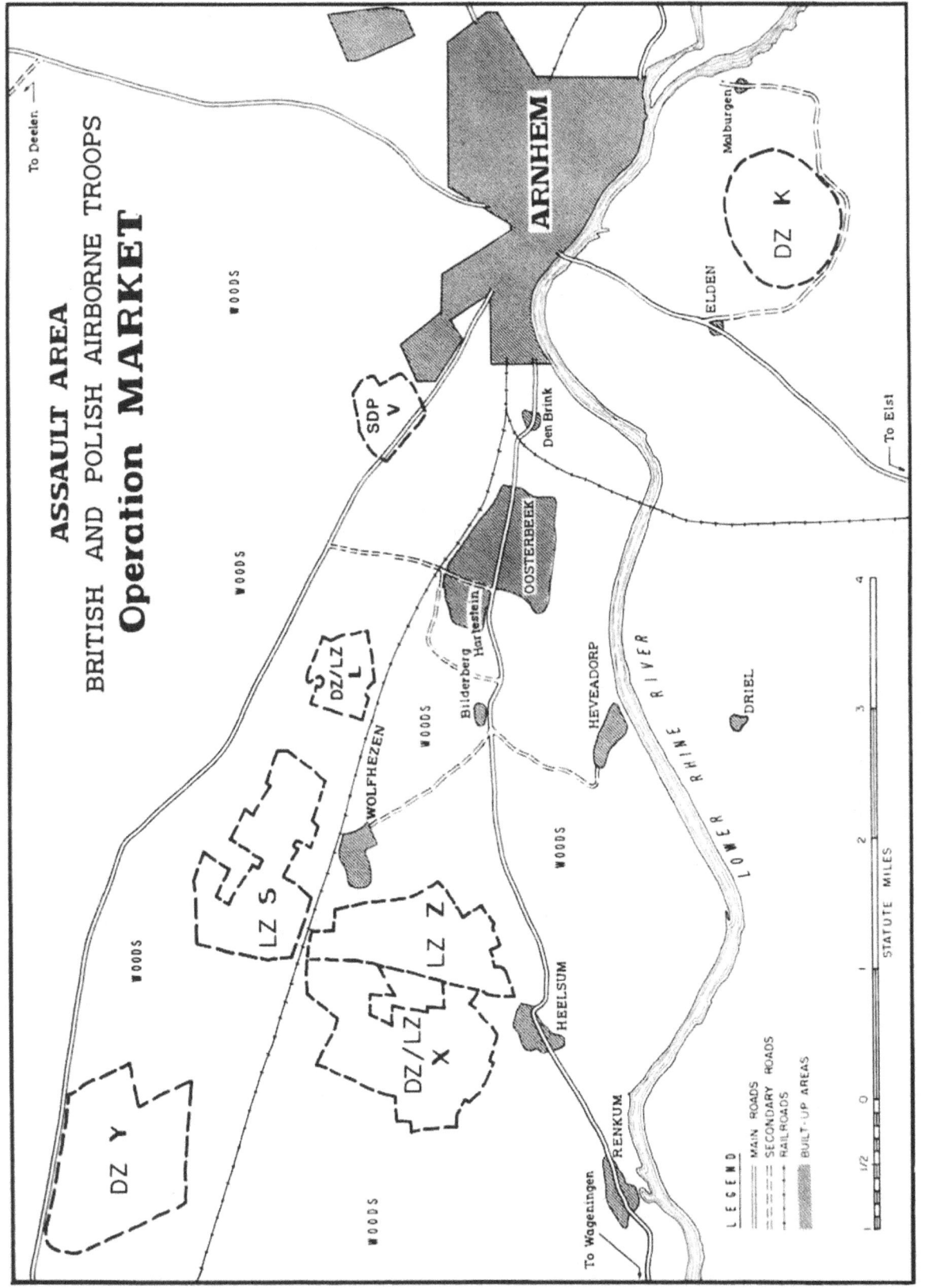

Map 9.

thereafter, although there was considerable small-arms fire near Arnhem. No planes were lost and only six were damaged.

The level of route accuracy was high. No pilot is known to have lost his way. The British attributed this success mainly to excellent visual navigation. Gee was unable in most cases to give a good target fix. This failure of what all the British pilots relied on as their primary radar aid was only partly due to jamming and partly to unspecified factors, one of which may have been distance. Less than half the fliers elected to use Rebecca. Good results were reported by most of those interrogating the Eureka on LZ S, but barely half of those attempting to pick up the one on LZ Z got satisfactory responses. American experience indicates this poor performance may have been due to imperfect calibration.

The zones were clearly recognized, and the landings were good. The colored panels, smoke and Very lights displayed by the pathfinders were quite visible, but the glider pilots do not seem to have paid much attention to them. They came down all over the zones, showing some tendency to overshoot in the light and variable breeze. Of 134 gliders which reached the Arnhem area on their way to LZ S, 132 certainly landed on or very near that zone. Of the 150 remaining gliders headed for LZ Z, 116 landed on the zone and 27 were located very near it. The most serious accident was the loss of two guns when the Hamilcars carrying them stuck in soft ground and turned over.[21]

The paratroop mission to Arnhem, flown by two serials of the 314th Troop Carrier Group and two from the 61st Group, began its take-offs from Saltby and Barkston Heath at 1121 and had all its planes in the air by 1155. They assembled smoothly and had a rather uneventful trip over the northern route. Slight and ineffectual flak greeted them as they reached the continent and there was some flak from near Elst and Wageningen in the Arnhem area. However, not a plane was shot down and only five were damaged. The formation leaders reported their Gee sets were badly jammed, but Rebecca guided them well. The white panels on the zones showed up clearly and the blue smoke was particularly effective in the still air.

Between 1353 and 1408 all but four of the 2,283 paratroops in the aircraft made their jump at altitudes of 700 to 900 feet and all but 35 of the 680 parapacks carried were released. One of the packs had fallen earlier and the other 34 stuck, although several of the pilots made extra passes in attempts to get them loose.[22]

The accuracy of the paratroop drop was almost perfect, and the troops were assembled and ready to move by 1500 hours. The plans had provided that a glider-borne reconnaissance squadron would race ahead in jeeps and seize the highway bridge. The 2d Battalion of the Parachute Brigade would follow on foot to reinforce this advance party. Unfortunately, so many of the gliders carrying the reconnaissance squadron failed to reach the landing zone that the unit was unable to operate. However, the paratroop battalion set out from Heelsum at 1530 and headed east down the Utrecht highway toward the road bridge six miles away. During the first four miles throngs of cheering Dutchmen were the greatest impediment encountered. On the outskirts of the city Company C was detached to turn right along the railway and seize the railroad bridge over the river. Some men had actually sprinted onto the bridge when the German guards set off their charges and the main span curled skyward.* The company then moved into Arnhem, attacked German positions near the railway station, was cut off, and, a day or so later, destroyed.

Soon after Company C left them, A and B Companies were halted by fire from an armored car and from machine guns and mortars on a rise called Den Brink. An antitank gun was brought up to deal with enemy armor; B Company was detached to neutralize Den Brink, and A Company pressed on as quickly and unobtrusively as possible. On reaching the bridge about 2000, it seized the north end unopposed but an attempt to send a platoon to the south end was driven back by fire from SS troops supported by two antitank guns and an armored car. The Germans had just arrived. A Dutch constable who walked across the bridge at 1930 stated after the war that the guards usually placed there were not on duty and that no one was there to defend it when he crossed. Never was the value of a *coup de main* more evident. A force landed or dropped near the south end of the bridge that afternoon could have secured it without a blow.

---

*The pontoon bridge was already unusable. The Germans had removed the center portion a day or two before.

The company at the bridge was reinforced soon after arrival by battalion headquarters and later by part of brigade headquarters. Radio failure thwarted attempts to summon B Company to the bridge, but it got there at dawn on the 18th, having lost one platoon in the dark. About 100 men of other units also marched in about that time after bypassing German strongpoints during the night. Their arrival raised the force at the bridge to a strength of approximately 550 men.

The struggle of this little band, led by Lt. Col. J. D. Frost, holds a place in British history like that occupied in American tradition by the battle of the Alamo, but in both cases the result was inevitable unless substantial reinforcements reached the defenders—and no help came. The paratroops held a perimeter around the bridge until driven from it by tanks on the 19th. On the 20th tanks and mobile guns moved to within a range of 30 yards and shelled the houses still occupied by the battalion until all were burning and only one was standing. Then German infantry began infiltration of what remained of the paratroops' positions. Less than 100 men were still able to fight, and their ammunition was almost gone. Early on the 21st the survivors were ordered to split up and escape by hiding or filtering through the German lines. Hardly any succeeded.

What had happened to all the other troops landed and dropped outside Arnhem on 17 September? The answer is that most of the gliderborne troops had to stay where they were to guard drop and landing areas for the next day's missions, and that the rest of the paratroops had been stopped short of the bridge. Divisional Headquarters had opened at 1430 on D-day and by 1600 some 1,400 troops of 1 Airlanding Brigade had assembled to the strains of a bagpipe and moved into position around the zones. Although opposition had been negligible during landing, they were harassed during the night by aggressive patrols and mortar fire, indications of hard fighting to come. The 3d Parachute Battalion had followed the 2d down the Utrecht highway but had been slowed by strong resistance. At dawn on the 18th it was still on the western side of Arnhem, heavily engaged and unable to advance. The 1st Battalion was supposed to take high ground on the north side of the city. Therefore, after a splendid drop some 200 yards from its rendezvous, the unit moved north from the zone onto the Ede-Arnhem road and started down that road at practically full strength. Slowed by heavy sniping and by a halt to take defensive positions after sighting German tanks, it was unable to reach the city before nightfall. About 0100 the commander decided to push on into Arnhem and join forces with the other battalions, but the night advance proved costly, and at first light his troops were at a standstill somewhat north of the railway station with the road in front of them effectively blocked.[23]

The Balance for D-day

At the end of D-day MARKET-GARDEN seemed to be going well. With powerful air support to clear their path the American and British troop carriers had been successful beyond all expectations. The airborne commanders were unanimous and fervent in their praise of the accurate and efficient delivery of their troops.[24]

The ground thrust by the British Guards Division had failed to reach Eindhoven; the Zon bridge had been blown; and no bridges over the Waal or the Rhine had yet been taken. On the other hand, the Guards delay did not seem serious; the span at Zon would soon be usable; and paratroops had driven close to the still-intact highway bridges at Nijmegen and Arnhem. Except at Best and in Nijmegen resistance to the American airborne had been limited, as expected, to feeble attacks by small, nondescript groups. The plight of the British at Arnhem was desperate, but as yet they did not know it.

What made their situation so bad was the presence of overwhelming numbers of German guns and tanks near Arnhem. The Germans had recently moved both the 9th and 10th SS Panzer Divisions into that area to refit. Dutch agents reported their presence to the Allies but, although the 82d Division appears to have received and to some extent accepted the report, British intelligence experts dismissed it as incredible. They judged that the Germans could muster at Arnhem no more than 3,000 disorganized men with very few tanks and guns.

The Germans were further favored by the presence of their commanding general, Field Marshal Walter Model, who had his headquarters at Oosterbeek within three miles of the British landing zones. Without lingering in his ringside seat Model leaped into his car as soon as the landings began,

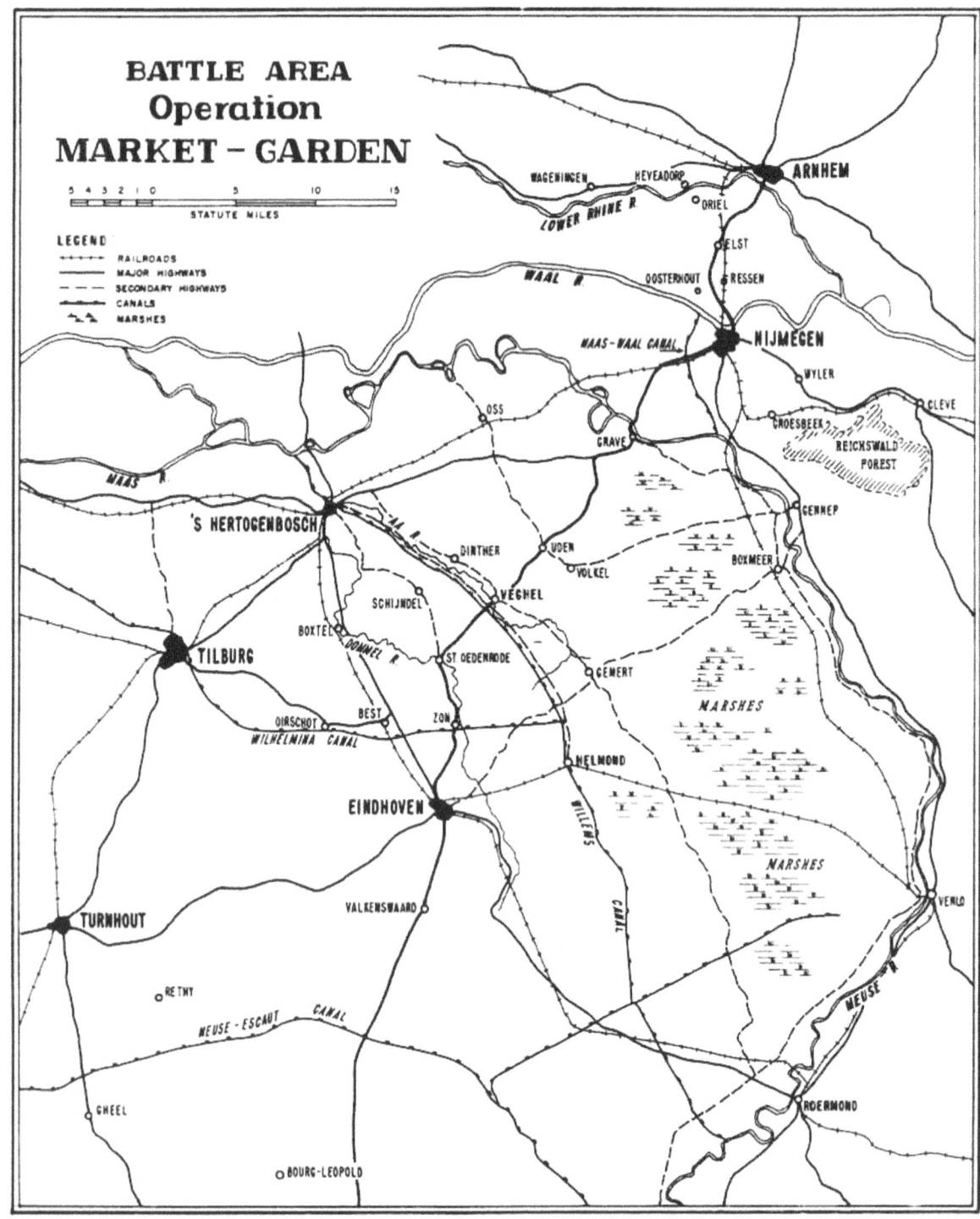

Map 10.

drove full speed into Arnhem and summoned his panzers into action. Thus before the British had finished assembling, superior German forces were deploying against them.

It has been suggested that the Germans were able to plan a trap at Arnhem because the plans for MARKET had been betrayed to them. Betrayal there certainly was, but it probably made little difference. A Dutch leader, Christian Lindemans, had been sent by SHAEF to Eindhoven on 14 September to warn the resistance group there of an Allied attack. Lindemans, however, had turned informer six months before to save his brother from the clutches of the Gestapo and now, faithful to his new masters, told all he knew of the operation to the head of German Army Intelligence at Driebergen on 15 September and was also questioned at Vught by staff officers of General Kurt Student's First Parachute Army, which was defending that sector. This can be reconciled with Student's post-war statement that he was completely surprised by the airborne operation by assuming that Lindemans' message merely referred in general terms to an attack through Eindhoven. Lindemans seems to have had only an inkling that airborne troops would be used. To have told him more would have been not only unwise but unnecessary.

A ground attack up the Eindhoven road had seemed quite likely to the Germans, and the reconnaissance activity which they observed along the Eindhoven-Arnhem road tended to confirm such an hypothesis. Apparently they even mistook the preparatory bombing and strafing on the morning of the 17th for an interdiction operation in support of a ground assault. Student, Germany's leading airborne expert, could hardly fail to see that the Zon bridge was a logical objective for an airborne mission, but since he is said to have regarded deep airborne penetrations as inconsistent with Allied policy and Montgomery's cautious character, he probably did not expect such an operation north of the Wilhelmina Canal.

All the German dispositions are consistent with the view that they anticipated an attack but had no specific knowledge of an airborne operation. Steps taken in accordance with that expectation would account for the stiff resistance facing the Guards on their way to Eindhoven, the promptness with which the Zon bridge was blown, and the ferocious fighting around the bridge at Best.

On the other hand, if the Germans had had definite knowledge of the 101st Division drop plans, they would surely have had a reception committee on the drop zones, and if they had realized that Arnhem was in danger, the all-important bridges at Nijmegen and Arnhem would not have been left intact and almost unguarded. As for the two panzer divisions at Arnhem, they had been ordered to that area as far back as 8 September, a week before Lindemans did his Judas work. The evidence, then, points to an Allied blunder rather than a German trap. German intelligence had not discovered the MARKET plan. Allied intelligence had disastrously erred in ruling out the presence of the panzers at Arnhem.[25]

On the evening of D-day 10 planes of the RAF Bomber Command dropped dummies and firing devices west of Utrecht and another 10 did so near Emmerich in an attempt to divert enemy forces from the MARKET area. The Germans were sufficiently deceived to send troops into the supposed drop areas, and as late as D plus 4 they listed the drops as genuine. However, capture of an Allied field order on the evening of D-day revealed to the Germans the true location and objectives of MARKET and thereby destroyed most of the value of the deception.[26]

D plus 1, Plans and Auxiliary Air Action

About 1800 on D-day General Brereton decided to postpone H-hour on D plus 1 from 1000 to 1400 hours and to send all his missions that day over the southern route. The delay was determined by predictions that fog would cover the take-off fields during the early morning and that there would be rain and low clouds over the Channel and the Low Countries until about noon. The change in route was made to avoid flak. If the British and the 101st Division progressed as expected, the southern route would be in friendly hands as far as Nijmegen.

Early on the 18th the weather appeared to be developing as predicted, but by late morning dense masses of low-lying clouds were threatening to make the southern route unusable. Therefore Brereton hastily ordered all missions to fly along the northern route.* The arrival time was left at 1400 hours.

---
*See Map No. 6, p. 92.

The effect of these changes was to mass four missions on one route at one time, an achievement made possible by the prior arrangements for three-lane traffic. Serials for the 101st Division would fly in the right lane and head right at the IP to LZ W. Those for the 82d Division would be in the center, and American planes carrying British paratroops to Arnhem would use the left lane and turn left at the IP. Overhead at 2,500 feet would be British planes towing gliders to the Arnhem area. In all, 1,336 American troop carrier planes, 340 British troop carriers and 1,205 gliders would be dispatched. Immediately after them 252 B-24's on the bomber resupply mission would fly over the same route to get the benefit of the anti-flak operations set up to protect the troop carriers.

Orders to use the northern route reached the troop carrier fields at the last minute. When the news arrived at Chilbolton 20 minutes before take-off time, the crews of the 442d Group were already aboard their planes and the group had only enough time to brief the flight leaders on the new plan. The lead serial crews of the 313th Group also had to be called from their aircraft about half an hour before take-off to get the news. Warnings to swing wide at the IP to avoid flak had to be sent by radio.[27]

The airborne missions on 18 September were protected on the same massive scale as before. Air Defense of Great Britain sent 277 fighters to guard the troop carriers between England and the IP. Of these, 16 Spitfire squadrons gave escort and area cover, while three squadrons of Spitfires, five of Tempests, and three of Mustangs attacked flak positions from Schouwen island to the IP. Six fighters were lost.

The Eighth Air Force had 397 fighters make sorties in support of MARKET. As on D-day, two groups of P-51's flew perimeter patrols on a line curving from Hasselt through Wesel to the Zuider Zee. Between the IP and the zones six P-51 groups, most of them guided by MEW, flew area cover at and above 2,500 feet, while two P-47 groups and the rocket squadron loaned by the Ninth Air Force attacked flak batteries and other ground targets.

On the 18th the Allied fighters had to contend with the first strong effort made by the Germans to intercept an Allied airborne mission. This effort was made in accordance with decisions taken by Hitler at a conference on the night of the 17th. The Nazi dictator had decided that since ground reserves were inadequate for a large-scale counterattack, the Luftwaffe would have to make an all-out effort to tip the scales against MARKET.

The German airmen were met on D plus 1 by the 357th and 359th Fighter Groups. The 359th Group, patrolling the perimeter with 57 planes, fought and repelled 35 FW-190's about 15 miles northeast of Arnhem, shooting down three of them and losing two of its own aircraft. The 357th Group, which was supposed to cover the Eindhoven area, was vectored out onto the perimeter about 40 miles southeast of Eindhoven to meet an attack. There, at 1505, while troop carrier operations were at their height its 52 planes battled about 60 enemy fighters. The pilots claimed 26 of the Germans destroyed at a cost of two of their own planes. None of the Nazis got through to strike at the troop carrier columns that day.

Operations against flak batteries did not go as well as on D-day. Since it was impossible to know with any accuracy what positions the airborne troops would be holding, the fighters had orders to attack only when fired upon. The Germans quickly learned to hold their fire until the P-47's were almost past, give them a short burst from the rear, and cease fire. These tactics made it very difficult to locate hidden batteries or to make sure that a suspected position was hostile. Haze and low clouds further hampered identification and greatly impeded bombing. Out of 95 P-47's three were lost and 10 damaged. Only 49 dropped bombs. The pilots claimed 33 flak positions destroyed, 4 damaged, about 37 silenced, and several secondary targets hit. They were skeptical as to their own effectiveness under such baffling conditions particularly in the case of the "silenced" batteries. However, their purpose was achieved. The troop carriers were able to fly in daylight over more than 80 miles of enemy territory with losses of less than two percent.[28]

D plus 1, Eindhoven Sector

In the 101st Division's area of responsibility the 506th Parachute Infantry Regiment marched south at dawn, reached Eindhoven at 0900, and took the town before noon over the resistance of about a battalion of Germans. The bridges there were unharmed. Two British armored cars on reconnaissance got through to the 506th about 1230, but the rest of the British armor was still five miles to the south, bumping along from roadblock to roadblock. Not until 1830 did the Guards reach Eindhoven, and they halted for the night outside Zon on the south side of the Wilhelmina Canal while their engineers laid a Bailey bridge over the center trestle of the damaged highway bridge there.[29]

The 501st PIR had a relatively easy day. It repulsed four or five feeble attacks made by improvised German forces gathered west of it at Schijndel and 's Hertogenbosch. Much more serious was the situation of the 502d PIR. Its 3d Battalion began the day in battle with superior forces at the Best highway bridge. The rest of the regiment, excepting the 1st Battalion, which remained at St. Oedenrode, moved to assist it and was also engaged and pinned down. Early in the afternoon the Germans attacked with artillery and tank support against the paratroops, who were still without artillery. "Enemy closing in, situation getting desperate," reads the entry in a battalion journal.[30] Bombing and strafing by five P-47's, which arrived in the nick of time, enabled the troops to repel that attack, but bitter and indecisive fighting continued throughout the day in the Best sector, within 1,000 yards west and southwest of LZ W. This situation presented an unexpected hazard to the glider missions landing on W that afternoon.[31]

The 101st Division was to be reinforced on the 18th by a 450-plane mission of the 53d Wing bringing Waco gliders to LZ W. The mission was divided into an A Section and a B Section, each made up of six serials, one from each of the groups at the Wing's disposal. Aboard the gliders were 2,656 troops, 156 jeeps, 111 trailers full of supplies, two bulldozers, and no guns.* Again one notes the assumption that the 101st would be able to get along without artillery, but would need great mobility to cover its long perimeter. The troops carried were principally from the 327th Glider Infantry Regiment (minus the 1st Battalion), the 326th Airborne Engineer Battalion, and the 326th Airborne Medical Company. Among the remainder was a detachment of divisional headquarters including the divisional artillery commander, Brig. Gen. Anthony C. McAuliffe, who rode in the lead glider of the lead serial.

Take-offs began about 1120, and the serials assembled over the Greenham Common area, took their positions at Hatfield, and proceeded 83 miles northeast to Aldeburgh. From there they followed the northern route to the IP below 's Hertogenbosch and turned south southeast on their final run to LZ W. The weather was good, except for a thick haze, which in places limited visibility to a couple of miles.

Despite the favorable weather 10 gliders failed to leave England; five of them had structural failures and five broke loose or were prematurely released. Two of the 10 crashed. Three Wacos were ditched in the Channel, but alert rescue work saved all aboard them. Another became uncontrollable, was released over Schouwen Island, and glided to probable destruction in a heavily fortified area.

In general ground fire was unexpectedly slight and inaccurate, and no German planes were sighted. The first serial suffered worst, two of its planes being shot down after their gliders were released, and 21 others being damaged, generally after they passed the IP.

The other 11 serials in the mission lost only two planes between them. One of those was hit about 15 miles short of the zone, caught fire, released its glider and crashed. The other ditched on the way back but the crew were saved. Casualties among the troop carrier crews totalled only eight dead or missing and about that number wounded or injured. Out of 112 aircraft damaged, 108 were readily repairable. Four, two of which had collided while landing, had to be salvaged.

As mentioned above, one glider had to be cut loose prematurely when its tug plane was set afire. Another Waco was hit by flak three miles from the zone and disintegrated. Three others were prematurely released over enemy territory and not heard of again. Another three reached the zone but crashed upon it. The remaining 428 gliders landed safely on or near LZ W between 1430 and 1620. The serials arrived at very irregular intervals with two apparently out of sequence. Naturally this led to confusion and interference at the release point, and some units reported being forced to release their gliders at altitudes of 1,200 and even 1,500 feet. However, by daylight with plenty of landing room this mix-up produced only

---

*Hq 101st Abn Div, Report on Operation MARKET Troop Carrier figures list 2,624 troops, 167 vehicles and 9 guns, which probably were heavy weapons of the 327th Glider Infantry. (Hist 53d TC Wg Sep 44).

minor inconvenience. Captain E. C. Thornton, an airborne observer, called the landings splendidly executed.

The focus of the landings was at the extreme west end of the zone, and many were made somewhat further west. In such cases the planes and gliders came within range of the German troops massed in the vicinity of Best, and some of the glider-borne troops were pinned down by rifle and mortar fire as they emerged from their gliders.

Assembly on the whole went quickly and well. The men formed in small groups and moved east onto the highway where they were sorted out with the aid of a control section established by divisional headquarters. When the returns were in, 2,579 troops had been mustered and 151 jeeps and 109 trailers had been reported on hand and usable. Only 54 of the airborne were dead or missing and 23 were injured. Only five of the jeeps and two of the trailers were lost or damaged. The mission had been about 95 percent successful. A carrier pigeon was dispatched to bring the good news to the 101st's headquarters in England.[32]

D plus 1, Nijmegen Sector

The 82d Division was faced on D plus 1 with a threat which for a time was serious indeed. At first everything seemed promising. The 508th PIR had extended its lines westward to make contact with the 504th at the site of Bridge 9, thus giving the division a neat sausage-shaped perimeter with its north side on high ground and its south protected by the Maas. Except for Nijmegen the enemy had shown little strength, and the 508th was deploying for a stronger thrust at the Nijmegen bridge. Then between 0800 and 1000 the Germans surged down the road from Wyler, pushed back the one company of the 508th which had been left to guard LZ T, and seized an ammunition dump. About the same time, other forces attacked out of the Reichswald Forest and overran DZ N.

The 82d seemed close to disaster. If the Nazis held the zones when the gliders landed there would be a slaughter which would make that on LZ W in Normandy seem insignificant. If the attackers broke through the perimeter into the woods around Groesbeek, it would scarcely be possible to drive them out, and with enemy troops at its center, the division's carefully chosen ring of defensive positions would become precarious. Fortunately the German troops involved were a hastily gathered assortment, no match for the paratroops in either quality or quantity, and the postponement of the glider missions to 1400 gave sufficient time to counterattack and clear the landing zones. News of the change in schedule had reached the division at 0840 about the same time as the first reports of the German attacks.

General Gavin threw his only ready reserve, two companies of the 307th Engineers, into the gap between the 505th Regiment and the 508th, and ordered the two regiments to hold their lines along the ridge at all costs and to retake their landing zones, T and N, in time for the glider missions. The 508th pulled back its companies in the Nijmegen area, redeployed on the ridge, and at 1310 launched an attack on LZ T; by 1400 it had regained that area and captured 149 prisoners and 16 guns. The 1st Battalion of the 505th was directed to attack eastward at 1240 and clear LZ N. Already engaged in stiff fighting at Riethorst and Mook, the battalion could spare only Company C to do the job. However, with help from Company I they were able by 1350 to push off the zone the relatively weak enemy force. At 1415 the Nazis again attacked out of the Reichswald with three companies supported by 11 armored vehicles. The 3d Battalion of the 505th repelled this thrust with the help of artillery support, which knocked out five of the vehicles. The landing zones had been saved, but they were far from safe. The Germans had dug in near enough to both LZ T and LZ N to rake them with small arms fire and bombard them with mortars.

While carrying on a defensive battle around its zones, the 82d captured another bridge over the Maas-Waal Canal, valuable insurance in case anything happened to the one at Heumen. During the morning a patrol of the 508th PIR pushed north to Honinghutie, the point where the main highroad crossed the canal. Checked by stubborn resistance on the approaches to the east end of the bridge, it called for assistance from the 504th, which sent a platoon to assist it. About noon this unit moved stealthily onto the west end of the bridge, took the Germans by surprise, and slaughtered them. However, the Nazis damaged the structure making it unsafe for heavy vehicles.[33]

The glider mission dispatched by the 50th and 52d Wings to the 82d Division on the 18th was originally to consist of 11 serials with 50 aircraft in the first and 40 in each of the rest, but two planes had been added to the second and fourth serials, making a total of 454. Like that of the 53d Wing, the mission was divided into two sections with one serial from each of six groups in the lead section and one from each of them except the 439th Group in the rear section. Every plane towed a Waco. In the gliders were 1,899 troops—nearly three quarters of whom were artillerymen—206 jeeps, 123 trailers and 60 guns.* The great difference between this load and that of the 101st's mission was in the emphasis on artillery. From past experience and in view of its exposed position, the staff of the 82d rightly judged it would need its guns and had therefore packed into the gliders the 319th, 320th and 456th Field Artillery Battalions, Battery B of the 80th Antitank Battalion, and Headquarters Battery of Divisional Artillery.

As take-off time approached, fog and low clouds hung over the Grantham area, necessitating a further delay of some 50 minutes before starting.† The first plane took off at 1109, and it was nearly two hours before all tugs and gliders were in the air. A serial which could assemble and set out on course within half an hour of its first take-off was considered to be doing well. The clouds were still low enough to impede assembly, and one serial of the 313th Group had to rendezvous over Cottesmore instead of its own base, Folkingham. However, beyond the coast the weather was good, though somewhat hazy, and the flying was smooth.

While still over England one glider began to disintegrate in mid-air, a not uncommon trick of the Waco, and another was loosed by a hysterical soldier who reached forward and yanked the release handle. Both landed safely. Over the Channel two other gliders, caught in prop-wash, lurched suddenly and snapped their cables. They ditched, and the occupants were quickly rescued. At least one of these ditchings was caused by some of the four-engined British planes which were supposed to be towing their gliders a thousand feet overhead but had failed to keep their prescribed altitude. There was also some tendency for the serials of the two American glider missions to get in each other's lanes, but except for one plane of the 313th Group which fell in with a serial of the 53d Wing and released its glider on LZ W no mix-up or serious confusion resulted. Three other gliders were released after landfall and before reaching Grave because of accidents or flak damage. Personnel and cargo from two of the three later reached the airborne.

Many glider pilots who did complete their sorties did so under difficulties. The plexiglass windows of some gliders blew out, letting a hundred-mile-an-hour wind blow through the cockpit. Over 20 percent of the interphones between plane and glider failed or worked badly. Several glider pilots reported that the lack of co-pilots greatly increased the strain of the three-hour flight.

Althiugh aircraft losses ran a little higher than those in the parallel mission of the 53d Wing, they were low nevertheless, only ten planes in all. One pilot, who had endangered himself by slipping slightly off course, was brought down by flak on Schouwen, and one other probably went down in that locality. From the coast to the IP, opposition was slight, but flak near 's Hertogenbosch blasted the wing off a C-47 and sent it crashing. The machine guns and light flak of German troops gathering in the Schijndel-Uden area accounted for two more planes, and two others were shot down within half a minute after releasing gliders over LZ T. Considering how close the Germans were to the zones, it is remarkable that the bag there was no bigger. Three additional aircraft were shot down in flames several miles southeast of the release area because of a costly mistake. Their squadron had missed its zone and had flown over strong German forces near Gennep.

At the end of October, 23 troop carrier men on this mission were dead or missing; half a dozen had wounds or injuries; the rest had reported back. The fate of the gliders whose tugs were lost near the coast or over Germany was unknown, but the occupants of the other five reached the Allied lines, as did four of their cargoes.

Over 90 percent of the returning planes were operational and none had to be salvaged. However, about 100 of them had been damaged by ground fire. Since more than half the damage was concentrated in three serials, portions of which had missed their zones and had flown from three

---

*These statistics are taken from the divisional history. The troop carrier figures are 1,779 troops, 201 jeeps, 55 guns and about 210 tons of other supplies and equipment, including trailers. The principal differences are in the data for the two serials flown by the 61st Group. Some guns seem to have been added to the loading lists shortly before the mission.

†Perhaps because of the weather the serial of the 439th Group which was to lead the first section appears to have gone at the end of that section, giving the lead to the 313th Group.

to 12 miles beyond them, it can be assumed that if all serials had stayed on course, the repairs resulting from the mission would have been relatively light.[34]

The lead serial in the column was one from the 313th Group, which was flying its first glider mission. As it approached the release area, the formation split down the middle into two columns of pairs far enough apart so that all the glider pilots could make a left turn without causing too much congestion. At 1431 the lead glider cut loose at an altitude of 800 feet and descended in a 360° spiral to the left. The others followed, most of them holding formation in two parallel spirals which fanned out as they approached the ground. On the downwind leg they passed over the panels and smoke, which had been set out by the pathfinders about a mile southwest of LZ N because the zone itself was a battlefield. The landing was made directly into a gentle northeast wind.

Most of the 313th's landings were slow and good. Almost every glider incurred some damage in landing on the soft, rough, ground, but only one glider was wrecked and damage to passengers and cargo was slight. Mortar and rifle fire from German positions less than a mile away, supplemented occasionally by a shell from some distant gun, delayed the unloading of the gliders but did little real harm. One glider pilot in the serial was killed by a mortar and two or three of the airborne were wounded.

The experience of the 313th was fairly typical of the mission as a whole. In all, 385 gliders landed within the lines of the 82d Division. Releases were made consistently at heights of 800 and 1,000 feet. A majority of the gliders came down in orderly fashion. Comparatively few of the glider pilots saw smoke signals and very few sighted panels. Some, seeing the fighting beneath them, chose to come in fast, but most made conservative landings at speeds of 60 to 75 miles per hour. There were cases of gliders being brought to a stop within as little as 50 feet. The arrestor parachutes, which had been installed on about half the gliders, proved very effective brakes, and many pilots who used them urged later that they be made standard equipment. Although most of the gliders nosed over or suffered some damage to their landing gear, less than 20 of those in the landing area had been destroyed. Not a single glider pilot is known to have been killed in landing accidents, but two were slain by enemy fire, seven injured and 10 wounded during or soon after landing. Thirty-five were missing. Of the airborne only 3 were killed and 42 wounded or injured during flight or landing, but 117 were missing. Not a single gun was reported to have been damaged in landing, although six of them came down far outside the 82d Division's area and could not be used by it. Only 29 of the jeeps and 17 of the trailers were either damaged or missing, so the division was able to employ 85 percent of the vehicles which had been loaded.

Of 212 gliders supposed to land on LZ N about 150 landed within a circle a half-mile in radius centered on the hamlet of Knapheide a mile southwest of the zone. All but a handful of the other gliders in those serials either landed within 1½ miles of Knapheide or stuck to their instructions and landed on LZ N. The 242 intended for LZ T did not fare so well. However, approximately 90 of them did land on the zone and 52 of them west of it but within a mile of the panels and smoke, which had been set out by the pathfinders exactly on its western edge. Another 19 were well bunched slightly over a mile west of LZ T, and 19 were scattered in German-held territory between 1 and 4 miles northeast of the zone.

While the sources are sometimes obscure or contradictory, it seems fairly clear that, excepting a few individual errors, seriously inaccurate releases were confined to three serials. In the third serial, which was flown by the 316th Group, a flight leader loosed his glider prematurely over LZ O and half the serial followed his example out of obedience and a desire to keep its gliders together. One explanation given was that other gliders had been seen landing on LZ O, but indications are that up to that time only one glider had landed there. A dozen glider pilots attest that a panel T was visible near Overasselt and this may well have caused the release. Whether the panels were carelessly left from the day before or set out again by order of someone in the 82d, which was taking every action it could think of to keep the gliders from landing in the battle area, their effect was harmless, even beneficial, since the landings were made in a safe and suitable area. The other half of the serial reached LZ T, but only six released gliders there. Eight kept on going and deposited their gliders between Wyler and Zyfflich northeast of the LZ. This error was costly. From the gliders beyond Wyler the 319th Field Artillery lost 5 officers and 40 men dead or captured and the cargoes of all eight gliders.

The eighth serial, which was flown by the 61st Group and carried Battery B, 320th Glider Field Artillery, also did badly. The glider of one of its flight leaders cut loose about 45 miles short of the zone as a result of flak damage. The tow pilot turned out of formation, circled to watch the glider land, and then went home. The pilot who took the lead went by pilotage alone after passing the IP and got lost. Followed by eight others he curved southward, missed the zone, and released his glider inside Germany 12 miles east-southeast of LZ T. Not one man from the gliders in that formation reached the 82d Division. The lead elements of the other squadron in this serial overshot the zone, with the result that nine of their gliders came down in the Wyler area. Although the Germans attacked this concentration and destroyed the gliders by shelling, most of the troops and glider pilots took cover and held out till nightfall. They then worked their way back to the Groesbeek area. The other 21 gliders in the serial landed on or near the zone.

The following serial may well have been influenced by the errors of its predecessor. It was also handicapped by the fact its Gee sets were jammed and its Rebeccas for some reason were not picking up signals from the Eureka on the landing zone. Of 38 gliders in that formation when it reached the Grave-Veghel area, at least 24 and probably 30 made a deviation to the south. However, they recognized their error sooner than those in the eighth serial and made their release between three and five miles south of LZ T in the general vicinity of Gennep. Some ran into close-range fire from antiaircraft batteries and others into automatic and small arms fire. Three planes were brought down and two gliders crashed. Most of the glider pilots protected themselves by slipping or diving to minimum altitude before attempting to land. Gliders landing safely were attacked almost as soon as they hit the ground. Remarkable leadership by some officers of the 320th Field Artillery saved the situation. They gathered together about four separate groups which defended themselves until nightfall and then worked their way north to the American lines. Saved in this way were approximately 160 of the airborne and at least 10 jeeps, 2 guns and 22 glider pilots. Only four glider pilots and nine of the airborne were missing. Of the other gliders in the serial one cut over LZ O after a flak hit, six or seven landed in the vicinity of LZ T and one which had overshot the zone landed in the Wyler area. Its occupants were able to reach friendly territory but had to abandon their cargo.[35]

D plus 1, Resupply by Bomber

The bomber resupply mission to the 82d and 101st Divisions was to arrive 20 minutes after the troop carriers, drop time being set for 1557. It was to be flown by 252 B-24's of the 2d Bombardment Division from bases in Norfolk and Suffolk. Supplies were trucked in on the night of the 17th. The ball turrets were removed, and each plane was loaded in bomb racks, waist, and bomb bay with about two tons of supplies packed in 20 containers. A trained dropmaster of the 2d Quartermaster Battalion* was assigned to each plane to direct the pushing of bundles through the turret well and the rear hatch.

The bomber staff, new to this sort of mission, had been in great doubt as to tactics, and particularly as to what would be the best altitudes for the bombers to maintain. Finally it decided to imitate the troop carriers by having the planes fly at 1,500 feet to the IP, descend to about 300 feet for the drop, and make a climbing turn to 1,500 feet or higher for the trip back. Formations would be nine-ship V's in trail at 30-second intervals. The speed would be 165 miles an hour along the route and 150 miles when dropping. Except for leaving England at Orfordness, a headland two miles south of the troop carrier departure point, the Liberators would follow the northern troop carrier route out and back in order to benefit from the marker boat, anti-flak operations, and air-sea rescue facilities provided for their predecessors. At the IP the 20th Wing with 131 planes would proceed to DZ N with supplies for the 82d Division, and behind it 121 aircraft of the 14th Wing would turn southward to drop on DZ A and DZ W for the 101st.

The same visual aids set out on the zones for the troop carriers were to be provided for the bombers, but since the B-24's were not equipped

---
*This SOS unit, which had absorbed the 490th QM Depot Company and two other quartermaster companies, was attached to IX TCC and was under operational control of IX TCC Service Wing.

with Eureka, the pathfinders were to provide radio "buncher" beacons to guide them. Each flight was to drop its loads when its leader dropped, and he was to do so directly over the T.[36]

The bombers were given fully as much support as the transports. The ADGB fighters covering the troop carrier missions were in a position to protect the Liberators over most of their way to the IP, and four of the P-51 groups flying area cover around Eindhoven and Nijmegen remained throughout the supply drop. Two groups of P-38's and P-51's flew 104 sorties as close escort from landfall to drop zone, and two groups of P-47's bombed and strafed flak positions between IP and drop zones five minutes before the bombers were due to arrive. No hostile planes were sighted, but the flak-busters had a hard time. Clouds were rolling in below 1,000 feet; the haze was thickening as the afternoon wore on; and the German gunners were perfecting their hit-and-hide tactics. In 88 sorties the P-47 group lost 21 planes and had many damaged, while destroying only 6 gun positions and damaging about 15.[37]

The bombers were handicapped before they started by a curious staff error. After most of the briefing was done, it was discovered that the 2d Bombardment Division had sent 20th Wing data to the 14th Wing and vice-versa. Since the correct maps and photographs were flown in just as the planes were warming up, pilots and navigators had to familiarize themselves with their route as they went along.

Another untoward incident occurred over the middle of the Channel. The 20th Wing made a 360° turn to the left and the 14th, anxious to keep its assigned position, turned with it. The turn, which was made to avoid running into a belated serial of the 442d Troop Carrier Group, caused delay and confusion, particularly since the haze made it easy for a group which lagged a little to lose sight of the one ahead. In the 20th Wing the 448th Group became separated from the others and proceeded independently, and five pilots in the 93d Group lost their way and had to go home. Thanks to good navigation, greatly aided by Gee, all but those five appear to have reached the IP.

The 20th Wing had some trouble locating DZ N. The radio beacon was not on, and most formations saw neither panels nor smoke. Part of the 489th Group missed the zone on its first run, circled, turned away on its second run to avoid other formations, and dropped on the third try. The 448th Group, probably misled by evidences of paratroop operations on DZ O, dropped five miles short near that zone at 1630 hours. Some incoming flights had to swerve to avoid those returning. Many appear to have used glider concentrations as drop points, and since the gliders were spread up to 3,000 yards north, west and south of DZ N, the drop was similarly dispersed. The prescribed altitude was well maintained, almost all drops being made from heights between 250 and 400 feet. Most of the bundles landed within the lines of the 82d Division, and about 80 percent of the 258 tons dropped were recovered. Estimates vary as to the percentage collected, but the value of the ammunition and other items delivered was unquestionably great. General Gavin considered them "vital to our continued combat existence."[38]

The 446th Group experienced an easy approach over several miles of friendly territory dotted with waving paratroops and Dutch civilians, and it returned almost unscathed. The others reported small arms and light flak, which in places was intense and accurate. The wing lost 4 planes, had about 38 damaged and had at least 16 men wounded.

The flights of the 14th Wing had overrun each other in the haze and reached the IP in great disorder at altitudes ranging from 500 to 1,500 feet. They received little or no assistance from the pathfinders, who apparently got their equipment into operation too late to be of use. However, with one exception, all the 121 pilots found their way to the general vicinity of DZ's A and W and dropped their loads. Most dropped from about 300 feet as prescribed, but some flights came in on the deck as low as 50 feet, too low for accuracy. For the others, as photographs show, the gliders on DZ W were the most obvious landmarks.

The results were not good. Even the wing commander admitted that the bundles were badly scattered. Some 238 tons were dropped. On DZ W, where 108 of the Liberators were to drop, only about 20 percent of the supplies were recovered. This is less damning than it appears, since the gliders used as checkpoints were at the west end of the zone and a deviation of less than a mile to the west of them would suffice to put the bundles in the hands of the Germans in the Best sector. The failure, however understandable, caused the

101st Division serious shortages of food and other essentials.

The 501st PIR had been given a drop on DZ A by 13 planes. Although the supplies they brought were rather scattered, they were centered 1,000 yards west of the zone. A small-scale German attack in this area had been routed about an hour earlier, and the 501st had both time and men to spare for collection details. Under these relatively favorable conditions it was able to retrieve slightly over 50 percent of its bundles.

The 14th Wing had had very little trouble with ground fire on the way in, and some flights which stayed low and skimmed out on the deck came back untouched. However, most pilots who had dropped on DZ W made a climbing turn to the right, as planned. This tactic posed them like clay pigeons directly over the guns of the Germans at Best. For a minute or two the Nazis gave the wing what even the bomber men regarded as a very rough time. Three of their planes were shot down, one crash-landed at Brussels, and four crash-landed in England fit for nothing but salvage. At least 32 others received some damage. Next day the returned pilots agreed unanimously that the climbing turn was a mistake.[39]

D plus 1, Arnhem Sector

While the American airborne were having hard fighting on D plus 1, the British had worse. Frost's paratroops at the highway bridge were penned in by German guns and armor and suffered severely. The 1st and 3d Parachute Battalions spent a nightmare day struggling forward down city streets flanked by well chosen and strongly manned German positions. By evening they had gained only a few hundred yards and had been whittled down to about 100 fighting men apiece. To make matters worse, the divisional commander and the commander of 1 Parachute Brigade had been cut off from their men while following the 3d Battalion in its house-to-house fighting.

Back in the drop and landing areas the glider troops were having a hard fight to hold their perimeter and even had to use the bayonet to throw back attacks in some places. Nevertheless, the commander of 1 Airlanding Brigade ventured to send half a battalion of the South Staffordshire Regiment down the Heelsum-Arnhem road to reinforce the paratroops. Like their predecessors they reached the western outskirts of Arnhem, ran into strong opposition, and could go no farther. No more troops could be spared until that day's missions arrived, and their arrival had been postponed four hours; a painful delay for the British airborne.[40]

The lift to Arnhem on D plus 1 was led by 126 American planes, two serials of 36 aircraft from the 314th Group and two of 27 from the 315th Group. They were to drop 2,119 British troops of 4 Parachute Brigade on DZ Y and with them 51 tons of supplies, including 407 parapacks and 24 door bundles.

From the initial take-off at 1123 their trip over the northern route went smoothly, until they reached Oss, six miles beyond the IP. There, one plane hit by small arms crashed with all aboard and flak set another afire. Its occupants all jumped and made their way to the Allied lines. Another C-47 was hit about 10 miles further on and began to burn. The paratroops and at least one of the crew got out safely and were guided to Nijmegen by the Dutch. The most intense fire, including much light flak, came from Wageningen about five miles short of the drop zone. Two planes which caught fire there attempted crash landings, but one of them hit a power line and exploded, and the other was probably destroyed. Most of the troops had been standing on the alert and were able to jump, but only one of the troop carrier men got back. At Wageningen the mission turned due north, then made a right-angle turn and crossed DZ Y heading east. Another aircraft was hit and set on fire by Germans on the edge of the drop zone. All troops were dropped, but plane and crew crashed in flames. On the way back, danger spots were carefully avoided, and no more losses were incurred. However, at least 24 of the returning planes had been damaged. The returnees blamed part of their losses on lack of fighter-bomber assistance, and claimed they had seen no friendly fighters beyond the IP.

Landmarks and navigational aids combined made it relatively easy for most pilots in the mission to locate DZ Y. They made their drop in a shower of tracers between 1406 and about 1420 from heights of 800 to 1,000 feet. All but a couple of parapacks and six paratroops, who were prevented from jumping by wounds or snarled equipment, were dropped. About 90 percent of the drops were, as a British participant put it, "slap in the right place." However, one nine-plane flight in the last serial, having become somewhat separated from the rest of the formation, dropped its loads a mile or two from the zone. A ten-mile breeze was blowing, and the troops came down rather roughly in brush and trees. Moreover, substantial numbers of enemy troops were in the drop area. One battalion bagged 80 prisoners before it reached its rendezvous. Despite these minor blemishes and inconveniences, the drop was rightly regarded as very successful.[41]

The paratroop mission to DZ Y was followed by 295 British aircraft towing gliders to LZ S and LZ X.* In the gliders was the second echelon of 1 Airlanding Brigade Group. The glider column, supposed to fly at 2,500 feet, ran into $5/10$ to $8/10$ cloud as low as 2,000 feet with the result that nine of the gliders broke loose over England and two over the North Sea. Ground fire over Holland was thicker than it had been on the day before, especially in the 's Hertogenbosch area, where heavy flak was seen bursting, and several gliders were hit. Only one of the tugs was shot down, but 30 were damaged. The glider of the destroyed plane may have reached the Arnhem area. A total of 13 gliders were loosed over Holland and one, badly damaged, over friendly Belgium. Some may have snapped their cables, but at least 9 of these 14 releases were caused or necessitated by ground fire.

As on the first day the accuracy of the British fliers was very good. All the pathfinders' beacons and markers were functioning, but again Rebecca-Eureka worked badly. Less than half of those interrogating the Eureka on LZ X received responses. Of 73 glider-tug combinations sent to LZ S, 69 reached the landing area, and at least 67 put their gliders on or near the zone. Of 223 dispatched to LZ X, 203 reported success, and photographs showed 189 of their gliders on or close to the zone. The principal flaw in the performance was that most of the glider pilots ignored the T's laid out to show wind direction. In spite of this, serious accidents were rare and caused less damage than the German forces just outside the zones. It was estimated that while only 39 of the 533 gliders accounted for in the first two lifts were wrecked, at least 47 of the 332 gliders on and around LZ's X and Z were destroyed by mortar fire or burned to prevent their falling into the hands of the enemy.

A third mission, flown from Harwell by 35 Stirlings of 38 Group, was to drop supplies on DZ L at about 1500. Two of those converted bombers failed to return and 14 others were damaged. One returning pilot reported dropping by mistake on LZ S, which was about a mile west of L. All but two of the others believed they had made accurate drops, generally from heights of about 500 feet. Actually the 803 panniers and containers dropped were rather widely scattered, and many drifted southwest of the zone into enemy territory, probably because the planes from which they fell had flown too high. The net weight of supplies dropped was 87 tons and of this only 12 tons were recovered. In contrast, two bulk-loaded Hamilcar gliders yielded 14 tons of supplies between them.[42]

No time was lost in utilizing the troops delivered in the second lift. As soon as the second half of the South Staffordshires had assembled after landing, they were sent into Arnhem to join the rest of the battalion; and at 1515 the divisional operations officer, appearing on DZ Y, ordered the 11th Parachute Battalion to follow the South Staffordshires to town. However, the eight miles between DZ Y and Arnhem could not be covered at a bound. Not until late that evening after a march through Wolfhezen and Hartestein did the paratroops catch up with the Staffordshires near a hospital on the west side of Arnhem. By then the latter had made contact with the remnants of 1 Parachute Battalion, and in a conference at about 2000 the commanders of the three units laid plans for an attack toward the highway bridge at 0400 next morning.

The main body of 4 Parachute Brigade minus the 11th Battalion moved south of its zone to the Utrecht-Arnhem railway and advanced down the railway with the purpose of taking positions on high ground north of Arnhem as specified in the original plan. However, it halted because of darkness near Wolfhezen, which was at the southeast corner of LZ S. The battalion of glider troops which had held DZ Y during the drop also moved along the railway, stopped near the brigade, and was attached to it next morning.

The rest of the division abandoned LZ's S, X, and Z by nightfall on the 18th had moved

---

*In order to bring in the loads of gliders aborting on the prevous day the number dispatched was increased from 270 to 296. One crashed on take-off because of an engine failure.

into positions further east centered on Hartestein, which was on the highway two miles west of Arnhem, and extending to Heveadorp on the Rhine a mile and a half southwest of Hartestein. Thus the lines held by the main body of First Division roughly resembled an arrowhead with the shaft along the highway, the point at Hartestein and the barbs at Wolfhezen and Heveadorp.[43]

The Balance for D Plus 1

During the second day of MARKET the Allies had fallen seriously behind schedule, but success still seemed within their reach. Few of their difficulties could be ascribed to the air side of the venture. The glider mission for the 101st Division had delivered over 95 percent of its loads accurately and safely, an unprecedented achievement. In spite of enemy attacks on the landing zones and despite some pilot errors, the mission for the 82d Division had been about 85 percent successful. Incomplete data on the paratroop and glider missions to the British that day indicates their score was better than 85 percent. The supply drops had been less satisfactory, but shortages were still not critical. As yet enemy aircraft had not fired a shot at the troop carriers, and losses from ground fire continued low.

The British tanks were still at Zon, awaiting the repair of the bridge; the 82d Division had had to pull out of Nijmegen; and the situation of the British paratroops in Arnhem was known to be serious. However, the big bridges at Arnhem and Nijmegen were still intact, and the British airborne and the 82d Division were preparing to attack toward them next day. Though the British had suffered cruelly, the Polish paratroops due on the 19th would compensate for their losses. If British intelligence was right, the Germans at Arnhem had already committed everything they had and were near the end of their resources. In that case tenacity would win.

D Plus 2, Plans and Auxiliary Air Action

Weather and tactical developments produced several changes in the plans for D plus 2. On

Figure 9. Paratroop Drop near Grave, Holland, during Operation MARKET, 23 September 1944.

the evening of the 18th General Brereton decreed that all airborne missions next day would take the southern route and that the drops and landings would begin at 1500 hours instead of 1000. His preference for flight over friendly territory dictated selection of the southern route. Predictions of extensive fog in northern areas and almost unbroken low clouds further south on the morning of the 19th account for the postponement. By afternoon, the fog would be gone and the clouds were expected to lift somewhat.

The 101st Division had decided it wanted artillery in the third lift, so the five serials originally slated to drop supplies to it were transformed into glider serials to bring in guns and gunners. Instead

Figure 10. Resupply drop from B-24's over Holland during Operation MARKET, 18 September 1944.

of 191 Wacos the division would receive 382 and to this were added three more carrying the loads of gliders which had aborted earlier. In addition, the low attrition rate in the previous missions made it possible to increase the number of gliders going to the 82d Division from 209 to 219, the resupply aircraft for that division from 142 to 167, and the planes carrying Polish paratroops to Arnhem from 108 to 114. The RAF would send to Arnhem a parachute resupply mission of 163 planes and a glider mission of 52 planes, including seven added to bring in replacements for gliders which had aborted on previous missions.[44]

Weather conditions proved to be much worse than had been predicted. Throughout the day haze and stratus blanketed the Grantham area, and great masses of low cloud persisted over the Channel and the Low Countries. Along most of the troop carrier route haze limited visibility to about half a mile. The only area on the route with even relatively good weather was that around Arnhem.[45]

Lavish air support had again been planned, but, because of the widespread bad weather, very few of the support missions could be flown. Escort and cover duties between England and the southern IP near Gheel had been assigned to 15 Spitfire squadrons of ADGB, but only one of those squadrons carried out its mission as planned, and only 68 of the Spits made sorties. The rest had to turn back. Of seven groups of P-51's which the Eighth Air Force was to furnish for perimeter patrols and area cover,* five groups were able to reach the battle area and make a total of about 180 sorties. Two of these groups had to battle German fighters which were seeking to penetrate the perimeter. At 1445 near Wesel the 364th Group sighted and engaged more than 30 enemy aircraft. It reported the destruction of five of them and the loss of one of its own. The 357th Fighter Group, which had 54 planes on patrol in the Arnhem area, had four such clashes. It encountered 25 Messerschmitts at 1610 hours, about 30 Focke Wolfes at 1620, between 20 and 30 assorted fighters at 1705, and 15 Messerschmitts at 1720. The group claimed to have shot down 18 of the enemy and lost five of its aircraft. Except for the fight near Wesel these air battles were fought after the troop carrier serials had left the combat area, but they undoubtedly saved the airborne troops some punishment. If the Nazis had struck earlier, their chances of getting at the troop carriers would have been better, since because of the weather two P-51 groups on area patrol were late in getting into position.

The Eighth Air Force had also agreed to send two P-47 groups and the rocket squadron for anti-flak work south of 's Hertogenbosch, but they were unable to make any sorties. Flak neutralization beyond 's Hertogenbosch for missions to Nijmegen and Arnhem was a responsibility of Ninth Air Force units based in northern France. These dispatched 171 aircraft, but few of the planes reached the front, and none of them went into action. The principal reason for their failure was the impossibility of attacking ground positions through low clouds and thick haze. Thus weather

---

*Escort duty between 's Hertogenbosch and Arnhem had originally been delegated to the Ninth Air Force, but on the morning of the 19th all responsibility for protection of the troop carriers from air action beyond Gheel was given to Eighth Air Force.

D Plus 2, Eindhoven Sector

An encouraging feature of D plus 2 was the progress made by the British ground forces. At 0615 their lead tanks rumbled over the bridge at Zon. Half an hour later they rolled into Veghel. By 0830 they had burst across the 10 miles of hostile territory north of Veghel and made contact with the 82d Divison at Grave. This was the sort of dash Montgomery had hoped for.

However, the contact of both American divisions with Dempsey's army still hung by a thread. Therefore the 101st Division had to retain responsibility for the whole long stretch of road from Veghel to Eindhoven. The 506th PIR, reinforced by a couple of squadrons of British tanks, held the sector south of Zon. Although the Luftwaffe bombed Eindhoven heavily that night, the regiment was outside the town and had only a handful of casualties. The 501st PIR continued to have a relatively easy time around Veghel and sent a company on patrol to Dinter four miles northeast of that town. The 502d sent its second battalion at 0600 to make another assault on the bridge at Best, but once again the attack was beaten back. At 1415 the whole regiment, excepting the 1st Battalion, which was still defending St. Oedenrode, was thrown into a coordinated attack on the enemy position. This attack, supported by a squadron of British tanks, smashed through to victory over numerically superior opponents. By 1600 the paratroops had taken the bridge and with it fifteen 88-mm. guns and 1,056 prisoners. Over 300 German dead were found on the field.[47]

The glider mission flown on D plus 2 by the 53d Wing and 442d Group for the 101st Division took off between about 1130 and 1320 in ten serials containing 385 plane-glider combinations. The weather over the assembly area around Greenham Common was barely passable with visibility poor and clouds closing in at about 1,200 feet. Beyond Hatfield conditions deteriorated rapidly, and before reaching the coast the serials ran into deep, dense clouds in which visibility was zero. Glider pilots unable to see their tugs had to guide their craft by the tilt of the tow rope and by telephone conversation with the plane crew. At most points over the Channel it was possible to get under the clouds by going down to about 200 feet, but even then visibility was generally half a mile or less.

Many gliders broke loose, cut loose* or were brought back; the whole last serial was called back after it was well out over the Channel. Of these gliders, 80 landed more or less smoothly in England and two in the last serial collided over their base, killing their pilots and six troops. Another 17 gliders had to be ditched in the Channel, but were located by rescue launches in time to save all personnel. During the flight over friendly Belgium 31 more gliders broke loose or were released, all presumably as a result of the weather. Three of them crashed, killing five men, injuring four, and putting two jeeps out of action. The rest landed well, and all the troops and materiel aboard them reached the 101st within a week.

Contrary to expectations, the route instead of passing over the new salient ran just west of it, and with visibility so low, the airmen probably blundered over some strongpoints they would normally have avoided. In spite of clouds and mist Nazi gunners sent up intense and accurate light flak from Rethy, Moll, and Best. Small-arms fire, probably aided by the fact that the mission had to fly low, also took its toll. The troops on LZ W could see the formations approaching over the battlefield between Best and the zone and could certainly have saved some losses by recommending a detour if a ground-air radio had been provided. As it was 17 aircraft, 7 percent of those making sorties, were destroyed,† and 5 others had to be salvaged after landing at friendly bases. Almost all had received the fatal damage before reaching the LZ. Among the crews 31 men were dead or missing. Approximately 170 of the returning planes had been damaged, but this ratio, some 70 percent of those exposed, is offset by the fact that in most cases the damage was slight.

About half of the pilots whose planes were shot down managed to release their gliders on or close to LZ W. Among the bravest and the luckiest were 1st Lt. Jesse M. Harrison of the 435th Group and his co-pilot. Although their aircraft was already on fire, they brought their glider over the zone for a good release, then jumped through the flames,

---

*When a plane banked in the overcast its glider was apt to turn on its back and go out of control, necessitating release.

†Another 17 landed at Brussels, partly because of damage and partly because of the weather. These planes were at first listed as missing.

and lived. Many gliders were shot loose, broke loose or were prematurely released as a result of enemy action. One squadron in the next-to-last serial released 15 gliders by mistake nearly 10 miles west of the zone. Since the ceiling in the release area was about 600 feet and visibility less than a mile, the wonder is not that they went wrong, but that so many went right. In all, 16 gliders landed safely in enemy territory, their occupants and most of their cargoes eventually reaching the 101st Division. Another 26 Wacos were unaccounted for, almost certainly because they had come down in hostile territory and all aboard them had been killed or captured.

Of 213 gliders reaching the drop zone one was shot down, two or three crashed, and 209 made good landings with very little damage, a remarkable performance under the circumstances even if some allowance be made for the smooth and spacious character of the landing zone. Landings began at 1437 and ended about 1600.

The mission had carried 2,310 troops, of whom 1,341 reached their destination in safety, 11 were dead, 11 were injured, and 157 were missing. The remainder had been returned to England or landed safely somewhere short of the zone. Out of 136 jeeps loaded into the gliders 79 arrived at the zone in good condition, as did 49 out of 77 trailers and 40 out of 68 guns. By far the most depleted unit was the 907th Field Artillery Battalion, which had been carried by the last two serials and one flight of the serial preceding. Of its 89 gliders 57 had been returned to England, 4 had ditched, and about 17 were missing or down in enemy territory. Only 24 men of the battalion and none of its twelve 105-mm. howitzers were landed in the vicinity of LZ W.* The other units carried were the 81st Airborne Antitank Battalion, the 321st Glider Field Artillery Battalion, and portions of the 327th Glider Infantry Regiment, the 377th Parachute Field Artillery Battalion, and divisional artillery headquarters. These came in at between 55 and 95 percent of strength. The antitank battalion had on hand only 14 of the 24 guns with which it had started, but the 377th Field Artillery had all 12 of its 75-mm. howitzers in position and ready to fire by 1710, an hour and forty minutes after it landed.

The guns which did arrive proved their worth almost immediately. About 1700 a German force with tanks and self-propelled guns struck at Zon from the east and got to within a few hundred yards of the Zon bridge, which the 502d PIR had left lightly defended while it concentrated on winning its battle at Best and guarding its landing zone. Since by that time the landings were over and victory had been won at Best, the 502d had ample resources to counter the threat. Antitank guns of the 81st Battalion knocked out two German tanks, and the rest retreated. Had this thrust come a couple of hours earlier, it might have achieved the destruction of the bridge, a most serious possibility.[48]

D Plus 2, Nijmegen Sector

At Nijmegen on the morning of the 19th the 82d Division eagerly awaited the coming of the British tanks. Browning had told Gavin on the previous evening that the Nijmegen bridge must be taken on the 19th or, at the latest, very early on the 20th. With tank support this seemed possible. Paradoxically, although the bridge was the main objective of his division, Gavin could spare only one battalion to attack it. He had a 25-mile perimeter to defend, and the glider-borne reinforcements scheduled to join him that day failed to arrive.

Why the Germans had not already blasted the highway bridge at Nijmegen is uncertain. General Gavin, who should know, claims that Dutch guerrilla fighters kept the Nazis from placing charges on the span. The resistance forces in Nijmegen certainly did a magnificent job of harassing the garrison, but the Germans did have access to the bridge and could probably have blown it had they resolved to do so. This lends weight to a post-war statement by General Student that Model, who believed the bridge could be held, had prohibited its demolition.

The medium tanks of the Guards moved over secondary roads to the Maas-Waal Canal and crossed on the bridge at Heumen about 1000. An hour later a battalion of tanks, a company of British armored infantry, and the 2d Battalion of the 505th PIR headed north to make a renewed bid

---
*In order to give the airborne more firepower the 105-mm. howitzer had been redesigned so it could enter a C-47 or a Waco without being disassembled. Its dimensions had been cut from 238 x 82 x 60 inches to 157 x 67 x 55 inches, and through the use of light alloys its weight had been reduced from 4,235 pounds to 2,500 pounds. The 907th had been chosen to give the new weapon its first combat test in MARKET, so the ill-fortune of the serials carrying it was particularly regrettable. (Maj T. F. Walkowicz, *Future Airborne Armies*, A Report for the AAF Scientific Advisory Group, Sep 45, pp. 21, 59 in AU Library M-30484-S)

for the Nijmegen bridges. They attacked early in the afternoon and penetrated to the center of the town without opposition except for some artillery fire. There they split, one paratroop company and seven tanks heading for the railway bridge, while the rest struck at the road bridge. Neither group succeeded. The main body ran into forces ensconced in revamped Dutch fortifications in a park at the south end of the bridge and were stopped about 400 yards short of their goal. Repeated assaults lasting well into the night produced nothing but heavy losses. At the close of its third day of operations the 82d Division had 649 casualties in its hospital at Groesbeek and over 150 dead.[49]

Lowering clouds over the bases of the 50th and 52d Wings forced them to postpone the glider mission which had been prepared to deliver the 325th Glider Infantry Regiment and some other troops to the 82d Division at 1000 on the 19th. A few planes and gliders got off the ground but were recalled almost immediately.

The resupply mission of 167 planes, which was to drop 265 tons of supplies to the 82d, did somewhat better, because it staged from the bases of the 53d Wing in southern England and two serials had been sent to those bases on the day before. One serial of 25 aircraft flown by the 439th Group ran into heavy cloud off the Belgian coast and broke up. One of its planes followed the gliders going to LZ W and dropped its bundles near there. Another got far enough to be damaged by antiaircraft fire.* The rest apparently turned back before reaching the Continent. The other serial, 35 planes of the 61st Group, began taking off from Aldermaston at 1250. They flew across the Channel through dense haze under a 200-foot ceiling. Over Holland the weather improved greatly, but flak was thick, and no friendly fighters were sighted north of Gheel. Two planes were shot down, one west of Veghel, and another shortly after making its drop. Fifteen were damaged, and five men were missing, including a quartermaster bundle-dropper who fell out the door of his aircraft.

As a result of its struggle for LZ's N and T on the previous day, the 82d Division had decided to use DZ O as both drop and landing zone for the time being, so its pathfinders set out their aids on that zone. Although one squadron claimed it got

*One of the crew bailed out in the mistaken belief the plane was about to blow up.

no response, the Eureka was probably functioning effectively. The panels and smoke on the zone were clearly visible. One pilot dropped his bundles prematurely near 's Hertogenbosch, and another straggled off and followed a British formation to Arnhem. However, 32 planes reached the vicinity of DZ O at 1530.

Remembering their stinging reception on the previous day, the troop carriers made a fast, high drop. Authorized to go in at 1,000 feet, they let go their bundles at speeds up to 135 miles an hour from as high as 2,500 feet. The results were decidedly unsatisfactory. The airborne called the amount recovered negligible, and official estimates put it at only 20 percent of the quantity dropped. The failure of this mission was a real blow to the 82d Division, since it was becoming critically short of both food and ammunition.[50]

D Plus 2, Arnhem Sector

To the British troops at Arnhem 19 September was a day of disaster. Their attacks failed, and by nightfall it was evident that the initiative had passed to the enemy.

At dawn on the 19th a last attempt was made to break through to the bridge. The Staffordshires advanced down the Heelsum-Arnhem highway, followed by 11 Parachute Battalion, while the remnants of 1 and 3 Parachute Battalions moved along the riverbank, which was only a couple of hundred yards to the right of the road. They battled onward for about half a mile to a point called The Monastery, where after exhausting their supply of antitank ammunition, they were overrun by tanks. They fell back, engaged enemy forces flanking them on the slopes of Den Brink, and were again terribly mauled by mortar fire and tanks, followed up by infantry. Barely 400 survivors of the four battalions were able to withdraw to Oosterbeek, a mile further west, where they had the support of divisional artillery.

At 0500 that morning 4 Parachute Brigade had attacked from the Wolfhezen area in an effort to take high ground at Koepel, just beyond which lay Drop Point V. The attack stalled more than half a mile west of Koepel, leaving the drop point in enemy hands. By mid-afternoon it was all too clear that the brigade could get no further, so it was ordered to fall back on Wolfhezen and thence south to the main divisional position around

Hartestein. Thus it happened that the gliders which were to land on LZ L, a mile east of Wolfhezen, came down at 1600 in the front lines of a force attempting to disengage under heavy pressure.

Perhaps even worse than these reverses was the fact that the 114 planes of the 52d Wing which were to carry the bulk of the Polish Parachute Brigade to DZ K south of the Arnhem bridge were grounded by the impenetrable overcast in their area. Had the Poles arrived at 1000 that morning as planned, they might conceivably have saved the bridge or at least rescued what was left of 2 Parachute Battalion. It was not until that afternoon that German tanks were able to close in on Frost's men and begin systematic destruction of their positions dominating the north end of the span, and up to that time the Nazis appear to have had few troops and no tanks on the south bank of the river. When the Poles did come two days later, bridge and battalion were lost beyond redemption.

Also postponed were glider missions by 80 American and 10 British planes to land the 878th (US) Aviation Engineer Battalion on LZ's X and L. Their gliders stood ready; the weather at their bases was favorable; but the land on which to build an airstrip outside Arnhem had not been won and, indeed, never was won; so the engineers waited, and their planes stood idle.

The British were able to send out a resupply mission and a small glider mission from their bases in southern England, but those, too, were jinxed. They dispatched 35 Horsas carrying Polish headquarters and artillerymen to LZ L, and also 8 to LZ X and one to LZ S with cargoes returned from previous missions. Of these gliders, five broke loose over England, two over the sea and five more over Belgium and Holland. The pilots reported seeing considerable flak, especially near the zones, and had no fighter support at all. One glider was shot loose and another was so damaged it had to be released. None of the tug aircraft were lost, but nine of them were damaged.

The pathfinders had all their equipment including Eureka working nicely on LZ L and 28 pilots reported releasing gliders there. However, the Horsas had to land in the middle of a battle. Some were hit by shells and others had to be abandoned with their cargoes. A majority of the Polish troops were able to report for duty, but losses were heavy.

Only two or three of the gliders bound for LZ's S and X reached the Arnhem area, and they probably fell into enemy hands, since little, if any, of those zones was held by the British.

As for the resupply mission, every effort had been made to deflect it from Drop Point V to a safe point south of Hartestein, but in vain. A message sent on the 18th was not received. The airborne set up a Eureka in a tower at the new point, but that could be used only intermittently for fear of exhausting the battery. Although about half of the pilots interrogating it reported success, it seems to have done them singularly little good. This may have been partly due to the set being turned on late and partly to the tendency of the blips on a Rebecca screen to merge when it was within about two miles of its Eureka. The old drop point was less than a mile and a half northeast of the new one. Smoke, panels, and Very lights were also used, but because of trees surrounding the new DP an aerial observer would have had to be almost directly overhead to see them. Almost none of the pilots on the mission did pass close enough to the spot to sight the visual aids.

The upshot of these failures in communication was that the resupply mission headed for its original DP, crossed the enemy lines at about 1,000 feet through intense flak, and dropped most of its supplies in the Koepel area. Out of 100 Stirlings of 38 Group and 63 Dakotas of 46 Group, 13 were destroyed and 97 damaged. The heroic persistence of the pilots, one of whom won the Victoria Cross, only ensured that their loads would go to the Germans. Out of 388 tons of supplies dropped, only 21 tons, less than six percent, was recovered. Most of this was probably from five planes which dropped their loads by mistake near Wolfhezen and from an extra couple of Stirlings which had been sent to drop on DZ L and appear to have done so.

By nightfall on 19 September the main body of the British airborne, terribly short of ammunition, food and water, held an area of less than two square miles between Oosterbeek and Hartestein on the east and Heveadorp and Bilderberg on the west. The glider battalion which had been with 4 Parachute Brigade entered the perimeter that night. The brigade itself was still near Wolfhezen and in danger of being cut off.

General Urquhart, seeing no hope of rescuing

his battalion at the Arnhem bridge, decided to have the Polish paratroops dropped on the south bank of the river opposite his positions at Heveadorp, since the ferry there might yet be used to effect a crossing. Messages requesting this change, use of the Hartestein drop point for supply drops, and selection of LZ Z for further glider landings were sent and reached Eastcote. It seems doubtful whether the division actually held LZ Z at the end of the 19th, but the enemy in that sector had been inactive enough to make occupation of the zone seem feasible. The power of German attacks on the north and east made it certain the other zones could not be used.[51]

The Balance for D Plus 2

Whether fair weather on the 19th would have brought success to MARKET is far from certain. All one can say is that it might possibly have done so. The arrival of the 325th Glider Infantry Regiment at 1000 hours as planned might have enabled the 82d Division to take the Nijmegen bridge that day. Had the Polish brigade dropped at the south end of the Arnhem bridge they might have been able to secure it and join forces with Frost's battalion before the latter had been crippled by losses. Even so, they might not have been able to hold the north end of the bridge against German tanks and artillery for the time which it would probably have taken the British ground forces to get there from Nijmegen. What is certain is that after the 19th the Allied chances of getting a bridgehead across the Rhine were very, very small.

D Plus 3

The fortunes of the airborne divisions on the 20th varied greatly. The 101st continued to have a fairly easy time. Its only important action was the repulse of an attack by the 107th Panzer Brigade* from Nunen toward the Zon bridge at 0630. This came near enough to interrupt traffic before being driven back. A battalion of the 506th PIR riding British tanks, tried to intercept the Nazis' retreat, but they got away with little loss. In the Veghel area, the 1st Battalion of the 501st PIR occupied Dinter and pushed on to Heeswijk,

some five miles northeast of Veghel. The German losses of about 40 killed and 418 captured in this operation and the fact that almost all the captives were from improvised units composed of air force personnel led the 501st momentarily to the rash conclusion that it had destroyed the enemy forces in its vicinity.[52]

For the 82d Division 20 September was a strenuous day on which, while undertaking the capture of the Nijmegen bridge, it had also to beat back the first major counterattack against the Allied corridor. The attack was made by the 6th Parachute Division. After pushing the 508th PIR out of advanced positions near Wyler during the morning one regiment supported by armor attacked it at Beek about noon, while at Mook on the southern side of the perimeter another regiment with strong artillery support drove against the lines of the 505th PIR. In bitter fighting, which raged far into the night, the Germans penetrated as much as 1,000 yards in both sectors but failed in their purpose, which was to pinch off the whole east end of the area held by the 82d Division and seize the Groesbeek ridge. The situation that night was so critical that 185 glider pilots were hurried to the front near Mook to reinforce the 505th PIR.

While holding off a German division on its right, the 82d jabbed ferociously to its left. On the night of the 19th Browning, Gavin, and Lt. Gen. B. G. Horrocks of XXX Corps had worked out a plan to take the Nijmegen bridge from the rear by sending the 504th PIR across the Waal in assault boats about a mile downstream from the town. At the same time a new frontal attack by the 2d Battalion of the 505th and tanks of the Grenadier Guards would hit the south end of the bridge.

Early on the 20th British troops of 32 Brigade and the Coldstream Guards relieved units of the 504th which were holding the bridges at Grave and Heumen, and the regiment assembled in woods east of the Honinghutie bridge. It had seen little fighting since D-day and was in good shape. At 1400 the battalion of the 505th engaged the German defenders in the strong points south of the bridge, and at 1500, exactly on schedule, the first boats, carrying the 3d Battalion of the 504th, pushed out into the river. The 1st battalion was to follow with the 2d standing in reserve.

At that point the stream was about 1,000 feet

---

*This unit had been on its way from East Prussia to Aachen by rail on 17 September but had been diverted to Venlo for use against the 101st Division.

across, and the enemy held the opposite shore in strength. Artillery, mortars and British fighter-bombers had hammered their positions and smoke had been used to obscure the crossing. Nevertheless, their fire was effective. Many men were hit before the boats left the bank, and only 11 of the 26 boats in the first wave got back to make a second trip. Not much more than a battalion of paratroops got across, but their peerless fighting qualities enabled them to sweep through the German defenders. By 1600 they had a beachhead 1,000 yards deep. By 1700 they had taken the north end of the railroad bridge. By 1830 they had the highway bridge itself under fire. At that moment five British tanks broke through onto the south end of the bridge. Two were hit, but the others, raking the span from end to end, abruptly terminated the battle. The Nijmegen bridge had been taken and none too soon. Nazi tanks heading south had begun crossing the Arnhem bridge three hours earlier.[53]

At Arnhem, where the day was one of defeat in all sectors for the British airborne, the Germans had won access to the bridge during the afternoon after pointblank fire from tanks and artillery had reduced Frost's positions to a flaming shambles. The two battalions of 4 Parachute Brigade isolated near Wolfhezen had to run a terrible gauntlet to get back to the division, and only about 130 of their men reached the Hartestein perimeter. Into that perimeter the Germans, seeing they had their foe at bay, directed all the artillery and mortar fire they could muster until mortar shells were pouring down at a rate of 50 a minute. At intervals German infantry, supported by tanks, would close in for the kill. Their attacks did not break the lines of 1 Airborne, but bit by bit they bent them inward. The only good news for the division was a message received that night that the Nijmegen bridge had been captured intact.[54]

As revised on the evening of the 19th, plans for troop carrier operations on D plus 3 called for all missions to take the southern route and for four of them to arrive simultaneously at their zones at 1500 hours. Again the timing was dictated by predictions of extensive fog throughout the forenoon. The original southern route was modified to permit the missions to fly up the British salient and pass close to Eindhoven with missions to the Arnhem and Nijmegen sectors using Schijndel as their IP. At the last minute Eindhoven was made IP for all airborne missions that day, Schijndel being regarded as too hot a spot.

In an effort to make up for lost time 1,047 aircraft and 405 gliders were to be dispatched, with all the gliders and 317 resupply craft going down the center lane to DZ/LZ O for the 82d Division. A 51-plane paratroop and resupply mission for the 101st would follow the right lane to DZ W, and 114 planes of the postponed Polish paratroop mission to Arnhem would use the left lane. Overhead would fly 160 RAF planes with supplies for 1 Airborne Division.

Escort as far as Schijndel was to be furnished by Air Defense, Great Britain. The Eighth Air Force was to fly its usual perimeter patrols between Maastricht, Wesel, Apeldoorn and Zwolle, supply area cover beyond the IP, and attack flak positions between the IP and Nijmegen. The Ninth Air Force was to neutralize flak batteries between the IP and Arnhem, but it does not seem to have gotten a clear statement of its assignment until 1430 on the 20th.[55]

Once again unfavorable weather greviously curtailed the troop carrier operations. On the morning of the 20th the weathermen decided that the overcast would lift later than they had thought, so arrival time for the missions was set back from 1500 to 1700 hours. Then in view of the urgent need of the British at Arnhem it was decided to split the RAF resupply mission and send 67 of its planes to drop at 1345. Arrival time for the other missions was moved to 1720.

Although at take-off time ceilings over eastern England were between 1,000 and 2,000 feet and visibility was only one or two miles, the first wave of 67 Stirlings departed for Arnhem. Area cover was provided by 46 P-51's of Eighth Air Force, while ADGB furnished a total of 65 planes from 3 Spitfire and 3 Mustang squadrons for escort and anti-flak operations. Visibility in the Arnhem area was poor, making an already difficult operation even more difficult. One Spitfire and one Mustang were lost.

The later missions were given escort and cover to the IP by 17 squadrons of Spitfires, of which one squadron ran into bad weather over the Channel and turned back. The rest made 173 sorties but saw no action and had no losses. The Eighth Air Force had five P-51 groups on area cover beyond the IP and six flying the perimeter. These flew 430 uneventful sorties, losing only one plane and that by accident. Because the Ninth Air Force was unable to contribute its quota of fighters, the Eighth had to handle all flak suppression beyond the IP. It sent four groups of P-47's and the rocket squadron to do the job. They flew 179 sorties, but, hampered by bad visibility and by lack of briefing in the case of those substituting for Ninth Air Force units, they were able to claim only two gun positions destroyed and two others damaged. They had no losses and not very much damage.[56]

The second wave of British supply planes to Arnhem numbered 97 aircraft. Since available British sources lump this drop and the earlier one together, they must be treated as one. Out of 100 Stirlings and 64 Dakotas dispatched only 2 Stirlings aborted. Flak was reported as very heavy, especially in the target area. It brought down 9 planes and damaged 62. Of the remainder, 30 Stirlings were scheduled to make their drop on DZ Z, and their pilots reported doing so. That zone was entirely held by the Germans, and all that was dropped on or near it probably fell into their hands. At the Hartestein drop point a Eureka and visual aids had been set out despite the incessant bombardment, and 122 pilots reported dropping supplies there. Although only 13 of them picked up the Eureka and 32 sighted visual aids (Very lights being much the most effective, probably because they rose above tree-top level), results were decidedly better than on the day before.

Out of 386 tons of supplies dropped, about 300 tons was intended for the Hartestein drop point and 41 tons or about 14 percent of this was reported as collected. Considering that recovery was possible only within an area of about one square mile, and that in the turmoil of battle much that was recovered was never reported, the precision of the drop was greater than the statistics indicate. Assuredly, the rations which were recovered were worth their weight in gold to the airborne, most of whom had had almost nothing to eat for 24 hours or more.

The Polish paratroop mission was again postponed because of fog, which persisted until late in the day in the Grantham area. The planes were loaded and warmed up, ready to go if there was the slightest break in the overcast, but the opportunity never came. Finally, five minutes before take-off time the mission was delayed another 24 hours.[57]

The big glider mission marshalled for the 82d Division was also grounded by the fog in the Grantham area. Fortunately the resupply mission to that division had been delegated to the 53d Wing, and its bases in the south were comparatively clear. Beginning about 1430 the wing put 310 planes in the air with the 434th, 435th, and 438th Groups contributing one serial each and the 436th and 437th Groups two apiece.* They carried a cargo of 441 tons, of which the greater part was ammunition.

One plane had to turn back with pararack trouble. The others flew over the southern route, close to Eindhoven, past Best, then up the highway to DZ O. Fighter cover was good, and in spite of the lack of antiflak activity, ground fire was conspicuous by its absence. Some serials could report that not a shot was fired at them. Not a plane was lost and only six were damaged. This experience, so different from that of the British mission that day, can be attributed to the fact that the Americans were over friendly territory almost all the way to their drop zone.

The lead serial reached DZ O at 1648, and the others followed at extremely irregular intervals, some arriving almost simultaneously, others as much as 20 minutes apart, with the last one turning up at 1749. In addition, most of the serials were loose or broken, probably because of bad weather en route. However, since the pilots and navigators of the 53d Wing had become fairly familiar with the southern route as far as Best, and the way from there up the highroad to the Grave bridge was unmistakable, none of the stragglers lost their way.

As might be expected, the drop was disorganized and spasmodic with each serial or separate element using its own tactics. Some released their bundles as low as 400 feet, others as high as 1,800 feet. Although there was the usual difficulty getting bundles out the door in time, and 14 parapacks stuck, over 99 percent of the cargo was delivered. Its concentration, however, was most unsatisfactory. The bundles landed in a pattern about two miles wide and six miles long centered considerably northwest of the zone. The 82d Divi-

---

*Two P-51's and one P-47 got back but had to be salvaged.

*One additional aircraft towed a Waco, which had been on call, with a ton and half of supplies, making the total dispatched 311.

sion reported recovering 60 percent of these supplies with Dutch assistance, and according to some estimates 80 percent was ultimately recovered, but the hunt was long and difficult. It was sheer good luck that most of the supplies landed in friendly territory. The value of the mission was very great nevertheless. The supply dumps of the 82d were running low, and it had not yet received any supplies by road. Indeed, the first truck convoys for the division had just reached the Meuse-Escaut Canal; some of those first trucks had been loaded with shells of the wrong caliber; and others by some strange oversight were empty.[58]

The 101st Division, being in firm contact with the Allied ground forces, had much less need of supply by air. However, 35 aircraft of the 442d and 439th Groups took off from Greenham Common with 17 tons of supplies for that division. They flew unharmed over the new southern route to DZ W and dropped their loads at 1748. Again the drop was inaccurate, and only about 30 percent of the bundles were reported as recovered.*

A miniature paratroop mission was also flown to DZ W by 12 planes of the 442d Group carrying Battery B of the 377th Parachute Field Artillery. The planes had to fly to Ramsbury to take on their load, 125 artillerymen and six 75-mm. howitzers. Somewhat late in arriving, the planes were not loaded until about 1500, and in the turmoil the pilots were not informed of the changes made in the southern route. They therefore took the D-day route west of the salient and ran into intense light flak and small-arms fire which damaged five of the planes, one severely. The mission did not reach the zone until 1831 by which time the sun was setting and the haze was growing thick. In the face of these difficulties the pilots made an accurate and very compact drop from perfect formation. An hour after its jump the battery had assembled 119 men and almost all its equipment, including five howitzers, ready for action. The other howitzer was ready by morning.[59]

At the close of D plus 3, the Allied commanders believed success was still within their reach, provided that the ground forces could strike north from the captured Nijmegen bridge and reach the British airborne troops at Arnhem next day. So far as they knew the Arnhem bridge was still in British hands. Defense of the salient against German counterattacks was obviously a prerequisite to a sustained advance toward Arnhem, but no serious threat to the salient was in sight. Troop carrier delivery of the Polish brigade and the 325th Glider Infantry was expected to offset British losses at Arnhem and provide the weary 82d Division with fresh infantry for either defense or offense.

D Plus 4

On 21 September ground operations went uniformly well south of Nijmegen and very badly north of it. By evening British units of VIII Corps advancing east of Eindhoven had taken the town of Geldrop and pushed on to the Wilhelmina Canal, thus belatedly freeing most of the 506th PIR for use elsewhere. In the St. Oedenrode area German activity was limited to one small, sharp, probing attack in the afternoon. The 501st PIR continued to expand westward from Veghel, and its 1st Battalion entered Schijndel with only scanty resistance. The 82d Division had to cope with continued attacks in the Beek and Mook sectors, but these made little headway and by noon had subsided.

On the previous evening, as soon as the capture of the Nijmegen bridge seemed assured, Browning and Horrocks had agreed to rush forward a tank brigade of the Guards at dawn to take the Arnhem bridge before the paratroops at the north end were overwhelmed. The attack, too late to save the bridge, was foredoomed to failure. Between the Waal and the Rhine the road and railroad ran on embankments bordered by marshy, heavily ditched land impassable to armor. Near Ressen, scarcely three miles north of Nijmegen, the Guards were stopped by well-sited antitank guns which smashed every attempt to move up the causeway. Attempts to try other routes met a similar fate. The tanks could not leave the embankments to get at the guns. The radio of their air support party was out of order, so they could not call on air to remove the obstacles, although British fighter-bombers were overhead. As for infantry with which to storm the German positions, they had none.

The 82d Division, exhausted by four days of fighting, and still lacking the 325th Glider Regiment, had all it could do to hold its own lines. The nearest British infantry, the 43 Division, did

---

*This figure represents an average for several categories of supplies, a few items in one category being counted as equal to tons in another. It is further distorted by the fact that hardly any of the rations which were dropped were reported as collected.

reach Nijmegen that day, but too late to participate in the northward thrust. It had taken three days to move less than 60 miles by truck. One cause of this lagging was the excessive caution of British drivers, who caused interminable traffic jams by refusing to pull off the narrow road onto the grass for fear of mines. Sharing the widespread conviction that the war was practically won, they could not sense the need for haste—nor, it seems, could their commanders. Other and inevitable delays had been imposed by the Luftwaffe night attack on Eindhoven, which blocked the streets for several hours, by the German tank attacks at Zon on the 19th and 20th, and occasionally by shelling at other points.

Meanwhile, outside Arnhem 1 Airborne Division stubbornly defended its perimeter between Hartestein and Heveadorp. Tanks overran its lines at some points, and at others infantry charges had to be met with the bayonet. Food, water, and ammunition were increasingly scarce, and the ammunition dump, set afire by shelling, was saved only by the most strenuous efforts. Still the division fought on.* In the city the remnants of the paratroops at the bridge made one last attack at 0500 in the hope of winning defensible positions and after the failure of that effort scattered to escape as best they could.[60]

The plans laid on the 20th for airborne operations on D plus 4 called for 117 British resupply sorties to a drop point near Hartestein about 200 yards east of that used on D plus 3. To reduce the flak hazard the planes were to be sent in four waves, really separate missions, with the first arriving at 1315 and the last not until 1615. The American troop carriers were to send 806 planes. Of these, 114 carrying Polish paratroops would fly in the left lane. In the center lane would fly 419 planes with gliders for the 82d Division, 82 towing gliders to the 101st Division, and a parachute resupply mission of 191 planes for the 101st Divison. The glider and resupply serials for the 101st Division were sandwiched in between the first four and the last four serials going to the 82d, probably to give the latter division time to clear its landing zone before the second batch of gliders

arrived. At first the lead plane was scheduled to arrive at LZ O at 1515, but the time was later changed to 1615. All missions, both British and American, were to fly the southern route and use Eindhoven as their IP.

Protection of the first three waves of British resupply planes was to be handled by six Spitfire squadrons of ADGB. One P-51 group from Eighth Air Force would provide area cover. The last wave of British aircraft and the long American column were to be guarded from the Belgian coast to Eindhoven by 15 squadrons of fighters from ADGB; between Eindhoven and their destinations protection would be by 15 fighter groups of Eighth Air Force.

The weather was almost identical with that on the preceding day. Thick fog was general over England during the morning but had lifted in the south before the first resupply wave began taking off at 1100 hours. However, low stratus persisted between 600 and 1,200 feet, and haze restricted visibility to as little as a mile in some areas. Conditions were much better outside England, and over Holland there was only $4/10$ to $7/10$ cloud at about 3,000 feet.

All of the 64 Stirlings dispatched by 38 Group in the first three RAF resupply waves reached Holland, and 61 are believed to have accomplished their mission. However, the weather kept all but 19 of their Spitfire escorts from leaving England, and they did not catch up with the misison until after it had reached the Arnhem area. Although the 56th Fighter Group of Eighth Air Force sent 34 P-47's as area cover, they also arrived late.

This inadequate fighter protection gave the Luftwaffe its first good chance to attack an Allied airborne mission, and it made the most of the occasion. Thirteen Stirlings failed to return, and most of them had fallen prey to the Nazi fighters. One squadron of Focke-Wulf's swooping down out of the clouds shot down 7 out of a sequence of 10 Stirlings within a few moments. The Spitfires do not appear to have engaged the enemy. Some of their pilots sighted German planes but mistook them for P-51's on area cover until it was too late to catch them. Near Lochem about 1505 the 56th Group did intercept 22 or more German fighters (mostly Focke-Wulf's with square wingtips somewhat resembling P-51's) on their way back to Germany from the Arnhem area. The group claimed to have destroyed 15 of them at a

---

*It was heartened by remarkably accurate artillery support from the guns of the 64th Medium Regiment, Royal Artillery. This unit 10 miles away in a suburb of Nijmegen had established radio contact with an artillery control set of 1 Airborne and used it not only to lay down a screen of protecting fire but also to provide a much-needed link between Browning and the commander of First Airborne Division.

cost of two missing and one salvaged. Thus, although the raiders had done their mischief, they paid high for the opportunity.

Escort for the main troop carrier effort that day was also much curtailed because of weather. Five out of 15 British fighter squadrons failed to leave England because of the overcast and the 118 ADGB fighters which did make sorties sighted only a few German planes, which made off as fast as they could. As for Eighth Air Force, it cancelled the missions of 13 of its 15 supporting groups, leaving one group of P-47's and one of P-51's to perform area patrol.* The P-51's ran into low clouds over their base during assembly and were recalled. This left only 36 planes of the 353d Fighter Group under MEW guidance to protect the troop carriers beyond Eindhoven.

The 353d patrolled the Eindhoven-Arnhem area faithfully from 1610 to 1650. At 1630 about 5 miles southwest of Nijmegen it came upon approximately 30 German fighters, some attacking C-47's while others acted as top cover. After a sharp clash in which the enemy displayed considerable skill the 353d Group drove them off. One P-47 had been lost and six Nazi fighters were reported shot down.

The 53 Dakotas of 46 Group which flew the last wave of the British resupply lift suffered almost as severely as the Stirlings preceding them. They lost 10 aircraft to flak and fighters. In all, out of 117 planes dispatched by 38 Group and 46 Group on the 21st, 23 were missing and 38 were damaged, a disturbingly high proportion.[61]

Once again 1 Airborne Division had a Eureka beacon functioning, at least some of the time, on the roof of its headquarters, but only a couple of navigators are known to have signalled it, and neither got responses. The lack of use may be attributed to the pilots' growing familiarity with the route and to the relatively good flying conditions over Holland. Again panels, Very lights, smoke, and an Aldis lamp were used to mark the drop point, and once again the Very lights were by far the most effective with 30 pilots sighting them as compared to 14 seeing panels, and one seeing smoke.

Although 91 crews reported successful drops and some others probably reached the drop point, the intense fire of the German forces surrounding 1 Airborne effectively disrupted the drop. Out of 271 tons of supplies parachuted, only about 11 tons or 4 percent was officially recovered. It is, however, likely that the starving and desperate troops picked up some food and ammunition which they did not declare or turn in.[62]

The boldest venture of the day was made by the 52d Wing, flying the Polish paratroops. Layer upon layer of clouds from 150 feet above the ground to heights of 9,000 feet pressed down on its bases. Visibility in the Grantham area was close to zero. These conditions were outweighed by the desperate need of 1 Airborne Division for immediate assistance, which only the Poles could provide. As one flier wrote, "The weather was impossible. No one believed until actual take-off that the mission would actually run."[63] But run it did.

The mission was arranged in serials of 27, 27, 27 and 33 planes, the first two serials being flown from Spanhoe by the 315th Group and the other two from Saltby by the 314th Group. The lead serial of the 314th began taking off at 1310 with instructions to assemble at the 1,500-foot level, which was believed to be clear. The serial assembled successfully and started out, but soon found itself in a blind alley, completely blocked by cloud. The only thing to do was disperse and try to climb out of the overcast. In this attempt 25 pilots lost their bearings and returned to base. The other two after long circling above the clouds sighted a later serial and joined it.

By 1405 when the next take-offs were made, tactics had been revised. The planes took off in single file, spiralled up to 10,000 feet, and assembled there on top of the clouds. This worked. Only 6 of the 87 aircraft in the last three serials became detached from their mates and had to return to base. However, at 1545 while crossing the Channel a flight leader in the 314th Group repeatedly received a message on the flight control frequency which he was unable to decode. Deciding it must be a recall, he brought his 10 planes back to Saltby.

Over the first part of its route the mission remained close to 10,000 feet, but near the Belgian coast the clouds thinned and broke, enabling the formations to descend to the 1,500-foot level. One straggler, hit by flak near the mouth of the Scheldt, had to drop its troops near Ghent and limp home

---

*Another group, the 359th, was to escort the Polish paratroop mission. It managed to get 20 picked pilots into the air, but conditions were so bad that they had to be recalled. (Hist 359th Ftr Gp Sep 44)

on one engine. The rest swung up the west side of the salient to the drop zone, a large area of open, ditched land northeast of the town of Driel on the south side of the Rhine opposite Heveadorp. No pathfinders had been sent to mark the zone, but the leaders found their way to it by good visual navigation, checked occasionally by Gee, which was functioning well and without much jamming.

The mission had neither anti-flak patrols nor fighter cover to protect it over Holland. The one fighter group on patrol beyond Eindhoven left the area just before the troop carriers arrived. Fortunately no hostile fighters spotted the serials, but there was some ground fire along the way and much light flak and small arms fire near the zone. Several planes were hit and at least one very hard hit during the approach, but all managed to make their drops. The three serials passed over the zone at 1708, 1712 and 1715 at altitudes between 700 and 850 feet. The Poles, who were overloaded with equipment and were making their first drop into combat, were a little slow in getting out. This caused many of them to jump several hundred yards beyond the zone. It also prevented the troop carrier formations from turning homeward as soon as they had intended. As a result, several flights after turning south passed over Elst, a Nazi stronghold bristling with antiaircraft guns. So many were the guns and so incessant their firing that the little town reminded one flier of "a pinball machine gone mad." The formations exposed to this barrage disintegrated instantaneously. Most of the pilots dived onto the deck and flew across Holland at minimum altitude and maximum speed. Very few planes returned to base that night. However, next day it was found that only five, all from the 315th Group, had been destroyed. The other missing aircraft had had to land in Belgium or southern England because of damage, darkness, and thickening fog. Some pilots landing at Bradwell had to have the aid of a fog dispersal unit. German fire had damaged 33 planes, 14 of them so severely that they had to be turned over to service groups for repair. Casualties were 11 men dead or missing and at least 10 wounded or injured.

The mission had set out with 1,511 Polish troops and around 100 tons of supplies and equipment. Of this load 998 troops and 69 tons of supplies were dropped in the vicinity of the prescribed zone. About 750 paratroops, three-quarters of those who had been dropped, were able to assemble that evening. Statistically speaking, then, the mission was only about 50 percent effective. In terms of difficulties and hazards overcome it was a brilliant performance. The Polish brigade commander wrote "I cannot praise too much the perfect dropping, which in difficult weather conditions and in spite of strong enemy antiaircraft fire over the D.Z. was equal to the best dropping during any exercise this Bde. Gp. has ever had."[64]

If the British airborne had been able to hold their ground, the mission might have saved them, perhaps even enabled the Allies to retain a foothold across the Rhine. At 2100 that night Polish troops reached the bank of the river, only to find the ferry sunk and the opposite shore in enemy hands. The Germans had taken Heveadorp two hours before. At 2230 the brigade liaison officer, who had crossed the river further down with Dutch assistance, notified the Poles that 1 Airborne was preparing to counterattack Heveadorp and was collecting boats and rafts to bring them across. The attack came to nothing; the boats failed to appear; and the Polish brigade fell back on defensive positions at Driel.[65]

Needless to say, the appalling weather in the Grantham area made it impossible to dispatch the gliders marshalled for the 82d Division. Although conditions at the bases of the 53d Wing in southern England were better, they were bad enough to ground the gliders intended for the 101st Division also, particularly since the 101st was in no great need of reinforcement. The parachute resupply mission set up for the 101st was sent, but it was reduced to two small serials. Another serial with emergency supplies was arranged for the 82d Division.

The 438th and 437th Groups dispatched 15 planes apiece carrying about 16 tons of rations to LZ W for the 101st. During the early part of their flight they had to contend with haze, which limited visibility to as little as half a mile, and with $7/10$ cloud between the altitudes of 500 and about 6,000 feet. Three pilots straggled, lost their way, and returned because of the weather, and three others turned back because of mechanical difficulties. The remainder, 12 in each serial, flew unopposed over the southern route and dropped their loads over DZ W at 1631 and 1640. Although as a result of the weather the drop was not well concentrated, it was fairly accurate, and about 31 percent of the rations were recovered. All planes returned undamaged, having probably been over friendly territory all the way.

Another 33 planes with about 15 tons of rations were dispatched by the 438th Group to DZ O for the 82d Division. Two of them aborted on account of the weather. The rest reached the drop zone at 1700 after a difficult but uneventful trip and made a somewhat scattered drop from a height of 1,500 feet.[66]

D Plus 5

On 22 September the weather was very bad and, after waiting until midday, Airborne Army cancelled all its missions.* Fog had been widespread over England and the Low Countries throughout the morning and was replaced in the afternoon by stratus with ceilings about 1,000 feet and in places as low as 300 feet. In the course of the afternoon rain spreading over England from the west lowered the ceiling to between 500 and 1,000 feet and reduced visibility to between 1,000 and 2,000 yards. Although 38 Group stated in its report that resupply missions could have been flown, the advancing disturbance could have made the return to base very hazardous, and this risk may have been the decisive consideration. The Eighth Air Force did dispatch two groups of P-47's to patrol the Arnhem area. They flew 77 uneventful sorties and returned safely.[67]

The ground fighting on 22 September was made memorable by a German offensive which cut the Allied corridor near Veghel, and by the efforts of British infantry to break through to the Rhine. While British forces had moved up to buttress both flanks of the corridor as far as the Wilhelmina Canal, the road from there to Grave was defended only by the 101st Division and by the British convoys moving along the highway. Over most of that stretch no man's land began at the edge of the road; off it in fields and farmyards and on obscure back roads the enemy was concentrating his forces for a typical German pincer attack to snap the stem of the Allied salient. Veghel was the natural objective for such an attack, since destruction of the bridges there would block traffic for days no matter how soon the Allies retook the town. Furthermore, Veghel was lightly held. Its garrison, the 501st Parachute Regiment had detached its 1st and 3d Battalions to carry on a little offensive of their own five miles away at Schijndel, leaving only Headquarters and the 2d Battalion to hold Veghel. The nearest source of reinforcements was the 502d PIR at St. Oedenrode, and since it was needed to garrison that sector any substantial help would have to come from the Zon area seven or eight miles away. The Germans could fairly hope that by the time a relief column reached Veghel they would have the town.

On the night of the 21st and early on the 22d General Taylor, sensing the threat to his northern flank, gave orders for the 327th Glider Infantry Regiment to move to Veghel, and for the 506th PIR, minus the 1st Battalion, to occupy Uden four miles north of Veghel. About 1000 the regimental headquarters of the 506th rolled through Veghel, followed a little later by 175 men of the 2d Battalion, and drove peacefully on to Uden. The rest of the 506th was still south of St. Oedenrode, and the 327th, which had not received its orders until 0930, was just starting. Only its 3d Battalion was to go by truck. The others were to march up back roads, so as not to block traffic on the highway.

About 1100 the Nazis attacked Veghel in strength from the east, using the 107th Panzer Brigade and the 280th Assault Gun Brigade. This formidable force very nearly overwhelmed the single battalion opposing it, but the arrival at 1215 of part of the 2d Battalion of the 506th somewhat stabilized the situation. By frantic efforts the 3d Battalion of the 327th, the 3d Battalion of the 506th, and a battery of antitank guns were rushed in during the next couple of hours, and none too soon. At 1400 the Germans attacked again on the northeast, and at the same time the other arm of their pincer, several battalions of infantry supported by tanks and artillery, pressed from the west toward the canal bridges. Company D of the 506th, which had just ridden into town, was hastily dispatched to stop them and managed to do so with the support of a British tank squadron. Considerable British armor and artillery enroute to Nijmegen had been held up in Veghel by the German offensive and played an important part that day in saving the town.

Unable to break through into Veghel, the Ger-

---
*There are some references to missions being flown on the 22d, but the weight of the evidence is overwhelmingly against them.

mans used their superior numbers to work their way around the defenders and cut the highway both north and south of the town. Then they renewed their offensive, and very nearly reached one of the railroad bridges before being stopped. The pressure on the south was relieved about 1600 by the arrival of the main body of the 327th Glider Infantry and the 321st Glider Field Artillery Battalion. They fought their way into the town and took over the defense of its southwest side. Further insurance was provided by the return of the 3d Battalion of the 501st, which had been recalled from Schijndel at noon and marched into Eerde about 1630 after making a wide circle to the south. The crisis was over, but for several hours the enemy had been dangerously close to success, and the 101st Division had had to concentrate over half its strength to beat them off. Also the road was still blocked north of Veghel, and the detachment of the 506th in Uden was isolated under heavy pressure.[68]

While the tide of battle surged around Veghel the 82d Division had a comparatively quiet day. It pushed along the south side of the Waal to Pals, about three miles east of Nijmegen to provide a buffer of friendly territory around the bridge. The Germans offered stiff resistance to patrols of the 508th PIR and made several attacks on a hill which it held south of Beek. Elsewhere the divisional perimeter was quiet.[69]

After tanks had failed to break through to the Rhine, the task of doing so had been turned over to the British infantry of 43 Division. This division was to send one brigade at dawn up the Arnhem highway through Elst and a second on a road further west through Oosterhout. The assault did not get started until 0830, and Elst, held by two SS battalions with about 20 tanks and numerous guns, seemed so formidable that the British decided to concentrate on the other route. That should have been easier, as Oosterhout was very weakly held, but 43 Division treated it as though it contained an army. The attack was made with such careful deliberation that not one of the division was killed, but it took all day to capture the village. Meanwhile 1 Airborne, which had radioed on the evening before that relief within 24 hours was vital, hung on as best it could.

Finally the way was clear, and a supply column with several DUKW's set out northward at 1800. An hour later it reached the Polish positions at Driel. However, darkness had fallen, and no place could be found on the steep, muddy banks of the river from which to launch the DUKW's. All that could be done was to ferry about 50 Polish paratroops and small amounts of food and ammunition across the Rhine on improvised rafts.[70]

D Plus 6

On 23 September the tense ground situation between Veghel and Grave resolved itself in the Allies favor. The German offensive against Veghel had lost its impetus and dwindled into two or three small thrusts which were easily parried. At 1500 the 101st Division counterattacked, using the 506th PIR. This regiment advanced northward, met only feeble resistance, and was halfway to Uden when about 1800, it made contact with 32 Guards Brigade, which had slashed down the highway from Grave. It had found the paratroops in Uden still holding their own. As soon as the highway was open the trucks began to roll, but for more than 24 hours traffic had been at a standstill.

The worst effect of the German roadblock was that it delayed the arrival of assault boats. The only ones available were a handful at Nijmegen which had come through the Waal crossing of the 504th PIR in usable condition. Too few for an assault, they were used on the night of the 23d to ferry essential supplies and 250 Polish paratroops across the river. By that time the Germans had almost complete control of the north bank, and only about 150 of the Poles got through to 1 Airborne. During the day sustained attacks by a brigade of 43 Division took most of Elst, but the Nazis still clung to enough of it to bar the highway. This was an inconvenience, since the Oosterhout road was a bad one. However, even had Elst been taken, the Rhine could not be crossed without boats.[71]

The renewed activity of the Allied air forces was a bright feature of D plus 6. Weather at last was favorable. In England the day was fair, the clouds high and broken, and only a few patches of light rain marred the prospect. Fog and overcast lingered over the Low Countries during the morning but were swept away early in the afternoon by a cold front, which left behind it clearing skies and brisk westerly winds.

Plans called for all missions to the airborne to fly the revised southern route, via Bourg Leopold and Eindhoven. The postponed glider missions to the American airborne were to fly the center lane to LZ's O and W with the lead glider reaching LZ O at 1400. Again the two glider serials for the 101st Division were to go from England to Eindhoven in the middle of the glider column slated for the 82d Division. One plane had been added, and 14 of the 442d Group withdrawn from the 82d Division's mission, giving it a total of 406. The gliders going to the 101st had been increased from 82 to 84, and the 442d Group, formerly scheduled to tow a serial, had been replaced by the 434th, which was more experienced in glider work.

The Polish troops who had been returned to base on D plus 4 were to be dropped on DZ O at 1447 by a 42-plane serial, flying the left lane. The ground situation no longer required a drop at Driel, and a drop at DZ O was safer for the troop carriers. A resupply drop to 1 Airborne would be made at 1400 by 123 aircraft of 38 and 46 Groups, flying at 2,500 feet. After reconnaissance by weather planes on the morning of the 23d, all arrival times were postponed two hours to give the weather on the continent more time to clear after the cold front passed.

From England to Eindhoven and back the troop carrier columns were to be given cover by 14 Spitfire squadrons of ADGB, and four more squadrons would fly area patrol between Bourg Leopold and Eindhoven. Between Eindhoven and Volkel (west of Uden) three Mustang squadrons of ADGB would be on area patrol. Eighth Air Force was to provide 13 groups and one squadron of fighters. Three P-51 Groups were to fly area patrol and escort between Bourg Leopold and Arnhem at heights of 2,500 to 5,000 feet. One group of P-51's and one of P-47's would fly high cover in those areas. A perimeter connecting Maastricht, Cleve, and Zwolle was to be guarded by 5 groups of P-51's and one of P-38's, under MEW direction. Two groups of P-47's and the rocket squadron were to neutralize flak between Nijmegen and Arnhem. All Eighth Air Force units were to be in position by 1530.

The RAF fighters flew 193 sorties without meeting air opposition but lost one or two planes. The Eighth Air Force units made 580 sorties and suffered 16 losses, largely from ground fire. The pilots reported sighting at least 185 enemy fighters, generally in groups of about 35, and claimed to have shot down 27 at a cost of 6 of their own. Out on the perimeter in the Geldern-Wesel area the 339th Fighter Group had three clashes with Nazi fighter formations and the pilots claimed to have destroyed six enemy planes while losing three. These interceptions occurred when the troop carriers were over Holland and may have been important in protecting them from Nazi forays. In another big battle the 353d Group, flying high cover southeast of Arnhem, met some 50 enemy fighters. Its pilots reported shooting down 19 aircraft and losing three. This fight came at 1745, by which time the last troop carriers had passed Eindhoven on their way home.

Anti-flak sorties were made by 88 aircraft, which fired 23 rockets, dropped 85 bombs, mainly 260-pound fragmentation bombs, and did much strafing. Although still restricted by the rule that they should not attack until fired upon, the flak-busters had a good day. They reported 18 gun positions destroyed and 17 damaged. One of the planes was shot down and 22 damaged. The 78th Fighter Group, which neutralized many German positions in the drop area of the British resupply mission, probably saved that mission from disastrous losses.[72]

The great array of gliders which had stood marshalled on the airfields of the 50th and 52d Wings in the eastern midlands since 19 September finally began taking off at 1210 on the 23d. In the 406 Wacos were 3,385 troops, 104 jeeps, 59 loaded trailers and 25 pieces of artillery.* The units involved were the 325th Glider Infantry, four batteries of the 80th Airborne Antiaircraft Battalion, two companies of engineers, the divisional reconnaissance platoon, and an MP platoon.[73]

As usual when large numbers of gliders were involved, assembly was a tedious business taking from 40 to 60 minutes. However, it was well handled, and only three gliders aborted, one breaking loose over England and two turning back with mechanical difficulties. Inevitably there was a certain amount of jostling and trouble with prop wash. The tugs and gliders in the rear were particularly affected. As formations tightened or loosened they had to vary their speed, from 110 to as much as

---

*The figures used are those given by the airborne, but they correspond quite closely to the totals of 3,378 men, 100 jeeps, 38 pieces of artillery and 253 tons of supplies and equipment (presumably including the artillery and jeeps) reported by the troop carriers.

160 miles an hour. To avoid prop wash rear elements flew above those preceding, and some got well over 2,000 feet up. It is not surprising that a few of them were jolted by wash from the RAF Stirlings at 2,500 feet. The intercom sets worked better than in the past, but over 20 percent of them failed or worked poorly. Although for most of the way visibility was over five miles and cloud bases over 2,500 feet, the column did pass through slight rain at some points. When all these difficulties have been noted, the fact remains that for most pilots the trip across the Channel and over Belgium went quite smoothly. Only one glider, which ditched successfully, went down in the Channel; and none did so in Belgium.

The mission apparently turned north at Gheel rather than Bourg Leopold, flew outside of the Allied salient, and as a result was subjected to some small-arms fire in an area west of Eindhoven. Five gliders were released in that area, one because of flak damage, one because it was out of control, the others for unspecified reasons. Real trouble came when the column reached the Veghel area. The Germans, beaten back from the highway, were still massed in strength along its flanks. The earlier serials flew over them for a distance of about five miles, and while doing so received a barrage of accurate and intense light flak and automatic weapons fire. Nine planes were shot down on the mission and 96 were damaged, about 20 percent of the damage being serious enough to require repair by service groups. Casualties aboard the planes were 13 dead or missing and about 17 wounded or injured. Nearly all of this toll was inflicted in the general vicinity of Veghel and Uden.

The first serial was especially hard hit, three of its planes going down and several gliders being shot loose or forced to release because of damage. The two lead gliders of the 29th Squadron had to cut loose, and this set off a succession of premature releases from its half of the formation. In some instances the tug flashed the green light; in some the glider pilot released of his own accord or at the request of the airborne. The upshot was that 21 gliders in that serial came down prematurely between Veghel and Grave. None were demolished and only a couple made rough landings. Except for three or four which landed on an airstrip near Volkel, they were strung out close to the highway in friendly territory or so near it that with Dutch assistance and some rescue work by Allied troops it proved possible to bring in all occupants and cargoes.

A similar situation occurred in the fourth serial when a squadron leader, whose plane was about to crash, released his glider near Veghel. His men faithfully followed his example with the result that 18 gliders in that formation came down within about six miles of Veghel. Six of these landed in hostile territory, and all aboard were lost.

The last three serials while still over Belgium received radio reports from returning formations on the danger spots ahead and adjusted their course accordingly with such beneficial results that they had only one plane shot down and two gliders released in the Veghel sector.

Some 348 gliders were brought as far as Grave. The Eureka on the zone was not functioning, probably because the batteries were worn out, but none of the pilots appear to have had trouble finding their way there. In the northwest part of the LZ near Overasselt, the pathfinders had laid out panels and sent up smoke signals which were sighted by most of the formations.

The first serial reached LZ O at 1603 and during the next seven minutes released its gliders there at altitudes of 900 to 2,500 feet. The second serial had already reached the zone and made its release between 1602 and 1607 from heights of 600 to 1300 feet. This overlapping would probably have caused confusion had not half the first serial released before reaching the zone and the remainder been much dispersed. Both timing and formation left something to be desired. Two more serials arrived out of sequence, and only the last two, which arrived at 1710 and 1717, were exactly on schedule. However, there seems to have been no serious interference between serials, and approximately three-quarters of the gliders descended in formation after release somewhere between 800 and 1,200 feet, and took a 90° or 180° turn to the left (depending on their angle of approach) so as to land into the wind. A minority of stragglers and non-conformists followed widely divergent patterns, making turns of 360° or more after high releases, turning right when the rest went left, or pulling away from their mates to avoid crowded fields. Nevertheless, the results compared very favorably with those in previous glider operations.

The main focus of the landings was in an oval a mile across and 1½ miles long lying northwest of Overasselt, and centered on the pathfinders. Within that area were some 210 gliders. A looser concentration of about 100 gliders gathered in an open area of similar size and shape along the riverbank opposite Grave. Of the rest, all but one were on or close to the zone and all but about six were within half a mile of one of the mian concentrations.

Although LZ O had the great advantage of being out of range of the enemy, landing on it was no easy matter. The zone had originally been regarded as unsuitable for gliders because so much of it consisted of very small or narrow fields bordered by fences, hedges and drainage ditches. Large numbers of livestock grazing in the fields created an additional hazard. Most of the glider pilots came in at speeds of 55 to 75 miles per hour, frequently using arrestor chutes to great advantage. They had to do a great deal of dodging and hedgehopping, but found that they could smash through the hedges and light fences almost unscathed. Only about eight of the gliders landing on the zone were destroyed, almost all by running into ditches. At least 102 received damage. Noses and wings were battered, wheels and undercarriages smashed, but the contents of the gliders came through almost intact. Out of 24 guns, 82 jeeps and 47 trailers put down on the LZ, only one jeep was unusable. Of over 2,900 troops landed there all but 10 were fit for duty.

The last gliders carrying the 325th Glider Regiment had landed at 1703. By 1800 the Regiment was assembled at 75 percent of strength and was moved immediately to the Groesbeek area to take up positions on the east flank of the 82d Division. Most of the missing personnel reported in during the next two days. It was a most welcome reinforcement, but the time when it could have any significant effect on the outcome of MARKET was already past.[74]

For much of the way the little 53d Wing glider mission to LZ W was flown in conjunction with that just described. Its 84 tug-glider combinations took off from the bases of the 436th and 438th Groups with 395 troops and 100 tons of supplies and equipment, including 15 guns, 13 trailers, and 23 jeeps. Four gliders aborted over England, one because a nervous soldier pulled the release handle. The rest flew to Bradwell Bay and there fell into position between the 5th and 6th serials of the mission to the 82d Division. One more glider was released over Belgium. The other 79 went almost unopposed to LZ W and were released there from a height of about 600 feet at 1632 and 1636 with excellent results. On the zone, fit for action, landed 338 troops, 14 guns, 12 trailers and 22 jeeps. Two gliders had crash-landed killing three soldiers and injuring nine.[75]

The repeat mission bringing in the Polish paratroops consisted of 41 planes of the 315th Group loaded with 560 troops and 28 tons of supplies and equipment. It arrived over LZ O at 1643 without loss, damage, or casualties after a milk run which stands in singular contrast to the experience of the glider serials which had flown to that zone just ahead of it. Whether this was because it flew the left hand lane 1½ miles west of the gliders or for some other reason is nowhere explained.

A green light, flashed too early, made 10 troops jump about five miles short of the zone, and two others were brought back. The remaining troops and all but 12 out of 219 parapacks dropped on or close to the zone. Most were well concentrated near the pathfinders northwest of Overasselt. About 18 pilots, impressed by the concentration of gliders, troops, and vehicles near the riverbank opposite Grave, dropped their loads there. The troops were quickly assembled, but spent the night in the Groesbeek area as reserves for the 82d Division.[76]

The 73 Stirlings and 50 Dakotas dispatched by the RAF to bring supplies to 1 Airborne had a most difficult mission. The area still held by British troops had shrunk to 1,000 yards in diameter and was ringed with enemy guns. Two planes aborted. Six were shot down, all apparently in or near the drop area, and 63 were damaged. Had not the 78th Fighter Group been on hand to keep down the fire the toll would have been much larger.

The drop point was even harder to locate than before. The Eureka was not working because the batteries were dead, and the Germans had captured the pathfinders' reserve stock. Parties attempting to use visual signals were harrassed by snipers, by mortars, and twice by strafing. Moreover; the Germans seem to have used bogus signals to mislead the pilots. Very lights were seen by 22 crews and other signals by 13, but only a handful dropped their loads within the British lines. Even well-placed bundles were hard to retrieve, since much of the terrain still held by the British was under observed fire, and hardly any vehicles were left for supply details to use. No doubt some were recovered by individuals and small units and used on the spot without any accounting. Even if we assume arbitrarily that four times as much was picked up as was ever reported, the amount reaching the troops was still less than 10 percent of what was sent. There was no alternative. Landing gliders in such a situation was out of the question.[77]

D Plus 7

Bad weather on 24 September once again halted all troop carrier missions from England. In the morning, rain lashed England and the Continent, overcast hung unbroken at 300 to 800 feet, and winds of 25 to 30 miles per hour swept across the airfields. Conditions improved somewhat over southern England in the afternoon, but not enough to warrant a mission.

However, as a result of the losses suffered on D plus 4, the commander of 46 Group had moved one of his squadrons to Brussels on the 23d, so that it could be escorted throughout its missions by fighters of 83 Group. This squadron dispatched 21 Dakotas escorted by 36 Spitfires on a supply mission to the Hartestein pocket. The weather was so unfavorable that only four got there and only two of them dropped more or less at random without sighting any signals. They must have been over enemy territory for 1 Airborne was unaware that any drop had been made. The other 17 planes gave up at Nijmegen, 15 of them dropping their supplies to the 82d Division, and 2 airlanding them at a newly discovered airstrip near Grave. All returned safely, but four had been damaged by flak.[78]

About 0900 on the 24th the Nazis attacked at Eerde in a new attempt to cut the highway. The attack was repelled, although it took all three battalions of the 501st PIR to handle it. The front appeared to have been stabilized, and truck convoys were pouring up the highway. Encouraged by this turn of events, Dempsey and Horrocks, meeting early in the afternoon at St. Oedenrode, decided to make one more bid for victory. That night the balance of the Polish Brigade and two companies of 43 Division would cross the Rhine in assault boats to buttress the lines of 1 Airborne.

On the next night there would be a crossing in strength to make the foothold secure. There was no expectation of taking the Arnhem bridge, which by that time was strongly held.

Hardly had the plan been made when it was upset. At 0430 the Germans slashed across the highway three miles south of Veghel. They brought up guns and tanks, and dug in for a long stay. It took 40 hours to pry them off the road, and during that time MARKET strangled to death. The northward movement of all supplies and reinforcements was halted, but by far the most serious effect was the delay in the arrival of assault boats, without which even a medium-sized landing was impossible.

On the night of the 24th all 43 Division had for its crossing were four boats already on hand and five which got through before the road was cut and reached the river shortly before midnight. With these about 250 men of the 4th Dorset Regiment made a brave attempt to reach 1 Airborne. The boats scattered in the darkness; most of them landed at points held by the Germans; and almost all the little force was mopped up before it could organize.[79]

D Plus 8

The operations of the troop carrier units on 25 September were restricted, mainly it seems because of unfavorable weather. Ceilings over the Channel and the Low Countries were between 1,000 and 1,500 feet and, although England had satisfactory weather in the morning, rain and low clouds with bases between 600 and 1,000 feet spread over the island from the west during the afternoon.

One composite resupply serial of 34 aircraft of the 434th, 435th and 436th Groups was loaded at Ramsbury with 49 tons of howitzer ammunition for the 101st Division. It flew unopposed over the southern route to Hechtel and from there up the highway to DZ W, the only damage being caused by a rough landing on the return. The formation shifted at the IP from the V of V's to a column of three-plane V's, and at 1641 made a very good drop. Each plane had carried 6 parapacks and three door bundles. Practically all of the former landed in a small area and were recovered. None of the latter were found, probably because it took too long to shove them out.[80]

The squadron of 46 Group based at Brussels

sent seven Dakotas with medical supplies and food over the southern route to a drop point at Heveadorp. One was shot down and three damaged by flak. At least six planes dropped their loads, and four did so within sight of 1 Airborne, but the troops were so pinned down that they could not recover a single bundle.

The resupply missions were protected by 60 Spitfires and 36 Mustangs of ADGB. These encountered about 50 enemy fighters near Arnhem and about 40 near Hengelo and claimed four destroyed at a cost of two Mustangs. Antiaircraft fire against the British missions was probably reduced by 7 Typhoons, 54 Mitchells, and 24 Bostons of 2 TAF which were operating against enemy guns in the Arnhem area, primarily to ease the pressure on the airborne.[81]

The blocked highway, the lack of assault boats, and reports that the Germans were moving up panzer units to cut off 1 Airborne from the Rhine forced the Allied generals to give up hope of holding a bridgehead at Arnhem. On the morning of the 25th Montgomery ordered that his airborne troops be withdrawn south of the river, and at 0605 a messenger informed Urquhart of the decision. The latter replied that the move would have to be made that night. His men could endure no more.

Indeed they could not. During the day the Germans infiltrated the Hartestein perimeter in many places, and in one instance so strongly that the airborne had to call down artillery fire from Nijmegen on the center of their own positions. The beleaguered force survived only because the enemy, confident of victory and awed by the ferocity of the airborne troops, hesitated to close with them. Instead the Nazis wasted time calling on a loud speaker for them to surrender.

The weather, which had played so important a part in the defeat of the British airborne, saved them in the end from annihilation. On the night of the 25th in rain and howling wind the division stealthily made its way to the river, leaving its wounded to man the defenses. The Germans, apparently unaware of what was going on, made no effort to intervene. Before morning 1,741 men of 1 Airborne, 422 glider pilots, 160 Polish troops and 75 of the Dorsets had swum or been ferried across the Rhine. About 110 hid or escaped and crossed the river later, thanks to heroic efforts by the Dutch. The rest had to be written off as lost.

An estimated 1,130 British and Polish troops perished in the battle of Arnhem and some 6,200 were taken prisoner. Through 25 September the 101st Division had 315 dead, 547 missing and 1,248 wounded; the 82d Division had 215 dead, 427 missing and 790 wounded in that period.[82]

Thus ended in failure the greatest airborne venture of the war. Although General Montgomery asserted that it had been 90 percent successful, his statement was merely a consoling figure of speech. All objectives save Arnhem had been won, but without Arnhem the rest were as nothing. In return for so much courage and sacrifice, the Allies had won a 50-mile salient — leading nowhere.

D Plus 9 and After

Allied ground operations after the evacuation of 1 Airborne may be disregarded, since the main objective of MARKET-GARDEN had been abandoned, and the American airborne were fighting as ground troops under Second Army control. It should be noted, however, that the fate of the salient they had created was still in doubt. The Germans subsequently made strenuous efforts to cut it by seizing or destroying the Nijmegen bridges. Savage attacks on a divisional scale were made out of the Reichswald Forest against the 82d Division on 28, 29, and 30 September and southward from Arnhem on 1 October. Meanwhile the Luftwaffe made repeated attempts to bomb the bridges. These failed, but on the night of 28 September swimmers with demolition charges did manage to destroy the railway bridge and put the highway bridge out of commission for 24 hours. Coming when it did this had little effect, but it serves as a reminder that the Allies had on the whole been lucky in securing bridges. If the Grave or Nijmegen bridges had been destroyed early in the operation, MARKET would have fared much worse than it did.

It was by no means certain on the morning of the 26th that another troop carrier effort might not yet be called for. The project in view was an airlanding of 52 Division near Grave. During the first six days of MARKET, plans to fly in that unit had been in abeyance for lack of a suitable field. On the 20th the divisional commander had proposed to Browning that one of his brigades be brought in by glider. Browning graciously declined the offer, partly because of ignorance as to the plight of I Airborne Division, but also no doubt because such an operation would have been risky and difficult to improvise. The tragedy was that a field existed on which infantry could have been landed with ease and safety, but in spite of extensive aerial reconnaissance nobody in authority knew of it.

Not until 21 September* did Airborne Corps discover a good grass fighter strip at Oud Keent only 2¼ miles west of Grave. Permission to use the strip was requested that night through Second Army but was not granted until the morning of the 23d. Browning's headquarters then called on FAAA for a mission to fly in an airfield control unit, the British air supply organization known as AFDAG (Airborne Forward Delivery Airfield Group) and an antiaircraft battery as soon as possible, obviously in preparation for bigger landings to follow. Meanwhile fences and other obstacles had been removed and a strip 100 yards wide and 1,400 yards long had been marked out.

Bad weather made it impossible to send the mission on the 24th and unsafe to do so on the 25th, but on the latter day a pathfinder team, equipped to operate a rudimentary control tower was flown in to the airstrip, and plans were laid to deliver the requested units and the 878th Engineer Battalion at noon on the 26th.

The heavy equipment of the engineers and the Bofors guns of the artillerymen were to go in 12 Horsas and 10 Hamilcars, towed by Stirlings of 38 Group. Most of the engineers and the control unit would be flown from Boreham and Chipping Ongar by four glider serials of the 61st and 437th Groups towing a total of 157 Wacos. The gliders would land in fields east of the airstrip. The antiaircraft battery and AFDAG were to be landed on the Grave strip by one 30-plane serial, followed by five 36-plane serials, all contributed by units of the 52d Wing.

Weather over England was passable all day, but in the morning predictions of rain and low ceilings over Holland led Brereton to order about 0800 that the operation be postponed 24 hours. By mid-morning prospects of improvement led him to decide that the airlanding serials could go

in that day, two hours later than previously planned. The gliders would have to wait.[83]

At 1115 the first plane was in the air, but the last did not set out until after 1400. It was necessary to have an average interval of at least half an hour between serials, because the dispersal area at the strip would hold only 70 aircraft, and once that number was down no more could be accommodated until some had unloaded and departed.

The trip along the southern route to Hechtel and up the highway was an easy one through clear air with broken clouds well overhead. There was occasional slight ground fire when planes flew too near the edge of the salient, but only one plane was damaged.

Close cover from England to the landing strip and back was furnished by 20 Spitfire squadrons and three Mustang squadrons of ADGB, which flew a total of 271 sorties without seeing action. The Eighth Air Force sent eight fighter groups, one at the head of the troop carrier column, 3 in relays over the landing area, 2 on area patrol in the Arnhem area, one on area patrol around Nijmegen, and one to the east to watch a perimeter from Maastricht through Venlo to Arnhem. Most of their 326 sorties were uneventful, but at 1600 when the Grave strip was already crammed with troop carrier craft and more serials were approaching it, the 479th Fighter Group flying area patrol near Haltern, about 50 miles east of Nijmegen, intercepted over 40 German fighters. The pilots claimed to have destroyed 28 enemy planes while losing only one, and that probably to flak. Another group, vectored to the scene before the fight ended, claimed to have shot down four more. No raiders got through to strike at the troop carriers.

Of 209 aircraft taking off on the mission to Grave, all reached the zone and landed on it safely between 1350 and 1740. The improvised control tower worked well, and teams of British and American glider pilots did yeoman service in the unloading of the 882 troops and 379 tons of cargo aboard the planes.* This was the closest the Allies came in World War II to airlanding in an airhead. The operation was successful, but it should be noted that the approach was over

---

*Air Commodore Darvall stated that he and the Corps Engineer "found" the strip on the 23d, but it is probable that they were sent to examine its usefulness after others had found it. Darvall, being on a hasty visit to the Nijmegen area, could easily have been unaware of a previous reconnaissance.

*Figures for individual serials as given in the report of the 52d Wing give a total of 873 troops and 410 tons of supplies. That report and IX TCC statistics state that the supplies included 134 jeeps, 73 trailers, and 31 motorcycles.

friendly territory and that the nearest enemy troops were several miles away.

Airborne Army's plans for use of the Grave strip were crushed on the 27th. At 0450 in the morning Second Army informed them that Luftwaffe strength in the area had been built up to such a point that no more troop carrier missions to the strip could be allowed, and that evening, orders came that the field was to be taken over by 83 Group as an advance fighter base. The group moved in next day. These actions were taken without consulting Airborne Corps or determining whether an additional strip might not be laid out, as in fact it quite easily could have been.[84] If fear of the Luftwaffe dictated the closing of Grave to IX TCC, the Luftwaffe was being much overrated. From the logistical point of view it was absurd to have supplies flown in to Brussels, reloaded onto trucks and carried at a snail's pace over 100 miles of congested roads to Nijmegen when they could just as well have been landed directly at Grave.

The effect was that the glider mission set up to carry the 878th Engineers was cancelled, the fly-in of 52 Division was never made, and AFDAG was dispersed to do odd jobs for Second Army. Instead of having up to 800 tons of supplies a day airlanded at Grave the troops in the salient were short of supplies for many weeks. Instead of being relieved, as they might have been, by 52 Division and prepared for future missions, the 82d and 101st Divisions were held in the line until late November on the pretext that they could not be spared. As for IX TCC, it was removed from airborne missions and training and turned for the time being into an aerial trucking service for the ground forces. As an ironic anticlimax it was allowed to send two insignificant supply missions to Grave on the 29th and 30th. In the first, five planes landed with 20 troops and 16 tons of supplies. In the second, three soldiers and 56 tons of supplies were airlanded from 22 planes.

Under pressure from General Arnold, who had been much dissatisfied with glider recovery from Normandy, Brereton made a strenuous effort to retrieve as many as possible of the gliders used in MARKET. He secured the services of Company A of the 876th Aviation Engineer Battalion to construct temporary strips near Zon (on LZ W) and near Grave from which gliders could be towed after being made flyable. Those flyable gliders were to be taken to Denain/Prouvy near Valenciennes on the northern border of France for final repairs which would restore them to operational status. After that they were to be redistributed to the troop carrier units.

Between 25 September and 1 October three repair teams of about 150 men apiece were flown to the Continent to repair the gliders at Zon. On 20 October one of these teams and two others arrived at Grave to begin repairing the gliders in that area. That same day the 61st Group began flying repaired gliders from Zon to Denain/Prouvy where another team, which had moved there on the 19th, set to work to make the patched-up Wacos operational.

Logistical support of the repair teams, especially those at Zon and Grave, involved great difficulties. Practically all supplies and equipment for the repairmen had to be flown from England. At first cargoes had to be landed at Brussels and delivered by truck over roads heavily congested with traffic for the front. Later landings were made at Eindhoven. By 8 October 202 flights had already been made to the Continent on behalf of the troop carrier repair effort, and hundreds more flights were made after that.*

Also, the task of glider repair was greatly impeded by enemy action, vandalism and bad weather. The British gliders beyond the Rhine were of course in German hands. The landing zones of the 82d and 101st Division were for several weeks within two or three miles of the front. During these early operations the glider mechanics came under small arms fire and even took some prisoners. The Grave area was still under artillery fire in December.

While the battle was raging around the drop zones the gliders could not be protected and until late October the gliders around Grave had to be guarded by Dutchmen, whose orders were cheerfully ignored by the Allied soldiery. Consequently, by the time repair work began everything removable had been taken from the gliders, and even their fabric had been ripped off in great chunks for foxhole covers.

The autumn rains turned the flat, boggy fields of the Netherlands into quagmires. At Zon steel matting had to be placed under the gliders to keep them from sinking into the mud, and planes assigned to tow out the Wacos stuck fast and had

---

*Part of this traffic was in support of men repairing damaged C-47's in and around Brussels.

to be hauled out by a crane. By mid-November the Zon strip was almost entirely under water and had to be closed. Thereafter all gliders from Zon had to be picked up by aircraft in flight. A particularly severe setback to the program was an October gale which wrecked 115 gliders that had been more or less completely repaired.

Because of these difficulties in the forward areas orders were issued in November for the removal of all flyable gliders from Zon, Grave and Denain/Prouvy to troop carrier bases near Chartres, and on the 22d of the month 111 repaired gliders were flown to those fields. On 28 December, most of the work being completed, the glider repair teams were removed, leaving only small clean-up detachments. The final total of gliders recovered was 281. Rickety and badly weathered, they were regarded with suspicion by the troop carrier units and were not much used. Although 90 fuselages and 373 tons of metal were also salvaged, these results hardly justify the use of 900 skilled men for three months, nor the effort needed to support them in a remote and exposed position.[85]

Conclusions

An appraisal of MARKET-GARDEN may well start with the question of why it did not succeed. Considering the complexity of the operation there is a remarkably high measure of agreement on this matter.

First and foremost comes the extraordinary revival of German fighting capacity brought about by General Model. Intelligence reports of over-all enemy strength were quite accurate, but as late as 14 September a Second Army estimate described the Nazis as weak, demoralized, and likely to collapse entirely if confronted with a large airborne attack. Had that been so, MARKET would have been a sure thing. No amount of bad luck could have done more than delay its success.

One step in the German reorganization was the movement of two panzer divisions into the Arnhem area. This movement, and the failure of Second Army Intelligence to assess information on it correctly was the second factor making for failure. If, as supposed, the Germans had had no more than a brigade group at Arnhem, the British airborne could have taken city and bridge and held them until relieved. Had the concentration of guns and armor there been recognized, the plans would doubtless have been changed.

A third factor, which enabled the Germans to bring their strength to bear, was General Urquhart's error in locating his zones between five and eight miles from the objective. This was contrary to all airborne doctrine and he later admitted that it had been an unnecessary and fatal error. It cost the division the advantage of surprise and compelled it to divide its forces in the face of the enemy in order to keep possession of the landing zones for later missions. The consequence was the frittering away of six battalions in futile attempts to reach and hold the bridge. To be fair, one must remember that flak estimates for the vicinity of Arnhem were very pessimistic and that the polder land near the bridge was considered dangerously swampy. Still, the Polish paratroops were scheduled to jump into the polders south of the bridge on D plus 2 and might just as well have done so on D-day. Considering what Frost's troops achieved, it seems that they and the Poles combined might have held the bridge until help came, especially if a few pieces of artillery had been dropped or landed with them.

Next in order, and first in General Montgomery's estimation, was the effect of bad weather in delaying the arrival of the Poles from D plus 2 to D plus 4 and that of the 325th Glider Regiment from D plus 2 to D plus 6. He believed that if the two units had arrived on schedule, the Poles could have broken through to Frost's positions and the 325th might have provided the extra infantry needed to win the Nijmegen bridge and fight through to Arnhem, presumably before nightfall on the 20th. Such an achievement by those two units could perhaps have made the difference between defeat and victory.

From one point of view the real culprit in this matter was not the weather, but the plan of operation which, by distributing the delivery of the troops over a period of three days, not only put MARKET at the mercy of the weather but also forced the airborne to waste much of their strength in guarding drop or landing zones for the later missions. All concerned would have much preferred to complete the lift in one or two days, but that was easier said than done.

The troop carriers could not have speeded up the operation by using more or larger planes, since they had put into MARKET almost every plane and crew they had. The C-46 was not yet available to IX TCC and the C-47 units of the 302d Transport Wing were neither trained nor available for airborne missions. One remedy for this limited capacity would have been to fly two sets of missions in one day as had been done in southern France over a course comparable to that flown in MARKET. However, even in retrospect IX TCC held that this expedient would have done more harm than good, since the September days were too short for adequate rest and servicing between the missions.* The American glider missions could have been completed on D plus 1 by using Horsa gliders or by flying Wacos in double tow, but the Americans had acquired an aversion to the Horsa, and double-tow, though used later in VARSITY, was a perilous novelty in 1944. The time which might have been spent in practicing it had been eaten up by bad weather and the air supply effort. Double-tow from England would also have involved a fuel problem, but this could have been met by the use of extra tanks or by allowing the units involved to land at bases in Belgium.

A partial solution would have been possible if the three groups which were moving to bases near Reims when preparations for MARKET began had been retained there. Flying from northern France they could easily have accomplished two missions in a day and would have been much less handicapped by bad weather than they were in the Grantham area. However, to do this large amounts of troop carrier materiel and all the airborne troops with their supplies and equipment would have had to be flown in from England. It is hardly conceivable that this movement could have been made in time if MARKET had begun on the 14th or 15th as originally contemplated. It might possibly have been done before the 17th, but IX TCC would have had to divert to the staging operation hundreds of planes which were bringing supplies to Brussels for Montgomery. Furthermore, bad weather could have disrupted MARKET as badly by interrupting the staging process as it did by grounding missions. Although it can be argued that some troop carrier and airborne units should have been already deployed in northern France, the logistical situation there would probably have made such a move an excessive strain on available resources. Under the circumstances, the decision to fly all missions from England must be regarded as logical.

The final straw which tipped the scales against MARKET was the slowness of the British ground troops. The delay of the Guards Armored Division in reaching Eindhoven made little difference, since if it had gone faster it would have had to wait longer before crossing the bridges at Zon and Nijmegen. What did hurt was the failure of 43 Division to move up fast enough to give infantry support to the Guards at Ressen on the 21st and its lack of aggressiveness on the 22d. To this may be added the failure of British units in VIII and XII Corps to advance up the flanks of the salient in time to prevent the Germans from cutting the highway as they did briefly at Zon and more seriously on the 22d and 24th near Veghel. The two corps averaged only three miles a day against feeble resistance. Unquestionably they were impeded by difficult terrain and by lack of transportation and supplies, but even British observers felt that they might have done better had they felt a greater sense of urgency. Better footwork by Second Army might possibly have saved the Arnhem bridge, or, more probably, have brought help to 1 Airborne soon enough to preserve a foothold across the Rhine.[86]

Weaknesses in communications, air support, resupply and the combat qualifications of American glider pilots have also been regarded as contributing to defeat in MARKET. While the signal organization of Airborne Corps was new and not wholly adequate, its radio communication was generally satisfactory except in the case of 1 Airborne Division, which from D-day to D plus 5 had very little contact with the outside world. Interference by a powerful British station drowned it out on one frequency. To prevent compromise the division had been given no data on ground force frequencies or procedure so it could not send messages through Second Army. Its long-range radios would sometimes reach England, but would not pick up Airborne Corps. Its short-range sets were too weak to begin with and after the move to Hartestein were muffled by the woods in that area. Some sets failed altogether, and others were knocked out by enemy action. The effect of all this was to keep Browning in comparative ignorance of the plight of the division until it was too

---

*It will be recalled that the troop carrier groups of IX TCC had received almost double the standard number of aircraft without any compensating increase in ground personnel.

late to do much about it. Had he known, he might have called in 52 Division or ordered 1 Airborne to move to Renkum, where it could have held out with comparative ease.

Another weakness in communications was the lack of ground-air radio contact with incoming troop carrier missions at the drop and landing zones. The greatest value of such a system would have been in steering missions away from danger points like Best and providing information on changes of zone like that which caused the British resupply mission on D plus 2 to miscarry so badly, but it would also have provided traffic control and warnings on sudden changes in the weather. Before the year was out those directing the destinies of Airborne Army had agreed that in future operations troop carrier representatives would be brought in with the airborne to provide ground-air communication with command ships in subsequent missions.[87]

Air support for the airborne troops after they landed was the responsibility of the Second Tactical Air Force, RAF. In contrast to the massive support given to the troop carrier operations, this was small in scale and ineffective, the reasons being bad weather, faulty support arrangements, and lack of planned interdiction.

Apparently no plans were made for interdiction of German troop and supply movements, and none was attempted, although a good deal of impromptu harassing was done.* Both Allied and German experts felt that interdiction would have been worth while, and one look at the map of Holland is sufficient to show why they thought so. Marshy soil and a multitude of waterways created bottlenecks for German armor and vehicles just as they did for those of the Allies. Surely the importance of MARKET warranted the stoppering of certain of those bottlenecks, even at some inconvenience to future ground operations. As it was, the Germans were able to move troops to the MARKET area much faster than they got them to Normandy at the time of the Allied landings. Two divisions moved from the Dutch coast 98 miles away and reached the battlefield on D plus 5.[88]

Two air support parties with SCR-193 were allotted to each of the airborne divisions and to Browning's headquarters. They were to send their requests to Second Army, which would turn them over to Second TAF's control center for consideration and forwarding to 83 Group. The support parties had SCR-522 sets for direct ground-air communication by VHF radio. In addition, two light warning radar sets and one GCI set were flown in. The GCI party landed in hostile territory and had to destroy its set. The personnel with the light warning units landed with 1 Airborne Division but were almost wiped out by German fire and were never able to operate their equipment.

The air support parties were frustrated by two basic difficulties. Their SCR-193 sets would not reach Second Army, which was 50 to 85 miles away, and, try as they would, they could make no effective contact with support aircraft with their SCR-522 sets. On D plus 1 the 101st Division and Airborne Corps Headquarters made contact with a mobile listening set of XXX Corps and were able to relay requests to Second Army through that. Both SCR-193 sets with the 82d Division were inoperative because of landing damage, but Browning's Corps Headquarters, which was in the 82d's area, sent requests on its behalf, and on the night of the 18th loaned the division one of its sets.

The great misfortune was that 1 Airborne was unable to put through any requests to anyone up to the time its only functioning VHF set was knocked out by a shell on D plus 2. Enemy fire had damaged the set very early and killed the only three well-trained operators. After making contact on 21 September with the short-range radio of 64 Regiment, the division sent some requests through that regiment to Airborne Corps to XXX Corps to 2 Army to Second TAF to 83 Group to the supporting units, or in other words, all around Robin Hood's barn. Other requests were originated by Airborne Corps on the basis of 1 Airborne's general situation, but Second TAF frequently objected to these on the grounds that it needed more precise information on where to strike. This was reasonable, although the airborne, so desperate that they called down artillery fire on their own positions, said later that they would rather have had inaccurate support than none. If only a "cab rank" patrol of fighters and fighter-bombers had been provided, prepared to take their

---

*Fighter and fighter bomber units of the Eighth Air Force, dispatched to protect the troop carrier missions from flak and enemy aircraft, claimed to have destroyed 3 tanks, 35 trucks, 127 motor vehicles, 10 locomotives and 118 railroad cars between 17 and 26 September. (8th AF, Special Rpt on MARKET, p. 42).

missions directly by ground-air radio from controllers on the spot, the problem of getting requests through to 83 Group would have ceased to be serious, and instructions could have been given with all necessary precision. In the opinion of 1 Airborne close support thus provided would have been invaluable in the initial phase of MARKET and might have swung the scale from defeat to victory.[89]

In justice to Second TAF it should be said that it was gravely handicapped by orders not to send support missions over the MARKET area when airborne missions were in progress. This restriction, intended to reduce congestion and prevent possible clashes between friendly forces, was transformed by weather conditions, repeated short postponements of airborne missions and Second TAF's remoteness from Brereton's headquarters, into something like a prohibition. Over and over again support units would be grounded in the early morning by bad weather, and after that by the prospect of an airborne mission, which they would belatedly learn had been postponed a few hours. By the time the actual mission had come and gone the evening mists would be gathering or the clouds rolling in. Had support missions been flown like those of the troop carriers over a specified corridor and had they been under effective ground-air control at destination, the restriction might have been dispensed with, making it possible to send planes to the aid of the airborne whenever weather permitted.

Instead direct air support during the nine decisive days of MARKET was decidedly inadequate except in a handful of cases. On 18 September 97 Spitfires and Mustangs were sent to help the 82d Division beat off the German attacks out of the Reichswald, and on 22 September 119 planes were sent to the assistance of the 101st Division, probably in response to a specific request from the division which Second TAF had accepted. The first direct support at Arnhem came on 24 September when 22 Typhoons attacked German positions around 1 Airborne, and on the 25th when 7 Typhoons and 74 Mitchells and Bostons did likewise, all to very good effect but much too late to win. Some armed reconnaissance was also flown but to comparatively little avail, since the Germans simply silenced their guns until the planes were past and waited until the coast was clear before sending in their own planes in repeated hit-and-run attacks, principally against 1 Airborne and the 82d Division. All in all, it must be said that ground support in MARKET was a difficult task badly handled, and that the support provided was too little and too late.[90]

The British glider pilots, who were organized as ground troops in a special glider pilot regiment, made a much better combat showing in MARKET than the American glider pilots, who were simply an element within the troop carrier squadrons. This contrast gave rise to proposals that the American glider pilots be put under the command of the airborne divisions to make good soldiers of them. A conclusive answer to that was given by General Ridgway, who observed that since the primary duty of glider pilots was to fly gliders, they belonged with the troop carriers.[91]

The idea has been advanced that, had the American glider pilots been comparable to the British as soldiers, the 82d Division could have sent them to the front in place of a regimental combat team and could have used the RCT to take the Nijmegen bridge on 19 September.[92] This theory apparently rests on the fallacious assumption that the Americans, like the British, had co-pilots in their gliders, and that therefore over 900 glider pilots were available. Since only a handful of co-pilots were used, it is clear after allowance for wounds, accidents, and releases in distant or hostile territory that the 82d Division could not possibly have mustered as many as 450 glider pilots at any time up to the afternoon of D plus 6. Moreover, a large proportion of those it did have were engaged in essential duties, which someone would have had to do. Thus the net gain to the division from having the glider pilots organized as infantry would have been on the order of a company rather than a regiment.

The question of why they did not do better should be considered in connection with the situation then existing. It was standard procedure to collect both British and American glider pilots at divisional CP's, use them for guard and supply duties, and evacuate them as soon as possible for employment in subsequent missions. Instructions for MARKET specified that they were to be used at the front only as a last resort. Nevertheless, they should have been trained for such an emergency and were not.

The equipment and briefing of the glider pilots was also unsuitable for a mission such as MAR-

KET. They were given no compasses; about half of them got no maps of their destination; and the others received only a single map on a scale of 1:100,000. Most seem to have had a rather indistinct blow-up of a high-altitude photograph of the landing area. The briefings were more concerned with the landing fields than with the surrounding terrain and said little of how and where the airborne units intended to deploy.

The 101st Division, which had a broad, open zone and an efficient glider reception party, assembled its glider pilots quite successfully, but most of the 82d Division's gliders on D plus 1 had to land in rough, partly wooded areas some distance from their zones and in circumstances of great confusion because of the enemy offensive out of the Reichswald. Since the pilots of those gliders commonly had little knowledge of the terrain, very little idea of where they were, and no maps or compasses with which to orient themselves, it is not surprising that many, having been separated from their comrades by some mishap, wandered about for as much as a day before finding their way to the CP.

Once assembled, the glider pilots were an amorphous mass, almost without organization, and hard to handle because few knew any one outside the 70 or 80 men from their own group. The senior glider officer in the 82d Division's area attempted to exercise authority, but he had little to build on. He had no staff and no formal chain of command. The group and squadron staffs who ordinarily administered and commanded the glider pilots were back in England. He was from the 50th Wing, and the bulk of the pilots, being from the 52d Wing, did not know him, questioned his authority and had no faith in his competence. After all, even the most disciplined infantry do better with officers whom they know.

Because of the lack of organization, and because the officer in command could not be everywhere, details were sent out on the authority of junior airborne and glider officers without record or coordination. Furthermore, although few glider pilots left the assembly or bivouac areas without permission, a pilot not on detail could almost always get permission from someone, usually the ranking officer of his squadron or his group, to set out for home in accordance with the policy of quick evacuation. Thus many glider pilots were freed from military control to wander about on their own, hitchhiking, fighting, and sometimes just sight-seeing.

The fact remains that over 90 percent of the glider pilots did their best in a difficult situation and served faithfully on guard and supply details and even as infantry. At midnight on the 20th, when the Germans were pressing the 82d Division very hard, some 300 glider pilots then in their bivouac, a barracks about a mile north of Mook, were called out, organized into companies and used as infantry at the front or in reserve. Most of them did not see much action, but about 100 men of the 313th and 61st Groups under able leadership from Capt. E. D. Andross took over a section of the front near Mook for the 505th PIR and held it until relieved late on the 23d by other glider pilots, who in turn were relieved next day by the 325th Glider Infantry. Living in foxholes, under frequent shelling and mortaring, soaked by repeated rains, almost without food except for raw carrots and turnips grubbed from the fields around them, Andross and his men did their best for three days and nights in the unfamiliar role of combat infantry. On 24 September they were being evacuated by truck when the Germans ambushed their convoy south of Veghel. The drivers dived for cover, but the glider pilots fought back, turned the trucks around under point-blank fire and drove 15 of them to safety. Theirs was a performance which would seem to call for some commendation.

On the record then the American glider pilots in MARKET were under handicaps which made them seem less disciplined and competent than they were. They did need more infantry training. They did need to have a coherent and effective organization of their own instead of being the fifth wheels of the troop carrier squadrons. They also needed compasses, detailed maps, and a more efficient assembly system. Had these needs been met their performance would probably have satisfied their critics. One step in that direction was taken when, shortly after MARKET, General Brereton ordered that all glider pilots be given broader and continuing combat training.[93]

MARKET was the first major test of resupply by air, and the test demonstrated that it was, though practicable, both inefficient and hazardous and beset with unsolved problems. One problem was capacity. Approximately 200 C-47's were required to carry the 265 tons a day of automatic supply set up for the 82d Division. Stirlings could carry three tons apiece, but 38 Group had scarcely enough of them to meet the needs of one British division. While 250 converted B-24's had supplied the two American airborne divisions fairly well on D plus 1 and could have done better with a little more experience, the Eighth Air Force, which felt its participation in MARKET had seriously interrupted its bombing program, could not be expected to loan its B-24 groups frequently or for long.

The tendency to dispersion inherent in a paradrop was accentuated by the multiplicity of small bundles and containers and by delays in getting bundles out the relatively small side door of the C-47 without the help of conveyors.* As a result supply collection consumed an excessive amount of manpower. General Gavin was not exaggerating much when he estimated that prompt and efficient collection would take a third of his men. Obviously nothing like that number could be spared during a battle.

No such supply fiasco as had occurred in NEPTUNE took place in MARKET. However, at the most generous estimate 1 Airborne Division got less than 15 percent of the supplies dropped to it, the 101st Division got less than 50 percent of its supplies, and the 82d less than 70 percent. Much less would have been retrieved, particularly in the case of the 82d Division, had not the Dutch been exceptionally helpful and honest. All three airborne divisions concluded that the bulk-loaded glider was a far more efficient means of supply than the parachute. However, gliders were so expensive and so vulnerable to bad weather or enemy action that parachute resupply still had to be relied on.

One of the features of a resupply schedule to isolated troops is its inflexibility. The missions must be flown or the men will die. The British learned at Arnhem just how risky such missions could become. Out of 630 planes sent on resupply missions they lost 52, an average of 8.5 percent and had 281 planes, 44 percent of the total, damaged. They considered losses on this scale unacceptable except in emergencies. Suggested remedies included high-altitude dropping, which was notoriously inaccurate with the techniques then used,* and drops from a pull-up after a low-level approach, a tactic which made navigation very difficult and was unlikely to reduce losses when the enemy was massed near the drop point. Probably aware of such objections, the RAF commanders arranged to have supplies delivered in the bomb racks of fighter-bombers of 83 Group, and were about to try this experiment when 1 Airborne was evacuated. This abdication by the British troop carriers is striking evidence that the hazards of resupply had not been sufficiently appreciated.[94]

In spite of its failure and in spite of some mistakes, MARKET was from the troop carrier point of view a brilliant success. The divisional commanders and the Polish brigade commander were unanimous in praising the skill and courage of the troop carrier crews and in calling the missions the best they had ever had in combat or even in training.[95]

The bold decision to fly by daylight had proven safe and successful. In the first two days, before the enemy could react effectively, troop carrier losses had averaged less than 3 percent, and only one major American mission had losses heavier than 5 percent. Operation by daylight not only brought a tremendous increase in navigational accuracy, it also cut the assembly time of the airborne to one-third that normally required at night. The average assembly time for a regiment was 45 minutes, and almost all regiments and smaller units were able to assemble at 80 to 100 percent of strength within an hour of arrival. The excellent drop given the 376th Field Artillery was especially noteworthy as proving that by daylight artillery could be dropped successfully to support paratroop infantry.

Cautious critics qualified their praise of this achievement by noting that crushing air superiority had been needed in MARKET to protect airborne missions in daylight from enemy aircraft and flak. Some 5,200 sorties had been flown to protect the troop carriers from the remnants of the Luftwaffe and to neutralize antiaircraft batteries.† Flak suppression had proven both difficult and dangerous against well-camouflaged opponents who knew

---

*Lateral dispersion could be reduced by flying in a column of V's instead of the V of V's. This had been done with good results in a resupply mission on D plus 8, but in a large mission that formation produced too long a column.

*That winter pilots of 38 Group under the direction of a control team using "talking Eureka" made successful test drops from 7,000-10,000 feet with modified bomb sights and parachutes set to open at 1,500 feet.

†The Eighth and Ninth Air Forces devoted 836 out of 3,352 sorties to flak neutralization. The ratio for ADGB seems to have been similar, but since some of its missions were for both cover and flak protection a precise breakdown of its effort is not feasible.

when to hold their fire. Nevertheless, the guns had been silenced. As for the Luftwaffe, it was never able to break through the cordon of Allied fighters. Its only successful attacks against the troop carriers were made on one occasion when arrangements for escort and cover had broken down.[96]

Helpful as daylight was, it did not eliminate the need for pathfinders. The three serials which missed the mark in the initial paratroop drops were all trying to hit unmarked zones. The British, as a result of their difficulties in locating obscure supply drop points, were emphatic in recommending maximum use of visual aids.[97]

Among the most significant and successful innovations were the use of alternate routes and multiple traffic lanes. The former had paid high dividends on D plus 1 when shifting from the southern to the northern route saved that day's missions from being grounded. The latter had proven that it was possible to cut the long troop carrier columns in half or even in quarters and send the segments in abreast so that a whole division might be landed in an hour.

When all is said, it is not the monumental size nor the operational intricacies of MARKET which linger longest in the memory. It is the heroism of the men who flew burning, disintegrating planes over their zones as coolly as if on review and gave their lives to get the last trooper out, the last bundle dropped. It is the stubborn courage of the airborne troops who would not surrender though an army came against them. In the sense that both troop carrier crews and airborne troops did all that men could do, there was, as Gavin said, no failure in MARKET.

CHAPTER V

Varsity--The Airborne Assault Across The Rhine

Preliminary Planning

AFTER MARKET the next Allied airborne operation in the ETO was VARSITY, an enterprise designed to facilitate a crossing of the Rhine in the Wesel area. General Bradley had stated on 5 September that he wanted an airborne assault to help him hurdle the river. He had hopes of a breakthrough at Aachen followed by a drive toward Cologne, and with this in view Airborne Army prepared an outline plan for an operation called NAPLES II, the seizure by two airborne divisions of a bridgehead between Cologne and Bonn.

On 17 October Brereton's staff learned that Bradley was contemplating an additional new offensive on his left flank to reach the Rhine near Wesel. They examined the terrain north of Wesel, and, having found it for the most part very well suited to airborne operations, produced on 7 November a short staff study containing the original plan for VARSITY. This entailed the use of the 17th Airborne Division and the British 6 Airborne under command of XVIII Corps to take bridgeheads east of Emmerich, east of Rees, or in both areas in support of a prepared crossing by Ninth Army.[1]

It was originally supposed that the Rhine might be crossed before the end of November. However, Ninth Army plagued by bad weather, supply shortages, and revived German resistance, was stopped at the Roer River, and on 20 November a meeting at SHAEF set New Year's Day as the target date for either VARSITY or NAPLES II. This schedule was swept into the wastebasket by the German Ardennes offensive which began on 16 December, and during the ensuing Battle of the Bulge Allied planning was necessarily defensive in character.

By mid-January a full-scale counteroffensive was under way, and with the initiative once more in their hands Eisenhower and his staff again turned their attention to the question of how to secure decisive and final victory.

They decided on a three-phase campaign, first an advance to the Rhine on so broad a front as to take the entire Rhineland and give the Allies the west bank of the river from Holland to the Alps, then assaults across the Rhine north of the Ruhr between Emmerich and Wesel and south of the Ruhr between Mainz and Karlsruhe, and finally a dual thrust into the heart of Germany. To satisfy Montgomery and the British Chiefs of Staff, who wished to concentrate on a single drive into northern Germany, the Supreme Commander agreed that the northern assault should be given maximum strength and should be launched as soon as possible, even before operations west of the river were concluded. Thus the main effort to cross the Rhine was to be made in the very area for which VARSITY had been proposed. On 2 February the Combined Chiefs of Staff gave their approval to this strategy.[2]

The firm decision by SHAEF to proceed with VARSITY and to give it priority over other proposed airborne operations was apparently taken about a week later. On 8 February Brereton was called in to confer on the subject with Eisenhower, and a day or so after that Ridgway was accorded an interview with the Supreme Commander, during which he was notified that the airborne troops in VARSITY would be commanded by XVIII Corps. On 10 February Airborne Army dusted off the November staff study and reissued it with remarkably few changes as an outline plan.[3]

The greatest change was in the surface forces

whose crossing VARSITY was intended to support. The sphere of 21 Army Group had been extended to include the Wesel area, displacing the United States Ninth Army southward so that its objectives beyond the Rhine lay between the Lippe river and the Ruhr. In addition Montgomery had been given operational control of Ninth Army, so all operations north of the Ruhr were in his hands. Already, on 4 February he had issued instructions which called for the Second British Army under Dempsey to secure crossings at Xanten 7 miles west of Wesel and at Rees, 12 miles northwest of the city in conjunction with a crossing by Ninth Army at Rheinberg, which was about 8 miles south of Wesel. The British amphibious operations were given the code name of PLUNDER. The Rheinberg operation was later called FLASHPOINT.

To the two airborne divisions originally selected for VARSITY was added the American 13th Airborne. This was an inexperienced outfit which had just arrived in France; no other divisions were available. The British 1 Airborne had been shattered at Arnhem, and the American 82d and 101st Divisions, having been held in the line almost continuously since September on what General Brereton considered very dubious grounds, would need several months to retrain and refit for airborne missions.[1]

Development of the Assault Plan

The main features of VARSITY were shaped during the last half of February and the first week in March by the Second Army, Airborne Army, and XVIII Corps commanders, Dempsey, Brereton, and Ridgway, with a minimum of participation by Montgomery. Detailed planning between the troop carriers and the airborne appears to have begun with a conference on 21 February and to have been almost completed inside a fortnight, although IX TCC did not issue its field order until 16 March. In this process the principal participants were IX TCC, 38 Group, and XVIII Corps, assisted by representatives of 46 Group, the troop carrier wings, and the airborne divisions.

During February Air Staff, SHAEF* blocked out an outline plan for the employment of cooperating air forces in VARSITY. On the 28th representatives of 21 Army Group, Airborne Army, Second Army, and the various air forces concerned met at SHAEF Forward to discuss their tasks and requirements. At that meeting responsibility for directing subsequent planning was given to Second Tactical Air Force, to which SHAEF, influenced by the evident need for more unified control of cooperating air forces than in MARKET, had delegated operational control of all such forces in VARSITY. At a meeting at Headquarters, Second TAF on 17 March plans were completed for all auxiliary air operations with the exception of some newly proposed by 21 Army Group, and on 20 March Second TAF issued its Air Plan, a most complex and comprehensive document.

It was clear from the start that there was barely enough lift for two divisions, so the 13th Airborne was placed in reserve. Employment of the unit in missions east of Wesel a few days after the original drops and crossings was considered and rejected, partly because the objectives were unsuitable, and partly because such a commitment would leave hardly any troops or gliders on hand for other airborne operations. Therefore on 6 March Brereton asked that the 13th Division be released from VARSITY. SHAEF agreed and reallocated the division to CHOKER II, an airborne operation to help the United States 7th Army cross the Rhine at Worms. However, by getting a foothold across the river between Worms and Mainz on the night of 22 March, a week before the target date for CHOKER, General Patton's 3d Army rendered that airborne enterprise unnecessary and, indeed, impracticable, because at that moment the troop carriers were marshalling for VARSITY. Several operations involving the 13th Airborne were planned later, but all were cancelled for one reason or another, leaving it the only American division in the ETO which did not see action in World War II.[5]

Mindful of the way weather had disrupted the missions scheduled for the third day of MARKET, Brereton and his colleagues were anxious to deliver all the airborne troops for VARSITY in one lift. However, it was not until 5 March that they felt sure they had the means to do this. Never before had two divisions been flown into battle in one single continuous effort. Larger numbers of troops had been delivered in both NEPTUNE and MARKET, but those operations had been extended over several days so that planes and crews could be used more than once.

---
*Air Staff, SHAEF had assumed responsibilities of headquarters, AEAF, which had been dissolved 17 October 1944.

At the end of February IX TCC had on hand 1,264 C-47's, 117 C-46's, 1,922 CG-4A gliders, and 20 CG-13 gliders. Roughly speaking the C-46 was equivalent in capacity to two C-47's and the CG-13 to two Wacos. The commanders decided against using the CG-13's because there were not enough of them to warrant the complications their inclusion would produce in the flight plan and because they had arrived so recently that the troop carriers were still unfamiliar with them. Also they required exceptionally good and large landing fields, since their minimum landing speed was 80 miles an hour.

At a meeting of airborne and troop carrier representatives on 26 February, General Williams proposed to dispatch 400 paratroop aircraft and 588 tug aircraft towing 660 Wacos for the American airborne and 243 more planes to carry the British paratroops. The spokesman for the 17th Airborne considered that 370 C-47's would be enough to lift its two parachute combat teams but asked for more gliders than Williams had offered. They finally agreed that the American airborne should have a paratroop lift of 226 C-47's and 72 C-46's, the equivalent of 370 C-47's, and a glider lift of 906 Wacos towed by 610 C-47's. Since the C-46 could tow no more Wacos than the C-47 but could carry twice as many paratroops, its use for the latter purpose was logical.

The 50 percent increase in glider lift was made possible by a decision to make extensive use of double-tow, a tactic which had never been successfully used in combat,* although it had been known for some time that the C-47 could tow two Wacos at once. The flying personnel of IX TCC had been familiarized with double-tow during the winter and had not found it unduly difficult. A C-47 with two extra fuel tanks could fly 315 miles with two Wacos in tow. Insufficient for missions mounted from England, this range was adequate for planes based in the Paris area.

The British with their very limited troop carrier force had great difficulty in finding enough lift for 6 Airborne. On 26 February the division asked for 275 American aircraft to carry its paratroops. Williams responded that 243 planes was all he could spare, and that was all the division got. The airborne wanted between 406 and 425 planes from 38 and 46 Groups to tow their gliders, but the two groups estimated that they could provide no more than 350 aircraft between them. Airborne Army raised 46 Group's quota from about 100 to 120 aircraft by insisting that SHAEF pry 25 of its planes away from transport work for service in VARSITY. The commander of 38 Group appealed to the Air Ministry on 1 March to give him 104 converted Stirlings and Halifaxes as soon as possible. He got enough of them to raise his group's contribution from 240 to 320 planes.

By using every qualified man including those whose tours of duty had expired and those assigned to training units the two groups managed to scrape up crews for the extra planes. The British airborne, having expended their glider pilots freely at Arnhem, had only 712 men left in the Glider Pilot Regiment. To provide a pair of pilots for each of the 440 British gliders in VARSITY the regiment had to take pilots from the RAF and retrain them in glider flying and infantry tactics.

The Americans would have had an adequate number of glider pilots had they not been required to keep a sufficient reserve to fly 926 gliders in CHOKER. Thus they too had to use converted power pilots as glider pilots. About half of the co-pilots for the Wacos in VARSITY were drawn from this source.⁶

It had been decided between 25 January and 8 February that in any of the airborne operations then under consideration the British troops would be flown from England and the Americans from the Continent.* Early in October 38 Group had been moved to bases in Essex northeast of London, a shift which put it about 100 miles nearer the VARSITY area and within reasonable range of its objectives in that operation. It would obviously have been preferable to base it on the Continent, but runways capable of handling its Halifaxes and Stirlings were not obtainable in France.

One American troop carrier wing, the 50th, had been located since late September in territory southwest of Paris with its headquarters at Chartres, the 439th Group at Chateaudun, the 440th Group at Bricy, the 441st at Dreux, and the 442d at St. André-de-l'Eure.

On or about 7 February the 53d Wing was informed that it would soon be moved to France. On 9 February orders were given to IX TCC and

---

*An attempt to use double-tow for an airborne mission in Burma in March 1944 had gone very badly.

*For route orientation refer to Map No. 11, p. 162.

IX Engineer Command to repair and expand 15 French airfields before 15 March for troop carrier use. On 11 February IX TCC issued movement orders directing the 53d Wing to begin moving to France next day and be fully established by the end of the month with headquarters at Voisenum, the 434th Group at Mourmelon-le-Grand, the 435th at Brétigny, the 436th at Melun, the 437th at Coulommiers and the 438th at Prosnes. These bases were dispersed over a wide area southeast of Paris.

While all or most of the above actions had been decided on before the outline plan of 10 February was issued, the location of the 52d Wing and 46 Group had not been settled. Because the British needed every plane in 38 and 46 Groups to tow gliders, three groups of the 52d Wing were allocated to carry their paratroops. Picked for the job were the 61st, 315th, and 316th Groups, the first two of which had flown British paratroops in MARKET. It would be very difficult for those groups to fly their missions from their home bases in the Grantham area or for 46 Group to do so from its fields in south-central England. Therefore it was decided that they should stage from East Anglia where they would be near 38 Group, could operate under its direction, and would have substantially shorter distances to fly.

The question of which airfields would be used for the purpose was not settled until 2 March when the Eighth Air Force agreed to loan Gosfield, Birch, Boreham, Chipping Ongar, and Wethersfield. The first two went to 46 Group. The 315th got Boreham, and the 61st received Chipping Ongar. After some uncertainty as to whether Wethersfield would be usable that base was assigned to the 316th Group.

The rest of the 52d Wing was slated to move from England to a group of bases between 60 and 90 miles north of Paris, but its shipment was delayed presumably because of doubt as to whether the bases would be ready in time. Finally on 23 February IX TCC ordered wing headquarters to Amiens, the 313th Group to Achiet and the 314th Group to Poix. Three neighboring fields, Abbeville-Drucat, Amiens/Glisy and Vitry-en-Artois, were being repaired for use by units of the 52d. At a conference on 26 February the wing commander successfully insisted that his three groups flying British troops from the United Kingdom be allowed to land at those bases after the operation instead of having to go back across the Channel.

Up to that time the role of the pathfinder group in VARSITY had remained in doubt. The objectives were so close to friendly territory that use of pathfinder teams would hardly be necessary, and so close to German positions that an advance drop by such teams would be suicidal. However, another group was wanted to fly paratroops for the 17th Division, and to fill that need the pathfinders were ordered on 27 February to move from Chalgrove to Chartres.[7]

Plans for the exercise of command and control were complete by the end of February. General Brereton would command Airborne Army with Williams heading its troop carrier component and Ridgway its airborne. Since both Brereton and Ridgway would be on the Continent, operational control of the troop carrier missions to be flown from England was delegated to AOC, 38 Group. Air Marshal Sir Arthur Coningham, AOC of the Second Tactical Air Force, RAF, was to command all cooperating air forces except bombers on resupply missions, which, of course, would be under Brereton's jurisdiction. Coningham delegated control of the air over the battle area to the AOC, 83 Group so that quick changes could be made there if the tactical situation dictated. Coningham and Brereton together would coordinate the airborne missions with the auxiliary missions and would decide whether VARSITY was to be cancelled or postponed.

The headquarters from which VARSITY was to be directed were distributed of necessity among three widely separate places, Paris, Brussels, and Mark's Hall, the 38 Group headquarters. Most of the troop carrier bases in France were fairly near Paris, so on 18 February Airborne Army moved its headquarters to Maison Lafitte on the outskirts of that city. On 22 February the troop carrier headquarters at Ascot detached a group of plans and operations men for duty at the Chateau de Prunay in Louveciennes, about six miles from Maison Lafitte, and on the 24th, Forward Headquarters, IX TCC, was officially opened at the chateau.

Although XVIII Corps had its headquarters at Épernay about 70 miles from Paris, it was able to maintain close liaison with Airborne Army. Not so with Second TAF. Coningham's large headquarters was firmly established in Brussels beside that of Montgomery. Since Coningham and Brereton would have to decide jointly on whether to postpone VARSITY and might have to make joint decisions during the operation, it was decided that the latter, accompanied by a small staff, would go to Brussels shortly before the launching of VARSITY and set up a Command Post at Headquarters, Second TAF. This CP, officially called FAAA TAC, was opened on 22 March. The operations center at Maison Lafitte was then designated FAAA CCP. Routine control and supervision of the airborne missions would be exercised partly from Maison Lafitte and partly from Mark's Hall. Command decisions would be made in Brussels and transmitted to the distant controllers for implementation. It was certainly an awkward arrangement, and although it worked without a hitch during the execution of VARSITY, everyone seems to have been rather relieved that it did so.[8]

Obviously PLUNDER and VARSITY could not be launched until the enemy had been driven from the Rhineland. In early February Montgomery believed that the crossing might be made by 15 March, but stubborn German resistance caused the target date to be set back to the 25th and then to the 31st of March. Finally, late in February, the Nazis cracked, and on 2 March Ninth Army broke through to the Rhine at Neuss.

The army commander, Lt. Gen. William H. Simpson, seeing little opposition ahead of his forces, proposed to make a surprise crossing. Montgomery, always inclined to prefer a "set piece" to impromptu action, vetoed the suggestion, but he did decide to advance the target date for VARSITY to 24 March, and he seems to have seriously considered launching it on short notice in the event of a breakthrough near Wesel. On being asked how long it would take to mount a "hasty" VARSITY, Airborne Army replied on 3 March that it would need at least a week to do a good job. No such haste was required. The Germans facing Second Army continued to fight with desperate fanaticism and held the west bank of the Rhine until 10 March. Then they withdrew across the river under cover of bad weather, blowing the last bridge behind them. Since by that time it was clear that a crossing in the Wesel area would meet substantial opposition, Montgomery adhered to his plans for an overwhelming blow requiring a fortnight for deployment. Accordingly on 8 March SHAEF officially set the 24th of that month as the target date for VARSITY.[9]

In order to launch VARSITY on the day prescribed, Airborne Army required visibility of at least three miles, a ceiling above 1,500 feet, and winds less than 20 miles an hour. In addition the planners wanted at least two days of good weather immediately before D-day for preliminary air operations. In northwest Germany March is not a pleasant month. Weather experts estimated that between 15 March and 15 April only about half the days would meet FAAA requirements and that there would be only two periods of three successive days suitable for air operations. So essential did Montgomery consider his airborne cohorts that on 19 February his chief of staff told Brereton that if the troop carriers were grounded by bad weather PLUNDER would be postponed until they could go. Later he agreed that a postponement of up to five days would be acceptable.[10]

Barely a week before D-day, representatives of 21 Army Group, probably speaking on Dempsey's behalf, asked for preparation of an alternate airborne operation ready to fly on 24-hour notice in support of PLUNDER in case bad weather did force cancellation of VARSITY. By 21 March Airborne Army had drawn up plans for an alternate operation in the vicinity of Erle, a town 12 miles east of the Wesel area. However, both Coningham and Brereton insisted on 48 hours notice to provide for rebriefing and anti-flak operations.[11]

General Dempsey of Second Army gave VARSITY its objective, the Diersfordter Wald, a wood between three and five miles east of the Rhine on the crest of a gentle rise. Though scarcely 100 feet above the river, the high ground provided the only good natural observation points in that area and the trees provided cover from which artillery could rake the stream. Until the wood was taken no bridge could be expected to last long.

Consequently Dempsey urged that instead of being put down close to the river as proposed in the outline plan, the airborne should be placed further east, close to the Diersfordter Wald, and out of the field of fire of artillery supporting the amphibious assault. Brereton and Ridgway agreed, and the trio decided to drop and land the troops as near the wood as possible, thereby eliminating long marches such as had cost the British so dearly in MARKET. After occupying the wood XVIII

Corps was to push west to make contact with Second Army, then south to the Lippe to seal off Wesel and make contact with the Ninth Army. After that it would prepare to advance eastward as part of Dempsey's forces.

According to the initial plans the airborne and amphibious assaults were to be launched simultaneously and at night. With the change in objectives went a change in timing. The open fields by the river might well be attacked at night, but it would be tempting fate to make a night attack on prepared positions in the depths of a wood. Also, whereas the river bank would have had to be taken early to aid the surface assault, there was no necessity to take the Diersfordter Wald until bridging operations began. On such grounds as these General Dempsey recommended that the airborne attack go by daylight after PLUNDER had begun. For reasons of his own Brereton agreed. Besides a conviction that troop carrier operations would be much more accurate by day, he had a strong expectation that they would be safer. By day the Allies ruled the skies challenged only by a handful of jet fighters. After dark the German night-fighter force, conserved for the defense of the Reich, was still a serious threat.* Accordingly the plans were drawn for an amphibious assault an hour or two before dawn, followed at 1000 hours by the airborne attack. Since hitherto the airborne phase had ordinarily begun first, this timing offered a fair prospect of catching the Germans in the Diersfordter Wald by surprise.[12]

Drop and landing zones† were selected on the basis of previous studies of the VARSITY area by IX TCC. Eight were on or near the east side of the Diersfordter Wald, and two, both for paratroops, were set into indentations on the west side of the wood at its northern and southern tips where it was relatively narrow. None of the eastern zones was more than 200 yards from a neighbor, and even those on the west side were within a mile of other zones. All 10 were packed into an area less than six miles long and five miles wide, an unprecedented degree of concentration. The chance that any airborne unit would be isolated was remote, but the risk of overlapping and confusion was considerable.

Almost all of the drop and landing area was firm, level ground, and the zones consisted of fields and meadows averaging 200 to 300 yards in length. Hedges were small and fences light, about half of the latter being made of wire. Ditches were few and small. There was no sign that the enemy was preparing landing obstacles. Aside from the Diersfordter Wald itself, there were five notable features. A double-tracked railroad to Wesel cut diagonally across the area from northwest to southeast. A few hundred yards to the east of the railroad was a high-tension power line on 100-foot pylons, a major hazard to gliders and paratroops. Bordering the eastern edge of the area and running south-southeast was the Issel River, a water barrier 60 feet wide. Just east of the river lay a half-completed autobahn (trunk highway) 150 feet wide, heavily embanked at some points, and lined with construction equipment. About a mile inside the northeast corner of the area was the little town of Hamminkeln. There were many minor hazards, tree-bordered roads, local power-lines, windmills, and the like, but it was most important to avoid depositing the airborne in the woods, in or beyond the Issel, or against the high-tension line.[13]

In November the Operational Plans Officer of IX TCC had proposed that the VARSITY missions follow a route from England to Blankenberge on the Dutch coast and from there to an IP at Goch, about 10 miles west of Rees. This way was short and straight with plenty of natural check points, but it involved a long overwater flight and was too far north to be convenient for units based around Paris. In March a course which would be about equally feasible for all units was finally chosen.* The British and American troop carriers based in East Anglia would use Hawkinge near Folkestone on the Kentish coast as their departure point and would fly from there to the tip of Cape Gris Nez, an overwater leg of only 27 miles to an easily recognizable landmark. Thence they would go east-southeast for 51 miles to Bethune and from there 87 miles east-northeast to Wavre, a rail and highway junction 11 miles southeast of Brussels. A straight flight from Gris Nez to Wavre had to be avoided because it would pass within radar range of German forces holding out at Dunkirk, and so involved the risk of premature discovery. Wavre was to be the Command

---

*It should also be noted that the bad condition and short runways of some troop carrier fields in France made them unsuitable for glider operations at night. (Notes of Group Commanders' Mtg, 50th TC Wing, 8 Feb 45 in Hist 50th TC Wg, Feb 45.)

†For DZ and LZ orientation, refer to Map No. 12, p. 175.

*See Map No. 11, p. 162.

Operation VARSITY
TROOP CARRIER ROUTES

Assembly Point. This location involved the least possible detour for the troop carrier wings in France and could be reached by all of them without their crossing each other's courses or wing assembly areas. At the same time it was far enough from the front so that the troop carrier columns could be massed on one route under full escort before coming within range of enemy fighters.

From Wavre the course went straight for 92 miles to the northeast, passing over the road and rail junction of Diest 27 miles from Wavre and over the hamlet of Marheeze 32 miles beyond Diest, to Weeze, a village on the Nierse River about a dozen miles west of the Rhine. Weeze was chosen as the principal Initial Point and was given the code name YALTA.

The system of multiple traffic lanes used in MARKET had been proposed for VARSITY in November and was embodied in the final plan. There were to be three lanes spaced 1½ miles apart. The contingent bringing 6 Airborne Division from the United Kingdom would follow the northern lane to their Initial Point, head from there for the six northernmost zones, and turn north onto a reciprocal course after delivering their troops. Their IP, (YALTA NORTH) was located beside a railroad north of Weeze, and east of an oxbow loop in the Nierse River. It lay between 15 and 18 miles from the zones.

Actually there were two northern routes, lying at different levels. The American C-47's flying paratroops were to fly at 1,500 feet until nearing the IP, while the British glider stream would keep to an altitude of 2,500 feet. This would enable the American serials flying British paratroops at 140 miles an hour to pass under the Dakotas of 46 Group, towing Horsas at 115 miles per hour, and make their drop ahead of them. The British had some tug-glider combinations in 38 Group cruising at 135 miles per hour and others at 145 miles an hour. In order to get a continuous stream at the IP the slow units were given a head start at Hawkinge such that by holding to the proper speed the faster ones would catch up with them at Weeze.

The American glider serials would occupy the center lane and use a bridge over the Nierse on the east side of Weeze as their IP. The paratroop serials of the 17th Airborne would follow the southern lane to their IP (YALTA SOUTH), a castle beside the Nierse 1½ miles south of Weeze. Although the last two paratroop serials in the south lane would fly for a while parallel to the first glider serial in the center, the former because of greater cruising speed were expected to pull ahead by five minutes before reaching their Initial Point.* All the American airborne were to be dropped or landed on the four southernmost zones, after which the planes bringing them would make a 180 degree turn to the right onto a reciprocal course for the return trip.

These arrangements made it possible to deliver the two divisions simultaneously, and, by the use of tight spacing, to compress the whole operation within a period of 2 hours and 37 minutes. The paratroop serials, formed as usual of 9-aircraft V's of V's in trail, were to be spaced at 4-minute intervals if numbering more than 40 aircraft and at 3-minute intervals if smaller than that. American glider serials would fly in pairs of pairs in echelon to the right with a 1,500-foot interval between successive elements. Single-tow serials were to be seven minutes apart. Double-tow serials got 10 or 12 minutes depending on whether they contained as many as 40 planes, because the novelty of double-tow made it advisable to allow margin for error. The British glider stream, flying in loose pairs at 10-second intervals, had a time length of only 39 minutes as compared to 2 hours and 6 minutes for the American gliders. However, the former had only 440 big gliders to deliver, while the latter had 906 Wacos.[14]

Navigation in VARSITY would be relatively easy, since flight was to be by day, over a straight course from Wavre to Weeze, and in friendly territory to within six miles of the objectives. Notwithstanding this, navigational aids were to be installed at 17 places including all turns. The longest unmarked stretches were one of 89 miles between Laon and Wavre and one of 87 between Bethune and Wavre. Beyond Wavre the longest gap was a mere 33 miles. From Wavre on, the missions would never be out of range of a Eureka beacon. All check points were to have Eurekas. Beacon lights of the type known as pundits were to be used at wing departure points and at Bethune, Wavre, and the IP. Cape Griz Nez, St. Quentin, and all points from Wavre to the Rhine inclusive were to have M/F beacons. In addition

---

*All American gliders were limited to the pace of the double-tow serials, 110 miles an hour. Two of the last three paratroop serials were made up of C-46's travelling at 165 miles an hour, the other of C-47's at 140 miles an hour.

smoke signals and colored panels were to be set out at LAST LAP, L, K, M and N, the points where formations would cross the west bank of the Rhine. All parties operating navigational aids were kept in contact with FAAA by radio or telephone, so that they could be notified of any change of schedule.

Separate pathfinder operations were omitted. They were regarded as unnecessary because navigation was so easy, as suicidal because the zones were in a strongly defended area, and as harmful because they would forfeit all chance of surprise. However, the lead aircraft in the first serial to pass over each of the four British and American drop zones was to drop a stick of pathfinder troops who were to set out colored panels and smoke but no beacons for the initial missions. Each airborne division was to bring in two M/F beacons and have one in operation on its supply drop zone in time to guide in the B-24 resupply mission. Eureka beacons were to be used on the zones for the D plus 1 resupply missions if IX TCC so desired. To avoid flak on its resupply mission 38 Group had worked out a plan to drop from around 8,000 feet on verbal directions from the pathfinder party by "talking Eureka" (Eureka with voice hook-up) to personnel in a "master" plane who in turn would direct the drop verbally over VHF radio. Three sets of "talking Eureka" were brought in, but the group never got a chance to try its scheme.

One promising type of radar, the SCR-717 was rejected, because the terrain along most of the route was not such as would show up well on its scope and because the BUPS beacons which could be used with it were not available. Gee, however, would be employed. Good coverage was available from three existing chains and another was about to open. Instructions for use of Rebecca followed the sensible pattern adopted after NEPTUNE. Only flight leaders or their substitutes were to operate Rebecca unless the formations broke up, in which case the leader of each separate element was to turn on his set. Use of IFF by flight leaders or stragglers when above overcast was authorized, but it was made unnecessary on D-day by the imposition of rigid restrictions on antiaircraft fire and by the clear weather then prevailing.

Communication between aircraft during VARSITY was limited to extreme emergencies and exercise of command functions at or above wing level until planes were at least 40 miles along on their homeward way. Then navigational information might be requested. This air-to-air communication was to be by VHF. A special ground-air W/T station was to be operated by IX TCC Forward. Over it, if necessary, recall signals could be sent to serials anywhere on the route. Two aircraft in each flight were to watch that frequency.

Two new organizations, the combat control team and the forward visual control post, had recently been created to remedy the communications deficiencies which had played so serious a part in MARKET. Both were used in VARSITY.

The troop carrier command had begun in January to organize combat control teams from its glider pilots and enlisted technicians on the basis of two teams for each American airborne division. The function of the teams was to inform headquarters and incoming serials of conditions in the battle area, particularly weather and enemy resistance, and to notify the airborne in turn of any changes in troop carrier plans, especially regarding timing, course or zones. Each team was composed of five men with a jeep and a quarter-ton trailer, modified to hold a power unit, an SCR-399 or 499 for communication with headquarters, and an SCR-522 for VHF radio conversation with missions overhead. In the coming operation two teams, one a spare in case of accidents or casualties, were to be landed at opposite ends of LZ N to operate for XVIII Corps. Each was to go in three Wacos, one for the jeep, one for the trailer, and one containing equipment for medical evacuation by glider pick-up. Two gliders loaded with wounded had been "snatched" very successfully from the Remagen bridgehead, and the troop carriers were prepared to evacuate large numbers of patients by glider in VARSITY under the direction of a combat control team if conditions warranted.

The forward visual control posts were fighter control teams with the primary purpose of directing close support aircraft. They had recently been organized by 38 Group. Each team had a jeep and a trailer and for VARSITY was equipped with two VHF sets, one for ground-to-ground communication by which to call for support aircraft and one for air-to-air communication by which to direct the planes to their targets. A whole team could fit in one Horsa. In VARSITY three FVCP's were to be flown in to 6 Airborne Division. One would serve that division, one would move south to work for the 17th Airborne, and one would act as a reserve. Because the FVCP's had been created only a short time before the operation, their personnel had very little training in either airborne operations or close support. Notwithstanding this handicap they were to prove very valuable.[15]

Although Airborne Army expected its troops to link up with the British ground forces within a few hours, it regarded resupply by air as highly desirable, because Second Army probably could not put more than one bridge in operation on D-day and at first would need everything that could be brought in by bridge or boat. However, it was in the critical early hours of the operation that the airborne, too, most urgently would need supplies, particularly ammunition. On D plus 1 resupply might be too late or might be prevented by bad weather. Resupply at night might be inaccurate and surely would be hard to recover. On D-day itself the troop carriers would be fully occupied with the initial missions. The solution was to fly the supplies in by bomber as had been done on the second day of MARKET. On 28 February Airborne Army asked USSTAF to have Eighth Air Force dispatch 240 Liberators from England on D-day with 540 tons of supplies for its troops. The request was granted.

The supply drop was scheduled to occur at 1300 hours, about 20 minutes after the last gliders landed. So early a drop involved some risk that zones still would be in enemy hands, but it also had great advantages. The same air effort set up to protect the troop carriers from enemy air and ground action would serve to protect the bombers; and the airborne, instead of keeping large numbers of fighting men waiting for hours to guard zones and pick up supplies, could collect their bundles soon after assembling and go about their business. Both troop carrier and resupply missions were to follow the same route. Primarily intended to simplify control of fire from Allied antiaircraft batteries, this plan also facilitated fighter protection and use of navigational aids.

Remembering the miscarriage of MARKET, Brereton and Ridgway were anxious to provide against the contingency, however remote, that the Second Army assault might be contained, leaving the airborne cut off from supplies. Therefore on 5 March the two agreed to have a resupply mission ready to go on D plus 1 unless cancelled. In final form this consisted of 440 C-47's of IX TCC carrying 550 tons of materiel and 240 planes of 38 Group carrying 530 tons, enough to last the two divisions for two days. If bad weather in England or over the Channel grounded 38 Group, a substitute force of 75 Dakotas of 46 Group would take off from Nivelles near Brussels with high-priority items for the British airborne. Likewise, if the troop carrier units on the Continent were grounded, C-47's from England would fly a one-day level of supplies to the 17th Division. In addition, preparations were made to deliver on request an additional two-day level of supplies for 6 Airborne and a one-day level for the 17th Airborne.[16]

Not until after the middle of March were decisions reached on how to protect the troop carrier missions from being fired on in error by Allied gunners, but the action finally taken was very thorough as far as the D-day missions were concerned. Fighter Command, RAF, agreed to prohibit antiaircraft fire near the troop carrier path in England from 0700 to 1500 hours. A representative of the naval commander concerned made a like promise for naval antiaircraft in the Thames estuary and within a 10-mile belt along the troop carrier route across the Channel. The 21 Army Group directed that on the Continent within a strip 30 miles wide centered on the route no flak was to be fired west of the Maas between 0700 and 1500 or east of it between 0900 and 1400. Outside the prohibited zone no guns were to fire on aircraft during the period of the missions unless they committed a hostile act.

On the Second Army front no guns or mortars near the troop carrier lanes were to fire on trajectories higher than 500 feet between 0958 and 1330 hours. As further insurance the artillerymen were to detail a special watch to report on approaching formations and on such damaged aircraft as might dip low over the guns on their return.

During the resupply mission on D plus 1 antiaircraft batteries were to fire only on planes committing hostile acts, except that within 12,000 yards of the Rhine crossings at Xanten and Rees they might fire on aircraft definitely recognized as hostile. This exception destroyed most of the value of the protective clause, for within the 12,000-yard radius around the crossings was the very area where battle-smoke and battle-tension might cause the supply formations to be fired upon. The determination of Second Army to protect its pontoon bridges from German bombers was reasonable enough, but the fact remains that the D plus 1 mission in VARSITY was to have no more protection from Allied antiaircraft fire at the front than the unfortunate follow-up mission to Sicily, which had been smashed by friendly guns.[17]

Planning for Auxiliary Air and Artillery Action

Traditionally the most important task of cooperating air units in an airborne operation was to protect it from enemy air. This was not so in VARSITY, for the German Air Force was in eclipse. Its maximum 24-hour effort against VARSITY had been estimated in November as 365 sorties by day and 265 by night. On 16 March IX TCC rated its capacity as 425 by day and 410 by night.[18]

Weak as it was, German air could inflict great damage by night attacks on troop carrier fields during the marshalling period. A survey made late in February showed that the small size and bad condition of many troop carrier fields in France made dispersion impossible. Thus a few raiders sweeping over a crowded parking area could put a whole group out of operation. On 3 and 4 March the Germans demonstrated their ability to make such a raid. Night fighters sneaked in behind homeward-bound British bombers, inflicted substantial losses on the British, and did some damage in secondary attacks at Cottesmore and Barkston Heath. Action to meet the threat was initiated by IX TCC on 6 March with the result that at least one automatic antiaircraft battery was stationed at every troop carrier base in France, and Ninth Air Force agreed to hold night-fighter units on call during the critical marshalling period after 20 March to defend those airfields.[19]

The Luftwaffe did have a new and formidable weapon, the jet fighter. About 80 jets, able to fly rings around all Allied fighters then in action, had been accumulated during the winter at a group of airfields near Rheine within easy range of the Wesel area. The best way to stop the jets was on the ground. Once they were in the air, at least a few of them could probably outrace escorting fighters and make a stab at the troop carriers. Therefore on 17 March the Eighth Air Force was given the task of bombing the five jet bases and 10 others within 25 miles of Wesel which were suitable for jets. This was to be done on D minus 3 or as soon thereafter as weather permitted. Since some damaged fields might be repaired within 36 hours, the bombing was to be repeated on D-day before 0915, subject to confirmation by Second TAF. To make sure no jets got away, RAF fighters of 83 Group would patrol over the jet bases from first light on D-day until the bombers arrived. On confirmation by Second TAF, Eighth Air Force was also to bomb German night-fighter bases just before dark on D-day. This action, however, was intended to protect the troops on the ground, rather than the troop carriers.[20]

Escort and cover were to be provided on a massive scale. The troop carrier stream from the United Kingdom would be escorted as far as the Rhine and back by 11 Group, RAF. Units based in France would be escorted to and from the river by fighters of Ninth Air Force. Beyond the Rhine there would be no escort, but a system of standing patrols would be maintained on D-day from dawn to dark. Responsibility for the VARSITY assault area rested on 83 Group, RAF, which was to patrol a zone 50 miles deep bounded by the Lippe, the Rhine, and a line touching Emmerich, Enschede, Münster, and Hamm. Similar zones to the north and south would be patrolled by 84 Group and the XXIX Tactical Air Command respectively. Fighters of the Eighth Air Force would patrol east of the three zones to intercept enemy aircraft approaching the battle area from other parts of Germany.[21]

Diversionary feints in the direction of Borkum, an island off the German coast, were to be flown by Coastal Air Command, RAF, and certain missions by Bomber Command, RAF, against targets on the northern edge of the Ruhr had in part a diversionary purpose. These thrust were well suited to draw off interceptors which might be used against the troop carriers. Although Fifteenth Air Force agreed to send a very large bomber force from Italy against Berlin, Munich and other targets in Central Europe, the direction of approach and the fact that all its objectives were over 300 miles from Wesel make it difficult to regard this effort as diversionary in the strict sense of the word. It may have been meant to discourage redeployment of German fighter units to the western front. A diversionary dummy-dropping mission by Bomber Command was considered but not attempted, partly because that kind of deception was considered useless by day, which was when VARSITY would need it most, and partly because units previously used in such work were not available.[22]

Flak was the weapon most feared by the planners of VARSITY. This fear was due as much to the nature of the operation as to the weakness of the Luftwaffe. There was no way for the troop carriers to fly around the enemy strong points. Those strong points were their objectives. In December the A-3 of IX TCC had warned that antiaircraft fire might inflict losses such as the command had never before encountered. In March Air Marshal Coningham called flak his chief anxiety. On 19 March intelligence experts reported a very considerable build-up of German antiaircraft artillery in the VARSITY area.[23]

The situation had one advantage in that over 2,000 Allied guns were massed within range of the German batteries. Second and Ninth Armies agreed to neutralize flak within range of their field artillery. German batteries further away or masked from artillery fire were to be dealt with by air action. The line dividing the two areas of attack split the drop and landing area approximately in half, providing an opportunity to compare the results of shell-fire and bombardment.

Known enemy batteries were to be left strictly alone until D-day so they would not go into hiding. On the 24th, an hour before the troop carrier columns arrived, medium bombers of the Ninth Air Force and 2 Group, RAF, would begin a half-hour attack on antiaircraft positions beyond the artillery boundary, using fragmentation clusters and proximity fuses as far as possible to avoid cratering the drop and landing zones. Between the departure of the mediums and the arrival of the airborne missions Allied artillery would hammer flak positions within its sector. Flak-busting fighter-bomber patrols contributed by 83 and 84 Groups and XXIX TAC would arrive at 0930 as the mediums left and would be maintained over the area until 1300 in readiness to silence batteries observed firing on the troop carrier missions.[24]

As to the German ground forces opposing PLUNDER and VARSITY, Allied hopes that they had been shattered in the Rhineland gave way as D-day approached to a sober conviction that the enemy had extricated much more than anticipated, and that there would be a real fight ahead. Aware that Wesel was a logical place to cross the Rhine the Nazis had, it was estimated, massed about 10 of their best remaining divisions within 20 miles of the area selected for Montgomery's assaults. However, they had been so reduced by attrition as to number less than 50,000 combat effectives. Among them were two or three panzer divisions with perhaps 100 tanks and self-propelled guns, but these were reported to be near Duisburg, Isselburg, and Bocholt, more than 10 miles away from the assault area. Brereton kept order of battle teams on duty 24 hours a day up to the last minute before VARSITY was launched, undoubtedly to prevent panzer units from surprising the airborne at Wesel as they had done at Arnhem.

A maximum of 12,000 troops including two divisions and a brigade group were thought to be within a 10-mile radius of the airborne assault. If they concentrated in the Diersfordter Wald to oppose the amphibious landings the airborne, arriving in their rear and on their flanks, would cut them off. Since the German commanders reputedly anticipated an airborne operation and had even rehearsed defense measures against one, it was more likely that they would place only a holding force in the wood and keep their main strength back of the Issel River to await developments. In that case the airborne might be the ones encircled.

Whatever the defense plan, it was evident that as little as five minutes after arrival the paratroops and glider men might be in combat with substantial German forces in well-prepared positions. The initial fighting might be hard. Thereafter the duration and severity of the battle would probably depend on the extent to which the Nazis could bring up reinforcements. To stand a chance of winning they would need to get half a dozen of their depleted divisions into the battle area. The Allies proposed to stop any such movement through the use of their superior airpower.[25]

In contrast to MARKET, which had no systematic interdiction, VARSITY was the beneficiary of four interdictory operations. The original program asked for and obtained by Second Army and FAAA was short, small, and efficient. It called for bombing a dozen vital communications centers within 15 miles of the assault area* late on

---

*Dinslaken, Anholt, Isselburg, Dingden, Brunen, Raesfeld, Bocholt, Borken, Dorsten, Gladbeck, Sterkrade, and a bridge near Sterkrade.

D minus 1 or on D-day. If successful, this would block every good way by which German reinforcements could approach the battle area. On D-day armed reconnaissance patrols of 83 and 84 Groups and XXIX TAC would sweep the highways clean of military traffic west of Zwolle, Münster, Hamm, and Siegen and similar patrols of Eighth Air Force fighters would do so east of that line.

To supplement this plan 21 Army Group proposed on 17 March that, since the Germans obviously would not be taken by surprise, they should be softened up by several days of preparatory bombing directed against barracks and military installations within a 30-mile radius of Wesel. Next day Second TAF, and the air forces concerned agreed to bomb 26 such targets north of the Lippe and 16 south of it at least twice every 24 hours from D minus 3 through D minus 1, preferably both by day and by night so that the enemy could get no rest. This program was aimed solely at German reserves. The assault areas were excluded for fear of damage to zones or riverbanks. Most of the places already on the interdiction list were included, and the general effect was to reinforce the interdiction of the VARSITY area. It should, however, be noted that about half the targets named were too far away to affect the airborne operation, important as they might be to later phases of 21 Army Group's offensive.* The same thing applies to the interdiction patrols flown by the fighters of Eighth Air Force. Their effect was to prevent creation of a second line of defense rather than reinforcement of the front.

Even more remote from VARSITY, though not without influence on it, was a project proposed early in February by Lt. Gen. Hoyt Vandenberg, commander of the Ninth Air Force, to isolate all territory between the Rhine and an arc from Bremen along the Weser and Lahn rivers to Coblenz by bombing 18 bridges and viaducts, and then to paralyze the railroads in that area by destroying their rolling stock. The operation was approved, mainly, it appears, for its economic and general strategic value, and not as direct tactical assistance to VARSITY.

It began on 21 February and by 21 March the only remaining serviceable bridges were three at the northern extremity of the arc; 20 out of 25 marshalling yards had been knocked out; and railroad traffic was at a standstill. This situation must have hampered Nazi efforts to build defenses along the Rhine, but, even if the way had been clear, they had almost no reserves east of the Weser. The industries of the Ruhr were strangled, as Vandenberg had intended they should be. The tactical value of the operation as far as VARSITY is concerned is uncertain but probably rather limited.[26]

One other air operation was a bombing of Wesel itself. Second Army asked for this very urgently on 17 March, and Bomber Command, RAF, was given the assignment of attacking the city on D minus 1. Dempsey had decided to take Wesel by a commando assault at 2230 on the 23d and considered bombing essential to soften up the defenders. Since the flak batteries in Wesel were a threat to the troop carrier missions, this decision to hit the city hard and take it early would be of real assistance to VARSITY.[27]

Close support of the airborne troops was to be divided between artillery and air units in much the same way as flak suppression. A "cab rank" of rocket-firing Typhoon fighter-bombers dispatched in relays of four every 15 minutes was to be maintained throughout the day over the Wesel area, ready to attack targets on requests received by radio from control parties with the troops. Requests for additional aircraft to fly close support were to be made through the control parties to an advanced control center of 83 Group.

Artillery support was to play a role never before possible in an airborne operation. At 1000 hours on D-day XVIII Corps was to receive operational control of 104 guns for direct support of 6 Airborne Division and 88 guns for direct support of the 17th Airborne plus a battery of heavy antiaircraft guns for each division. An additional 176 guns including 155-mm. pieces and 240-mm. howitzers were to be under corps control for general support. Since only 51 guns were to be flown in for the 17th Division and only 24 for 6 Airborne, it is easy to see that the ability to call on ground artillery multiplied the firepower of the airborne force many times over.[28]

Training

In contrast to the vestigial training for MARKET, preparation for VARSITY included a rehearsal, a short period of intensive joint training,

---

*Tedder, Spaatz, and Vandenberg expressed the opinion on 21 March that this operation should have been concentrated against reserves near the front, omitting several objectives deep in the rear.

and, before that, a systematic training program designed to maintain proficiency. Particular credit for this last feature should probably be given to Brereton's insistence that his troop carriers be given adequate opportunity to practice troop carrier operations. In the face of ground pressure for more air supply SHAEF was persuaded to agree that between 17 December 1944 and 17 January 1945 only two troop carrier groups need be held on reserve for CATOR and later that only three would be reserved between 17 January and 17 February. The other groups were slated to go into training, but emergency air supply and transport work during the Battle of the Bulge occupied them during the latter part of December.

Early in January the battle subsided and training went into full swing. During that month and the next about two thirds of the aircraft dispatched by IX TCC were on training flights, and about 50,000 hours of flying time were devoted to such flights. Most attention was given to formation flying, which took up some 21,000 hours. Glider towing occupied over 9,000 hours, and glider landing was stimulated by a requirement that every glider pilot make at least five landings a month. Navigational and instrument flights were also stressed, and the large number of replacements, especially in the 52d Wing, necessitated a great deal of transition flying. Joint training with the airborne was necessarily on a low level, because the troops were in action or otherwise unavailable. Only 101 paratroops jumped during the two-month period.

Plans for three weeks of intensive combined troop carrier-airborne training in preparation for VARSITY were discussed and approved on 28 February. Among other things they called for five jump exercises by regimental combat teams. Training was to end on 20 March, about 10 days before the operation, and was to culminate in a rehearsal.

What was conceived as a well-rounded program was in fact seriously curtailed. When VARSITY was moved up to 24 March, it became necessary to terminate training on the 15th. According to troop carrier statements, all other cancellations and changes were made at the request of airborne representatives. The principal change was the reduction of the paratroop exercises to one of 135 planes for the 507th PIR of the 17th Airborne and one of 154 aircraft for the 13th Division, which, incidentally, came after that unit had been diverted to CHOKER. One exercise was eliminated by the shortening of the program. The 17th Airborne cut out another because of staging difficulties, caused by the fact that its quarters near Chalons were over 50 miles away from all but one operational troop carrier base. Many training flights for the division were staged from two small, unoccupied strips at Chambry and Malmaison, but this expedient would not do for large exercises. Also abandoned was a paratroop exercise by the 52d Wing with paratroops of 6 Airborne Division.

No glider exercises were planned or attempted. At most of the fields, facilities for mass glider landings were so inadequate that General Williams had limited non-tactical glider lifts from any base to 16 at a time. As for the rehearsal, the airborne declined to participate in it for fear of possible losses. It developed into a mere simulated exercise by a skeleton force to test troop carrier command arrangements and tactics.

The American troop carriers did accomplish a great deal. During the period of joint training they dropped 19,678 paratroops, and carried 26,666 glider troops. Almost all of this, however, was done by eight of IX TCC's 15 groups*. The 50th Wing, already established in its French bases made 4,329 glider tows between 1 and 18 March, and on the 9th its A-3 Officer boasted that the wing was giving the airborne three times as much practice as they had asked for. Three groups of the 53d Wing were also active, especially the 435th, which carried 15,642 glider troops, and the 438th, which dropped 6,649 paratroops between 10 and 15 March. The 436th also did its share.

In the 52d Wing only one whole group, the 313th, engaged in joint training, and it had to, because it was equipped with the new and unfamiliar C-46. General Williams had wanted to have two paratroop regiments familiarized with the Commando and, if possible, to have it tested in an exercise. Busy until 10 March in moving to Achiet and in competing transition training on the new craft for its crews, the 313th Group then sent out 125 planes over a five-day period and dropped 3,246 men of the 513th PIR, its partner in the coming operation, to familiarize them with the characteristics of the C-46, especially its double jump-doors. The group did not attempt any mass drops. On 9 March a dozen planes of the 315th

---
*Counting the pathfinders as a group.

Group were sent from Spanhoe to Nether Avon to give jump training to paratroops of 6 Airborne. Before returning on the 15th they dropped 4,128 men, and the divisional commander expressed himself as well satisfied.

The other groups of the command did little or no joint training. The 434th Group was unable to participate because its base at Mourmelon was not ready for it to begin moving there until 10 March. Why the others did not do so is not clear, although both movement to new bases and distance from airborne units undoubtedly were inhibiting factors. Besides the American units, 46 Group, RAF, was also very short of training; 90 percent of it was retained on transport work until D minus 2.

Since these seemingly undertrained units did well in VARSITY, one may hazard the conclusion that joint training with airborne troops before an operation is not essential for experienced troop carrier units. What counted in VARSITY was the recovery of proficiency in troop carrier tactics and navigation by hard training during January and February in IX TCC and at regular intervals by relays in 46 Group.[29]

Special attention was given to the role glider pilots were to assume after landing. Their status as integral components of the troop carrier squadrons was not changed. However, for combat purposes the glider pilots of each troop carrier group were organized into units equivalent to infantry companies. The wing glider officer and a small staff would act as a battalion headquarters exercising tactical and administrative control of those companies during the ground phase. Training in infantry tactics was conducted by the 17th Airborne Division, and the glider pilots were provided with such infantry equipment as compasses, canteens, entrenching tools, and light sleeping bags, the lack of which had been felt in MARKET.

It is significant that glider pilot employment was to be much as before. On landing they would assist in unloading, then proceed to the assembly area of the airborne unit carried, assemble there into their own tactical organizations and move as units to a specified wing assembly area. There after mustering them by squadrons the wing glider officer, working in conjunction with a previously delegated representative of the airborne commander, was to assign them to such tasks as guard duty, supply collection and, circumstances permitting, to protection of usable gliders from vandalism. In spite of all the talk of using them to reinforce the infantry, it was specified that the glider pilot units were not to be committed to battle except in extreme emergency, and then only in a defensive role. Furthermore, they were to be evacuated from the combat area on the highest possible priority. Evidently Airborne Army had not been convinced that trained pilots were as expendable as riflemen.[30]

The rehearsal, appropriately called TOKEN, was postponed by unfavorable weather from 16 March to 17 March. Command arrangements, communications, navigational aids and tactics were like those planned for VARSITY. However, each serial in the coming operation was represented by a single element, including the leader and assistant leader of the serial. The VARSITY route was used as far as Wavre, after which a similar course with modified headings was used to zones near Montlaucon and back on a reciprocal route. No troops were carried and no gliders released, except that two gliders with a combat control team were landed on Villeneuve-Vertus airfield to test the functioning of the team.

While results were generally very good, an unexpected tail wind of 20 miles an hour upset the timing and caused some elements to reach their objectives as much as 12 minutes ahead of schedule. Reception of the M/F beacons along the route was poor in many cases, and the signals of the Ruhr Gee chain showed a tendency to fade. There were also failures in land-line communications with the troop carrier forces in England. The signal lines were speedily repaired, since even a brief loss of contact with 38 Group during the actual operation could have been serious. Another significant result of the rehearsal was a decision by General Williams that after passing the command departure point at Wavre the troop carrier serials would adhere to indicated air speeds instead of attempting to reach each checkpoint at a scheduled time. This change was intended to prevent the confusion which might result if some groups interfered with others by excessive slowing or speeding in an effort to meet their schedule.[31]

Briefing and Security Measures

Because VARSITY was a set piece scheduled well in advance, there was plenty of time to prepare orders and conduct briefings. On 16 March, D minus 8, IX TCC issued its field order. In accordance with instructions in a recent letter from Airborne Army, this set briefing times as late as possible. Wing commanders were to be briefed on D minus 3, group and squadron commanders and key personnel on D minus 2, and combat crews not until D minus 1. However, the practical advantages of obtaining more time to prepare outweighed these adjurations. Indications are that the wing commanders all had a good working knowledge of the operation many days before the 16th. The American wings briefed the commanders and key personnel of their groups and squadrons on D minus 5 and D minus 4; 38 Group, RAF, had held a similar briefing at Mark's Hall on 18 September, D minus 6. A majority of the combat crew briefings were held on D minus 1, but in many cases, especially where space limitations prevented a group from briefing all its squadrons at once, crew briefings had begun on the 22d.

The briefings, carefully prepared and embodying the accumulated experience of previous operations, were generally held to be excellent. The extent and quality of the intelligence provided was a source of surprise and satisfaction to the recipients. All pilots and glider pilots got maps of the route on scales of 1:500,000 and 1:250,000 and a map of the Wesel-Diersfordt area on a scale of 1:100,000. Maps and defense overprints of the DZ-LZ area on a scale of 1:25,000 were distributed for briefing in quantities of 20 or more for each group and with them numerous overlays of the area on the same scale showing the DZ's and LZ's, landmarks and obstructions, known flak positions, and the German order of battle. Photographic cover, though not complete, was very good. Every group got two sets of lithographed mosaics of the DZ-LZ area on a scale of 1:8,000 and one run-in mosaic on a scale of 1:33,000. Enlarged vertical photographs of the various zones were also distributed and in such quantity that every glider pilot received a picture of his landing zone blown up to page size. Each group was given a set of oblique photographs of the run-in strip and several of oblique panoramas of the DZ-LZ area.[32]

The security precautions taken for VARSITY were intended to conceal the composition of the attacking force and the exact time and place of the operation. The fact that an assault would soon be made across the Rhine north of the Ruhr was clear to any skilled observer of the military situation and was made even more obvious by Montgomery's massive preparations and by reports in the newspapers.

Particular pains were taken to conceal changes in radio traffic from which the enemy might deduce what was brewing. The movement of the airborne divisions to the airfields was done as unobtrusively as possible with identification marks removed from uniforms and equipment. The ground echelons of those divisions were disguised as Communications Zone troops during their move up to the front. At the airfields the precautions taken were like those before the invasion of Normandy, though not quite as stringent. On the arrival of the troops, traffic in and out of the bases was restricted and the troops were sealed in their bivouac areas. Briefed troop carrier personnel were segregated from those unbriefed, telephone service was curtailed and calls monitored, and outgoing mail was stored in special bags until after the operation.[33]

Auxiliary Air Operations

By rare good fortune VARSITY had favorable weather, not only for its grand finale but also for the three days of preparatory air operations. The opportunity was used to the full. On 21 and 22 March 1,744 Fortresses and Liberators of the Eighth Air Force, escorted by 752 fighters, dumped about 4,000 tons of bombs on the 5 jet bases and 10 other airfields which they were to put out of action. Almost all the runways attacked were thoroughly cratered. Approximately 5 bombers and 11 fighters were lost, but reports indicated that at least 62 enemy fighters had been destroyed, most of them on the ground.

On D-day 1,452 B-17's and B-24's escorted by 95 fighters dropped slightly over 4,000 tons more. In the morning they hit the jet fields again, and during the morning and afternoon they hammered a dozen additional bases, mostly night-fighter fields. Photographs showed that all the targets were badly cratered and apparently out of operation. Somehow the Germans did put jet fighters in the air on D-day, but they were a mere handful of survivors flying not as units but as individuals. The price of the D-day attacks on airfields was eight bombers all of which so far as is known, fell victim to flak, not to the Luftwaffe.[34]

Interdiction and harassing operations by the Allied air forces between first light on D minus 3 and dawn on D-day were monumental in size and complexity. In 3,471 effective bomber sorties some 8,500 tons of bombs were dropped against communications targets. Barracks and other military installations received some 6,600 tons of explosive, delivered by 2,090 bombers. Most notable of these missions against the German ground forces was the accurate dropping of 1,090 tons of bombs about 2230 on D minus 1 by 195 Lancasters and 23 Mosquitoes of Bomber Command, RAF on Nazi positions on the northwest side of Wesel only 1,500 yards ahead of British commando troops poised for assault. In addition to specific bomber missions, fighter bombers swept on armed reconnaissance over the railroads and highways, the pilots claimed a total of 215 rail cuts, 80 locomotives, 2,383 railroad cars, and 318 other vehicles.[35]

Certain bombing missions on D-day were primarily interdictory. In a morning attack on the edge of the Ruhr 506 Halifaxes and Lancasters of RAF Bomber Command dropped over 1,900 tons of bombs on marshalling yards at Sterkrade, troops near Gladbeck and industrial plants near Bottrop and Dortmund, in an operation which was at once diversionary, strategic, and interdictory. That afternoon 317 medium bombers of IX Bombardment Division were sent on a turnaround mission with the dual purpose of finishing off bridges at Colbe, Pracht, and Vlotho under the Vandenberg plan,* and hitting Borken, Bocholt, and Dorsten, these latter being among the 12 targets originally selected for interdiction on behalf of VARSITY. The bridges were hit and smashed by 173 of the 202 bombers dispatched against them. For some reason Borken and Bocholt were not attacked, but Dorsten and secondary targets at Stadtlohn, Aalten, and Dulmen were severely damaged by 120 tons of bombs dropped by 100 planes between 1500 and 1531.

Brunen and Raesfeld, two more of the original 12 interdiction targets, were also hit on the 24th by 66 medium bombers of Second TAF with 98 tons of bombs. Troop concentrations in Brunen, which was only five miles east of the Diersfordter Wald, would have been in a particularly favorable position for a counterattack against the airborne.

The bombing of flak positions prior to the arrival of the VARSITY missions was greatly handicapped by smoke and haze. Although IX Bombardment Division dispatched 433 medium and light bombers (plus 11 carrying WINDOW) for that purpose, only 285 bombed their primary objectives, and most of them had to rely on radar (Oboe) in making their attacks. Of the rest, 8 bombed other gun positions, 73 struck at miscellaneous targets, and 67 made no attack. In all, 799 tons of fragmentation and 13 tons of general purpose bombs were dropped on that mission between 0744 and 0904.* About the same time 71 medium bombers of 2 Group, RAF, were dropping 109 tons of bombs on four other antiaircraft positions. They, too, were hampered by low visibility but claimed hits on two of their objectives.[36]

On D-day escort and cover west of the Rhine were provided for the airborne missions by 213 planes of 11 Group, RAF, and by about 330 American fighters under IX Tactical Air Command.† Since in most areas relays of fighters were used to maintain protection throughout the operation, no more than a dozen American fighter squadrons and half a dozen from the RAF were guarding the route at any one time. To avoid boundary problems, the RAF fighters kept their patrols on the north side of the troop carrier lanes between Wavre and the Rhine, while the Americans stayed on the south side.

East of the Rhine, 83 and 84 Groups had five squadrons on patrol after dawn at altitudes of 5,000 and 12,000 feet over the strip bounded by Wesel, Arnhem, Winterswijk, and Dorsten. They added two more at 0930 and kept seven on the watch until after 1300. The Spitfire squadrons which formed the bulk of this force had to be replaced at one-hour intervals because of their limited fuel capacity.†† Additional fighter cover south of Wesel was provided by XXIX TAC, which had one fighter squadron on duty from 0630

---

*See above, p. 168.

*The figures given above are taken from the history of the bombardment division. Most reports rely on its operations summary, which states that 327 planes dropped 695 tons of bombs on flak positions.
†Both IX TCC and FAAA report that 676 American fighters were used as escort and cover for the troop carriers, but that figure appears to include 273 sorties by XIX TAC in the Mainz-Mannheim area more than 150 miles south of the VARSITY objectives.
††In escort, cover, and fighter sweeps 83 and 84 Groups made some 900 fighter sorties that day.

to 1000 and three during the airborne assault for a total of 72 sorties.

All the escort and cover sorties were uneventful. Only a few German planes were seen, and all kept their distance.[37]

During the airborne assault, flak positions in the vicinity of the drop and landing areas were attacked by fighter-bombers of Second TAF. Seventeen British planes were lost in this anti-flak operation.

Working south of Wesel along the exit route from the southern zones and occasionally attacking guns in the assault area itself was the 406th Fighter Group from XXIX TAC. This group made 48 sorties in relays of 12,* and lost 3 planes but claimed hits on 36 gun positions. As in MARKET the task of hunting out mobile flak batteries was difficult and dangerous; low-flying decoys had to coax the gunners into revealing their position.[38]

Besides protecting the troop carriers with air cover and anti-flak patrols, Second TAF provided all air support in the battle waged by the airborne troops. Its light bombers and fighter bombers made 412 sorties against prearranged targets, including three German headquarters. Operating partly from "cab rank" and partly on special request, 254 rocket-firing Typhoons gave close support. Meanwhile, fighters prowling north and east of the assault area flew 212 sorties on armed reconnaissence. Another 180 planes made regular reconnaissance flights.[39]

East of Münster, the Eighth Air Force made 1,158 sorties during the day in fighter sweeps against air and ground targets. Its pilots intercepted a formation of 20 German fighters about noon and another of 30 about 1530, and claimed to have destroyed 53 enemy aircraft in combat. The intercepted formations, which were both headed west, probably represented feeble efforts at air action against VARSITY. Some of the sweeps were directed against ground transportation and reportedly destroyed 8 locomotives and 132 other vehicles.[40]

---

*Widely accepted reports that 121 American fighters flew anti-flak sorties for VARSITY have a basis in Ninth Air Force totals, which probably lumped some other missions under that heading (Hq. 9th AF, Air Summary of Operation, 24 Mar 45, in 533.332).

The Final Decision and The Ground Assault

The decision on whether or not VARSITY would be launched on schedule was made by Brereton and Coningham at 1600 on 23 March. This time there was no question of postponement. The meteorologists predicted fine weather for the next day. There would be rather thick haze in the Wesel area during the early morning, but this would clear before the troop carriers' approach, giving them visibility of at least two miles there and over four miles elsewhere. Surface winds would blow at 10 to 15 miles an hour at the bases and about 10 miles an hour on the drop and landing zones. Accordingly the commanders directed that VARSITY proceed as scheduled with P-hour, the moment of the first drops, set at 1000A on 24 March. ("A" Time was Greenwich Mean Time plus one hour.) The decision was reaffirmed at 0600 on the 24th after receipt of another forecast issued at 0400. The predictions closely followed those of the previous evening. VARSITY could go as planned.[41]

Presumably General Montgomery had authorized the launching of PLUNDER, his amphibious assault, the moment he had the air commanders' assent to VARSITY. He has written that he gave the orders at 1530 on the 23d. The operation went with the textbook precision that was his trademark. At 2100, exactly as scheduled, the first wave of assault boats pushed out into the Rhine, carrying the first elements of four battalions of 51 Division. Their objective was Rees, 12 miles downstream from Wesel. At 2200 the Commando Brigade began its crossing about two miles west of Wesel. At 0200 a crossing in the Xanten area midway between Wesel and Rees was begun by four battalions of 15 Division. The 9th Army assault south of the Lippe also began at 0200. All these crossings were completely successful. Everywhere the opposite bank proved thinly held, initial resistance was feeble, and the initial artillery reaction slight.

Fierce fighting did develop at some points. German paratroops facing the northern prong of the assault held Rees throughout D-day and kept 51 Division pinned close to the river. With artillery and mortars still in positions from which they could rake the river in that sector, the Nazis prevented any bridge-building there and made ferry operations difficult. No help would reach the airborne from 51 Division, but it was engaging its share of the German defense force. The commando brigade also had its hands full. Despite the severe pounding received from Bomber Command, the garrison of Wesel clung stubbornly to portions of the town throughout the day. However, in the center 15 Division did well and by 1000 hours on D-day was in a position to capitalize on the airborne assault which was to strike the hilltop positions ahead of it.[42]

The Lift and Initial Operations of the British Airborne Division

The first mission in VARSITY to get under way was that of the 61st, 315th, and 316th Troop Carrier Groups carrying the paratroop echelon of 6 Airborne Division from Chipping Ongar, Boreham and Wethersfield. They were favored with almost perfect weather, clear skies and excellent visibility. Emplaning at Boreham was briefly delayed while the British finished their inevitable tea, and a flurry of excitement was produced at Chipping Ongar by a buzz-bomb which passed overhead and exploded near the base. However, take-offs went off about on schedule with the first plane in the air at 0709 and the last shortly after 0740. Of 243 aircraft slated to go, only one failed to depart and that because no load had been provided for it. Aboard the rest were close to 3,900 troops and 137 tons of supplies.

As usual the planes assembled into elements, the elements into flights, and the flights into serials, which then swung over their bases and headed for the departure point at Hawkinge. They reached there approximately on schedule after sighting more robot missiles en route, missiles immune to antiaircraft fire because they were in the troop carrier lane.

From England to the Rhine everything went smoothly. No navigational problems arose. The 213 planes of RAF Fighter Command guarding that part of the route had little to do, for not one enemy aircraft came within sight of the mission that day. The only flaw was an error in timing which caused the various serials to arrive from 6 to 10 minutes ahead of schedule. The crews were aware of their true position and the red warning lights flashed as usual four minutes before the actual arrival time. However, this premature arrival did cut out nearly a third of the artillery bombardment of German flak batteries which had been scheduled to last from 0930 to 1000 hours.

Near the Rhine an unexpected navigational difficulty arose. Montgomery had shielded his amphibious operations with a huge smoke screen extending for nearly 50 miles along the Rhine. Although the generators were turned off early on D-day after reconnaissance pilots reported that unfavorable flying conditions were developing, the smoke did not have time to clear. Borne on the southeast wind it covered the visual aids at Last Lap so they could be seen only from directly overhead and combined with local haze to reduce visibility between the river and the drop zones to one mile or even less. Fortunately the distance was short, less than three miles to one zone, five miles to the other; landmarks on the run-in were plentiful and not such as to be readily obscured by haze; and good Gee fixes were available in case of need. In addition some pilots were helped by the visual aids set out on the zones by the pathfinders from the lead serials. At any rate both supplies and troops were dropped with great accuracy.

Of the first three serials all reached the zone except two which had to turn back for mechanical reasons. At 0951 the rest, 80 planes of the 61st Group and 39 of the 316th began their drop of 1,920 men of 3 Parachute Brigade on or near DZ A, an irregular area about 1½ miles in diameter on the west side of the panhandle which formed the northern end of the Diersfordter Wald. The British troops showed a tendency to become entangled, with the result that some jumped late, others required a second pass, and at least 13 were brought back. Some formations, probably in the rear, came in much too high and dropped their troops from heights up to 1,150 feet. Until after the drop, flak was insignificant, but thereafter it thickened and brought down three aircraft and damaged about 30.

The next three serials had a much harder time. Their objective was DZ B, an irregular area 1½ miles long on the east side of the wood about two miles beyond DZ A. The Nazis in the wood put up surprisingly little fire. All the planes, 40 from the 316th Group and 81 from the 315th, are believed to have reached the zone and dropped at least some of their troops, although at least two aircraft were hit and burning before the jump began. The lead formation reached the zone at 1003, and during the next quarter-hour 1,917 men of

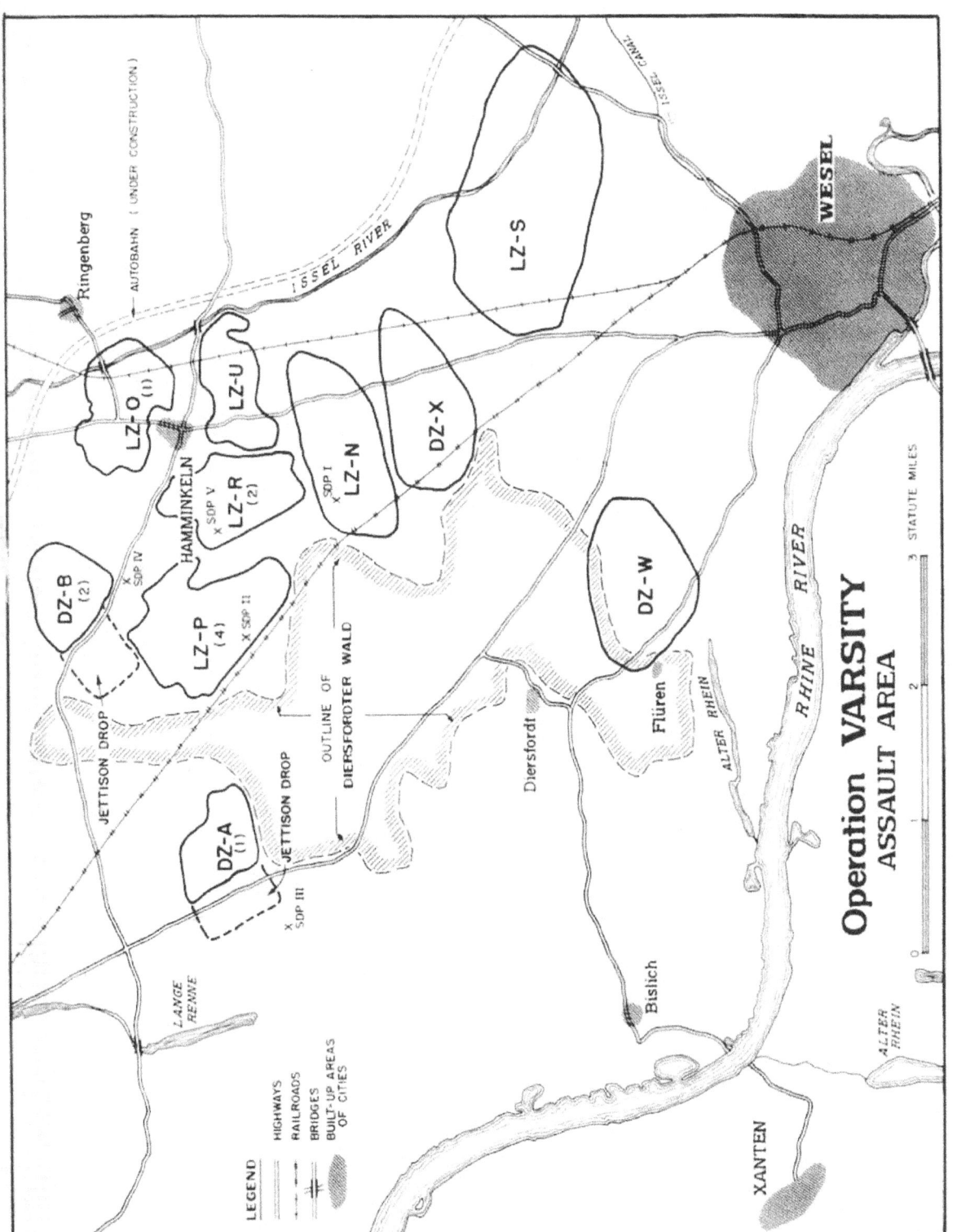

Map 12.

5 Parachute Brigade were dropped from altitudes between 700 and 1,000 feet. The troops testified that the pilots flew straight and true and gave them an accurate and generally excellent jump. Only seven soldiers were returned, all because of fouled equipment.

As the formations swung left onto a homeward course after leaving the zone, sudden blasts of intense and accurate light flak swept the serials. Of the 121 planes which had reached DZ B, 10 were shot down east of the Rhine, and 7 others crash-landed in friendly territory in such condition that only one or two of them were ever repaired. An additional 70 were damaged, most of them severely enough to make them temporarily non-operational. Troop carrier casualties amounted to only 6 dead, 20 missing, and 15 wounded or injured. However, many crews came down just behind the front; others were rescued by the rapid Allied advance after a brief term as prisoners of war.

The high ratio of aircraft losses deserves sober consideration. The losses were inflicted in a comparatively small area from which flak had supposedly been eradicated by the systematic use of overwhelmingly superior airpower. As Airborne Army analysts noted, the batteries doing the bulk of the damage were too far east to be affected by the artillery barrage. Some may well have been mobile pieces brought in at the last minute in spite of the elaborate interdiction program. Others may have eluded observation or been unsuccessfully attacked. Anyway, there they were, painful proof that flak suppression is a difficult and uncertain business.

The 61st Group returned to Abbeville-Drucat, the first plane landing at 1125. Plans to have the 315th and 316th Groups land in France had been abandoned on 22 March because their new bases there were not ready, so they had to make the long flight back to their home fields, Spanhoe and Cottesmore, at which most of their members arrived about 1300.[43]

At 1021, as soon as the British paratroops had finished jumping, the glider echelon of 6 Airborne Division was to arrive, borne by 440 gliders of 38 and 46 Groups. Of these, 370 were to carry Divisional Headquarters and 6 Airlanding Brigade to four landing zones, LZ's O, R, and U, bunched within a one-mile radius around Hamminkeln, and LZ P, an irregularly shaped area about 1½ miles long from north to south which was just west of those zones and just south of DZ B. The other 70 gliders were to land reinforcements for the paratroops on DZ's A and B. Actually, the outlines of the zones had little significance, because the commanders of 38 Group and 6 Airborne Division had decided on the advice of the commander of the glider pilot regiment to make many small, separate, precision landings as close as possible to tactical objectives instead of the massed landings employed hitherto. Speed was to be sought at the expense of concentration. Although in a sense this meant that *coup de main* procedure would be generally used, two special *coup de main* parties were to land on the eastern edges of LZ's O and U to seize bridges over the Issel.

The first tug and glider took off at 0600. This early start, over an hour ahead of the paratroop aircraft, was necessary because it took about an hour to get a batch of 60 gliders into the air and more time still to haul them up to the prescribed altitude. Only one of the tugs failed to take off. However, the heavy Horsas and Hamilcars were very apt to abort, and in this case, despite the superlatively good weather, 35 broke loose or had to be released prematurely. Two of them ditched in the Channel, but all aboard were speedily rescued.

Two hostile planes were sighted, but none attacked and the high-flying British column suffered little from flak. It lost only seven planes and had 32 damaged. At least 402 of the gliders were successfully released in the combat area. Haze, smoke and dust from the artillery and air bombardments reduced visibility to between 1,000 and 3,000 yards but helped to some extent to shield the fliers. Releases began about 10 minutes early and ranged from the planned height of 2,500 feet to 3,500 feet. So accurate were the releases that about 90 percent of the gliders landed on or very near their zones, many of them within 100 yards of their objectives. Only half a dozen missed the landing area by more than a mile, and those landed to the south in the territory of the American airborne.

The Horsas and Hamilcars fared much worse than their tugs. About 10 of them were shot down and 284 were damaged by flak. The high releases gave German gunners plenty of time to get their sights on the gliders, and they made the most of it. About half of the gliders were damaged in landing, which is not surprising considering the brittle nature of the Horsa, the inexperience of many of the pilots, and the difficulties of landing through smoke and under severe fire.

Ground resistance in many parts of the landing area was at first vigorous and effective. Artillery and incendiary bullets destroyed 32 gliders and the occupants of 38 others were so pinned down by German gunners that they could not unload. That unloading went as well as it did was attributed to the fact that most of the gliders were Mark II Horsas which had hinged noses as well as detachable tails. Only 88 gliders, less than a quarter of those reaching the battle area came through unscathed. As for their pilots, 38 were killed, 37 were wounded, and 135 were missing, a casualty rate of 28 percent.

The glider contingent would have had a much harder time had it not been for the presence of British paratroops on DZ's A and B and of American paratroops, dropped by mistake, on zones west of Hamminkeln. Thus it cannot be said that the British operations in VARSITY provide a good precedent for glider landings on zones not previously occupied by paratroops. However, the gliders did bring into the assault area a force of 3,383 airborne troops with 271 jeeps, 275 trailers, 66 guns, ranging in size from 6-pounders to 25-pounders, and a wealth of other equipment including trucks and bulldozers.

Perhaps the most successful of the three British airborne brigades was that on DZ A. It cleared the zone within an hour of its drop and by 1400 had occupied all objectives in its sector, which was on the northwest side of the Diersfordter Wald. About 1500 a battalion of 15 Division pushed up the hill and entered the paratroop positions. East of the wood the troops on DZ B suffered about 300 casualties in hard fighting around their drop zone and were not able to take their assigned place on the north flank of the division until about 1530.

The two *coup de main* parties were landed with great accuracy, and each speedily took the bridge assigned to it. The resistance encountered by the other glider troops varied tremendously from place to place. However, by nightfall all organized resistance in the British sector from the western edge of the woods to the Issel had been broken, six bridges across the river had been seized intact, and over 600 prisoners had been taken. The cost to 6 Airborne was 347 dead, 731 wounded, and 319 missing, but many of those missing soon rejoined their units.[44]

The Lift and Initial Operations of the American Paratroops

The lift of the American troops began at 0725 on the 24th when a plane of the pathfinder group, which was to fly the lead serial, took off from Chartres with the group commander, Colonel Crouch, as pilot and Col. Edson D. Raff, commander of the 507th Parachute Infantry Regiment, as a passenger. Raff had commanded the paratroops who made the first American combat jump outside Oran during the invasion of North Africa. Crouch had led the pathfinders in missions to Italy, Southern France, Normandy, and Holland. Now, appropriately enough, the two men held the place of honor in the last major airborne operation of the war.

The 46 planes in Crouch's serial flashed into the air in less than five minutes, and assembled so rapidly that they swept over the field in formation on their way to the command assembly point only 10 minutes after the last aircraft left the ground. From Prosnes, Mourmelon, and Achiet six other paratroop serials proceeded to Wavre to take their positions behind the serial from Chartres.

Over northern France and the Low Countries the sky was clear and visibility unlimited. At Achiet, which had only one usable runway, gusts of wind, blowing at 10 to 15 miles an hour across the runway caused one C-46 to swerve and crash on take-off. Only deft handling kept others from a similar fate. Not one of the C-47's in the paratroop formations failed to take off or had to turn back. However, engine trouble and a flat tire kept two C-46's from taking off, and another with engine trouble had to return after take-off. Except for three men injured in the crash, all troops in the aborting planes were transferred to four substitute aircraft, which were standing by, and flew after the rest. The last left Achiet about 0930, half an hour behind schedule.

The C-46 serials from Achiet were scheduled to reach Wavre at 0934 and 0938. In order to take their place in the right-hand lane, they would have to cross the path of the leading American glider serial, which was to enter the center stream from their right at 0936. The remedy prescribed for this awkward situation was to have the C-46's fly in the left lane, then temporarily free of British traffic, until their greater speed put them well ahead of the gliders, after which they would shift to the right-hand lane. Ingenious as it was, the arrangement left too little margin for error, considering that two very different types of formation, employing different types of planes, were to converge on the Wavre area from widely separate starting points.

What happened was that, as the C-46 pilots approached Wavre, they beheld the glider column crossing directly in front of them. The lead serial turned left, outpaced the gliders, and swung around them into its assigned lane, but it had had to make a considerable detour to do so. The second climbed to 2,000 feet and went over the gliders without changing course. Troop carrier records barely mention the incident and indicate pretty clearly that the Achiet serials quickly recovered their proper course and altitude. However, the commander of the paratroops aboard them, the 513th PIR, believed that the first serial at least never did get fully reoriented and that the subsequent inaccurate drop of his men was a result of this episode.[45]

The first four paratroop serials, a force of 181 C-47's, were to carry 2,479 troops of the 507th PIR and its teammate, the 464th Parachute Field Artillery Battalion, to DZ W. The drop zone was an egg-shaped area of fields and bottom land with a main axis about 2,000 yards long parallel to the direction of approach and with a maximum width of 1,500 yards. It nestled against the south side of the Diersfordter Wald east of the hamlet of Flüren and 2½ miles northwest of Wesel. To reach it the troop carriers would cross the Rhine at a sharp bend in the river near Xanten and from there would fly east-northeast for about three miles to the zone. During most of the run-in they would have on their right a natural pointer, the Alter Rhein, a long, straight, narrow lake in an old riverbed parallel to their course. Shortly before reaching the zone the fliers would pass for a few hundred yards over a hook of woodland projecting from the southwest corner of the Diersfordter Wald.[46]

Given even passable visibility the drop was almost bound to be accurate, but DZ W lay under a pall of smoke blown by the southeast wind from the bombed ruins of Wesel and from Second Army smoke pots along the river, only a mile south of the run-in. The fliers could glimpse colored panels at Last Lap and see the Rhine. Beyond the river the ground was invisible except through an occassional rift in the smoke.

Enemy action had little or no effect on the drop. Since the Germans had already been driven from the open land near the river, ground fire was negligible west of the woods. The first two serials found it everywhere very slight, probably because they took the enemy by surprise. They lost only one plane, hit on its homeward turn, and had five or six damaged. The other two serials bound for DZ W received more fire, mostly from small arms, but, although 29 planes were hit not one was shot down. There was no air opposition although one or two hostile planes were seen on the way back.[47]

The lead serial, which carried the 1st Battalion, lost its way in the smoke, and at about 0950* its first three flights dropped Raff and 493 men on the western edge of the Diersfordter Wald more than two miles northwest of DZ W. This placed them in the sector allotted to the 513th PIR and a little way northeast of the fortress known as Schloss Diersfordt, a major objective, the taking of which had been delegated to the 3d Battalion of the 507th. The rear elements of the serial held closer to course and dropped 200 men of the 1st Battalion somewhat to the south of the castle.

Instead of attempting a trek to the drop zone, both groups went into action on the spot. Raff's men drove confused and wavering German troops out of good positions in the nearby woods, killing some 55, taking over 300 prisoners, and capturing a battery of 150-mm. howitzers. Then they marched south to attack the castle where at about 1100 they found the rest of the battalion already engaging the German occupants.

The second and third serials, both flown by the 438th Group, approached DZ W accurately in good formation and placed the 2d and 3d Battalions of the 507th squarely on the zone. The 2d Battalion came down under heavy fire from German troops concentrated in the woods north and west of it. Nevertheless, the paratroops assembled quickly into platoons and companies, moved against the enemy strongpoints, and by 1100 had taken them in a series of short, fierce actions. Their biggest prize was a battery of 81-mm. mortars which had been zeroed in on the zone. The

---

*Troop carrier and airborne sources give times ranging from 0948 to 0957, but this is considered most likely. (Hist 1st TC Pfdr Sq, Mar 45.)

3d Battalion also had to conduct a fighting assembly, in the course of which it took about 150 prisoners. However, within 45 minutes after its jump 75 percent of the battalion had been concentrated in readiness to move to Schloss Diersfordt. Altogether, the regiment is reported to have had 90 percent of its personnel assembled within an hour and a half after its jump. Under the circumstances this indicates a high degree of concentration in all three drops as well as excellent performance by the troops.

The fourth serial, which reached the zone about 1005*, was fairly accurate, but its drop of the 464th Field Artillery Battalion was somewhat dispersed. Elements of the battalion were dropped as much as 1,500 yards northwest of the DZ. Under brisk fire from the woods as they hit the ground, the artillerymen hastily set up three 50-cal. machine guns and three howitzers and laid direct fire on the most troublesome enemy positions. After the fighting around them died down, they moved according to plan to the northeast end of the zone and by 1300 hours had 9 of their 12 howitzers set up there. The other 3 had been damaged in landing because the parachutes did not open properly. The battalion only fired 50 rounds that day, most of them during the afternoon in a difficult but successful duel with an 88-mm. gun, two 75's, and a mortar located around a house which the 464th had intended to use as its command post. Maj. Gen. William M. Miley, the divisional commander, jumped with the artillery, but was little more than an observer during the initial stages of the battle. High-level coordination of the innumerable small-unit actions was neither possible nor necessary.

During the afternoon German morale weakened, and resistance in the 507th's sector almost vanished. The last big fight was at the castle. The 3d Battalion arrived there at 1200 after a rapid march through the woods, relieved the 1st Battalion, excepting Company A, which was already deployed, and launched an attack. Within an hour they had taken all the fortress but an isolated turret, bagging some 500 prisoners and five medium tanks.† Evidently German hope and fighting spirit were vanishing together.

Within 3½ hours after its jump the 507th had taken all its assigned objectives, and it appears to have done so in the face of numerically superior forces. It captured that day approximately 1,000 prisoners* belonging to three regiments of the German 84th Division, an artillery regiment, a GHQ battalion and an antiaircraft battery.

What remained to be done was to link up with the ground forces and other airborne units. Contact with elements of the 194th Glider Infantry east of DZ W was achieved early in the afternoon. At 1300 Company D met advance elements of 15 Division, and Company F reported contact with that division at 1434. At 1803 the paratroops joined forces with the British airborne on the northern boundary of their sector, and at 0200 next morning a patrol to the southeast reached the British troops in the Wesel area. In contact with friendly forces on all sides the 507th had nothing more to do in its sector except a little mopping up.[48]

The last three of the seven serials carrying American paratroops were to bring the 513th Parachute Infantry Regiment and the 466th Parachute Field Artillery Battalion to DZ X. This zone was a rough quadrangle, some 2,500 yards long from east to west and about 1,000 yards wide, consisting mostly of small, flat fields. The double-track railway to Wesel ran just inside its western boundary, making an excellent checkpoint for the drop. DZ X was set against the east side of the Diersfordter Wald about 1¼ miles east-northeast of DZ W and 2½ miles north-northwest of Wesel. For more than a mile before reaching the zone the troop carrier formations would have to fly over the central portion of the wood.

The whole air echelon of the 513th PIR, 2,071 men with 64 tons of supplies and equipment, had been lifted from Achiet by 72 C-46's of the 313th Group, 35 in the lead serial, 34 in the second and 3 substitutes flying many miles behind them. Because of the speed of the C-46 the verbal warning was given 15 minutes before the jump instead of 20, and the red light 3 instead of 4 minutes in advance. There was much jostling within the serials, probably because the 313th Group had had insufficient opportunity to fly their new planes in large formations. One jam which occurred as they approached the Rhine may have played its

---
*Again there is disagreement on the time.
†The paratroops knocked out one tank with a Gammon grenade and two with recoilless 57-mm. guns. The other two were destroyed by the fire of heavy artillery from across the Rhine.

*There are very large discrepancies in the POW figures reported by the airborne troops. The captives had come in so rapidly that it was hard to keep track of them.

part in throwing them off course. The pilots all appear to have believed that they crossed the river at the proper point, but their crossing place was not particularly distinctive, and it is perhaps significant that only one crew reported seeing the panels set out near the west bank to mark it. East of the Rhine the visibility was about half a mile, very bad, though a little better than that on the approaches to DZ W.

Moderate and rather inaccurate light flak and small-arms fire met the two serials as they passed over the wood. Several planes, including the lead ship, flown by Lt. Col. William L. Filer, commander of the 313th, burst into flames, but all were able to continue. Although no one bailed out or turned back the plight of the leader may have affected the accuracy of the drop.

At 1008 the first serial of the 313th reached what appeared to be the drop zone. As they let down to make their drop they were raked by intense and accurate light flak and small-arms fire from positions on their left and received some heavier flak from the right. Suddenly the sky seemed full of burning and exploding planes. The formations began to break up and congestion forced some pilots to slow to as little as 80 miles an hour. The C-46's displayed remarkable resistance to stalling, but one, apparently unhit, did dive into the ground with all its crew and troops. The other 68 in the serials dropped their troops from heights of 600 to 1,000 feet. Of three stragglers, two dropped behind the seventh serial at 1023, and the other after running into interference in two passes over the zone dropped its troops on the west bank of the Rhine. On one plane a bundle stuck in the door prevented a dozen men from jumping, and eight others were brought back, most of them because of wounds. Several paratroops made the jump in spite of being already wounded.

Accurate and intense ground fire, especially from positions along the Issel, continued while the C-46 serials were making their right turn after the drop, and some shooting followed them until they got back to the Rhine. As the remnants of the 313th trickled into Achiet between 1110 and 1147 it became evident that the group had suffered a disaster. The German guns had taken a toll of 19 planes destroyed or fit only for salvage and another 38 damaged, many of them severely. Personnel losses, though less than at first expected, stood a week later at one dead, 22 wounded or injured, and 33 missing.

Of the 19 planes lost, 14 had gone down in flames. Participants in the mission agreed that the C-46 seemed to catch on fire every time it was hit in a vital spot. The 313th Group blamed this inflammability on the plane's complex hydraulic system. The technicians of the 52d Wing attributed it to the arrangement of the wing tanks which, when they were hit, caused gasoline to travel along the inside of the wing toward the fuselage.

In other respects the C-46 showed it could endure punishment very well. One Commando received a direct flak hit on the left engine, then three in the fuselage, and glided to a landing after another hit stopped the right engine. The crew tried to count the small holes in the plane from bullets and shrapnel, but quit when they reached 200. Another plane landed safely at a friendly base with two large shell holes in the left wing, one in the right stabilizer, and major flak damage to the left propeller, the controls, the fuselage, the tail wheel nacelle, and the wheel itself, not to mention numerous bullet holes, some of which had punctured a gas tank.[49]

Unlike the pilots of Crouch's serial, who were vaguely aware that they had missed their mark, those of the 313th were sure that they had either hit their zone or come extremely close to it. Actually they had deposited their paratroops between 1½ and 2 miles north of DZ X in fields southwest of Hamminkeln. Where they crossed the Diersfordter Wald the wood was about as wide as on their proper course, and the relative position of the double-track railroad beyond it was similar to what it was on the true zone. Thus such glimpses as the fliers had of these landmarks merely confirmed them in their error. Indeed, the commander of the 513th PIR was equally deceived and supposed himself to be on the drop zone for quite a while after he reached the ground. The puzzling aspect of the situation is not the failure of visual navigation but the failure of radar to correct it. The 313th reported that its navigators made frequent and successful use of Gee both along the route and in the DZ area, relying principally on the Ruhr chain. As observed earlier, pinpoint accuracy in the use of Gee was not easy to attain, but in this case a single good fix should have sufficed to show that the 313th was too far to the north.⁵⁰

Most of the 513th Parachute Infantry came down within an area approximately the same size as their intended zone. The drop pattern was such that they were able to concentrate within an hour into about six large groups. The greater part of the 2d Battalion assembled and organized within thirty minutes under intense small-arms fire.

Once assembled the paratroops engaged the enemy in their vicinity and disposed of them effectively. The British airborne into whose sector they had descended testified that the Americans were excellent fighters and very helpful. Fighting and reconnoitering in the drop area occupied a majority of the 513th PIR until after noon. Not until after 1230 did three groups of its men, one from the 1st Battalion, one from the 2d, and another led by the regimental commander, join forces about a mile southwest of Hamminkeln. This regimental nucleus then reorganized and prepared to fight its way south into its assigned area. The movement was sharply contested and had to be interrupted several times for operations against strongpoints along the line of advance. However, the main body of 513th reached DZ X about the middle of the afternoon. Other portions of the regiment made their way to the zone independently against opposition varying from fierce to feeble. First to reach it was a group from the 3d Battalion which had oriented itself quickly, moved south immediately after assembly and reached the drop zone about 1300. Other bodies of men arrived at 1330 and 1530. Because the regimental objectives in the Diersfordter Wald had already been cleared by the 1st Battalion of the 507th PIR and those east of the wood had been taken by members of the 194th Glider Combat Team, the 513th after reaching DZ X was able to deploy almost unopposed into its assigned positions in the northern portion of the 17th Division's sector. In spite of, or perhaps because of, its peregrinations the regiment had destroyed two tanks and two batteries of 88-mm. guns and captured about 1,150 prisoners during the day.

One question which had perplexed the leaders of the 513th PIR during the morning was the whereabouts of their supporting artillery unit, the 466th Parachute Field Artillery Battalion. They were all completely out of contact with it. The reason was that the battalion had come down where it was supposed to, on DZ X. The last parachute serial, a formation of 45 C-47's from the 434th Group, had flown accurately to the drop zone and dropped 376 artillerymen and 12 howitzers* there at 1023. Nine overeager men had jumped west of the Rhine, and two wounded men were brought back. Ground fire against that serial was nowhere more than moderate. It caused the loss of only one plane and damage to 17. This record suggests that if the two preceding serials had followed the proper course their losses would have been much less than those they did incur.⁵¹

At first the fighting in the drop area was severe, and the artillerymen with only a couple of sticks of infantry to assist them were in a difficult position. All the officers in one battery were killed or wounded within a few minutes after they hit the ground. However, the 466th fought manfully to clear its zone and was greatly aided by glider troops landed north of it on LZ N and south of it on LZ S. Here is a case in which the closeness of the zones and the decision to bring in the gliders immediately after the paratroops was beneficial and may have saved the artillerymen from heavy losses. The amount of infantry fighting that the artillerymen had to do is shown by the fact that they killed some 50 Germans, took 320 prisoners and captured ten 76-mm. guns, eight 20-mm. guns and 18 machine guns.

Within 30 minutes after its jump the battalion had some howitzers in operation. Except for one piece which had been damaged by enemy fire, all its 12 howitzers were in position and ready to fire by 1300 hours. Radio contact with the 513th Regiment was made about noon, and during the regiment's move south the 466th gave it effective artillery support against several German strongpoints. The gunners' performance was the more creditable in that they were in the strange situation of firing from behind the enemy toward their own attacking infantry.⁵²

The Lift and Initial Operations of the American Glider Troops

A *Stars and Stripes* headline on the day after VARSITY proclaimed that "All Was Clockwork" in the American glider operations. Successful they

---
*Three howitzers landed by glider on LZ N joined the battalion later.

Figure 11. Troop Carrier Aircraft Carrying Paratroops in Operation VARSITY, 24 March 1945.

certainly were, but like most combat missions, they did not go with metronomic smoothness.

Of the 610 C-47's and 906 Wacos scheduled to go, 8 planes and 14 gliders had to be replaced by substitutes, either because of unfitness to take off or because they aborted soon after starting. An additional 21 gliders dropped out along the route, principally on account of loose or ill-balanced loads, but also because of structural weaknesses and towing difficulties. Three pairs of Wacos flying in double-tow had the short-tow glider foul its mate's rope, with the result that two lost wings and crashed and three had to be cut loose. Aside from these accidents, double-tow worked well. Although the slowness with which double-tow combinations took the air, even on runways close to 6,000 feet long, made observers hold their breath, there were no crashes on take-off. Formation flying along the way was made difficult by extreme turbulence, which Col. Adriel N. Williams of the 436th Group called the worst he had ever experienced. So strenous was the task of holding the gliders in position that many of their pilots and co-pilots were glad to be able to alternate in 15-minute stints at the controls. As a further complication, the prescribed air speed of 110 miles an hour turned out to be too slow, causing some near stalls and much jockeying for position. Thanks to the clear skies, the simple course, and the effective system of beacons no serious navigational problems appeared until the formations reached the Rhine. The intercom sets, as usual, proved unsatisfactory. In the 50th Wing less than half of them functioned.

The first contingent, two serials apiece from the 437th, 436th, 435th, and 439th Troop Carrier Groups (the last being under the control of the 53d Wing for the operation), all used double-tow, and were the only ones to use it. They flew the 194th Glider Infantry Regiment, the 680th and 681st Field Artillery Battalions and four batteries of the 155th Antiaircraft Battalion to LZ S. The zone was a crude rectangle more than two miles long and more than a mile wide, with its long axis tilted east-southeast. It was about half a mile southeast of DZ X and about two miles northeast of Wesel. The double-track railroad ran just to the west of it. The most obvious landmark on the LZ itself was the Issel, which curved across the zone, isolating the eastern quarter from the rest.

The standard procedure was take-off at 30-second intervals from static hook-up. At Melun and Brétigny the 435th and 436th groups were able to use two runways, one for each serial, but the 437th at Coulommiers and the 439th at Chateaudun had to get along with a single runway apiece. Nevertheless, the 437th Group, which began its take-offs at 0734 had its first serial as-

Figure 12. Paratroop Drop near Wesel, Germany, during Operation VARSITY, 24 March 1945.

sembled and swinging over the field onto course at 0823. The rest followed it to Wavre and down the center lane to the Rhine. Their performance en route was good but, for reasons already noted, by no means perfect. The commander of the 53d Wing, while expressing himself later as very well pleased with his men, considered that even the best formation could have been improved.

The run-in from the bend in the Rhine near Xanten to LZ S was about six miles long. It touched the southern edge of DZ W. There the column was to split in two, one line heading for the northern part of the landing zone and one for the southern part, so that the gliders in each serial could avoid congestion by landing in pairs in two separate patterns. In order to land into the wind they were to make a 270° turn to the left after release.

The glider formations met with the same smoke and haze which had proved such an obstacle to the paratroop echelon. Visibility over parts of the run-in area was reported to be as low as an eighth of a mile, and the landing zone itself was very hard to see. However, only a fraction of one or two serials appear to have gone off course. Possibly the pilots could observe the landmarks better than the faster-moving paratroop formations, or possibly the zone was far enough to the southwest to be somewhat in the lee of the smoke.

During the approach ground fire brought down two planes in the lead serial, forcing their gliders to cut and land about a mile short of their destination. However, the thickest fire was at the LZ and on the turn and consisted at worst of moderate light flak and intense automatic and small arms fire. In all, out of 295 planes entering the battle area on their way to LZ S, 12 were shot down, one lost by accident on its return, and about 140 damaged. Although 14 of the damaged planes were forced to make emergency landings and about that many more needed 3d or 4th echelon repairs, a great many had nothing but harmless bullet holes. Of the crews, four men were known to be dead, seven wounded, and 23 missing at the end of the month.

The lead serial made its release at 1036, the last at 1140. Within little more than an hour they delivered approximately 572 gliders containing 3,492 troops and 637 tons of cargo, including 202 jeeps, 94 trailers, and 78 mortars and artillery pieces, to the vicinity of LZ S.*

As usual that day most of the serials appear to have reached the zone between 5 and 10 minutes ahead of schedule. An exception to this was the 436th Group, which was 14 minutes early. It overran the rear formations of the 437th Group, causing a jam. As a result about half the pilots of the 436th had to climb and release their gliders from altitudes between 1,000 and 1,700 feet. The other serials maintained safe intervals and with few exceptions released in formation from heights of 400 to 800 feet.

Once Wesel was passed, the return was unopposed. The planes swept back across the Rhine, dropped their tow ropes in a specially designated zone five miles south of Xanten,† and headed home on the prescribed reciprocal course. The first planes of the lead serial reached Coulommiers on schedule at 1225, and by 1345 most formations had landed. The flow of stragglers continued until 1500. At least 37 of them had simply stopped at authorized emergency fields to refuel.

In accuracy and concentration the glider landings compared favorably with those in previous operations. Since the conditions were far from favorable, the improvement may be attributed to better training and especially to the rule that every glider pilot make at least five landings a month. Of 157 loads delivered by the first two serials, 139 were well concentrated at their proper destination, the east end of LZ S, 11 landed within a mile of the zone, 4 fell short as a result of enemy action, 2 were missing, and 1 straggler landed several miles to the north. A sequence of 15 gliders at the tail of the lead serial achieved the feat of packing themselves into a strip a quarter-mile long, and the first dozen of the next serial did equally well in a neighboring area.

In the four middle serials the Wacos were spread loosely all over the zone, about a dozen outliers were scattered up to a mile away from it, and two landed more than two miles off in the British sector. After the last two serials split at DZ W, part of the left-hand line deviated too far to the north.

In consequence, of 141 gliders brought across the Rhine by those two serials, only 58 landed as they were supposed to on the west end of the zone, a couple of others were on other parts of the LZ, about 50 within a mile of it, mostly to the northwest, 21 between 1 and 2 miles northwest, 4 slightly further in that direction, and 6 were missing.

This error by the 439th Group, the only significant inaccuracy by American glider formations in VARSITY, was less serious than it might have been. Since most of the territory for three miles northwest of LZ S was occupied by other drop and landing zones, most of the misplaced glider men found themselves among friendly troops.

As the gliders swooped down in their 270° turn, they ran into savage fire from flak and small arms. According to one prisoner, the Germans had fused their shells to burst at 500 feet, a little low for most of the planes but effective against the gliders. Also, it was observed that the gunners seemed to concentrate on the gliders rather than on the planes. Over 50 percent of the descending craft were hit by flak and a similar proportion by small arms. Less than a third were unhit. The gliders given high releases by the 436th Group seem to have suffered a little more than the rest from flak, but otherwise all serials fared approximately the same. Never had the toughness and stability of the Wacos shown to better advantage. Though most of them were hit, only a few, perhaps half a dozen, were shot down.

The enemy had set up no landing obstacles worthy of mention, but many gliders were wrecked on landing, usually by collision with trees, phone poles or other gliders. Wounded pilots and damaged controls were contributing factors in some cases. The report on one glider was "Controls hit by flak in air. Wings and nose gone. Pilot and co-pilot hit. 12 EM WIA." "Wing tip shorn on telephone pole. Landing gear shorn in trees. Flak hit tail in air. Load and personnel O.K." was the laconic entry on another.* As usual a majority of the Wacos suffered minor damage to landing gear, nose or wings, generally from landing on soft ground or hitting fences or hedges. Such accidents, however, rarely harmed occupants or cargo. One glider plunged through three fences without damaging its contents.

---

*The initial load had been 592 Wacos with 3,594 troops and 654 tons of cargo including 208 jeeps, 101 trailers and 84 mortars and guns.

†Similar areas had been designated for other glider missions, but this was the first in which friendly territory could be used for the purpose. Tow ropes were too valuable to be dropped at random or over enemy territory if it could be avoided. At the same time, falling ropes were too dangerous to allow their being dropped on the zones or near the troop concentrations on the west bank of the Rhine.

*Report of Glider Operation, 24 Mar 45, Serial #10, in KCRC, files of 17th Abn Div.

The moment after landing was the most perilous of all. The zone was infested with entrenched riflemen and machine gunners. Every building in sight seemed to house its crew of snipers. There were several batteries of 20-mm. flak guns, at least four 75-mm. and 88-mm. pieces and innumerable mortars in action. At least nine gliders were destroyed on the ground by shells and tracers. Several other Wacos were so raked by machine guns and rifle fire that all or most of the occupants were hit before they could take cover. Under the circumstances fighting came first and assembly second.[53]

The role of the 194th Glider Infantry and its attendant artillery was to occupy the southeast corner of the divisional sector bounded on the east and south by the Issel River and Canal. It was to make contact with the British commandos on the southwest, the 507th PIR to the west and the 513th PIR on the north.

At first LZ S was a scene of the wildest confusion with at least 150 small battles raging at various points. In these fights concentration counted heavily. The 2d Battalion with 90 percent of its gliders on the zone, most of them well grouped, was off to the best start. Its companies had assembled and were advancing on their objectives within 45 minutes after landing. Fastest of all was half of Company E. Thanks to exemplary performances by pilots and glider pilots of the 437th Troop Carrier Group in the second serial it was able to assemble within a quarter of an hour, taking 50 prisoners in the process. Shortly thereafter it and part of Company F converged upon a German regimental CP and took it with a rush. So bewilderingly swift had been their onslaught that as the German commander was going out the door of the dugout under guard, an orderly, unaware that the CP had been captured, dashed out of an inner room calling "Sir, you forgot your maps."

By noon the 194th Glider Regiment was 73 percent assembled, and German resistance was beginning to crumble. The defenders' efforts had been directed principally at knocking out the airborne forces as they landed. Once the speed and size of the attack and the aggressiveness of the attackers made it evident that that was a vain hope, most of the Nazis saw no point in further resistance. The only area in which substantial counterattacks were attempted was to the south. In that sector the Germans struck back, using several Mark IV tanks. Four of the tanks were knocked out by bazookas, but Company G was repeatedly pinned down and had some of its positions overrun. Not until sundown did a patrol get through to Wesel to make contact with the commando troops. That night much of the area between the landing zone and the city was still a no-man's land. Out of it about midnight emerged a force of about 150 Germans with two or three tanks and self-propelled guns. They ran into the glider pilots of the 435th Group, who, organized as an infantry company, and with the help of a couple of antiaircraft batteries, were guarding a crossroad northeast of Wesel. The defenders held their fire until the enemy was close, then smashed the attack with a single volley, which killed about 50 men and knocked out a tank. The Germans stumbled off into the darkness, ran against a position manned by glider infantry and broke up. So ended organized resistance in the territory allotted to the 194th Glider Regiment. The regiment had taken about 1,150 prisoners and had destroyed or captured 10 tanks, 2 flak wagons, 37 artillery pieces and ten 20-mm, antiaircraft guns. The airborne units on LZ S had had over 50 dead and 100 wounded or injured during the landings and the initial assembly period. Of the glider pilots accompanying them 18 were killed, 80 wounded or injured, and 30 still missing three weeks later.

It is to be noted that the first artillery support received by the 194th Glider Infantry came not from the guns landed with it but from British guns across the Rhine, against targets given them over the radio of the 681st Field Artillery. They went into action soon after the landings, at a time when assistance was particularly welcome, and continued to good effect throughout the day. In some contrast to this was the effort of the 680th Field Artillery which fired only three missions totalling 20 rounds that day, although it did manage to get eight guns into position after a dispersed landing and some hard infantry fighting. Two of its guns had been landed too far away to reach the unit on D-day, and two had been destroyed by enemy fire. The 681st was firing coordinated missions within two hours after landing and executed six missions that day, firing a total of 79 rounds. It had assembled 10 usable guns. Another, landed beyond the Issel, was fired, but later abandoned. All of the antiaircraft guns appear to have arrived safely.[54]

The last seven American glider serials were to go to LZ N. This zone, about 1½ miles long and half a mile wide, lay against the east side of the Diersfordter Wald about 4 miles north of Wesel. It was tightly sandwiched between DZ X on the south and two British landing zones to the north. Once again the principal landmark on the zone was the ubiquitous double-track railway, which slanted across its western end.

The 440th Group was to send two 45-plane serials to LZ N from Bricy, the 441st one of 48 from Dreux, the 442d one of 48 from St. André de l'Eure, and the 441st and 442d would each contribute half of another 48-plane serial from Chartres. These were all from the 50th Wing and would fall into line at Pontoise, the wing departure point. Two 40-plane serials of the 314th Group from Poix in the 52d Wing area would take position behind them at Wavre. All were to haul Waco gliders in single-tow. Bricy had a giant runway 7,700 feet long, but the other bases were unsuitable for double-tow operations, either because of short runways or lack of marshalling facilities.

The load going to LZ N amounted to 1,321 troops and 382 tons of supplies and equipment, including 143 jeeps, 97 trailers and carts and 20 guns and mortars. The troops consisted of the 139th Engineer Battalion and a mélange of medics, signal men and staff personnel. These specialists had been protected as far as possible by sending them last and by providing that the 513th PIR should occupy the landing zone before they arrived. However, at the time of the landings the 513th was still pulling itself together after its unexpected drop near Hamminkeln.

Take-off and assembly was punctual and without serious accidents, although the strong wind created difficulties, especially at St. André de l'Eure, where it blew at right angles to the runway. The leader of the 440th Group took off from Bricy at 0831, and all 90 of his group's tug-glider combinations were in the air within 38 minutes, having taken off at 20-second intervals.* The 442d Group's 48-plane serial from St. André began its take-offs at 0900 and swung over the field in full formation headed for Pontoise at 0935.

Wind, turbulence, prop-wash, and the unduly slow air speed specified in the orders gradually distorted the glider formations, and caused the rear elements of the serials to stack up until they were some 400 feet or more above the leaders. On the other hand, all but one glider, which was cut loose because of structural weakness, arrived at the Rhine squarely on course, within sighting distance of the white panels and yellow smoke which marked the point where they were to cross the river. Excellent fighter cover, both above and below their level, protected them as they approached the battle area. Between Wavre and the Rhine eight flights of fighters were seen, and protection by one flight or more was continuous. No German fighters came forth to challenge them.

Ground fire between the Rhine and the landing zone was remarkably meager and ineffective. There was only an occasional rattle of small-arms fire as the serials crossed the concave waist of the Diersfordter Wald. Most of the enemy in that part of the wood had already been dealt with by the 507th Parachute Infantry. Fire from the zone itself was hot enough to make Lt. Col W. H. Parkhill of the 441st Group describe it as a flaming hellhole, but the shooting was directed at the gliders. The planes were mostly left alone.

Between 1404 and 1505 the serials returned to their bases almost intact amid a festive atmosphere at opposite poles from the anxiety and sorrow in the 313th Group. Out of 313 planes winging over or near LZ N only 3 were lost and 44 damaged. Moreover, only 9 of the damaged craft needed 3d or 4th echelon repairs. Not a man in their crews was killed or missing and just 3 were wounded. All losses and most of the damage appear to have been incurred during the turn, a mile or more beyond the zone at points where the formations came temporarily within range of enemy positions beyond Issel.

The first glider release over LZ N was made at 1155, five minutes ahead of schedule, and subsequent releases ran from three to six minutes early. The seven-minute interval allotted each serial proved a little too tight for 48-plane formations, and one or two of them overran their predecessors. This happened to the 441st Group's serial from Dreux, and probably accounts for the fact that it released too soon and too high, at the west end of the zone instead of the east and at 1,000 to 2,000 feet instead of 600 feet above the ground. In other serials the lead elements generally came in at about the right height, but the rear usually slanted up to over 1,200 feet and in the last serial as high as

---
*Two had to return with engine trouble and were replaced by substitutes.

2,500 feet. Such differences in altitude made it impossible to follow a uniform landing pattern. Many gliders were so high that their pilots felt it necessary to make more than the prescribed 270 degree left turn, and some in the 441st Group made one or even two complete circles before beginning that turn.

Haze and smoke, which still held visibility to about half a mile, also disrupted the landings. The glider pilots could see the ground beneath them quite well but could make out very little ahead of them or to the side until they were about 200 feet from the ground. Men who did not know exactly where they were on release needed a rare eye for terrain to orient themselves on the basis of a few fields and farm buildings. Many had no idea where they were when they landed.

Intense fire, mainly from small arms, met the gliders as they coasted down. As a rule, whether by design or because they could not see through the smoke, the Germans held their fire until the Wacos were below the 500-foot level, so the high releases did not produce appreciably greater damage or casualties than the normal ones. Only one glider is known to have been shot down, but at least a quarter of them were hit, producing some damage and several casualties.

Every one of the serials intended for LZ N appears to have released over or very near that zone.* This is sufficiently demonstrated by the fact that of 302 gliders, the positions of which are recorded, about 200 landed on the zone, not more than 15 landed over 1,000 yards away from it and none more than a mile and a half away. The south wind combined with the low visibility to produce a tendency to land further north than was proper. In the first five serials only 6 gliders landed south of the zone and 61, including 5 outside the 1000-yard mark, landed to the north. The last two serials, which had been allotted the southwest portion of the zone, released over or outside the edge within sight of panel markings and smoke set out on DZ X. As a result none of their gliders came down north of LZ N but about 31 landed south of it, 7 of them far enough south to be on or near LZ S.†

Although accuracy was fairly good, concentration was poor. The first two serials, scheduled to land in the north central part of the zone, spread out quite evenly all over it. The next, supposed to use the east end of the LZ, put 15 gliders at its western end and scattered many others. The last four serials were likewise dispersed, but with a tendency to string out from north to south. It was exceptional for a sequence of more than four gliders to land together. Thus, whereas initial assembly of the airborne on LZ S was frequently by platoons and pairs of platoons, on LZ N it had to be by squads and pairs of squads. Although there were some complaints that the glider pilots had lacked air discipline and had gone on the principle of every man for himself, the prevailing view was that they had landed as well as could be expected, considering that they had to contend with low visibility and intense ground fire and that so many of them had been released from faulty formations at improper altitudes. Those in the later serials had the added excuse of having found the best of their assigned fields already occupied not only by American gliders but by several British Horsas.

Unwilling to serve as targets any longer than necessary, a large proportion of the glider pilots dove down in tight spirals and made fast, rough landings. Over 50 percent of the gliders were damaged in accidents, but once again almost all their loads came through intact. While some gliders landed among friendly troops north or south of LZ N, the zone itself was enemy territory. No advance party of paratroops had arrived to neutralize it. The Germans seemed to have a detachment in every building or patch of woods, and although loath to venture from cover, they maintained a steady fire. Many glider men were slain in their seats, and many loads were burned or destroyed by mortars. In several cases the airborne were pinned down for as much as two hours. As of early April, glider pilot casualties stood at 14 dead, 26 wounded, and 51 missing, a ratio indicating resistance almost as severe as that on LZ S. Actually the defending force in the vicinity of LZ N appears to have been relatively small and lacking in artillery* but its opponents, not much more numerous, were mostly semi-combatant specialists, and rather widely dispersed. Fighting lasted

---

*As on LZ S, the formations were to split as they approached the zone and release in columns of pairs 600 yards apart. Elements of these columns may have spread too widely.

†The three landing farthest south had made a right turn instead of a left turn on release. (MR 50th TC Sq, 24 Mar 45; Hq 50th TC, Operation VARSITY, Composite Narrative of Squadron Glider Pilots, 30 Mar 45.)

*A single 88-mm. gun is said to have been the only piece of sizable artillery on the zone. (Hist 97th TC Sq; Mar 45.)

until about 0530 with the 139th Engineer Battalion doing the lion's share of the work in clearing the zone. That day its men killed 83 Germans and captured 315.[55]

Resupply

Close behind the last troop carrier formation came the bombers engaged in the D-day resupply mission. In contrast to the bombers' supply drop in MARKET, this had been planned well in advance. The Second Air Division had been told in general terms by the Eighth Air Force on 9 March to prepare for such a mission. On the 14th in collaboration with Eighth Air Force planners the Division had blocked out a tentative plan which called for a run on a south-to-north heading followed by a quick left turn into friendly territory. However, in the big conference at Second TAF on the 17th the plan was changed to give the bombers the same route as the troop carriers as far as the drop zones and a right turn after the drop to take advantage of measures to be taken against flak in the Wesel area.

The field order issued by the Division on the 22d called for 240 B-24's to take off from East Anglia and pick up the troop carrier route at Hawkinge. The bomber force was to keep in the right-hand lane from Wavre on and was to descend gradually from heights of 3,000 feet over England, 1,500 feet over the Channel, and 1,000 feet at Wavre to a drop altitude between 300 and 500 feet. From a cruising speed of 160 miles an hour at Wavre the B-24's were to slow to 155 miles per hour at the IP and to 150 or under for the drop. Any danger that they would overrun the much slower glider formations was to be reported by the escort commander in time for the bombers to regain a proper interval by making a circle or a dogleg. At Wavre the nine groups committed were to fall into trail and at the IP the individual flights would do so. The basic formation would be the nine-plane V of V's, loose en route and tightened for the final run. Two weather planes 20 minutes ahead were to report on conditions at the destination.

At 1257 the first planes were to begin dropping supplies for the 17th Airborne to Supply Drop Point W. This was an oval about 2,000 yards long from east to west and 1,500 yards from north to south, roughly identical with DZ W. It may be recalled that the big bend in the river near Xanten, the lake known as the Alter Rhein, and the southern edge of the Diersfordter Wald provided convenient landmarks on the way to that zone. Airborne troops on the spot were to mark the zone with a red T, white letter W and red smoke and were also to have an M/F beacon in operation. The 120 planes in the rear of the column were to deliver their loads to 6 Airborne Division on SDP B. This was a diamond-shaped area about 2,000 yards across located about 4½ miles east of the Rhine and about ¾ of a mile west of Hamminkeln with the double-track railroad on its southwest edge. It was to be marked with a yellow T, green smoke, and a white letter B, supplemented by an M/F beacon. In addition a VHF landing beacon (SCS-51) was to be set up at the IP and aimed at SDP B so that the bombers could ride along its beam to their objective. After completing the drop the bombers were to turn to the right, climb to 2,500 feet and return along the troop carrier route to Wavre. From there they would make almost a bee-line return to their bases by way of Ostend.

Supplies for the airborne had been requisitioned well in advance. Those for the Americans had been packed by the 490th Quartermaster Depot Company and those for the British by the Air Dispatch Group. The packages were then sent to the Third Strategic Air Depot at Neaton, and from there between 20 and 23 March they were distributed to the bomber bases, all of which were within 30 miles of the depot. At 1430 on the 23d loading began. Thanks to careful preparation this unfamiliar task was accomplished without difficulty. The Second Air Division had conducted tests and issued a special letter of instructions; the 490th Quartermaster Company had provided two-instructor-demonstrators and the personnel of the bomb groups had been given special training in loading and dropping procedure.

Each plane was to carry about 2½ tons of cargo, wrapped in 20 or 21 bundles, a dozen forward in the bomb racks, five or six in and around the ball turret well (the turret having been removed), and three at the emergency escape hatch in the tail. Because their load was abnormally light, the Liberators tended to be tail-heavy. Consequently ammunition and other heavy articles were concentrated forward. All bundles of gasoline cans were placed at the turret well. Some indestructable items were to be allowed to fall free, but most were to have parachutes, each of the four classes being distinguished by a chute of a different color.[56]

The first bombers rose into the air from their East Anglia bases at 0910. Take-off and group assembly were fast and efficient. The big planes rolled away at average intervals of considerably less than a minute apiece. Briefing errors caused some groups to take wrong positions in the line, and though attempts were made to correct this situation, the confusion thus created seems to have caused recurrent overrunning and stringing out. Most inconvenienced by this was the 491st Group, which was to lead the drop at SDP B. It had to make several "S's" and doglegs to keep behind the 44th Group and had to swerve again to avoid it as they reached the Rhine. At least one group went down on the deck to avoid the prop wash of its predecessor.

Navigation was very good, and unintentional deviations from course were few and generally unimportant. Two flights of the 389th Group did find themselves heading to the south of SDP W and had to circle for a second pass. In the 448th Group, headed for SDP B, an accidental drop west of the Rhine by one plane caused four more to drop all or most of their loads west of the river. Two other pilots in that group reported dropping at random in the American sector. The first formation made its drop at 1310 and the last about 1330. There seem to have been no major errors, but minor ones were sufficient to spread supplies all over the Diersfordt area. Fortunately, few pilots overshot the mark by so much as to put them beyond the territory held by the airborne, so almost all the bundles were recoverable.

The bomber men blamed the dispersion of the supplies on haze and smoke so thick that a formation half a mile ahead was invisible. Because the bombers were making their run at speeds 20-30 percent faster than those of the troop carriers and were engaged in an unfamiliar type of operation, this short field of vision was a particularly serious handicap for them. They also complained that reception of the M/F beacons had been poor. However, their Gee sets had functioned perfectly, the VHF beacon beamed at SDP B had worked very well, and the columns of colored smoke at the drop points had been plainly seen by many pilots.

Probably the biggest source of error was approach from too low an altitude. Many flights came in at altitudes between 100 and 300 feet, and some pilots had to zoom to clear the high tension line. This sort of hedge-hopping was not conducive to accurate navigation, nor could pilots coming in on the deck have a right to expect much assistance from either radio beacons or visual aids. Another factor contributing to dispersion was the time taken to eject the bundles. Bundles in the bomb bay could be released by turning a switch, and those in the rear of the plane could, if all went well, be shoved out in six seconds after the men there were notified by the alarm bell, but a balky bundle or a fouled line could easily cause enough delay for a plane moving at 150 miles an hour to go a mile or two. There was also an element of risk inhibiting hasty movement around an open hole. One man was whisked through the turret well along with the bundles he was pitching out.

The 17th Division G-4 was unable to collect more than about 50 percent of 306 tons of supplies dropped for that division. However, it was known that many bundles had been picked up and used on the battlefield without any report. The British airborne reported that about 85 percent of their 292-ton consignment landed in the divisional area and 10 percent to the north of it. On 7 April they reported having recovered about 80 percent, a very high ratio for parachute resupply. Probably the actual recovery ratio for the 17th Division was equally good.

The Liberators met no opposition until after the supplies were dropped, but after that they ran into light flak and small-arms fire which in the opinion of some participants surpassed anything they had encountered on bombing missions. In spite of their armor 15 of the B-24's were shot down* and 104 of them were damaged. Astonishing to relate, the bombers' loss ratio was seven times that of the C-47's which had flown to LZ N only a few minutes earlier. The losses and damage were so distributed that no single battery could have caused more than a small fraction of them. Some planes were hit very near their zones, others near Wesel after turning homeward. Seven of the 15 lost aircraft were missing and unaccounted for. It seems possible that in some cases the momentum of the relatively fast and heavy Liberators carried them beyond the Issel before they could complete their turns, thus giving German gunners who had

---

*One may have hit a mast or other obstacle.

never had a shot at the C-47's nor revealed themselves to the flak eradicators of 83 Group an opportunity to spray the bombers at close range.[57]

Before the last bomber dropped its load of supplies, the airborne troops had made contact with advance elements of Second Army. As the afternoon advanced other contacts were made, and German resistance disintegrated at an accelerating tempo. Accordingly, although 6 Airborne Division requested that the resupply mission for D plus 1 be sent as scheduled, Second Army cancelled it about 1600 on the 24th on the grounds that it was not needed. VARSITY was over.[58]

The Exploitation of VARSITY

Although the airborne troops employed in VARSITY had been integrated into the ground offensive before the end of D-day, and although no further airborne or resupply missions were flown, a brief look at subsequent events is necessary to reveal the results of the operation.

As recorded earlier, the fighting done by the airborne during the first few hours had been on a small-unit basis, with regimental headquarters gradually establishing control. Corps and divisional staffs did not begin to function until after mid-afternoon. General Ridgway and a small staff from XVIII Corps reached DZ W at 1526 hours after having crossed the Rhine by assault boat. The 17th Division opened its CP at Flüren at 1600 hours, and the corps headquarters shared its facilities.

After beating off counterattacks east of Wesel and west of Ringenberg on the night of the 24th both airborne divisions spent most of D plus 1 in mopping up very feeble resistance. The front ran from the Rhine about a mile north of Bislich to the Issel River, a mile north of Hamminkeln, along the river to the Issel Canal, and along the canal to the outskirts of Wesel. It included several Allied bridgeheads on the far side of the river and the canal. In Wesel itself the commando brigade, which became attached to XVIII Corps on the morning of the 25th, continued to have hard fighting throughout the day at some places but had nearly finished its task by nightfall.

During the afternoon and night of D plus 1 the 17th Airborne moved quietly across the Issel and into positions along the autobahn. At 0900 on the 26th it attacked with ample artillery and tank support, swept ahead easily, and by 1100 had reached points six miles east of Wesel. That afternoon elements of the 507th PIR took a bridge over the Lippe outside Krudenburg seven miles east of Wesel and made contact there with units of Simpson's Ninth Army. The British airborne also pushed between two and three miles eastward but were unable to take Ringenberg on their northern flank.

On the 27th General Miley gave the order "Advance to Dorsten. This is a pursuit." At midnight a British armored brigade passed through the positions of the 17th Division, and next day troops of that division rode tanks into the outskirts of Dorsten, some 14 miles east of Wesel. All German lines had been broken, and Montgomery's armored columns, sweeping through the gaping hole, were free to drive into the heart of Germany. On the 29th a spearhead plunged 16 miles to Haltern and Dulmen. On the 30th XVIII Corps Headquarters closed its command post and retired to the rear. A few days later the 17th Division was also withdrawn.

Nothing shows the collapse of German resistance after the first few hours of fighting more strikingly than the Allies' casualty figures. Up to 2400 on D plus 2 the 17th Division had 231 men reported killed in action and 670 wounded, exclusive of injuries. Most of these casualties had been suffered in the first five hours of the operation. During the five days from D plus 2 through D plus 7 only 74 more were reported killed and 102 more wounded, including about 40 men who had been previously listed as missing. On 31 March the division reported a total of 284 men missing and 182 injured, only 20 of the injuries being serious. Since few were injured and hardly any cut off after the initial phase of the operation, these figures probably approximate the toll of injured and captured resulting from the VARSITY drops and landings.

The Americans on their part took about 3,000 German prisoners on D-day. During the spectacular advances of the next four days they took less than 1,000, and most of those were overrun rather than overcome. During much of that time there was no contact with organized enemy forces. Resistance consisted of little more than sniping and the defense of a few roadblocks. Meanwhile, the American Ninth Army had been moving rapidly, despite stiff opposition in some places, and by the 28th had pushed its front to a line extending from Dorsten south to Gladbeck. On the northern flank, however, Montgomery's troops in the Rees area were held close to the Rhine throughout four days of hard fighting. They were able to advance on the 28th as far as Emmerich on the north and the Issel on the east, but even this success must be discounted, because by then their opponents' position had been rendered untenable by the deep penetration of the Allied airborne troops south of them. While it seems impossible for the Germans to have stopped the massive forces arrayed for PLUNDER, the slow costly progress around Rees indicates that they might have contained a purely amphibious assault by Second Army for several days. If so, VARSITY deserves recognition as the decisive stroke which brought about a quick breakthrough.[59]

Special Features of VARSITY

Some aspects of VARSITY, notably the roles of the forward visual control posts, the combat control teams, the glider pilot "companies," and glider salvage, require special mention. The Horsas carrying the three forward visual control units landed safely and accurately. However, the equipment for one team burned after being hit by German artillery. A second team was in operation at the 6 Division CP within two hours after its landing. It quickly made radio contact with the Forward Ground Control Center and that afternoon directed fighters from 83 Group's "cab rank" against four targets given it by the G-3 Air of 6 Division. Next day the team handled 22 accurate and generally successful missions against targets which were sometimes within as little as 300 yards of the British positions. On an average requests took only about five minutes to go from the troops to brigade to G-3 for evaluation and another five for transmission to the pilots by the forward visual control post (FVCP) with the forward ground control center monitoring and assigning priorities. The plan to have the other FVCP join the 17th Airborne after landing on a zone in the British sector proved unrealistic. The difficulties of moving for several miles across an area in which fighting was going on prevented the unit from reporting until the morning of D plus 1. After it did arrive it was not much needed and directed only four strikes. While the employment of the FVCP's was limited, their success, particularly in the British sector strongly indicated the value of having such a system to provide for the airborne troops, through precise and punctual air support, the firepower which they themselves lacked. Tanks were the worst enemy of the airborne, and in its brief period of operations the FVCP with 6 Division was credited with calling down aerial destruction on 16 German tanks.[60]

The two combat control teams landed at opposite ends of LZ N, took cover for an hour, and then unloaded their equipment. Thanks to the policy of duplication they were able to function although one of their six gliders had crashed and the radio aboard another had been damaged. Both teams reported to the 17th Division CP at 1700 hours that afternoon. Next morning at 0800 they went on the air, made contact with the Combined Command Post at Maison Lafitte half an hour later, and continued in operation until 1050 on D plus 2. Cancellation of all airborne missions after D-day deprived them of their planned function of coordinating troop carrier traffic. They might have had difficulty in exercising that function, for they did not receive any messages from FAAA, although seven out of nine radio messages sent by them were received by FAAA.[61]

The discipline and combat effectiveness of the glider pilots won high praise from the airborne. On both American landing zones they did a good job under fire which was everywhere harassing and frequently intense. A majority participated in the initial assembly and came under the control of the wing organizations before nightfall. The senior glider officer on LZ S sent 50 pilots to guard the CP of the 17th Division, two "companies," to hold positions along the railroad embankment at the west end of the zone, one "company" to guard a crossroad, and one to guard prisoners. As noted earlier, the unit at the crossroad performed like veterans that night in beating off a German force of superior size. The rest had a surprisingly quiet night. They were relieved at 0900 next morning and marched back to the Rhine, 583 strong, as escort for 2,456 prisoners. After delivering the prisoners they were taken by DUKW's across the Rhine and to a British artillery base, where they were given refreshments, put aboard trucks and transported to an airfield at Helmond. From Helmond troop carrier planes flew them back to their home stations.

Most of the glider pilots landing on LZ N were organized into "companies" under the command of the 53d Wing CP and did guard duty or held defensive positions during the night for the 513th Parachute Infantry. One of their units had a brisk fight in the dark with German troops and did well. They were not relieved until 1530 on D plus 1, and did not leave the battle area until 1730, too late to reach Helmond that day.

Despite some delays at Helmond three quarters of the glider pilots were returned to their units before the end of D plus 4, and almost all who were fit to travel were back within six days. As of 9 April only 55 out of about 1,770 American glider pilots reaching the combat area were still missing. Only 35 glider pilots had been killed, 85 wounded and 21 injured.

Although the low casualty rate suggests that landing gliders in the midst of an enemy line of defense was much less dangerous than had been expected, the glider pilots expressed a preference for having paratroops on the landing zone ahead of them. If assault landings were to be made, they recommended that the gliders be provided with more and better exits and with some armor or at least flak curtains. Also, if they were to play the part of combat troops they wanted some heavy weapons such as bazookas and BAR's. Once again they called for better maps of the landing area, preferably on a scale of 1:25,000. In spite of all precautions, scattered landings and battlefield confusion had forced large numbers of the glider pilots in VARSITY to find their own way, and in such cases possession of an adequate map was a life and death matter. On the whole, however, they felt that the planning and execution of the glider side of VARSITY was the most efficient to date and that the problems raised by previous missions had mostly been solved.[62]

The gliders in VARSITY had fared much worse than their occupants. A caretaker detachment sent in on D plus 2 found them in bad shape with most of their clocks and compasses gone. Some 600 repairmen arrived on 4 April and repaired 148 Wacos enough so they could be "snatched" and flown to Grimberghen for complete overhaul. In the case of the big British gliders, pick-up tactics were not considered feasible. Of those conveniently located and in good condition, 24 were disassembled and hauled away by road to a base where they could be repaired, reassembled, and flown back. The rest of the American and British gliders were salvaged. Salvaged materiel from the Wacos alone filled 47 trucks and 30 trailers. Nevertheless, the fact remains that less than 17 percent of the American gliders and 6 percent of the British gliders which had landed east of the Rhine were recovered in usable condition.[63]

Conclusions

General Brereton described VARSITY as a "tremendous success" and rated it the most successful airborne operation hitherto attempted. Through the use of multiple traffic lanes, the C-46 aircraft, and double-tow, nearly 17,000 well-equipped airborne troops had been poured into an area of less than 25 square miles within four hours. This concentration in time and space was decisive.

Captured documents, the testimony of prisoners, and the postwar statements of German generals agree that the defenders had anticipated an airborne assault in the Wesel-Emmerich sector and had prepared for it. They appear to have had at least 10,000 men in carefully organized defensive positions in the Diersfordt area. An initial attack by one airborne division or less might have been resisted stubbornly, as was the assault at Rees. Instead the unprecedented and unexpected weight of the blow overwhelmed resistance and shattered the precarious morale of the defenders. Contributing to this was surprise as to the precise location of the assault area and paralysis produced by the terrific Allied air support effort. The Germans had kept their reserves several miles back. When the day came only one regiment was able to make its way to the assault area. Without sufficient reinforcements for holding operations, let alone a counterattack, the Nazis were unable to prevent a complete breakthrough. The airborne also aided in the progress of PLUNDER as planned by covering the flank of the commandos at Wesel and by preventing observed artillery fire at British pontoon bridges across the Rhine above Bislich, but these effects were insignificant compared to their success in smashing a hole through the German lines.[64]

The fact that the Diersfordt area was only three miles away from ground troops who had successfully pushed across the Rhine, even before VARSITY began, undoubtedly facilitated the task of the airborne troops. On the afternoon of D-day advance elements of XII Corps eliminated any serious threat to their rear by linking up with them at several points. That night the guns massed west of the Rhine shielded them with a massive barrage which not only multiplied their effective firepower, but also enabled the airborne artillerymen to conserve their scanty ammunition. While the batteries of the 17th Airborne were firing 15 missions, the supporting artillery of the Welsh 53 Division fired 29.* In terms of rounds the disparity was probably much greater, since the latter had 88 guns, and the American airborne had only 42 in action out of the 51 they had brought with them.[65] Finally, the arrival of ground reinforcements, particularly tanks, on D plus 1, enabled the airborne to exploit their initial success to the full.

All concerned agreed that the air side of the operation had gone with remarkable smoothness and that General Williams and his command deserved great praise. Of 540 planeloads of paratroops every stick had been brought to the combat area and less than 1 percent of the troops had been brought back because of sickness, accidents, wounds, or refusals. Of 908 American gliders, about two-thirds of which were in double-tow, all but 23, or 2.5 percent, reached the Rhine despite windy, turbulent weather. Of the British gliders 36 or 8.2 percent of their quota of 440 failed to get there. Although this figure might have been lower if they had had substitute aircraft available, one may infer that it was easier to manage Wacos in double-tow than a Horsa in single tow. Whether the difference lay in the size of the British gliders, the greater prop-wash of 38 Group's four-engine planes, or some other factor is an open question.

Route, schedule, and tactics had proved sound. Not one pilot had failed to follow the simple, well-marked course to the IP. The 43 serials had flown from 23 bases spread over an area which was about 300 miles long and divided by the English Channel. They reached their destination in proper sequence within 10 minutes of schedule, in spite of their adherence to specified air speeds† instead of arrival times. Some flaws there were. The confusion created by the crisscross of the 313th Group at Wavre might possibly have been avoided.

Probably the Waco serials would have been able to keep better formation had their time intervals been slightly longer and their prescribed flying speed five miles an hour faster—adjustments which might well have been made before the operation had there been even one realistic, large-scale glider exercise.

The accuracy of the drops and landings in VARSITY was much better than in NEPTUNE or even in MARKET. Except for 1½ sticks of paratroops dropped west of the Rhine and less than a score of gliders, all appear to have come within about two miles of their zones and most within a mile of them.

However, the low visibility contributed to some serious errors. Exposure to smoke during the last three to five miles of their flight caused three paratroop serials to make their drops approximately two miles north of their true zones. It is of course possible that they were off course before reaching the Rhine, but then they could have corrected themselves by the Eureka beacons at the IP and on the west side of the river. The visual aids on the riverbank were at times obscured by the smoke; the M/F beacons performed erratically and were not much relied on; but the Eurekas were working beautifully at an average range of 16 miles with no jamming or failure.

Beyond the Rhine the leaders of the paratroop serials had to judge their position by visual navigation, compass, and Gee. The most likely culprit for the three inaccurate drops is visual navigation, since in the smoke and haze east of the river mistakes in observation would be easy to make and hard to check. The wind was stronger than predicted, but hardly enough so to cause significant deflection from course between the Rhine and the drop zones. Gee was reported to have worked very well. Signals from the Ruhr and Reims chains came in strong and clear at all points on the route. Although the enemy used both jamming and decoy signals as countermeasures, the latter were easily recognized, and the former were disposed of in most cases by employment of the antijamming switch or by shifting from one chain to the other. However, Gee signals were not easy to interpret precisely, especially under combat conditions. Two of the three inaccurate paratroop serials had special grounds for error. The lead plane of the 313th Group had been set afire soon after crossing the Rhine, a circumstance likely to

---
*The fire of the British artillery was controlled by radio instructions from forward observers who had gone in with the airborne infantry battalions.

†Seven different air speeds had been prescribed, each for a different type of formation.

interfere with accurate navigation, and the pathfinder serial had tried to use the new Münster Gee chain for which they had not yet received charts and may thereby have gotten a bad fix. Whatever the causes of deflection, it is evident that the problem of ensuring accuracy in an airborne mission was still not fully solved.[66]

With the exception of one serial, the concentration and pattern of the paratroop drops ranged from good to excellent. It is significant that the 507th PIR was able to assemble 90 percent of its strength within an hour and a half and the 513th did almost as well, although both had had to spend much time and effort in fighting during the period of assembly. Indeed, since they were dropped in the presence of strong enemy forces, good initial concentration had been a prerequisite to their success. The formation flying which produced that concentration deserves praise, but with the qualifications that it was done by daylight and that during the approach to the zones little resistance was encountered.

The glider serials were more accurate but less orderly than the paratroop formations. Except for about four flights and a handful of individuals, all seem to have released their gliders over or very near their proper zones. Ragged formations, overrunning of some serials by those behind them, and a general tendency of rear elements to climb to avoid prop wash produced considerable confusion, with American gliders being released at altitudes varying from 500 to 2,500 feet and British gliders at 2,500 to 3,500 feet. This situation coupled with the inability of the glider pilots to get a good view of the terrain until they were below the 200-foot level prevented a majority from landing in their assigned fields and caused dispersion all over the landing zones and the adjoining area. Enough gliders were able to land in sequence in the proper spot to show that it could be done, given a good release and the luck to sight a few landmarks on the way down. It should also be said that, especially on LZ S, the units that were well concentrated on landing played a disproportionately important part in the early stages of the fighting.

The extreme inflammability of the C-46's pushed their loss rate (including salvaged craft) to an unhealthy 28 percent. No doubt some C-47's were saved from fire by their new self-sealing fuel tanks. Yet the ratio of losses to damage among C-47's was almost exactly what it had been in MARKET.* A substantial proportion of the American losses, though not of the damage, was caused by a few light flak batteries which by camouflage or movement had escaped the preliminary anti-flak effort. Such guns were probably responsible for the heavy losses among planes dropping troops on DZ B. Had that one trouble spot been removed and no C-46's been used, IX TCC might have lost less than 2 percent of its planes. Had the Germans had a few more batteries in action and the troop carrier command been fully equipped with C-46's, VARSITY could have been extremely costly. So delicate is the balance in airborne operations.

The over-all cost of VARSITY was moderate, 7 British troop carrier aircraft destroyed, 46 American craft destroyed (plus 9 salvaged), and 15 of the bombers in the resupply mission destroyed. Damaged were 32 British craft, 339 from IX TCC, and 104 of the bombers. The loss ratios for planes crossing the Rhine were 1.7, 5.0, and 6.4 percent, and damage ratios 8, 31, and 44 percent. However, only 100 of IX TCC's planes needed 3d or 4th echelon repair. The rest had received minor damage, mainly from small arms.

The British attributed their comparative impunity to keeping above an altitude of 2,500 feet, out of effective range of small-arms fire. At that height, too, they may have been shielded by the smoke, and perhaps they benefitted from German gunners' instructions to concentrate on low-flying planes and gliders. That height was a protection is confirmed by the fact that the high-flying American glider serials over LZ N had even smaller losses than the British and that the low-flying resupply mission suffered worst of all.

Flak neutralization had, as in MARKET, been difficult but on the whole successful. Interdiction and close support had worked wonders, and the British FVCP's had proved the value of having fighter control teams with the airborne. Perhaps the most brilliant achievement of the Allied air forces was the complete neutralization of the Luftwaffe on its own home ground. Less than 20 German planes came within sight of the troop

---

*The 313th Group did not have self-sealing tanks. It appears that a majority of the other groups in the command had them, but the author has not found any statement of the number installed before VARSITY. Although 599 such tanks had been received by the end of February, a large proportion of them needed modification. Only 76 had been installed as of 5 March. (Hist IX TCC, Jan-Feb 45, Pt VIII, Sec 5 and 6.)

carrier formations, and there is no evidence that any of them were able to make a kill or even a pass. The weather for once had been on the side of the Allies. Five days of clear skies, an extraordinary phenomenon for that time and place, had enabled them to use their aerial superiority to the full. However, the planners had been careful to allow leeway for bad weather, and, thanks to the concentration of the airborne missions and initial resupply within a four-hour period, any two consecutive favorable days between the 23d and 28th of March would have sufficed for the execution of PLUNDER, VARSITY, and all essential supporting operations.

CHAPTER VI

Conclusions Regarding Large-Scale Airborne Operations

THE MOST IMPORTANT lesson taught by VARSITY, MARKET, and airborne operations in NEPTUNE was that airborne assaults on a corps scale could be successfully executed, something which had been seriously doubted after the painful experiences in Sicily. While in Normandy and Holland the lift had to be spread over several days, that for the Rhine crossing was concentrated into a four-hour period, greatly increasing the impact of the assault, and reducing escort requirements and the risk that bad weather would ground important elements of the force. It also freed the airborne troops from the need to keep a large part of their men guarding drop and landing zones for subsequent missions.

In all three cases troop carrier resources were stretched to the limit. However, had IX TCC been fully equipped with C-46's in time for VARSITY, it could have added a third division to the two actually carried on D-day. Larger planes would also have reduced the number of bases needed to accomplish a given lift. Lack of forward bases was a grave handicap to MARKET and caused a very awkward dispersal of the take-off fields in VARSITY. On the other hand, it was much easier to find bases suitable for the C-47, which could take off within 3,000 feet from an unsurfaced runway, than it was for four-engined aircraft or even for the C-46. This was why a dozen fields in France could be allotted to American troop carrier units at a time when none were available for the converted heavy bombers of 38 Group.

Massive paratroop assaults in MARKET and VARSITY had achieved a success which disarmed criticism. The principal doctrinal change in that field was the reaction against night paratroop operations after NEPTUNE. The dissatisfaction of both troop carrier and airborne leaders was focused on the means of supplying and reinforcing the paratroops. The principal means of reinforcement and of bringing in heavy equipment was the glider, a neglected step-child which had never been popular.

Gliders used up shipping space, cluttered up airfields, deteriorated rapidly and were destroyed by hundreds in storms. They required large numbers of glider pilots and glider mechanics, unassimilated specialists whose presence created problems of employment and morale within the troop carrier squadrons.* Glider operations were inherently wasteful in that they required two aircraft and two crews to do the work of one. To keep gliders under control and in close formation required good light and almost perfect weather. Glider missions occupied about 50 percent more air space and moved 30 to 40 miles an hour more slowly than equivalent paratroop formations. During the tow, in landing, and immediately after landing, gliders were much more vulnerable than paratroops, hence their relegation to follow-up missions rather than to the initial assaults. Furthermore, experience had shown that in most combat operations at least 80 percent of the gliders

---

*If the glider pilots had been organized in separate groups, as was done on a provisional basis in the Mediterranean Theater they would have been able to follow a coherent and continuous training program of their own, working with whatever troop carrier units were engaged in glider training and spending slack periods on realistic infantry practice instead of stagnating during the long periods when the squadrons they were assigned to were preoccupied with non-glider activities. The advantage of permanently teaming tug and glider pilots together was in practice largely lost in every big operation by massive shifts of glider pilots from units not scheduled for glider missions to others that were.

used would have to be written off afterwards as destroyed or irrecoverable.

In rebuttal it should be said that the light, durable Waco had certain advantages that other types of assault craft have not achieved after 10 years of postwar experimentation. It could land safely in smaller, rougher fields than an assault plane. It had no engine to hit, no fuel to catch fire. It could be towed at twice the speed of present-day helicopters. Above all, it could be produced in great numbers for as little as $15,000 apiece. One wonders whether the Allies would have accepted the cost and the risk of crash-landing a thousand assault planes among the swamps and hedge-rows of Normandy or of setting down a thousand helicopters within point-blank range of enemy guns as they did gliders in VARSITY. Gliders did those difficult and dangerous jobs acceptably and could be assigned to do them in the reassuring certainty that they were expendable. The British even dared to use their gliders for *coups de main* against bridges and other key objectives and found them very satisfactory for the purpose.

One drawback of the American gliders was their small size. Instead of the Waco with its 3,750-pound load the airborne wanted a glider which would carry a truck or a 155-mm. howitzer. By the end of the war they were thinking in terms of gliders with 4, 6 and even 8-ton payloads. However, no large gliders except the CG-13A (which proved unfit for tactical operations) was sent overseas or even placed in production by the United States during World War II. Even if a suitable glider in the 4-ton class had been available the C-47 would probably have been incapable of towing it. The Americans might have made some use of the Horsa in MARKET and more in VARSITY, but their experience in Normandy with its brittleness and other peculiarities seems to have given both troop carriers and airborne a lasting prejudice against it.

Resupply by parachute avoided the difficulties of a glider tow and the hazards of a glider landing, but it was inefficient and wasteful. A C-47 capable of carrying about three tons could deliver little more than a ton by parachute from its pararacks or in bundles pitched out its side door. Installation of conveyor belts in the cabin was helpful in handling bundles but such conveyors did not go into production in the United States until the spring of 1945. Moreover, the bundles had to be small to get out the door or fit the pararacks. Even the 75-mm. howitzer had to be broken down into several parts to be dropped. New techniques were on the horizon. The British had used parachute clusters to drop whole jeeps and artillery pieces from the bomb bays of Halifaxes. However, even with them the dropping of heavy equipment was still in the experimental stage. Not until after the war, when they received the C-82 with its big cargo door in the rear, were the American troop carriers able to make such drops.

Further weaknesses of parachute resupply were inaccuracy and dispersion. Supplies were rarely dropped with precision by either the British or the Americans and were usually scattered over several miles of ground. The task of collecting the scattered bundles was difficult and hazardous. General Gavin estimated after MARKET that to get proper recovery of the supplies dropped for his division in that operation he would have had to put a third of his force on supply detail, something not usually practicable in the presence of the enemy. Even after a vigorous collection program under relatively favorable conditions as in VARSITY at least 20 percent of the bundles would probably be lost. A force hemmed in by the enemy as the British were at Arnhem might recover very little of what was dropped for them. For instance, on D plus 1, in MARKET, 1 Airborne Division got more supplies from three bulk-loaded Hamilcar gliders than it did from a parachute drop by 33 four-engined aircraft.

The use of B-24 bombers for resupply was a valuable supplement to the American troop carrier effort in MARKET and VARSITY. However, it was equally wasteful in that the big aircraft capable of carrying six tons of bombs could deliver less than 2½ tons in a parachute drop. Also, the bombers had to be withdrawn from their primary mission several days before an operation for modification, loading and other preparations. The performance of the bomber crews was roughly similar to that of the troop carriers, but their loss rate was relatively high. With more experience in resupply work they might have reduced their losses by shifting to drops from medium altitude or by other changes in tactics, such as avoidance of climbing turns after completion of their drops.

The value of airborne forces striking close behind enemy lines to pave the way for a ground assault was demonstrated in Normandy and again on the Rhine. In Holland an attempt to employ them in a more independent role some 60 miles beyond the front failed, but by so narrow a margin as to indicate that such ventures were feasible. Had German strength and dispositions been as expected, MARKET would almost certainly have been a decisive victory. As it was, success would probably have been achieved had the British airborne picked zones close to their objective, had the weather been favorable on D plus 2, and had the British ground forces advanced more aggressively.

Many people, including General Arnold, felt that more and bigger airborne operations should have been attempted.[1] The reasons why more were not made are many and complex. Assuredly it was not for lack of eagerness on the part of Airborne Army and the airborne planners who preceded it. Dozens of plans were made which never won SHAEF approval, and over a dozen were cancelled after reaching the stage of detailed planning.

Much of the time the means for a large airborne mission were not available. During periods of heavy fighting as in Normandy, Holland, and the Ardennes, airborne divisions were kept at the front for months at a time and when relieved were in need of recuperation and retraining. For this reason the three weeks before MARKET and the month before VARSITY were the only times after the invasion of Normandy when a three-division operation would have been possible. Whenever a breakthrough did occur, the leaders of the advancing armies clamored for air supply to the exclusion of all airborne operations, regardless of the needs of other ground commanders. Thus Third Army bitterly opposed Montgomery's request for MARKET and later did the same to Seventh Army's request for EFFECTIVE.

When plans were made to exploit a victory by airborne action, the final planning and preparations were usually so slow and the objectives so close to the front that advancing ground troops reached the area before the missions were launched. The resultant cancellations represented a great waste of time and effort at critical moments. To some extent this was inevitable. Large operations did require time for preparation. It was risky, as MARKET proved, to strike far beyond the front on the assumption that an advance would continue. On the other hand, the rewards of success in a venture like MARKET might be complete and final victory, a prize worth gambling for. It should also have been possible to pre-package small missions in readiness to seize key points on short notice ahead of the most rapid ground thrust.* After all, a regiment had been dropped at Salerno on less than 12-hours notice, under difficulties greater than usually prevailed in the ETO.

Another factor which limited the use of the airborne and made ground commanders reluctant to rely on them was weather. Even paratroop missions could not risk a 20-mile wind or low clouds at the drop zone. Stormy weather was a major factor in the defeat of the airborne in Holland, almost grounded them in the invasion of Normandy, and was a source of worry to the planners of VARSITY. Purely local and temporary weather conditions could have serious results. Such phenomena were the cloudbank over the Normandy coast that scattered the first four missions in NEPTUNE, and the pall of smoke hanging over the objectives in VARSITY. To avert such unpleasant surprises, systematic weather reconnaissance was provided during MARKET and VARSITY, and periodic weather reports were sent out during VARSITY by radio teams with the airborne. Such warnings might make it possible to avoid unfavorable conditions, but sooner or later in all three of IX TCC's airborne operations the command had to accept marginal weather, and that acceptance usually brought trouble in its wake.

Clouds might disperse formations; wind could render gliders unmanageable; but the greatest weather hazard was low visibility, since not merely the success of the mission but the survival of the airborne troops depended on the accuracy with which they were delivered. When, as on the first day of MARKET, the fliers could see their route and observe panels and smoke signals set out by pathfinders on the drop zones, they could carry out a most exacting mission with more than sufficient accuracy. When they could not see their way, they were inaccurate because they had to depend on two unreliable guides, dead reckoning and

---

*One or two such operations were planned in the closing weeks of the war, but the only one carried out was AMHERST, a harassing operation in Holland executed on the night of 7 April by 38 Group, RAF, and French troops of the Special Air Service (a kind of air commando organization). (Air Ministry, A.H.B. Airborne Forces, 1951, pp. 199-203.)

radar. The troop carriers had learned the pitfalls of dead reckoning as early as TORCH and never relied on it thereafter when they could help it. Radar, although helpful, had serious limitations.

Responsor beacons to mark points in hostile territory had to be set up by agents, partisans or pathfinders. Such episodes as the Lindemans case* show that the first two methods involved a grave risk of discovery or betrayal. Preliminary pathfinder flights also reduced the chance of surprise for the main force. In addition, pathfinder planes might be shot down, as happened in Holland, or miss the zone by a wide margin, as some did in the invasion of southern France; and pathfinder troops might be neutralized by enemy action after reaching the ground, as many were in Normandy and most would have been in VARSITY, had they been used. The Rebecca-Eureka beacon, in standard use by the troop carriers had a range of less than 30 miles at the altitudes below 2,500 feet which were usually flown in airborne missions. More serious was the difficulty in making precise readings of the Rebecca scope when near the beacon. This made the normal margin of error with that equipment greater than a mile.

Certain airborne radars, including the SCR-717, produced a rough map of the terrain on a scope. Since only coastlines and large cities showed up well, such instruments were of limited value in airborne operations. The SCR-717 did prove helpful in making an accurate landfall in NEPTUNE and in MARKET.

A third type of radar (or radio) was used to establish the position of a plane in relation to a chain of stations in friendly territory. The British system of this type known as Gee was used by all airborne missions in the ETO. However, the effectiveness of Gee depended on the skill of the navigator reading it, the plane's distance from the stations, and, especially, the plane's azimuth. Since Gee chains were bulky and complex installations, requiring months to establish, airborne operations which were small or were flown on short notice would seldom have a Gee chain ideally situated for their use. Thus, although in theory Gee could be accurate to within 100 yards, it was rarely precise to within a mile in operations. In AMHERST the average Gee error was over three miles, and this was condoned as inevitable.[2]

Except in unusually open country a small error might put the airborne on dangerous ground or place difficult obstacles in their path. Notable examples would be the drop of paratroops in NEPTUNE into the swamps of the Merderet and on the far side of the Douve. Apart from these risks the difficulty of a contested advance across unfamiliar terrain made it likely that every mile of inaccuracy would cost hours of delay in reaching the objectives. Thus, although radar could remedy gross errors, it was not sufficiently precise to justify sending airborne missions in darkness or low visibility if that possibly could be avoided.

Another consideration restricting the employment of airborne forces was their vulnerability, both in the air and on the ground. This vulnerability is indicated in the case of the troop carriers not by the over-all losses, which were kept so low as to make pessimists like Leigh-Mallory seem absurd, but by the way loss rates shot up on occasions when something went wrong.

In every airborne operation in the European Theater the combined losses of British and American troop carrier aircraft were less than 4 percent of those employed; less than 2 percent of the crews were killed or missing; and less than 1 percent of the troops were shot down or incapacitated by enemy action before they jumped or their glider was released.* On the other hand, some formations in each operation were very roughly handled. In several instances exposure for two or three minutes to light flak and small arms fire caused the loss of between 10 and 20 percent of the planes exposed. One small British mission attacked by German fighters lost 20 percent of its aircraft.

The degree of air superiority which enabled the United States and Great Britain to send 10,000 sorties over France and western Germany on the day of VARSITY while the Luftwaffe could make less than 100 sorties against them made it possible to protect an airborne mission very thoroughly. It was standard procedure to destroy or neutralize enemy airfields within fighter range, set up perimeter patrols to intercept fighters flying in from outlying areas, and provide the troop carrier formations with extensive escort or area cover to dispose of the few foes who might manage to ap-

---
*See above, p. 117.

*Planes were seldom much exposed to enemy fire before approaching their objectives, so if they were hit short of the assault area the pilot could usually coax them to it and deliver his troops. More than half the crew members who bailed out or crash-landed were saved by the proximity of Allied troops, the efficiency of the Air Sea Rescue Service, or the assistance of friendly civilians, particularly the Dutch underground in MARKET.

proach them. Except for the one episode in MARKET when defensive measures were in abeyance it is doubtful whether German fighters ever got close enough to an Allied airborne mission to make a pass at it.

If an air attack was deadly but preventable, ground fire, other than heavy flak, which the troop carriers carefully avoided, was indecisive but galling. In VARSITY missions were flown in broad daylight right over the enemy's main line of defense with quite moderate losses in most cases. A C-47 could take hundreds of bullets and keep flying. Light flak was much more dangerous than small arms. The guns were mobile, hard to locate, and dangerous to attack. Anti-flak operations in MARKET almost ruined two good fighter groups, and even in VARSITY, where the area to be neutralized was relatively small, the batteries few in number, and the weather favorable, such operations were only moderately successful. In the latter operation some troop carrier formations suffered severe losses in passing over a handful of 20-mm. batteries which had survived all efforts to suppress them. Thus, even though light flak could theoretically be neutralized, its presence in quantity was a strong deterrent.

Airborne troops were most vulnerable immediately after arrival on the ground. Paratroops could be picked off while they were still dispersed and shaken. Gliders made splendid targets for mortars and machine guns. Even the low-grade, defeatist forces encountered in VARSITY made the period of initial assembly difficult and costly. Kesselring later expressed the opinion that had they been first-rate troops the operation would not have succeeded. On the other hand, drop or landing zones which, like those in MARKET, were virtually undefended, could seldom be found near really valuable objectives, and the long distance between zones and objectives at Arnhem proved a fatal barrier to success. At Ste Mère Eglise, the Grave bridge, and a score of other places it was proven that by far the best way for the lightly armed airborne troops to take an objective was to rush it before a strong defense could be organized. The question was whether the airborne could be delivered within quick striking distance without suffering defeat or crippling losses during assembly and unloading.

A second weakness was vulnerability to counterattacks supported by tanks and armor. Once the airborne troops were assembled, their fighting qualities made them a match for superior numbers of infantry and for almost any amount of militia. They showed remarkable ability to dispose of individual tanks and guns. However, their extremely limited firepower could be outmatched by a comparatively small artillery concentration, and they were altogether unable to cope with panzer divisions in the open field. That was demonstrated at Arnhem, when the crack troops of 1 Airborne Division were terribly mauled by depleted, war-weary panzer units.

Sometimes, as in VARSITY and the last stages of MARKET, ground artillery could provide a protective barrage for the airborne. Also in VARSITY, interdiction and close air support proved effective means to prevent counterattacks. However, there was the chance in any operation far beyond the front that the artillery would not get within range and that supporting air units would be grounded or rendered ineffective by unfavorable weather. These considerations help to explain why no serious consideration was given in the ETO to any airborne operation in which the ground forces were not scheduled to make contact with the airborne within three days, nor to any in which the airborne troops were expected to encounter considerable numbers of tanks before ground reinforcements reached them. Violation of these rules in MARKET was not intentional but the result of faulty intelligence and errors of judgment.

Another way to give the airborne the firepower they needed was to establish an airhead, that is, to seize an airfield on which to land reinforcements and supplies. The C-47 mission to the Grave landing strip on D plus 9 in MARKET showed that this kind of mission was perfectly feasible on a small scale with small planes. It doubled the payload carried in parachute resupply and eliminated dispersion, loss, and drop damage. It also eliminated use of the glider with all its overhead and tactical inefficiency.

However, the defense and maintenance of an independent airhead required a very massive lift, able to handle many more and bigger guns that had hitherto been assigned to the airborne, other heavy items, particularly engineer equipment, and a resupply level of some 400 tons (mainly ammunition) per division per day, instead of the 250 tons which had been customary. Such an operation called for big planes, long, hard-surfaced runways to receive them, and specially equipped supply units. Except for fewer than 200 C-46's acquired near the end of the war, IX TCC had to rely entirely on the relatively small C-47. Large airfields were usually well defended if in good condition and, once destroyed, required extensive reconstruction operations. As for airhead supply units, the Americans had nothing of the sort, and the British experimental unit known as AFDAG was allowed to disintegrate after MARKET.

Assuming that an airhead was established, it would have to be firmly held. A breakthrough like those achieved by the Germans around Veghel during MARKET would probably mean disaster. Indeed, the operation would be imperilled if the enemy simply got near enough to the airfield to place observed artillery fire on it or to rake missions with close-range antiaircraft fire during landing or take-off. The report of the 101st Division on MARKET expressed the opinion that in an airhead operation one entire airborne division would be needed exclusively for the defense of one airfield. Also, normal fighter escort and cover would have to be extended to protect the airfield at all times, especially during the hours of unloading. Despite these considerations, FAAA did toy with the idea of engaging in independent airhead operations far beyond the front, but the tactical and logistical problems involved were such as to cause the rejection or shelving of most such projects at an early stage.*

The only enterprise of this kind to approach completion was EFFECTIVE, a plan to put down the 13th Airborne Division near Bisingen, a village about 30 miles south of Stuttgart, seize an airfield, and establish an airhead over 50 miles in the rear of the German forces opposing Seventh Army in the Black Forest area. On 9 April 1945 SHAEF tentatively approved the operation and ordered completion of detailed plans. A week later, Seventh Army, which was still facing stubborn resistance, announced that it wanted EFFECTIVE. SHAEF agreed to set 22 April as the target date. Once again an airborne attack was forestalled by German collapse. On the 18th a breakthrough by armored units ensured the encirclement of the Black Forest region, and late on the 19th EFFECTIVE was cancelled.[3]

After dwelling on the limitations and vulnerability of the airborne forces, it is well to emphasize that these were comparable to those of amphibious forces, except perhaps in the field of logistics. If lift for three divisions was hard to find before OVERLORD, assault boats for five divisions were even harder to get.* Storms could halt amphibious operations on an unsheltered coast about as easily as they did airborne and resupply missions. The June gales in Normandy proved that. While troop carrier navigation was not precise, it compares reasonably well with that of the naval forces which missed UTAH Beach by a mile and a half. Vulnerable as the airborne were during delivery and assembly, their worst initial losses were paralleled by the casualties in certain amphibious assaults.† Even in ability to cope with counterattack, the record of the three airborne divisions in MARKET compared favorably with that of the three beach-landed divisions which were bottled up at Anzio. Any airborne operation larger than a raid required air superiority, but throughout the war that was a prerequisite, not only for amphibious operations, but for all ground offensives, except perhaps the German drive in the Ardennes.

At the end of World War II airborne and troop carrier commanders alike were convinced that airborne operations would play an important part in future wars. However, there were good reasons for qualifying such opinions. In a major war such operations could be no more than auxiliary to traditional ground warfare until airborne forces gained the firepower and logistical capabilities to maintain themselves for long periods against first-rate opposition. As General Gavin put it "We have . . . barely begun to solve the problems of airborne transport and equipment."[4] Today many of those problems have been solved. More serious was the fact that without air superiority, airborne warfare involved excessive risk. To ensure superiority fighter planes and bombers would have to

---

*One spectacular plan which died an early death was that for ARENA. The objective of this operation was the seizure by four airborne divisions of an area near Kassel containing several airfields to which several infantry regiments would subsequently be transported by air. The plan involved as many as 2,500 air landings and 1,000 parachute resupply sorties a day. (SHAEF G-3, Operation ARENA GCT/370-44/Plans, 2d Draft, 15 Mar 45, in 505.61-3.)

*Moreover, troop carrier aircraft could be moved from theater to theater for an assault within a few days, as was done for DRAGOON, while landing craft took months to assemble.
†By far the heaviest initial losses by Allied airborne divisions were in Normandy where the 82d Division had 156 men killed, 756 missing, and 347 wounded on D-day, and the 101st had 182 killed, 501 missing, and 557 wounded in that time. The 2d Marine Division had 913 killed and missing and 2,037 wounded during its assault on Tarawa. (Harrison, *Cross-Channel Attack*, pp. 284, 300; R. W. Shugg and H. A. DeWeerd, *World War II* [Washington, 1946], p. 242.)

receive priority over troop carriers in the postwar budget. Finally—and most important of all to the future of airborne warfare—the advent of the atomic bomb, by giving strategic bomber forces the power to win a war overnight, threatened to render all other means of warfare secondary, if not superfluous. Although the role of airborne forces in an atomic war is still in dispute, their value in non-atomic warfare under suitable conditions was demonstrated in World War II—and is certainly much greater now than it was when they flew to victory in VARSITY.

Footnotes

Chapter 1

1. Gordon A. Harrison, *Cross-Channel Attack* (Washington, 1951), p. 47; Hq 8th AF, Flow Chart 5 Apr 43, in USAFHD 505.24-1A. (Unless otherwise noted, documents cited in this study are identified by their file number in USAFHD.)

2. Frederick E. Morgan, *Overture to OVERLORD* (Garden City, 1950), pp 27, 29, 41; Hq AEAF, Historical Data, US Component Allied Expeditionary Air Force, in 505.24-1A.

3. W. F. Craven and J. L. Cate, *The Army Air Forces in World War II*, II (Chicago, 1949), 635-37; CCS 244/1, ann IV, app A, 25 May 43 (excerpt) in USAFHD files; Hq 8th AF, Flow Chart, 5 Apr 43 (pencilled note "Brought to U.K. by Stratemeyer."); ltr, Brig Gen R. C. Candee, CG VIII ASC, to CG 8th AF, subj: Flow Chart for Tactical Air Force, 15 May 43; Hq VIII ASC, Tactical Air Force Tentative Proposed Troop Basis Amended, 24 May 43, all above in 505.13-5; Hq VIII ASC Tactical Air Force Tentative Proposed Troop Basis, 21 May 43, in 505.13-4 (see also table, same title and date in 505.13-5).

4. Harrison, *Cross-Channel Attack,* pp 72-75, 183; min of COSSAC Staff Confs, 2, 9, and 23 Jul 43, in 505.10-7; COSSAC(43) 28, App O, Operation "OVERLORD" Airborne Forces, 15 Jul 43, in 505.14-3; COSSAC(43) 32 (Final), Digest of Operation "OVERLORD," 27 Jul 43, in 505.12-7; COSSAC(43) 36, Transport Aircraft and Gliders for Operations "OVERLORD," 28 Jul 43; memo for C/AS et al from Lt Col S. R. Richards, subj: European Theater Troop Carrier Requirements, 17 Aug 43, in 505.14-2; ltr, AM T. Leigh-Mallory, CG AEAF, to AOC-in-C Br TAF and CG 9th AF, subj: Preparation of Tactical Air Forces for Operation "OVERLORD," 6 Oct 43, in 505.33-11; Hq AEAF, Airborne Forces and Air Supply in Operation "OVERLORD" and "RANKIN," Position as of the 12th October 1943, 18 Oct 43, in 505.14-23; ltr, Air C-in-C AEAF to AOC 2d TAF and CG 9th AF, Directive to Tactical Air Forces Operation "OVERLORD," 6 Dec 43, in 505.25-31; memo for CG AAF from Brig Gen G. C. Jamison, subj: Troop Carrier Requirements First Half 1944, 29 Dec 43, in USAFHD files; msg OP 544, MAAF Adv to CG 12th AF and CG XII TCC, 8 Jan 44, in 650.1622.

5. Lecture, Col J. T. Dalbey, C/S Abn Comd, subj: Airborne Troops in a Landing Assault, 28 May 43, in 502.141; min, COSSAC Staff Conf, 2 Jul 43; min of Meeting Held at Norfolk House on August 10th [1943] to Discuss Future Policy Relating to the Employment of Air Borne Forces, in 505.10-6; Hq AEAF, Airborne Forces and Air Supply in Operation "OVERLORD," 18 Oct 1943.

6. Craven and Cate, *The Army Air Forces in World War II*, II, 455-6; Air Ministry, A.H.B., *Airborne Forces* (1951), pp. 96-7, 246-49; min of Meeting Held at Norfolk House on August 10th (1943) to Discuss Future Policy Relating to the Employment of Airborne Forces; Hq AEAF, Airborne Forces and Air Supply in Operation "OVERLORD," 18 Oct 43; COSSAC 3140/Sec, Annex, Operation "OVERLORD" Points for Further Investigation as a Result of COS(43) 180th Meeting, and JP(43) 260(Final), 7 Aug 43, in 505.12-7; lecture, Brig Gen P. L. Williams, The Airborne Assault Phase of the Sicilian Campaign, 17 Aug 43, in 611, 452-1; Lt Col S. R. Richards, Capt R. K. Ward and Capt J. L. Morris to CG VIII ASC, subj: Board Findings on Towing of Horsa Glider with C-47A Airplane, 24 Aug 43, in 505.14-22; War Cabinet, Chiefs of Staff Committee, Airborne Forces, Joint Memorandum by the General and Air Staffs, 20 Sep 43, in 505.06-1; NJC5 (Final) "Neptune" Zero Hour for the Assault, Covering Recommendations by Principal Staff Officers, app D, Airborne Considerations, 14 Dec 43; NJC (Final) "OVERLORD" The Effect of Weather, 14 Dec 43, both in 505.25-2.

7. *Airborne Forces,* pp. 107-8; AEAF/MS399/Air Plans, Air Plan—Operation "OVERLORD," app B, Airborne Tasks, 7 Dec 43, in 505.33-25; min of Meeting at AEAF Headquarters, Stanmore, To Discuss the Employment of Airborne Forces in Continental Operations, 9 Dec 43, in 505.27-11; min of Conference Held by Air C-in-C AEAF at Bentley Priory, Stanmore, 20 Dec 43, in 505.25-3.

8. Ltr, Maj Gen L. H. Brereton to Maj Gen I. C. Eaker, 19 Sep 43, in 519.818.

9. Hist IX TCC, 16 Oct-Dec 43; Hist 50th TC Wg, Oct-Dec 43; Hist 434th TC Gp, 9 Feb-Dec 43; Hist 435th TC Gp, 25 Feb-Dec 43; Hist 315th TC Gp, 17 Feb 42-30 Nov 43.

10. Ltr, Air C-in-C AEAF to AOC 2 TAF and CG 9th USAF, subj: Directive to Tactical Air Forces Operation "OVERLORD," 6 Dec 43, in 505.25-31; Agenda for Meeting of Joint Commanders-in-Chief at St. Paul's, 7 Dec 43, in 505.25-2; min of Meeting at AEAF Headquarters to Discuss the Employment of Airborne Forces in Continental Operations, 9 Dec 43, in 505.27-11.

11. Incomplete file of min of Airborne-Air Planning Committee AEAF, in 505.27-11.

12. Craven and Cate, *The Army Air Forces in World War II*, IV, 109-10; ltr, Lt Gen C. Spaatz to CG 9th AF, subj: Control of the Ninth Air Force, 24 Feb 44; ltr, Maj Gen L. H. Brereton, CG 9th AF, to Air-C-in-C AEAF, subj: D-Day Fitness of IX Troop Carrier Command, 29 Apr 44, both in 505.25-31.

13. Hq AEAF, Memo Book, in 505.19-1; min of Meeting Held at AEAF Headquarters to Discuss and Agree the Requirements of a Joint Troop Carrier Command Post and Operations Room, 19 Feb 44; min of 8th and 9th mtgs of Airborne-Air Planning Committee AEAF, 14 and 29 Apr 44, both in 505.27-11.

14. Morgan, *Overture to OVERLORD*, pp. 190-91, 203; COSSAC(43), 26th and 29th rpts to Sec C/S Com, War Cab, 11 Oct and 1 Nov 43, in 505.10-8; memo for AEAF Chief of Operations from Lt Col J. H. Reynolds, subj: Visit to Airborne Forces Development Center, 24 Dec 43, and 1st ind, Brig Gen A. C. Strickland, AEAF Chief of Operations, to Lt Col S. Q. Wentz, 1 Jan 44; in 505.33-67.

15. James M. Gavin, *Airborne Warfare* (Washington, 1947), pp. 40-42; 21 Army Gp, "NEPTUNE" Study No. 5, Tentative Assault Plan (1st draft), 27 Dec 43, in 506.451-313; AEAF "NEPTUNE" Study No. 6, Delay of Enemy Reserves (2d draft), 4 Jan 44, in 505.34-4.

16. Harrison, *Cross-Channel Attack*, pp. 158, 165-67; Dwight D. Eisenhower, *Crusade in Europe* (Garden City, 1948), pp. 208, 217; Bernard L. Montgomery, *Normandy to the Baltic*, (Germany, 1946), pp. 5-14; Hq 9th AF, Planning Journal, 6 and 7 Jan 44, in 533.305C.

17. Harrison, *Cross-Channel Attack*, pp. 168, 173; min of Supreme Commander's Conferences, mtgs 1 and 2, 21 Jan 44; memo for C-in-C (Air) from Air Commodore, Head of Plans, 23 Jan 44, and Addendum, 24 Jan 44, all in 505.25-6; Hq AEAF, Operation "OVERLORD" initial Joint Plan—Programme of Work, 18 Jan 44; NJC 1003 (Revised) Notes on Planning Procedure, 15 Jan 44, both in 506.451-313.

18. Omar N. Bradley, *A Soldier's Story* (New York, 1951), p. 232; Gavin, *Airborne Warfare*, pp. 42-44; Hq 9th AF, Planning Journal, 15 Jan 44, in 533.305C; min of Supreme Commander's Conferences, mtg 1, 21 Jan 44.

19. NJC 1004, NEPTUNE—Initial Joint Plan, 1 Feb 44, in 533.451; min of mtg (AEAF Air Plans) at Norfolk House, 22 Jan 44, in 505.25-13; min of Supreme Commander's Conferences, mtg 3, 24 Jan 44, in 505.25-6; memo for Col Cole, Dep C/S Plans 9th AF, from Maj D. W. Bostwick, 29 Jan 44, in 533.451.

20. *Airborne Forces*, pp. 106, 123; Winston S. Churchill, *Closing the Ring* (Boston, 1951), pp. 443, 587-88; Hq AAF Plans Div, Daily Activity rpts, 29, 31 Jan 44, in USAFHD files; min of 6th, 7th, and 8th Conferences Held by Air C-in-C AEAF, 9, 16, and 23 Feb 44, in 505.25-3.

21. Ltr, Gen G. C. Marshall to Gen D. D. Eisenhower, 12 Feb 44, in 506.451-322B; Hq AAF Plans Div, Daily Activity rpts, 7 and 9 Feb 44, in USAFHD files.

22. Harrison, *Cross-Channel Attack*, pp. 185-86; min of Supreme Commander's Conferences, mtg 5, 18 Feb 44, in 505.25-6.

23. Bradley, *A Soldier's Story*, p. 234; min of a Meeting at St. Paul's to Discuss the Employment of Airborne Forces, 22 Feb 44, in 505.33-67; Hq 9th AF, Planning Journal, 23 Feb 44; NEPTUNE—Initial Joint Plan, Amdt 1, 2 Mar 44, in 533.451.

24. Min of 9th AF Commanders' mtg, 3 Mar 44, in 533.142; journal, IX TCC A-3, 17 Mar 44, in 546.305; Hq IX TCC, Tactical Air Plan for Operation NEPTUNE, 2 May 44, (Annex 12 to 9th AF Tactical Air Plan for Operation NEPTUNE) in 533.451; min of 10th mtg of Airborne-Air Planning Committee, 18 May 44, in 505.27-11.

25. Min of Meeting Held at Norfolk House to Discuss the Employment of Airborne Forces in Operation OVERLORD, 25 Mar 44, in 505.33-67; Hq AEAF, Operation "NEPTUNE" Overall Air Plan, 15 Apr 44, in 506.451.317; journal, IX TCC A-3, 22 Mar 44.

26. Min of 7th, 8th, and 9th mtgs of Airborne-Air Planning Committee, 14, 19, and 28 Apr 44, in 505.27-11; memo for CG AAF from AC/AS Plans, subj: OVERLORD Air Plans, 26 May 44, in 145.96-223C; Hq AEAF, Operation "NEPTUNE" Overall Air Plan, 15 Apr 44; min of Supreme Commander's Conference, mtg 16, 24 Apr 44, in 505.25-6; min of 9th AF Commanders mtg, 5 May 44, in 533.142.

27. Hq IX TCC, Tactical Air Plan for Operation NEPTUNE; min of AEAF mtg, 17 May 44, in 506.451-322C; min of 10th mtg of Airborne-Air Planning Committee, 18 May 44, in 505.27-11; Hq IX TCC FO 1, 31 May 44, App D3, in 533.451.

28. Harrison, *Cross-Channel Attack*, pp. 258-60.

29. Gavin, *Airborne Warfare*, pp. 46-48; Harrison, *Cross-Channel Attack*, pp. 249-50, 263-64.

30. Harrison, *Cross-Channel Attack*, p. 260; memo for Gen Nevins from Air Commodore C. B. Pelly, AEAF Head of Plans, 26 May 44; memo for C/S SHAEF from Maj Gen H. R. Bull, subj: Implication of Reported Enemy Reinforcements of the Cotentin Peninsula, 28 May 44, both in 505.33-37.

31. Harrison, *Cross-Channel Attack*, p 186; Gavin, *Airborne Warfare*, pp. 52-3; R. G. Ruppenthal, *UTAH Beach to Cherbourg* (Washington, 1947), pp. 8-10; journal, IX TCC A-2, 26-31 May 44, in 546.604; memo for CG AAF from AC/AS Plans, subj: OVERLORD Air Plans, 26 May 44, in 145.96-223C.

32. Gavin, *Airborne Warfare*, pp. 47-8, 53.

33. Eisenhower, *Crusade in Europe*, pp. 246-47; Harri-

son, *Cross-Channel Attack*, p. 186; min of Supreme Commander's Conferences, mtg 20, 29 May 44, in 505.25-6.

34. AC/AS Intelligence Analysis Div, European Br, Status of Air Prerequisites for Operation "OVERLORD," 29 Mar 44, in 142.132; Hq AEAF Operation "NEPTUNE" Overall Air Plan, 15 Apr 44; Hq IX TCC FO 1, 31 May 44, ann 1.

35. Hq AEAF, Operation "NEPTUNE" Overall Air Plan, 15 Apr 44; journal, IX TCC A-3, 26 Mar, 6, 8, 12, 16 Apr 44; Hq IX TCC, Tactical Air Plan for Operation NEPTUNE, 2 May 44; min of 9th mtg of Airborne-Air Planning Committee, 28 Apr 44.

36. Ltr, Hq AEAF to Distr, subj: Operation "NEPTUNE"—Employment of U.S. Airborne Forces, 31 May 44, in 505.34-12; memo for Gen Smith from Col R. B. Bagby, 31 May 44; ltr, Hq AEAF to Dist, subj: Operation "NEPTUNE," U.S. Troop Carrier—Airborne Forces, 1 June 44, both in 505.34-12; Hq IX TCC FO 1, 31 May 44, app D1 and D3, in 533.451.

37. Report by the Allied Naval Commander-in-Chief Expeditionary Force on Operation "NEPTUNE," Oct 44, in 506.451-490A.

38. Hq AEAF, Signals Report on Operation "NEPTUNE"—Planning and Assault Phase, Jul 44, in 505.29-32; ltr, Hq AEAF to Distr, subj: Use of IFF in Operation "OVERLORD," 10 May 44, in 505.451-161.

39. Hist IX TCC, May, Jun 44; Hist 52d TC Wg, Jun 44; Hist 45th TC Sq, Jun 44; Hist 49th TC Sq, Jun 44; Hist 62d TC Sq, June 44; Hist 97th TC Sq, Jun 44; memo for Col M. M. Frost from Lt. Col W. R. Carter, subj: Painting of Aircraft and Gliders, 13 May 44, in 505.25A; min of 19th Conference Held by Air C-in-C AEAF, 17 May 44, in 505.25-3.

40. Min of 9th mtg of Airborne-Air Planning Committee, 28 Apr 44; Hq IX TCC, Tactical Air Plan for Operation NEPTUNE, 2 May 44; Hq IX TCC FO 1, 31 May 44, in KCRC, files of 82d Abn Div.

41. Planning Journal, Hq 9th AF, 24 and 25 Mar 44, in 533.305C; journal, IX TCC A-3, 25 and 26 Mar, 12 Apr 44; min of 9th AF Commanders' mtg, 14 Apr 44, in 533.142; Hq IX TCC, Tactical Air Plan for Operation NEPTUNE, 2 May 44; Hq 9th AF Adv, Minutes of AEAF mtg, 16 May 44, in 506.451-322C.

42. Min of 7th-10th mtgs of Airborne-Air Planning Committee, 24 Mar, 14 and 28 Apr, and 18 May 44, in 505.27-11; ltr, ACM T. Leigh-Mallory to Deputy SCAEF, subj: Operation "OVERLORD" Preparatory Air Operations, 30 Apr 44, in 506.451-161; ltr, Hq AEAF to Distr, subj: Operation "TITANIC," 18 May 44, in 505.34-12; ltr, Brig Gen F. H. Smith, Jr., AEAF Chief of Operations to Hq BC, subj: Operation "NEPTUNE" Diversionary Operations in Support of Airborne Forces (Operation "TITANIC"), 25 May 44, in 505.34-12.

43. Hq IX TCC, Tactical Air Plan for Operation NEPTUNE, 2 May 44; memo for Hq 100 Gp from Hq BC, subj: R.C.M. Role for Nos. 199 and 803 Squadrons, Operation "OVERLORD," 26 May 44 in 505.451-161; msg, AC 84, Hq AEAF to 8th AF A-3, 3 Jun 44, in 505.451-161.

44. Hq AEAF, Air Signals Report on Operation "NEPTUNE," Jul 44, Sec X.

45. Hq 9th AF Adv, min of AEAF mtg, 16 May 44, in 506.451-322C; ltr, Brig Gen F. H. Smith, Jr., AEAF Chief of Operations, to Distr, subj: Operation "OVERLORD" Night Fighter Support for Airborne Operations, 20 May 44, in 505.34-12; ltr, Maj Gen E. R. Quesada, CG IX FC to CG 9th AF, subj: Rpt, Conference AEAF, May 22, 1944, 23 May 44, in 506.451-322C; directive, Maj Gen E. R. Quesada, CG IX FC and AVM J. V. Saunders, 11 Gp, to Distr, subj: Operation "NEPTUNE" Day and Night Fighter Support for Airborne Operations, 1 Jun 44, in 506.451-329; ltr, Lt Gen J. H. Doolittle, CG 8th AF, to CG USSTAF, subj: Role of Eighth Air Force in Operation "OVERLORD," 31 May 44; ltr, Hq AEAF to CG USSTAF, subj: Bombing Operations in Support of "OVERLORD," 1 Jun 44, both in 506.451-161.

46. Hq IX TCC FO 1, 31 May 44, App 4 (Schedule of Navigational Aids) to Ann 3, and App B (IX Troop Carrier Routes); Hq IX TCC FO 1, 31 May 44, amdt 1, 4 Jun 44 (this cancelled plans for another marker boat at SPOKANE).

47. Hq AEAF, Air Signals Report on Operation "NEPTUNE," Jul 44, Sec VI; memo for Distr from Hq AEAF, subj: Organization and Operational Employment of "Gee" in the AEAF, 29 Jan 44, in 505.27-27; ltr, Maj Gen B. M. Giles, C/AS, to CG 9th AF, subj: Status of Troop Carrier Training, 4 Feb 44, in 546.712; min of 8th mtg held by Air C-in-C AEAF, 23 Feb 44, in 505.25-3; min of 9th AF Commanders' mtg, 25 Feb 44, in 533.142; journal, IX TCC Communications Officer, 8, 11, 16, 27 and 31 Jan 44, in 546.901A; journal, IX TCC A-3, 9 Apr 44, in 546.305; journal, IX TCC A-4, 15 Apr 44, in 546.801; ltr, Lt Gen J. H. Doolittle, CG 8th AF, to CG USSTAF, subj: Use of PPF Equipment to Make Initial Attack on Assigned Target Areas on "D" Day, 26 May 44, in 506.451-161; ltr, Hq IX TCC Adv to C/AAF, Report of Operation (NEPTUNE), 13 Jun 44, in 245.631-1; ltr, IX TCC Communications Officer to CG IX TCC, Report of Signal Communications D-1/D plus 3, Operation "NEPTUNE," 15 Jun 44, in 546.451A-1; rpt, Dr. A. W. Lines, D.C.D. to AEAF, subj: The Use of Radar Aids in Operation NEPTUNE," 14 Jul 44, in 506.451-313A (hereinafter cited as Lines, Report on Radar Aids in NEPTUNE).

48. Hq IX TCC, Teletype Conference, 31 Mar 44, in 519.255.4(E); Hq AEAF, Air Signals Report on Operation "NEPTUNE," Jul 44.

49. Min of 8th mtg Held by Air C-in-C AEAF, 23 Feb 44; min of 7th and 8th mtgs of Airborne-Air Plan-

ning Committee, 24 Mar and 14 Apr 44; journal IX TCC A-3, 17 and 22 Mar 44; Hq IX TCC, Teletype Conference, 31 Mar 44; Hq IX TCC FO 1, Ann 3, 31 May 44; Lines, Report on Radar Aids in NEPTUNE; memo for Brig Gen P. L. Williams, CG IX TCC, from L. N. Ridenour, Advisory Specialists Group, subj: Radar Aids to Operations of IX Troop Carrier Command, 19 Apr 44, in 519.255-A(E); Hq 101st Abn Div Pfdr Gp (Prov), FO 1, 31 May 44, in KCRC files of 101st Abn Div.

50. SHAEF, Op Memo 12, Standard Operating Procedure for Airborne and Troop Carrier Units, 13 Mar 44, in 507.301; Hq IX TCC FO 1, 31 May 44; ann 3; Hq 101st Abn Div Pfdr Gp (Prov) FO 1, 31 May 44; Hq IX TCC Adv, Report of Operation (NEPTUNE), 13 Jun 44.

51. Hq IX TCC, Rosters, 12 Jan-Jun 44, in 546.116.

52. Hq IX TCC GO's 8, 10, 11, and 20, 25 Feb, 1 and 6 Mar, and 18 Apr 44, in 546.02; Hq IX TCC, SO 46, 12 Dec 43, in 546.02; Hist IX TCC, Oct 43; journal, IX TCC Comm Sec, 3 and 4 Feb 44; journal, IX TCC A-3, Mar-Jun 44.

53. Hist IX TCC, Jan-May 44; Incl, Tab "B": Aircraft Strength—Ninth Air Force Target vs Actual, in ltr, Maj Gen H. S. Vandenberg to CG USSTAF, subj: Interim Program Report on Equipment, Training and Manning of Ninth Air Force, 1 Apr 44, in 505.30-1.

54. Ltr, Giles to CG 9th AF, subj: Status of Troop Carrier Training, 4 Feb 44; journal, IX TCC A-1, 16 Mar, 10 Apr, 10, 16, 23-31 May 44, in 546.122; Hq IX TCC, Statistical Summary for the Year 1944, in 546.308.

55. Hq IX TCC Adv, Report of Operation (NEPTUNE), 13 Jun 44; rpts, IX TCC A-1, 20 Apr and 20 May 44, in 546.116.

56. Hist 53d TC Wg, May 44; journal, IX TCC A-4, 7, 11 and 16-19 Feb, 12, 14, 16 and 21-23 Mar, 14, 16 and 23-25 Apr, 4 May and 22 June 44; rpts, IX TCC Ordnance Section, 30 Apr, 10 and 20 May 44, in 546.116.

57. Ltr, Lt Gen J. L. Devers to Gen H. H. Arnold, 3 Jul 43; ltr, Arnold to Devers, 1 Aug 43, both in USAFHD files; ltr, Giles to CG 9th AF, subj: Status of Troop Carrier Training, 4 Feb 44; journal, IX TCC A-3, 30 May 44; Hq IX TCC, Statistical Summary for the Year 1944.

58. Ltr, Lt Gen I. C. Eaker to Maj Gen B. M. Giles, 28 May 43, in USAFHD files, Hist IX AFSC, 16 Oct 43-9 May 45, pp. 31-39, 108; Hq IX TCC, Statistical Summary for the Year 1944; journal, IX TCC A-3, 20, 27-30 Mar 44; journal, IX TCC A-4, 26 and 28 Mar, 1, 10, and 29 Apr 44.

59. *Airborne Forces*, p. 247; Hist, 437th TC Gp, May 44; journal, IX TCC A-4, 28 and 29 Apr; journal, IX TCC A-3, 22, 24-26 May, 2 and 4 Jun 44; rpts, IX TCC AC Engineer, 30 Apr, 20 and 30 May 44, in 546.116.

60. Hist IX AFSC, 16 Oct 43-9 May 45, p. 121; Hist IX TCC, Apr 44; journal, IX TCC A-4, 23 and 25 Mar, 20 Apr, 8-11 May 44; journal, IX TCC A-3, 21 May 44; rpt, IX TCC AC Engineer, 30 Apr 44; rpts, IX TCC AC Supply, 10, 20, and 31 May 44.

61. Ltr, SHAEF to C-in-C 21 Army Gp and C-in-C AEAF, subj: Training Program Troop Carrier—Airborne Combined Training, 6 Feb 44; ltr, SHAEF to C-in-C 21 Army Gp and C-in-C AEAF, subj: Troop Carrier-Airborne Combined Training, 31 Mar 44, both in 505.30-1; ltr, Brig Gen H. A. Johnson to DC AEAF, subj: Troop Carrier Exercises, 26 Feb 44; all three in 505.30-1; min of 10th mtg Held by Air C-in-C AEAF, 8 Mar 44, in 505.25-3.

62. Hist IX TCC, Feb, Mar 44; ltr, Johnson to DC AEAF, 26 Feb; memo for DC AEAF from Brig Gen H. A. Johnson, subj: Will Units Assigned to the AEAF Be Training and Equipped by May 1st or June 1st, 1944, 31 Jan 44, in 505.30-1; journal, IX TCC A-4, 27 Jan, 1, 15, 17, 19 and 20 Feb. 44; min of 9th AF Commander's mtgs, 3 and 9, Mar 44, in 533.142; min of Meeting at Training Branch to Discuss Selection and Assignment of Additional Aerodromes for Glider and Fighter Operation, 16 Mar 44, in 505.25-23; bi-weekly log of Brig Gen H. A. Johnson, 16-18 Mar 44, in 505.30-1; min of 7th mtg of Airborne-Air Planning Committee, 24 Mar 44, in 505.27-11; ltr, Hq AEAF to Under Secretary of State, Air Ministry, DDO, subj: Operation "OVERLORD"-Airfield Dispositions, 27 Mar 44, in 505.33-31; journal, IX TCC A-4, 26-31 Mar, 1 and 3 May 44.

63. Leonard Rapport and Arthur Northwood, Jr., *Rendezvous with Destiny, A History of the 101st Airborne Division* (Washington, D.C., 1948), pp. 40, 44-45, 57-58; Gavin, *Airborne Warfare*, p. 39; rpt, Hq 82d Abn Div, The 82d Abn Division, Action in Normandy, France, Jun-Jul 44, p. 1, in 533.451-451.

64. Hist 53d TC Wg, Feb, Mar 44; Hist 434th TC Gp, Oct 43-Mar 44; Hist 435th TC Gp, Oct 43-Mar 44; Hist 436th TC Gp, Feb and Mar 44; Hist 437th TC Gp, Feb and Mar 44; Hist 438th TC Gp, Feb and Mar 44; journal, IX TCC A-4, 8, 10 and 15 Feb, 5 23 Mar 44; ltr, Giles to CG 9th AF, subj: Status of Troop Carrier Training, 4 Feb 44.

65. Hist IX TCC, Mar, Apr 44; Hist 53d TC Wg, Mar, Apr, and May 44; Hist 434th TC Gp, Mar 44; Hist 437th TC Gp, Mar 44; Hist 435th TC Gp, Apr 44; Hist 75th TC Sq, Apr 44; Hist 506th PIR, Activation—Apr 44, in KCRC in regimental files; ltr, Brig Gen M. D. Taylor, CG 101st Abn Div, to Col M. M. Beach, 24 Mar 44, in hist file 53d TC Wg; journal, IX TCC A-3, 21 and 26 Mar, 4 and 27 Apr 44; rpts, IX TCC A-3, 12 Mar, 11 Apr 44, in 546.116; Hq IX TCC FO 6 (Exercise MUSH), 12 Apr 44; Hq 9th AF Adv to AEAF, COSUM 21 (Exercise MUSH), 21 Apr 44, both in 546.717D; ltr, Brig Gen P. L.

Williams to CG AAF, subj: Troop Carrier Training for Operation "NEPTUNE," 14 Jun 44, in 546.452G.

66. Hist IX TCC, Feb, Mar 44; Hist 52d TC Wg, Feb, Mar, Apr 44; Hist 315th TC Gp, Feb, Mar 44; Hist 442d TC Gp, 1 Sep 43-1 Apr 44; Hist 305th TC Sq, 1 Sep 43-1 Apr 44; Hist 306th TC Sq 1 Sep 43-1 Apr 44; journal, IX TCC A-3, 18, 26 Mar 44; journal, IX TCC A-4, 15, 19 Feb 44; ltr, Maj R. M. Stewart, Jr. to Chief of Training, AEAF, subj: The 52d Troop Carrier Wing, 11 Apr 44, in 505.30-1.

67. Hist IX TCC, Apr and May 44; Hist 52d TC Wg, Apr and May 44; Hist 316th TC Gp, Mar and Apr 44; Hist 315th TC Gp, Apr and May 44; Hist 442d TC Gp, Apr and May 44; Hist 14th TC Sq, Apr 44; Hist 53d TC Sq, Apr 44; Hist 43d TC Sq, Apr and May 44; wkly ops rpts (hereinafter cited as opreps: All opreps and mission reports will be found in unit history files unless otherwise noted.), 315th TC Gp, 8 Apr-7 May 44, opreps 442d TC Gp, 8 Apr-7 May 44; journal, IX TCC A-3, 13 and 21 Mar, 9, 12, 24 and 27 Apr, 1, 9, and 15 May 44; rpt, IX TCC A-3, 11 Apr 44; Hq 9th AF Adv COSUM 21, 21 Apr 44; ltr, Maj R. M. Stewart to Chief of Training AEAF, subj: The 52d Troop Carrier Wing, 11 Apr 44; ltr, Brig Gen P. L. Williams to CG AAF, subj: Troop Carrier Training for Operation "NEPTUNE," 14 Jun 44.

68. Hist 50th TC Wg, Feb and Mar 44; Hist 439th TC Gp, Feb and Mar 44; Hist 440th TC Gp, Feb and Mar 44; Hist 441st TC Gp, Feb and Mar 44; Hq IX TCC, GO's 9 and 14, 25 Feb and 21 Mar 44, in 546.193; ltr, Maj R. M. Stewart to Chief of Training AEAF, subj: The 50th Troop Carrier Wing, 11 Apr 44, in 505.30-1.

69. Hist IX TCC, Apr 44; Hist 50th TC Wg, Apr and May 44; Hist 440th TC Gp, Apr and May 44; Hist 441st TC Gp, Apr 44; Hist 439th TC Gp, May 44; Hist 441st TC Gp, May 44; wkly opreps, 441st TC Gp, 1-29 Apr 44, in unit hist files; journal, IX TCC A-3, 11, 17, 18, 27 Apr 44; journal, IX TCC A-4, 17, 19 May 44; rpt, IX TCC A-3, 21 Apr 44; in 546.116; rpt, IX TCC Engineer, 10 Apr 44, in 546.116; ltr, Williams to CG AAF, 14 Jun 44.

70. Hist IX TCC, Feb 44; journal, IX TCC Communications Officer, 12, 13, and 22 Feb 44, in 546.910A; journal, IX TCC A-3, 21 and 23 Mar 44; journal, IX TCC A-4, 25 Mar 44; rpt, IX TCC A-3, 5 Mar 44, in 546.116; ltr, Williams to CG AAF, 14 Jun 44.

71. Lines, Report on Radar Aids in NEPTUNE; ltr, Williams to CG AAF, 14 Jun 44; ltr, Col J. L. Crouch to CG IX TCC, Attn A-3, subj: Report Pathfinder School, 13 Jun 44, in 546.072A; Hq IX TAC (Rear) Opnl Res Sec, Rpt 47, Report on the Mission of the Pathfinder Aircraft of the Pathfinder School, IX Troop Carrier Command, During Operation NEPTUNE, Jun 5/6, 1944, 25 Jun 44, in 546.310A.

72. Hist IX TCC, Apr and May 44; Hist 50th TC Wg, May 44; Hist 52d TC Wg, May 44; Hist 53d TC Wg, May 44; Hist 315th TC Gp, May 44; Hist 434th TC Gp, May 44; Hist 437th TC Gp, May 44; Hist 439th TC Gp, May 44, Hist 440th TC Gp, May 44; Hist 442d TC Gp, May 44; min of 9th and 10th mtgs of Airborne-Air Planning Committee, 28 Apr and 18 May 44; Hq 52d TC Wg FO 6 Exercise EAGLE, May 44 in unit hist file; oprep EAGLE, Hq 314th TC Gp, 12 May 44; Consolidated Mission Report (hereinafter cited as CMR) EAGLE, Hq 314th TC Gp, undated; oprep EAGLE, Hq 315th TC Gp, 13 May 44; oprep EAGLE, Hq 442d TC Gp, 12 May 44; ltr CG 21 Army Gp to Hq AEAF, subj: Exercise "EAGLE" Airborne Rehearsal, 20 Apr 44, in 505.89-11; Hq IX TCC FO 8, Operation EAGLE, 7 May 44, in 505.89-11; Hq 50th TC Wg FO 11, Exercise EAGLE, 8 May 44, in 535.717D; oprep 1, Hq IX TCC Pfdr Force, Mission EAGLE, 12 May 44, in 546.3062A.

73. Hist 50th TC Wg, Jun 44; Hist 52d TC Wg, Jun 44; Hist, 53d TC Wg, Jun 44; Hist 442d TC Gp, Jun 44; journal, IX TCC A-3, 17 and 26 Mar 44; journal, IX TCC A-2, 29 Apr, 4 and 31 May and 3 Jun 44.

74. Hist 52d TC Wg, Jun 44; Hist 313th TC Gp, Jun 44; Hist 439th TC Gp, Jun 44; Hist 33d TC Sq, June 44; Hist 47th TC Sq, Jun 44; Hist 49th TC Sq, Jun 44; Hist 59th TC Sq, Jun 44; Hist 61st TC Sq, Jun 44; Hist 62d TC Sq, Jun 44; Hist TC Sq, Jun 44; Hist 95th TC Sq, Jun 44; Hist 98th TC Sq, Jun 44; Hist 309th TC Sq, Jun 44; journal, IX TCC A-2, 14, 18 and 31 May 44; ltr, Exec 0 50th TC Wg, to Hist 0 50th TC Wg, subj: Planning of "Operation Neptune," 9 Jun 44, in wing hist file; ltr, Hq AEAF to Distr, subj: Briefing of Key Personnel, 31 May 44, in 505.27-18.

75. Hist 50th TC Wg, Jun 44; Hist 52d TC Wg, Jun 44; Hist 53d TC Wg, Jun 44; Hist 34th TC Sq, Jun 44; ltr, Col B. A. Dickson, 1st Army S-2 to Distr, subj: Security in Airborne Mounting, 15 May 44; ltr, Hq IX TCC to CG 52d Wg and CO's 50th and 53d TC Wgs, subj: Security Directive for Operation "NEPTUNE," 21 May 44, in hist file 50th TC Wg.

76. Eisenhower, *Crusade in Europe*, pp. 250-51; Harrison, *Cross-Channel Attack*, pp. 273-76; dispatch, ACM T. Leigh-Mallory, Air C-in-C AEAF to SAC, subj: Air Operations by the Allied Expeditionary Air Force in Northwest Europe from November 15th, 1943 to September 30th, 1944, Nov 44, in AU Lib 940.54 G 786 1, no. 37839; Hq AEAF, A Report of Air Operations Preparatory to and in Support of Operation "NEPTUNE," in 506.306A (There is a very close relationship between this report and corresponding portions of Leigh-Mallory's dispatch.); Report by the Allied Naval C-in-C Expeditionary Force on Operation "NEPTUNE," I, 10, 44-46, in 506.451-490A.

77. Craven and Cate, *AAF IN WW II*, III, 172, 188, 195; Harrison *Cross-Channel Attack*, pp. 275, 278, 293, 297-98; Hq AEAF, Air Signals Report on Operation "NEPTUNE"—Planning and Assault Phase,

Jul 44, Sec VIII; dispatch by Leigh Mallory on Air Operations by AEAF; Hq AEAF, A Report of Air Operations Preparatory to and In Support of Operation "NEPTUNE"; Report by Allied Naval Commander-in-Chief on Operation "NEPTUNE"; Dept of the Army, Airborne Operations, A German Appraisal (Pamphlet 20-232), Oct 51, in 170.132-232; Telephone Log of the German Seventh Army from June 6 to June 30, 1944, in 512.621 (British Air Min, German Translations, v.13), in 512.621 VII/70; lecture by Lt R. C. Smith, 23 Jun 44, in 248.532-49.

Chapter II

1. Leonard Rapport and Arthur Northwood, Jr., *Rendezvous with Destiny*, pp. 93-94; Hq AEAF, Air Signals Report on Operation "NEPTUNE" Jul 1944; rpt, Dr. A. W. Lines, D.C.D. to AEAF, subj: The Use of Radar Aids in Operation "NEPTUNE," (hereinafter cited as Lines, Report on Radar Aids in NEPTUNE); Hq IX TAC (REAR) ORS Report 47, Report on IX TCC Pathfinder Mission During Operation NEPTUNE, 25 Jun 44; IX TCC Pfdr Gp, Oprep BOSTON, 6 Jun 44, and Oprep ALBANY, 11 Jun 44, both in 546.3062A; rpt, Hq 82d Abn Div, Action in Normandy, France, June-July 44, ann 4a, in 533.451.451.

2. SHAEF, Opr Memo 12, SOP for Airborne and Troop Carrier Units, 13 Mar 44, in 507.301; Hq IX TCC, Memo 50-21, SOP for Troop Carrier-Airborne Operations, 2 May 44, in 505.34-12; Hq IX TCC FO 1, NEPTUNE-BIGOT, 31 May 44; Hist 88th TC Sq, Jun 44; Hist 301st TC Sq, Jun 44.

3. Hq 101st Abn Div, Airborne Operation Neptune-101st Abn Div, 19 Jul 44, in KCRC divisional files.

4. Hist 438th TC Gp, Jun 44; Hist 441st TC Gp, Jun 44; Hist 310th TC Sq, Jun 44; journal, 9th AF Dep C/S, 5 Jun 44, in 533.305B.

5. Lt S. S. Cromie, 438th TC Gp, quoted in S. Levitt, "Down and Go," *Stars and Stripes*, 2 Jul 44, in Hist file 438th TC Gp; Air Ministry, A.H.B., *Airborne Forces* (1951), pp. 125, 129-30; Hist 98th TC Sq, Jun 44; journal, 506th PIR S-3, 5-6 Jun 44, in KCRC regimental file.

6. Hist 53d TC Wg, Jun 44; Hist 436th TC Gp, Jun 44; Hist 438th TC Gp, Jun 44; Hist 79th TC Sq, Jun 44; Hist 80th TC Sq, Jun 44; Hist 81st TC Sq, Jun 44; Hist 90th TC Sq, Jun 44; oprep 1, 436th TC Gp, Mission Neptune, 6 Jun 44; oprep 1, 438th TC Gp, Mission Neptune, 6 Jun 44; Hq 9th AF, "First Reports over Phone" (handwritten notes) in 533.4511; Hist 502d PIR, (Jun 44) in KCRC, unit files.

7. Rapport and Northwood, *Rendezvous with Destiny*, Maps p. 102 and 104; R. G. Ruppenthal, *UTAH Beach to Cherbourg* (Washington, 1947), Map p. 16 and Map V; Hq 101st Abn Div, Airborne Operation Neptune—101st Abn Div, 19 Jul 44.

8. Gordon A. Harrison, *Cross-Channel Attack* (Washington 1951), pp 280-82, 329; Ruppenthal, *UTAH Beach to Cherbourg*, pp. 16-20, 51, 54; Rapport and Northwood, *Rendezvous with Destiny*, pp. 103-10, 121-27.

9. Ruppenthal, *UTAH Beach to Cherbourg*, pp 20-21, Map p. 22 and Map V; Rapport and Northwood, *Rendezvous with Destiny*, pp. 96-97, 101; Hist 50th TC Wg, Jun 44; Hist 435th TC Gp, Jun 44; Hist 439th TC Gp, Jun 44; Hist 75th TC Sq, Jun 44; Hist 76th TC Sq, Jun 44; Hist 77th TC Sq, Jun 44; Hist 78th TC Sq, Jun 44; Hist 91st TC Sq, Jun 44; Hist 92d TC Sq, Jun 44; Hist 93d TC Sq, Jun 44; Hist 94th TC Sq, Jun 44; oprep 50th TC Wg, Mission ALBANY, 6 Jun 44; aprep, 435th TC Gp, Mission 13 Operation Neptune, 6 Jun 44; MR 439th TC Gp, Neptune Bigot, 6 Jun 44; interrogation of Lt Col C. H. Young, in hist file 439th TC Gp; Lines, Report on Radar Aids in NEPTUNE; Hq 101st Abn Div Airborne Operation Neptune—101st Abn Div, 19 Jul 44; ETOUSA Hist Sec, The 506th Parachute Infantry Regiment in the Normandy Drop, in 502.04B-3.

10. Harrison, *Cross-Channel Attack*, pp. 282-84; Ruppenthal, *UTAH Beach to Cherbourg*, pp. 20-23, 51-53; Rapport and Northwood, *Rendezvous with Destiny*, pp. 95-103, 128-31, 134; journal, 506th PIR. S-1, 6 Jun 44; journal, 506th PIR S-2, 6 Jun 44; journal, 506th PIR S-3, 6 Jun 44, all in KCRC, regimental files.

11. Hq 501st PIR FO 1, 24 May 44; Hq 506th PIR FO 1, 24 May 44; Hq 101st Abn Div FO 1, 18 May 44; amdt 1, 27 May 44, in KCRC, divisional files.

12. Ruppenthal, *UTAH Beach to Cherbourg*, pp. 23-27; Hist 50th TC Wg, Jun 44; Hist 440th TC Gp, Jun 44; Hist 441st TC Gp, Jun 44; Hist 95th TC Sq, Jun 44; Hist 96th TC Sq, Jun 44; Hist 97th TC Sq, Jun 44; Hist 98th TC Sq, Jun 44; Hist 99th TC Sq, Jun 44; Hist 301st TC Sq, Jun 44; Hist 302d TC Sq, Jun 44; DZ Europe, The Story of the 440th TC Gp, in unit hist files; Lines, Report on Radar Aids in NEPTUNE; oprep, 50th TC Wg, ALBANY; Hq 101st Abn Div, Airborne Operation Neptune-101st Abn Div, 19 Jul 44.

13. Rapport and Northwood, *Rendezvous with Destiny*, pp. 60, 93, 111-20, 132-38; Ruppenthal, *UTAH Beach to Cherbourg*, pp. 25-30 and Map V; Harrison, *Cross-Channel Attack*, pp. 286-88; Hq 101st Abn Div FO 1, 18 May 44 and amdt 1, 27 May 44, in unit files in KCRC; Hq 101st Abn Div, Airborne Operation Neptune-101st Abn Div, 19 Jul 44, in unit files in KCRC; ltr, Capt C.G. Shettle to CG 506th PIR, subj: Report on Activities of 3d Battalion, 24 Jun 44; ltr, Shettle to Co 506th PIR, subj: Unusual Incident, 8 Jul 44, both in files of 506th PIR in KCRC.

14. Ruppenthal, *UTAH Beach to Cherbourg*, pp. 72-74, 77-78; Harrison, *Cross-Channel Attack*, pp. 239, 293, 297-98, 347-48, 356-57; journal, 506th PIR S-3, 8 Jun 44.

15. Lines, Report on Radar Aids in NEPTUNE; Hq 82d Abn Div, Action in Normandy; Hist 52d TC Wg, Jun 44; Hist 315th TC Gp, Jun 44; Hist 316th TC Gp, Jun 44; Hist 34th TC Sq, Jun 44; Hist 36th TC Sq, Jun 44; Hist 37th TC Sq, Jun 44; Hist 43d TC Sq, Jun 44; Hist 44th TC Sq, Jun 44; Hist 45th TC Sq, Jun 44; Hist 309th TC Sq, Jun 44; Hist 310th TC Sq, Jun 44; oprep, 315th TC Gp, Mission NEPTUNE-BOSTON, 6 Jun 44; oprep, 316th TC Gp, Mission Neptune-Boston, 6 Jun 44.

16. Ruppenthal, *UTAH Beach to Cherbourg*, Map on p. 32 and Map VI.

17. Harrison, *Cross-Channel Attack*, pp. 289-97, 342-44; Ruppenthal, *UTAH Beach to Cherbourg*, pp. 30-39, 61-65; James M. Gavin, *Airborne Warfare* (Washington, 1947), pp. 60-61; Hist Sec ETO, Regimental Study 6, The Capture of Ste Mere Eglise, in 502.04B-6; Hist 505th PIR, 6 Jun-15 Jul 44; journal, 505th PIR S-1, 6 and 7 Jun 44; journal, 505th PIR S-3, 6 and 7 Jun 44; msgs, Hq 2d Bn, 505th PIR, to CO 505th PIR, 0820, 1215 and 2030, 6 Jun 44; msg, Hq 1st Bn, 505th PIR, to CO 505th PIR, 0930, 6 Jun 44, all above in USAFHD, Microfilm Box 2058, Item 2141.

18. Ruppenthal, *UTAH Beach to Cherbourg*, Map VI; Lines, Report on Radar Aids in NEPTUNE; Hist 313th TC Gp, Jun 44; Hist 314th TC Gp, Jun 44; Hist 32d TC Sq, Jun 44; Hist 47th TC Sq, Jun 44; Hist 49th TC Sq, Jun 44; Hist 50th TC Sq, Jun 44; Hist 61st TC Sq, Jun 44; Hist 62d TC Sq, Jun 44; Hq 52d TC Wg FO 1, Operation NEPTUNE, 1 Jun 44; oprep, 313th TC Gp, Neptune Bigot 1, 6 Jun 44; oprep, 314th TC Gp, BIGOT NEPTUNE 1, 6 Jun 44; MR, 47th TC Sq, 6 Jun 44, MR 48th TC Sq, 6 Jun 44 Narrative of Capt C. S. Cartwright in hist file 62d TC Sq.

19. Ruppenthal, *UTAH Beach to Cherbourg*, pp. 30, 40-41, 119-20; Harrison, *Cross-Channel Attack*, pp. 293, 400-1; S.L.A. Marshall, "Affair at Hill 30," *Marine Corps Gazette*, Feb 48, pp. 8-20, Mar 48, pp. 20-25.

20. Ruppenthal, *UTAH Beach to Cherbourg*, Map p. 36, and Map VI; Hist 61st TC Gp, Jun 44; Hist 442d TC Gp, Jun 44; Hist 14th TC Sq, Jun 44; Hist 15th TC Sq, Jun 44; Hist 53d TC Sq, Jun 44; Hist 59th TC Sq, Jun 44; Hist 61st TC Sq, Jun 44; Hist 303d TC Sq, Jun 44; Hist 304th TC Sq, Jun 44; oprep, 61st TC Gp, Mission Neptune Boston, 6 Jun 44; oprep, 442d TC Gp, Mission Bigot Neptune, 6 Jun 44; CMR 303d TC Sq, 6 Jun 44; CMR 304th TC Sq, 6 Jun 44.

21. Ruppenthal, *UTAH Beach to Cherbourg*, pp. 37-40, 119-27; Harrison, *Cross-Channel Attack*, pp. 290-92, 396-401; Hist Sec ETO Regt Unit Study 4, The Forcing of the Merderet Causeway at La Fière France, in 502.04B-4; Hist, 325th Gl Inf Regt 6 Jun-14 Jul 44. in Box 2055, AGO Microfilm Item 2121; journal, 325th Gl Inf Regt, 7-11 Jun 44; journal, 325th Gl Inf Regt S-3, 7-9 Jun 44, above three in Box 2055, AGO Microfilm Item 2121; journal, 82d Abn Div S-2, 6-10 Jun 44; Statement by Maj D. E. Thomas, 15 Jun 44, both in Box 2007, AGO Microfilm Item 2029; journal, 82d Abn Div S-3, 6-10 Jun 44; Strength Rept, 505th, 507th and 508th PIR's and 325th Gl Inf Regt, 9 Jun 44, both in Box 2030, AGO Microfilm Item 2047.

22. Journal, 9th AF Dep C/S, 11 Jun 44, in 533.305B.

23. Hist 50th TC Wg, Jun 44; Lines, Report on Radar Aids in NEPTUNE.

24. Rapport and Northwood, *Rendezvous with Destiny*, pp. 74, 132; IX TCC Adv, Report of Operation (NEPTUNE), 13 Jun 44, in 245.631-1; Incl, "Timing for Night of D-1/D, U.S. Troop Carrier Revised Schedule of 30 May 44" to ltr, Hq AEAF to Distr, subj: Operation "NEPTUNE"—Employment of U.S. Airborne Forces, 31 May 44, in 505.34-12.

25. Rapport and Northwood, *Rendezvous with Destiny*, pp. 97, 119 (Map 15), 130-33; Hist 434th TC Gp, Jun 44; Hist 73d TC Sq, Jun 44; oprep, 434th TC Gp, Mission Neptune-Bigot, 6 Jun 44; Hq IX TCC, Tactical Air Plan for Operation NEPTUNE, 2 May 44; journal, 506th PIR S-3, 6 Jun 44; Hq 506th PIR, Operations of the 506th Parachute Infantry in the Invasion of Western Europe, in KCRC unit files; Lines, Report on Radar Aids in NEPTUNE.

26. Hist 437th TC Gp, Jun 44; Interrogations of glider pilots, 437th TC Gp, in unit hist file (Some of these erroneously titled as relating to other missions.); Hq 82d Abn Div, Action in Normandy; Lines, Report on Radar Aids in NEPTUNE; Hq Btry A, 80th Abn AA Bn, Action Rpt, 6-8 Jun 44, in Box 2044 AGO Microfilm Item 2074.

27. Rapport and Northwood, *Rendezvous with Destiny*, pp. 131-33; Hist 434th TC Gp, Jun 44; oprep 434th TC Gp, Mission Neptune-Bigot-Keokuk, 7 Jun 44.

28. Ruppenthal, *UTAH Beach to Cherbourg*, pp. 53-54; Hq, 82d Abn Div, Action in Normandy; Hist 437th TC Gp, Jun 44; Hist 438th TC Gp, Jun 44; Hist 87th TC Sq, Jun 44; Hist 88th TC Sq, Jun 44; Hist 89th TC Sq, Jun 44; Hist 90th TC Sq, Jun 44; oprep 2, 437th TC Gp, Mission NEPTUNE ELMIRA, 7 Jun 44; oprep 2, 438th TC Gp, Mission ELMIRA, 6 Jun 44; MR 88th TC Sq, 7 Jun 44; narratives of Capt W. W. Bates and Capt W. J. Adams, in Hist 53d TC Wg, Jun 44; Hist 505th PIR, 6 Jun-15 Jul 44; Operations Overlay, 505th PIR, 1830 6 Jun 44, in Box 2058 AGO Microfilm Item 2141; Statement by Major Silvey in Hist 320th Gl FA Bn, 6 Jun-11 Jul 44, in Box 2049, AGO Microfilm Item 2101.

29. Hist 435th TC Gp, Jun 44; Hist 436th TC Gp, Jun 44; Hist 75th TC Sq, Jun 44; Hist 76th TC Sq, Jun 44; 77th TC Sq, Jun 44; Hist 78th TC Sq, Jun 44; Hist 79th TC Sq, Jun 44; Hist 80th TC Sq, Jun 44; Hist 81st TC Sq, Jun 44; Hist 82d TC Sq, Jun 44; oprep 2, 435th TC Gp, Ser 33 of FO 1—Neptune, 7 Jun 44; oprep 2, 436th TC Gp, Mission Neptune, 7 Jun 44; interrogations of glider pilots, 82d TC Sq; Hq 53d TC Wg, Statistical Analysis, First Year in ETO, 13 Mar 45, in unit hist file.

30. Hq 82d Abn Div, Action in Normandy, ann 5; Hist, 505th PIR, 6 Jun-15 Jul 44; opr Overlay, 505th PIR, 1830 6 Jun 44; Hist 82d Abn Div Arty 25 May-15 Jul 44, in Box 2046, AGO Microfilm Item 2079; Hist 319th Gl FA Bn, 6 Jun-12 Jul 44, in Box 2048, AGO Microfilm Item 2096; Hist 320th Gl FA Bn, 6 Jun-11 Jul 44; journal, 320th Gl FA Bn, 6-8 Jun 44; Table of Glider Landing Statistics (320th Gl FA Bn), all in Box 2049, AGO Microfilm Item 2101.

31. Hist 434th TC Gp, Jun 44; Hist 437th TC Gp, Jun 44; Hist 73d TC Sq, Jun 44; oprep, 434th TC Gp, Mission Neptune-Bigot, 7 Jun 44; oprep, 437th TC Gp, Mission Neptune No. 3, 7 Jun 44; interrogations of glider pilots, 437th TC Gp, in unit hist files (only 14 available); Hq 82d Abn Div, Action in Normandy, ann 5.

32. Ruppenthal, *UTAH Beach to Cherbourg*, p. 65; Hist 50th TC Wg, Jun 44; Hist 439th TC Gp, Jun 44; Hist 441th TC Gp, Jun 44; Hist 91st TC Sq, Jun 44; Hist 92d TC Sq, Jun 44; Hist 93d TC Sq, Jun 44; Hist 94th TC Sq, Jun 44; Hist 99th TC Sq, Jun 44; Hist 100th TC Sq, Jun 44; Hist 301st TC Sq, Jun 44; Hist 302d TC Sq, Jun 44; oprep, 50th TC Wg, Mission HACKENSACK, 7 Jun 44; oprep, 439th TC Gp, Mission HACKENSACK, 7 Jun 44; oprep, 441st TC Gp, Mission HACKENSACK, 7 Jun 44; Hq 441st TC Gp, Aircraft Order, Operation OVERLORD, in unit hist file; Hist 325th Gl Inf Regt, 6 Jun-14 Jul 44; journal, 325th Gl Inf Regt, 7 Jun 44, both in Box 2055, AGO Microfilm Item 2121.

33. Memo Rpt, Maj W. C. Lazarus, ATSC Eng Div subj: Study of Airborne Requirements in the European Theater of Operations, 30 Nov 44, in R. J. Snodgrass, *The AAF Glider Program November 1944-January 1947*, Nov 47, II, Doc 118 in 201-51.

34. Hist 53d TC Wg, Jun 44; Hist 75th TC Sq, Jun 44; interrogations of glider pilots, 82d TC Sq, in unit hist file; interrogation of Capt W. T. Evans, in hist file 437th TC Gp; interrogation of Capt William W. Bates in hist file 53d TC Wg; ltr, Maj Gen M. B. Ridgway to CG IX TCC, subj: Operations, 8 Jun 44, in hist file 437th TC Gp; rpt IX TCC A-1, 10 Jun 44, in 546.116; Combat Casualty Rpt, Hq IX TCC, 14 Jun 44, in 546.3911; rpt, Hq IX TCC, subj: Troop Carrier Operational Activities, 29 Nov 44, in 546.02.

35. Hq 52d TC Wg, FO 2, Operation NEPTUNE, 3 Jun 44, and amdts 2 and 3, 3 and 5 Jun 44, in unit hist file; rpt, Hq IX TCC, Supply By Air, 20 Nov 44, pp. 30, 33, 34, in 546.461; min of mtg held at Norfolk House, subj: Operation "OVERLORD"—Specialized Equipment for Troop Carrier Operations and Supply by air, 8 Mar 1944, in 505.33-67.

36. Hist 52d TC Wg, Jun 44; Hist 61st TC Gp, Jun 44; Hist 313th TC Gp, Jun 44; Hist 314th TC Gp, Jun 44; Hist 316th TC Gp, Jun 44; Hists 14th, 15th, 53d and 59th TC Sqs, Jun 44, in Hist file 61st TC Gp; Hist 29th TC Sq, Jun 44; Hist 32d TC Sq, Jun 44; Hist 36th TC Sq, Jun 44; Hist 37th TC Sq, Jun 44; Hist 44th TC Sq, Jun 44; Hist 45th TC Sq, Jun 44; Hist 47th TC Sq, Jun 44; Hist 48th TC Sq, Jun 44; Hist 49th TC Sq, Jun 44; Hist 61st TC Sq, Jun 44; Hist 2d QM Depot Supply Sq, Apr, May and Jun 44; oprep, 61st TC Gp, Mission Neptune Freeport, Serial 38, 7 Jun 44; oprep, 313th TC Gp, Mission Neptune Bigot #2, 7 Jun 44; oprep, 314th TC Gp, BIGOT-NEPTUNE #2, 7 Jun 44; oprep, 316th TC Gp, Neptune Bigot Freeport, 7 Jun 44; CMR, Hq 314th TC Gp, NEPTUNE #2, 7 Jun 44; CMR Hq 14th TC Sq, Mission Neptune Freeport, (n.d.); CMR Hq 15th TC Sq, Mission Neptune Freeport, (n.d.) CMR Hq 48th TC Sq, Mission NEPTUNE II Resupply, 7 Jun 44; CMR Hq 50th TC Sq, NEPTUNE-BIGOT Resupply, 7 Jun 44; Hq 82d Abn Div, Action in Normandy, p. 9, ann 2; Hq IX TCC, Supply By Air, 20 Nov 44, p. 2; Hq XVIII Corps, Airborne Resupply Operations, 30 Oct 44, in 507.301; Hist 407th Abn QM Co., 6 Jun-15 Jul 44, in AGO Microfilm Box 2061, Item 2162.

37. Hist 50th TC Wg, Jun 44; Hist 440th TC Gp, Jun 44; Hist 442d TC Gp, Jun 44; Hist 95th TC Sq, Jun 44; Hist 96th TC Sq, Jun 44; Hist 97th TC Sq, Jun 44; Hist 98th TC Sq, Jun 44; Hist 303d TC Sq, Jun 44; Hist 304th TC Sq, Jun 44; Hist 306th TC Sq, Jun 44; DZ Europe, The Story of the 440th TC Gp; Hq 50th TC Wg, Opn O 158, 6 Jun 44; Hq 440th TC Gp, FO 2 Memphis, 6 Jun 44; oprep, 440th TC Gp, Mission Memphis, 7 Jun 44; oprep, 442d TC Gp, Mission Memphis, 7 Jun 44; weekly oprep, 439th TC Gp, 11 Jun 44; rpt, Hq IX TCC, Supply By Air, 20 Nov 44, p. 2; Hq XVIII Corps, Airborne Resupply Operations, 30 Oct 44, in 507.301.

38. Hist 50th TC Wg, Jun 44; Hist 80th TC Sq, Jun 44; Hist 81st TC Sq, Jun 44; Hist 82d TC Sq, Jun 44; oprep, 441st TC Gp, Neptune #3 Resupply, 8 Jun 44; opreps, 436th TC Gp, Neptune #4, 5, 6 and 7, 10, 12, and 13 Jun 44; Hq IX TCC, Opr Flashes U 53 C and U 55 C, 10 and 12 Jun 44; rpt, Hq IX TCC, Supply By Air, 20 Nov 44, p. 2.

39. *Airborne Forces*, pp. 124-36, 139, 284; Hq AEAF, Air Signals Report on Operation "NEPTUNE," Jul 44; Hq 38 Gp, Report on the British Airborne Effort in Operation "NEPTUNE" by 38 and 46 Groups, R.A.F., 14 Nov 1944, in 512.452.

40. Bernard L. Montgomery, *Normandy to the Baltic* (Germany, 1946), pp. 71, 73; *Airborne Forces*, pp. 147-48; Hist 50th TC Wg, Jun 44; Hist 52d TC Wg, Jun 44; Hist 53d TC Wg, Jun 44; Hist 315th TC Gp, Jun 44; Hist 435th TC Gp, Jun 44; Hist 52d TC Wg, FO 1, Opr NEPTUNE, 1 Jun 44; ltr, IX TCC Adv to CG's 52d, 50th and 53d TC Wgs, subj: Operation WILDOATS, 12 Jun 44 and enclosures, in 546.452D.

CHAPTER III

1. W. F. Craven and J. L. Cate, *The Army Air Force in World War II*, III (Chicago, 1951), 244-45; Air Ministry, A.H.B., *Airborne Forces*, (1951) pp. 141-44; Lewis H. Brereton, *The Brereton Diaries* (New York, 1946), pp. 308-9, 322; ltr, Gen H. H. Arnold

to Lt Gen Carl Spaatz, 28 Dec 43, in USAFHD files; memos for ACM Leigh-Mallory from Secy Gen Staff, SHAEF, subj: Summary of Decisions Made by Chief of Staff and Deputy Chiefs of Staff, 20 Jun, 13 Jul and 1 Aug 44, in 505.17-11.

2. Ltr, SHAEF AG to Distr, subj: Reorganization of Airborne Forces, 8 Aug 44, in 145.81-69; ltr, SHAEF AG to Lt Gen L. H. Brereton, subj: Directive, 8 Aug 44; ltr, SHAEF AG to Air C-in-C AEAF, subj: Redesignation of Combined Airborne Forces, 16 Aug 44, both in 505.80-1.

3. Memo for C/AS from Lt Col A. C. Carlson *et al*, subj: Report of Observations of Airborne Operations in the ETO, 30 Oct 44, Tab E, Operations Planned by First Allied Airborne Army Prior to MARKET, and Tab G, Airborne Planning, in 506.452A.

4. Ltr, SHAEF AG to Air C-in-C AEAF, subj: Assignment of Units, 16 Aug 44; Hq AEAF, Org Memo 134/ORG/1944, 22 Sep 44, in 505.80-1.

5. Hist IX TCC, Sep 44; Hist IX TCC Service Wing (Prov), Sep 44; USSTAF GO 59, 1 Sep 44, in hist file of IX TCC; ltr, Hq IX TC Sv Wing (Prov) to CG IX TCC, subj: Activities of IX TROOP Carrier Service Wing (Prov) in Operation "Market," 20 Oct 44.

6. Hist IX Pfdr Wing (Prov), 14-30 Sep 44.

7. Hist IX TCC, Aug, Sep 44.

8. *Airborne Forces*, p. 148; Bernard L. Montgomery, *Normandy to Baltic*, (Germany, 1946), pp. 96-97; SHAEF AEAF Air Plans Branch, Position of Planning Reports, 5 Jul, 18 Jul, and 1 Aug 44, in 505.25-13; SHAEF AEAF Staff, Activity Rpts, 5, 11, 14, 18, 21, and 29 Jul 44, in 505.30-7.

9. James M. Gavin, *Airborne Warfare*, (Washington, 1947), p. 62-63; min of 9th AF Commanders mtgs, 7 Jul 44, in 533.142.

10. USAF Historical Study 74, Airborne Missions in the Mediterranean, 1942-1945, pp. 178 and 192; Hist IX TCC Jul and Aug 44.

11. Hist IX TCC, Jun and Jul 44; wkly opreps, 50th TC Wg, 10 Jun-29 Jul 44; wkly opreps, 52d TC Wg, 10 Jun-29 Jul 44; wkly opreps, 53 TC Wg, 10 Jun-29 Jul 44; CATOR Wkly Load Summaries, 10 Jun-29 Jul 44; memo for Vandenberg from Bagby, 24 Jun 44, both in 505.27-30A.

12. Hist 50th TC Wg, Aug; Hist, 53d TC Wg, Aug 44; Hq 53d TC Wg FO 2, 15 Aug 44, in hist file 434th TC Gp; Report of Observations of Airborne Operations in the ETO, 30 Oct 44, Tab E; ltr, Brig Gen H. L. Clark to Brig Gen P. L. Williams, 11 Aug 44 in 546.452B; ltr, Hq AEAF to Dist, subj: Operation "TRANSFIGURE"—Air Support, 17 Aug 44, in 505.61-48.

13. Report of Observations of Airborne Operations in the ETO, 30 Oct 44, Tab E; SHAEF Air Plans Branch, Position of Planning on 17 August 1944, in 505.25-13.

14. Omar N. Bradley, *A Soldier's Story*, (New York, 1951), pp. 385-86; 401-4; *The Brereton Diaries*, p. 339; Chester Wilmot, *The Struggle for Europe*, (New York 1952), pp. 471-2, 476, 484-85, 529-30; Report of Observations of Airborne Operations in the ETO, 30 Oct 44 and Tabs H and I; rpt, Hq IX TCC, Supply By Air, 20 Nov 44, pp. 4-5, 9, 15, 18, 24-25, in 546.461; ltr, Brig Gen R. G. Moses, 12 Army Gp G-4 to CG TCC, subj: Supply by Air, 11 Sep 44, in hist 50th TC Wg, Sep 44; journal, IX TCC A-3, 1-4 Sep 44, in 546.305; Hist 50th, TC Wg, Sep 44; Hist 52d TC Wg, Sep 44; Hist 53d TC Wg, Sep 44; Hist 438th TC Gp, Sep 44.

15. Bradley, *A Soldier's Story*, pp. 398-400; Montgomery, *Normandy to the Baltic*, pp. 148-153; Wilmot, *The Struggle for Europe*, p. 468; ltr, Eisenhower to Brereton, 29 Aug 44, in Report of Observations of Airborne Operations in the ETO, 30 Oct 44, Tab C.

16. Bradley, *A Soldier's Story*, pp. 401-3; Montgomery, *Normandy to the Baltic*, pp. 158-59; *The Brereton Diaries*, pp. 336-38; Report of Observations of Airborne Operations in the ETO, Tab E; Hist IX TCC, Aug and Sep 44; ltr, Hq FAAA to Lt Gen F. A. M. Browning, subj: Task Force for Operation LINNET, 27 Aug 44; Hq FAAA Outline Plan for Allied Airborne Operation LINNET, 29 Aug 44; Hq IX TCC FO 3, 31 Aug 44, all three in 546.452J.

17. Report of Observations of Airborne Operations in the ETO, Tabs E and G; Hist 52d TC Wg, Sep 44; Hq IX TCC Adv, Warning Order for Airborne Operation, 6 Sep 44; ltr, Hq IX TCC Adv to Distr, subj: Routing and Times of Troop Carrier Forces, 7 Sep 44; Hq 52d TC Wg, FO 6, 7 Sep 44, all three in 546.452I.

18. Dwight D. Eisenhower, *Crusade in Europe*, (Garden City, 1948), p. 307; Montgomery, *Normandy to the Baltic*, pp. 165-66; 170-74; Wilmot, *The Struggle for Europe*, pp. 487-92; msgs, 13765 and 14764, SHAEF Fwd to CG FAAA et al, 9 and 13 Sep 44; both in Report of Observations of Airborne Operations in the ETO, Tab C.

19. *The Brereton Diaries*, pp. 341-42; Gavin, *Airborne Warfare*, pp. 72-75, 85-86; Leonard Rapport and Arthur Northwood, Jr. *Rendezvous with Destiny* (Washington, 1948), pp. 255, 263, 267; rpt, Hq FAAA, Operations in Holland, Sep-Nov 44, pp. 9-11, in 545.01A; Hq 8th AF, Special Report of Operations in Support of First Allied Airborne Army 17-26 Sep 44, 31 Oct 44, pp. 1-2, in 520.452 (hereinafter cited as Hq 8th AF, Special Report on MARKET); ltr, Brereton to Arnold, 24 Oct 44, in 545.452C; Hq IX TCC, FO 3, 31 Aug. 1944; Hq IX TCC, FO 4, 13 Sep 44, in 546,452K; Hq 82d Abn Div, FO 11, ann la, 11 Sep 44, in Hist IX TCC, Sep 44, App 4; ltr, Hq FAAA to Lt Gen F. A. M. Browning, subj: Task Force for Operation "MARKET," 11 Sep 44·

msg, VX 25218, CG FAAA to CG USSTAF *et al*, 1900 10 Sep 49, both in 520.452.

20. Gavin, *Airborne Warfare*, pp. 86, 88.

21. Hq IX TCC, Air Invasion of Holland, IX Troop Carrier Command Report on Operation MARKET, 2 Jan 45, pp. 9-15, in 546.452K; Hq IX TCC, FO 4, 13 Sep 44, Hq 8th AF, Special Report on MARKET, pp. 4-6; Hq 38 Gp, Opn 0526, 12 Sep 44, in Hist IX TCC, Sep 44, App 4.

22. Hilary St. G. Saunders, *The Red Beret*, (London 1950), pp. 227-30; Wilmot, *The Struggle for Europe*, pp. 499-500; Gavin, *Airborne Warfare*, pp. 111-112; *Airborne Forces*, pp. 152, 155-56 and Fig. 6; Hq British Airborne Corps, Report of Allied Airborne Operations in Holland, Sep-Oct 44, p. 2 and App B, Map 2, and Apps C and D; in 545.452E.

23. Gavin, *Airborne Warfare*, pp. 86-88, 97-98; Hq 82d Abn Div, FO 11, 11 Sep 44.

24. Rapport and Northwood, *Rendezvous with Destiny*, pp. 263, 265, 275 and maps 34-36 (The maps are not entirely consistent with each other.); Hq IX TCC, FO 4, 13 Sep 44; Hq 101st Abn Div, FO 1, BIGOT MARKET, 14 Sep 44, in Hist IX TCC, Sep 44, App 4.

25. Gavin, *Airborne Warfare*, pp. 87-89; Rapport and Northwood, *Rendezvous with Destiny*, pp. 263, 265, 275; *Airborne Forces*, pp. 151-58; Hq. IX TCC FO 4, 13 Sep 44 and amdts 1, 2 and 3, 16, 17 Sep 44, in 520.452; Hq 38 Gp, Opn 0 526, 12 Sep 44; rpt Hq FAAA, Operations in Holland Sep-Nov 44, pp. 11-12; Hq IX TCC, Air Invasion of Holland, pp. 9-15, and 59; min of Meeting at Main Hq, 2d Army, 14 Sep 44, in 520.452; Report of Observations of Airborne Operations in the ETO, 30 Oct 44; Tab D, Intelligence Plans and Estimates; ltr, Hq IX TCC to CG 9th AF, subj: Navigational Radar Aids, 18 Jun 44; ltr, Hq 9th AF to CG USSTAF, subj: Navigational Radar Aids, 1 Jul 44, and 1st, 2d and 5th ind, 16, 21 Jul and 2 Aug 44, both in 519.255-4; msg, S-221, IX TCC Adv to Hq 8th AF, 16 Sep 44; msg, K-13, Hq 21 AG to Hq 2 Gp RAF *et al*, 16 Sep 44, both in 520.452.

26. Hq IX TCC, FO 4, 13 Sep 44; min of mtg at Main Hq, 2d Army, 14 Sep 44; Hq Brit Abn Corps, Opr Instr 2, 14 Sep 44, in Hist IX TCC Sep 44, app 4.

27. Hq 8th AF, Special Report on MARKET, pp. 2-7; journal 9th AF Oprs Div, 15 Sep 44, in 533.305E; msgs, AC-106 and AC-110, Hq AEAF Rear to Hq USSTAF *et al*, 15 and 16 Sep 44; msg, MC 38, Hq AEAF Adv to Hq 9th AF Adv, 16 Sep 44; telet, 48, Hq 9th AF Adv to CG IX TAC, (16) Sep 44, all in 533.452M; msg, S-5386, Vandenberg to Spaatz, 16 Sep 44; msgs, D-61078 and D-61108, Doolittle to Vandenberg, sig Spaatz, 16 and 17 Sep 44, all in 520.452.

28. Hist 442d TC Gp, Sep 44; Hq IX TCC, FO 4, 13 Sep 44; Hq 38 Gp, Opn 0 526, 12 Sep 44; Report of Observations of Airborne Operations in the ETO, 30 Oct 44, Tab E; Hq IX TCC, Air Invasion of Holland, pp. 54, 55, 57; Hq 50th TC Wg, Report of Operation MARKET, 23 Oct 44, in unit hist file; rpt, IX TCC Engr Sec, 10 Sep 44, in 546.115.

29. Hist IX AFSC, 16 Oct 43-9 May 45, pp. 147-48, and 190, in 540.01; Hist 26th Mobile R and R Sq, Sep 44; rpt, ASC USSTAF Statistical Office, Status of Aircraft and Combat Crews as of 16 Sep 44, 18 Sep 44, in 546.245; rpt, Hq IX TCC, Statistical Summary for the Year 1944, (n.d.) in 546.308; rpt, IX TCC A-1, 10 Sep 44, in 546.115; rpt, IX TCC Air Corps Engr Sec, 30 Aug 44, in 546.116.

30. Hq IX TCC, Air Invasion of Holland, p. 56; min of 9th AF Commanders Mtgs, 16 and 23 Jun 44, in 533.142; journal, IX TCC A-4, 22 Jun and 3 Sep 44, in 546.801.

31. Report of Observations of Airborne Operations in the ETO, 30 Oct 44, Tab 1, Statistical Summary of the Activities of the IX Troop Carrier Command (4 Jun-7 Oct 44); Hist 50th TC Wg, Jun-Sep 44; Hist 52d TC Wg, Jun-Sep 44; Hist 53d TC Wg, Jun-Sep 44; Hist 315th TC Gp Sep 44; Hist 316th TC Gp, Sep 44; wkly opreps, 50th TC Wg, 5 Aug-16 Sep 44, in app E to wg hists, Aug and Sep 44; wkly opreps, 52d TC Wg, 17 Jun-26 Aug 44; table, subj: Operations for period 29 Jul through 2 Sep, in app B to Hist 50th TC Wg, Aug 44.

32. Hq IX TCC, Air Invasion of Holland, pp. 20, 47; Hist 50th TC Wg, Sep 44; Hist 52d TC Wg, Sep 44; Hist 53d TC Wg, Sep 44; Hist 440th TC Gp, Sep 44; Hist 442d TC Gp, Sep 44; Hist 99th TC Sq, Sep 44; rpt, Hq 52d TC Wg, Operation "MARKET," Sep 44, (n.d.), pp. 6, 9, 60, in unit hist file.

33. Hq FAAA, Operations in Holland Sep-Nov 44, p. 14; Hq IX TCC, Operation MARKET Weather Summary, in Hist IX TCC, Sep 44, App 5; rpt, IX TCC Staff Weather Officer, Weather Outlook for the Period 16-20 Sep 44 for Southern England, Channel and Battle Areas, 1630, 16 Sep 44, in Hist IX TCC, Sep 44, app 5; Hq 8th AF, Special Report on MARKET, ann 55, Operational Possibilities Based upon Weather for the Period 17-25 Sep Inclusive.

34. Hq FAAA, Operations in Holland Sep-Nov 9 44, pp. 15-16; Hq IX TCC Air Invasion of Holland, ann 5, Air Support Activity in Connection with Operation "MARKET"; Hq 8th AF, Special Report on MARKET, pp. 8-10; 8th AF Opnl Research Sec, Report on Operation by Eighth Air Force Heavy Bombers in Support of Nijmegen and Arnhem Operations—17 Sep 44, 10 Oct 44, in Hq 8th AF, Special Report on MARKET, ann II; Hq USSTAF Intopsum 815, 18 Sep 44, in 519.3071.

CHAPTER IV

1. James M. Gavin, *Airborne Warfare*, (Washington, 1947), pp. 98-99; Hist IX TCC Pfdr Gp, 14-30 Sep 44, in 546.072A; Hq IX TCC, Air Invasion of Holland, IX Troop Carrier Command Report on Opera-

tion MARKET, 2 Jan 45, pp 59-62, and p. 72 (ltr, Gavin to Williams, 25 Sep 44,), in 546.452K; Hq 82d Abn Div, Graphic History of the 82d Airborne Division Operation "MARKET" (hereinafter cited as Hq 82d Abn Div, Graphic History of "MARKET") Pt III, in Hist IX TCC, Sep 44, app 5; J. A. Huston, Airborne Operations (Draft Hist, Dept of the Army, OCMH) ch. VII.

2. Hilary St. G. Saunders, *The Red Beret* (London, 1950), pp. 231-32; Hq 38 Gp, Report on the British Airborne Effort in Operation MARKET, 1 Jan 45, pp. 10-11, in 505.54-3.

3. Hist 53d TC Wg, Sep 44; Hist 435th TC Gp, Sep 44; Hist 442d TC Gp, Sep 44.

4. Hist, IX TAC, Sep 44; Hist 4th Ftr Gp, Sep 44; Hist 361st Ftr Gp, Sep 44; Hq 8th AF, Special Report of Operations in Support of First Allied Airborne Army 17-26 Sep 44, 31 Oct 44, pp. 11-12, and ann 1, Map 3, in 520.452 (hereinafter cited as Hq 8th AF, Special Report on "MARKET"); oprep, 48th Ftr Gp, 17 Sep 44; oprep, 366th Ftr Gp, 17 Sep 44; oprep, 367th Ftr Gp, 17 Sep 44; oprep, 474th Ftr Gp, 17 Sep 44.

5. Leonard Rapport and Arthur Northwood, Jr., *Rendezvous with Destiny* (Washington, 1948), pp. 268-69; Hist 53d TC Wg, Sep 44; Hist 434th TC Gp, Sep 44; Hist 435th TC Gp, Sep 44; Hist 436th TC Gp, Sep 44; Hist 438th TC Gp, Sep 44; Hist 442d TC Gp, Sep 44; Hist 304th TC Sq, Sep 44; Hq IX TCC, Air Invasion of Holland, pp. 25-26; Hq 101st Abn Div, Report on Operation MARKET, 12 Oct 44, pp. 1-2, in 545.452D; Hq, 506th PIR, After Action Report, 10 Dec 44, in KCRC unit files, msg, S24B, IX TCC Adv to Hq 8th AF, 18 Sep 44, in 520.452.

6. Rapport and Northwood, *Rendezvous with Destiny*, pp. 275-79; Hist, 442d TC Gp, Sep 44; Hq IX TCC, Air Inxasion of Holland, pp. 25-26, 71; Hq 501st PIR, Summary of Operations 17-18 Sep 44, and attached overlay of paratroop drops, in KCRC unit files; 501st PIR S-2, Report 1305-2400, 17 Sep 44, in KCRC unit files.

7. Rapport and Northwood, *Rendezvous with Destiny*, pp. 271-74; Chester Wilmot, *The Struggle for Europe* (New York, 1952), pp. 506-8; Hq IX TCC, Air Invasion of Holland, pp. 26 and 70-71; Hq 506th PIR, After Action Report, 10 Dec 44; Hq 506th PIR, Unit Journal Operation "MARKET," 17 Sep 44; "Regimental History 506th Parachute Infantry Journal" (handwritten notebook), all three in KCRC unit files.

8. Rapport and Northwood, *Rendezvous with Destiny*, pp. 280 ff.; Hist 435th TC Gp, Sep 44; Hist 438th TC Gp, Sep 44; Hist, 75th TC Sq, Sep 44; Hist 89th TC Sq, Sep 44; Hq IX TCC, Air Invasion of Holland, pp. 26, 70; 502d PIR S-3, Report, 17 Sep 44; journal, 3d Bn, 502d PIR, S-3, 17 Sep 44, both in KCRC regimental files; ltr, Capt E. C. Thornton to CG IX TCC, subj: Operation MARKET, 1 Oct 44, in hist IX TCC, Sep 44, app 5.

9. Rapport and Northwood, *Rendezvous with Destiny*, pp. 269-71; Hist 53d TC Wg, Sep 44; Hist 437th TC Wg, Sep 44; Hq IX TCC, Air Invasion of Holland, p. 27; Hq 101st Abn Div, Report on Operation MARKET, 12 Oct 44, pp 1, 3, and ann 2 (Report on Operation Market 101st Airborne Division Glider Echelon).

10. Gavin, *Airborne Warfare*, p. 98; Hist 99th TC Sq, Sep 44; Hist 100th TC Sq, Sep 44; Hist 301st TC Sq, Sep 44; MR 29th TC Sq, 17 Sep 44; MR 47th TC Sq, 17 Sep 44; MR 48th TC Sq, 17 Sep 44; Hq 82d Abn Div, History of "MARKET," pp. 1-2, 7, Pt III, and Pt IV; Hq IX TCC, Air Invasion of Holland, pp. 22-24; rpt, Hq 52d TC Wg, Operation "MARKET" Sep 44, n.d., pp. 12, 21-22; Hq 50 TC Wg, Report of Operation "MARKET," 23 Oct 44, p. 7 and Stat Summary, in Hist IX TCC, Sep 44, app 5.

11. Hq IX TCC, Air Invasion of Holland, ann 5, Air Support Activity in Connection with Operation "MARKET"; Hq 8th AF, Special Report on MARKET, pp. 11-12, and ann 1, Map 3; Hist 78th Ftr Gp, Sep 44; rpt Col F. C. Gray, Summary of 78th Fighter Group's Operations in Support of Allied Airborne Operations in Arnhem-Nijmegen Area, in hist file 78th Ftr Gp.

12. Gavin, *Airborne Warfare*, p. 100; Hist 50th TC Wg, Sep 44; Hist 52d TC Wg, Sep 44; Hist 439th TC Gp, Sep 44; Hist 440th TC Gp, Sep and Oct 44; Hist 441st TC Gp, Sep 44; Hist 313th TC Gp, Sep 44; Hist 315th TC Gp, Sep 44; Hist 316th TC Gp, Sep 44; Hist 34th TC Sq, Sep 44; Hist 36th TC Sq, Sep 44; Hist 49th TC Sq, Sep 44; Hist 99th TC Sq, Sep 44; Hist 100th TC Sq, Sep 44; Hist 301st TC Sq, Sep 44; Hist 302d TC Sq, Sep 44; Hq 50th TC Wg, Report of Operation "MARKET," 23 Oct 44, p. 7 and Stat Summary; rpt, 52d TC Wg, Operation "MARKET" Sep 44, pp. 21-22, 56-7, 64.

13. Gavin, *Airborne Warfare*, pp. 98, 101, 104; Hist 45th TC Sq, Sep 44; Hq IX TCC, Air Invasion of Holland, pp. 22-23; Hq 82d Abn Div, History of "MARKET," pp 1-2, Pt III and Pt IV; rpt, Hq. 52d TC Wg, Operation "MARKET," Sep 1944, p. 21; MR 29th TC Sq, 17 Sep 44; MR 48th TC Sq, 17 Sep 44; Hist, 505th PIR, 17 Sep-31 Dec 44, in Box 2059. Microfilm Item 2143; journal, 82d Abn Div G-3, 17, 18 Sep 44, in Box 2032, Microfilm Item 2048; journal, 505th PIR S-1, 17 Sep 44, in Box 2059, Microfilm Item 2143; msg, Cider Sunray, minor to Cider Sunray, 17 Sep 44, in Box 2056, Microfilm Item 2136.

14. Msg, CO 2d Bn 504th PIR, to Hq 504th PIR, 1650 17 Sep 44 in Box 2056 Microfilm Item 2136.

15. Gavin, *Airborne Warfare*, pp. 99, 102-3; Ross S. Carter, *Those Devils in Baggy Pants* (New York, 1952), pp. 140-42; Hq 82d Abn Div, History of "MARKET," pp. 1-2, Pt III and Pt IV; ltr, Col Reuben H. Tucker to CO 315th TC Gp, subj: Commendation, 23 Sep 44, in hist file 43d TC Sq; Hist 17

Sep 4-Nov 44; journal 504th PIR S-3, 17-18 Sep 44; both in Box 2056, Microfilm Item 2136.

16. Hq 82d Abn Div, History of "MARKET," pp. 1, 3, Pt III and Pt IV; Hq 50th TC Wg, Report of operation "MARKET," 23 Oct 44, p. 7 and Opnl Summary; rpt, 307th Abn Engr Bn S-3 to Hq 82d Abn Div, 19 Sep 44, in Box 2022, Microfilm Item 2037.

17. Gavin *Airborne Warfare*, pp. 102, 104-5; Hist 440th TC Gp, Sep 44; Hist 441st TC Gp, Sep 44; Hist 100th TC Sq, Sep 44; Hist 301st TC Sq, Sep 44; Hist 302d TC Sq, Sep 44; Hq 82d Abn Div, FO 11, 13 Sep 44, and ann 1b, 1b(3) and 1c, in Hist IX TCC, Sep 44, app 5; Hq 82d Abn Div, Graphic History of "MARKET," pp. 1-2, Plate 1, Pt III, and Pt IV; Hq 508th PIR, SITREP, 18 Sep 44, in Box 2022, Item 2037; ltr, Lt Col L. G. Mendez to Lt Col Krebs, 8 Oct 44, in hist file 440th TC Gp.

18. Gavin *Airborne Warfare*, pp. 103-4; Hist 440th TC Gp, Sep 44; DZ Europe, The Story of the 440th TC Group, pp. 63-66, in unit hist file; Hq 82d Abn Div, Graphic History of "MARKET," pp. 1, 3, Pt III and Pt IV.

19. Hist 439th TC Gp, Sep 44; Hist 92d TC Sq, Sep 44; Hq IX TCC, Air Invasion of Holland, p. 21; Hq 50th TC Wg, Report of Operation "MARKET," 23 Oct 44, p. 7 and Stat Summary; Hq 82d Abn Div, History of "MARKET," pp. 1, 3, Pt III and Pt IV.

20. R. J. T. Hills, *Phantom Was There* (London, 1951), pp. 252-54; Hq 38 Gp, Report on the British Airborne Effort in Operation "MARKET," pp. 7, 11; Hq British Abn Corps, Airborne Operations in Holland, Sep-Oct 44, p. 7 and Pt III, Index C, in 545.452E; Hq FAAA, Operations in Holland Sep-Nov 44, p. 29; journal, 82d Abn Div G-3, 17-20 Sep 44.

21. Hq 38 Gp, Opn O 526, 12 Sep 44, in 546.02; Hq IX TCC, FO 4, 13 Sep 44, amdt 2, 16 Sep 44, in 520.452; Hq 38 Gp, Report on the British Airborne Effort in Operation "MARKET," pp. 9-11, 24-25, Tables II and IV and Fig. 4.

22. Hist 61st TC Gp, Sep 44; Hist 314th TC Gp, Sep 44; MR's 14th, 15th 53d and 59th TC Sqs, 17 Sep 44 all in hist 61st TC Gp; MR 50th TC Sq, 17 Sep 44; MR, 62d TC Sq, 17 Sep 44.

23. Saunders, *The Red Beret*, pp. 232-39, 242-43, 251-55; Wilmot, *The Struggle for Europe*, pp. 503-5; John North, *North Europe, 1944-5* (London, 1953), pp. 105-9; Hq 1 Abn Div, Report on Operation "MARKET," 10 Jan 45, pp. 3-6, 12-13, in 545.452A.

24. Ltr, Gavin to Williams, 25 Sep 44; ltr, Maj Gen R. E. Urquhart to Brig Gen Harold L. Clark, 6 Oct 44, in Hist IX TCC, Sep 44, app 5; msg, GRC 163, IX TCC Adv to Hq 53d TC Wing, 20 Sep 44, in hist file 53d TC Wg.

25. Saunders, *The Red Beret*, pp. 277-8; Wilmot, *The Struggle for Europe*, pp. 501-3; North, *Northwest Europe*, pp. 104-5, 110; H. J. Giskes, *London Calling North Pole* (N.Y. and London, 1953), pp. 140-46, 170-72; Orestes Pinto, *Spy-catcher* (New York, 1952), pp. 154, 174-5; 181-7, 191-2; J. A. Huston, Airborne Operations (Draft), ch 7, p. 61; memo for C/AS from Lt Col A. C. Carlson *et al*, subj: Report of Observations of Airborne Operations in the ETO, 30 Oct 44, Tab D, Incl 1, (Hq FAAA, Enemy Situation on Second Army Front, 15 Sep 44), in 506.452A; Hq 82d Abn Div FO 11, 11 Sep 44, ann 1c (Order of Battle Summary), 11 Sep 1944; Hq Abn Corps (Brit), Opn Instr 1, Operation "MARKET," 13 Sep 44, both in Hist IX TCC Sep 44, app 4.

26. Hq 8th AF, Special Report on MARKET, p. 12; Dept of Def, WSEG, Staff Study 3, A Historical Study of Some World War II Airborne Operations, p. 160, in 160.804-3.

27. Hist 442d TC Gp, Sep 44; Hist 47th TC Sq, Sep 44; ltrs, amdt Reg 249 and 251, Hq TC Forces to Dist, subj: Amendment of Timing Schedule for Operation MARKET, 18 Sep 44, in 520.452; Hq FAAA, Operations in Holland Sep-Nov 44, pp. 18-19; msgs, AX (sic) 113, and AC 114 and 117, Hq AEAF (Rear) to Hq 8th AF *et al* 17 and 18 Sep 44; msg, VX 25308, Hq FAAA to Hq 8th AF *et al*, 2025 17 Sep 44, all three in 520.452; msg, D 61116, Hq 8th AF to Hq 9th AF Adv, 18 Sep 44, in 533,452M; rpt, IX TCC Staff Weather Officer, Final Operational Forecast for 1000 to 1900, 18 Sep 44, in Hist IX TCC Sep 44, app 5.

28. Wilmot, *The Struggle for Europe*, p. 508; Hist 357th Ftr Gp, Sep 44; Hist 359th Ftr Gp, Sep 44; Hq 8th AF, Special Report on MARKET, pp. 14-16 and ann VI (Report from P-47 Groups).

29. Rapport and Northwood, *Rendezvous with Destiny*, pp. 301-306; Wilmot, *The Struggle for Europe*, pp. 507-8; Hq 506th PIR, After Action Report, 10 Dec 44; Hq 506th PIR, Unit Journal Operation "MARKET," 18 Sep 44; "Regimental History 506th Parachute Infantry Journal," 18 Sep 44.

30. Journal, 3d Bn, 502d PIR, S-3, 18 Sep 44.

31. Rapport and Northwood, *Rendezvous with Destiny*, pp. 298 ff.; Hq 101st Abn Div, Report on Operation MARKET, 12 Oct 44, ann 4, p. 1, and ann 4A (Situation May 17 Sep 44); Hq IX TCC, Air Invasion of Holland, p. 71; Hq 501st PIR, Summary of Operations 17-18 Sep 44; 501st PIR S-2, Reports, 18, 19 Sep 44; 502d PIR S-3, Rpt, 18 Sep 44; journal, 3d Bn, 502d PIR, S-3, 18 Sep 44.

32. Rapport and Northwood, *Rendezvous with Destiny*, pp. 299-301; Hist 53d TC Wg, Sep 44; Hist 434th TC Gp, Sep 44; Hist 435th TC Gp, Sep 44; Hist 436th TC Gp, Sep 44; Hist 437th TC Gp, Sep 44; Hist 438th TC Gp, Sep 44; Hist 442d TC Gp, Sep 44; Hq IX TCC, Air Invasion of Holland, pp. 30-32, 52, 71; Hq 101st Abn Div, Report on Operation MARKET, 12 Oct 44, ann 4, p. 2; ltr, Capt. E. C. Thornton to CG IX TCC, subj: Operation MARKET, 1 Oct 44.

33. Gavin, *Airborne Warfare*, pp. 107-8; Hq 82d Abn Div, Graphic History of "MARKET," p. 3 and Plate 1; Hist 505th PIR, 17 Sep-31 Dec 44; journal, 82nd Abn Div G-3, 18 Sep 44; journal, 505th PIR S-3, 18 Sep 44; Hq 508th PIR, SITREP, 1, 18 Sep 44.

34. Hq 50 TC Wg, Report of Operation "MARKET," 23 Oct 44; Hq 52d TC Wg, Operation "MARKET" Sep 1944, pp. 13, 23-27 and 64; Hist 61st TC Gp, Sep 44; Hist 313th TC Gp, Sep 44; Hist 316th TC Gp, Sep, Oct 44; Hist 439th TC Gp, Sep, Oct 44; Hist 440th TC Gp, Sep, Oct 44; Hist 441st TC Gp, Sep 44; Hist 15th TC Sq, Sep 44; Hist 29th TC Sq, Sep 44; Hist 36th TC Sq, Sep, Oct 44; Hist 45th TC Sq, Sep, Oct 44; Hist 49th TC Sq, Sep, Oct 44; Hist 50th TC Sq, Sep 44; Hist 53d TC Sq, Sep, Oct 44; Hist 61st TC Sq, Sep 44; Hist 62d TC Sq, Sep 44; Hist 319th FA Bn, 13 Sep-16 Oct 44, in Box 2048, Microfilm Item 2097; interrogation of 2d Lt J. M. Rice, in hist file 316th TC Gp; interrogation of FO Irby, in hist file 313th TC Gp.

35. Hist 316th TC Gp, Sep, Oct 44; Hist 36th TC Sq, Sep 44; Hq 82d Abn Div, Graphic History of "MARKET," pp. 3-4, Pt III and Pt IV; Hq 52d TC Wing, Operation "MARKET" Sep 44, pp. 24-26, 33-43; interrogation of glider pilots, 61st TC Gp, 313th TC Gp, and 316th TC Gp, in unit hist files; MR 59th TC Sq, 18 Sep 44, and Suppl Rpt, 20 Sep 44, in hist file 61st TC Gp; Hist 319th FA Bn, 13 Sep-16 Oct 44; Hist 320th FA Bn, 17 Sep-16 Oct 44.

36. Hq 8th AF, Special Report on MARKET, pp. 16-17; and Route Chart of D plus 1 Supply by Heavy Bombers in ann I; directive, Hq FAAA, subj: MARKET, Bomber Supply D plus 1, 17 Sep 44; msg, VX 25282, Hq FAAA to Hq IX TCC et al, 16 Sep 44, both in 502.452; Hq 14th Combat Bomb Wg, Min of Critique of 19 Sep 44, in unit hist files; Route Chart of 448th Bomb Gp Mission, 18 Sep 44, in unit hist files.

37. Hq 8th AF, Special Report on MARKET, pp. 17-18; Hist 56th Ftr Gp, Sep 44; Hist 78th Ftr Gp, Sep 44.

38. Hq IX TCC, Air Invasion of Holland, p. 74, (ltr, Gavin to Williams, 25 Sep 44).

39. Rapport and Northwood, *Rendezvous with Destiny*, p. 299; Hq 8th AF, Special Report on MARKET, p. 17; Hq 101st Abn Div, Report on Operation MARKET, 12 Oct 44, ann 7 (Resupply); rpt, Hq IX TCC, Supply By Air, 20 Nov 44, pp. 5, 36, and app A (Hq 2d Bomb Div, Air Supply and Resupply by B-24 Aircraft), in 546.461; Hq IX TCC, Air Invasion of Holland, p. 74 (ltr, Gavin to Williams, 25 Sep 44); Hq 82nd Abn Div, Graphic History of "MARKET," p. 4; Hist 14th Comb Bomb Wg, Sep 44; Hist 20th Comb Bomb Wg, Sep 44; Hist 44th Bomb Gp, Sep 44; Hist 93d Bomb Gp, Sep 44; Hist 330th Bomb Sq, Sep 44; Hist 392d Bomb Gp, Sep 44; Hist 446th Bomb Gp, Sep 44; Hist 448th Bomb Gp, Sep 44; Hist 489th Bomb Gp, Sep 44; Hist 491st Bomb Gp, Sep 44; Hist 2d QM Bn, Sep 44; Hq 501st PIR, Summary of Operations, 18 Sep 44; rpt, Hq XVIII Corps, Airborne Resupply Operations, 30 Oct 44, in 507.301; Hq 14th Comb Bomb Wg, Min of Critique of 19 Sep 44, in unit hist files; Hq 448th Bomb Gp, Air Commanders' Report, Mission of 18 Sep 1944, and Report of 1st Lt O. C. Munns, Navigator, in unit hist files.

40. Saunders, *The Red Beret*, pp. 236-7, 239-40, 242-3; Hq 1 Abn Div, Report on Operation "MARKET," pp. 6-10.

41. Saunders, *The Red Beret*, pp. 244-45; Hist 314th TC Gp, Sep 44; Hist 315th TC Gp, Sep 44; Hist 34th TC Sq, Sep 44; Hist 43d TC Sq, Sep, Oct 44; Hist 50th TC Sq Sep 44; Hist 61st TC Sq, Sep 44; Hist 62d TC Sq, Sep 44; Hq 52d TC Wg, Operation "MARKET," pp. 23-4; Hq 1 Abn Div, Report on Operation "MARKET," p. 10; MR 50th TC Sq, 18 Sep 44; MR 61st TC Sq, 18 Sep 44; MR 62d TC Sq, 18 Sep 44.

42. *Airborne Forces*, pp. 165-66; Hq 38 Gp, Report on the British Airborne Effort in Operation "MARKET," pp. 12-14, 24-25; Table 3 and Fig. 4; Hq 1 Abn Div, Report on Operation "MARKET," Pt II, app D (Aircraft losses) and E (Tonnage of Resupply Collected Daily).

43. Saunders, *The Red Beret*, p. 245; Hq 1 Abn Div, Report on Operation "MARKET," pp. 9-12.

44. Rapport and Northwood, *Rendezvous with Destiny*, pp. 312-13; Hq IX TCC, FO 4, 13 Sep 44, ann 1a, amdts 1 and 2, 18 Sep 44, in 520.452; Hq 101st Abn Div, FO 1, 14 Sep 44, ann 5; Hq 38 Group, Report on the British Airborne Effort in Operation "MARKET," p. 16; rpt, Hq IX TCC Staff Weather Officer, Weather Outlook for the Period 18-22 September 1944 for Southern England and the Battle Area, 1700 18 Sep 44, in Hist, IX TCC Sep 44 App 5.

45. Hq IX TCC, Operation MARKET Weather Summary, p. 22.

46. Hq 8th AF, Special Report on MARKET, pp. 20-22; journal, 9th AF Opns Div, 18-19 Sep 44, in 533.305E; msgs, AC 120, 122, Hq AEAF (Rear) to Hq 8th AF et al, 0130, 1020 hours, 19 Sep 44, in 520.452; Hq IX TAC, Summary of Air Operations for 19 Sep 44, in 536.332; Hq XIX TAC, Morning Summary, 20 Sep 44, in 537.332; Hq 404th Ftr Gp, Opn Flashes, 19 Sep 44 in unit hist file; MR 357th Ftr Gp, 19 Sep 44; MR 364th Ftr Gp, 19 Sep 44.

47. Hq 101st Abn Div, Report on Operation MARKET, 12 Oct 44, ann 4, p. 2; Hq 504th PIR, SITREP 2, 18-19 Sep 44; journal, 504th PIR S-3, 19 Sep 44; both in Box 2056, Microfilm Item 2035.

48. Rapport and Northwood, *Rendezvous with Destiny*, pp. 312-13; Hist 53d TC Wing, Sep 44; Hist 434th TC Gp, Sep 44; Hist 435th TC Gp, Sep 44; Hist 436th TC Gp, Sep 44; Hist 438th TC Gp, Sep 44; Hist 442d TC Gp, Sep 44; Hist 71st TC Sq, Sep 44; Hist 73d TC Sq, Sep 44; Hist 74th TC Sq, Sep 44; Hist 75th TC Sq, Sep 44; Hist 76th TC Sq, Sep 44; Hist 77th TC Sq, Sep 44; Hist 78th TC Sq, Sep 44;

Hist 79th TC Sq, Sep 44; Hist 80th TC Sq, Sep 44; Hist 81st TC Sq, Sep 44; Hist 82d TC Sq, Sep 44; Hist 87th TC Sq, Sep 44; Hist 88th TC Sq, Sep 44; Hist 89th TC Sq, Sep 44; Hist 90th TC Sq, Sep 44; Hist 303d TC Sq, Sep 44; Hist 304th TC Sq, Sep 44; Hist 305th TC Sq, Sep 44; Hist 306th TC Sq, Sep 44; Hq IX TCC, Air Invasion of Holland, pp. 34-5, 64, 68; Hq 101st Abn Div, Report on Operation MARKET, 12 Oct 44, ann 1 (Report on Operation MARKET 101st Abn Div Glider Echelon) and ann 4, p. 2; Hq 377th Para FA Bn, After Action Rpt, 10 Dec 44, in KCRC unit files.

49. Gavin, *Airborne Warfare*, pp. 109-10; Wilmot, *The Struggle for Europe*, pp. 511-12; Hq 82d Abn Div, Graphic History of "MARKET," p. 4; journal, 82d Abn Div G-3, 18, 19 Sep 44; journal, 505th PIR S-3, 19 Sep 44, in Box 2059, Microfilm Item 2143; Hist 307th Abn Med Co, Sep 43-Feb 45 in Box 2061, Item 2153.

50. Hist 61st TC Gp, Sep 44; Hist 439th TC Gp, Sep 44; Hist 91st TC Sq, Sep 44; Hist 92d TC Sq, Sep 44; Hist 93d TC Sq, Sep 44; Hq 50th TC Wg, Report of Operation "MARKET," 23 Oct 44, p. 7; Hq 52d TC Wg, Operation "MARKET," Sep 44, pp. 13, 27; Hq 82d Abn Div, History of "MARKET," p. 5; MR's 53d and 59th TC Sqs, 19 Sep 44, in hist file 61st TC Gp; msg, AC 50th TC CP Eastcote to Hq 8th AF *et al*, 19 Sep 44, in 520.452.

51. *Airborne Forces*, pp. 167-68; Saunders, *The Red Beret*, pp. 245-8, 255-56; Wilmot, *The Struggle for Europe*, pp. 510-11, 526; Hq 1 Abn Div, Report on the British Airborne Effort in Operation "MARKET," pp. 16, 17 and 25.

52. Hq 101st Abn Div, Rpt on Operation MARKET, 12 Oct 44, ann 4, pp. 2-3; Hq 501st PIR, oprl sum, 20 Sep 44; 501st PIR S-2 Rpt, 20 Sep 44, both in KCRC unit files.

53. Wilmot, *The Struggle for Europe*, pp. 512-13; Hq 82d Abn Div, History of "MARKET," p. 5, Plate 2 and Sup to Plate 2; Hist 504th PIR, 17 Sep-31 Dec 44; journal, 504th PIR S-3, 20 Sep 44, both in Box 2056, Microfilm Item 2136.

54. Saunders, *The Red Beret*, pp. 253-4, 257-8; Hq 1 Abn Div, Rpt on Operation "MARKET," pp. 18-19.

55. Ltr, Hq TC Forces to Dist, subj: Amendment of Timing Schedule for Operation "MARKET," 19 Sept 44; Hq IX TCC FO 4, 13 Sep 44, ann 1A, amdt 2, 19 Sep 44, both in 520.452; journal, 9th AF Op Div, 20 Sep 44, in 533.305E; msgs, AC 127, 129, 132, 134, AEAF Rear to Hq 8th AF *et al*, 19, 20 Sep 44, in 520.452.

56. Hq 38 Gp, Report on the British Airborne Effort in Operation "MARKET," p. 19; Hq 8th AF, Special Report on MARKET, pp. 23-25; Hq IX TCC, Air Invasion of Holland, ann 5; ltr, Hq 8th AF to Hq FAAA, Attn: General Stearley, subj: Eighth Air Force Support in Operation "MARKET," 22 Sep 44, in 520.452 msgs, AC 132, 134, AEAF Rear to Hq 8th AF *et al*, 20 Sep 44.

57. *Airborne Forces*, pp. 168-69; Hist 34th TC Sq, Sep 44; Hist 43d TC Sq, Sep 44; Hq 38 Gp, Report on the British Airborne Effort in Operation "MARKET," pp. 18-19, 25 and Table VI; Hq 1 Abn Div, Report on Operation "Market," pp 19, 34, 35, 40; Hq 52d TC Wg, Operation "MARKET" Sep 44, p. 13.

58. Wilmot, *The Struggle for Europe*, p. 514; Hist 53d TC Wg, Sep 44; Hist 434th TC Gp, Sep 44; Hist 435th TC Gp, Sep 44; Hist 436th TC Gp, Sep 44; Hist 437th TC Gp, Sep 44; Hist 438th TC Gp, Sep 44; Hist 73d TC Sq, Sep 44; Hist 75th TC Sq, Sep 44; Hist 77th TC Sq, Sep 44; Hist 78th TC Sq, Sep 44; Hist 79th TC Sq, Sep 44; Hist 80th TC Sq, Sep 44; Hist 81st TC Sq, Sep 44; Hist 82d TC Sq, Sep 44; Hist 88th TC Sq, Sep 44; Hist 89th TC Sq, Sep 44; Hist 90th TC Sq, Sep 44; Hq IX TCC, Air Invasion of Holland, pp. 36-7, 74; Hq IX TCC, Supply By Air, p. 5; Hq XVIII Corps, Airborne Resupply Operations, 30 Oct 44; Hq 82d Abn Div, History of "MARKET," p. 6.

59. Hist 439th TC Gp, Sep 44; Hist 442d TC Gp, Sep 44; Hist 304th TC Sq, Sep 44; Hq 101st Abn Div, Report on Operation MARKET, ann 7; Hq XVIII Corps, Airborne Resupply Operations, 30 Oct 44; Hq 377th Para FA Bn, After Action Report, 10 Dec 44, in KCRC unit files.

60. Wilmot, *The Struggle for Europe*, pp. 513-17; Hq 1 Abn Div Rpt on Operation "MARKET," pp. 19-21; Hq 82d Abn Div, Graphic History of "MARKET," pp. 5-6; Hq British Airborne Corps, Airborne Operations in Holland, Sep-Oct 44, pp. 12-14.

61. *Airborne Forces*, p. 170; Hq 8th AF, Special Rpt on MARKET, pp. 26-28; Hq 38 Gp, Report on the British Airborne Effort in Operation "MARKET," p. 20; Hq IX TCC FO 4, ann 1A, 13 Sep 44, amdts 3 and 4, 20 Sep 44, in 520.452; MR 56th Ftr Gp, 21 Sep 44; MR 353d Ftr Gp, 21 Sep 44; msg AC 134, Hq AEAF Rear to Hq 8th AF *et al*, 21 Sep 44, in 533.452M (variant in 520.452).

62. Hq 38 Gp, Report on the British Airborne Effort in Operation "MARKET," pp. 20, 25; Hq 1 Abn Div, Report on Operation "MARKET," pp. 21, 34, 35.

63. Narrative of 1st Lt E. N. McKay, in hist file 314th TC Gp.

64. Ltr, Maj Gen S. Sosabowski to Brig Gen H. L. Clark, 16 Oct 44, in Hq 52d TC Wg, Operation "MARKET" Sep 44.

65. Hq 52d TC Wg, Operation "MARKET" Sep 44, pp. 14, 15, 28, 29, 64, 68; Hq British Abn Corps, Airborne Operations in Holland, Sep-Oct 44, p. 13; Hq 1 Abn Div, Report on Operation "MARKET," p. 21; Hist 314th TC Gp, Sep 44; Hist 315th TC Gp, Sep 44; Hist 34th TC Sq, Sep 44; Hist 43d TC Sq, Sep 44; Hist 50th TC Sq, Sep 44; Hist 309th TC Sq Sep 44; Hist 310th TC Sq, Sep 44; MR 50th TC Sq,

23 Sep 44; MR 62d TC Sq, 22 (sic) Sep 44; Narrative of 1st Lt E. N. McKay, in hist file 314th TC Gp.

66. Hq IX TCC, Air Invasion of Holland, pp. 37-8; Hq 101st Abn Div, Report on Operation MARKET, 12 Oct 44, ann 7; Hist 53d TC Wing, Sep 44; Hist 438th TC Gp, Sep 44; Hist 89th TC Sq, Sep 44; Hist 90th TC Sq, Sep 44.

67. Hq 8th AF, Special Report on MARKET, p. 30; Hq IX TCC, Operation MARKET Weather Summary, p. 23; Hq 38 Gp, Report on the British Airborne Effort in Operation "MARKET," p. 22; msg AC 141, AEAF Rear to Hq 8th AF *et al*, 1300 hours, 22 Sep 44, in 520.452.

68. Rapport and Northwood, *Rendezvous with Destiny*, pp. 338, 351-59; Hq 101st Abn Div, Report on Operation MARKET, 12 Oct 44, Ann 4, pp. 3-4; Hq 501st PIR, Summary of Operations, 22 Sep 44; Hq 506th PIR, After Action Rpt, 10 Dec 4; speech at U.S. Armed Forces Staff College, Maj Gen McAuliffe, subj: Airborne Operations, 15 May 47 in AU Library M36185-R.

69. Hq 82d Abn Div, Graphic History of "MARKET," p. 6.

70. Wilmot, *The Struggle for Europe*, pp. 518-19; North, *Northwest Europe, 1944-1945*, p. 118; Hq British Abn Corps, Airborne Operations in Holland, Sep-Oct 44, p. 15; Hq 1 Abn Div, Report on Operation "MARKET," p. 22.

71. Wilmot, *The Struggle for Europe*, pp. 519-20; Rapport and Northwood, *Rendezvous with Destiny*, pp. 360-61; Hq British Abn Corps, Airborne Operations in Holland, Sep-Oct 44, pp. 15-16; Hq 101st Abn Div, Report on Operation MARKET, 12 Oct 44, ann 4, pp. 4-5; Hq 506th PIR, After Action Rpt, 10 Dec 44.

72. Hq 8th AF, Special Report on MARKET, pp. 32-33; Hq IX TCC, Air Invasion of Holland, ann 5; Hist 78th Ftr Gp, Sep 44; Hist 339th Ftr Gp, Sep 44; Hist 353d Ftr Gp, Sep 44; Col F. C. Gray, Summary of 78th Fighter Group's Operation in Arnhem-Nijmegen Area, in hist file 78th Ftr Gp.

73. Hq IX TCC, Air Invasion of Holland, p. 64; Hq 82d Abn Div, History of "MARKET," p. 7 and Pt IV; Hq 50th TC Wg, Report of Operation "MARKET," 23 Oct 44, p. 8 and Stat Sum; Hq 52d TC Wg, Operation "MARKET," Sep 44, pp. 29-30; Hist 53d TC Wg, Sep 44.

74. Hq IX TCC, Air Invasion of Holland, p. 74 (ltr, Gavin to Williams, 25 Sep 44); Hq 82d Abn Div, Graphic History of "MARKET," p. 7, Pt III and Pt IV; Hist 61st TC Gp, Sep 44; Hist 313th TC Gp, Sep 44; Hist 316th TC Gp, Sep 44; Hist 440th TC Gp Sep 44; Hist 47th TC Sq, Sep 44; Hist 49th TC Sq, Sep 44; Hist 61st TC Sq, Sep 44; Hist 97th TC Sq, Sep 44; Hist 99th TC Sq, Sep 44; Hist 301st TC Sq, Sep 44; Hist 302d TC Sq, Sep 44; DZ Europe, The Story of the 440th TC Group, pp. 70-71; MR 14th TC Sq, 23 Sep 44; MR 29th TC Sq, 23 Sep 44; MR 49th TC Sq, 23 Sep 44; Glider Pilot Checks, 313th TC Gp and 316th TC Gp, for mission of 23 Sep 44, in unit hist files.

75. Rapport and Northwood, *Rendezvous with Destiny*, p. 361; Hq 101st Abn Div, Report on Operation MARKET, 12 Oct 44, p. 5 and ann 2B (Report on Glider Echelon); Hist 53d TC Wg, Sep 44; Hist 436th TC Gp, Sep 44; Hist 438th TC Gp, Sep 44; MR 89th TC Sq, 23 Sep 44.

76. Hq 52d TC Wg, Operation "MARKET" Sep 44, p. 30; Hist 315th TC Gp, Sep 44; Hist 34th TC Sq, Sep 44; Hist 43d TC Sq, Sep 44; Hist 310th TC Sq, Sep 44.

77. *Airborne Forces*, p. 171; Hq 38 Gp, Report on the British Airborne Effort in Operation "MARKET," pp. 22-23, 25; Hq 1 Abn Div, Report on Operation "MARKET," pp. 22, 34-35.

78. *Airborne Forces*, pp. 170-71; Hq IX TCC, Operation MARKET Weather Summary, p. 23; Hq 38 Gp, Report on the British Airborne Effort in Operation "MARKET," p. 23; Hq 1 Abn Div, Report on Operation "MARKET," pp. 34-35, 42; Hq 8th AF, Special Report on MARKET, pp. 34-35.

79. Wilmot, *The Struggle for Europe*, p. 520; Hq British Abn Corps, Airborne Operations in Holland, Sep-Oct 44, p. 17; Hq 1 Abn Div, Report on Operation "MARKET," pp. 22-23; Hq 101st Abn Div, Report on Operation MARKET, 12 Oct 44, ann 4, pp. 5-6; 501st PIR, oprl sum, 24, 25 Sep 44.

80. Hq IX TCC, Operation MARKET Weather Summary, p. 25; Hq 101st Abn Div, Report on MARKET, ann 7; Hist 53d TC Wg, Sep 44; Hist 435th TC Gp, Sep 44; Hist 436th TC Gp, Sep 44; Hist 71st TC Sq, Sep 44; Hist 73d TC Sq, Sep 44; Hist 75th TC Sq, Sep 44; Hist 78th TC Sq, Sep 44; msg AC 146, Hq AEAF Rear to Hq 8th AF *et al*, 25 Sep 44, in 520.452.

81. *Airborne Forces*, p. 171; Hq 38 Gp, Report on the British Airborne Effort in Operation "MARKET," p. 23; Hq IX TCC, Air Invasion of Holland, ann 5; Hq 8th AF, Special Report on MARKET, p. 36; Hq 1 Abn Div, Report on Operation "MARKET," p. 42.

82. Montgomery, *Normandy to the Baltic*, p. 184; Wilmot, *The Struggle for Europe*, pp. 521-22; Saunders, *The Red Beret*, pp. 264-65; Hq British Abn Corps, Airborne Operations in Holland, Sep-Oct 44, p. 18; Hq 1 Abn Div, Report on Operation "MARKET," p. 22.

83. Hq FAAA, Operations in Holland Sep-Nov 44, pp. 39, 42; Hq British Abn Corps, Operations in Holland, Sep-Oct 44, pp, 13, 16; Hq IX TCC, Air Invasion of Holland, ann 6 (Notes By A.O.C. NO. 46 Group (Air Commodore L. Darvall) on Visit to Belgium and Holland 26 Sep 44); Hq IX TCC FO 4, ann 1a, 13 Sep 44, amdt 6, 25 Sep 44, and ann 1C, 13 Sep 44, amdt 7, 25 Sep 44, both in 520.452; msgs, AC

76, 78, 148 and 149, AEAF Rear to Hq 8th AF et al, 25, 26 Sep 44, in 520.452.

84. Hq British Abn Corps, Operations in Holland, Sep-Oct 44, pp. 18-19; Hq IX TCC, Operation MARKET Weather Summary, p. 23; Hq 8th AF, Special Rpt on MARKET, pp. 37-38; Hq 52d TC Wg, Operation "MARKET" Sep 44, pp. 15-16, 31-32; Hist 313th TC Gp, Sep 44; Hist 314th TC Gp, Sep 44; Hist 315th TC Gp, Sep 44; Hist 316th TC Gp, Sep 44; Hist 479th Ftr Gp, Sep 44; Hist 43d TC Sq, Sep 44; Hist 48th TC Sq, Sep 44; Hist 50th TC Sq, Sep 44; Hist 61st TC Sq, Sep 44; MR 29th TC Sq, Sep 44.

85. Hist 15th TC Sq, Oct 44; Hq IX TCC, Air Invasion of Holland, p. 17; ltr, Brereton to Arnold, 24 Oct 44; Hq IX TCC Service Wg (Prov), Glider and Aircraft Recovery After Operation MARKET, 1 May 45, in unit hist file; ltr, Hq 50th TC Wing to Lt Col B. B. Price, subj: Evacuation of Gliders, 5 Dec 44; memo rpt, Lt Col B. B. Price, subj: Inspection of Gliders Used in MARKET Operation, 8 Jan 45, both in Hq AMC, The AAF Glider Program Nov 44-Jan 47, III, 22-23, in 201-51.

86. *The Brereton Diaries*, pp. 360-61, 363-64; Montgomery, *Normandy to the Baltic*, pp. 186-87; Gavin, *Airborne Warfare*, pp. 110, 112, 120; Wilmot, *The Struggle for Europe*, pp. 524-28; *Airborne Forces*, pp. 173-75; Hq British Abn Corps, Airborne Operations in Holland, Sep-Oct 44, pp. 21-22; Hq IX TCC, Airborne Invasion of Holland, p. 80; Hq 1 Abn Div, Report on Operation "MARKET," p. 43; Report of Observations of Airborne Operations in the ETO, 30 Oct 44, pp. 2-3, and Tab D.

87. Hq British Abn Corps, Operations in Holland, Sep-Oct 44, p. 23; Hq 101st Abn Div, Report on MARKET, p. 3; ltr, CG 101st Abn Div to CG FAAA (Thru CG XVIII Corps Abn) subj: Participation of the 101st Abn Division in Operation MARKET for the Period D-plus 10, 15 Oct 44; ltr, CG 82d Abn Div to CG XVIII Corps Abn, subj: Lesson of Operation MARKET, 3 Dec 44; ltr, CG XVIII Corps Abn to CG FAAA, subj: Operation MARKET, Airborne Phase D to D plus 10, Inclusive. 4 Dec 44. (Above letters in 545.452A). Hq 38 Gp, Report on the British Airborne Effort in Operation "MARKET" p. 29.

88. *Airborne Forces*, p. 178; Hq British Abn Corps, Operations in Holland, Sep-Oct 44, app G (Air Support Notes); Dept of the Army, *Airborne Operations. A German Appraisal* (DA Pamphlet 20-232) Oct 51, pp. 32, 35; Dept of Defense, WSEG Staff Study 3, A Historical Study of Some World War II, Airborne Operations, pp. 103-4, 126.

89. Hq Abn Troops, Opr Instr 1, and App E, 13 Sep 44, in Hist IX TCC Sep 44, app 4; Hq British Abn Corps, Operations in Holland, Sep-Oct 44, app G (Air Support Notes), Ind C (Course of Events) and Ind E (Air Support, Ground to Air Signals); Hq 1 Abn Div, Report on Operation "MARKET," p. 44; Hq 101st Abn Div, Report on Operation MARKET,

12 Oct 44, p. 3 and ann 6; ltr, CG 82d Abn Div to CG XVIII Corps (Abn), subj; Lessons of Operation MARKET, 3 Dec 44; 1st Lt B. E. Davis Report on Arnhem Operations, 18-25 Sep 44, in 145.81-69.

90. Hq British Abn Corps, Operations in Holland, Sep-Oct 44, app G; Hq 8th AF, Special Rpt on MARKET, pp. 18, 25, 28, 30, 34, 36; Hq IX TCC, Airborne Invasion of Holland, ann 6.

91. Ltr, CG 82d Abn Div to CG XVIII Corps (Abn), subj: Lessons of Operation MARKET, 3 Dec 44; ltr, CG XVIII Corps (Abn) to CG FAAA, subj: Operation MARKET, Airborne Phase, D to D plus 10, inclusive, 4 Dec 44.

92. Hq British Abn Corps, Operations in Holland, Sep-Oct 44, p. 22.

93. Hq British Abn Corps, Operations in Holland, Sep-Oct 44, pp 22-23; Hq IX TCC, Airborne Invasion of Holland, p. 47 and 75-76 (ltr, Gavin to Williams, 25 Sep 44); Hq 1 Abn Div, Report on Operation "MARKET," p. 44; Hq 101st Abn Div, Report on Operation MARKET, 21 Oct 44, p. 3; Hq Abn Troops Opr Instr 1, App F, Policy Regulating the Operational Role of Glider Pilots, 13 Sep 44; Hq 52d TC Wg, Operation "MARKET" Sep 44, pp. 17-18, 62-63; Hist 313th TC Gp, Oct 44 (313th Troop Carrier Glider Pilots in Combat); Hist 44th TC Gp, Sep 44; glider pilot narratives, 61st TC Gp, 313th TC Gp, and 316th TC Gp, all in unit hist files; narrative of 2d Lt A. Kaplan in hist file 92d TC Sq.

94. *Airborne Forces*, pp. 172, 175-77, 276-77; Hq British Abn Corps, Operations in Holland, Sep-Oct 44, App B, Results of Maintenance by Air; Hq 8th AF. Special Report on MARKET, p. 43; Hq IX TCC. Supply by Air, pp. 5-7, 23, 30-31 and app A, Air Supply and Resupply by B-24 Aircraft; Hq 38 Group. Report on the British Airborne Effort in Operation "MARKET," p. 29; Hq 1 Abn Div, Report on Operation "MARKET," pp. 28, 35, 46; ltr, CG 82d Abn Div to CG XVIII Corps Abn, subj: Lessons of Operation MARKET, 3 Dec 44; ltr, CG 101st Abn Div to CG FAAA (Thru CG XVIII Corps Abn), subj: Participation of the 101st Abn Division in Operation MARKET for the Period D-D plus 10, 15 Oct 44; ltr, CO 53d TC Wg to CG IX TCC, subj: Air Supply and Resupply Report, 29 Oct 44, in 507.301.

95. Hq 38 Gp, Report on the British Airborne effort in Operation "MARKET," p. 32; Hq IX TCC, Airborne Invasion of Holland, p. 76 (ltr, Gavin to Williams, 25 Sep 44); ltr, Brig Gen J. M. Gavin to Brig Gen H. L. Clark, 26 Sep 44; ltr, Maj Gen R. E. Urquhart to Brig Gen H. L. Clark, 6 Oct 44; ltr, Maj Gen St. Sosabowski to Brig Gen H. L. Clark, 16 Oct 44, above letters in Hq 52d TC Wg, Operation "MARKET" Sep 44; ltr, CG 101st Abn Div to CG FAAA (Thru CG XVIII Corps Abn), subj: Participation of the 101st Abn Division in Opera-

tion MARKET for the Period D-D plus 10, 15 Oct 44.

96. Dept of Defense WSEG, Staff Study 3, A Historical Study of Some World War II Operations, pp 52, 55; Hq IX TCC, Airborne Invasion of Holland, p. 80; Hq 8th AF, Special Rpt on MARKET, pp. 40-41, 43 and Ann VI; Report of Observations of Airborne Operations in the ETO, 30 Oct 44, p. 3; ltr, CG 82d Abn Div to CG XVIII Corps (Abn), subj: Lessons of Operation MARKET, 3 Dec 44; ltr, CG XVIII Corps to CG FAAA, subj: Operation MARKET, Airborne Phase D to D plus 10, Inclusive, 4 Dec 44.

97. Hq 38 Group, Report on the British Airborne Effort in Operation "MARKET," p. 29; ltr, CG 82d Abn Div to CG XVIII Corps (Abn), subj: Lessons of Operation MARKET, 3 Dec 44.

Chapter V

1. Air Ministry, A.H.B., *Airborne Forces* (1951), p. 179; Omar N. Bradley, *A Soldier's Story* (N.Y., 1951), pp. 426, 433-39; Hq FAAA, Report of Operation VARSITY, (19 May 45), pp. 3-4, in 545.452B; Hq FAAA, Planning Staff Study for Operation "VARSITY," 7 Nov 44, in 520.452.

2. Dwight D. Eisenhower, *Crusade in Europe* (Garden City, 1948), pp. 370-72; Forrest C. Pogue, *The Supreme Command* (Washington, 1954), pp. 409-14.

3. Lewis H. Brereton, *The Brereton Diaries* (New York, 1946), p. 396; Hist XVIII Corps Abn, 17 Jan 42-May 45, p. 28, in 585.18; Hq FAAA, Outline Plan for Operation "VARSITY," 10 Feb 45, in 520.452.

4. *The Brereton Diaries,* pp 361, 367, 371; Hq FAAA, Outline Plan for Operation "VARSITY," 10 Feb 45.

5. Hq FAAA, Outline Plan for Operation "VARSITY," 10 Feb 45; Hq FAAA, Report on Operation VARSITY, p. 11; min of mtg at Forward SHAEF, Reims, 28 Feb 45 to Discuss Air Plans for Operation "VARSITY," in 505.39-5; notes of Air Staff Meeting at Forward SHAEF, Reims, 16 Mar 45 to Discuss Air Plans for Operation "CHOKER II," in 505.39-3; notes of Air Staff Meetings at Forward SHAEF, Reims, 12, 13, 20 and 24 Mar 45, in 505.39-3; msg VX-27402, CG FAAA to SHAEF, 6 Mar 45, in 505.79-3; msgs FWD-17712, FWD-17818 and FWD-18137, SHAEF Forward to 6 Army Gp, *et al,* 9, 12 and 24 Mar 45, in 505.79-3; diary, C/S 7th Army, 7-9 Mar 45; Hq 7th Army Opr Instr 107, 24 Mar 45, both in KCRC 7th Army files.

6. *Airborne Forces,* pp. 179-80, 184-85; Hist IX TCC, Jan-Feb 45, Pt II, chap 3, in 546.02; Hq IX TCC, Tactical and Non-Tactical Operations During the Final Phase of the War in Europe Including Operation "VARSITY," 20 May 45 (hereinafter cited as Hq IX TCC, The Final Phase), pp. 28-30, 63-64 and App 4, in 546.452A; Hq IX TCC, Monthly Statistical Summary for March 1945, 17 Apr 45, in 546.308; Hq 53d TC Wg, Report on Operation "VARSITY," 19 Apr 45, p. 2, in unit hist files; notes of Air Staff Meeting at Forward SHAEF, Reims, 24 Feb 45, in 505.39-4; ltr, Hq FAAA to CG IX TCC, subj: Operation VARSITY, 6 Mar 45, in USAFHD files.

7. Hist IX TCC, Jan-Feb 45, Pt VIII, Sec 4; Hist 52 TC Wg, Feb-Mar 45; Hist 53d TC Wg, Feb 45; Hq IX TCC, MO's 5, 9, and 10, 11 and 23 Feb 45, in hist IX TCC, Jan-Feb 45 Pt X; notes of Group Commanders Meeting, 50th TC Wg, 8 Feb 45, in hist 50th TC Wg, Feb 45; Hq IX TCC, The Final Phase, pp. 28-30; Hq FAAA, Outline Plan for Operation "VARSITY," 10 Feb 45; min of Meeting at Forward SHAEF, Reims, 28 Feb 45, to Discuss Air Plans for Operation "VARSITY"; msg, OX 5734, Air Ministry to Hq 8th AF, 8 Mar 45, in 520.452.

8. Hist IX TCC, Jan-Feb 45, Pt II, pp. 66, 110-11; Hq FAAA, Report of Operation VARSITY, pp. 2, 33-35 and app 3; Hq Gp, RAF, Report on Operation "VARSITY," 20 May 45, p. 22, in 512.452A; msg, VX 27890, FAAA to SCHAEF *et al*, 21 Mar 45, in 520.452.

9. *The Brereton Diaries,* p. 398; Bernard L. Montgomery, *Normandy to the Baltic* (Germany, 1946), pp. 242-43, 247-48; Pogue, *The Supreme Command,* pp. 422, 430; notes of Air Staff Mtg at Forward SHAEF, Reims, 3 Mar 45, in 505.39-3; msg FWD-17538, SHAEF Forward to 21 Army Gp, 3 Mar 45, in 505.79-3; msg A-264, SHAEF Forward to RAF Coastal Command *et al*, 9 Mar 45, in 520.452; notes of Allied Air Commanders Conference held at SHAEF, Reims, 8 Mar 45, in USAFHD files.

10. *The Brereton Diaries,* p. 397; Hq FAAA, Report of Operation VARSITY, pp. 4, 11; Hq XVIII Corps FO 4, ann la, 7 Mar 45, in KCRC unit files; ltr, Hq IX TCC (Main) to CG AAF, Attn: Chief Weather Div, Office Asst C/S OC&R, subj: Report on Operation "Varsity," 31 Mar 45, in hist IX TCC, Mar-Apr 45, Pt I.

11. Hq FAAA, Report of Operation VARSITY, p. 11; min of Coordinating Meeting at Main Hq 2 TAF, 17 Mar 45, in 520.452; notes of Allied Air Commanders Conference at Forward SHAEF, Reims, 21 Mar 45, in USAFHD files.

12. *The Brereton Diaries,* pp. 396-97; Hq FAAA, Report of Operation VARSITY, pp. 2, 11; Hq FAA, Outline Plan for Operation "VARSITY," 10 Feb 45, app E (Possible LZ's and DZ's); Hist XVIII Corps Abn, 17 Jan 42-May 45, pp. 28-9; min of Meeting at Forward SHAEF, Reims, 28 Feb 45, to Discuss Air Plans for Operation "VARSITY."

13. Hq IX TCC FO 5, ann 1 (Int Ann) and ann 7 (Run In Diagram for Operation "VARSITY") 16 Mar 45, in hist IX TCC, Mar-Apr 45, Pt X Sec 5; notes of Group Commanders Meeting, 50th TC Wg, 22 Feb 45; min of Meeting at Forward SHAEF, Reims, 28 Feb 45 to Discuss Air Plans for Operation "VARSITY."

14. Hq IX TCC, The Final Phase, p. 7; Hq IX TCC FO 5, 16 Mar 45.

15. Hq IX TCC, The Final Phase, pp. 34-36; Hq IX TCC FO 5, ann 3 (Signal Communications-Nav Aids), 16 Mar 45, and amdts 1 and 2, 17 and 18 Mar 45; Hq 38 Gp, Report on Operation "VARSITY," p. 10 and app A (The Training and Operation of Forward Visual Control Posts), 20 May 45.

16. Hq FAAA, Report of Operation VARSITY, pp. 45-6 and app 9, ann B; Hq IX TCC FO 5, ann 2 (Administrative Order), 16 Mar 45; min of Meeting at Forward SHAEF, Reims, 28 Feb 45 to Discuss Air Plans for Operation "VARSITY"; notes of Air Staff Meeting at Forward SHAEF, Reims, 7 Mar 45, in 505.39-3; min of Coordinating Meeting at Main Hq 2 TAF, 17 Mar 45; ltr, Hq FAAA to CG IX TCC, subj: Operation "VARSITY," Administrative Annex, 15 Mar 45, in 520.452.

17. Min of Coordinating Meeting at Main Hq 2 TAF, 17 Mar 45; Hq 2 TAF, Air Plan for Operations "VARSITY," "PLUNDER," and "FLASHPOINT," 20 Mar 45; amdt 1, 22 Mar 45; and amdt 2, 23 Mar 45, in 520.452; Hq XII Corps, Opr Instr 29, app H, 21 Mar 45, in KCRC, XVIII Corps files.

18. Hq IX TCC, The Final Phase, p. 5; Hq IX TCC FO 5, ann 1, 16 Mar 45; Hq FAAA, Outline Plan for Operation "Varsity," App E, 3 Dec 44; Hq FAAA, Revised Outline Plan for Operation "VARSITY," app C, (Appreciation of the GAF) 5 Feb 45, app C Revised 2 Mar 45, app C amdt, 15 Mar 45, all in 520.452; Hq 2 TAF, FO 638, ann 1, 22 Mar 45, in 520.452.

19. Hq IX TCC, The Final Phase, pp. 24-5; Hist 52d TC Wg, Mar 45.

20. Hq FAAA, Report of Operation VARSITY, pp. 7, 14; min of Meeting at Forward SHAEF, Reims, 28 Feb 45 to Discuss Air Plans for Operation "VARSITY"; min of Coordinating Meeting at Main Hq 2 TAF, 17 Mar 45.

21. Min of Meeting at Forward SHAEF, Reims, 28 Feb 45 to Discuss Air Plans for Operation "VARSITY"; min of Coordinating Meeting at Main Hq 2 TAF, 17 Mar 45; Hq 2 TAF, Air Plan for Operations "VARSITY," "PLUNDER," and "FLASHPOINT," 20 Mar 45; Hq 9th AF Adv Opr 0 459V, 20 Mar 45, in 520.452.

22. Min of Meeting at Forward SHAEF, Reims, 28 Feb 45 to Discuss Air Plans for Operation "VARSITY"; min of Meeting at Forward SHAEF, Reims, 16 Mar 45 to Discuss Air Plans for Operation "CHOKER II," in 505.39-3.

23. Hq IX TCC, The Final Phase, p. 8; notes of Air Staff Meeting at Forward SHAEF, Reims, 19 Mar 45, in 505.39-4; R&R, IX TCC A-3 to FAAA G-3, subj: Operations "VARSITY," "NAPLES II," "CHOKER II," 12 Dec 44, in USAFHD files; notes of Allied Air Commanders Conference at Forward SHAEF, Reims, 21 Mar 45.

24. Min of Coordinating Meeting at Main Hq 2 TAF, 17 Mar 45; Hq 83 Gp Operational Instr for Operation "PLUNDER," 19 Mar 45, in 520.452; Hq 9th AF Adv Opr 0 459V, 20 Mar 45.

25. Hq FAAA, Report of Operation VARSITY, pp. 6-7, 25; Hq FAAA, Outline Plan for Operation "VARSITY," app A, Estimate of Enemy Situation, 6 Feb 45, app A Revised, 4 Mar, 17 Mar, and 21 Mar 45, and Addendum, 21 Mar 45, in 520.452; Hq IX TCC FO 5, ann 1, 16 Mar 45 and amdt 2 to ann 1, 22 Mar 45; notes of Air Staff Meeting at Forward SHAEF, Reims, 19 Mar 45; Hq XVIII Corps FO 4, ann 1a, 16 Mar 45.

26. W. F. Craven and J. L. Cate, eds, *The Army Air Forces in World War II*, III (Chicago, 1951), 736, 746; notes of Meeting at SHAEF, 10 Feb 45 to Discuss Plans for Interdiction of German Communications East of the Rhine, in 505.39-4; notes of Allied Air Commanders Conferences at SHAEF, Versailles, 8, 15 Feb 45 and at Forward SHAEF, Reims, 21 Mar 45, in USAFHD files, Agenda for Coordinating Meeting—Operation "VARSITY," in 545.452B; min of Coordinating Meeting at Main Hq 2 TAF, 17 Mar 45; Hq 21 Army Gp, Target Proposals "PLUNDER," Mar 45, in KCRC, XVIII Corps files; Hq 2 TAF, Operation "Plunder" Target List from D-3 to D-1 on 21 Army Group Front, 20 Mar 45, in 520.452.

27. Min of Coordinating Meeting at Main Hq 2 TAF, 17 Mar 45.

28. Hq XVIII Corps FO 4, ann 5, and 7, 20 Mar 45, in KCRC unit files; Hq 83 Gp, Operational Instr for Operation "PLUNDER," 19 Mar 45.

29. Hq IX TCC, The Final Phase, p. 31; Hq 38 Gp, Report on Operation "VARSITY," p. 25; Hists IX TCC, Jan-Mar 45; Hists 50th TC Wg, Jan-Mar 45; Hists 52d TC Wg, Jan-Mar 45; Hists 53d TC Wg, Jan-Mar 45; Hist 313th TC Gp, Mar 45; Hist 434th TC Gp, Mar 45; Hist 438th TC Gp, Mar 45; Hist 34th TC Sq, Mar 45; Hq IX TCC, Consol Monthly Tng Rpts, Feb-Mar 45, in 546.02; ltr, Hq IX TCC Fwd to Dist, subj: Combined Troop Carrier-Airborne Training, 27 Feb 45, in hist IX TCC, Mar-Apr 45, Pt VI; ltr, Hq IX TCC Fwd to CG FAAA, subj: Combined Troop Carrier-Airborne Training, 21 Mar 45, in hist IX TCC, Mar-Apr 45, Pt. VI; ltr, Maj Gen E. Bols to Brig Gen H. L. Clark, 23 Mar 45, in hist file 34th TC Sq.

30. Hq IX TCC, The Final Phase, pp. 68-70; Hq FAAA, Report of Operation VARSITY, App 10; Hq IX TCC FO 5, amdt 2, 18 Mar 45.

31. Hq IX TCC, The Final Phase, pp. 39-43; Hq 50th TC Wg, Int Rpt, Operation "TOKEN," 18 Mar 45, in hist file; Hq IX TCC, FO 5, amdt 2, 18 Mar 45.

32. Hq FAAA, Report of Operation VARSITY, pp. 25, 29-30; Hq 52d TC Wg, Report on Operation "VARSITY," p. 4, in unit hist file; Hq 53d TC Wg, Report

on Operation "VARSITY," pp. 3, 18, in unit hist file; Hist 50th TC Wg, Mar 45; Hist 52d TC Wg, Mar 45; Hist 53d TC Wg, Mar 45; Hist 61st TC Gp, Mar 45; Hist 313th TC Gp, Mar 45; Hist 441st TC Gp, Mar 45; Hist 442d TC Gp, Mar 45; Hq IX TCC FO 5, 16 Mar 45; ltr, Hq FAAA to CG IX TCC and AOC's 38 and 46 Gps, subj: Security in Mounting an Operation, 3 Mar 45, in hist file 442d TC Gp.

33. Hq FAAA, Report of Operation VARSITY, pp. 28-29, 38-40; Hist 50th TC Wg, Mar 45; Hist 42d TC Wg, Mar 45; Hist 53d TC Wg, Mar 45; Hist 442d TC Gp, Mar 45.

34. Hq FAAA, Report of Operation VARSITY, pp. 14-15 and app 5, ann B; Hq 8th AF Intopsum 325, 326, 328, 21, 22 and 24 Mar 45, in 520.02-86.

35. Hq FAAA, Report of Operation VARSITY, pp. 14, 18, and app 5, ann A.

36. Hq FAAA, Report of Operation VARSITY, pp. 16-17, and app 5, ann C; Hq 9th AF, Air Summary of Operations, 24 Mar 45, in 533.322; Hist IX Bomb Div, Mar-Apr 45, I, 159-62, in 534.02; Hq IX Bomb Div Opr Sums 193, 194, 24 Mar 45, in 533.332.

37. Hq IX TCC, The Final Phase, p. 76; Hist IX TAC, Mar 45, in 536.02; Hist 354th Ftr Gp, Mar 45; Hist 362d Ftr Gp, Mar 45; Hq 2 TAF, Air Plan for Operations "VARSITY," "PLUNDER" and "FLASHPOINT," 20 Mar 45; Hq 83 Gp, Opr Instr for Operation "PLUNDER," 19 Mar 45; Hq 9th AF Adv, Opr 0 459V, 20 Mar 45; Hq IX TAC, Opr 0 "VARSITY," 23 Mar 45; Hq XXIX TAC, Opr 0 177, Operation FLASHPOINT and VARSITY, 21 Mar 45, all three in 533.452V; Hq IX TAC, Opr Sum 289, 24 Mar 45; Hq XIX TAC, Opr Sum 225, 24 Mar 45; Hq XXIX TAC, Opr Sum 83, 24 Mar 45, all three in 533.332.

38. Hq FAAA, Report of Operation VARSITY, p. 16 and app 5, ann C; Hist XXIX TAC, Mar 45, in 538.02; Hist 406th Ftr Gp, Mar 45; Hq XXIX TAC, Opr Sum 83, 24 Mar 45; dairy, Brig Gen R. E. Nugent, CG XXIX TAC, 24 Mar 45, in 533.13B; notes of Allied Air Commanders Conference at Forward SHAEF, Reins, 29 Mar 45 in USAFHD files.

39. *Airborne Forces*, pp. 191-92; Hq FAAA, Report of Operation VARSITY, p. 16; Hq 9th AF, Air Summary of Operations, 24 Mar 45.

40. Hq 8th AF, Intops Sum 328, 24 Mar 45.

41. Hq IX TCC FO 5, 16 Mar and amdt 3, 21 Mar 45; min of Coordinating Meeting at Main Hq 2 TAF, 17 Mar 45; msgs AO 319 and 329, Main Hq 2 TAF to Hq 8th AF *et al*, 23 1810A and 24 0625A Mar 45, in 520.452; Hq IX TCC, Operation VARSITY Weather Summary, 31 Mar 45, in hist IX TCC Mar-Apr 45, Pt X.

42. Montgomery, *Normandy to the Baltic*, pp. 255-58; Hq FAAA, Report of Operation VARSITY, pp. 8, 21-22.

43. Hq 52d TC Wg, Report on Operation "VARSITY," pp. 15, 18, 20-30; Hist 61st TC Gp, Mar 45; Hists 315th TC Gp, Mar, Apr 45; Hist 316th TC Gp, Mar 45 ; Hist 14th TC Sq, Mar 45; Hist 15th TC Sq, Mar 45; Hist 29th TC Sq, Mar 45; Hists 34th TC Sq, Mar, Apr 45; Hist 36th TC Sq, Mar 45; Hist 37th TC Sq, Mar 45; Hists 43d TC Sq, Mar, Apr 45; Hist 44th TC Sq, Mar 45 (A particularly vivid account); Hist 45th TC Sq, Mar 45; Hist 59th TC Sq Mar 45; Hists 309th TC Sq, Mar, Apr 45; Hists 310th TC Sq, Mar, Apr 45; MR 14th TC Sq, 24 Mar 45, in unit hist file; MR 59th TC Sq, 24 Mar 45; Hq IX TCC FO 5, amdt 4, 22 Mar 45; Hq FAAA, Analysis of Losses, Operation VARSITY, 28 Mar 45, in 145.81-69.

44. Air Ministry, *By Air To Battle* (London, 1945), pp. 141-44; Hilary St. G. Saunders, *The Red Beret* (London, 1950), pp. 303-7; Hq FAAA, Report of Operation VARSITY, pp. 21-23; Hq 38 Gp, Report on Operation "VARSITY," 20 May 45, pp. 6-9, 12-14, 18, 19, 23, 24, Tables III-VII and Fig. 5.

45. James M. Gavin, *Airborne Warfare* (Washington, 1947), pp. 135-36; Hq IX TCC, The Final Phase, p. 65; Hist IX TCC Pfdr Gp (Prov), Mar 45; Hist 313th TC Gp, Mar 45; Statements of 1st Lt A. C. Braem and 1st Lt W. C. Howell, 28 Mar 45, in hist 47th TC Sq, Mar 45.

46. Hq IX TCC FO 5, ann 1, 16 Mar 45.

47. Hq 53d TC Wg, Report on Operation "VARSITY," 19 Apr 45, pp. 5-7, 10-12; Hist 434th TC Gp, Mar 45; Hist 438th TC Gp, Mar 45; Hist IX TCC Pfdr Gp (Prov), Mar 45; Hist 1st TC Pfdr Sq (Prov), Mar 45; Hist 2d TC Pfdr Sq (Prov), Mar 45; Hist 3d TC Pfdr Sq (Prov), Mar 45; Hist 4th TC Pfdr Sq (Prov), Mar 45.

48. Hq 17th Abn Div FO 1, 18 Mar 45; Hq 507th PIR, Historical Report on 507th Combat Team During Operation "VARSITY" (n.d.); journal, 17th Abn Div G-1, 24 Mar 45; journal 507th CT S-3, 24 Mar 45; 507th PIR S-3 Rpt 24-25 Mar 45; 507th PIR S-3 Rpt 24-25 Mar 45; Hq 3d Bn, 507th PIR, Record of Events for the D-Day Jump Across the Rhine River in the Wesel Area (n.d.), all in KCRC, 507th PIR files; Hq 464th Parachute FA Bn, After Action Report, 1 Apr 45; Hq 17th Abn Div Arty, After Action Report Narrative (sic), 1 Apr 45; Hq 464th Parachute FA Bn, Unit Journal, 24 Mar 45, above three in KCRC 464th FA Bn files. Hq 17th Abn Div, Div Report of Operation "VARSITY," 3 May 1945, pp. 1-2, in AU Library, M-30394R.

49. Statements of 1st Lt E. C. Koenig and 2d Lt N. Driggers, 29 Mar 45; Statements of 1st Lts E. Hammesfahr and W. C. Rowley, 29 Mar 45; ltr, 1st Lt E. Hammesfahr to CO 313th TC Gp, subj: Aircraft Damage, 2 Apr 45, all in hist file 47th TC Sq.

50. Hq 52d TC Wg, Report on Operation "VARSITY," pp. 15, 32-35; Hist 313th TC Gp, Mar 45; Hist 29th TC Sq, Mar 45; Hist 47th TC Sq, Mar 45; Hist 48th TC Sq, Mar 45; Hist 49th TC Sq, Mar 45; MR, 29th

TC Sq, 24 Mar 45; MR 48th TC Sq, 24 Mar 45; Statements of pilots, 47th TC Sq, in unit hist files.

51. Hq 53d TC Wg, Report on Operation "VARSITY," 19 Apr 45, pp. 6, 7, 10; Hist 434th TC Gp, Mar 45.

52. Gavin, *Airborne Warfare*, pp. 135-37; journal, 17th Abn Div G-1, 24 Mar 45; Hq 17th Abn Div Arty, After Action Report Narrative, 1 Apr 45. Hq 17th Abn Div, Division Report on Operation "VARSITY," 3 May 45, pp. 2-4.

53. Hq 53d TC Wg, Report on Operation "VARSITY," 19 Apr 45, pp. 5-15 and Exhibits A and B; Hist 50th TC Wg, Mar 45; Hist 435th TC Gp, Mar 45; Hist 436th TC Gp, Mar 45; Hist 437th TC Gp, Mar 45; Hist 439 TC Gp, Mar 45; Hist 79th TC Sq, Mar 45; Hist 80th TC Sq, Mar 45; Hist 81st TC Sq, Mar 45; Hist 82d TC Sq, Mar 45; Hist 83d TC Sq, Mar 45; Hist 84th TC Sq, Mar 45; journal, Maj H. J. Nevins, 50th TC Wing Glider Officer in hist file 50th TC Wg.

54. Hq 17th Abn Div FO 1, 18 Mar 45; Hq 17th Abn Div, Div of Operation "VARSITY," 3 May 45, pp. 4-6; 1st Lt F. Langston, Airborne Invasion Glider Style, in KCRC, 17th Abn Div files: ltr, Hq 507th PIR to CG 17th Abn Div, subj: Report Glider Operation, 3 Apr 42 (sic) in KCRC, 507th PIR files; Hq 17th Abn Div Arty, After Action Rpt Narrative, 1 Apr 45.

55. DZ Europe, The Story of the 440th TC Group, pp. 89-91, 98, 103; Hist 50th TC Wg, Mar 45; Hist 52d TC Wg, Mar 45; Hist 314th TC Gp, Mar 45; Hist 440th TC Gp, Mar 45; Hist 441st TC Gp, Mar 45; Hist 442d TC Gp, Mar 45; Hist 97th TC Sq, Mar 45; Hist 99th TC Sq, Mar 45; Hist 301st TC Sq, Mar 45; Hist 302d TC Sq, Mar 45; Hq 52d Wg, Report on Operation "VARSITY," pp. 15, 36-45; MR's, 314th TC Gp, VARSITY Serials A-21 and A-22, 24 Mar 45; MR's 32d, 50th and 62d TC Sqs, VARSITY, 24 Mar 45, in hist file 314th TC Gp; ltr, CO 441st TC Gp to All Members 441st TC Gp, subj: Commendation of Glider Pilots, 28 Mar 45, in unit hist gle, ltr, Glider Officer 52d TC Wg to CO 52d TC Wg, subj: Narrative on Glider Activities in Operation "VARSITY," 29 Mar 45, in unit hist file; Hq 50th, 61st and 62d TC Sqs, Operation VARSITY, Composite Narratives of Squadron Glider Pilots, 30 Mar, 30 Mar and 27 Mar 45, in hist file 314th TC Gp; Narratives of Glider Pilots, 100th TC Sq and 302d TC Sq, Operation VARSITY, in unit hist file.

56. Hq FAAA, Report of Operation VARSITY, pp. 45-46; Hist 2d Air Div, Jan 44-Apr 45, Pt II, pp. 256-59; Hq FAAA, Administrative ann to Letter of Instructions, "Operation VARSITY," 15 Mar 45; Hq 2 Air Div FO 638, 22 Mar 45; ltr, Hq 2 Air Div to Dist, subj: Material Instructions for Operations "VARSITY," US Loadings, 22 Mar 45; msgs, VX-27792 and 27930, FAAA to Hq 8th AF *et al*, 18 and 23 Mar 45; msg G-19, Hq 6 Abn Div to Hq 8th AF *et al*, all six in 520.452.

57. Hq FAAA, Report of Operation VARSITY, pp. 17, 21, 46-47; Hist 2d Air Div, Jan 44-Apr 45, Pt II, pp. 257-59; Hist 2d Combat Bomb Wg, Mar 45; Hist 14th Combat Bomb Wg, Mar 45; Hist 20th Combat Bomb Wg, Mar 45; Hist 389th Bomb Gp, Mar 45; Hist 448th Bomb Gp, Mar 45; ltr, Hq 2d Air Div to CG 8th AF, subj: Tactical Report of Operation VARSITY—24 Mar 1945, 30 Mar 45, in 526.331A; ltr, Hq 2d Air Div to CG's All Combat Wings, This Division, subj: Tactical Analysis of Operation VARSITY, 24 Mar 45, 7 Apr 45, in 526.331A; Final Mission Statistics on "VARSITY" Operation, in hist file 448th Bomb Gp; ltr, Hq 2d Combat Bomb Wg to CG 2d Air Div, subj: Report on Mission of 24 March 1945—Wesel Area, 26 Mar 45, in wg hist file; min of Critique at Hq 14th Combat Bomb Wg, 26 Mar 45, in unit hist file.

58. Hq FAAA, Report of Operation VARSITY, p. 21; msg VX-28045, Hq FAAA to Hq 8th AF *et al*, 1900 24 Mar 45, in 520.452.

59. Montgomery, *Normandy to the Baltic*, pp. 258-59; Hq FAAA, Report of Operation VARSITY, pp. 22-4 and app 7; journal, 17th Abn Div G-1, 24-28 Mar 45; 17th Abn Div G-1, After Action Rpt VARSITY Operation, 1 May 45; 17th Abn Div Adj Gen, After Action Rpt for the Period 24 Mar 1945 thru 31 Mar 1945 (n.d.) both in KCRC divisional files; Hq 507th PIR, Historical Report on 507th Combat Team During Operation "VARSITY"; journal 507th PIR S-3, 25-28 Mar 45; 507th PIR S-2, Rpts, 25-28 Mar 45; 507th PIR S-3, Rpts, 24-27 and 28-29 Mar 45; Langston, Airborne Invasion Glider Style.

60. Hq 38 Gp, Report on Operation "VARSITY," pp. 16, 17, 21 and app A.

61. Hq FAAA, Report of Operation VARSITY, pp. 31, 36; Hq IX TCC, The Final Phase, pp. 82-83; memo for CO 8th Hist Unit, from IX TCC A-3, subj: Combat Control Teams, 5 Apr 45, in 546.302A.

62. Hq IX TCC, The Final Phose, p. 89; Hq 53d TC Wg, Report on Operation "VARSITY," pp. 13-15; journal, Maj H. J. Nevins, 50th TC Wg Glider Officer, VARSITY Operation; 52d TC Wg Glider Officer, Narrative on Glider Activities in Operation "VARSITY" 29 Mar 45, in unit hist file.

63. Hq IC TCC, The Final Phane, pp. 84-85, 88; Hq FAAA, Report of Operation VARSITY, p. 48.

64. Pogue, *The Supreme Command*, p. 429; Hist XVIII Corps Abn, 17 Jan 42-May 45, p. 31; Hist 52d TC Wg, Mar 45; Dept of the Army Pamphlet 20-232, Airborne Operations, A German Appraisal, Oct 51, p. 35, in K-170.131.232; ltr, Lt Gen L. Brereton to Gen H. H. Arnold, 25 Mar 45, in USAFHD files; ltrs, Brereton to Arnold, 28 Mar and 9 Apr 45, in 145.81-69; Generalfeldmarshall A. Kesselring, Comments on MS #P-51a, Airborne Operations, in 577.051-37.

65. Hq FAAA, Report of Operation VARSITY, p. 23; Hq 17th Abn Div Arty, After Action Rpt, 1 Apr 45,

in KCRC files of 464th FA Bn Hq XVIII Corps, FO 4, ann 5, 20 Mar 45.

66. Hq FAAA, Report of Operation VARSITY, pp. 32, 41-42; Hq 52d TC Wing, Report on Operation "VARSITY," p. 14; SHAEF Air Staff, Air Signals Report on Operation "OVERLORD" from the Assault to the Cessation of Hostilities, June 1945, Sec XXII pp. 6-7 and Map 3, in 506.451-901B.

CHAPTER VI

1. Henry H. Arnold, *Global Mission* (New York, 1949), pp. 398, 521-22; Lewis H. Brereton, *The Brereton Diaries* (New York, 1946) 365.

2. *Airborne Forces*, pp. 201-2; memo Hq AEAF, subj: Organization and Employment of "Gee" in the AEAF, Mar 44, in 505.29-11.

3. Hq IX TCC, The Final Phase, pp. 111-14; Hq IX TCC FO 7, 20 Apr 45, in 546.452H; notes of Air Staff Mtgs at SHAEF and at Forward SHAEF, 4, 13, 17, and 18 Apr 45, in 505.39-3; Hq 10th Armored Div, After Action Reports, 16-9 Apr 45, in 585.010; diary, 7th Army C/S, 9-20 Apr 45, in KCRC, 9th Army files; msgs Fwd 19393 and 19507, SHAEF Forward to 6 Army Gp *et al*, 18 and 19 Apr 45, in 520.452.

4. Gavin, *Airborne Warfare*, pp. 159-60.

Appendix

Appendix I

STATISTICAL TABLES—OPERATION NEPTUNE
5-13 June 1944

I. Paratroop Operations of IX Troop Carrier Command

	ALBANY	BOSTON	TOTAL
Aircraft			
dispatched (1)	433	378	821
effective (2)	436	377	813
abortive (3)	2	1	3
destroyed or missing (4)	13	8	21
damaged	81	115	196
Plane crewmen			
wounded or injured	4	11	15
killed or missing (1 Jul 44)	48	17	65
Troops			
carried	6,928	6,420	13,348
dropped (5)	6,750	6,350	13,100
Artillery			
carried (6)	12	2	14
Cargo			
tonnage carried (7)	211	178	389

(1) Including pathfinders
(2) Included if any troops jumped or cargo was dropped over France
(3) Unable to fly or returning with load
(4) Excluding aircraft in BOSTON destroyed before take-off
(5) An approximation
(6) Including howitzers only
(7) Short tons

II. Glider Operations of IX Troop Carrier Command

	CHICAGO	DETROIT	KEOKUK	ELMIRA	GALVESTON	HACKENSACK	TOTAL
Aircraft							
dispatched (1)	52	52	32	177	102	101	516
effective	51	52	32	175	100	101	511
abortive	1	—	—	2	2	—	5
destroyed or missing	1	1	—	5	—	—	7
damaged	7	38	1	92	26	11	175
Horsas							
dispatched	—	—	32	140	20	30	222
abortive	—	—	—	2	2	—	4
Wacos							
dispatched	52	53	—	36	84	70	295
abortive	1	1	—	—	2	—	4
Plane crewmen							
killed or missing							
(1 Jul 44)	4	4	—	1	—	—	9
wounded or injured	1	3	—	8	—	—	12
Glider pilots							
dispatched	104	106	64	352	208	200	1,034

II. Glider Operators of IX Troop Carrier Command—Continued

dead or missing (1 Jul 44)	14	14	—	26	—	3	57
Troops							
carried	155	220	157	1,190	968	1,331	4,021
landed	153	209	157	1,160(2)	927	1,331	3,937
landing casualties							
Waco troops	27	30(2)	—	15	35	16	123
Horsa troops	—	—	44	142	80	74	340
Artillery pieces							
carried (3)	16	16	6	37	20	—	95
Vehicles							
carried	25	27	40	123	41	34	290
Cargo							
tonnage	14	10	19	131	26	38	238

(1) Including one paratroop plane carrying 16 troops in ELMIRA, two gliders and planes of the 435th Group in GALVESTON and a pathfinder plane without troops in HACKENSACK.
(2) Estimate.
(3) Howitzers and antitank guns.

III. Resupply Operations of IX Troop Carrier Command

	FREEPORT	MEMPHIS	MISSIONS ON CALL (8-13 June)
Aircraft			
dispatched	208	119	34
effective	153	117	34
abortive	55	2	—
destroyed or missing	11	3	—
damaged	94	35	—
Plane crewmen			
dead or missing (1 Jul 44)	29	2	—
wounded or injured	22	4	—
Troops			
carried (1)	76	—	15
dropped	22	—	15
Cargo tonnage			
carried	211	221	7
dropped	156	215	7
recovered (2)	100	(?)	7
Gliders			
dispatched	—	—	10
effective	—	—	10
Vehicles			
carried and landed	—	—	4
Cargo tonnage			
carried and landed	—	—	23
Troops			
carried and landed	—	—	44

(1) Included in FREEPORT total are 54 quartermaster personnel who did not jump.
(2) Probably included in FREEPORT total are some supplies sent in MEMPHIS.

Appendix 2

Statistical Tables—Operation Market
17-30 September 1944

I. Paratroop and Parachute Resupply Operations of IX Troop Carrier Command
A—Missions for 101st Division; B—Missions for 82d Division; C—Missions for British

	17 Sep A	17 Sep B	17 Sep C	18 Sep C	19 Sep B	20 Sep A	20 Sep B	21 Sep A	21 Sep B	21 Sep C	23 Sep C	25 Sep A	Total
Aircraft													
dispatched	428	482	143	126	60	46	311	30	33	114	41	34	1,848
effective	428	481	143	126	35	46	310	24	31	72	41	34	1,771
abortive	—	—	—	—	24	—	1	6	2	41	—	—	74
destroyed or missing (1)	17	10	—	6	2	—	—	—	—	5	—	—	40
damaged	101	131	5	24	16	5	6	—	—	33	—	—	321
Plane crewmen													
killed or missing (2)	26	25	—	22	5	—	—	—	—	11	—	—	89
Troops													
carried	6,735	7,274	2,283	2,119	—	125	—	—	—	1,511	560	—	20,607
dropped	6,712	7,229	2,279	2,110	—	125	—	—	—	998	558	—	20,011
drop casualties	109	124	(?)	(?)	—	2	—	—	—	(?)	(?)	—	—
Artillery													
carried	—	12	—	—	—	6	—	—	—	—	—	—	18
Cargo tonnage													
carried	167	247	57	51	71	47	442	16	15	66	28	49	1,256

(1) Out of 87 planes listed in these tables as destroyed or missing in MARKET, 19 were later repaired or salvaged.
(2) Total as of 31 Oct 44.

II. Glider and Aircraft-Land Operations of IX Troop Carrier Command
A—Missions for 101st Division; B—Missions for 82d Division

	A	B	A	B	A	A	B	26 Sep B	29 Sep B	30 Sep B	Total
Aircraft											
dispatched	70	50	450	454	385	84	406	209	11	22	2,141
effective	64	48	437	450	250(?)	79	402	209	5	22	1,972
abortive	6	1	13	4	130	5	4	—	6	—	169
destroyed or missing	6	1	4	10	17	—	9	—	—	—	47
damaged	42	5	112	100	169	—	96	—	—	—	524
Gliders											
dispatched	70	50	450	454	385	84	406	—	—	—	1,899
effective	62	48	429	424	225	79	351	—	—	—	1,618
abortive	6	1	13	4	130	5	4	—	—	—	163
Plane crewmen											
killed or missing(1)	18	4	8	23	31	—	13	—	—	—	97
Troops											
carried	311	216	2,624(?)	1,773(?)	2,310	395	3,378	882	20	3	11,912
landed	291	215	2,605	1,650(?)	1,363	350	3,000(?)	882	20	3	10,374
landing casualties	5	6	26	45	22	12	17	—	—	—	133
Artillery pieces											
carried	—	8	—	60	68	15	25	—	—	—	176
effective	—	8	—	54	40	14	24	—	—	—	140
Jeeps											
carried	43	28	156	206	136	23	104	134	—	—	830
effective	32	24	151	177	79	21	92	134	—	—	710
Trailers etc											
carried	19	7	124	123	77	13	59	104	—	—	526
effective	15	7	122	106	49	12	50	104	—	—	465
Cargo											
tonnage carried	77	10(?)	244	211	245	95	253	379	30(?)	56	1,600

(1) Total of 31 Oct 44.

III. Operations of 38 and 45 Groups, RAF

	D-day	D plus 1	D plus 2	D plus 3	D plus 4	D plus 6	D plus 7	D plus 8	TOTAL
Aircraft									
dispatched	371	329	209	164	117	123	21	7	1,341
effective	331	302	177	152	91	115	17	6	1,191
abortive	31	10	2	2	2	2	—	—	49
destroyed or missing	—	3	13	9	23	6	—	1	55
damaged	7	44	106	62	61	63	4	3	350
Paratroops									
dropped	186	—	—	—	—	—	—	—	186
Net tonnage dropped	(?)	87	388	386	271	291	—	8	1,431
Gliders									
dispatched	359	296	42						697
effective	319	372	30						621
abortive	31	9	2						42
Glider troops									
landed	2,908	1,200	107						4,215
Artillery pieces									
landed	44	52	9						105
Other vehicles									
landed	420	443	63						1,026

IV. Resupply Operation by 2d Air Division—18 September 1944

Aircraft (B-24)	
dispatched	252
effective	246
destroyed or missing	11
damaged	70
Tonnage	
carried	—
dropped	486

V. Casualties

	Killed	Missing	Wounded or injured
IX TCC Crews	31	155	66
IX TCC Glider Pilots	12	65	37
RAF TCC Crews	31	217	17
British Glider Pilots	59	636	35
2d Air Division	1	63	34(?)
TOTAL	134	1136	187

Appendix 3

Statistical Tables—Operation Varsity
24 March 1945

I. Operations of IX Troop Carrier Command

	DZ A	DZ B	DZ W	DZ X	DZ X	LZ N	TOTAL
Aircraft							
dispatched	121	121	181	45 (C-47) 74 (C-46)	300	314	1,082 (C-47) 74 (C-46)
effective	119	121	181	44 (C-47) 70 (C-46)	296	313	1,074 (C-47) 70 (C-46)
abortive	2	—	—	1 (C-47) 2 (C-46)	4	1	8 (C-47) 2 (C-46)
destroyed or missing	3	16	1	1 (C-47) 20 (C-46)	14	3	38 (C-47) 20 (C-46)
damaged	30	47	35	21 (C-47) 38 (C-46)	137	44	314 (C-47) 38 (C-46)
Paratroops							
carried	1,973	1,924	2,479	387 (C-47) 2,071 (C-46)			6,763 (C-47) 2,071 (C-46)
dropped	1,920	1,917	2,469	376 (C-47) 1,995 (C-46)			6,682 (C-47) 1,995 (C-46)
Para. Arty. carried	—	—	12	12			24 (C-47)
Cargo tonnage carried	71	66	105	111			353
Gliders							
dispatched					594	314	908
effective					572	311	883
abortive					17	1	18
Troops							
carried					3,594	1,321	4,915
landed					3,492	1,318	4,810
Artillery pieces carried					40	3	43
Jeeps carried					208	142	350
Trailers, and other vehicles carried					101	97	198
Cargo tonnage					654	382	1,036

II. Operations of 38 and 46 Groups, RAF

Aircraft	
dispatched	440
effective	402
abortive	35
destroyed or missing	7
damaged	39
Gliders	
dispatched	440
effective	392
abortive	35
Glider troops	
carried	3,383
Artillery pieces	
carried	66
Jeeps and trucks	
carried	285
Other vehicles	
carried	553
Tanks (Locust T9)	
carried	3

III. Resupply Operation by 2d Air Division

Aircraft	
dispatched	240
effective	237
abortive	—
destroyed or missing	15
damaged	104
Cargo tonnage	
carried	598
delivered	582

IV. Casualties

	Killed	Missing	Wounded or Injured
IX TCC Crew Personnel	8	108	47
IX TCC Glider Pilots	33	55	106
RAF TC Crew Personnel	7	—	20
British Glider Pilots	38	135	77
2d Air Division Crew Personnel	5	116	30
TOTAL	91	414	280

Glossary

AEAF	Allied Expeditionary Air Force
Airborne mission	Sequence of flights to and from an objective or group of objectives by aircraft engaged in an airborne operation
Airborne operation	Operation in which troops are transported by air for entry into combat
Airborne troops	Ground units organized and/or trained for airborne operations
Airhead	Isolated area within which airborne troops are reinforced and resupplied by airplanes landing on airfields or landing strips. Any isolated area held by airborne troops in hostile territory.
Airportable (airtransportable) troops	Ground units suitable for transportation by air, but not organized or trained for airborne operations
Aldis lamp	Powerful flashlight with a very narrow beam visible only from the point at which it is directed.
AMHERST	Small British airborne operation in Holland in April 1945
AOC	Air Officer Commanding
ARENA	Proposed airborne operation in 1945 to establish a large airhead in the Kassel area
BENEFICIARY	Proposed airborne and amphibious operation in June or July 1944 to take St. Malo
BOXER	Proposed airborne operation in August 1944 to take Boulogne
BUPS	Radar responsor beacon for use with SCR-717
CHOKER II	Proposed airborne assault across the Rhine near Worms

COMET	Proposed airborne operation in September 1944 to secure a bridgehead across the Rhine at Arnhem
Commando	C-46 two-engined medium transport
COSSAC	Chief of Staff, Supreme Allied Commander
CP	Command Post
Departure Point (DP)	Designated point from which all or part of the serials in an airborne mission set out on course at specified intervals.
Drop Zone (DZ)	Area designated for the dropping of troops and supplies by parachute or, in the case of some supplies, by free fall
Element	Smallest aerial formations; usually two or three aircraft
EFFECTIVE	Proposed airborne operation in April 1954 south of Stuttgart
FAAA	First Allied Airborne Army
FLASHPOINT	Amphibious crossing of the Rhine by Ninth Army near Rheinberg in conjunction with VARSITY-PLUNDER
Flight (troop carrier)	Formation usually composed of two or more elements and roughly equivalent to a squadron
FVCP	Forward Visual Control Post
GARDEN	Ground attack toward Arnhem in conjunction with MARKET
Gee	British radio/radar navigation system similar to LORAN
Hamilcar	British glider of 17,500 pounds carrying capacity
HANDS UP	Proposed airborne and amphibious operation in June or July 1944 to seize Quiberon Bay area
Holophane light	Powerful and highly directional electric light used to mark routes and drop zones

Horsa	British plywood glider of 6,900 pounds carrying capacity
IFF (identification friend or foe)	Radar system for identifying friendly aircraft
Initial Point (IP)	Designated point from which the formations on a mission set their final course to their objectives
Jumpmaster	Member selected to take charge of the jump of a plane load of paratroops
Landing zone (LZ)	Area designated for the landing of gliders
Liberator	B-24 four-engined bomber
LINNET I	Proposed airborne operation in Tournai area in September 1944
LINNET II	Proposed airborne operation in September 1944 to seize bridges over the Meuse north of Liege
Luftwaffe	German Air Force
MARKET	Airborne operation in September 1944 to secure a bridgehead across the Rhine at Arnhem
NAPLES II	Proposed airborne assault across the Rhine south of Cologne
NEPTUNE	The assault phase of OVERLORD
Occult	Aerial lighthouse
OVERLORD	Allied invasion of northwest Europe
Panzer Division	German armored division
Pararack	Rack in or under an aircraft in which supply bundles (parapacks) are carried and from which they may be salvoed by means of a release switch.
Paratroops	Units organized and/or trained to drop by parachute for entry into combat
Pathfinders	Force sent in advance of an airborne mission to set up navigational aids

PIR	Parachute Infantry Regiment
PLUNDER	Ground assault across the Rhine in conjunction with VARSITY
Rebecca-Eureka	Radar navigational aid. The Rebecca, an airborne sender-receiver indicates on its scope the direction and approximate range of the Eureka, a responsor beacon
SCR-717	Airborne radar scanner which produces a pattern on its scope corresponding to the topography of the landscape scanned
serial	Formation usually composed of several flights and separated from other formations by a specific time interval
SHAEF	Supreme Headquarters, Allied Expeditionary Force
Stick	Paratroops assigned to jump from a given exit on a single pass
SWORDHILT	Proposed airborne and amphibious operation to take Brest
TCC	Troop Carrier Command
TRANSFIGURE	Proposed airborne operation south of Paris in August 1944 to cut off German retreat
Tug	Aircraft towing a glider or gliders
VARSITY	Airborne assault across the Rhine near Wesel in March 1945
VHF	Very high frequency radio
Waco (CG-4A)	American glider of steel and canvas construction of 3,750 pounds carrying capacity. Called "Hadrian" by the RAF.
Window	Bits of foil dropped to obscure by their radio "echoes" the scopes of enemy warning radar sets. Also known as "chaff."

INDEX

A

Aa River, 94-95, 103
Abbeville-Drucat, 159, 176
Achiet, 159, 169, 177-80
Adams, Capt. William J., 52
Air Defense of Great Britain (AD-GB), 4, 96, 100, 107, 118, 124, 128, 134, 137-38, 142, 146-47, 154
Air Dispatch group (Brit.), 188
Air Forces (numbered):
  Second Tactical AF (RAF), 4, 96-97, 100, 146, 151-52, 159-60, 166, 168, 172-73, 188
  Eighth AF, 5, 15, 19, 29, 86, 96-97, 100, 102, 107, 118, 128, 134-35, 137-38, 140, 142, 147, 151, 154, 159, 165-66, 168, 171, 173, 188
  Ninth AF, 4-5, 11, 16-17, 27, 58, 81-83, 96-97, 102, 118, 128, 134-35, 154, 166-68, 173
  Fifteenth AF, 166
Air Ministry (Brit.), 4, 8, 158
Airborne-Air Planning Committee, 5, 9
Airborne Forward Delivery Airfield Group (Brit.) (AFDAG), 147-48, 201
ALBANY, paratroop mission, 33, 35-36, 38, 40-43, 45-46, 48, 55, 58-61, 63, 79
Aldeburgh, 90, 107, 120
Aldermaston, 19, 21-22, 61, 63, 65-66, 70, 131
Alderney, 11, 32, 64
Aldis lamp, 12, 35, 40, 138
Allied Expeditionary Air Force (AEAF), 4-5, 9, 14-15, 18, 29, 82-83, 96-97, 99
Allied Naval Commander of the Expeditionary Force (ANCXF), 12, 15
Alter Rhein, 178, 188
Amfreville, 56-57
AMHERST, airborne operation, 198-99
Amiens, 159
Andross, Capt. E. D., 153
Angoville-au-Plain, 43, 47
ANVIL. See DRAGOON.
ARENA, proposed airborne operation, 201

B

Bagby, Col. Ralph B., 18
Balderton, 23, 98, 111
Ballard, Lt. Col. Robert A., 46-47
Barkston Heath, 23, 48, 98, 114, 166
Basse Addeville, 43, 45-46
Bates, Capt. William W., 67
Battalions (numbered):
  2d QM Bn., 123
  80th Abn. AA Bn., 64, 66, 111, 121, 142
  81st Abn. AA Bn., 61, 130
  100th Panzer Repl. Bn. (Ger.), 51
  139th Engr. Bn., 186, 188
  155th AA Bn., 182
  307th Engr. Bn., 110, 120
  319th FA Bn., 68-69, 121, 123
  320th FA Bn., 68-69, 121, 123
  321st FA Bn., 130, 141
  326th Abn. Engr. Bn., 119
  376th Parachute FA Bn., 111, 154
  377th Parachute FA Bn., 36, 38, 64, 130, 136
  456th Parachute FA Bn., 48, 121
  464th Parachute FA Bn., 178-79
  466th Parachute FA Bn., 179, 181
  680th FA Bn., 182, 185
  681st FA Bn., 182, 185
  795th Georgian Battalion (Ger.), 51-52
  876th Avn. Engr. Bn., 148
  878th Avn. Engr. Bn., 88, 93, 132, 147-48
  907th FA Bn., 130
Baucke, Capt. Chester A., 51
Bayeux, 2, 6-7, 80
Beek, 133, 136, 141
BENEFICIARY, proposed airborne operation, 83
Best, 95, 103, 106, 115, 117, 119-20, 124-25, 129-30, 135, 151
Beuzeville-au-Plain, 38-39, 50, 52
Bidwell, Col. Bruce W., 8
Birch, 159
Birtwhistle, Lt. Col. Owen G., 18
Bocholt, 102, 167, 172
BOLERO, 1
Bomber Command (RAF), 4, 14, 29, 97, 117, 166, 168, 172, 174
Boreham, 98, 147, 159, 174
BOSTON, paratroop mission, 33, 46, 48, 50-51, 53-61, 79
Bottesford, 23-24
Boulogne, 15, 29, 87
Bourg Leopold, 141-43
BOXER, proposed airborne operation, 82, 87
Bradley, Maj. Gen. Follett, 2
Bradley, Lt. Gen. Omar N., 6-9, 47, 58, 82, 86, 156
Bradwell Bay, 91, 102, 144
Brereton, Maj. Gen. Lewis H., 4-5, 22, 27, 81-82, 85-89, 98-100, 117, 128, 147-48, 152-53, 156-57, 159-61, 165, 167-68, 173, 192
Brest, proposed airborne operations against. See SWORDHILT.
Bretigny, 159, 182
Bricy, 158, 186
Brigades (numbered):
  1 Airlanding Brig. (Brit.), 112, 115, 125-26
  1 Parachute Brig. (Brit.), 112, 114, 125
  3 Parachute Brig. (Brit.), 174

Armies (numbered):

First Allied Airborne Army (FAAA), 81-82, 85-88, 97, 99-100, 112, 140, 147-48, 151, 156-60, 164-65, 167, 170-72, 176, 191, 198, 201
First Army, 6-7, 10, 18, 27, 87
First Parachute Army (Ger.), 117
Second Army (Brit.) 6-7, 89-90, 95, 112, 146-51, 157, 160, 165, 167-68, 178, 190-91
Third Army, 85-87, 157, 198
Seventh Army, 157, 198, 201
Seventh Army (Ger.), 29, 30, 85
Ninth Army, 156-57, 160-61, 167, 173, 190
Army Air Forces Headquarters, 8
Army Groups (numbered):
  12th Army Gp., 82
  21 Army Gp., 5-7, 14, 82, 87, 95, 157, 160, 165, 168
Arnhem, 1, 87-91, 93, 97, 100-101, 112, 114-15, 117-18, 125-28, 131-38, 140, 142, 145-47, 149-50, 152, 154, 158, 167, 172, 200
Arnold, Gen. H. H., 5, 19, 81, 148, 198

4 Parachute Brig. (Brit.), 125-26, 131-32, 134
5 Parachute Brig. (Brit.), 176
6 Airlanding Brig. (Brit.), 176
32 Guards Brig. (Brit.), 133, 141
107th Panzer Brig. (Ger.), 133, 140
280th Assault Gun Brig. (Ger.), 140
Brigade groups (numbered):
  1 Airlanding Brigade Group. See 1 Airlanding Brigade.
Browning, Lt. Gen. F. A. M., 79, 81-82, 87-89, 93, 112, 130, 133, 136-37, 146-47, 150-51
Brussels, 88, 125, 129, 145, 148, 150, 159, 160, 165

C

C-46, 86, 158, 169, 180, 194, 196
C-47/C-53, 4, 21, 35, 74-75, 79, 86, 89, 153-54, 158, 196
C-82, 197
CG-13 glider, 158, 197
Caen, 2, 6-7, 9, 29
Cap d'Antifer, 15
Cape Gris Nez, 161, 163
Candee, Brig. Gen. Robert C., 2
Carentan, 2, 7, 9, 29, 45-48, 63
Carquebut, 52, 67, 72
Cassidy, Lt. Col. Patrick J., 39
Chalgrove, 98, 101, 159
Chappell, Col. Julian M., 71
Chartres, 149, 158-59, 177, 186
Chateau de Prinay, Louveciennes, 159
Chateaudun, 158, 182
Chef-du-Pont, 43, 45, 50-52, 54, 56-57, 69, 72
Cherbourg, 2, 7, 29
CHICAGO, glider mission, 42, 61, 63-65, 72
Chief of Staff, Supreme Allied Commander (COSSAC), 2-4, 6-7
Chiefs of Staff:
  British, 2, 156
  Combined, 1-3, 7, 156
Chilbolton, 98, 118
Chipping Ongar, 147, 159, 174
CHOKER II, proposed airborne operation, 157-58, 169
Churchill, Prime Minister Winston S., 8, 22
Clark, Brig. Gen. Harold L., 86
Coastal Air Command (RAF), 97, 166
Coldstream Guards Regiment, 133
Cole. Lt. Col. Robert G., 39
Combined Air Transport Operations Room (CATOR), 82, 86, 169

Combined Airborne Headquarters. See First Allied Airborne Army.
Combined Command Post, Maison Lafitte, 159-60, 191
Combined Control Center AEAF, Uxbridge, 15
COMET, proposed airborne operation, 87-91, 93, 95-96, 98
Commando Brigade (Brit.), 173-74, 185, 190, 192
Commands (numbered):
  VIII Fighter Comd., 15
  IX Air Force Service Comd., 19-20, 75, 83, 98
  IX Engineer Comd., 158
  IX Fighter Comd., 14-15
  IX Tactical Air Comd., 172
  IX Troop Carrier Comd., 4-5, 8-9, 11-12, 14-27, 50, 58, 61, 67-68, 72, 78-79, 81-82, 85-87, 89-90, 95, 97-99, 123, 148-49, 157-59, 161, 164-67, 169-72, 194, 196, 198, 201
  XII Troop Carrier Comd. (Prov.), 17-18
  XIX Tactical Air Comd., 172
  XXIX Tactical Air Comd., 166-68, 172-73
Companies (numbered):
  2d QM Depot Supply Co., 75
  326th Abn. Med. Co., 119
  490th QM Depot Supply Co., 123, 188
Coningham, Air Marshal Arthur, 159-60, 167, 173
Corey nose, 72, 99
Corps (numbered):
  I Abn. Corps, 81-82, 112, 147-48, 150-51
  V Corps, 47
  VII Corps, 10, 45, 47, 52
  VIII Corps (Brit.), 136, 150
  XII Corps (Brit.), 150, 193
  XVIII Abn. Corps, 82, 156-57, 159-60, 168, 190
  XXX Corps (Brit.), 133, 151
Cottesmore, 23-24, 26, 55, 98, 166, 176
Coulommiers, 159, 182, 184
Coutances, 15, 29
Crookham Common, 19, 83, 98
Crouch, Lt. Col. Joel L., 24, 32, 83, 177, 180
Culoville, 42, 64
Cutler, Brig. Gen. Stuart L., 81

D

Deception and diversion, 14-15, 29-30, 97, 100, 118, 166-67
Dempsey, Lt. Gen. Miles C., 6, 9, 89, 94, 129, 145, 157, 160-61, 168

Denain/Prouvy, 148-49
Depots (numbered):
  Third Strategic Air Depot, 188
DETROIT, glider mission, 61, 64-65, 69, 72
Diersfordt, 178-79, 192
Diersfordter Wald, 160-61, 167, 172, 174, 178, 180-81, 186, 188
Dinter, 129, 133
Divisions (numbered):
  1 Abn. Div. (Brit.), 9, 79, 83, 85, 87-88, 91, 93, 98, 115, 134, 137-39, 141-42, 144-47, 150-52, 154, 157, 197, 200
  2d Air Div. See 2d Bombardment Div.
  2d Bomb. Div., 86, 123-24, 188
  4th Armored Div., 52, 69
  6 Abn. Div. (Brit.), 83, 156, 158, 163-65, 168-70, 174, 176-77, 179, 188-91
  6 Parachute Div. (Ger.), 132
  7 Armored Div. (Brit.), 80
  IX Bomb. Div., 172
  9th Panzer Div. (Ger.), 115, 149
  10th Panzer Div. (Ger.), 115, 149
  13th Abn. Div., 157, 169, 201
  15 Div. (Brit.), 173-74, 177, 179
  17th Abn. Div., 156, 158-59, 163-65, 168-70, 181, 188-92
  43 Div. (Brit.), 136, 141, 145, 150
  51 Div. (Brit.), 173-74
  52 Light Div. (Brit.), 88, 93, 146, 148, 151
  53 Welsh Div. (Brit.), 193
  82d Abn. Div., 9-12, 16-17, 21-23, 25-27, 32-33, 38-39, 41, 48, 52-53, 56-59, 61, 64, 66-68, 70-79, 83, 87-88, 93-94, 97-98, 101, 107-12, 115, 118, 120-23, 127-31, 133-37, 139-42, 144-46, 148, 151-54, 157, 201
  84th Inf. Div. (Ger.), 179
  90th Inf. Div., 58
  91st Inf. Div. (Ger.), 10, 42, 51, 53-54, 59
  101st Abn. Div., 9-12, 17, 21-22, 24-26, 32-33, 35, 48, 50, 52, 54, 58-59, 61, 63-65, 74, 76-77, 83, 85, 87-89, 94, 98, 101-3, 106, 111, 116-20, 122, 126-29, 132-33, 136-37, 139-42, 145-46, 148, 151-54, 157, 201
  243d Div. (Ger.), 10
  709th Div. (Ger.), 10
Dommel River, 94, 106
Donalson, Lt. Col. John M., 36, 38
Dorsten, 167, 172, 190-91
Douve River, 7, 9, 12, 40, 42-43, 45-48, 53-55, 58, 69-70, 75, 77, 199
DRAGOON (ANVIL), invasion of

southern France, 1, 7, 61, 83, 89, 106, 150, 199, 201
Dreux, 158, 186
Dreux-Evreux area, proposed airborne missions to, 8
Driel, 139, 141-42
Duke, Col. James E., Jr., 18, 83
Dulmen, 172, 190

E

EAGLE, airborne rehearsal, 23-26, 28
Eaker, Lt. Gen. Ira C., 3
Eastcote. See Troop Carrier Command Post, Eastcote.
Eerde, 105, 141, 145
EFFECTIVE, proposed airborne operation, 198, 201
Eindhoven, 89-91, 94-95, 101-2, 105, 115, 117-19, 124, 129, 134-39, 142-43, 148, 150
Eisenhower, Gen. Dwight D., 6-8, 11, 14, 22, 28, 47, 81-82, 85, 87-88, 156
Elam, Maj. Dan, 103
ELMIRA glider mission, 53, 65-70
Elst, 114, 139, 141
Emmerich, 97, 118, 156, 166, 191-92
Erle, proposed airborne mission to, 160
Ernst, Lt. Col. Grant W., 83
Ewell, Lt. Col. Julian, 42
Evans, Brig. Gen. Frederick W., 8
Exeter, 21, 24, 42, 77-78, 98

F

Falley, Generalleutnant Wilhelm, 59
Fairford, 102
Fighter Command, RAF, 165, 174
Filer, Lt. Col. William L., 180
Fisher, Col. Ralph E., 18, 83
FLASHPOINT, 157
Flüren, 179, 190
Folkingham, 23, 76, 121
Foucarville, 39, 64
FREEPORT, resupply mission, 74-79
Frost, Lt. Col. J. D., 115, 125, 132-34, 149
Fulbeck, 23, 77-78, 98

G

GALVESTON, glider mission, 53, 68-70, 75
GARDEN, 88, 115, 146, 149
Gavin, Maj. Gen. James M., 10, 54, 56-57, 82, 93-94, 111, 120, 124, 130, 133, 154-55, 197, 201
Gennep, 121, 123
Gheel, 95, 101-2, 128, 131, 143
Ghent, 91, 102, 138

Giles, Brig. Gen. Benjamin F., 5, 18
Gladbeck, 167, 172, 191
Glider pilots, ground employment of, 73-74, 152-53, 170, 185, 191-92
Gliders, pick-up and recovery of, 72-73, 148-49, 164, 192
Gliders, shipment and assembly of, 19-20, 98
Gosfield, 159
Graham, Col. Robt. M., 18, 83
Grantham, 21, 23, 48, 98, 107, 121, 128, 135, 138-39, 150, 159
Grave, 88, 93-95, 101, 107, 110, 121, 123, 129, 133, 135, 140-41, 143-49, 200
Greenham Common, 21-22, 26, 35-36, 45, 66, 78, 98, 102, 119, 129, 136
Grenadier Guards Regiment, 133
Grimberghen, 192
Griswold nose, 20, 72, 99
Groesbeek, 93-94, 109-12, 120, 123, 131, 133, 144
Groups (numbered):
 2 Gp. (RAF), 167, 172
 4th Ftr. Gp., 102
 IX TC Pathfinder Gp. (Prov.), 24, 83, 98, 159, 177-78
 11 Gp. (RAF), 15, 166, 172
 38 Gp. (RAF), 4-9, 14, 79, 82, 88-90, 96-98, 102, 112, 126, 132, 137-38, 140, 142, 147, 154, 157-59, 163-65, 170-71, 176, 193, 196, 198
 44th Bomb. Gp., 189
 46 Gp. (RAF), 4-5, 9, 79, 82, 85-86, 88-90, 96-98, 112, 132, 138, 142, 145, 157-59, 163, 165, 170, 176
 56th Ftr. Gp., 137
 61st TC Gp., 18, 22-23, 48, 55-56, 75-76, 88, 114, 121, 123, 131, 147-48, 153, 159, 174, 176
 78th Ftr. Gp., 101, 107, 142, 144
 83 Gp. (RAF), 145, 148, 151-52, 154, 159, 166-68, 172, 190-91
 84 Gp. (RAF), 166-68, 172
 93d Bomb Gp., 124
 313th TC Gp., 18, 22-23, 53, 56, 75-76, 107-9, 118, 121-22, 153, 159, 169, 179, 180-81, 186, 193-94
 314th TC Gp., 18, 22-23, 26, 53-54, 56, 75, 114, 125, 138, 159, 186
 315th TC Gp., 3, 5, 18, 22-23, 26, 35, 48, 50-51, 97, 110, 125, 138-39, 144, 159, 169, 174, 176
 316th TC Gp., 18, 22-24, 48, 50, 55, 75-76, 109-10, 122, 159, 174, 176

339th Ftr. Grp., 142
353d Ftr. Gp., 138, 142
357th Ftr. Gp., 118, 128
359th Ftr. Gp., 118, 138
361st Ftr. Gp., 102
364th Ftr. Gp., 128
365th Ftr. Gp., 103
389th Bomb. Gp., 189
406th Ftr. Gp., 173
434th TC Gp., 5, 22, 26, 61, 65, 70, 97, 103, 135, 142, 145, 159, 170, 181
435th TC Gp., 5, 22, 40-41, 68-70, 80, 102, 106, 129, 135, 145, 159, 169, 182, 185
436th TC Gp., 18, 22, 36, 38, 68, 78, 105, 135, 144-45, 159, 169, 182, 184
437th TC Gp., 18, 22, 26, 64, 66-67, 70-71, 89, 106, 135, 139, 147, 159, 182, 184-85
438th TC Gp., 18, 35-36, 38, 45, 59, 66-67, 80, 106, 135, 139-40, 144, 159, 169, 178
439th TC Gp., 18, 23-24, 40-41, 70-71, 77, 98, 109-11, 120, 131, 136, 158, 182, 184
440th TC Gp., 18, 23-24, 26, 42-43, 45, 76-78, 80, 98, 107, 111-12, 158, 186
441st TC Gp., 18, 23-24, 35, 42-43, 45, 71, 78, 80, 98, 107, 112, 158, 186-87
442d TC Gp., 18, 23, 26, 35, 48, 55, 76-78, 88-89, 98, 102-3, 105, 118, 124, 129, 136, 142, 158, 186
446th Bomb Gp., 124
448th Bomb Gp., 124, 189
474th Ftr. Gp., 103
479th Ftr. Gp., 147
489th Bomb Gp., 124
491st Bomb Gp., 189
Guards Armored Division (Brit.), 105, 115, 117, 119, 130, 136, 150
Guernsey, 11, 32, 64
Gurecki, 1st Lt. John, 103

H

HACKENSACK, glider mission, 53, 69-71, 78
Haltern, 147, 190
Hamilcar glider, 4, 6, 79, 98, 176
Hamminkeln, 161, 176-77, 180-81, 186, 188, 190
HANDS UP, proposed airborne operation, 83
Harrison, 1st Lt. Jesse M., 129
Hartestein, 126-27, 132-35, 137, 145-46, 150
Harwell, 127

Hatfield, 102, 119, 129
Hattert, 110
Hawkinge, 161, 163, 174, 188
Headquarters Airborne Troops. See 1 Airborne Corps.
Hechtel, 145, 147
Heelsum, 91, 114
Helmond, 191-92
Heumen, 109-10, 120, 130, 133
Heveadorp, 91, 127, 132-33, 137, 139, 146
Hiesville, 42, 61, 64-65, 77
Hitler, Adolph, 10, 118
Hollinghurst, AVM L. N., 82, 95
Holophane lights, 15, 17, 32, 95
Honinghutie, 120, 133
Horrocks, Lt. Gen. B. G., 133, 136, 145
Horsa glider, 4, 68, 69, 72, 176, 177, 193, 197
HUSKY, airborne missions in, 3-4, 166, 196

I

Issel, River and Canal, 161, 176-77, 180, 182, 185-96, 189-91

J

Johnson, Col. Howard R., 42, 45-47, 58, 77
Jones, Col. Glynne M., 18, 83

K

Keevil, 97
KEOKUK glider mission, 63, 65-67
Kershaw, Lt. Col. Theodore, 42, 71
Kesselring, Fieldmarshal Albert, 200
Kinnard, Lt. Col. W. O., 95
Knapheide, 123
Koepel, 131-32
Krause, Lt. Col. Edward C., 50-51
Krebs, Lt. Col. Frank X., 107

L

la Barquette, 45-47, 77
la Fière, 43, 50-51, 53-57, 59, 65
La Haye du Puits, 9, 12
Langar, 23, 98, 107
Le Havre, 29
le Port, 45-47, 59
Lee, Maj. Gen. William C., 21
Leigh-Mallory, AM Trafford, 4-9, 11, 14, 26-28, 61, 80-82, 96, 199
les Droueries, 45-47, 66
les Forges, 40, 42, 47, 50, 52, 63, 66-68, 70, 73
Lindemans, Christian, 117, 199
Lindquist, Col. Roy, 54, 56
LINNET, 87, 89-90, 96, 98
LINNET II, 82, 87

Lippe River, 157, 160, 166, 168, 173, 190
Louveciennes. See Chateau de Prunay, Louveciennes.
Lovett, Robert A., 99

M

Maas River, 88, 93-94, 109-10, 120, 165
Maas-Waal Canal, 93-94, 109-10, 120, 130
Maastricht, 134, 142, 147
McAuliffe, Brig. Gen. Anthony C., 40-42, 119
McBride, Lt. Col. Francis A., 83
MacNees, Col. Frank J., 40, 106
Mainz, 156-57, 172
Maison Lafitte. See Combined Command Post, Maison Lafitte.
Malden, 108
Maloney, Lt. Col. Arthur, 56
March, 25, 107
MARKET, 59, 61, 72, 81-83, 86, 88-90, 94-101, 106, 115, 117-18, 127, 130, 133, 144-46, 148-57, 159-60, 163-65, 167-68, 170, 173, 188, 193-94, 196-201.
Mark's Hall, 159-60, 171
Marshall, Gen. George C., 1, 5, 8, 81
Melun, 159, 182
Membury, 21-22, 36, 45, 68, 76-78
MEMPHIS, resupply mission, 74, 76-78
Merderet River, 10-12, 33, 43, 45, 48, 50, 52-59, 64, 75-76, 199
Merryfield, 21, 24, 35, 42, 71, 98
Meuse-Escaut Canal, 88, 136
Miley, Maj. Gen. William M., 179, 190
Millett, Col. George V., Jr., 56-57, 94
Model, Field Marshal Walter, 115, 130, 149
Moelenhoek, 109
Montebourg, 32
Montgomery, Gen. Bernard L., 6-7, 82, 86-89, 129, 146, 149-50, 156-57, 159-60, 167, 171, 173-74, 190, 198
Montmartin-en-graignes, 55
Mook, 8, 120, 133, 136, 153
Morgan, Lt. Gen. Frederick E., 2, 5-6
Mourmelon-le-Grand, 159, 170, 177
Muir, Lt. Marvin F., 40
Münster, 166, 168, 173, 194
Murphy, Lt. Col. M. C., 18

N

NAPLES II, proposed airborne operation, 156
NEPTUNE, 7-9, 17, 21, 23, 25-26, 28, 50, 59-61, 72-73, 75-76, 78, 80-81, 90, 94, 97-99, 106, 154, 157, 164, 171, 193, 196, 198-99
Nether Avon, 169
Neuville-au-Plain, 50-52
Nierse River, 163
Nijmegen, 88, 90-91, 93-94, 97, 100-1, 107, 111-12, 115, 117, 120, 124-25, 127-28, 130-31, 133-34, 136-38, 140-42, 145-50, 152
Norfolk House, 2, 4, 7
North Foreland, 91
North Witham, 24-25, 32, 98
Northolt, 27

O

Oberdorf, Lt. Col. John W., 18
Occults (aerial lighthouses), 15, 48, 95
Oirchot, 103
Oosterbeek, 115, 131-32
Oosterhout, 107, 141
Ostberg, Lt. Col. Edwin J., 56
Oud Keent, 147
Overasselt, 110, 122, 143-44
OVERLORD, 1-8, 11, 17, 19, 21, 201

P

Paris, 158-59, 161
Parkhill, Lt. Col. W. H., 186
Parks, Brig. Gen. Floyd L., 81
Pathfinder School. See IX Troop Carrier Pathfinder Group (Prov.).
Pathfinders, 3-4, 15-16, 24-26, 32-33, 36, 40, 43, 48, 53, 55, 60, 65, 68-69, 71, 83, 88, 96, 101-3, 106, 109-10, 114, 122, 124, 131-32, 143-44, 147, 155, 159, 164, 174, 198-99.
Patton, Lt. Gen. George, 85-86, 157
Picauville, 53, 59, 75
PLUNDER, 157, 160-61, 167, 173, 191-92, 195
Poix, 159, 186
Polish Parachute Brigade, 83, 85, 87-88, 93, 98, 128, 132-34, 136-39, 141-42, 144-46, 149, 154
Pont l'Abbé, 40, 53-54, 58
Pontoise, 186
Portbail, 12
Portland Bill, 11-12, 32, 35, 56, 66, 70, 74-75, 77, 80
Pouppeville, 41-42
Pratt, Brig. Gen. Don F., 61, 64
Prosnes, 159, 177
Pruitt, Lt. Col. James C., 18
pundits, 163

Q

QUADRANT Conference, 3-4
Quesada, Maj. Gen. Elwood, 58

Quiberon Bay, proposed airborne operation against. See HANDS UP.

R

Radar:
  IFF, 12, 14, 96, 164
  WINDOW, 14, 29, 172
Radar countermeasures. See deception and diversion.
Radar and radio navigational aids:
  "buncher" beacons, 124
  BUPS beacon, 15-16, 25, 32, 53, 164
  Gee, 15-16, 24, 25, 32-33, 36, 38, 40, 43, 53, 55, 59-60, 67, 90, 95-96, 102, 107, 114, 123-24, 139, 164, 170, 174, 180-81, 189, 193-94, 199
  Loran, 95
  MF beacon, 95-96, 163-64, 170, 188-89, 193
  Oboe, 172
  Rebecca-Eureka, 3-4, 15-17, 24-26, 32, 36, 38, 40-41, 43, 48-49, 53, 55, 60, 63-64, 67-69, 75-76, 78-80, 95-96, 101-3, 106-7, 114, 123-24, 126, 131-32, 135, 138, 143-44, 154, 163-64, 193, 199
  SCR-717C, 16, 24-25, 32, 53, 59, 74, 79, 95-96, 164, 199
  VHF beacon, 188-89
Radio, 12, 17, 35, 52, 55, 63, 113, 133-34, 143, 150-52, 164, 171, 185, 191, 198
Raff, Col. Edson D., 67-68, 73, 177-78
Rambouillet, 85
Ramsbury, 21-22, 64-66, 70, 136, 145
Rask, Col. Peter S., 18
Rees, 156-57, 165, 173, 191-92
Regiments (numbered):
  4th Dorset Regt., 145-46
  6th Parachute Regt. (Ger.), 10, 47
  8th Inf. Regt., 39, 41-42, 52, 58, 67, 72, 77
  12th Inf. Regt., 39
  22d Inf. Regt., 39
  64th Medium Regt. RA, 137, 151
  191st Arty. Regt. (Ger.), 42
  194th Glider Inf. Regt., 179, 181-82, 185
  325th Glider Inf. Regt., 22, 52, 57-58, 70-72, 109, 131, 133, 136, 142, 144, 149, 153
  327th Glider Inf. Regt., 22, 119, 130, 140-41
  401st Glider Inf. Regt., 70-71
  501st Parachute Inf. Regt., 11, 22, 40, 42-48, 77, 103, 105-6, 119, 125, 129, 133, 136, 140-41, 145
  502d Parachute Inf. Regt., 22, 36, 38-39, 105-6, 119, 129-30, 140
  504th Parachute Inf. Regt., 22, 94, 109-10, 120, 133, 141
  505th Parachute Inf. Regt., 22, 48, 50-52, 54, 56-59, 67, 79, 109-11, 120, 130, 133, 153
  506th Parachute Inf. Regt., 11, 22, 39-42, 45-57, 64, 105-6, 118-19, 130, 133, 136, 140-41
  507th Parachute Inf. Regt., 22, 51, 53-58, 169, 177-79, 181, 185-86, 190, 194
  508th Parachute Inf. Regt., 22, 51, 53-57, 59, 110-11, 120, 133, 141
  513th Parachute Inf. Regt., 169, 178-81, 185-86, 192, 194
  1057th Grenadier Regt. (Ger.), 51, 54, 56-57
  1058th Grenadier Regt. (Ger.), 42, 46, 51-52
Reichswald Forest, 97, 107-9, 112, 120, 146, 152-53
Reims, 98, 150
Rethy, 103, 106, 129
Rheine, 166
Rhine River, 86-87, 91, 93, 115, 127, 136, 139-41, 145-46, 148, 150, 156-57, 160, 163-66, 168, 171-74, 178-80, 182-86, 190-93, 196, 198
Riethorst, 109, 120
Ridgway, Lt. Gen. Matthew B., 10, 22, 27, 48, 51-52, 57, 67, 73, 82, 152, 156-57, 159-60, 165, 190

S

St. André-de-l'Eure, 158-186
St. Arnoult-en-Yvellines, 85
St. Côme-du-mont, 43, 45-47, 64, 66-68, 70, 77
St. Germain-de-Varreville, 33, 36, 38-39, 41
St. Jores, 41
St. Lo, breakthrough at, 83, 85
St. Malo, proposed airborne operation against. See BENEFICIARY.
St. Marcouf Islands, 12, 35, 63, 66, 68, 70-71, 74-75, 77
St. Sauveur de Pierre Pont, 9, 43
St. Martin-de-Varreville, 7, 36, 38-39, 54
St. Oedenrode, 94, 106, 119, 129, 136, 145
Ste Marie-du-Mont, 40, 42, 47, 69-70
Ste Mere Eglise, 10-11, 29, 33, 36, 39, 41, 43, 47-48, 50-52, 54, 57, 64-70, 73, 76, 78, 200
Saltby, 23, 114, 138
Sass, Capt. Howard W., 76
Scheldt River, 88, 91, 138
Schijndel, 103, 119, 121, 134, 136, 140-41
Schouwen Island, 90, 107, 112, 118-19, 121
Schwartzwalder, Capt. F. V., 56-57
Seine River, 8, 85, 86
Seventh Army Sturm Battalion (Ger.), 52
Severn Estuary, 11
Shanley, Lt. Col. Thomas J. B., 53-58
's Hertogenbosch, 91, 107, 119, 121, 126, 128, 131
Shettle, Capt. Charles G., 46-47, 59
Shulman, 2d Lt. Herbert E., 103
Sicily, airborne missions to. See HUSKY.
Silvey, Maj. Robert W., 69
Simpson, Lt. Gen. William H., 160, 190
Sink, Col. Robert L., 40, 42, 47, 64
Spanhoe, 23, 138, 169, 176
South Staffordshire Regiment, 125-26, 131
Spaatz, Gen Carl, 168
Squadrons (numbered):
  21 Weather Sq., 99
  26th Mobile Reclamation and Repair Sq., 19, 98
  29th TC Sq., 143
  84th TC Sq., 65
  88th TC Sq., 67
  98th TC Sq., 77
  803d Special Sq., 15
Stanmore, 4, 80, 82, 87, 96, 97, 99
Stearley, Brig. Gen. Ralph S., 81
Stoddart, 1st Lt. Robert S., Jr., 103
Stratemeyer, Maj. Gen. G. E., 2
Student, General Kurt, 117, 130
Styles, Lt. Col. Clayton, 53
Sunnyhill Park, Ascot, 81, 88-89, 99-100
Supreme Commander Allied Expeditionary Force (SCAEF), 6, 11, 156
Supreme Headquarters, Allied Expeditionary Force (SHAEF), 6, 8, 12, 15, 20, 81-83, 85-89, 156-58, 160, 169, 198, 201
SWORDHILT, proposed airborne operation, 83

T

Tarrant Rushton, 98
Taute River, 7
Taylor, Maj. Gen. Maxwell D., 21, 38, 40-42, 47, 89, 94, 106, 140
Tedder, ACM Arthur, 168
Timmes, Lt. Col. Charles J., 56-57
Tournai, 87

TRANSFIGURE, proposed airborne operation, 85-86, 89
Transport Command (RAF), 4
Troop Carried Command Post, Eastcote, 5, 75, 80, 89-90, 93, 97, 99-100, 133
TRIDENT Conference, 1
Tucker, Col. Reuben, 94-95
Turqueville, 52, 66-68, 70, 76

U

Uden, 121, 140-41, 143
Upottery, 21, 24, 40, 70-71, 98
Urquhart, Maj. Gen. R. E., 93, 125, 132, 146, 149
USSTAF, 5, 82-83, 99, 165
UTAH Beach, 7-12, 30, 36, 39, 52, 65-71, 77, 201
Uxbridge, 5, 15, 17

V

Valkenswaard, 105
Valognes, 29, 33, 38, 54
Vandenberg, Lt. Gen. Hoyt, 168, 172
Vandervoort, Lt. Col. Benjamin H., 50-51
VARSITY, 59, 61, 150, 156-61, 163-64, 166-74, 177, 181, 184, 190-200, 202
Veghel, 89, 95, 101, 103, 105-6, 109, 123, 129, 131, 133, 136, 140-41, 143, 145, 150, 153, 201
Very pistol, 12, 96, 114, 132, 135, 138, 144

Vierville, 47
Vire River, 2, 7
Vitry-en-Artois, 159
Voisenum, 159
Volkel, 142-43

W

Waal River, 88, 91, 93, 111, 115, 133, 136, 141
Waco (CG-4A) glider, 4, 68-69, 72, 197
Wageningen, 114, 125
Walcheren Island, 88, 100
Wavre, 161, 163, 170, 172, 177-68, 183, 186, 188
Weeze, 163
Welford Park, 21-22, 40, 68, 76-77
Wesel, 1, 87, 102, 118, 128, 134, 142, 156-57, 160-61, 166-68, 171-74, 178-79, 182, 184-86, 188-90, 192
Wethersfield, 159, 174
WILDOATS, proposed airborne operation, 78-80, 83
Wilhelmina Canal, 94, 103, 105-6, 117, 119, 136, 140
Willems Canal, 94-95, 105
Williams, Col. Adriel N., 182
Williams, Maj. Gen. Paul L., 5, 10, 16, 18, 21, 24, 26, 27, 61, 83, 85-86, 89, 91, 95, 98, 158-59, 169-70, 193
Wings (numbered):
 2d Bomb. Wg. See 2d Bomb. Division.

IX TC Service Wg. (Prov.), 83, 123
14th Bomb. Wg., 123-25
20th Bomb. Wg., 123-24
50th TC Wg., 5, 11, 21, 23-27, 35, 74, 83, 98, 107, 120, 131, 142, 153, 158, 169, 182, 186
51st TC Wg., 1
52d TC Wg., 3, 11, 16-18, 21-26, 48, 74, 79-80, 83, 88, 98, 107, 112, 120, 131-32, 138, 142, 157, 153, 159, 169, 180, 186
53d TC Wg., 11, 18, 21-22, 25-26, 68-69, 83, 91, 98, 100, 102-3, 106, 119, 121, 129, 131, 135, 139, 144, 158-59, 169, 182-83, 192
302d Transport Wg., 150
325th Reconnaissance Wg., 100
Wolfhezen, 126-27, 131-32, 134
Worms, 157
Wyler, 94, 111, 120, 122-23, 133

X

Xanten, 157, 165, 173, 178, 183, 188

Y

Young, Lt. Col. Charles H., 40-41

Z

Zon, 94-95, 105-6, 115, 117, 119, 127, 129-30, 133, 137, 140, 148-50
Zuckerman, Lt. Col. Paul S., 18
Zwolle, 134, 142, 168

www.ingramcontent.com/pod-product-compliance
Lightning Source LLC
Chambersburg PA
CBHW050458110426
42742CB00018B/3301